WAR AND PEACE IN ISLAM

The Uses and Abuses of Jihad

WAR AND PEACE IN ISLAM

The Uses and Abuses of Jihad

Edited by
HRH Prince Ghazi bin Muhammad
Professor Ibrahim Kalin
Professor Mohammad Hashim Kamali

THE ISLAMIC TEXTS SOCIETY

This first edition published 2013 by
MABDA (The Royal Islamic Strategic Studies Centre) &
The Islamic Texts Society
Miller's House
Kings Mill Lane
Great Shelford
Cambridge CB22 5EN
United Kingdom

ISBN: 978-1-903682-83-8

Cover Design by Besim Bruncaj
Set in Minion
Printed in Jordan by National Press

CO-SPONSORS:
The International Institute of Advanced Islamic Studies (IAIS), Malaysia, and MABDA (The Royal Islamic Strategic Studies Centre), Jordan and The Institute of Strategic Thinking (SDE), Turkey.

CONTENTS

Part III: Beyond Peace: Forbearance, Mercy, Compassion and Love

ACKNOWLEDGEMENTS

All praise be to God, for allowing us to bring together this book. The editors also wish to thank the authors of the articles and those institutes or publishing houses that have allowed their writings to be reproduced herein. Particular thanks go to the MABDA staff for working on this book in various ways: Lamya Khraisha, Aftab Ahmad, Sulayman Hart, Besim Bruncaj and Zeinab 'Asfour. Fiona O'Brien also did excellent copy-editing.

A NOTE ON THE TRANSLATION OF THE QUR'AN

There are a number of English translations of the Qur'an; authors in this volume have not specified which they have used, and indeed in some cases may have provided their own translations. Some have translated the Divine Name '*Allah*' as 'God', and some have left it as '*Allah*'—we have respected this. The chapter and verse numbers refer to the original Arabic. We have also kept the authors' own preferences as regards modern or archaic English in translating the Qur'an.

In addition, aside from standard terms like Qur'an, jihad, etc., we have not standardised the transliteration throughout the text. The index alone has been standardised and fully transliterated.

FOREWORD

by His Eminence Alhaji Muhammad Sa'ad Abubakar, CFR, MNI Sultan of Sokoto and President-General Nigerian Supreme Council for Islamic Affairs

---

Let me first express my profound gratitude to the editors of this important volume for giving me the singular honor and privilege to write a foreword to this immensely valuable collection of researched articles and works on the very timely issues of war and peace. I have taken time to go through this wonderful collection of sixteen chapters, spanning some 400 pages that have literally explored every conceivable aspect of the subject 'War and Peace in Islam'. This is perhaps the first work of its kind where experts who have excelled in their different fields have come together to collaborate on such a crucial issue of our time as War and Peace.

This highly enlightening volume is astonishingly comprehensive, capturing the different aspects and perspectives of the subject matter: legal, philosophical, sociological, theological and indeed military dimensions of war and peace in Islam against a background of other major religions in the world. Expectedly the quality of research and analysis is evidently impressive. Indeed given the level of scholarship one would not expect any less; the past and present Shaykhs of the famous al-Azhar, distinguished legal experts like Prof. Hashim Kamali, Prof. Ibrahim Kalin and HRH Prince Ghazi, who is also a Professor of Islamic Philosophy, and a host of others all contributed in their different fields of expertise.

It is particularly interesting how each chapter reinforces the other, generating a compelling moment which demolishes a lot of the stereotyping that is today associated with war and peace in Islam. The contribution of Dr Joel Hayward, who is a scholar of warfare, on 'Warfare in the Qur'an' and that of David Dakake on 'The Myth of Militant Islam' having marshaled very powerful researched arguments were able to expose and demystify many of the current myths promoted by western media and other ignorant bigots. The contribution of Dr Naveed Sheikh on 'Body Count: A Comparative Quantitative Study of Mass Killings in History" was ingeniously crafted, having assembled almost fifty pages of empirical data on religious warfare from the Roman times to date, including such otherwise obscure groups as the Aztec of 15th Century Mexico and working out the figures to put our current discussions on religious conflict and warfare in a historical and global perspective, is simply disarming.

The systematic, evidence based, unassailably empirical researched contributions, carefully and painstakingly disentangling and explaining the prevailing confusion around the discussion on war and peace in Islam is perhaps the greatest contribution yet to peace in our contemporary troubled world. It recommends itself to all and sundry, but particularly young people, policy makers and political and business leaders. It is my honor and privilege to be associated with these great strides in the pursuit of peace in the globe.

Once again I wish to register special appreciation for the editors and indeed the authors of the various chapters, especially HRH Prince Ghazi with whom I have had the privilege of sharing a number of peace platforms.

His Eminence Alhaji Muhammad Sa'ad Abubakar, CFR, MNI
Sultan Of Sokoto and President-General Nigerian Supreme Council
For Islamic Affairs
May 2013

INTRODUCTION

Professor Mohammad Hashim Kamali

The book before us is presented in three parts, namely 'war and its practice', 'peace and its practice', and 'beyond peace: forbearance, mercy, compassion and love'. This volume's range is evidently not confined to the study of jihad, yet jihad remains its central concern—as indicated by its title. The main issue concerning jihad has been eloquently stated by Seyyed Hossein Nasr, who wrote: 'In modern times in the West no vocabulary in the Islamic religion has been so distorted, maligned, misunderstood, and vilified as the word jihad.'[8] Nasr added that this is due not only to Western media's demonising epithets and constructions, but also to those extremist Muslims who readily provide the latter with examples to justify their propagation of the distorted image of this term.

Taking a balanced approach to the understanding of words and concepts naturally begins with employing them for their true meanings. The essence of this requirement is captured in a Qur'anic directive to Muslims: *And when you speak—speak with justice* (*Al-An'ām*, 6:152).[9] Justice is inclusive of truth. The Qur'an seems here to be conveying the awareness that one can tell the truth in different ways, and that it is best if it is moderated with a sense of justice. The problem before us is one of widespread distortion in the uses of jihad, not just by the Western media, but by Muslims themselves, who have become a party to that distortion. The concept of *Jihad fī sabīl Allāh* (striving in the path of God) as contained in the Qur'an and Hadith has often been distorted and misused by the perpetrators of military violence and terrorism against Muslims and non-Muslims alike. Matters are made worse by the fact that the word has gained commercial appeal in Europe and the United States. A number of writers seeking to make their books commercially successful have been using jihad in their titles in any way possible. It is important therefore to explain what jihad stands for, through a careful reading of the Qur'an and Hadith. This is the basic theme and message of the book before us, one which is articulated in the writings of a number of outstanding scholars and opinion leaders on the subject. To restore moderation and balance to a distorted picture, one needs to begin with what one believes to be the truth about jihad.

Jihad derives from the root word *jahada*, which means to strive or to exert effort. Its translation in the Western media as 'holy war' would in Arabic be equivalent to *al-ḥarb al-muqaddasah*, which is totally unfamiliar and unknown to Arabic speakers. Jihad consists of the effort one makes to do something good and to prevent or oppose evil. The effort may be directed towards oneself or the outside world. The struggle to control and refine one's ego, to conquer ignorance, to discipline one's own base desires, to excel in the work undertaken to the best of one's ability are the jihad of the self (*jihad al-nafs*). In a similar vein, the Sufi contemplation used to combat the distractions of the soul is called *mujāhadah*. To combat poverty and disease, to build housing for the poor, or to fight corruption and abuse would all qualify as jihad that serves a social purpose of great benefit. We are cast into a world in which there is disequilibrium and disorder both externally and within ourselves. To create a life of equilibrium based on surrender to God and following His injunctions involves constant jihad. For ordinary Muslims, praying five times a day throughout their lives, or fasting from dawn to dusk during the month of Ramadan are certainly not possible without great effort, or jihad. A Muslim who works to earn a living and support his family is also engaged in jihad. It is now common to hear Muslim intellectuals speak of jihad in business, jihad in the acquisition of knowledge, and jihad against social ills afflicting young people, drug abuse and AIDS. Understood in its comprehensive sense, jihad is an inherent aspect of the human condition in facing the imperfections of this world. The Prophet Muhammad ﷺ has said that 'the *mujāhid* is one who wages a struggle against himself'.[10] The effort to facilitate a just system of rule is underscored in another hadith: 'the best form of jihad is to tell a word of truth to an unjust ruler.'[11] In a hadith al-Bukhari and Muslim have recorded, a young man asked the Prophet: 'Should I join the jihad?' that was apparently in progress at the time. In response, the Prophet asked him a question: 'Do you have parents?', and when the man said 'Yes', the Prophet told him, 'Then strive by serving them.'[12]

The Qur'an refers to jihad in twenty-four verses, most of which emphasise the spiritual and non-violent manifestations of jihad, such as being steadfast in the faith and sacrifice in its cause, migration from Mecca to Medina, and peaceful propagation of the faith. The reader will find comprehensive coverage of the Qur'an in the various chapters of this book. It is worth mentioning, however, that jihad as armed struggle against the aggressor occurs only in the Medinan verses of the Qur'an. During the first thirteen years of his campaign in Mecca, the Prophet was not permitted to use force even for self-defence. Islam was propagated only through peaceful methods. The idolaters of Mecca persecuted and forced a number of the Prophet's companions to migrate, initially to Abyssinia, and later to Medina. The Meccans not only continued but stepped up their hostility and attacked the Muslims, some 270km away, in the battles of Badr (624 CE) and Uhud (625 CE), with superior forces, inflicting heavy casualties on them. Only then was permission granted to: *Fight in the way of God those who fight you, but begin not hostilities. Verily God loves not the aggressors* (*Al-Baqarah*, 2:190).

When a legitimate jihad is waged, it must not be based on anger and hatred. The Qur'an thus warns: *Let not your hatred of a people cause you to be unjust. You must do justice* (*Al-Mā'idah*, 5:8). The believers were also directed to *repel the evil deed with one that is better, then verily he, between whom and thee there was enmity (will become) as though he were a protective friend* (*Fuṣṣilat*, 41:34).

Islamic law provides a clear set of rules that regulate military engagement, which have not, however, been consistently followed. The Prophet ﷺ instructed the warriors to avoid harming women and children, the aged, monks and priests, the blind and the insane, and refrain from acts of brutality and maiming. Destruction of livestock, trees and crops was also forbidden unless it was for the purpose of sustaining life. Innocent human life should be immune from all forms of unlawful aggression, as the Qur'an proclaims: *Whosoever kills a human being for other than manslaughter or corruption in the earth, it shall be as if he had killed all humanity* (*Al-Mā'idah*, 5:32).

The majority of Sunni and Shi'i jurists have held that jihad is legitimate only in defence against aggression. They also maintain that jihad must be declared by the legitimate leader. Hence no group, party or organisation has the authority to take up arms in the name of jihad without authorisation by lawful authorities. For there will otherwise be disorder and anarchy. This is the purport of the hadith which provides that: 'A Muslim ruler is the shield [of his people]. A war can only be waged under him and people should seek his shelter [in war].'[13]

From his reading of the source evidence, Ibn Qayyim al-Jawziyyah (d. 1350 CE/751 AH) divided jihad into four main varieties: i) jihad against the self; ii) jihad against the unbelievers; iii) jihad against the hypocrites; and iv) jihad against the agents of corruption.[14]

Each of these has been subdivided into four types: a) jihad of the heart; b) jihad of the tongue; c) jihad by wealth; and d) jihad by person. Thus a total of sixteen varieties of jihad come into the picture, most of which consist of peaceful struggle for a good cause. The last variety, that is, of jihad in person, includes military jihad, but also actions such as care for the ill and personal service.[15] Jihad against the self is the foundation of all jihad, for fighting an external enemy would not be possible without a successful engagement in inner jihad. Jihad by one's words consists of education and advice given to promote good and prevent evil. This is known in the present-day Arab countries as *jihad al-tarbiyah* (the education effort). In the Twelver Imami Shi'i doctrine, to quote Nasr again, 'all the eminent authorities have consequently maintained that jihad, except for self defence, is forbidden in the absence of the ma'sum, that is "the inerrant Imam"'.[16]

Western media is apt to associate war and violence with Islam. The book before us forcefully refutes this through a reading mainly of the Qur'an and Hadith—letting these sources speak for themselves, as it were, before the learned authors advance their own interpretations and insights. Some sections of the present volume also review factual historical evidence on warfare. 'The fact is,' as Ali Mazrui wrote, that 'in the last 100 years, western civilisation has killed millions more people than any other way of life in the annals of man in a comparable unit of time ... It has also been the West in the last 100 years which had made warfare less and less respectful of civilian life.'[17]

Mahmud Shaltut, the late Shaykh of al-Azhar from 1958 to 1963, and the contemporary Grand Mufti of Egypt, Shaykh 'Ali Gomaa, have shown in their writings in the book before us that the Qur'an only allows war for self-defence. Another Shaykh of al-Azhar, Muhammad Sayyid Tantawi, issued a fatwa in 2001 to condemn hostage taking in the Philippines: 'Islam rejects all forms of violence. These acts of violence have nothing to do with Islam.' He also condemned the terrorist act of September 11, 2001 in the United States.[18] The Chief Mufti of Saudi Arabia, Abdulaziz bin Abdallah Āl al-Shaykh, similarly declared in 2004:

> You must know Islam's firm position against all these terrible crimes. The world must know that Islam is a religion of peace ... justice and guidance ... Islam forbids the hijacking of airplanes, ships and other means of transport, and it forbids all acts that undermine the security of the innocent.[19]

Seyyed Hossein Nasr added his voice to say:

> Those who carry out terrorism in the West or elsewhere in the name of jihad are vilifying an originally sacred term, and their efforts have not been accepted by established and mainstream religious authorities as jihad.[20]

The Jeddah-based Islamic Fiqh Academy affiliated to the Organisation of the Islamic Conference (OIC), in its sixteenth session (5–10 January 2002) vehemently condemned all manifestation of terrorism and its attributions to Islam:

> Terrorism is an outrageous attack carried out either by individuals, groups or states against the human being. It includes all forms of intimidation, harm, threats, killing without a just cause, all forms of armed robbery, banditry, every act of violence or threat intended to fulfil a criminal scheme individually or collectively, terrify and horrify people by hurting them or by exposing their lives, liberty, and security to danger. It can also take the form of inflicting damage on the environment, a public or private utility— all of which are resolutely forbidden in Islam.

In her article *The Revolt of Islam*, Nikkie Kiddie, a US professor of Middle Eastern history, explains the rise of militancy among Muslims. She notes that with the exception perhaps of Wahhabism, militant jihad movements in the modern era began and grew mostly as a response to Western colonialism. The earliest examples in the eighteenth century in Sumatra and West Africa emerged in the face of 'disruptive economic change influenced by the West'. In the nineteenth century, broader waves of jihad movements cropped up in Algeria, Sudan, the Caucasus, and Libya as 'a direct response to French, British, Russian and Italian colonial conquest'.[21]

The remainder of this Introduction consists of a summary of the conditions under which military jihad may legitimately be waged. But it may be said in passing that the relationship of jihad to peace is one of means and end. Jihad is not an end in itself but a means towards peace, freedom of conscience and justice. Unlike the Romans, for example, who subscribed to the notion that *silent enim legis enter arma* (laws are silent during wars), Islamic law regulated war and proscribed acts of oppression and injustice in the name of jihad. A set of rules were thus formulated to be observed before the onset of war, during it, and after the war ends—which manifest in principle that laws are not silent during war. The book before us is an articulation of the conditions and restraints that the shariʿah imposes on jihad, just as it also underlines the message that the quest for peace and justice must be the overriding purpose of all jihad. Whereas jihad has been widely covered in the existing literature, this book is distinguished by the insight it offers into the source evidence, not only on jihad, but also on Islam's teachings on peace, fraternity and love.

To summarise the conditions of jihad:

1) First and foremost, every effort must be made to avoid war. War can only take place after all peaceful efforts to prevent it fail.
2) All war in Islam is defensive, a struggle for liberation to defend one's freedom of conscience, home, property or homeland from aggression.
3) Jihad must not be waged for ignoble purposes, personal objectives and revenge. No personal interest or private gain should be the aim of jihad.
4) Jihad must be declared by a legitimate ruler, but only after necessary consultation with people of specialised knowledge and technical know-how.
5) Justice must prevail during armed jihad. Excessive violence and acts of brutality, maiming and dishonouring the human dignity of the deceased must be avoided.
6) Action may be taken only against armed combatants. Civilians and persons who are neither involved nor trained to be engaged

in combat may not be targeted. Killing and harming women and children is prohibited.

7) Animals, crops and trees are to be spared unless it be for sustaining life. Polluting the environment, rivers, wells and demolition of houses is prohibited.
8) Treachery and deception, killing and attacking people by surprise is prohibited.
9) Looting and plunder are prohibited, and people's rights and properties may not be violated.
10) The enemy must be among those with whom fighting is permitted as compared to those with whom at truce has been agreed. Breach of valid international agreements and treaties is a violation of the rules of jihad.
11) It is impermissible to use human shields in jihad.
12) Even during conflict, all possible efforts must be made to end war.
13) Prisoners of war (POWs) must be treated humanely and their lives protected; they are entitled to dignified treatment, and fulfilment of their essential needs.
14) If ransom is paid for a POW, he or she must be freed. Ransom can consist of teaching ten Muslims to read and write.
15) Religious persecution and forced conversion cannot be the aim of jihad. On the contrary, jihad must seek to establish freedom of religion and enable people to practice their religious convictions freely.
16) Places of worship, churches and synagogues must not be targeted. Monks and priests who are not involved in violence must not be harmed.
17) If a prisoner of war embraces Islam freely and willingly, he or she must be freed.

Mohammad Hashim Kamali
International Institute of Advanced Islamic Studies (IAIS) Malaysia
Kuala Lumpur, May 2013

ABOUT THE CONTRIBUTORS (in Alphabetical Order)

Prof. Ismail Albayrak was born in Ankara in 1968. Upon receiving his primary and secondary education he began to study in the School of Divinity/Ankara where graduated in 1991. In 1994 he won a scholarship from the Turkish Higher Education Council to continue his postgraduate studies abroad. For this purpose, in 1995 he went to England. Ismail received his PhD degree from Leeds University in 2000. Since then he has been working at Sakarya University, Adapazarı/Turkey, where he teaches and writes on Qur'anic Studies, classical exegesis, contemporary approaches to the Qur'an and Orientalism. He is also interested in the place of Muslim communities and their activities in globalisation, together with the study of interfaith dialogue. In January 2008 he was appointed to the newly established Fethullah Gülen Chair in the Study of Islam and Muslim-Catholic Relations at the Australian Catholic University.

Dr Karim Douglas Crow is Principal Research Fellow at the International Institute of Advanced Islamic Studies (IAIS), Malaysia in Kuala Lumpur since 2008. He received his Doctorate in Islamic Studies from the Institute of Islamic Studies at McGill University in Montreal. Born in Beirut of Lebanese and American parents, he studied in Damascus and Cairo, and earned his BA and MA from the American University of Beirut. His research and publications centre on the functions of intelligence and rationality in Islam; metaphysical and spiritual topics in Asian societies; the Sunni–Shi'ah schism (his edited volume *Facing One Qiblah*, Singapore 2005); and Islamic Peace studies. Current research examines civilisational implications of globalising trends within Muslim societies; rationality and modernity; and ethical & philosophic dimensions of Muslim thinking (his edited volume *Islam, Cultural Transformation and the Re-emergence of Falsafah*, Tehran 2009). He is working on several books: *Consuming Islam: In Search of Islamic Lifestyle*; and *Lamp of Knowledge: Career & Teaching of Ja'far al-Ṣādiq* [IIP, forthcoming]. For the past sixteen years Professor Crow has served as advisor for non-governmental programs on Islamic peace education in the Arab world, the Caucasus, Iran, and Indonesia. He participates regularly in international colloquia in Asia and Europe.

Dr Caner K. Dagli is an Assistant Professor in the Department of Religious Studies at the College of the Holy Cross in Worcester, MA, USA. He is a general editor of the forthcoming *Study Quran*, and has published in the fields of Islamic philosophy and Sufism. In 2006–2007 he was an advisor for interfaith affairs to the Hashemite Royal Court of Jordan.

Dr David Dakake is an American Muslim specialising in comparative religion and Islamic philosophy. He has travelled extensively in Egypt and Iran and holds an MA in Religious Studies from Temple University. He has spent many years studying with traditional masters of Islamic philosophy, while publishing articles on Islamic history and philosophy. Formerly a consultant for the Islamic Research Institute in Washington D.C., he is currently employed as an Adjunct Professor in the Religious Studies Department at George Mason University in Fairfax, Virginia where he teaches classes on Judaism, Christianity, Islam and other world religions.

HRH Prince Ghazi bin Muhammad bin Talal (b. 1966) is the nephew of the late King Al-Hussein bin Talal of Jordan. He was educated at Harrow School; received his BA from Princeton University in 1988 *Summa cum laude*; his first PhD from Cambridge University, U.K., in 1993, and his second PhD from Al-Azhar University in Cairo 2010. Prince Ghazi has held many advisory official positions in Jordan including: *Cultural Secretary* to H.M. King Hussein; *Advisor for Tribal Affairs* to H.M. King Hussein; *Personal Envoy of and Special Advisor* to H.M. King Abdullah II, and *Chief Advisor for Religious and Cultural Affairs* to H.M. King Abdullah II. In 1996 Prince Ghazi founded the Al-Balqa Applied University, and in 2008 he founded the World Islamic Sciences and Education University (WISE). In 1997 he founded the National Park of the Site of the Baptism of Jesus Christ ﷺ, and in 2000 he established the Great Tafsir Project (www.Altafsir.com), the largest online project for exegesis of the Holy Qur'an. He was the author of 'Three Articles of the Amman Message' in 2005; the author of the historic open letter 'A Common Word Between Us and You' in 2007, and the author of the World Interfaith Harmony Week United Nations General Assembly Resolution in October 2010. In 2012 he established the Al-Ghazali Integral Professorial Chair in Al-Aqsa Mosque and Al-Quds University, and the Al-Razi Integral Professorial Chair in the King Hussein Mosque and Jordan University. Prince Ghazi is also Chairman of the Board of Trustees of The Royal Aal al-Bayt Institute for Islamic Thought. In 2012 he founded the Prince Ghazi Trust for Qur'anic Thought. Prince Ghazi is the author of a number of books and articles—including the widely-acclaimed work *Love in the Holy Qur'an*—as well as the recipient of a number of awards and decorations including the Eugen Biser Prize (2008) and the St. Augustine Award for Interfaith Dialogue (2012).

HE Shaykh Ali Gomaa is the former Grand Mufti of the Arab Republic of Egypt. He was the second highest Sunni authority in Egypt after Shaykh Ahmad al-Tayyeb and one of the foremost Islamic scholars in the world. Gomaa was responsible for Daral Ifta al Masriyyah, a leading institute for Islamic legal research, and the legal arm of the Egyptian Ministry of Justice, which is responsible for passing official religious rulings.

Prof. Joel Hayward is currently Professor of International and Civil Security at Khalifa University in Abu Dhabi. Previously he was a Senior Fellow at the Markfield Institute of Higher Education and a Fellow of the Cambridge Muslim College. His career highlights include having been the Dean of the Royal Air Force College for five years, a Director of the Royal Air Force Centre for Air Power Studies for four years, and the Head of King's College London's Air Power Studies Division for six years. Professor Hayward is the author or editor of nine books and monographs as well as many book chapters and journal articles, some of which have appeared in German, Russian, Portuguese, Spanish and Serbian translations. He is a member of the British Armed Forces Muslim Association and serves as Strategic Policy Advisor to Shaykh Dr Muhammad Tahir-ul-Qadri. Unusually for a social scientist, he is also active in the literary arts and has published both fiction and poetry.

His second collection of poetry was published in 2011. He writes regular columns in Emel and other Islamic magazines.

Prof. Ibrahim Kalin, PhD, is Chief Advisor to the Prime Minister of Turkey. Dr Kalin is the founding director of the SETA Foundation for Political, Economic and Social Research based in Ankara, Turkey and served as its director from 2005 to 2009. He is a fellow at the Prince Alwaleed Center for Muslim-Christian Understanding, Georgetown University. Professor Kalin has a PhD from the George Washington University and is a broadly trained scholar of philosophy and Islamic studies. He has taught courses on Islamic philosophy, comparative philosophy, Islam-West relations and Turkish foreign policy. His field of concentration is post-Avicennan Islamic philosophy with research interests in comparative philosophy and Muslim-Christian relations. He has served as spokesperson for the *A Common Word* Initiative.

Prof. Mohammad Hashim Kamali is the Founding Chairman and CEO of the International Institute of Advanced Islamic Studies (IAIS) Malaysia. He was Professor of Islamic Law and Jurisprudence at the International Islamic University Malaysia (1985-2004), and also Dean of the International Institute of Islamic Thought and Civilization (ISTAC) from 2004 to 2006. He was a member and sometime chairman of the Constitution Review Commission of Afghanistan (2003) and also served as a UNDP Advisor on constitutional reform in the Maldives (2004 and 2007). He advised on the new constitution of Iraq (2004-2005) and the proposed new constitution of Somalia. Professor Kamali is a member of the Shariah Advisory Council of the Securities Commission Malaysia, and also serves on the advisory boards of thirteen local and international academic journals. He has addressed over 150 national and international conferences and has published twenty books and over 140 academic articles. He is an original signatory of *A Common Word Between Us and You* (2007). Professor Kamali appears in The 500 Most Influential Muslims in the World, 2009 & 2010. He was a recipient of the 'Isma'il al-Faruqi Award for Academic Excellence' in 1995 and again in 1997. He received the King Abdullah II bin al-Hussein International Award 2010 from H.M. King Abdullah of Jordan, in recognition of his outstanding academic contributions towards serving Islam and the Muslims.

Dr Joseph Lumbard is an assistant professor of classical Islam at Brandeis University. Professor Lumbard researches Islamic intellectual traditions with an emphasis on Sufism and Islamic philosophy. He is the editor of *Islam, Fundamentalism, and the Betrayal of Tradition* (World Wisdom, 2004), a collection of essays that examines the religious, political and historical factors that have led to the rise of Islamic fundamentalism. Currently, Professor Lumbard is researching the development of Sufi theories of love in the early Islamic period and their influence on the Persian Sufi tradition. He completed his PhD at Yale University in 2003.

Shaykh Sayyid Hasan Saqqaf is Hasan ibn ʿAli ibn Hashim ibn Ahmad, Abu Hashim al-Saqqaf al-Husayni, a contemporary Shafiʿi scholar and professor of hadith. Based in Amman, Jordan, his shaykhs include Hashim Majdhub of Damascus in Shafiʿi jurisprudence, Muti' Hammami in estate division, and Muhammad Hulayyil in Arabic grammar. Shaykh Saqqaf has been given written authorisation in the Shadhili *ṭarīqah* and hadith from Shaykh ʿAbdullah Ghimari of Tangiers. He teaches a circle of students in Amman and has published over forty-five books and treatises of tenets of faith, jurisprudence, and heresiology.

Dr Reza Shah-Kazemi is an author who specialises in comparative mysticism, Islamic Studies, Sufism and Shi'ism. He is the founding editor of the Islamic World Report and is currently a Research Associate at the Institute of Ismaili Studies with the Department of Academic Research and Publications. He received degrees in International Relations and Politics at Sussex and Exeter University, before receiving his doctorate in Comparative Religion from the University of Kent in 1994. He later acted as a consultant to the Institute for Policy Research in Kuala Lampur. Dr Shah-Kazemi has authored several works including *The Spirit of Tolerance in Islam* (IIS/IB Tauris, 2012); *Spiritual Quest: Reflections on Qur'anic Prayer according to the teachings of Imam ʿAli* (IIS/IB Tauris, 2011); *Common Ground Between Islam and Buddhism* (Fons Vitae, 2010); *Paths to Transcendence: According to Shankara, Ibn Arabi and Meister*

Eckhart (World Wisdom, 2006); *Justice and Remembrance: Introducing the Spirituality of Imam 'Ali* (IIS/IB Tauris, 2006) and *The Other in the Light of the One: The Universality of the Qur'an and Interfaith Dialogue* (Islamic Texts Society, 2006).

Grand Imam Mahmoud Shaltut was born in 1893 and was a great Egyptian religious scholar, jurist, Qur'anic exegete and reformer. He was appointed by Gamal Abdel-Nasser to the prestigious position of Grand Imam of Al-Azhar at a key time in Egyptian history, from 1958 until Shaykh Shaltut's death in 1963. As Grand Imam of Al-Azhar, Shaltut's reforms focused on the separation of the state and religious institutions, particularly Al-Azhar. He also dedicated himself to showing the world that Islamic shari'ah law is not at odds with modern society and that it is a guiding light through the changes and challenges of contemporary life. Shaykh Shaltut strove to combat sectarianism in Islam and encouraged harmony in the interactions between Sunnis and Shi'ites. He was a powerful orator and his finely honed communication skills extended to his writing, particularly his Qur'anic exegesis. His writings are known for their straightforward language, eloquence and accessibility to the layperson. Imam Shaltut will always be remembered for his efforts to show the world that Islam is a religion of unity, flexibility, moderation and reason.

Dr Naveed Sheikh holds a First Class BA (hons) in Politics and Modern History from the University of Buckingham where he completed his degree in two years, received five merit prizes for academic excellence and graduated with the university's highest honour, the Edgar Palamountain Medal of Excellence, presented to him by Lady Thatcher in 1997. He also has an MA in International Relations (with distinction) from the University of Durham where his dissertation received the highest mark since the founding of the Department of Politics. He proceeded to enrol for a PhD at the Centre of International Studies at the University of Cambridge, working on a thesis on nuclear non-/proliferation and identity imaginaries. He has held fellowships at Harvard University (2001–02) and Hosei University in Tokyo (2003–4). He joined SPIRE as a permanent lecturer in International Relations in September 2005.

PART I: WAR AND ITS PRACTICE

CHAPTER ONE

THE QUR'AN AND COMBAT

Grand Imam Mahmoud Shaltut

Thanks be to God, and peace be upon His Messenger, Muhammad, who was sent by God as a mercy to all mankind. God revealed the Holy Qur'an to the Prophet Muhammad to clarify all things; it prescribes for humanity correct doctrine and high morality and shows us how to organise our relationships with each other in a manner that wards off tyranny and preserves rights.

This is a study of combat (*qitāl*) gleaned from the Holy Qur'an; it is from a series of lectures I delivered on Egyptian radio. I wished to present it again in written form so that people may read it and benefit and so that, if they are so inclined, people may also offer their opinions on the matter.

In the introduction I include what I see as the ideal approach to Qur'anic exegesis. I also discuss the reason that drove me to choose this subject in particular.

The research discusses the following subjects: the nature of the call to Islam (*da'wah*); the Holy Qur'an and the legitimacy of combat; and the Holy Qur'an and the organisation of combat and its rules. The research concludes that the practical combat which the Prophet ﷺ and his two caliphs undertook was an exact and correct application of what the Holy Qur'an prescribes in regards to legitimate combat, its organisation and its rules.

This is what you will read in this study and it is my fervent hope that God has inspired me to write with reason and with wisdom.

> *My success is only with God. In Him I trust and to Him I turn [repentant].* (*Hūd*, 11:88)

The Ideal Approach to Qur'anic Exegesis

There are two approaches to Qur'anic exegesis:

The First Approach: The exegete explains the verses and chapters of the Holy Qur'an in their traditional order and elucidates the meaning of words and the relationships between verses. This is the approach that people have become familiar with, as it is as old as Qur'anic exegesis itself. One characteristic of this approach is that exegesis is as varied as the exegetes who interpret the verses. For example, exegetes who are immersed in the sciences of rhetoric will employ rhetoric in interpreting the verses of the Holy Qur'an. Likewise, exegetes who are immersed in morphology and syntax will employ parsing words as a means of interpretation. Exegetes who are immersed in history will employ stories and news; they may even be tempted to take this too far and relate Judaica, or *Isrā'īliyyāt*; stories without due investigation or scrutiny. Furthermore, exegetes who are immersed in philosophy will enjoy discussing creatures and creation and this will be reflected in their exegesis. When they are immersed in theology and jurisprudence, their interpretation will no doubt be coloured by these things and so on and so forth. These varied approaches to Qur'anic exegesis may make it difficult for people who turn to Qur'anic commentaries for Divine Guidance, reassurance and wisdom to find these things.

As a result of this approach, verses are sometimes explained in ways that alter their true meaning or purpose; sometimes they are even considered to have been abrogated. Often verses are interpreted on the basis of fundamental rules derived from jurisprudential branches by heads of *madhāhib*. These rules are taken to be fundamentals, and are referred to in understanding the Holy Qur'an and the Sunnah and in deriving rules and laws. This does not stop at legislation, or at the Verses of Legislation, but encroaches into the area of beliefs and different groups' opinions. Thus we may hear them say: 'This verse does not agree with the Sunni *madhāhib* because its allegorical interpretation (*ta'wīl*) is such and such.' Or they may say: 'This verse does not agree with the Hanafi *madhab* as its allegorical interpretation is such and such.' Or they might say: 'This verse, or these verses—around seventy of them—are incompatible with the legitimacy of combat (*qitāl*) and are therefore abrogated.'

Thus the Holy Qur'an has become the branch after it was the root, a follower after it was followed, and something weighed on a scale after it was the scale on which all things took their measure. God says in the Holy Qur'an:

> *If you should quarrel about anything, refer it to God and the Messenger, if you believe in God and the Last Day.* (*Al-Nisā'*, 4:59)

Referring to God is referring to His Book, and referring to the Prophet ﷺ is referring to his Sunnah. But some have reversed this and have overturned legislation and referred God's Book and the Sunnah of His Prophet to their opinions and the *madhāhib* of their imitators. God says:

> *They have taken their rabbis and their monks as lords beside God …* (*Al-Tawbah*, 9:31)

In his exegesis of this verse al-Fakhr al-Razi related that his shaykh said: 'I witnessed a group of jurist imitators listen as verses from the Holy Qur'an were recited to them in relation to particular issues; their *madhāhib* were at odds with these verses and they did not accept them or pay them any heed. Instead, they continued to look at me in astonishment as if to say: "How can we comply with what these verses say when the narrative of those who came before us is at odds with them?"' As Razi related this about his shaykh, so have many other scholars such as Ghazali, al-Izz bin Abdul-Salaam and many others.

These circuitous methods of interpreting the Holy Qur'an, and this setback that the relationship between the Qur'an and jurisprudence and beliefs suffered, caused a kind of intellectual chaos towards the Holy Qur'an and the meanings of the Qur'an. This chaos had an impact in making people feel averse to the Holy Qur'an and listening to exegetes.

The Second Approach: The exegete collects all the verses pertaining to a particular subject and analyses them collectively, studying how they relate to each other. In this way he can arrive at a proper judgement of the verses and become clear on what the verses are saying. With this approach the exegete also cannot impose an interpretation on any verse, rather the verse reveals its meaning; and the exegete does not miss the wonders of the Divine Word. In our view, this second approach is the ideal approach to Qur'anic exegesis; particularly if the intent is to spread the Qur'an's guidance and to show that the topics the Qur'an deals with are not purely theoretical, with no practical application in everyday life.

This approach also enables the exegete to deal with many practical issues, each one separate and independent. This way people may know the subjects of the Holy Qur'an with their clear titles, and know how closely linked the Qur'an is to their practical daily lives. These subjects include: the Qur'an and the roots of legislation; the Qur'an and science, the Qur'an and the family, the Qur'an and the etiquette of social gatherings, the Qur'an and tourism, the Qur'an and economics, the Qur'an and sacrifice, the Qur'an and kindness and so on and so forth on subjects that build a strong and flourishing nation. In this way people are assured, in a practical and clear manner that the Holy Qur'an is not far removed from their lives or the way they think or their problems. They are assured that the Holy Qur'an is not just a spiritual book whose sole mission is to explain how to be closer to the Almighty without concerning itself with the practical exigencies of daily life. This false and pernicious notion is widespread, not only among the general public, but also among many people who claim, or whom others claim, to be scholars. In the eyes of such people the Holy Qur'an becomes merely a collection of texts to recite or listen to in times of meditation, or a tool through which to invoke God's protection or seek healing. This is an injustice to the Holy Qur'an, indeed an injustice to themselves, their minds and their chances for a good life which they have deprived of an unstinting source of knowledge, wisdom, legislation, politics, education, refinement and all one needs to manage the issues that life throws at humans. God says in the Holy Qur'an:

> *Truly this Qur'an guides to that which is straightest and gives tidings to the believers who perform righteous deeds that there is a great reward for them.* (*Al-Isrā'*, 17:9)

This approach that we have described bears generous fruit to those who follow it and protects them from thinking ill of the Holy Qur'an and its legislation. It also puts the exegete face to face with the subject he wishes to discuss and places him in an environment steeped in relevant verses; he may use one to understand another. The most correct explanation of the Holy Qur'an is the explanation the exegete absorbs from the Qur'an itself. It is often that an ordinary person perusing the Holy Qur'an misses the secret in a particular verse, but when he reads a sister verse discussing the same subject, the secret is unveiled and revealed to him.

It was our wish, and that of some men blessed with religious insight, to share this new approach to Qur'anic exegesis so that the topics of the Holy Qur'an may be known and studied purely, in a manner innocent of the impurities that may veil the Qur'an's truth or distort its beauty. Our wish is for the Qur'an to be studied far from the circuitous approach, and in a manner that transcends extrinsic tales and imaginings that no sound mind seeking truth could possibly believe. It is my hope that in this new approach to Qur'anic exegesis people may find what their souls yearn for, in terms of learning about the guidance of the Holy Qur'an and contemplating its secrets and its wisdom and benefitting from its principles and teachings.

Years ago, I applied this second approach to the subject of 'The Qur'an and Women' and I believe that those who read it with good intent met it with an open and assured heart. The topic I should now like to discuss, utilising the second approach, is 'The Qur'an and Combat'. Combat is a very real issue in these troubled times and many people disparage Islam, with regards to the matter of combat. Learning the Holy Qur'an's wise prescriptions and rules regarding combat, its justifiable causes and its purpose has never been more pressing. The Holy Qur'an proves to us that Islam loves peace and hates bloodshed and the loss of life for the sake of the transient and the ephemeral; it also hates greed, gluttony and love of killing. Those who terrorise the world with their lethal wars should know how far they have deviated from Islam, which they believe is the only religion of peace. They should ask themselves if it is logical that a religion which calls for peace and for people to devote what God has given them to good and to building, and not to what is harmful and destructive, would be a religion that approves of its followers terrorising the world and causing heartache and laying waste to once-flourishing cities and cultures. They even go so far as to say that their religion is the religion of peace and that other religions are religions of war established by the sword and coercion.

(*The section 'The Nature of Islamic Da'wah' has been omitted—an unabridged version of the text of Shaltut's* The Qur'an and Combat *can be found at www.mabda.jo.*)

There is absolutely no reason or justification for anyone to believe or presume that the Islamic *da'wah* forces people to believe in Islam by means of the sword and combat.

First: The nature of the Islamic *da'wah* is free of complexity, ambiguity and intellectual hardship that would require manifest or surreptitious coercion[22].

Second: Islamic shari'ah law, taken from the Qur'an, is not in contravention of, or in opposition to, God's cosmic Sunnah which He made the basis for the faith of the believers and the basis for the disbelief of the unbelievers i.e. man is free to choose for himself through examination and conviction.

Third: Islamic shari'ah law, taken from the precise and unambiguous verses of the Holy Qur'an, rejects the use of coercion as a means to call people to God, as do the laws of the other preceding (Divinely revealed) religions.

Fourth: The Prophet Muhammad ﷺ was the first person to take on the responsibility of *da'wah*, and as such he was responsible before God for the sole task of his Message which the Holy Qur'an expounded in both its Meccan and Medinan parts. The task was to convey and warn, not to use coercion and violence to demand faith from people.[23]

Fifth: The Holy Qur'an, which is the source of the Islamic *da'wah*, does not respect faith that has been coerced and forced and denies its validity on the Day of Resurrection. How then could it enjoin coercion or allow it as a method of calling people to believe in the Message of Islam?

We know these conclusions from the Qur'an itself and believing in them is part of believing in the Holy Qur'an. Here one may ask: 'Given these conclusions, what is the significance of the Verses of Combat (*Ayāt Al-Qitāl*) in the Holy Qur'an?'

This will be the subject of our next section.

The Verses of Combat (Āyāt Al-Qitāl)

In this chapter we will review the Verses of Combat in the Holy Qur'an in order to understand their meaning, significance, purpose and their relation to each other. Then we shall arrive at a conclusion regarding the verses which command combat and, together with the conclusions reached in the preceding section, we shall elucidate the verses.

The Holy Qur'an expounds two kinds of combat: the first is combat between Muslims and the second is combat between Muslims and non-Muslims.

First: Combat between Muslims is an internal matter of the Muslim Ummah and is governed by its own laws, relating only to the Ummah and no one else. The Holy Qur'an is clear about how to handle instances of rebellion and breach of public order, whether between subjects or between subjects and rulers. It legislates how to manage such situations in a manner that preserves the unity of the Muslim Ummah and the authority and standing of the ruling body in a manner that protects the community from the evils of aggression and hostility. This is clear in the following verses from *Sūrat Al-Ḥujurāt*:

> *And if two parties of believers fall to warfare, make peace between them. And if one of them aggresses against the other, fight the one which aggresses until it returns to God's ordinance. Then, if it returns, reconcile them, and act justly. Surely God loves the just. / The believers are indeed brothers. Therefore [always] make peace between your brethren, and fear God, so that perhaps you might receive mercy.* (*Al-Ḥujurāt*, 49:9–10)

These two verses discuss a situation where disagreement that cannot be solved by peaceful means breaks out between two groups of believers, and both groups resort to the use of force and the judgment of the sword. The verses stipulate that the Ummah, represented by its government, should investigate the causes of strife between the two groups and try to reconcile them. If this is achieved through negotiations, and both parties receive their dues, aggression is warded off and security restored; thus God saves the believers from combat. If, however, one of the groups continues to aggress against the other, refuses to comply with God's commands and attacks the authority of the believers, then it has become an aggressor that has rebelled against the rule of law and the system. In this case, the community of Muslims must fight (*qitāl*) it until it submits and returns to what is righteous. The verses then clarify the secret to successfully resolving any discord that might arise between different groups. The secret is that when a group returns to what is righteous, they may not be oppressed or deprived of their rights; indeed, justice must prevail and each group must be given its dues. Consider the end of the first verse (*Al-Ḥujurāt*, 49:9): *Surely God loves the just.* The verses tell us that the intention behind the legislation is the preservation of the unity and indivisibility of the Ummah and the safeguarding of religious brotherhood; one of the important matters of faith. The second verse says:

> *The believers are indeed brothers. Therefore [always] make peace between your brethren, and fear God, so that perhaps you might receive mercy.* (*Al-Ḥujurāt*, 49:10)

These wise Qur'anic legislations were revealed by an illiterate Prophet to ensure peace and bring an end to aggression and violence. They were revealed more than thirteen centuries before the human mind came up with the 'League of Nations' or the 'Security Council' as means to preserve peace and guarantee liberties and rights for people and states.

If nations understood these wise legislations properly, gave them the attention they deserve and followed them, they would never go astray from the path of wisdom and they would have been spared the repeated catastrophes caused by aggression and violence on the one hand and disagreement and division on the other. These are the rules legislated by the Holy Qur'an regarding combat between Muslims. This combat clearly has no bearing on the principles of Islamic *da'wah* and faith in its Message.

Second: Combat between Muslims and non-Muslims. The Holy Qur'an expounds in a comprehensive manner, in many verses and chapters, the legitimate causes and purposes of combat between Muslims and non-Muslims. It enjoins that when the purposes of legitimate combat are achieved, it must end. The Qur'an also elucidates what Muslims should be prepared for, and the necessary cautions they must take against an unexpected outbreak of war. The Holy Qur'an clarifies the rules and regulations of this kind of combat, in addition to those of truces and treaties. In the following we shall discuss the verses dealing with the causes of this kind of combat, and how it must stop when its purposes are achieved. We will then discuss the relationship between the Verses of Forgiveness and the Verses of Combat.

The early Muslims spent many years in Mecca suffering the worst kinds of punishment, they were not free to worship, were persecuted for believing in a creed that brought them reassurance and were terrorised with regard to property and personal safety. All this continued until they were forced to emigrate. They left their homes and settled in Medina, patiently accepting God's will. Whenever they felt the urge to resist oppression and seek revenge, the Prophet held them back and urged them to be patient and await God's will. The Prophet ﷺ said: 'I have not been ordered to fight (*qitāl*).' This lasted until they were almost overcome by despair and doubt. Just then God revealed the first Verses of Combat:

> *Permission is granted to those who fight because they have been wronged. And God is truly able to help them; / those who were expelled from their homes without right, only because they said: 'Our Lord is God'. Were it not for God's causing some people to drive back others, destruction would have befallen the monasteries, and churches, and synagogues, and mosques in which God's Name is mentioned greatly. Assuredly God will help those who help Him. God is truly Strong, Mighty—/ those who, if We empower them in the land, maintain the prayer, and pay the alms, and enjoin decency and forbid indecency. And with God rests the outcome of all matters.* (*Al-Ḥajj*, 22:39–41)

These verses discuss and justify permission for combat because of the injustices the Muslims faced, and because they were expelled from their homes and forced to emigrate. The verses then explain that this permission is in line with the Sunnah of people clashing, which maintains a certain equilibrium and averts oppression. It also allows the adherents of different faiths to perform their religious rituals and preserve the doctrine of monotheism. Finally, these verses show that it is God's Sunnah to help those who help Him, the pious who do not use war as an instrument for destruction and corruption, for subjugating the weak and satisfying their own desires and ambitions. The verses make it clear that God helps those who, if they are empowered in the land, cultivate it with goodness and obey God's orders, and are causes for goodness and righteousness and not causes for what is wicked and corrupt. Indeed, God knows who is destructive and who is a cause for good. God says at the end of these verses: *And with God rests the outcome of all matters.*

As we have said, these verses are the first Verses of Combat. They are very clear and do not contain even the slightest evidence of coercion. On the contrary, they confirm that people clashing with each other is one of God's cosmic Sunnahs, inevitable for the preservation of order and the continuation of righteousness and civilisation. Without this principle, the earth would be corrupted and all the different places of worship would be destroyed. Indeed, that would happen if tyrants had control over religion, free to abuse it without restraint, coercing people to convert without anyone standing in their way. These verses are not specific to Muslims, they are about humanity in general; they state clearly that destruction would have befallen monasteries, churches and synagogues.

Now let us consider the Verses of Combat in *Sūrat Al-Baqarah*:

> *And fight in the way of God with those who fight against you, but aggress not; God loves not the aggressors. / And slay them wherever you come upon them, and expel them from where they expelled you; sedition is more grievous than slaying. But fight them not by the Sacred Mosque until they should fight you there; then if they fight you, slay them—such, is the requital of disbelievers. / But if they desist, surely God is Forgiving, Merciful. / Fight them till there is no sedition, and the religion is for God; then if they desist, there shall be no enmity, save against evildoers. / The sacred month for the sacred month; holy things demand retaliation; whoever commits aggression against you, then commit aggression against him in the manner that he committed against you; and fear God, and know that God is with the God-fearing.* (*Al-Baqarah*, 2:190–4)

These verses command the Muslims to fight (*qitāl*) in the way of God those who fight against them, to pursue them wherever they are and to scatter them as they have scattered the Muslims. The verses prohibit unprovoked aggression and emphasise that God does not love aggression or aggressors. The verses then explain that expelling people from their homes, terrorising and preventing them from living peacefully without fear for their lives or possessions is sedition worse than murder and bloodshed. Therefore, those who practice or provoke these things must be fought in the same manner as fighters must be fought. The verses also prohibit combat in holy places and during holy periods, unless Muslims are under attack in holy places or during holy periods. In these cases, Muslims are allowed to retaliate in equal proportion. The verses then clarify that when the purposes of legitimate combat are achieved, it must end. These purposes are that there be no sedition in matters of religion and that people enjoy religious freedom without oppression or torture. When these purposes are accomplished and people feel safe, combat must cease.

These verses and the principles they expounded regarding the reasons and purposes of combat do not contain even the slightest trace of the idea of coercion. On the contrary, these verses, like the ones that precede them, state clearly and distinctly that the reason the Muslims were ordered to fight (*qitāl*) is the aggression they faced and the fact that they had been expelled from their homes, and because God's sacred institutions had been violated. Another reason explained in the verses is the many attempts to create sedition in the faith of the Muslims. The verses also clarify the purpose behind such combat, which is to end violence against Muslims and to establish religious freedom devoted to God, free from any pressure or coercion.

We see the principles expounded in these verses in many other Verses of Combat in the following surahs of the Holy Qur'an: *Al-Nisā'*, *Al-Anfāl* and *Al-Tawbah*. God says in *Sūrat Al-Nisā'*:

> *What is wrong with you, that you do not fight in the way of God, and for the oppressed men, women, and children who say, 'Our Lord, bring us forth from this town whose people are evildoers and appoint for us a protector from You, and appoint for us from You a helper'.* (*Al-Nisā'*, 4:75)
>
> *So fight in the way of God; you are charged only with yourself. And urge on the believers; maybe God will restrain the might of the disbelievers; God is mightier and more severe in castigation.* (*Al-Nisā'*, 4:84)
>
> *... And so if they stay away from you and do not fight you, and offer you peace, then God does not allow you any way against them. / ... So, if they do not stay away from you, and offer you peace, and restrain their hands, then take them and slay them wherever you come upon them; against them We have given you clear warrant.* (*Al-Nisā'*, 4:90–1)

Consider the following in these verses: ...maybe God will restrain the might of the disbelievers...and...if they do not stay away from you ...When we reflect on these verses we can understand the spirit of sedition that people harboured against Muslims and on account of which the Muslims were ordered to fight (*qitāl*) them. This is exactly the same principle that is expounded in the verses we sited from *Sūrat Al-Baqarah*, *Sūrat Al-Anfāl* and *Sūrat Al-Tawbah*. God says in *Sūrat Al-Anfāl*:

> *And fight them until sedition is no more and religion is all for God; then if they desist, surely God sees what they do.* (*Al-Anfāl*, 8:39)

This verse is similar to what God says in *Sūrat Al-Baqarah* and *Sūrat Al-Tawbah*:

> *But if they break their oaths after [making] their pact and assail your religion, then fight the leaders of unbelief—verily they have no [binding] oaths, so that they might desist. / Will you not fight a people who broke their oaths and intended to expel the Messenger—initiating against you first? Are you afraid of them? God is more worthy of your fear if you are believers.* (*Al-Tawbah*, 9:12–13)

> ... *And fight the idolaters altogether, even as they fight you altogether; and know that God is with those who fear Him.* (*Al-Tawbah*, 9:36)

Consider the following in these verses: *But if they break their oaths after [making] their pact and assail your religion* ... and *initiating against you first* ... and *even as they fight you altogether*. When we reflect on these verses we can understand that they were revealed about people who were recalcitrant in their sedition and in whom the elements of corruption were so deeply rooted that oaths had become of no value to them and virtue of no significance. There is no doubt that combat with these people, purifying the earth from them and ending their sedition is to serve the common good of mankind.

In *Sūrat Al-Tawbah*, after the verses we quoted above, there are two verses that at first consideration seem to contradict the principles regarding combat. We shall cite these two verses and clarify what they signify in light of the verses which precede, which are many and clear, and fundamental to the issue of the legality of combat (*qitāl*) and the reasons for it. Therefore, other verses must be compared to the principles contained in those verses and interpreted accordingly.

The first verse is:

> *Fight those who do not believe in God, nor in the Last Day, and who do not forbid what God and His Messenger have forbidden, nor do they practice the religion of truth, from among of those who have been given the Scripture, until they pay the jizyah tribute, readily being subdued.* (*Al-Tawbah*, 9:29)

The second verse is:

> *O you who believe, fight those of the disbelievers who are near to you, and let them find harshness in you, and know that God is with the pious.* (*Al-Tawbah*, 9:123)

The first verse commands the Muslims to fight (*qitāl*) a group that God describes as people who *do not believe in God*. This group has behaved towards the Muslims in a manner that is cause to fight them: they broke pacts, attacked the *da'wah* and placed obstacles in its path. However, the verses do not state that unbelief in God and the other descriptions mentioned are reasons for the Muslims to fight them; the verses only mention them as descriptions and clarifications. These descriptions are meant to serve as further incitement to fight them once their aggression materialises. For they changed God's religion to suit themselves and took their rabbis and monks as lords beside God (*Al-Tawbah*, 9:30), while allowing and forbidding things according to their whims, unbelieving in what God has decreed as forbidden or permissible. Nothing deters them from breaking pacts, violating rights and aggression. These are the people who, according to the above verses, must be fought continuously until they yield and desist from harm and spreading sedition. The Holy Qur'an introduces a symbol to signify this yielding; the payment of a tribute or poll tax (*jizyah*). The *jizyah* was a means through which people participated in shouldering the burdens of state and sharing the means for the common good of both Muslims and non-Muslims.[24]

The verse also indicates the reason for combat which we have already pointed out. The phrase *readily being subdued* shows us the state they will be in when the *jizyah* is collected from them, a state of yielding to the authority of the Muslims and living under their laws.

Doubtless this means that previously they had been recalcitrant and that there was good cause for the Muslims to fight them.

This is how this verse should be understood and its context brings it in line with the other verses. If the intention behind this verse was to have the Muslims fight them because of their unbelief and to show that unbelief was the reason why they were fought, then the verse would have stated that the purpose of this combat was to have them convert to Islam. In this case *jizyah* would not have been an acceptable result, nor indeed would allowing them to abide by their own religion.

The second verse, ... *fight those of the disbelievers who are near to you* ..., should not be compared with the previous verses which were revealed to clarify the reasons and causes for combat. This verse was revealed to show a practical war plan to be followed when legitimate combat breaks out. The verse guides the Muslims, stating that, when enemies are manifold, the nearest of them should be fought first and so on, in order to clear the road from enemies and to facilitate victory.[25]

This principle, established in the Holy Qur'an, is one of the principles followed today by warring states. No belligerent state attacks until it has cleared the path before it and until it is sure that all obstacles in its way have been removed. Thus, it is clear that these two verses have no link to the reason for combat as formulated by the other verses.

From what we have discussed one may infer:

—There is not a single verse in the Holy Qur'an that indicates that the aim of combat in Islam is conversion.

—The causes for combat—as seen in the preceding verses—are limited to fending off aggression, protecting the *da'wah* and safeguarding freedom of religion.

—When the Holy Qur'an prescribed combat, it distanced it from avarice, selfishness and the abasement of the meek. Indeed the Holy Qur'an intended combat (*qitāl*) only as a means to peace, security and a life of justice and equality.

—The *jizyah* was never intended as payment in return for one's life or retaining one's religion, it was intended as a symbol to signify yielding, an end of hostility and a participation in shouldering the burdens of the state.

After this has been explained, nobody can malign Islam or misinterpret the verses of the Holy Qur'an and assume what other ignorant people have assumed; that Islam has chosen combat (*qitāl*) as a means of propagating its *da'wah*, and that its calling was propagated by coercion and the use of force.

We shall now cite a verse from *Sūrat Al-Mumtaḥanah* that can be considered an Islamic ordinance regarding how Muslims should treat non-Muslims.

> *God does not forbid you in regard to those who did not wage war against you on account of religion and did not expel you from your homes, that you should treat them kindly and deal with them justly. Assuredly God loves the just. God only forbids you in regard to those who waged war against you on account of religion and expelled you from your homes and supported [others] in your expulsion, that you should make friends with them. And whoever makes friends with them, those—they are the wrongdoers.* (*Al-Mumtaḥanah*, 60:8–9)

Read this ordinance then recall *Sūrat Al-Mā'idah*, one of the last parts of the Holy Qur'an to be revealed, and note what it says about the relations between Muslims and non-Muslims:

> *Today the good things are permitted to you, and the food of those who were given the Scripture is permitted to you, and permitted to them is your food. Likewise, the believing married women, and the married women of those who were given the Scripture before you, if you give them their wages in wedlock, and not illicitly, or taking them as lovers. Whoever disbelieves in faith, his work has indeed failed, and in the Hereafter he shall be among the losers.* (*Al-Mā'idah*, 5:5)

When one considers these verses, one understands the sublime spirit that Islam possesses with regard to its relations with non-Muslims: kindness, justice, friendship and affinity. It is a relationship so magnificent that even the most modern principles of international relations known to man pale in comparison.

The Relationship between the Verses of Forgiveness and the Verses of Combat

It now behoves us to discuss an issue that has occupied the minds of many people while examining the Holy Qur'an and comparing its verses. These people fall into two categories:

A group that is antagonistic towards Islam and which searches the Holy Qur'an for faults.

A group of Qur'anic exegetes whose religious zeal drives them to reconcile between supposed inconsistencies within the Holy Qur'an.

This second group is inclined to consider that some verses abrogate others, and some of these exegetes allow themselves to get carried away to such an extent that they seem to have paved the road, unintentionally, for attacks by those who are antagonistic to Islam and to the Holy Qur'an.

The antagonists have examined the relationship between the different Verses of Combat (*Ayāt Al-Qitāl*) and the Verses of Combat as a whole; they have also examined the Verses of Pardon and Forgiveness. Their conclusion is that while some Verses of Combat permit combat, other verses urge combat and incite it. And while some verses order combat against those who aggress and forbid instigating aggression, other verses command that everyone be fought mercilessly, relentlessly and without distinction between aggressors and others. While these verses as a whole order and regulate combat, there are many other verses found in all surahs of the Holy Qur'an that command forgiveness, pardon, countering evil with good and a calling to the way of God with wisdom.

The antagonists claim that these are all contradictions incompatible with the idea that the Holy Qur'an was divinely revealed to the Prophet Muhammad ﷺ. As for those who love the Holy Qur'an and serve it, they hold that the Verses of Combat abrogate the Verses of Forgiveness and Pardon, even verses like (*Fuṣṣilat*, 41:34): *And they are not equal, the good deed and the evil deed. Repel with that which is better* ... and (*Al-Naḥl*, 16:125): *Call to the way of your Lord with wisdom and fair exhortation, and dispute with them by way of that which is best* .... They also say that (*Al-Tawbah*, 9:36): ... *fight the idolaters altogether, even as they fight you altogether* ... abrogates any preceding Verses of Forgiveness.

One of their more peculiar opinions is that (*Al-Baqarah*, 2:191): *And slay them wherever you come upon them* ... abrogates the immediately preceding verse (*Al-Baqarah*, 2:190): *And fight in the way of God with those who fight against you* ...' They also say that (*Al-Baqarah*, 2:193): *Fight them till there is no sedition* ... abrogates (*Al-Baqarah*, 2:191): ... *But fight them not by the Sacred Mosque until they should fight you there* ....

The above Qur'anic pericope from *Sūrat Al-Baqarah* is made up of four verses; two abrogating verses and two abrogated verses: the second verse abrogates the first and the fourth abrogates the third.

Al-Imam al-Razi commented on this opinion in his great work on Qur'anic exegesis *al-Tafsīr al-Kabīr*: 'It is improbable that the Wise One would combine verses in a row where each abrogates the other.' It is not improbable that this interpretation has paved the road for antagonists of Islam to say that the Holy Qur'an contains contradictions. They do not accept the notion of abrogation as claimed by lovers of the Holy Qur'an. Indeed how can they accept our claim when even some of our own scholars do not?

After this explanation, one can see that there is no contradiction or incompatibility between the different Verses of Combat and no room for the idea that some have been abrogated, because abrogation is only applied when there is contradiction. These verses are therefore fixed and unassailable; amounting to the same thing and establishing one rule, one reason and one purpose.

As for the Verses of Forgiveness and Pardon, they aim to shape morality and are to be followed in a context that does not infringe on pride and dignity. Every situation has its own legislation and these verses are also fixed and unassailable.

Legislation that is built upon consideration for different situations, and for the different conditions of individuals and groups, and asks of people that in each situation they follow what is most suitable, cannot be accused of being a contradictory legislation or that some parts of it abrogate others. Indeed, to people with sound minds, it is a wise and extremely precise legislation that promotes the interest of those who fall under its authority and brings happiness to the individual and the community.

The Verses that Organise Combat

In the previous sections we concluded that the Holy Qur'an gives only three reasons for combat: fending off aggression, protecting the *da'wah* and safeguarding freedom of religion. These are the only cases in which God makes combat (*qitāl*) lawful, urges it and considers it desirable. God also reveals many of the ethics and rules that guarantee victory. In this section we will discuss the verses that expound these aspects of combat.

When one studies these verses in the Holy Qur'an, one finds that Islam stipulates general principles that constitute an objective law for combat that is better than any other found in modern civilisation.

This objective law for combat for a nation that wishes for itself pride and dignity is based on three elements:

1) Strengthening the nation's morale.
2) Preparing material force.
3) Practical organisation for combat.

In outlining the ways in which people may enjoy a good life, the Holy Qur'an expounds these three elements in a manner that encompasses all the institutions and systems that humanity has produced in all its varied cultures and throughout the ages. These elements are powerful, extensive and dominate people's hearts and fill them with mercy, compassion, devotion and a desire for God's approval through purifying the earth from corruption and clearing it from tyranny and aggression. These notions are present in all three elements.

(*A section here has been omitted regarding the details of strengthening the nation's morale, preparing material force and practical details for combat. An unabridged version of the text of Shaltut's 'The Qur'an and Combat' can be found at www.mabda.jo.*)

Regarding declaration of war, the Holy Qur'an makes it a duty and warns against attacking the enemy unawares. God says in the Holy Qur'an: *And if you fear, from any folk some treachery, then cast it back to them with fairness. Truly God does not love the treacherous* (*Al-Anfāl*, 8:58). This verse commands that if there is fear that a party will be treacherous, any pact that has been made with them may be broken and cast back to them. The verse also asks that this be done in an explicit and clear manner lest the Muslims commit treachery, which God does not love and does not approve of.

Regarding meeting the call to jihad, the Holy Qur'an warns against tardiness and behaving as though it were a burden. God says in the Holy Qur'an:

> *O you who believe, what is wrong with you that, when it is said to you, 'Go forth in the way of God', you sink down heavily to the ground. Are you so content with the life of this world, rather than with the Hereafter? Yet the enjoyment of the life of this world is in the Hereafter but little. / If you do not go forth, He will chastise you with a painful chastisement, and He will substitute [you with] another folk other than you, and you will not hurt Him at all; for God has power over all things.* (*Al-Tawbah*, 9:38–9)

These verses warn that if we are tardy in meeting the call to jihad, we will suffer painful chastisement, humiliation, substitution and the transfer of power and authority to another people.

(*A section here has been omitted regarding purging the army of elements of sedition and betrayal. An unabridged version of the text of Shaltut's* The Qur'an and Combat *can be found at www.mabda.jo.*)

Regarding truce and peace treaties, the Holy Qur'an orders us to heed calls for peace and the termination of war if the enemy is so inclined and if the enemy shows signs of sincerity and fidelity. God says in the Holy Qur'an:

> *And if they incline to peace, then incline to it, and rely on God; truly He is the Hearer, the Knower. / And if they desire to trick you, then God is sufficient for you. He it is Who strengthened you with His help and with the believers.* (*Al-Anfāl*, 8:61-62)

Regarding taking prisoners and the treatment of prisoners of war, the Holy Qur'an says:

> *It is not for any Prophet to have prisoners until he make wide slaughter in the land.* (*Al-Anfāl*, 8:67)

If the imam decimates the enemy and takes prisoners, he may choose between liberating them without ransom and in return for nothing, or liberating them in exchange for money or men. The choice should be made based on the common good. God says in the Holy Qur'an:

> *So when you encounter [in battle] those who disbelieve, then [attack them with] a striking of the necks. Then, when you have made thoroughly decimated them, bind. Thereafter either [set them free] by grace or by ransom, until the war lay down its burdens ...* (*Muḥammad*, 47:4)

Regarding treaties and honouring them, the Holy Qur'an commands the honouring of treaties and forbids violating them. It teaches that the intention behind treaties is for security and peace to reign instead of disorder and war. It warns against using treaties as an artful means to deprive the other party of its rights or to oppress the weak. Consider God's words in the Holy Qur'an:

> *And fulfil God's covenant when you made a covenant, and do not break [your] oaths after pledging them and having made God surety over you. Truly God knows what you do. / And do not be like her who undoes her yarn after having made it strong, [breaking it up] into fibres by making your oaths a [means of] deceit, between you, so that one group may become more numerous than [another] group ...* (*Al-Naḥl*, 16:91–2)[26]

If the imam determines that Muslims will come to harm as a result of a treaty and that the harm exceeds the advantages to be gained by observing it, he is obliged to reject it. This rejection must be declared openly. God says in the Holy Qur'an:

> *A proclamation from God and His Messenger to mankind on the day of the Greater Pilgrimage that God is free from obligation to the idolaters, and [so is] His Messenger ...* (*Al-Tawbah*, 9:3)

These are the principles we were able to derive from the Holy Qur'an concerning the practical aspects of combat. The Holy Qur'an is an inexhaustible treasure, when we investigate its significations and examine its meanings, we will always arrive at something new. The best aid for the understanding of the Holy Qur'an is the observation of current events and historical facts, for they are the best interpreters and the clearest road to comprehension of its purposes and its principles. If one studies what the Holy Qur'an relates concerning the military activities of the Prophet ﷺ, one grasps many of these purposes and principles which will strengthen the faith of the believers that the Holy Qur'an is a revelation by the omnipotent and omniscient Creator who is cognizant of the intentions of our souls.

The Practical Application of the Qur'anic Rules of Combat

In this epilogue we shall present the practical application of the principles expounded by the Holy Qur'an regarding combat during the time of the Prophet ﷺ and his two successors (caliphs), Abu Bakr and 'Umar. After this period the Muslims were afflicted by internal and external affairs that prevented them from observing God's prescriptions and laws. These affairs also compelled them, especially where combat was concerned, to adopt practices of a much wider range than those which God had prescribed for jihad in His way.

The phases of the Prophet's life and the lives of the believers who were with him before combat began are due to:

The clandestine call (*da'wah*) which a small group of people believed in. They were bound to the Prophet by close family ties or friendship which revealed to them the sublime spirit and magnificent nature of the Prophet.

The public call (*da'wah*) directed to his clan and then to all mankind.

The temptations with which the Meccans tried to seduce the Prophet ﷺ, offering him as much property, power and sovereignty as he wished in exchange for him desisting from propagating the call (*da'wah*).

The violence and oppression which the Prophet and his companions suffered. History has recorded blood-chilling instances of torture.

The Hijrah to Abyssinia in order to save Islam and preserve lives.

The malefactions, maliciousness and conspiracies against the Prophet, the Muslims and even against all the descendants of 'Abd Manāf in order to prompt the latter to deliver the Prophet and his companions, and not to protect them from the aggression of the polytheists. One of these actions was the boycott of Abu Talib and his people, which—were it not for the Grace of God—nearly broke their spirit of resistance.

Seeking refuge in Al-Ta'if and seeking the help of Thaqīf who met the Prophet and his companions with mockery and derision and drove them away.

The Hijrah to Medina which was facilitated by delegations that had visited the Prophet, and by the pains taken by him to call the tribes to Islam. Both factors helped the spread of the noble calling of Islam and gained supporters among the Medinan youth who promised the Messenger they would propagate and protect the call to Islam until death. One of the consequences of this Emigration was that the fury and rancour of the polytheists increased as the opportunity to assassinate the Prophet passed them by.

The role of the enmity between the Muslims and the Jews in Medina. As soon as the Prophet settled in Medina it became clear to him that the Jews there denied his call and plotted against him and his companions. The Prophet had thought that the Jews would be his closest supporters because they were People of the Book and because they had previously asked for his assistance in their wars against the polytheists. This induced the Prophet to extend his hand to them in order to prevent sedition and strife and he concluded a treaty with them that left them to their religion. After concluding this treaty, the Prophet felt more secure and turned his attention to his original enemies who, after his Hijrah, were attacking his followers at every turn. His followers could not emigrate for financial reasons and their enemies waited for opportunities to oppose the call to Islam and scatter its adherents.

The harassment the Prophet and his companions faced at the hands of their enemies. The Prophet foresaw that unless he propagated his Call to Islam in Medina, which was the task entrusted to him by God, the Meccans would inevitably find a way to penetrate Medina and attack him by surprise, especially since the Jews with whom he had concluded a treaty were not to be trusted to keep their pledge. It was not improbable that the Medinan Jews would open up opportunities in Medina for the enemy outside and that they would subsequently join forces with them in order to expel the believers from Medina, just as they had been expelled from Mecca.

For all these reasons the Prophet and his companions prepared to resist those who opposed the call to Islam, the people of Mecca. The Prophet engaged in skirmishes with them and displayed his strength and determination to continue with his call and strive for its propagation and protection and indeed to save the meek men, women and children who say as is related in the Holy Qur'an:

> *...'Our Lord, bring us forth from this town whose people are evildoers and appoint for us a protector from You, and appoint for us from You a helper'.* (*Al-Nisā'*, 4:75)

It was in this spirit that combat between the believers and the polytheists began and battles between both parties took place; some of which are related in the Holy Qur'an. And God crowned all these confrontations with conquest and clear victory.

The Jews broke their pledge; they were not able to purify their hearts from rancour and envy. God's continuous favours to His Prophet and his faithful companions kindled the fire of antagonism in the hearts of the Jews until it induced them to break the pledges they had concluded with the Prophet. This was done by Banu Qaynuqā, Banu Al-Nadhīr and Banu Quraytha. They insulted the Prophet ﷺ and the believers at a time when the Prophet needed to keep enemies and battles at a minimum. But this was God's will and the Muslims had no choice but to reject the pledge they had with the Jews and after a phase of peace and treaties, enter a new phase in their relations, a phase of hostility and war.

These were the phases that the Prophet went through, before and after the Hijrah. From this it becomes clear to us that the polytheists of Mecca fought the Prophet from the start of his Mission. They were the first to commit aggression, chased the believers from their homes, tyrannised the meek and subjected them to all kinds of maltreatment and torture. It is also clear that the Jews of Medina were only attacked by the Messenger after they had broken their pledge to him and aggressed against him as the polytheists had done before.

It is also evident that the Prophet only fought those who fought him, and he only fought to end sedition in religion and to stave off and respond to aggression and violence. These are exactly the prescriptions for combat (*qitāl*) revealed in the Holy Qur'an, as we have discussed.

The wars that took place after the death of the Prophet were conducted by Abu Bakr and Umar and they were a continuation of something for which the groundwork had been laid by the Byzantines (*Al-Rūm*) and the Persians (*Al-Furs*) during the Prophet's lifetime. These two caliphs had no choice but to fend off evil and enable people to hear the call to Islam and to safeguard the security of the Muslims with regard to their religion and their homes.

As a Prophet and a Messenger of God, Muhammad ﷺ called the kings of the Byzantines and the Persians to Islam. To the king of the Byzantines he dispatched his famous missive in which he called him to Islam and held him, in the event of his refusal, answerable for the injustice he inflicted on his own people by keeping them from Islam. When the letter was translated for the king of the Byzantines, he assembled his patriarchs and high officials, submitted the letter to them and asked for their advice as to whether he should accept the summons or not. They turned stubbornly away and expressed their resentment of his attitude. The king of the Byzantines appeased them by saying: 'I only said what I said to test your resolve concerning religion and kingship'. So the king of the Byzantines abandoned his original intention, preferring kingship over Islam. Then the Byzantine high officials and patriarchs began to sow the venomous seeds of hatred against Islam and its Prophet in the hearts of commanders and subordinates. One of the consequences was that when Shurhabil al-Ghassani met the Prophet's envoy to the Prince of Basra at the Battle of Mu'tah, al-Ghassani gave orders to behead him. The Byzantines surmised that the Muslims would not tolerate such an attack on their honour. They therefore intensified their state of alert and assembled a force of Byzantines and Christian Arabs in an attempt to annihilate the Prophet ﷺ. When the Messenger of God heard about this, he prepared an army to confront those who rose against him and mocked his call to Islam. As soon as this army reached the place where the Muslim envoy had been killed, they found the Byzantine troops in a state of high alert. The two armies clashed and fought a fierce battle. Three Muslim heroes were killed and had it not been for a stratagem that God disclosed to Khalid ibn al-Walid, not a single soldier in the Muslim army would have survived. There were continuous reports that the Byzantines were assembling troops against the Muslims, determined to attack them. The Prophet prepared himself and set out with an army before they could attack him in his own land. When he reached Tabuk, he found that they had abandoned their plan. The Prophet remained there a few days, during which some princes concluded peace treaties with him. He then returned to Medina, thinking about those who had lost because of Khalid ibn al-Walid's stratagem and assuming that they would definitely fight back. Therefore, he equipped an army under the command of Usama ibn Zayd. Immediately after this army had set out, the Prophet ﷺ died and was succeeded by Abu Bakr who took over command of the Muslims. Abu Bakr was of the opinion that firmness, loyalty and wisdom required that he dispatch the army that the Prophet had assembled to counter the danger of the aggressors. This was followed by a rapid succession of wars between the Muslims and the Byzantines until the Muslims conquered their lands and enabled their people to find Islam.

The spirit of hostility displayed by the Byzantines was matched by the Persians, who were even more arrogant and powerful. For when the Prophet sent a missive to Khosrau (Kisra), the latter tore it to pieces and cast it on the floor. Indeed so haughty and arrogant was Khosrau that he sent word to his governor in Yemen to send two strongmen to the Prophet Muhammad ﷺ to bring him to Khosrau. They actually reached the Prophet and informed him of the mission they had been tasked with. The Messenger then said: 'This day Khosrau will be killed.' Once the two men learned that the words of the Prophet had come true, they became Muslims. Their conversion caused the conversion of the governor of Yemen to Islam. Following this, Bahrain and Oman—countries that were under Persian protection—became Muslim.

The Persians thought that the victory of the Muslims over the Byzantines was only due to the weakness of the Byzantine armies. The Persians began to attack their neighbouring Arab tribes, employing the kings of Al-Hīrah who attacked the Muslims forcefully. The Muslim army then marched to meet them and war broke out until the proxy of the Persians had to flee to Al-Mada'in and the kings of Al-Hirah surrendered to the Muslims. This ignited hatred for the Muslims in the hearts of the Persians; they recalled their might and equipped an army to expel the Muslims from their lands. Fighting broke out and in the end the Muslims advanced to the lands of the Persians. Khosrau's throne fell and all the Persian lands yielded to the Muslims.

From this brief description it will be clear that, in the first period, the Muslims only attacked people after they had shown hostility and opposition to the call (*da'wah*). It also shows that when such hostility became manifest and once the Muslims were convinced of its danger to themselves and to the call to Islam, they hastened to put out its fire and eliminate it before it became pervasive. The Muslims did not wait for their enemies to attack them in their own lands. This is in accordance with a natural and instinctive sociological rule: 'When people are attacked in their own home, they are inevitably humiliated.' Nevertheless, according to Islamic prescriptions, whenever the Muslims arrived in the land of an enemy whose hostility to them was evident, they let him choose one out of three things: conversion to Islam, poll-tax (*jizyah*) or combat (*qitāl*). These choices were offered in the hope that the enemy would come to his senses, look into his heart and replace aggression and antagonism with wisdom. The Prophet ﷺ enjoined the commanders of his army: 'If you meet your polytheist enemy, call on him to choose one of three things.' This shows us that the enemy's spirit of animosity preceded the dispatching of the Muslim army and that offering him choices was done in the hope for peace and the abandonment of hostility. It is also clear that the wars the Muslims fought in the first period of Islam were not aimed at forcing people to convert to Islam, nor at subjugating or humiliating them, neither were they prompted by greed for money or greater power.

It behoves us to return to the Qur'anic prescriptions regarding our behaviour with, and treatment of, the *ahl al-dhimmah*, who are not adherents of Islam. One must also read how the Rightly Guided Caliphs and the righteous army commanders dealt with those who were not adherents of Islam. Then we can learn, based on reason and evidence not supposition and conjecture, how lenient and magnanimous Islam is in the treatment of its non-Muslim subjects and how deeply it loves universal peace and human solidarity. We can also see how exalted Islam's universal human laws are; laws that have attracted people to the faith of Islam of their own free will and under the protection of which non-Muslims have lived for centuries, without any complaints of injustice.

After reading this, it is my fervent hope that the reader be left in no doubt that the Holy Qur'an and the life of the Prophet ﷺ together establish a theory concerning combat, as I have described in this treatise. May God guide us in spreading His laws and guidance which guarantee the dignity and honour of Muslims. He is the All-Hearing, the All-Answering.

Originally published as an unabridged booklet by the Royal Aal al-Bayt Institute for Islamic Thought in November 2012 (Translation: Lamya Khraisha).

CHAPTER TWO

WARFARE IN THE QUR'AN

Professor Joel Hayward

A frequently quoted saying, with slight variations, insists that, while not all Muslims are terrorists, all terrorists are Muslims. This is a great untruth. According to the American Federal Bureau of Investigation, Muslims have not been responsible for the majority of terrorist attacks identified and prevented, or committed throughout the world in the last twenty years.[27] Yet it is true that, even before the Bush administration initiated a concentrated campaign against anti-American terrorists around the world in 2001—a campaign which quickly came to be known as the War on Terror—several states including the United States and Israel had already experienced terrorism undertaken unmistakeably by Muslims. For example, the bombings of US embassies in Nairobi and Dar es Salaam in 1998 brought Osama bin Laden and Ayman al-Zawahiri to the focused attention of US security services for the first time. These terrorists and their ideological bedfellows embraced an extreme *minority* opinion within Islam. According to that opinion, militant opposition to any ostensibly oppressive political activity that weakens Islamic states and their interests constitutes a righteous struggle (*jihad*) on God's behalf (*fī sabīl Allāh*, literally 'in the path of Allah'). Yet these 'jihadists' (a phrase not widely used in those pre-9/11 days) did not garner much public interest until that dreadful day when nineteen of them hijacked four aircraft and carried out history's worst single terrorist attack.

No one can doubt that Western attitudes towards Islam changed for the worse at that time and have not returned to the way they were before 2001. Among widely held negative views of Islam is a perception (or at least a concern) that, while Western states adhere to the Just War tenets, other states and peoples, particularly Muslims in general and Arabs in particular, have no comparable philosophical framework for guiding ethical behaviour during international disputes and during warfare itself. According to this perception, the Western code of war is based on restraint, chivalry and respect for civilian life, whereas the Islamic faith contains ideas on war that are more militant, aggressive and tolerant of violence.

This article analyses the Qur'an and attempts to explain its codes of conduct in order to determine what the Qur'an actually requires or permits Muslims to do in terms of the use of military force. It concludes that the Qur'an is unambiguous: Muslims are prohibited from undertaking offensive violence and are compelled, if defensive warfare should become unavoidable, always to act within a code of ethical behaviour that is closely akin to, and compatible with, the Western warrior code embedded within the Just War doctrine. This paper attempts to dispel any misperceptions that the Qur'an advocates the subjugation or killing of 'infidels' and reveals that, on the contrary, its key and unequivocal concepts governing warfare are based on justice and a profound belief in the sanctity of human life.

The Importance of the Qur'an

Sadly, people do not tend to read the holy scriptures of other faiths so it is not surprising that, although Muslims constitute one-quarter of the world's population,[28] very few Muslims have studied the Jewish *Tanakh*, the Christian Bible or the Hindu Vedas, and equally few non-Muslims have taken the time to study the Qur'an. Not many people ever even 'dip' into other holy books to get a quick feel for the language, tone and message. Yet, given the geographical location of our major wars throughout the last two decades, the strategic importance of the Middle East and the cultural origin of some recent terrorist groups, it is surprising that very few non-Muslim strategists and military personnel have taken time to read the Qur'an alongside doctrine publications and works of military philosophy. The Qur'an is certainly shorter than Clausewitz's widely read and constantly quoted *Vom Kriege* (*On War*) and far easier to understand. The Qur'an is a relatively short book of approximately 77,000 words, which makes it about the size of most thrillers or romance novels and roughly half the length of the New

Testament or one-seventh the length of the Old.[29] It is not deeply complex in its philosophy or written as inaccessible poetry or with mystical and esoteric vagueness.

Muslims understand that the Qur'an was revealed episodically by the Angel Jibril (the biblical Gabriel) to Muhammad, a Meccan merchant in what is now Saudi Arabia, through a series of revelations from Allah (Arabic for 'the God'), over a period of twenty-three years beginning in the year 610. Muhammad's companions memorised and wrote down the individual revelations almost straight away and compiled them into the Qur'an's final Arabic form very soon after his death in 632. That Arabic version has not changed in the last fourteen hundred years. The Qur'an is therefore held by Muslims to be the very words of Allah, recorded precisely as originally revealed through Muhammad. This explains why most of the world's 1.6 billion Muslims[30] endeavour to learn at least the basics of Qur'anic Arabic so that they can read and more importantly *hear* Allah's literal words as originally revealed. This is also why they consider all translations into other languages to be decidedly inferior to the original Arabic. Muslims usually explain that these translations convey the 'meaning' of the revelations, and are therefore still useful, but not the exact word for word declarations of Allah.[31]

A fair and open-minded reading of the Qur'an will draw the reader's eyes to hundreds of scriptures extolling tolerance, forgiveness, conciliation, inclusiveness and peace. These are the overwhelming majority of the scriptures and the central thrust of the Qur'anic message. A clear indication of that message is found in the fact that every one of the 114 surahs (chapters) of the Qur'an except one opens with a reminder of Allah's loving and forgiving attitude towards humans: *bism Allāh al-Raḥmān al-Raḥīm* (In the name of God the All-Compassionate and the Ever-Merciful). Muslims understand that the compassion and forgiveness extended by God to humans must be mirrored as much as is humanly possible by their compassion and forgiveness to each other.

Yet readers will also find a few scriptures in the Qur'an that seem to be 'Old Testament' in tone and message and are more warlike than, for example, Christians are used to reading in the words of Christ and the New Testament writers. Critics of the Qur'an who advance what I consider to be an unsustainable argument that Islam is the world's most warlike major faith—among whom the US scholar and blogger Robert Spencer is both the most prolific and influential[32]—routinely highlight those Qur'anic passages to support their argument that Islam has a clear tendency towards aggressive war, not inclusive peace.[33]

Such writers commonly focus their attention on a few passages within the Qur'an which seem to suggest that Allah encourages Muslims to subjugate or drive out non-Muslims—and even to take their lives if they refuse to yield. The critics especially like to quote surah 9, *āyah* (verse) 5, which has become known as the 'Verse of the Sword' (*Āyat Al-Sayf*). This verse explicitly enjoins Muslims to kill *pagans wherever you find them, and seize them, beleaguer them, and lie in wait for them in every stratagem (of war)*. (*Al-Tawbah*, 9:5)[34]

The critics often add to their condemnation of the aforementioned surah 9:5 with equally strong attacks on surah 9:29. This verse directs Muslims to 'fight those who believe not in Allah' and the Day of Judgment, who do not comply with Muslim laws, as well as those Jews and Christians who reject the religion of Islam and will not willingly pay a state tax after their submission.[35] Many critics assert that this verse directs Muslims to wage war against any and all disbelievers anywhere who refuse to embrace Islam or at least to submit to Islamic rule.[36]

The critics also place negative focus on surah 2:190–4, which states:

> *Fight in the cause of Allah those who fight you, but do not transgress limits: for Allah loves not the transgressors. / And slay them wherever you catch them, and turn them out from where they have turned you out; for tumult and oppression are worse than slaughter; but fight them not at the Sacred Mosque [al-Masjid al-Ḥarām, the sanctuary at Mecca], unless they (first) fight you there; but if they fight you, slay them. Such is the reward of those who suppress faith. / But if they cease, then Allah is Oft-forgiving, Most Merciful. / And fight them on until there is no more tumult or oppression, and there prevail justice and faith in Allah; but if they cease, let there be no hostility except to those who practise oppression.* (*Al-Baqarah*, 2:190–4)

You could not imagine gentle Buddha or the peaceful, cheek-turning Jesus ever saying such things, the critics of Islam assert, ignoring the heavily martial spirit and explicit violence of some sections of the Old Testament; a revelation passionately embraced in its entirety by Jesus.

They also brush off some of Jesus' seemingly incongruous statements as being allegorical and metaphorical—such as Luke 22:36, wherein Jesus encourages his disciples to sell their garments so that they can purchase swords, and Matthew 10:34 ('Do not think I come to bring peace on earth. I did not come to bring peace, but a sword').[37]

When they read the Qur'an, the opponents of its message place little importance on the obvious differences of experiences and responsibilities between Jesus and Muhammad. Jesus was the spiritual leader of a small and intimate group of followers at a time of occupation but relative peace and personal security throughout the land. He suffered death, according to the Christian scriptures, but his execution by the Rome-governed state came after a short burst of state anger that actually followed several years of him being able to preach throughout the land without severe opposition and with no known violence. By contrast, the Prophet Muhammad (in many ways like Moses or Joshua) found himself not only the spiritual leader but also the *political* and *legislative* leader of a massive community that wanted to be moderate, just and inclusive but suffered bitter, organised persecution and warfare from other political entities which were committed to his community's destruction. His responsibilities (including the sustenance, education, governance and physical protection of tens of thousands of children, men and women) were very different.

A double standard also seems to exist. Many of the scholars and pundits who dislike the fact that Muhammad had to fight military campaigns during his path to peace, and who consider his religion to be inherently martial, overlook the fact that many biblical prophets and leaders—including Moses, Joshua, Samson, David and other Sunday School favourites—were also warriors through necessity. Despite our children's book image of these warriors, their actions included frequent killing and were sometimes couched in highly bloodthirsty language. For example, the Book of Numbers (31:15–17) records that Moses ordered war against the Midianites, but was gravely disappointed when, after having slain all the men, his warriors chose not to kill the women. He therefore instructed his warriors to kill every male child and to leave alive no females except virgins, whom the Israelites were allowed to keep as slaves. This hardly fits with our Charlton Heston-esque view of a very popular Jewish and Christian prophet.

It is worth observing that among the scriptures that form the bedrock and bulk of the Judeo-Christian tradition—the Old Testament—one can find numerous verses like these that explicitly advocate (or at least once advocated) large-scale violence incompatible with any codes of warfare that Jews and Christians would nowadays condone. For instance, when Joshua led the Israelites into the Promised Land and promptly laid siege to Jericho, which was the first walled city they encountered west of the Jordan River, 'they destroyed with the sword every living thing in it—men and women, young and old, cattle, sheep and donkeys' (Joshua 6:21). The lack of what we would today call discrimination between combatants and non-combatants accorded with God's earlier commandment that, in areas which God had set aside for their occupation, the Israelites were to ensure that, 'without mercy', they did not leave alive 'anything that breathed'.[38]

The ancient world was certainly brutal at times, with military excesses sometimes involving deliberate widespread violence against whole civilian communities. 'It is a wonderful sight,' Roman commander Scipio Aemilianus Africanus gushed in 146 BC as he watched his forces raze the enemy city of Carthage to the ground following his order that no trace of it should remain. 'Yet I feel a terror and dread lest someone should one day give the same order about my own native city.'[39]

No one can doubt that humanity has since made tremendous progress in the way it conceives the purpose and nature of warfare and the role and treatment of non-combatants. Yet we would be wrong to believe that the 'Carthaginian approach' has disappeared entirely. The Holocaust of the Jews in the Second World War, one of history's vilest crimes, involved the organised murder of six million Jews by Germans and others who considered themselves Christians or at least members of the Christian value system. Other crimes perpetrated by Christians during recent wars have included the (Orthodox Christian) Bosnian Serb massacre of 8,300 Bosnian Muslim men and boys in and around the town of Srebrenica in July 1995.

A fair assessment of historical evidence reveals that Christianity is a faith of justice that cannot reasonably be considered blameworthy in and of itself for the Crusades, the Holocaust, the Srebrenica massacre or the Timothy McVeigh terrorist attack in Oklahoma City in 1995, even though Christians committed those horrendous acts and many others. Similarly, a fair assessment of Islam reveals that it is equally a faith of justice that cannot fairly be seen as blameworthy in and of itself for the Armenian Genocide, the Iran-Iraq War, Saddam Hussein's invasion of Kuwait or the Al-Qaeda attacks on America in 2001, even though Muslims committed those disgraceful deeds. Certainly Islam's framing scripture, the Qur'an, contains no verses which are as violent as the biblical scriptures quoted above or any Qur'anic verses more violent than those already quoted. In any event, even the most ostensibly violent Qur'anic verses have not provided major Islamic movements, as opposed to impassioned minority splinter groups, with a mandate to wage aggressive war or to inflict disproportionate or indiscriminate brutality.

Understanding Abrogation

While Muslims hold the Qur'an to be God's literal, definitive and final revelation to humankind, they recognise that it is not intended to be read as a systematic legal or moral treatise. They understand it to be a discursive commentary on the stage by stage actions and experiences of the Prophet Muhammad, his ever-increasing number of followers and his steadily decreasing number of opponents over the twenty-three year period which took him from his first revelation to his political hegemony in Arabia.[40] Consequently, several legal rulings within the Qur'an emerged or developed in stages throughout that period, with some early rulings on inheritance, alcohol, law, social arrangements and so on being superseded by later passages; a phenomenon known in Arabic as *naskh* that the Qur'an itself describes. For example, surah 2:106 reveals that when Allah developed any particular legal ruling beyond its first revelation and He therefore wanted to supersede the original verses, He would replace them with clarifying verses.

The removal or annulment of one legal ruling by a subsequent legal ruling in some instances certainly does not mean that Muslims believe that all later scriptures automatically cancel out or override everything, on all issues, that had appeared earlier. The Qur'an itself states in several surahs that Allah's words constitute a universally applicable message sent down for *all of mankind* and that it was a *reminder* (with both *glad tidings and warnings*) to *all* of humanity.[41] With this in mind, Muslims believe that to ignore scriptures on the basis of a that-was-then-this-is-now reading would be as mistaken, as, conversely, would be believing that one can gain meaning or guidance from reading individual verses in isolation, without seeing how they form parts of consistent concepts which only emerge when the entire book is studied. Adopting either approach would be unhelpful, self-serving and ultimately misleading. It is only when the Qur'an's key concepts are studied holistically, with both an appreciation of the context of particular revelations and the consistency of ideas developed throughout the book as a whole, that readers will be able to understand the Qur'an's universally applicable ethical system.

Opponents of Islam take a different view. Embracing a view that all later Qur'anic scriptures modify or cancel out all earlier ones, they have devised an unusual narrative. They have routinely argued that, in the early years of his mission while still in his hometown of Mecca, the powerless Muhammad strongly advocated peaceful coexistence with peoples of other faiths, particularly Jews and Christians. Despite mounting resistance and persecution, some of it violent and all of it humiliating, Muhammad had to advocate an almost Gandhian or Christ-like policy of forbearance and non-violence. Then, after he and his followers fled persecution in 622 by escaping to Medina, where they had more chance of establishing a sizeable and more influential religious community, the increasingly powerful Muhammad became bitter at his intransigent foes in Mecca and ordered warfare against them.[42] Finally (the critics claim), following the surprisingly peaceful Islamic occupation of Mecca in 630, the all-powerful Muhammad realised that Jews and others would not accept his prophetic leadership or embrace Islamic monotheism, so he then initiated an aggressive war against all disbelievers.[43] The critics furthermore claim that, because Muhammad did not clarify or change his position before he died two years later, in 632, after Allah's revelation to mankind was complete, the verses encouraging the martial suppression of disbelief (that is, of the disbelievers) are still in force today. These supposedly include the so-called Verse of the Sword of surah 9:5 (and 29), quoted above and revealed to Muhammad in the year 631.[44] As scholar David

Bukay, a strong critic of Islam, wrote:

> Coming at or near the very end of Muhammad's life ... [surah 9] trumps earlier revelations. Because this chapter contains violent passages, it abrogates previous peaceful content.[45]

The critics of Islam who hold this view insist that these warlike verses abrogate (cancel out) the scores of conciliatory and non-confrontational earlier verses which had extolled spiritual resistance (prayer and outreach) but physical non-violence.

They note that Osama bin Laden and other leading radical 'Islamists'—who also insist that the later Qur'anic verses on war have cancelled out the earlier peaceful and inclusive verses—have justified their terror attacks on the United States and other states by quoting from the Verse of the Sword and the other reportedly aggressive scriptures mentioned above.

Bin Laden certainly did draw upon the Verse of the Sword and other seemingly militant Qur'anic scriptures in his August 1996 'Declaration of War against the Americans occupying the Land of the Two Holy Places'[46] as well as in his February 1998 fatwa.[47] The first of these *fatāwā* (verdicts) instructed Muslims to kill Americans until they withdrew from their occupation of Saudi Arabia, and the second more broadly instructed them to kill Americans (both civilians and military personnel) and their allies, especially the Israelis, for their suppression of Muslims and their exploitation of Islamic resources in various parts of the world.

Of course, the obviously partisan Bin Laden was not a cleric, a religious scholar or a historian of early Islam. He was an impassioned, violent and murderous extremist without judgement or moderation. He was not representative of Islamic belief or behaviour and he had no recognised status as an authority in Islamic Sciences that would have allowed him to issue a fatwa. His assertions that the Verse of the Sword and other martial Qur'anic verses are still in place and universally applicable therefore do not hold a shred of authority or credibility, except perhaps among already-radicalised fanatics who share his world view and consider him worth following. Thankfully they are very few in number.

Certainly most Islamic authorities on the Qur'an and Prophet Muhammad ﷺ today, as opposed to scholars from, say, the war-filled medieval period, are firm in their judgement that the most warlike verses in the Qur'an, even those revealed very late in Muhammad's ﷺ mission, do not cancel out the overwhelming number of verses that extol tolerance, reconciliation, inclusiveness and peace.[48] For example, according to British scholar Dr Zakaria Bashier (author of many books on early Islam including a thorough analysis of war), all the beautiful verses throughout the Qur'an which instruct Muslims to be peaceful, tolerant and non-aggressive are:

> *Muḥkam* [clear in and of themselves] verses, i.e. definite, not allegorical. They are not known to have been abrogated, so they naturally hold. No reason exists at all to think that they have been overruled.[49]

Bashier adds that even the contextual information revealed within the Qur'an itself will lead readers to the inescapable conclusion that the Verse of the Sword related only to a particular time, place and set of circumstances, and that, in any event, claims of it superseding the established policy of tolerance are 'not borne out by the facts of history'.[50] Prolific British scholar Louay Fatoohi agrees, arguing that an 'overwhelming number' of Muslim scholars reject the abrogation thesis regarding war. Fatoohi highlights the fact that throughout history the Islamic world has never acted in accordance with this extreme view. Fatoohi observes that Muslims have almost always coexisted very well with other faith communities and that the 1600 million peaceable Muslims in the world today clearly do not accept the view otherwise, if they did, they would all be at war as we speak.[51] Muhammad Abu Zahra, an important and influential Egyptian intellectual and expert on Islamic law, summed up the mainstream Islamic view by rejecting any abrogation thesis pertaining to conflict and stating that 'War is not justified ... to impose Islam as a religion on unbelievers or to support a particular social regime. The Prophet Muhammad ﷺ fought only to repulse aggression.'[52]

Explaining the Verse of the Sword

It is quite true that, taken in isolation, surah 9:5 (the Verse of the

Sword) seems an unusually violent pronouncement for a Prophet who had for twenty years preached tolerance, peace and reconciliation. Yet it is equally true that, when read in the context of the verses above and below surah 9:5, and when the circumstances of its pronouncement by Muhammad are considered, it is not difficult for readers without preconceptions and bias to understand it more fully. Here is the verse again:

> *But when the forbidden months are past, then fight and slay the pagans wherever you find them, and seize them, beleaguer them, and lie in wait for them in every stratagem (of war).* (*Al-Tawbah*, 9:5)

The fact that the verse actually starts with the Arabic conjunction *fa*, translated above as 'but', indicates that its line of logic flows from the verse or verses above it. Indeed, the preceding four verses explain the context.

Verse 1 gives the historical context as a violation of the Treaty of Hudaybiyyah, signed in 628 by the State of Medina and the Quraysh tribe of Mecca. In short, this was a peace treaty between Muhammad and his followers and those Meccans who had spent a decade trying to destroy them. Two years after the treaty was signed the Banu Bakr tribe, which had allied with the Quraysh, attacked the Banu Khuza'ah tribe, which had joined the side of the Muslims. Muhammad considered the Banu Bakr attack a treaty violation, arguing that an attack on an ally constituted an attack on his own community.[53] Then, following his extremely peaceful seizure of Mecca and his purification of its holy site (he destroyed no fewer than 360 idols in the Ka'bah), the Qur'anic revelation contained a very stern warning. (Other sources reveal that Muhammad then explained it publicly from the steps of the Ka'bah and sent out deputies to the regions around Mecca to destroy pagan shrines and idols and utter the warnings to local communities.[54]) The scriptural warning was clear: anyone wanting to undertake polytheistic pilgrimages to Mecca (or immoral rituals within it, such as walking naked around the Ka'bah[55]) in accordance with existing agreements with the Quraysh tribe or with Muhammad's own community should understand that henceforth they would not be permitted to do so. No polytheism (worship of more than one god) and idolatry (worship of any man or object instead of the one god) would ever again be tolerated within Islam's holy city. From that time on it would be a city devoted to Allah alone.[56] As surahs 9:17 and 18 say:

> *It is no longer proper for idolaters to attend Allah's mosques, since they have admitted to their unbelief. ... Allah's mosques should be attended only by those who believe in Allah and the Last Day, who observe prayer and give alms and fear none but God.* (*Al-Tawbah*, 9:17–18)

Verses 2 and 3 were revealed through Muhammad to give polytheists or idolaters living in Mecca and its environs, as well as any polytheistic or idolatrous pilgrims in transit along Muslim-controlled trade and pilgrimage routes, a clear warning that they should desist or leave. The scriptures generously included a period of amnesty that would last until the end of the current pilgrimage season. Thus, Arab polytheists and idolaters would gain a four-month period of grace. Verse 4 makes clear that during that period of amnesty, polytheists or idolaters were to be left untouched so that Muslims would not themselves become promise-breakers. (*So fulfil your engagements with them to the end of the term; for Allah loves the righteous.*) After clarifying that the threatened violence would apply only to those who had ignored the warnings and continued to practice polytheism or idolatry in and around the holy city and its sanctuary, and were still foolish enough not to have left after four months, verse 5—the Verse of the Sword—clearly warned them that there would be a violent military purging or purification in which they seriously risked being killed.

Although this is sometimes omitted by critics of the Verse of the Sword, the verse actually has a secondary clause which, after the direction to root out and kill anyone who had ignored the clear and solemn warnings and continued their polytheism or idolatry, enjoined Muslims to remember that they must be merciful (*to open the way*) to those who repented and accepted their penitent obligations in terms of Islam. Moreover, the Verse of the Sword is immediately followed by an unusually charitable one—again ordinarily left out of Islam-critical treatments—in which any of the enemy who asked for asylum during any coming violence were not only to be excluded from that violence, but were to be escorted to a place of safety.[57]

The rest of surah 9 contains more explanation for the Muslims as to why they would now need to fight, and fiercely, anyone who broke their oaths or violated the sanctity of holy places, despite earlier hopes for peace according to the terms of the Treaty of Hudaybiyyah. The 'controversial' verse 29, which talks of killing polytheists and idolaters, actually comes right after verse 28, which speaks specifically about preventing them from performing religious rituals or pilgrimages in or around the newly purified sanctuary in Mecca. Verse 29 thus also refers to the purification of Mecca and its environs as well as to the need to secure the borders of the Arabian Peninsula from greater external powers which might smother the Islamic ummah (community) in its infancy. The rest of surah 9 also apparently contains scriptures relating to the later campaign against Tabuk, when some groups which had treaty obligations with Muhammad broke their promises and refused to join or sponsor the campaign. It is worth noting that, in this context also, Muhammad chose to forgive and impose a financial, rather than physical, penalty upon those who genuinely apologised.[58]

It is clear, therefore, that the Verse of the Sword was a context-specific verse relating to the purification of Mecca and its environs of all Arab polytheism and idolatry so that the sanctuary in particular, with the Kaʿbah at its centre, would never again be rendered unclean by the paganism of those locals and pilgrims who had long been worshipping idols (reportedly hundreds of them) there.[59] It was proclaimed publicly as a warning, followed by a period of grace which allowed the wrongdoers to desist or leave the region, and qualified by humane caveats that allowed for forgiveness, mercy and protection. It is thus not bloodthirsty or unjust, as Robert Spencer and his colleagues portray it. Indeed, it is so context-specific that, even if it *were* still in force—and I share the assessment that it has not abrogated the scriptures encouraging peace, tolerance and reconciliation—it would only nowadays have any relevance and applicability if polytheists and idolaters ever tried to undertake and re-establish pagan practices in the Saudi Arabian cities devoted only to Allah: Mecca and Medina. In other words, in today's world it is not relevant or applicable.

Critics apparently fail to grasp the specific nature of the context—the purification of Mecca from polytheistic and idolatrous pilgrimages and rituals—and even misquote the famous medieval Islamic scholar Ismaʿil bin ʿAmr bin Kathir al-Dimashqi, known popularly as Ibn Kathir.

Spencer claims that Ibn Kathir understood the Verse of the Sword to abrogate all peaceful verses ever previously uttered by the Prophet Muhammad ﷺ.[60] Ibn Kathir said no such thing. He quoted an earlier authority, al-Dahhak bin Muzahim, who only stated that the Verse of the Sword cancelled out every treaty which had granted pilgrimage rights to Arab pagans to travel along Islamic routes, enter Mecca and perform unpalatable rituals there.[61] Because this earlier source referred to the Verse of the Sword 'abrogating' something, Spencer mistakenly extrapolates this to claim that this one single verse cancelled out all existing interfaith practices and arrangements and that it forever negatively changed attitudes to non-Muslims in general.

In case any readers are not convinced, there is another verse in the Qur'an—also from the later period of Muhammad's life—which (using words virtually identical to the Verse of the Sword) also exhorts Muslims to *seize and slay* wrongdoers *wherever you find them* (*Al-Nisā'*, 4:89). Yet this verse, surah 4:89, is surrounded by so many other explanatory and qualifying verses that its superficially violent meaning is immediately moderated by its context of tolerance and understanding. *First*, it threatened violence *in self-defence* only against those people or groups who violated pacts of peace with the Muslims and attacked them, or those former Muslims ('renegades') who had rejoined the forces of oppression and now fought aggressively against the Muslims. *Secondly*, it stated that, if those aggressors left the Muslims alone and free to practice their faith, and if they did not attack them, but offered them peaceful coexistence, then Allah would not allow Muslims to harm them in any way (*Allah has opened no way for you to war against them* (*Al-Nisā'*, 4:90). The verse went even further. It not only offered peaceful coexistence to those who formally made peace with the Muslims, but also to anyone, even Muslims who had slipped backwards and who merely chose to stay neutral; that is, who did not take either side in the tense relations between the Muslims on the one hand and the Quraysh and their allies on the other.[62]

The Origins of Self-defensive Concepts of War

It is worth remembering that, for the first fourteen years of his public life (from 610 to 624), Muhammad had practised and proclaimed a policy of peaceful non-resistance to the intensifying humiliation, cruelty and violence that the Quraysh, the dominant tribe of Mecca, attempted to inflict upon him and his fellow Muslims. Throughout that period he had strenuously resisted 'growing pressure from within the Muslim ranks to respond in kind' and insisted 'on the virtues of patience and steadfastness in the face of their opponents' attacks'.[63] The persecution at one point was so severe that Muhammad had to send two groups of followers to seek refuge in Abyssinia. Even after he and the rest of his followers fled the persecution in Mecca and settled in Medina in 622, the developing ummah (Islamic community) experienced grave hardship and fear. Some of the non-Muslims in Medina passionately resented the presence of Muslims and conspired to expel them. From Mecca, Abu Sufyan waged a relentless campaign of hostility against Muhammad and the Muslims, who had now become a rival power and a threat to his lucrative trade and pilgrimage arrangements. Abu Sufyan sought no accommodation with Muhammad. In his mind, and according to the norms of Arabic tribal warfare, the only solution was the ummah's destruction.[64]

In 624, two years after the migration of Muslims to Medina—two years in which the Quraysh continued to persecute them and then led armies against them—Muhammad finally announced a revelation from Allah that Muslims were allowed physically to *defend* themselves to *preserve* themselves through the contest of arms. Most scholars agree that surah 22:39 contains that first transformational statement of permission.[65] Including the verses above and below, it says:

> *Verily Allah will defend (from ill) those who believe: verily, Allah loves not any that is a traitor to faith, or shows ingratitude. / To those against whom war is made, permission is given (to fight), because they are wronged—and verily, Allah is Most Powerful for their aid. / (They are) those who have been expelled from their homes in defiance of right (for no cause) except that they say, 'Our Lord is Allah'.* (*Al-Ḥajj*, 22:38–40)

These verses continue by pointing out that, had not Allah in previous eras allowed people to defend themselves from the aggression and religious persecution of others, there would surely have been the destruction of '*monasteries, churches, synagogues and mosques, in which the name of Allah is commemorated in abundant measure*'. The verses add that Allah will surely aid those who aid him, and that he is truly mighty and invincible.

The references to defending the faithful from harm in verse 38, to those on the receiving end of violence in verse 39 and those who have been driven from their homes in verse 40 reveal very clearly that Allah's permission to undertake armed combat was not for offensive war, but *self-defence* and *self-preservation* when attacked or oppressed. Interestingly, it even extols the defence of all houses of worship, including the churches of Christians and the synagogues of Jews.

This permission for self-defensive war-fighting (the Arabic word is *qitāl*, or combat) corresponds precisely with the first Qur'anic passage on war that one reads when one starts from the front cover: surah 2:190, which, as quoted above, states: *Fight in the cause of Allah those who fight you, but do not transgress limits: for Allah loves not the transgressors* (*Al-Baqarah*, 2:190). Thus, the purpose of armed combat was self-defence and, even though the need for survival meant that warfare would be tough, combat was to adhere to a set of prescribed constraints.[66] The following verse's instruction to *slay them* wherever they turn up commences with the conjunction *wa*, here translated as 'and', to indicate that it is a continuation of the same stream of logic. In other words, Muslims were allowed to defend themselves militarily from the forces or armies which were attacking them wherever that happened. Tremendous care was to be taken not to shed blood in the environs of Mecca's sacred mosque, but if Muslims found themselves attacked there, they could kill their attackers while defending themselves without committing a sin. This series of verses actually ends with instructions that, if the attackers ceased their attacks, Muslims were not to continue to fight them because Allah is *Oft-Forgiving, Most Merciful* (*Al-Baqarah*, 2:192). Thus, continued resistance could—and nowadays can—only be a proportionate response to continued serious direct oppression.[67] In every Qur'anic example in which war-fighting (*qitāl*) is encouraged for protection against serious direct oppression or violence, verses can be found that stress that, should the wrongdoers cease their hostility, Muslims must immediately cease their own fighting.

The Qur'anic permission for defensive resistance to attacks or serious direct oppression does not mean that Muhammad enjoyed war, or took pleasure whatsoever in the fact that defensive warfare to protect his ummah from extinction or subjugation would involve the loss of even his enemies' lives. He was no warmonger and forgave and pardoned mortal enemies whenever he could. This 'reluctant warrior', to quote one scholar, urged the use of non-violent means when possible and, often against the advice of his companions, sought the early end of hostilities.[68] At the same time, in accordance with the revelations he had received, he accepted that combat for the defence of Islam and Islamic interests would sometimes be unavoidable. One of Muhammad's companions remembers him telling his followers not to look forward to combat, but if it were to come upon them then they should pray for safety and be patient.[69]

Critics of Islam are fond of quoting surahs that seem to reveal a certain savagery that today seems bloodcurdling to them. *When you meet the unbelievers*, the Qur'an says in surah 47:4, *strike at their necks until you weaken them [that is, defeat them] and then bind the captives firmly. Thereafter you may release them magnanimously or for a ransom* (*Muḥammad*, 47:4). In *Sūrat Al-Anfāl*, 8:12 the Qur'an likewise commands soldiers in battle to strike at necks and fingers. Although these verses may seem out of place in a religious text, they are not out of place within advice given by a military commander before a battle. That *was* precisely the context of those particular revelations. Muhammad's community had not yet fought a battle or formed an army and those Muslims who were about to become warriors needed to be taught how to kill immediately and humanely. Decapitation, as opposed to wild slashes at limbs or armoured bodies, ensured humane killing instead of ineffective and brutal wounding. Even better, if a soldier could make an enemy drop his weapon by striking at his hands, he might be able to take him prisoner. Having him alive as a captive who could later be freed, even with a wounded hand, was preferable to leaving him as a corpse.

Today all military or security forces in the world teach weapon-handling skills with the same focus. Recruits and officer cadets are taught how to kill or wound on firing ranges where instructors teach them which target areas will bring humane death and which ones will cause someone's incapacitation without death. The two Qur'anic passages mentioned above should be read in that light. Moreover, they do not represent an instruction to all Muslims anytime to kill or wound all non-Muslims anywhere. That would violate every concept of justice embedded within Islam. The instructions were to one group of Muslims (the nascent ummah, which had not yet experienced combat) in anticipation of a specific conflict: the Battle of Badr fought in March 624.

The fact that these combat-related instructions are contained within a religious book which has powerfully clear central messages of forbearance, toleration and inclusiveness is easily explained by the fact that the Qur'an, revealed episodically over decades, was (and is) considered by Muslim's to be God's word. *Every* revelation on every issue was thus faithfully recorded and retained, including ones dealing with all sorts of things—war, combat, diplomacy, finance, marriage, child-rearing, divorce, death, education, science and so forth—with which the first Muslims had to deal. It is thus a manual for life, with sections on war and combat which are relevant when Muslims go to war for defensive reasons, and on, say, pilgrimage when Muslims go on the Hajj for spiritual fulfilment.

The Qur'an and the Hadith (the recorded words and actions of Muhammad) show that Muhammad took no pleasure in the fact that—as also taught in later Western Just War theory—the regrettable combatant-versus-combatant violence inherent within warfare would sometimes be necessary in order to create a better state of peace. Explaining to fellow Muslims the need in some situations to undertake combat, Muhammad acknowledged Allah's revelation that warfare was something that seemed very wrong, indeed a 'disliked' activity, yet it was morally necessary and thus morally right and obligatory under some circumstances.[70] Warfare was frightening and dreadful, but in extremis better than continued serious persecution and attack.[71]

Muhammad's greatest triumph—his eventual return to his hometown Mecca in 630 at the head of an army of 10,000—was itself a bloodless affair marked by tremendous forgiveness and mercy. After his forces entered the city, the panicked Quraysh tribe, which effectively surrendered after realising that resistance to the Muslim army was futile, anticipated that their leaders and warriors would be slain.[72] After all, for two decades they had humiliated, persecuted and tried to assassinate Muhammad and had maltreated and even waged savage war against his followers. Yet, aside from four murderers and serious oath-breakers who were judged to be beyond rehabilitation, Muhammad chose to forgive them all in a general amnesty. There was no blood-bath. He reportedly asked the assembled leaders of Quraysh what fate they anticipated. Expecting death, but hoping for life, they replied: 'O noble brother and son of a noble brother! We expect nothing but goodness from you.' This appeal must have relieved Muhammad and made him smile. He replied: 'I speak to you in the same words as Yusuf [the biblical Joseph, also one of Islam's revered prophets] spoke unto his brothers. ... "No reproach on you this day." Go your way, for you are the freed ones.'[73] He even showed mercy to Hind bint Utbah, Abu Sufyan's wife, who was under a sentence of death for having horrifically and disgracefully mutilated the body of Muhammad's beloved uncle Hamzah during the Battle of Uhud five years earlier. Hind had cut open Hamzah's body, ripped out his liver and chewed it.[74] She then reportedly strung the ears and nose into a necklace and entered Mecca wearing it as a trophy of victory. When justice finally caught up with her five years later she threw herself upon Muhammad's mercy. Extending clemency of remarkable depth, Muhammad promised her forgiveness and accepted her into his community.[75]

Proportionate Response, Last Resort and Discrimination

Mercy between humans, based on forgiveness of someone else's acknowledged wrongdoing, was something that Muhammad believed precisely mirrored the divine relationship between the Creator and humans. The concepts of patience, forgiveness and clemency strongly underpinned the early Islamic practice of warfare. Proportionality—one of the core principals of Western Just War—also serves as a key foundational principle in the Qur'anic guidance on war. Doing no violence greater than the minimum necessary to guarantee victory is repeatedly stressed in the Qur'an (and described as 'not transgressing limits'). So is the imperative of meeting force with equal force in order to prevent defeat and discourage future aggression. Deterrence comes by doing to the aggressor what he has done to the innocent: *Should you encounter them in war, then deal with them in such a manner that those that [might have intended to] follow them should abandon their designs and may take warning* (*Al-Anfāl*, 8:57). With this deterrent function in mind, the Qur'an embraces the earlier biblical revelation to the Israelites, which permits people to respond to injustice eye for eye, tooth for tooth. Yet, like the Christian Gospels, it suggests that there is more spiritual value (bringing 'purification') in forgoing revenge in a spirit of charity.[76] This passage, interestingly, is from the same period of revelation as the Verse of the Sword, which further weakens the abrogation thesis mentioned above. Moreover, even on this matter of matching one's strength to the opponent's strength,[77] the Qur'an repeatedly enjoins Muslims to remember that, whenever possible, they should respond to provocations with patience and efforts to facilitate conciliation. They should avoid fighting unless it becomes necessary after attempts have been made to achieve a peaceful resolution (which is a concept not vastly different from the Western Just War notion of Last Resort) because forgiveness and the restoration of harmony remain Allah's preference.[78]

Dearly wanting to avoid bloodshed whenever possible, Muhammad created a practice of treating the use of lethal violence as a last resort which has been imitated by Muslim warriors to this day, albeit at times with varying emphasis.[79] Before any war-fighting can commence—except for spontaneous self-defensive battles when surprised—the leader must make a formal declaration of war to the enemy force, no matter how aggressive and violent that enemy is. He must communicate a message to the enemy that it would be better for them to embrace Islam. If they did (and Muhammad liked to offer three days for reflection and decision[80]) then the grievance ended. A state of brotherhood ensued. If the enemy refused, then a proposal would be extended that offered them peace in return for the ending of aggression or disagreeable behaviour and the paying of a tax. If the enemy refused even that offer, and did not cease their wrongdoing, they forfeited their rights to immunity from the unfortunate violence of war.[81]

Islamic concepts of war do not define and conceptualise things in exactly the same way as Western thinking has done within the Just War framework. Yet the parallels are striking. The reasons for going to war expressed within the Qur'an closely match those within *jus ad bellum*, the Just War criteria which establishes the justice of a decision to undertake combat. The criteria include Just Cause, Proportionality and Last Resort. The behaviour demanded of warriors once campaigning and combat have commenced also closely match those within *jus in bello*, the Just War criteria which establishes the proper behaviour of warriors that is necessary to keep the war just. The Qur'an described this as a prohibition against 'transgressing limits'.[82] Ibn Kathir, a famous and relatively reliable fourteenth-century scholar of the Qur'an, accepts earlier interpretations that the 'transgressions' mentioned in the Qur'an refer to 'mutilating the dead, theft (from the captured goods), killing women, children and old people who do not participate in warfare, killing priests and residents of houses of worship, burning down trees and killing animals without real benefit'.[83] Ibn Kathir points out that Muhammad had himself stated that these deeds are prohibited. Another source records that, before he assigned a leader to take forces on a mission, Muhammad would instruct them to fight honourably, not to hurt women and children, not to harm prisoners, not to mutilate bodies, not to plunder and not to destroy trees or crops.[84]

In the year after Muhammad's death in 632, his close friend and successor Abu Bakr, the first caliph, compiled the Qur'an's and the Prophet's guidance on the conduct of war into a code that has served ever since as the basis of Islamic thinking on the conduct of battle. In a celebrated address to his warriors, Abu Bakr proclaimed:

> Do not act treacherously; do not act disloyally; do not act neglectfully. Do not mutilate; do not kill little children or old men, or women; do not cut off the heads off the palm trees or burn them; do not cut down the fruit trees; do not slaughter a sheep or a cow or a camel, except for food. You will pass by people who devote their lives in cloisters; leave them and their devotions alone. You will come upon people who bring you platters in which are various sorts of food; if you eat any of it, mention the name of God over it.[85]

There is no explicit statement within the Qur'an that defines the difference between combatants and non-combatants during war, so readers might think that any man of fighting age (children, women and the aged having been excluded) is considered fair game. The Qur'an does not allow this. The verses that talk of combat are clear that war is only permissible against those who are waging war; that is, those in combat. Aside from those combatants and anyone acting unjustly to prevent Muslims from practising their faith or trying to violate the sanctity of Islam's holy places, *no one* is to be harmed.

The rationale for this is clear. Central to the Qur'anic revelation and stated unequivocally in many passages is the message that the decisions that pertain to life and death are Allah's alone, and that Allah has proclaimed that human life—a 'sacred' gift—may never be taken without 'just cause'.[86] In the Qur'anic passages narrating the story of Cain and Abel (surah 5:27–32, revealed very late in Muhammad's life) one can read an explicit protection of the lives of the innocent. *Sūrat Al-Mā'idah*, 5:32 informs us that, if anyone takes the life of another human, unless it is for murder, aggressive violence or serious persecution, it is as though he has killed all of humanity. Likewise, if anyone saves a life, it is as though he has saved all of humanity. To discourage war, the very next verse is clear: those who undertake warfare against the innocent do not count as innocent, nor do those who inflict grave injustice or oppression upon the innocent. They forfeit their right to what we would nowadays call 'civilian immunity', and are liable to be killed in battle or executed if they are caught and have not repented.[87]

Jihad

It should already be clear that, far from serving as the foundation of a callous faith in which human life is not respected, or a bellicose faith in which peace is not desired, the Qur'an presents warfare as an undesirable activity. It should be undertaken only within certain constrained circumstances and in a manner that facilitates the quick restoration of peace and harmony and minimises the harm and destruction that war inevitably brings. An analysis of such matters would not, of course, be complete without making some sense of jihad, that famous word and concept that nowadays is most controversial and misunderstood.

Interestingly, given that jihad is now associated with extremists who are full of hatred, like Osama bin Laden and other terrorists, the Qur'an does not allow hatred to form the basis of a military or other armed response to perceived injustices. It explicitly states that the hatred of others must not make anyone *swerve to [do] wrong and depart from justice. Be just* (*Al-Mā'idah*, 5:8 and see 5:2). The Qur'an likewise praises those who *restrain their anger and are forgiving towards their fellow men* (*Āl 'Imrān*, 3:134).[88] These and other verses communicating the same message are clear enough to prevent crimes perceived nowadays by Muslims from turning them into criminals.[89] They certainly made an impact on Muslims during Muhammad's lifetime. During the Battle of Khandaq in 627, for example, 'Ali ibn Abi Talib (who later served as caliph) reportedly subjugated 'Amr ibn 'Abd al-Wudd, a powerful warrior of the Quraysh. 'Ali was about to deal a death blow when his enemy spat in his face. 'Ali immediately released him and walked away. He then rejoined battle and managed to slay his enemy. When later asked to explain why he had released his foe, 'Ali replied that he had wanted to keep his heart pure from anger and that, if he needed to take life, he did it out of righteous motives and not wrath.[90] Even if the verity of this story is impossible to demonstrate (it is first found in a thirteenth-century Persian Sufi poem), its survival and popularity attest to the perceived importance within Islam of acting justly at all times, even during the heightened passions inevitable in war.

Despite some popular misperceptions that jihad is based on frustration or anger that many non-Muslims consciously reject the faith of Islam, the Qur'an is quite clear that Islam can be embraced only by those who willingly come to accept it. Islam cannot be imposed upon anyone who does not. Surah 2:256 is emphatic that there must be *no compulsion in religion* (*Al-Baqarah*, 2:256). Truth is self-evident, the verse adds, and stands out from falsehood. Those who accept the former grasp *the most trustworthy hand-hold that never breaks*. Those who accept falsehood instead will go forth into *the depths of darkness*: the same hell that Christ had preached about. The fate of individuals, based on the choice they make, is therefore Allah's alone to decide. The Qur'an repeats in several other verses that coerced religion would be pointless because the submission of the heart wanted by Allah would be contrived and thus not accepted as genuine. When even Muhammad complained that he seemed to be surrounded by people who would not believe, a divine revelation clarified that Muslims were merely to turn away from the disbelievers after saying *peace* to them *for they shall come to know*

(*Al-Zukhruf*, 43:88–9). The Qur'an itself enjoins believers to invite disbelievers *to the Way of thy Lord with wisdom and beautiful preaching; and argue with them in ways that are best and most gracious ... if you show patience, that is indeed the best (cause) for those who are patient. ... For Allah is with those who restrain themselves, and those who do good* (*Al-Naḥl*, 16:125–8). At no point in Muhammad's life did he give up hope that all peoples would want to get along harmoniously. Despite his grave disappointment whenever communities competed instead of cooperated, in one of his later public sermons he revealed the divine message that Allah had made all of mankind *into nations and tribes, that you may know each other* (not: 'that you may despise each other'*)*.[91]

This desire for tolerant coexistence even included other faiths and Muhammad never stopped believing in the commonality of belief between Muslims and the God-fearing among those who identified themselves as Jews and Christians (*Ahl al-Kitāb*, the People of the Book). They shared the same prophetic line of revelation, after all. Despite rejection by several powerful Jewish tribes, and frustration over trinitarian concepts, Muhammad remained convinced that the Jewish and Christian faith communities (as opposed to some individual tribes which acted treacherously) were eminently acceptable to Allah if they followed their own scriptures. Verses saying precisely this were revealed very close in time to the Verse of the Sword. The verses encourage the Jews and Christians to believe (submit to God) and act faithfully according to their own scriptures, the Torah and the Gospel. The verses state that, if they do so, they, along with Muslims (fellow submitters (*Al-Baqarah*, 2:62)), will have no need to fear or grieve (*Al-An'ām*, 5:69). The revelation of these religiously inclusive verses late in Muhammad's life further undermines the thesis that the verses revealed late in his life undid all of the interfaith outreach that Muhammad had preached years earlier.

So what, then, is jihad and why does it seem so threatening? The answer is that jihad, far from meaning some type of fanatical holy war against all unbelievers, is the Arabic word for 'exertion' or 'effort' and it actually describes any Muslim's struggle against the things that are ungodly within him or her and within the wider world. One major form of jihad is the Muslim's struggle against his or her *nafs*: an Arabic word that may be translated as the 'lower self' and refers to the individual's ego, carnal nature and the bad habits and actions that come from failure to resist temptation or desire.[92] For example, a Muslim who consciously strives to break the habit of telling white lies, or the drinking of alcohol, or who struggles against a bad temper, is involved quite properly in a jihad against those unfortunate weaknesses. In surah 29:6 the Qur'an explains this by pointing out that the striving (jihad) of individuals against their personal ungodliness will bring personal, inner (that is, spiritual) growth. Yet the very next verse goes further by exhorting believers not only to work on their personal faith, but also to do 'good deeds' to others. Devoting time and giving money to the welfare of the poor and needy (of all communities, not just Muslims), and to the upkeep and governance of the ummah, is mentioned in several scriptures as this type of divinely recommended effort (jihad). Winning souls to Islam through peaceful preaching is likewise a worthy effort. Muhammad himself revealed a divine exhortation to *strive* with *all effort* (*Al-Furqān*, 25:52) (in Arabic it uses two forms of the same word jihad) using the powerful words of the Qur'an to convince unbelievers.

Jihad is also used in the Qur'an to mean physical defensive resistance to external danger. It appears in thirty verses, six of them revealed during Muhammad's years in Mecca and twenty-four revealed during the years of armed attack by the Quraysh tribe and its allies and then the protective wars to create security within and around the Arabian Peninsula.[93] Critics of Islam claim that this ratio reveals that jihad and *qitāl* (war-fighting) are effectively synonymous regardless of context. This is incorrect. The struggle against ego and personal vice is a greater, non-contextual and ever-required struggle, as Muhammad revealed. After returning from a battle he told his supporters: 'You have come back from the smaller jihad to the greater jihad.' When asked what the greater jihad was, Muhammad replied: 'The striving of Allah's servant against his desires' ('*mujāhadāt al-'abd li-hawah*').[94]

Moreover, the Verse of the Sword and the other supposedly bloody verses quoted in this article do *not* use the word jihad for the recommended defensive war-fighting. They use *qitāl*, which simply means fighting or combat. Yes, *qitāl* is permitted as part of a defensive struggle against serious oppression or persecution, but that does not mean that all jihad is fighting. That would be using logic similar to saying that, because all fox terriers are dogs, all dogs are fox terriers. All lawful *qitāl* is jihad—a legitimately approved and rigorously constrained military struggle against evil—but not all jihad (or even much of it or the 'greater' type) is warfare. Questions about who can legitimately call for or initiate *qitāl* as part of any jihad, in a world which no longer has caliphs leading the ummah, are debated by Islamic scholars, with a vast majority arguing that only state leaders in Islamic (or Muslim-majority) lands would be legitimately able to do so if a genuine just cause emerged. The fact that *fatāwā* and other calls for fighting made in recent years by Al-Qaeda and Taliban leaders have not been accepted by the overwhelming majority of the world's 1.6 billion Muslims is a clear sign that few Muslims see them as legitimate leaders or agree that armed fighting would be a just and appropriate response to the alleged grievances.

Interestingly, all the verses mentioning jihad as armed struggle in defence of the Islamic people and polity are exhortative in nature: with pleas for effort, urgings of courage and a fighting spirit, assurances of victory and promises of eternal rewards for those who might die in the service of their community. This emphasis reveals that Muhammad recognised that wars were so unpalatable to his peace-loving community that, even though the causes of Muslim war-fighting were just, he had to go to extra lengths—much as Winston Churchill did during the dark days of the Second World War—to exhort frightened or weary people to persevere, to believe in victory and to fight for it. On 4 June 1940 Churchill gave a magnificent speech to inspire the British people to continue their struggle against the undoubted evils of Nazism, even though the German armed forces then seemed stronger and better in battle. His speech includes the fabulous warlike lines:

> We shall fight on the seas and oceans,
> We shall fight with growing confidence and growing strength in the air,
> We shall defend our island, whatever the cost may be,
> We shall fight on the beaches,
> We shall fight on the landing grounds,
> We shall fight in the fields and in the streets,
> We shall fight in the hills,
> We shall never surrender.[95]

No one would dream of calling Churchill warmongering, much less murderous. Muhammad's exhortations for Muslims to do their duty—a phrase used by Churchill in that speech and others—and to struggle against the threat of defeat at the hands of the Muslims' enemies are best seen in the same light. Indeed, most of the verses which urge *qitāl* as part of the struggle (jihad) against enemies relate to the self-defensive wars mentioned above, with the remaining verses relating to the broader need to protect the nascent ummah from both the local spiritual pollution of intransigent Arab polytheism and idolatry as well as the external threat to unsafe borders around the perimeter of the ummah. No verses in the Qur'an encourage or permit violence against innocent people, regardless of faith, and no verses encourage or permit war against other nations or states that are not attacking the Islamic ummah, threatening its borders or its direct interests, or interfering in the ability of Muslims to practice their faith. Armed effort against any states that might do those oppressive things would still be permitted to this day, at least according to a fair reading of the Qur'an[96]—just as it is within Western Just War theory. Yet such a situation would involve a very different set of circumstances to those existing in the world today; those which somehow wrongly prompted a very small number of radicalised terrorists to undertake aggressive and offensive (not justly motivated and defensive) struggles. Their reprehensible actions, especially those that involve the taking of innocent lives, fall outside the behaviours permitted by a reasonable reading of the Qur'an.

Conclusion

This paper is not an attempt at religious apologetics. It is written by a scholar of military strategy and ethics for a general audience in an endeavour to demonstrate that the world's second largest religion (only Christianity has more adherents) includes at its core a set of scriptures that contains a clear and very ethical framework for understanding war and guiding the behaviour of warriors. That framework only supports warfare when it is based on redressing substantial material grievances (especially attack or serious direct persecution), when it occurs after other means of addressing the grievances have been attempted, and when it includes the cessation of hostilities and the restoration of peace as soon as a resolution has been attained. It demands of warriors that they uphold the concepts of proportionality (doing no more harm than is necessary) and discrimination (directing violence only at combatants whilst minimising harm to civilians and their possessions and infrastructure). That framework is very compatible with the Western Just War philosophy that, for example, gave a moral underpinning to the United Kingdom's war against Argentinean troops occupying the Falkland Islands in 1982, the US-led Coalition's eviction of Saddam Hussein's troops from Kuwait in 1991, and NATO's seventy-eight-day air war against Slobodan Milošević's Yugoslavia in order to protect Kosovars from ethnic violence in 1999.

So, then, if the Qur'an itself condemns any violence that exceeds or sits outside of the framework for justice revealed within its verses, how can we explain the barbarous 9/11 attacks, the home-grown 7/7 attacks and other suicide-bombing attempts within the United Kingdom and the murder of civilians by terrorists in other parts of the world who claim to act in the name of Islam? British scholar Karen Armstrong answered this obvious question so succinctly in the days after 9/11 that her words make a fitting conclusion to this article. During the twentieth century, she wrote, 'the militant form of piety often known as fundamentalism erupted in every major religion as a rebellion against modernity'. Every minority fundamentalist movement within the major faiths that Armstrong has studied 'is convinced that liberal, secular society is determined to wipe out religion. Fighting, as they imagine, a battle for survival, fundamentalists often feel justified in ignoring the more compassionate principles of their faith. But in amplifying the more aggressive passages that exist in all our scriptures, they distort the tradition.'[97] Armstrong is correct, but her word 'distort' is too weak for Al-Qaeda-style terrorists. They have not merely distorted the Qur'anic message; they have entirely perverted it and in the process created additional unhelpful hostility towards Islam—a faith of justice which seeks to create peace and security for its believers and a state of harmony and peaceful coexistence with other faiths.

CHAPTER THREE

JIHAD AND THE ISLAMIC LAW OF WAR

Dr Caner Dagli

Overview

Introduction

1) Does jihad mean 'holy war'?
2) What is the role of non-violent jihad?
3) Do Muslims go to war against others merely because they are non-Muslim?
4) What are the Five Basic Rights of Islamic law, and how do they relate to war?
5) What does the Qur'an say about jihad and fighting?
6) When do Muslims make treaties?
7) What is the distinction between pre-emption and aggression?
8) What is the difference between 'The Abode of Islam' and 'The Abode of War'?
9) Is forced conversion an Islamic teaching?
10) What is the 'sword verse'?
11) What are the basic rules of combat as laid down in Islam's authoritative texts?
12) What is the status of non-Muslims under Islamic rule?
13) What is the *jizyah*, or poll tax, on non-Muslims?
14) Does orthodox Islam sanction rebellion against political authority?
15) How does the Islamic law of war come to be violated?

Conclusion

Further Reading

Introduction

What is the Islamic law of war and peace? This crucial question underlies all discussion of jihad, perhaps the most misrepresented of ideas in the West's understanding of Islam. 'Holy war',[98] 'a faith spread by the sword',[99] 'Islamo-fascism',[100] 'infidel',[101] and many of the other catchphrases so popular in the uninformed debate on this topic only serve to muddle the issue. It is therefore useful, and even imperative, to explain what jihad is, what it means to Muslims, and how it relates to the concrete issues of war and peace. Since one cannot hope to understand a law by studying the actions of those who break it, we will not discuss here the actions of individuals, but focus on the very sources of Islamic law itself as they relate to jihad, war and peace. Acts of violence and situations of peace can only be judged, from the point of view of Islam and the shari'ah (Islamic law), on how fully they accord with the principles set down by the Qur'an, the teachings of the Prophet, and the precedent set by the tradition of religious scholars through the centuries.

Naked assertions by individuals who claim to speak in the name of Islam without a foundation in these authoritative sources and principles must be examined in light of these very sources and principles, and not accepted at face value. What follows is an attempt to describe the most important issues surrounding the Islamic law of war and peace, and to lay out the mainstream, traditional Islamic position, comprised of three essential principles:

- Non-combatants are not legitimate targets.
- The religion of a person or persons in no way constitutes a cause for war against them.
- Aggression is prohibited, but the use of force is justified in self-defence, for protection of sovereignty, and in defence of all innocent people.

We will expand upon these principles in what follows.

Question 1: Does 'Jihad' Mean 'Holy War'?

Although very often the Arabic word jihad is glossed as 'holy war', if we were to translate 'holy war' back into Arabic we would have *al-ḥarb al-muqaddasah*, a term which does not exist in any form in the Islamic tradition. Jihad, both linguistically and as a technical term, means 'struggle', and is etymologically related to the words *mujāhadah*, which also means struggle or contention, and *ijtihād*, which is the effort exerted by jurists to arrive at correct judgments in Islamic law.

'Holy war' is actually a term that comes out of Christianity. Until its acceptance by the Emperor Constantine in the fourth century, Christianity was a minority religion that was often persecuted and which grew only through preaching and missionary activity. Christians were in no position to make war, and indeed Christ's teaching to turn the other cheek kept them from retaliation against their persecutors in most cases. When Christians came to possess real military power, however, they were faced with the task of fighting wars and of deciding when, if ever, a Christian could fight in a war and still be considered a true follower of Christ. Augustine was one of the earliest of Church thinkers to address this question in detail, discussing it under the general rubric of 'just war'. Both he and his mentor Ambrose of Milan described situations in which justice would compel Christians to take up arms, but without forgetting that war should only be seen as a necessary evil, and that it should be stopped once peace is achieved. Such ideas were later elaborated upon by such figures as Thomas Aquinas and Hugo Grotius.

It was with the rise of the Papal States and ultimately with the declaration of the Crusades that the concept of 'holy war' came to be an important term. It is noteworthy that the earliest 'holy wars' were often wars by Christians against other Christians, in the sense that the protagonists saw themselves as carrying out the will of God. However, it was with the 'taking of the cross' by the Christian warriors sent by Pope Urban in the eleventh century that 'just war' became 'holy war' in its fullest sense. It was only with the authorisation of the Pope that a knight could adopt the symbol of the cross. 'Holy war', as a term, thus has its origins in Christianity, not Islam.

This gradual transition from total pacifism to just war to holy war did not occur in Islam. The non-violent period lasted only until the Prophet emigrated to Medina, after which the community was forced to ponder the conduct of war. The early history of Islam, unlike that of Christianity, was marked by overwhelming military and political success. However, rather than stamp a permanently warlike character on Islam, the very fact that Muslims received revelation and guidance from the Prophet on matters of war established a set of rules and legal precedent that set clear and unmistakeable boundaries. As Christians came to learn after they had gained political power, in a world full of evil and human passions war was inevitable, and even followers of Christ's teaching of turning the other cheek were forced to formulate a concept of 'just war'. They lacked, however, the advantage of a clear and binding precedent that not only provided that *jus ad bellum*, or the conditions under which a just war could be waged, but *jus in bellum*, the rules on how the fighting itself is carried out. This is precisely what the Qur'an, the life and teachings of the Prophet and the actions of the early community gave to Islamic law.

The term 'holy war' is thus inaccurate and unhelpful, implying that for Muslims war has a kind of supernatural and unreasoned quality removed from the exigencies of the world. On the contrary, Islamic law treats war as a sometimes necessary evil, whose conduct is constrained by concrete goals of justice and fairness in this world. If warfare has any worth (and indeed, those martyred while fighting justly in the way of God are promised paradise), it comes from what is fought for, not from the fighting itself. Jurists of Islamic law never ask whether war is 'holy'. Rather, they determine, based on Islamic teaching, if it is right and just. An unjust attack by a group of Muslims acting outside of the law might be called war, but it is not jihad in the eyes of traditional Islam. Moreover, as the verses of the Qur'an and sayings of the Prophet below will show, jihad is also a name for a spiritual struggle, or taking a principled stand in a difficult situation.

Thus, not all war is jihad, and not all jihad is war.

Question 2: What is the Role of Non-Violent Jihad?

The history of the Muslim community under the Prophet is normally divided into two periods, the Meccan and the Medinan. Qur'anic chapters and verses are normally classified accordingly, depending on when the verse was revealed. The Muslim hijri calendar begins with the emigration (Hijrah) of the Prophet and his companions from Mecca to Medina, where they established the first Islamic political entity. The

Meccan period begins with the Prophet's first revelation from the archangel Gabriel, and ends thirteen years later with the Hijrah, while the Medinan period begins with Hijrah and ends ten years later with the Prophet's death in 632 of the Common Era.

In the Meccan period the Muslims were a minority religious community amongst the primarily polytheistic pagan Arabs, and possessed no political power or protection aside from that which was provided by their familial bonds. They did not constitute a formal organisation, but rather were a self-selected group of individuals who were bound to each other spiritually, and who were often verbally and physically abused for their practices and their belief in the one God. During this period the Prophet was neither judge nor ruler, but guide and teacher, and brought news of the true nature of things, especially as it concerned the oneness of God and the inevitable Day of Judgment. The commands and prohibitions during these years were of a spiritual nature, such as performing prayer and keeping away from unclean things, and there was no earthly punishment for going against them.

Once the Prophet and his companions emigrated to Medina, the Prophet took on the power to govern politically over the Muslims and non-Muslims of Medina. He became both a spiritual and temporal leader, and as such became responsible for both the spiritual and material needs of the people, whereas in the Meccan period his primary mission was to be *a bearer of good tidings, and a warner* (*Fāṭir*, 35:24). These material needs included the defence and maintenance of the new Islamic state, by force of arms if necessary. While the Muslims in the Meccan period were expressly forbidden to take up arms against their persecutors, in the Medinan period they were given permission to fight their enemies militarily, as will be discussed below.

Some have speculated that the Muslim community was not permitted to take up arms in the Meccan period because they were weak and outnumbered, but this is to forget that they were outnumbered three to one at the Battle of Badr, which took place in the Medinan period. Moreover, this explanation contradicts Qur'anic verses such as,

> *If there are ten steadfast among you, they will defeat two hundred, and one hundred among you will defeat one thou-*

> *sand of those who disbelieve, for they are a people who do not understand.* (*Al-Anfāl*, 8:65)

or,

> *How many a small party has defeated a larger party by God's leave! God is with the steadfast.* (*Al-Baqarah*, 2:249)

Still, we find that in this period of non-violent steadfastness, under the frequently violent persecution of the Meccan pagans to the new religion, the Muslims are commanded to carry out struggle, or jihad:

> *Do not obey the disbelievers, and struggle against them with it a great struggle.* (*Al-Furqān*, 25:52).

> *Then indeed your Lord—for those who emigrated after they were put through tribulation, then struggled and were patient—indeed your Lord, after that, is forgiving, merciful.* (*Al-Naḥl*, 16:110).

Verse 25:52 is universally considered to be Meccan by traditional exegetes of the Qur'an,[102] and Ibn 'Abbas pointed out that *struggle ... with it* means to struggle using the Qur'an, that is, with the truth contained therein against the false beliefs of the pagans. Verse 16:110 is thought by some to be Medinan, but the majority of exegetes consider the emigration mentioned to refer to the flight of some of the Muslim community to seek asylum with the King of Abyssinia, which occurred in the Meccan period.

The Prophet himself praised non-violent jihad. He said, 'The best struggle (jihad) is to speak the truth before a tyrannical ruler,'[103] and, 'The best struggle is to struggle against your soul and your passions in the way of God Most High'.[104] Some have questioned the authenticity of the hadith which describes the Prophet returning from a battle with the companions and saying, 'We have returned from the lesser struggle to the greater struggle', which is often cited by those seeking to recover the traditional meaning of jihad. If the hadith is indeed inauthentic, the meaning is still found in the aforementioned hadith that places the struggle against the soul above all other struggles. Moreover there are numerous other hadith which place the efforts required in the spiritual life above the rewards of physical combat. The Prophet once said, 'Shall I tell you of your best deed, the most pleasing to your King, the loftiest in your ranks, better than the giving of gold and silver, and better than meeting your enemy in battle, beheading him whilst he beheads you? The remembrance of God *(dhikr Allāh).*'[105]

Indeed, so important is the spiritual element of struggle that even when Muslims are commanded to fight they must first insure that the truth does not die with those who put their lives at risk in battle.

> *It is not for the believers to go forth altogether: why should not a party of every section of them go forth so that they may become learned in religion and that they may warn their folk when they return to them, so that they may beware?* (*Al-Tawbah*, 9:122)

The superior and inherent worth of spiritual struggle over armed struggle is an immutable value in Islam, but placing the spiritual above the worldly does not erase worldly concerns. It is universally agreed that Islamic law came to sanction armed struggle and war, but this sanction came with a law of war which is binding for Muslims. This law of war answers two fundamental questions: Why do we fight? How should we fight?

In almost all cases during the career of the Prophet, armed combat and war took place with Muslims on one side and non-Muslims on the other. These were not tribal battles, since members of the same tribe and often the same family fought on opposite sides. Nor were they religious battles in the sense that Muslims fought non-Muslims for the mere fact of their being non-Muslims. As we shall see, Muslims fought for the protection of their basic rights: the right to life, property, honour and most importantly the right to believe and practice their faith. Their grievances against their enemies were expulsion from their homes and seizure of their property; persecution in the form of torture and murder; and pressure to give up their faith in the one God and the Prophet Muhammad ﷺ.

A cursory knowledge of the life of the Prophet will show that one need not go into theology to explain why Muslims fought their enemies. The fact that Muslims were persecuted, reviled, tortured, pitted against their own families, exiled, ostracised and killed provides more than enough justification for their resort to force.

Question 3: Do Muslims go to War against Others Merely Because they are Non-Muslim?

Most scholars agree that the first verses to permit fighting were:

> *Indeed God protects those who believe. Indeed God does not love the treacherous, the ungrateful. Permission is granted to those who fight because they have been wronged. And God is truly able to help them; those who were expelled from their homes without right, only because they said: 'Our Lord is God'. Were it not for God's causing some people to drive back others, destruction would have befallen the monasteries, and churches, and synagogues, and mosques in which God's Name is mentioned greatly. Assuredly God will help those who help Him. God is truly Strong, Mighty—those who, if We empower them in the land, maintain the prayer, and pay the alms, and enjoin decency and forbid indecency. And with God rests the outcome of all matters.* (*Al-Ḥajj*, 22:38–41)[106]

It is of the greatest significance that the verses finally giving Muslims permission to use force to defend themselves should make mention of the houses of worship of other religions. God not only protects Muslims by repelling some by means of others, He also protects religion as such, which is described here in terms of the places wherein the name of God is remembered. As will be made clear below, it is not the religious identity of people which justifies the use of force against them, but their aggression and crimes against the Muslim community and, by extension, other religious communities under Muslim rule.

Question 4: What are the Five Basic Rights of Islamic Law, and How Do they Relate to War?

The question of protecting religion in war is a crucial one, for indeed the law of war in Islam is a subset of all Islamic law (the shari'ah), and as such it must conform to the principles of that encompassing law. Jurists of the (overwhelming majority) orthodox tradition have, in codifying the law, identified those fundamentals which the law must protect and which Muslims cannot violate. These are usually called 'The Aims of the Law' (*maqāṣid al-sharī'ah*), but in effect they amount to the Five Basic Rights. They are: (1) Religion; (2) Life; (3) Mind; (4) Honour; (5) Property. Muslims have always understood the value of the outward (the restrictions and prohibitions of the law) to derive ultimately from its protection of the inward (the human being's relationship with God and his own true nature), hence the traditional place of religion as the first Basic Right before the law. It is one reason why the Prophet placed the remembrance of God above all other acts. Yet Islamic law, and ipso facto the law of war, must take into account the other Basic Rights. The Right to Life includes safety from murder, torture, terror, and starvation. The Right to Mind encompasses the Islamic prohibition of intoxication, and more generally can be extended to those things which hinder human objectivity, such as misinformation, mis-education, and lying in general. The Right to Honour exists in what has come to be known in the modern world as 'human dignity', which in the Islamic context begins with the integrity of the family (and particularly of one's lineage) and extends to the protection of one's good name and an environment of mutual respect in society. The Right to Property protects against theft, destruction, and dispossession.

These Five Basic Rights all pertain to the conduct of war, enshrining the principle that the material is ultimately justified in light of the spiritual, and that the spiritual must guide the conduct of the material. In other words, morality and ethics apply to war, equally and according to the same principles, as they apply to economic transactions, marriage and sexuality, and government. Indeed, it is an abuse of good sense to suppose that a civilisation which developed a highly sophisticated law and system of justice, an international system of trade and credit, peaks of art and philosophy and major advances in science and technology—all within a world view formed by the Qur'an and the teachings of the Prophet—could somehow have omitted to address justice, harmony, and fairness when it came to questions of war and peace.

Question 5: What Does the Qur'an Say about Jihad and Fighting?

Below are some Qur'anic verses pertaining to jihad and fighting. Care has been taken to quote these at some length, as the relevant passages are often abbreviated and quoted out of context in much of the discussion about the Qur'an and jihad. When read as a whole, the justice and fairness of the Qur'anic commands speak for themselves:

And fight in the way of God with those who fight against you, but aggress not; God loves not the aggressors. And slay them wherever you come upon them, and expel them from where they expelled you; sedition is more grievous than slaying. But fight them not by the Sacred Mosque until they should fight you there; then if they fight you, slay them—such, is the requital of disbelievers. But if they desist, surely God is Forgiving, Merciful. Fight them till there is no sedition, and the religion is for God; then if they desist, there shall be no enmity, save against evildoers. The sacred month for the sacred month; holy things demand retaliation; whoever commits aggression against you, then commit aggression against him in the manner that he committed against you; and fear God, and know that God is with the God-fearing. (*Al-Baqarah*, 2:190–4)

Prescribed for you is fighting, though it be hateful to you. Yet it may happen that you hate a thing which is good for you; and it may happen that you love a thing which is bad for you; God knows, and you know not. They ask you about the sacred month, and fighting in it. Say, 'Fighting in it is a grave thing; but to bar from God's way, and disbelief in Him, and the Sacred Mosque, and to expel its people from it—that is graver in God's sight; and sedition is graver than slaying'. They will not cease to fight against you until they turn you from your religion if they are able; and whoever of you turns from his religion, and dies disbelieving—their works have failed in this world and the Hereafter. Those are the inhabitants of the Fire, abiding therein. (*Al-Baqarah*, 2:216–7)

God does not forbid you in regard to those who did not wage war against you on account of religion and did not expel you from your homes, that you should treat them kindly and deal with them justly. Assuredly God loves the just. God only forbids you in regard to those who waged war against you on account of religion and expelled you from your homes and supported [others] in your expulsion, that you should make friends with them. And whoever makes friends with them, those—they are the wrongdoers. (*Al-Mumtaḥanah*, 60:8–9)

Say to the disbelievers, that if they desist, that which is past will be forgiven them; but if they return, the way of [dealing with] the ancients has already gone before! And fight them until sedition is no more and religion is all for God; then if they desist, surely God sees what they do. (*Al-Anfāl*, 8:38–9)

Read as a whole, and not selectively quoted out of context, these verses make it clear that Muslims fight because they have been wronged; because they have been persecuted, which is seen as worse than killing; because they have been made to renounce their religion; and because they have been driven out of their homes. Muslims must fight their enemies not because of who they are, but because of what they have done to them and continue to do to them.

It must be remembered that the Prophet began preaching while still a respected and admired member of his community. It was the teachings he brought which the Quraysh saw as a threat, not the Prophet himself as a man, nor his followers as a group. He never threatened the Quraysh (other than warning them of the Day of Judgment) or used any kind of coercion whatsoever. The young Muslim community began to suffer persecution under the Quraysh because Islam was seen as a threat to its own pagan religion and to Mecca's role as a place of pilgrimage (and hence to the tribe's economic prosperity). The first reactions of the Muslims were to endure, then to flee, since they were not yet permitted to fight back. It was only after the Quraysh had made life unbearable—by ostracising the Muslims and finally even attempting to assassinate the Prophet—that the young community finally migrated to Medina. Indeed, the Muslims had exhausted all other options before resorting to force.

Question 6: When Do Muslims Make Treaties?

Though Muslims were eventually given permission to retaliate, in Islamic law the goal of redressing grievances is not mere revenge, but the establishment of peace. For this reason the Qur'an often makes mention of treaties of peace with non-Muslims, including the polytheists. The following verses are examples from the Qur'an involving treaties and agreements of peace with non-Muslims, again quoted at length so as to show their context:

> *They long that you should disbelieve as they disbelieve, so then you would be equal; therefore do not take friends from among them until they emigrate in the way of God; then, if they turn away, take them and slay them wherever you find them; and do not take any of them as a patron, or as a helper. Except those who attach themselves to a people between whom and you there*

is a covenant, or come to you with their breasts constricted about the prospect of fighting you, or fighting their people. Had God willed, He would have given them sway over you, so that assuredly they would have fought you. And so if they stay away from you and do not fight you, and offer you peace, then God does not allow you any way against them. You will find others desiring to have security from you and security from their own people; yet whenever they are returned to sedition, they are overwhelmed by it. So, if they do not stay away from you, and offer you peace, and restrain their hands, then take them and slay them wherever you come upon them; against them We have given you clear warrant. (*Al-Nisā'*, 4:89–91)

But if they break their oaths after [making] their pact and assail your religion, then fight the leaders of unbelief—verily they have no [binding] oaths, so that they might desist. Will you not fight a people who broke their oaths and intended to expel the Messenger—initiating against you first? Are you afraid of them? God is more worthy of your fear if you are believers. Fight them, and God will chastise them at your hands, and degrade them, and He will give you victory against them, and He will heal the breasts of a people who believe. And He will remove the rage in their hearts. God turns [in forgiveness] to whomever He will. And God is Knowing, Wise. Or did you suppose that you would be left [in peace] when God does not yet know those of you who have struggled and have not taken, besides God and His Messenger and the believers, an intimate friend? And God is aware of what you do.(*Al-Tawbah*, 9:12–6)

Those of them with whom you have made a pact, and then break their pact every time, and they are not fearful. So if you come upon them anywhere in the war, [deal with them so as to] cause those behind them to scatter, so that they might remember. And if you fear, from any folk some treachery, then cast it back to them with fairness. Truly God does not love the treacherous. And do not let those who disbelieve suppose that they have outstripped [God's purpose]; indeed they cannot escape. Make ready for them whatever force you can and of horses tethered that thereby you may dismay the enemy of God and your enemy, and others besides them, whom you know not: God knows them. And whatever thing you expend in the way of God shall be repaid to you in full, and you will not be wronged. (*Al-Anfāl*, 8:56–60)

The next verse clarifies that if they do maintain their treaties, then the treaties are to be honoured.

> *And if they incline to peace, then incline to it, and rely on God; truly He is the Hearer, the Knower.* (*Al-Anfāl*, 8:61)

The principles surrounding treaties is also seen in this verse:

> *Say to the disbelievers, that if they desist, that which is past will be forgiven them; but if they return, the way of [dealing with] the ancients has already gone before! And fight them until sedition is no more and religion is all for God; then if they desist, surely God sees what they do.* (*Al-Anfāl*, 8:38–9)

To command the state of non-violence through the observance of an established treaty with non-Muslim polytheists shows that the Muslim community was willing, and indeed commanded, to live in a state of peace with its neighbours even if those neighbours practiced a religion other than Islam. When the Muslims are commanded to fight those who break their treaties, it is the breaking of the treaty that invites warfare, not the fact that the treaty-breakers are polytheists.

The Prophet made several important treaties with the non-Muslim communities around Medina, and these were of more than one kind. Perhaps the best known is the treaty of Hudaybiyyah, where the Muslim community made a truce with the Quraysh tribe allowing the Muslim community to make a pilgrimage to Mecca the following year. This treaty was noteworthy for its pragmatism: the Prophet made certain concessions in favour of a greater good. Though they had set out to make a peaceful pilgrimage during the holy months when fighting was forbidden, they were met on the road by the Quraysh and ultimately did not reach Mecca that year as part of the treaty terms. Moreover, the Quraysh even demanded that the Prophet remove the Divine Name *Al-Rahmān* and the title of 'Messenger of God' from the treaty, which the Prophet agreed to despite the dismay of prominent companions such as 'Ali ibn Abi Talib, and even as staunch a Muslim as 'Umar ibn al-Khattab bristled at what he saw at the time as humiliating terms. Yet the Qur'an referred to Hudaybiyyah in these terms: *Verily We have given you a clear victory* (*Al-Fatḥ*, 48:1). Although the Muslims did not achieve their immediate aims of pilgrimage, the treaty of Hudaybiyyah created an environment of free travel and peace which served to strengthen the Muslim community's position in Arabia.

Thus Muslims sought peace with non-Muslims, and in no case is the reason for Muslim armed struggle against non-Muslims the mere fact of their religious identity. As is made clear in the passages from the Qur'an cited above, the reason for armed struggle is a state of war (*haraba*) originating in the concrete actions taken by the non-Muslims to harm the Muslim community, not their state of disbelieving in God (*kufr*) or of belonging to another religion. As the example of the Prophet shows, Muslims can make treaties with their enemies, even if they are polytheists, and they are expected by God to keep to their treaties. If hostilities resume with treaty-breakers, it is not because the treaty- breakers are non-Muslim but because they have re-entered a state of hostility. This in fact occurred on more than one occasion, notably the treaty of Hudaybiyyah, which was meant to last ten years but which was rendered void by Meccans' actions against the Muslim community.

In short, in Islam treaties are not predicated on theology or religious identity. Rather, like treaties anywhere, they rely on the two parties faithfully adhering to the terms. As in all transactions in Islamic law, such as buying and selling, and even marriage, the religion of the person making a treaty has no legal bearing on the force of the treaty. An agreement with a Muslim is no more or less binding than an agreement with a non-Muslim, whether it is a rental contract or the United Nations (UN) Charter.

Question 7: What is the Distinction between Pre-Emption and Aggression?

Some have sought support for the idea that Muslims can kill disbelievers for their disbelief in the Prophet's hadith during the Al-Ahzab campaign, 'Now we campaign against them but are not campaigned against by them. We are going to them.'[107] A similar type of support is sought in the battle of Khaybar, where the Muslims mounted a surprise attack against the Jews there, or at the battle of Mu'tah, where Muslims attacked the Byzantines.

If one restricted the meaning of hostility to shots being fired, then these examples might show that Muslims claim the right to unprovoked attack against others by reason of their being non-Muslims. However, an enemy need not be storming the gates in order to pose a grave and imminent danger. An enemy can have the intent to cause harm, or can be planning to cause harm, or can be conspiring with others who are already causing harm.

Indeed while there were several cases in which the Muslims 'campaigned when they were not campaigned against', there were nevertheless reasons why this cannot be considered aggression but rather pre-emption against a clear danger coupled with an intention of future aggression. In the case of Banū Mustalaq, it came to the Prophet's attention that they were conspiring against the Muslims. In the case of Khaybar, the Prophet learned that Banū Khaybar had made a secret agreement with Banū Ghaṭafān to unite against them. In order to pre-empt this action, the Prophet staged a surprise attack. In the case of the attack at Mu'tah, tribes to the north (which were under the protection of the Byzantines) showed their hostility towards the Muslims by taking the egregious step of killing the Prophet's emissary. In the Tabuk campaign Muslims set out based on information that the Byzantines were preparing to attack.

There exists a saying in Arabic, 'When the Byzantines are not campaigned against, they campaign.' This saying should remind us that the modern concepts of pre-emptive war and aggression must be understood in their proper context. Until the twentieth century, war was an accepted right of all states. Indeed, in 1928 the Kellogg-Briand Pact was the first major systematic attempt to renounce war as an instrument of national policy. Over the course of the twentieth century the Kellogg-Briand Pact was followed by the Nuremberg Principles, the Charter of the United Nations, and the Geneva Conventions, all of which laid the foundation for current international law. These agreements constitute binding treaties between the signatories. They make military aggression between states illegal, and among other things forbid the acquisition of territory by war, define war crimes during the conduct of war, and govern the treatment of prisoners, civilians, and combatants.

Such questions had already been an important part of Islamic law for more than a thousand years. Though the content of the law was different—reflecting a different international environment—the effort to regulate relations between states was well-established in Islam long before the treaties of the twentieth century. Indeed, while Islamic law flowed from principles laid down in the Qur'an and the life of the Prophet as part of a larger ethical law, the international treaties of the twentieth century were, it must be said, fuelled largely by the horror of the two World Wars and the fear of having such episodes repeated.

Question 8: What Is the Difference Between 'The Abode of Islam' and 'The Abode of War'?

From the point of view of Islamic law, any Muslim signatory to the Charter of the UN and the Geneva Conventions is just as bound to abide by them as the Prophet was to abide by the treaties he completed with the pagan Quraysh and with other tribes of Arabia and beyond. The military encounters between political entities in the past cannot be judged by the same standards that we judge such encounters today, because in the absence of an explicit renunciation of international agreements all nations are in a de facto treaty with all others, though the situation is not usually framed in those terms. The classical laws of jihad assumed—correctly—that the default position between states was a state of war, hence the name *Dār al-Ḥarb*, or Abode of War, which is usually set in contrast to *Dār al-Islām* or the Abode of Islam. This has been widely understood to mean that Muslims consider themselves obligated to wage war on all non-Muslim lands until they become part of *Dār al-Islām*, but this is not at all the case. The label 'the abode of war' signifies that the land in question is not in treaty with the Muslims and that hostilities can break out at any time. Recall that war was universally acknowledged as something states did to get what they wanted; there was no idea of violating international law or of becoming a 'rogue' state. From the point of view of current international law, all states were in a sense rogue states because there was no mechanism for enforcing or even defining the rules of war, aside from customary practices such as the receiving of emissaries.

Thus the explicit rules of the Islamic law of jihad were not imposed from without, as has been the case for states in the twentieth century, but were realised from within. The state of affairs in seventh century Arabia and the surrounding areas made this 'state of war' the rule rather than the exception. Unless an explicit treaty was made between two groups—in the case of Arabia, these fundamental units were usually tribes—then one could expect an attack at any time. The Qur'an reflects the early Muslim community's awareness of its weak and uncertain position in this hostile state of affairs:

> *Or is it that they have not seen that We have appointed a secure Sanctuary, while people are snatched away all around them? …* (*Al-'Ankabūt*, 29:67)
>
> *And remember when you were few and oppressed in the land, and were fearful lest men should snatch you away …* (*Al-Anfāl*, 8:26)
>
> *And they say, 'If we were to follow the Guidance with you, we will be deprived from our land'…* (*Al-Qaṣaṣ*, 28:57)

Muslims are described as *Those to whom people said, 'The people have gathered against you, therefore fear them' …* (*Āl 'Imrān*, 3:173)

The Surah of Quraysh also testifies to the risks of living on the Arabian Peninsula:

> *[In gratitude] for the security of Quraysh, their security for the journey of winter and of summer, let them worship the Lord of this House, Who has fed them against hunger and made them secure from fear.* (*Quraysh*, 106:1–4)

The separation of the world into the Abode of Islam and the Abode of War reflects the reality, brutal and unavoidable, that the world was not always governed by the universal treaties of today. The terms *Dār al-Islām* and *Dār al-Ḥarb* are not terms from the Qur'an or from the teachings of the Prophet, but grew out of the work of jurists coming to terms with the new international profile of Islam. As such, they also coined terms such as *Dār al-Ṣulḥ* ('Abode of Reconciliation') and *Dār al-'Ahd* ('Abode of Treaty'), referring to those lands not ruled by Islam but with which the Islamic state had some sort of peace agreement. Such designations were common from the Abbasid period all the way through to the Ottoman Empire in the twentieth century.

From the point of view of Islamic law, the gradual adoption and advancement of moral principles in international law is a welcome development, and brings the world closer to the Qur'anic ideal of non-aggression and peaceful coexistence. *And if they incline to peace, then incline to it, and rely on God; truly He is the Hearer, the Knower*

(*Al-Anfāl*, 8:61). This idealisation of peace is also echoed in the Prophet's command, 'Do not be hopeful of meeting the enemy, and ask God for well-being'.[108]

Question 9: Is Forced Conversion an Islamic Teaching?

Some texts exist which would, if misunderstood, seem to contradict the spirit of the Qur'anic verses and hadith mentioned above regarding the role of one's religion in war. One of these is the hadith which reads: 'I have been commanded to fight the people until they bear witness that there is no divinity but God and Muhammad is God's Messenger, perform the Prayer, and pay the Alms. When they have done this, their blood and property are safe from me, except by the right of Islam and their reckoning with God.'[109]

Three main questions are raised. First, who are the people whom the Prophet is commanded to fight? Second, what is the defining characteristic of these people, which makes them subject to the Prophet's fighting them? Third, and less obviously, is this hadith universal in its temporal scope, or is it limited to a specific time and situation?

A minority position holds that this hadith points to the fact that although in the beginning the Muslims were commanded to spread the truth of Islam peacefully, at a certain point this command was abrogated and from that point forward Muslims were commanded to fight non-Muslims until they accepted Islam. Abrogation (*naskh*) means that the legally binding status of a Qur'anic verse is superseded by the legally binding authority of a verse that is revealed later. For example, one verse of the Qur'an prohibits Muslims from praying while intoxicated, while a later verse abrogates this verse by promulgating an absolute prohibition on the consumption of alcohol. At issue here is whether a previous command to preach peacefully is cancelled by a later command to fight people until they accept Islam.

Among the verses which refer to preaching the truths in the Qur'an and inviting non-Muslims to Islam are the following:

> *So remind. For you are only an admonisher; you are not a taskmaster over them. But he who turns away and disbelieves, God will chastise him with the greater chastisement.* (*Al-Ghāshiyah*, 88:21-24)

> *But if they are disregardful, We have not sent you as a keeper over them. Your duty is only to deliver the Message...* (*Al-Shūrā*, 42:48)
>
> *And whether We show you a part of that which We promise them, or We take you [to Us], it is for you only to convey [the Message], and it is for Us to do the reckoning.* (*Al-Raʿd*, 13:40)
>
> *And obey God and obey the Messenger, and beware; but if you turn away, then know that Our Messenger's duty is only to proclaim plainly.* (*Al-Mā'idah*, 5:92)

Some of these verses are Medinan, which means that they were revealed after permission was given to the Muslim community to struggle through force of arms.

This makes it clear that the preaching of Islam is a question of allowing the truth to reach the ears of those who have yet to hear it, not of forcing others to accept it. Indeed, to force another to accept a truth in his heart is impossible, as acknowledged clearly in the Qur'anic verse *There is no compulsion in religion. The right way has become distinct from error* (*Al-Baqarah*, 2:256). This verse was revealed in Medina and was in fact directed at Muslims who wanted to convert their children from Judaism or Christianity to Islam.[110] As the Qur'an is so clear that the Prophet's only responsibility as regards bringing others to the truth is only to preach it to them, to bring the good news of paradise and to warn of hell, we are left with the hadith which claims that the Prophet has been commanded to fight until '*the people*' accept the oneness of God, the Messengerhood of the Prophet, perform the canonical prayer, and pay the Alms, all of which is tantamount to their becoming Muslims. The majority of the scholars of Qur'anic exegesis and law hold that the command to preach peacefully and to never coerce a person in his choice of religion was never abrogated and continued to hold sway up until the end of the Prophet's life and beyond. Amongst this majority there are two main positions. Some hold that the people referred to in the verse are the Arabian idol-worshippers, while all others fall into a separate category addressed by such verses as *God does not forbid you in regard to those who did not wage war against you on account of religion and did not expel you from your homes, that you should treat them kindly and deal with them justly. Assuredly God loves the just* (*Al-Mumtaḥanah*, 60:8). A second group of scholars holds that the command enshrined in 'There is no compulsion in religion' is universal and applies to everyone, be they idol-worshippers or Jews or Christians. In both cases the only possible scope for '*the people*' is limited to those with whom the Prophet was engaged in conflict at the time. The majority of scholars thus do not consider that 'the people' in this hadith refers to all people everywhere.

Question 10: What is the 'Sword Verse'?

One source of some controversy is the so-called sword verse, which reads:

> *Then, when the sacred months have passed, slay the idolaters wherever you find them, and take them, and confine them, and lie in wait for them at every place of ambush. But if they repent, and establish prayer and pay the alms, then leave their way free. God is Forgiving, Merciful.* (*Al-Tawbah*, 9:5)

There is no disagreement that indeed this verse commands the Muslims to kill the polytheists, but the question remains as to whether they are to be killed because they are disbelievers or because of their enmity towards the Muslims. Are they to be fought because they are hostile to the Muslims or because they reject Islam? The second part of the verse, which names repentance and the performance of the Prayer and the giving of alms as a condition by which the polytheists can save themselves from the Muslims, would seem to indicate that it is their unbelief, not their hostility, which is the motivation for Muslims to kill them. However, the next verse reads,

> *And if any one of the idolaters seeks your protection, then grant him protection so that he might hear the words of God and afterward convey him to his place of security—that is because they are a people who do not know.* (*Al-Tawbah*, 9:6)

This second verse commands Muslims to receive a polytheist if he seeks asylum, to preach the truth to him, and then to let him go safely. It sets no condition that he should repent or accept Islam. It is not a condition for the asylum seeker's safe return that he become a Muslim. Indeed, these two verses present not one but two possibilities for the non-Muslim to escape armed conflict with the Muslim community: the first is to accept Islam, as mentioned in the first verse, and the second is to seek asylum with the Muslims, as mentioned in the second verse.[111]

Some have tried, creatively and erroneously, to assert that the second verse is abrogated by the first, but this is an abuse of the principles of abrogation, and twists verses of the Qur'an to mean what we want them to mean. In fact, it would be impossible for *Al-Tawbah*, 9:5 to call for fighting against others solely based on their belief without it abrogating no less than 140 other verses calling for peace with those who do not fight against Muslims, even if they are pagans. Indeed, it would have to abrogate the verse immediately following it, 9:6. The verse *There is no coercion in religion* is not a command, but a statement of fact, of the same grammatical form as *There is no god but God.* Recall that this verse, according to one account, was revealed in the context of people over whose religious preferences the Muslims had no control—children of theirs who were among an exiled tribe. It is a description of what religion is in relation to the human will. In Qur'anic exegesis, only commands can be abrogated, not truths. Thus by definition there is no way that '*There is no coercion in religion*' (a statement, or *khabar*) can become 'Let there be coercion in religion' (a command, or '*amr*). In fact, among the four Sunni schools of jurisprudence only one, the Shafi'i school, contains the view that a person's belief can be a reason for fighting against them. This view, however, is mitigated by the fact that an opposite view, in agreement with the majority, is also attributed to Shafi'i.

Moreover, it is also important to note that two similar sounding but distinct words are used in the Qur'anic verse which says *slay the idolaters wherever you find them* and the hadith which reads, 'I have been commanded to fight with the people until …'. In the Arabic, the two verbs in question are *qatala*, which means to fight, kill, or murder, and *qātala*, which means to fight, to combat, or to contend with something. The resulting verbal nouns are *qatl* for *qatala* and *qitāl* for *qātala*. *Qatl* means killing, while *qitāl* means combat. *Sāḥat al-qitāl*, for example, means 'battlefield'. The difference is crucial and is sadly sometimes ignored. This is a case which demonstrates the importance of mastering Arabic before deciding on matters of Islamic law.

The Prophet did not say, 'I will kill/slay/murder the polytheists until …' He said, '*I will fight with them/ combat them/contend with them …*' *Qatl* is an action which, both linguistically and practically, requires only one agent. *Qitāl* implies two agents, each contending with or resisting the other. The use of *qitāl* implies a state of mutual hostility, or, from the Prophet's point of view, of a response to the polytheists' hostility.

Misunderstanding concerning such texts as these can be corrected easily by referring to the traditional law. It is one thing to hunt for quotes which serve a predetermined purpose, and quite another to understand a text in its proper context and in light of the tradition that has dwelt upon it for over 1400 years. Such problems become compounded through mistranslation and, in some cases, deliberate misinformation.

Question 11: What are the Basic Rules of Combat as Laid Down in Islam's Authoritative Texts?

The fundamental rules of combat are not academic extractions cleverly derived from history, but are explicitly laid out in Islam's authoritative texts:

> *And fight in the way of God with those who fight against you, but aggress not; God loves not the aggressors.* (*Al-Baqarah*, 2:190)

When the Prophet dispatched his armies he would say, 'Go in the name of God. Fight in the way of God [against] the ones who disbelieve in God. Do not act brutally. Do not exceed the proper bounds. Do not mutilate. Do not kill children or hermits.'[112] Once, after a battle, the Prophet passed by a woman who had been slain, whereupon he said, 'She is not one who would have fought.' Thereupon, he looked at the men and said to one of them, 'Run after Khalid ibn al-Walid [and tell him] that he must not slay children, serfs, or women.'[113] In another hadith the Prophet says clearly, 'Do not kill weak old men, small children, or women.'[114]

Abu Bakr al-Siddiq, the first caliph, gave these instructions to his armies:

> 'I instruct you in ten matters: Do not kill women, children, the old, or the infirm; do not cut down fruit-bearing trees; do not destroy any town; do not kill sheep or camels except for the purposes of eating; do not burn date trees or submerge them; do not steal from the booty and do not be cowardly'.[115]

Hasan al-Basri, one of the most important and influential of the second generation of Muslims, described the following as violations of the rules of war:

> ... mutilation (muthla), [imposing] thirst (ghulūl), the killing of women, children, and the old (shuyukh)—the ones who have no judgment for themselves (lā ra'yy lahum), and no fighters among them; [the killing of] monks and hermits, the burning of trees, and the killing of animals for other than the welfare [of eating].[116]

The principles here are clear. The Islamic law of war prohibits naked aggression, the harming of non-combatants, excessive cruelty even in the case of combatants, and even addresses the rights of animals and the natural environment.

Question 12: What is the Status of Non-Muslims under Islamic Rule?

An integral part of any law of war is the law of peace. It has already been established that the mere fact of a people being non-Muslim cannot constitute a legally sanctioned reason to go to war with them, and it thus follows that there must be a legally sanctioned way of living together with peoples who are non-Muslim. Mention has already been made of the possibility and legitimacy of treaties with non-Muslims, even with pagans who are not enemies and are not planning hostilities. Treaties can obviously also be made with the People of the Book—a term usually understood to be Jews and Christians but which in practice has applied to other religious traditions with which Islam has come into contact, such as Buddhism, Hinduism, and Zoroastrianism.

In Islamic law the People of the Book who live under the political rule of Muslims are called *ahl al-dhimmah*, literally 'people of protection', or often simply *dhimmī* ('protected person'). The doctrine of *dhimmah* is a natural outgrowth of the verse,

> *God does not forbid you in regard to those who did not wage war against you on account of religion and did not expel you from your homes, that you should treat them kindly and deal with them justly. Assuredly God loves the just.* (*Al-Mumtaḥanah*, 60:8)

As mentioned above, that area where Muslims are sovereign and where Islam provides the law for the rulers is referred to as *Dār al-Islām*, usually translated as the Abode of Islam, but sometimes left untranslated or referred to, rarely, as Islamdom, to parallel the term Christendom. In fact, often when the term 'Islam' is used in Western writings, popular and scholarly, what is being referred to is in fact *Dār al-Islām*, which is the political entity and not the religion itself. Indeed, a population need not be majority Muslim in order for it to be *Dār al-Islām*, and a population may be mostly Muslim without the area they inhabit being a part of *Dār al-Islām*.

Broadly speaking, there are two ways in which a given people may be considered *ahl al-dhimmah*. In one case, the dhimmis live amongst the Muslim population and share the same streets, markets, and neighbourhoods. In the second case, the dhimmis live in a land which is separate and where they run most of their own affairs. There are naturally degrees in between these two categories, but these are the two general types.

In the first case the dhimmis live under the laws and within the framework provided by the Islamic state, but with a substantial amount of autonomy as regards religious and cultural matters, often with the power to adjudicate certain disputes in their own separate system of courts. This was an extremely common arrangement, which began from the time of the Prophet and the first caliphs and continued until the dissolution of the Ottoman Empire in the twentieth century. The protected people were not required to contribute to the military protection of *Dār al-Islām*, but they were subject to a poll tax specific to them, most commonly known as the *jizyah* but which had other names as well.

In the second case, there exists an arrangement with the Islamic state that the dhimmi state will exist in peace with the Islamic state and will not help or support any enemy of Islam. Examples of this include the Prophet's arrangement with the people of Bahrain, who were Zoroastrians, and with the Christians of Najran. Under such an arrangement, the people remain completely autonomous and run their own affairs. They remain under the protection of the Islamic state, with no responsibility to provide active protection in return. The Islamic state has no right to any of their wealth or property except for the *jizyah*. The following is the text of the agreement between the Christians of Najran and the Prophet:

> Najran and their followers are entitled to the protection of God and to the security of Muhammad the Prophet, the Messenger of God, which security shall involve their persons, religion, lands, possessions, including those of them who are absent as well as those who are present, their camels, messengers, and images [*amthilah*, a reference to crosses and icons]. The state they previously held shall not be changed, nor shall any of their religious services or images be changed. No attempt shall be made to turn a bishop, a monk from his office as a monk, nor the sexton of a church from his office.[117]

Such agreements were commonplace in the early conquests, such as the agreements that the Muslim commanders made with the Christian population of Aleppo, Antioch, Ma'arret Masrin, Homs, Qinnasrin, and Baalbek. Upon the surrender of Damascus, the general Khalid ibn al-Walid wrote the following to the inhabitants of the city:

> In the Name of God, the Compassionate, the Merciful. This is what Khalid ibn al-Walid would grant to the inhabitants of Damascus, if he enters therein: he promises to give them security for their lives, property, and churches. Their city shall not be demolished, neither shall any Muslim be quartered in their houses. Thereunto we give to them the pact of God and the protection of his Prophet, the caliphs and the believers. So long as they pay the poll tax, nothing but good shall befall them.[118]

Perhaps most famous of all is the agreement between 'Umar ibn al-Khattab and the people of Jerusalem:

> This is the assurance of safety (*amān*) which the servant of God 'Umar, the Commander of the Faithful, has granted to the people of Jerusalem. He has given them an assurance of safety for themselves, for their property, their churches, their crosses, the sick and healthy of the city, and for all the rituals that belong to their religion. Their churches will not be inhabited [by Muslims] nor will they be destroyed. Neither they, nor the land on which they stand, nor their crosses, nor their property will be damaged. They will not be forcibly converted ... The people of Jerusalem must pay the poll tax like the people of [other] cities, and they must expel the Byzantines and the robbers ...[119]

Such agreements also applied to other religions as well. This is the treaty made between the Prophet's companion Habib ibn Maslamah and the people of Dabil:

> In the Name of God, the Compassionate, the Merciful. This is a treaty of Habib ibn Maslamah with the Christians, Magians [i.e., Zoroastrians], and Jews of Dabil, including those present and those absent. I have granted for you safety for your lives, possessions, churches, places of worship, and city wall. Thus ye are safe and we are bound to fulfill our covenant, so long as ye fulfil yours and pay the poll tax ...[120]

The main advantage of the *ahl al-dhimmah* over Muslims was the guarantee of their protection without the responsibility to actively engage in that protection themselves. Thus a dhimmi was not required to go to war to defend the Islamic state. The main disadvantage was the *jizyah*, a tax which Muslims did not pay.

Dār al-Islām is an Islamic polity ruled by Muslims in accordance with Islamic law, where the sovereignty and primacy of Muslim power is to remain undisputed, and the protected peoples live under this arrangement in a state of mutual agreement, with certain advantages given and others taken. Under the dhimmi arrangement a protected people is subjected to Muslim power in terms of political power only, while their identity, their language, their culture and most importantly their religion remain intact and under their control. This means that aside from paying the *jizyah* and obeying the overarching laws applying to people living in *Dār al-Islām*, the protected people are left alone to live their lives as they see fit. This includes the education of their children, the maintenance of their houses of worship, and even the handling of their own affairs (especially matters such as marriage, divorce, and inheritance). Under Islamic rule, dhimmis enjoyed true cultural and religious independence, and were in no way compelled to adopt the culture or religion of their rulers. Despite their theological differences with members of other faiths, Muslims did not consider the conquered peoples to be fundamentally inferior and in need of edification in order to be truly civilised. Military conquest did not entail or require the conversion of the conquered people. Islamic law provided Muslims with a ready-made and legally binding way of dealing with non-Muslims without robbing them of their selfhood, their language, or their religion.

Question 13: What is the Jizyah, or Poll Tax, on Non-Muslims?

One source of confusion is the misapplication of the verse ... *until they pay the jizyah tribute, readily being subdued* (*Al-Tawbah*, 9:29). A misunderstanding similar to the one which affects the Qur'anic verses pertaining to jihad occurs over the phrase *wa hum ṣāghirūn*, or 'in a state of humility, lowness'. That is to say, it is often thought that they pay the *jizyah* in a state of humility for being non-Muslims, but the state of being non-Muslim applies only to the giving of the *jizyah*, whereas the state of being humbled is a result of the previous hostility and enmity exhibited by the group against the Muslim community.

This is not to say that in Islamic history some rulers have not enforced a kind of humiliation to accompany the paying of the *jizyah* by the dhimmi communities, but in doing so they go against the established precedent and legal opinion. For example, Imam Nawawi, commenting on those who would impose a humiliation along with the paying of the *jizyah*, said, 'As for this aforementioned practice (*hay'ah*), I know of no sound support for it in this respect, and it is only mentioned by the scholars of Khurasan. The majority (*jumhūr*) of scholars say that the *jizyah* is to be taken with gentleness, as one would receive a debt (*dayn*). The reliably correct opinion is that this practice is invalid and those who devised it should be refuted. It is not related that the Prophet or any of the rightly-guided caliphs did any such thing when collecting the *jizyah*.[121] Ibn Qudamah also rejected this practice and noted that the Prophet and the rightly-guided caliphs encouraged the *jizyah* to be collected with gentleness and kindness.[122]

In a letter that 'Umar ibn 'Abd al-'Aziz sent regarding the *jizyah*, he gives the following instructions,

> Look to the protected people around you who are old and weak and who are no longer able to earn a living and pay them from the treasury of the Muslims such as will do them good. For indeed I have learned that the Commander of the Believers 'Umar ibn al-Khattab once passed an old man who was begging at people's doors. He said, 'We have been unfair to you. We used to take *jizyah* from you

> when you were young, then neglected you when you were old.' Then he said, 'Pay him from the treasury of the Muslims such as will do him good.'[123]

Moreover, the word *jizyah* itself simply derives from a root meaning 'part', referring to the fact that it is taken as a part of the wealth of the protected peoples. In fact, the use of the word *jizyah* is not even required. The historian al-Tabari relates that some members of the Christian community asked 'Umar ibn al-Khattab if they could refer to the *jizyah* as *ṣadaqah*, literally 'charity', which he agreed to.

It is also worth noting in this context that in most cases the *jizyah* taken was actually less than the zakat, or alms, paid by Muslims, which the dhimmis were not required to pay since the zakat is a religious requirement for Muslims only.

Another aspect of the debate over the status of protected peoples is the practice of requiring protected peoples to dress in some way that was recognisably distinct from Muslims (such as a sash around the waist which Muslims would then not be allowed to wear). In Islamic law such a ruling is the prerogative of the ruler, who may impose it for reasons of security, order, or for other reasons, though it is not required by Islamic law. It is worth noting that this practice was by no means universal and there is no record that the Prophet himself ever required it.

The classical law governing protected peoples was developed in a world where religious communities were also political communities. Some have said that the protected peoples were 'second-class' citizens, but this is to assume that all political arrangements can be compared to the modern nation-state and its concept of 'citizenship'. Indeed, many of the forms of independence the protected peoples enjoyed, such as independence of education and having religious courts, would scarcely be possible in the context of the modern nation state. In fact, the laws for protected peoples protected the very same Five Basic Rights (Religion, Life, Mind, Honour, and Property) which apply for Muslims, and the rights granted to the protected peoples were generally the most one could expect, short of granting them total sovereignty, which would negate their connection with *Dār al-Islām* in the first place.

In previous times Islamic law saw dominance within *Dār al-Islām* as the only guarantee for these rights, but the demand for obedience and deference from the protected people was geared, not towards some egotistical exaltation of Islam, but towards a just order where everyone's rights could be protected without undue advantage being taken. In the modern context, there is nothing in Islamic law that would preclude Muslims living as equal citizens in a state run by a democratically elected government, so long as their fundamental religious rights were protected.

Question 14: Does Orthodox Islam Sanction Rebellion Against Political Authority?

The relationship of the Muslim believer to those in political power reaches back to the beginning of Islam, when the Prophet became not only the spiritual guide of the new community but its political leader as well.

The question that Muslims have had to wrestle with since then concerns the legitimacy of political authority. Even though there was never a separation of church and state in Islam, there has always been, since the advent of the Umayyad caliphate thirty years after the death of the Prophet, a de facto separation of power between the ulama, or scholarly class, on the one hand, and the various caliphs, sultans, and kings on the other. One might call this a separation between court and mosque, between secretaries and scholars. What connected them was the duty of the ruler to dispose of the affairs of state in accordance with Islamic law and not his personal whim, and to do his part in maintaining the religion. It was the scholars who determined what that law was, and they functioned in various degrees of independence from the political rulers throughout most of Islamic history. That is to say, the rule of Islam is not the rule of God directly, nor even the rule of the clerics, but the rule of law—a law whose form is independent of the ruler whose role it is to carry it out.

In the context of traditional Islamic law, the question arises as to when it is permissible or even mandatory to take up arms against political authority. Spiritual or armed rebellion against the Prophet in the name of Islam would have been an absurdity, as he was God's chosen prophet and ruler and was thus universally acknowledged by anyone who called himself Muslim. However, after the Prophet, legitimacy and rebellion become real questions.

In a situation where a Muslim country is being ruled by a Muslim according to traditional Islamic law, if a ruler openly declares *kufr* ('unbelief') in a way that is plain and not open to any reasonable doubt, then traditional Islam holds that it is a duty to rise up against him. The declaration of *kufr* must be clear, however. For example, the ruler may openly deny Islam and the veracity of the Prophet's claim to being a Messenger of God. He may openly mock and degrade some fundamental pillar of religion like the pilgrimage to Mecca or the fasting in Ramadan. He may also act in a way that conclusively proves his *kufr*, such as openly worshipping an idol. Such words and actions, if not mitigated by other factors, would constitute proof of the ruler's state of unbelief.

However, it is crucial to make a distinction, as traditional Islam does, between apostasy, which is a denial of truth, and sin or even simple error, which is a failure to live up to it. Thus, rejecting the principle of the five daily prayers (which are performed with some variations amongst all Muslims) constitutes a negation of Islam itself, while being too lazy to pray is a sin. Mocking and degrading the Prophet is a rejection of Islam, but calling the mufti a silly fellow is, at worst, a sin. Prostrating before an idol in worship is a rejection of Islam, but rising when a respected elder enters the room is religiously neutral or even commendable. In traditional Islam, the sinner is allowed to respect the law and regret his weakness; by contrast, the disbeliever disregards the law in order to indulge his weakness. In any ethical system, the 'should' or 'ought' follows the 'is', which is to say that the truth always precedes and determines moral judgment. *Kufr* endangers that truth, and destroys the basis for morality, while sin is a failure to live up to that truth. Indeed, the very identification of an act as a sin is a kind of affirmation of the truth which that sin fails to live up to.

Having said that, traditional Islam has recognised three ways in which a ruler may legitimately come to power: (1) through receiving the allegiance *of ahl al-ḥall wa al-'aqd*; (2) by being chosen as a successor by the previous ruler; (3) or by force, on the condition that this is not to unseat a legitimate ruler but rather occurs in the absence of one. *Ahl al-ḥall wa al-'aqd* literally means 'people who untie and bind' or those with the authority to contract agreements. In the Islamic context they are those with religious and political authority, namely the ulama and others who are the de facto representatives of the interests of the people. Imam al-Nawawi said of political rulers,

> 'As for rising up against them and fighting them, this is forbidden by the consensus of Muslims, even if they are sinful tyrants (fāsiq, ẓālim) … The scholars have said that the reason why one should not separate from him and why it is forbidden to rise against him is the resulting strife, bloodletting, and corruption.'[124]

This statement reflects the general consensus amongst traditional scholars, which is based on hadith of the Prophet such as,

> 'After me there will be rulers (*ā'immah*, sing. *imām*) who will not follow my guidance or practice my Wont (Sunnah). Among them men will rise with the hearts of devils and the bodies of men.' He was asked, 'What should we do if we encounter that?' He said, 'Listen and obey their command. Even if they beat you and take your wealth, listen and obey.'[125]

In another hadith he was asked, 'Messenger of God, should we not oppose him by the sword?' He said,

> 'No, not so long as the Prayer is established among you. If you see something you hate in your ruler, hate his action, but do not cease to be obedient.'[126]

Islamic law does not expound a utopian ideology of a perfect world order. The Islamic tradition places paradise in the hereafter, not in this world, and recognises that it is only within men's power to maximize the level of justice in the world while maintaining a balance between the spiritual and the worldly. In a perfect world, the ruler would be just, wise, and pious, and would deal fairly with people while doing his part to protect their spiritual welfare. However, in such cases where a choice must be made between spiritual well-being and worldly justice, Islam chooses the former. Man may gain the world and lose paradise, while a man who gains paradise loses nothing in the ultimate sense. Thus a tyrant who taxes excessively and unreasonably punishes dissent, while maintaining the structure and tradition of faith (*so long as the Prayer is established among you*), is superior to a ruler who makes the trains run on time but whose programme uproots the very pillars of faith.

But this perspective is not merely a matter of placing the spiritual over the material. It is based upon a common sense approach that acknowledges that revolutions often bring about a sum total of suffering much greater than the previous order they seek to overturn. Muslims do not advocate doing nothing in the face of tyranny, but rather believe that non-violent methods of counsel and protest are ultimately better ways of improving the existing order. Indeed, Muslim jurists such as al-Juwayni and al-Ghazali and many, many others have discussed the conditions under which a ruler could be deposed and replaced by a new one, and it was typical in Islamic law for this function of replacing an evil (or insane) ruler to be seen as the role of the *ahl al-ḥall wa al-ʿaqd* (see above). This is considered different from open rebellion by the population at large, which would entail not only the replacement of the ruler but an upheaval affecting the broader society and destroying the order of that society. In the chapter on 'Enjoining Right and Forbidding Wrong' (*al-Amr bil-Maʿrūf wa al-Nahy ʿan al-Munkar*) in his seminal work *Iḥyāʾ ʿUlūm al-Dīn*, al-Ghazali describes the levels of enjoining right and forbidding wrong: the first is the identification of a wrong being committed, followed by friendly counsel and advice for the wrongdoer, beyond which one can engage in a harsh critique and public protest against the action, and in the most extreme cases one can resort to physical intervention to stop the wrong, but even in the case of the use of force a distinction is also to be made between intervening to stop a mugger, for example, and taking up arms against the sultan. Al-Ghazali states: 'As for intervening through force, that is not for subjects to undertake against the sultan, because it would lead to civil strife (*fitnah*) and generate harm, and that to which it would give rise would be worse than the initial difficulties. As for verbal condemnations such as 'O tyrant!' or 'O you who does not fear God' and the like, if such words leads to civil strife (*fitnah*) against others than this is not permissible, but if one fears only for oneself that is permissible and indeed commendable.' He quotes the famous hadith of the Prophet, 'The best struggle (*jihad*) is a true word spoken in the presence of a tyrannical ruler'. At the same time, jurists such as al-Mawardi and others have laid out the ethics of how rulers should deal with those who oppose them, setting out conditions on what is expected of a ruler who encounters non-violent resistance, violent rebellion, and situations in between. Such issues are extremely complex, but as a general principle force should be used by the ruler against his opponents as a last resort, when to do otherwise would result in even greater killing, fear, and harm to the population. If a ruler can bring about a resolution to a standoff or a conflict through persuasion or through addressing grievances then he must do so. Moreover, those who oppose the ruler 'with an interpretation', meaning on the principled basis of their understanding of what Islam requires, should be treated differently and more leniently than those who destabilise the existing order simply for personal gain and whose legal status would be that of a bandit or highwayman.

There is no doubt that some forms of tyranny impose upon the population a state of fear, suffering, and death that is so extreme that such a tyranny constitutes that very state of civil strife (*fitnah*) and social disintegration or 'corruption in the land'(*al-fasād fi al-arḍ*) which Islamic law seeks to avoid by discouraging precipitous revolution or open rebellion. In cases where there is already so much killing and mayhem that the conditions are already as bad as that of a civil war or even lawlessness, and where peaceful means such as counsel and protest have been exhausted (according to the traditional Islamic ethical principle of 'enjoining right and forbidding wrong'), and where the *ahl al-ḥall wa al-'aqd* cannot or will not intervene, then rebellion may be the only option. Also, some jurists (such as 'Abd Allah bin Bayyah and 'Ali Gomaa) have distinguished between starting a rebellion on the one hand and joining in one that is already underway on the other; the initiator bears responsibility for whatever follows, but in the case of an already ongoing civil war one may have to choose a side so that justice and order can be established and the conflict and instability can come to an end.

Muslims are expected to resist a ruler insofar as he commands them to go against the shari'ah; for example, a Muslim should not obey a command to refrain from praying the five canonical prayers. But this is not the same as rebelling against a ruler who himself does not completely enact the shari'ah, especially since Islamic law allows Muslims to live in a society in which Islamic law is not sovereign so long as their own religious rights are not violated. Those who advocate the overthrow of a ruler who does not rule in accordance with their view of the shari'ah are a tiny minority within Islamic law. They often make a compound error:

first they accept only their own vision of Islamic law, then they consider deviation from this vision to be a sin, and then they conflate this sin with unbelief, thus making the ruler subject to rebellion.

It should also be noted that some have engaged in guilt by association or 'unbelief (*kufr*) by association' to the absurd and vicious degree that employees of the state, and people who simply pay taxes, are considered to be complicit in the crimes of that state. Others have even gone so far as to say that anyone who merely lives in a society which does not conform to their vision of Islamic law is guilty of *kufr* (unbelief), since they passively accept it instead of actively fighting against it. There is no basis for this in Islamic law whatsoever.

Question 15: How Does the Islamic Law of War Come to be Violated?

Islam is the second largest religion in the world and in history after Christianity. It is also today the world's fastest growing religion, with 1.6 billion adherents all over the world. As of 2007 CE, some 25 percent or so of the world's population is Muslim. There were, historically, three main doctrinal and juridical branches of the religion: Sunni, Shi'ite and Khawarij. Currently (2007 CE) approximately 90 percent of all Muslims are Sunni, 9% are Shi'a, and less than 1 percent are Ibadi. The Sunnis (which include the Sufis or Mystics) are mostly followers of the four recognised schools (Hanafi, Maliki, Shafi'i and Hanbali) of law, and a minority are Salafi/Wahhabi, who historically arose from one of the four schools (the Hanbali), but today are Sunnis who sometimes follow their own interpretations outside of the 'four schools'. Amongst the Shi'ites, the Ja'faris or *Ithna 'ashari* ('Twelver') are the biggest group, followed by the Zaydis and the Isma'ilis. The Ibadis are descended from the original community of Khawarij, but the original radical Khawarij died out and were replaced by today's moderate Ibadis.

Aside from Islam's doctrinal and juridical divisions, a typical understanding of the spectrum in Islam, even within the Islamic world itself, places the fundamentalists on one side and the modernists on the other. The modernists are seen as open-minded, tolerant, peace-loving, and respectful of human rights. The fundamentalists are seen as fanatical, warlike, obscurantist, backwards, and tyrannical. Above all, from the Western point of view the modernists are 'like us' and hence are not threatening, while the fundamentalists are inherently dangerous and different.

In fact, a more helpful and accurate description of the spectrum of the world's Muslims would be the following five categories, from extreme secularism on one end to extreme sectarianism on the other. Understanding the differences is crucial to understanding jihad and the law of war.

SECULAR FUNDAMENTALISTS: A complete rejection of Islam as a substantial force in guiding society. At a maximum, religion is a private affair, and should have nothing to say about human relations. Islamic civilisation is something to be left behind, while modern Western civilisation is to be emulated, to the extent possible.

MODERNISTS AND MODERN SECULARISTS: Islam must adjust and change and learn the lessons of modernity; apologists holding that faith is valuable as a guide to ethics, but Islamic teachings should 'change with the times'. The values of the modern West are generally seen as the 'norm' to which the Islamic world should adjust itself.

TRADITIONALISTS: Islam is the source of meaning and guidance for the inward and outward life. Islamic civilisation is a source and treasure of intellectual, spiritual, and artistic nourishment. Loyalty to this tradition in no way precludes living sensibly and justly in the today's world, and indeed the tradition offers considerable flexibility in terms of forms of government and is a guarantor of basic rights.

PURITANICAL LITERALISTS: (Usually referred to as 'religious fundamentalists' or 'Islamists'). Both traditional Islamic civilisation and secular ideologies are failures. Muslims must pass over most of the civilisation and tradition after the first century or two after the Prophet. The state created by the Prophet and his successors was a golden age, and Muslims must duplicate it to the extent possible. Society must be cleansed of those elements which are 'innovations' from the pure state of the early Muslim community.

TAKFIRIS: (Sometimes called 'jihadists' or 'militant religious fundamentalists'). Those who do not follow true Islamic teaching (as defined by them) are no longer actually Muslim and fall outside of the protection of the law. Most self-identified Muslims and all non-Muslims are legitimate targets of violence, because they stand in the way of a very narrowly defined vision of Islam. *Takfir* means 'to declare another to be an unbeliever/apostate'. There are now both Sunni and Shi'ite takfiris—or rather, some takfiris consider themselves to be Sunnis and others consider themselves to be Shi'ites.

In reality the modernists and the puritanical literalists (the 'fundamentalists') represent only a small percentage of the population of the Muslim world, perhaps less than 10 percent combined. The majority of people—90 percent—in the Islamic world fall within a range which should be called 'traditional' and which itself encompasses a certain range of religiosity, but which is neither a complete affirmation of the post-religious values which are so powerful today, nor of the religious extremism of the fundamentalists. The takfiris and the secular fundamentalists represent a still smaller sliver of the world's Muslim population. All told, there are no more than 150,000 militant takfiris (including both the Sunni and 'Shi'ite strands) worldwide. These are thus less than one hundredth of one percent of all Muslims (that is, less than 0.01 percent), or less than one in every ten thousand Muslims. Secular fundamentalism also usually has little traction with the general population and is—paradoxically—limited to small rebel groups, such as the Kurdistan Workers' Party (PKK) in Turkey and the Mujahedin-e khalq (MEK) in Iran, and various establishment elites in a small number of Muslim countries.

That which we call 'fundamentalism' today (puritanical literalism) has several salient characteristics vis-à-vis traditional Islam. First, puritanical literalists generally ignore or explicitly reject most of the classical learned tradition of jurists and theologians, and limit themselves to their own interpretation of the Qur'an, the Hadith, and the first three generations of Muslims, which they take as authoritative (as do all Muslims). Second, they ignore or reject most of the philosophy, mysticism, and artistic production of Islamic civilisation. This results in a kind of anti-intellectualism and in a dry literalism. Third, they view religion almost entirely as a project of social engineering combined with a rigid obedientialism. Religion is thus reduced to a system of commands and prohibitions, with an excessive emphasis on outward conformity. Even worse, often these ideas are little more than a theological veneer for a crude ethnic chauvinism which seeks to universalise a tribal culture.

The modernists, for their part, generally share with the fundamentalists an aversion to the spiritual, artistic, and intellectual accomplishments of Islamic civilisation, and have an undiscerning 'West is best' approach to Islamic reform. Yet they both readily celebrate Islam's advances in science in technology and readily accept any modern technological innovation the West has to offer. These shared characteristics can be explained in light of the fact that both modernism and fundamentalism, in the Islamic world, are largely responses to the loss of power to the West over the last two hundred years. Thus, both modernism and fundamentalism blame traditional Islam for this failure, and both seek to re-establish the balance. The modernists hope to accomplish this by imitating their conquerors, while the fundamentalists hope to emulate the successes of the first generations of Muslims.

The secular fundamentalists and the takfiris, at the two extremes, are both intrinsically utopian in their outlook, the former striving to create a yet unseen paradise on earth while the latter hope to emulate a once realised golden age.

Falling into the fatal trap of any utopian ideology, both the secular and religious fundamentalists invert the traditional priorities and subjugate all values to the attainment of utopia. Robespierre's notorious statement, 'You cannot make an omelette without breaking eggs' enshrines the notion that the perfect world—here on earth—justifies any crime, and describes the authoritarian approach of these two extremes to the rest of the world. Thus, the bombing of innocent Muslims by a Muslim or non-Muslim state can be justified in the name of democracy and freedom (or in another context the liberation of the world's workers, or the ascendancy of the Arian race) which means that some are chosen to die so that the rest may live 'in freedom'. Also, the bombing of innocent Muslims by non-state actors can be justified because they stand in the way of establishing an 'Islamic state', or, in a perverted twist of spiritual logic, the killing of innocent Muslims in a terrorist attack is not really a crime because they will go to paradise as a result of being innocent victims in an attack justified by its ends.

Neither secular fundamentalists nor their religious counterparts can reasonably claim an ultimate set of values by which to act, despite appearances to the contrary. When one can justify any act in the name of a worldly utopia then one has passed into pure utilitarianism. This utilitarianism allows the secular fundamentalist to declare, without a hint of irony, that freedom (the lives of some) must be sacrificed for the sake of freedom (the liberty of others). It also allows the religious fundamentalist to assert, with the same obtuseness, that justice must be suspended (by taking innocent life) in order to preserve justice (the protection of innocent life).

What does all this mean for the law of war? In Islamic history, the law of war, though based on the Qur'an and the life of the Prophet, was constantly adapted to deal with new situations. Was it permissible to use fire as a part of a catapult weapon? What does one do in case of civilians inside of a citadel under attack? What constitutes the violation of a treaty? Questions such as these were always asked and answered in the context of the greater law, which was governed by immutable moral principles. This law, moreover, grew and was nurtured in an environment of spirituality, beauty, and the accumulated wisdom of the centuries beginning with the Prophet and continuing generation after generation. Islamic civilisation grew more experienced and sophisticated, and individuals lived in a world where tradition was alive, and the experience (and mistakes) of the past were always available to learn from.

Though the modernists and puritanical literalists do not necessarily espouse the unjust use of violence (and indeed, the vast majority of modernists and 'fundamentalists' are explicitly non-violent in their methods), their belief system removes the safeguards provided by centuries of tradition by rejecting that tradition or treating it as irrelevant. Even though Islamic law declares attacks against non-combatants, forced conversion and naked aggression to be illegal, life within traditional Islamic civilisation, with its integrated spirituality and nobility, would have made them generally unthinkable as well.

The case of Osama bin Laden's fatwa ordering Muslims to kill both soldiers and civilians is illustrative of the problems involved. Bin Laden was trained as a civil engineer, not an authority in Islamic law, and it takes little investigation to uncover that his interpretations of Islamic law are uninformed and self-serving. He can only draw the conclusions he draws by utterly ignoring everything Islamic law has had to say about such questions. Using Bin Laden's takfiri cut-and-paste method, one can make the Qur'an and Hadith say anything at all. That every top authority on Islamic law in the world rejects both Bin Laden's conclusions and his temerity in declaring a fatwa is, lamentably, often never mentioned in the West.

But such condemnation is not necessarily a problem for Bin Laden and his compatriots, because they never felt obligated to pay attention to traditional Islamic law in the first place. Ostensibly they claim to be following the Qur'an and the teachings of the Prophet, but their method amounts to a cherry-picking of sources to arrive at a conclusion that was decided beforehand. It is misleading to present Bin Laden, and others like him, as men steeped in their religious tradition who take Islam's teachings to their logical conclusions. For all the talk about 'madrasahs', which is simply the word for 'schools', it is important to note that the terrorists who claim to fight in the name of Islam today are almost entirely men educated in medicine, engineering, mathematics, computer science, etc. It is striking how absent graduates of recognised madrasahs or Islamic seminaries (such as Al-Azhar in Egypt) are among the ranks of the terrorists. It is not difficult to understand why: anyone who is exposed to the established traditional law could never, with honesty and good conscience, conclude that non-combatants are legitimate targets, or that other Muslims become unbelievers through mere disagreement with a certain interpretation of Islam.

Indeed, being steeped in the tradition of Islamic law is the best inoculation against the illegal use of force. Traditional Islam would not, and does not, recognise a civil engineer (Bin Laden) or a physician (Ayman al-Zawahiri) as competent to decide the rules of combat. Those who follow them do so for other reasons, or are much misled as to the orthodoxy of their leaders. Unburdened by precedent, whether through ignorance or disavowal, these rebellious upstarts are free to pursue their goals unrestrained by morality or justice. This is the sad legacy of both modernism and puritanical literalism: in seeking to reform Islam, they throw the baby out with the bath water, losing the natural checks against aggression and injustice in the process of jettisoning those aspects of the tradition they find unhelpful to their projects. Though not advocating such abuses themselves, the modernists and puritanical literalists leave the door open to the violation of basic human rights at the hands of the takfiris and the secular fundamentalists. Modernism did not create Hitler, but it removed the barriers, religious and cultural, which would have made his rise an impossibility. Similarly, puritanical literalism did not create Bin Laden, but it weakened the immune system, as it were, of Islamic society, leaving some within it susceptible to the contagion of takfirism.

By marginalising traditional, mainstream Islam, one does not wipe out the poison. One loses the antidote.

Conclusion

As with any religion or system of law, when it comes to the Islamic law of war there is a gap between the ideal and its application in the world. It is possible to sift through the long history of war and peace in Islamic civilisation and find examples where political powers and even religious scholars have acted and espoused views which are antithetical to the spirit and letter of the teachings of Islam regarding war and peace outlined above. Indeed, it has happened that Muslims have created situations amounting to forced conversion, or killed innocents in battle, or treated the members of other religions with contempt and cruelty. Yet there is an important difference between the flouting of high ideal and the institution of a vicious teaching. If abuses have occurred in the application of the Islamic laws of war, these exist in spite of those teachings, not because of them. Moreover, a fair reading of Islamic history will show that in the majority of cases the Islamic law of war—with its principles of justice, sparing of innocents, and idealisation of peace—were largely held to, and very often the conduct of Muslims in war exhibited the highest standards of chivalry and nobility.

Moving forward from the time of the Prophet and companions to the Crusades, we observe the figure of Salah al-Din al-Ayyubi, known to the West as Saladin, a figure of almost proverbial gallantry in battle and kindness in victory. The reconquest of Jerusalem by Saladin was as memorable for its mercy as was the initial Christian conquest for its brutality, mirroring the mercy the Prophet showed to his enemies when he entered victorious into Mecca near the end of his life. But one need not go so far back in history to find such examples. In the colonial era several Muslim resistance movements distinguished themselves by their high standards of conduct in their opposition to European aggression.

Among them were Imam Shamil (d.1871), the 'Lion of Daghestan', in his thirty year war against Russian domination, and Emir 'Abd al-Qadir al-Jaza'iri (d.1883), in his battle against French imperialism. Both men were distinguished scholars of Islam and spiritual leaders, in addition to being almost legendary military commanders. Steeped in the legal and spiritual tradition of Islam, these heroes won the grudging admiration of their enemies. Emir 'Abd al-Qadir, having fought the French for so many years, risked his life defending the Christians of Damascus, and made no distinction between his defence of Algerian Muslims and his protection of the Christians of Damascus against his fellow Muslims. For these warriors, their wise courage and stern compassion were necessary outgrowths of the Qur'an and the teachings of the Prophet. They would not have recognised the Islamic principles of combat they so steadfastly followed were they to witness some of the aberrations of the modern age.

In Islamic law, the ends do not justify the means, and justice is not predicated on creating a paradise on earth, whether that paradise is an imagined future or a recaptured past. The Islamic law of war has often come to be ignored, sadly, in the name of a totalitarian mindset which seeks to crush everything in its path for the sake of achieving its ultimate ends. According to such a view, compassion, nobility, beauty, and fairness are all to be sacrificed and then somehow recaptured later when the fighting ends. In this respect, the utopian rebels of today—whatever their religion or ideology—have much more in common with Lenin than with Saladin.

If we have not dwelt on historical battles or the minutiae of legal discussions through the centuries it is because the principles are so clear, even self-evident. The rules of war and peace in Islam can be distilled into three principles: (1) Non-combatants are not legitimate targets, and as we have seen this not only includes women, children, and the elderly but also animals and the natural environment. (2) The fact of someone's being non-Muslim does not make them a legitimate target of attack. The Islamic conquests were political in nature, and large areas under Muslim rule remained non-Muslim for centuries. The agreements cited above show that the Muslims' intention was never to convert by force. (3) Muslims are expected to live in peace with their neighbours whenever possible, and must respect treaties, but this never precludes the right to pre-emptive or responsive self-defence. Indeed, fourteen centuries ago Islam drew a line between pre-emption and aggression, allowing the former (as in the Prophet's campaigns at Khaybar and Mu'tah) and condemning the latter *(And fight in the way of God with those who fight against you, but aggress not; God loves not the aggressors* (*Al-Baqarah*, 2:190). In sum, God asks neither that Muslims be belligerent nor that they be pacifist. Rather, they must love peace but resort to force when the cause is just.

FURTHER READING (IN ENGLISH)

David Dakake, 'The Myth of a Militant Islam', in Joseph Lumbard, ed., *Islam, Fundamentalism, and the Betrayal of Tradition* (Bloomington, Indiana: World Wisdom, 2004), pp.3–37. Discusses the Bin Laden fatwa, the nature of authority in Islam, and the laws of jihad.

Khaled M. Abou El Fadl, *The Great Theft: Wrestling Islam from the Extremists* (HarperCollins, 2005). Valuable for its discussion of puritanical literalism versus traditional law.

Mohammad Hashim Kamali, *Principles of Islamic Jurisprudence* (Islamic Texts Society, 2005). One of the most complete and accessible introductions to Islamic law. Also valuable for its discussion of the 'sword verse' (pp. 223–5).

Reza Shah Kazemi, 'Recollecting the Spirit of Jihad', in Joseph Lumbard, ed., *Islam, Fundamentalism, and the Betrayal of Tradition* (Bloomington, Indiana: World Wisdom, 2004), pp.121–42: Addresses the spiritual dimensions of jihad and the case of Emir 'Abd al-Qadir's resistance against the French and his protection of Syrian Christians.

Vincenzo Oliveti, 'The Myth of 'the Myth of a Moderate Islam', in *Islamica Magazine*, no.15 (2006). An excellent treatment of common allegations of Islamic endemic violence.

Rudolph Peters, Jihad *in Classical and Modern Islam: A Reader* (Princeton, 1996). A sampling of some classical and contemporary treatises pertaining to jihad.

FURTHER READING (IN ARABIC)

Abdullah Bin Bayyah, Al-Irhāb, *Al-Tashkhis wa'l-hulul.* A discussion of terrorism. See also: www.binbayyah.net

Muhammad Sa'id Ramadan al-Buti, *Al-Jihad fi'l-Islam* (Damascus: Dar al-Fikr, 2005): An excellent overall discussion of the issues pertaining to jihad, from an eminent scholar and recognised authority, including the laws of war, protected peoples, political rebellion, preaching Islam (*da'wah*), treaties, and forced conversion.

Ali Gomaa, *Questions and Answers on* Jihad *in Islam* (Egypt: Supreme Council for Islamic Affairs, n.d.).

Originally published by the Royal Aal al-Bayt Institute for Islamic Thought as a booklet in 2007. The author wishes to state that his views have developed further since writing this essay.

CHAPTER FOUR

THE MYTH OF A MILITANT ISLAM

Dr David Dakake

In the post-September 11th environment there is an urgent need for a clear enunciation of the views of traditional Islam in regard to jihad, so-called holy war. The first matter which needs to be made clear is that jihad is not simply fighting or holy warfare. In Arabic, jihad literally means 'effort', that is, to exert oneself in some way or another. Within the context of Islam, jihad has the meaning of exerting oneself for the sake of God, and this exertion can be in an infinite number of ways, from giving charity and feeding the poor, to concentrating intently in one's prayers, to controlling one's self and showing patience and forgiveness in the face of offences, to gaining authentic knowledge, to physical fighting to stop oppression and injustice. Generally speaking, anything that requires something of us—that is, that requires that we go beyond the confines of our individual ego and desires—or anything that we bear with or strive after for the sake of pleasing God can be spoken of as a jihad in Islam.[127] This understanding of jihad is such that when the 'five pillars'[128] of the faith are taught, jihad is sometimes classified as a 'sixth pillar' which pervades the other five, representing an attitude or intention that should be present in whatever one does for the sake of God.

This being said, there is no doubt that jihad has an important martial aspect. To understand this we should remember that within the Islamic tradition the term jihad has been understood to possess two poles: an outward pole and an inward pole. These two poles are illustrated in the words of the Prophet of Islam when he said to his companions, after they had returned from a military campaign in defense of the Medinan community: 'We have returned from the lesser (*aṣghar*) jihad to the greater (*akbar*) jihad.'[129] Here the lesser jihad refers to physical fighting, whereas having come back to the relative physical safety of their city of Medina, the Muslims faced yet a greater jihad—namely, the struggle against the passionate, carnal soul that constantly seeks its own self-satisfaction above all else, being forgetful of God. This famous saying of the Prophet emphasises the hierarchy of the two types of jihad, as well as the essential balance that must be maintained between its outward and inward forms,[130] a balance often neglected in the approach of certain modern Islamic groups that seek to reform people and society from without, forcing change in the outward behaviour of men and women without first bringing about a sincere change in their hearts and minds. This is the lesson of the words of the Qur'an when God says, *We never change the state of a people until they change themselves* (*Al-Ra'd*, 13:11).[131] This lesson, as we shall see when we examine the earliest military jihad, was not lost on the first Muslims.

In the present crisis, the pronouncements of many self-styled Middle East 'experts' and Muslim 'authorities' who have dealt with the subject of jihad have generally been of two kinds. There have been those who have sought, in a sense, to brush aside the whole issue and history of military jihad in Islam in favour of a purely spiritualised notion of 'striving' in the way of God, and there have been those, both Muslim and non-Muslim, who have provided literal or surface readings of Qur'anic verses related to jihad and 'fighting' (*qitāl*) in an attempt to reduce all of Islam to military jihad.[132] The first view represents an apologetic attitude that attempts to satisfy Western notions of non-violence and political correctness but, in so doing, provides an 'understanding' that lacks any real relationship to the thought of the majority of Muslim peoples throughout Islamic history. The second view, which would make Islam synonymous with warfare, is the result either of sheer ignorance or of political agendas that are served by the perpetuation of animosity between peoples. This second position ignores entirely the commentary and analysis of the Islamic intellectual tradition that has served for over one thousand years as a key for Muslims to understand Qur'anic pronouncements related to jihad. In this essay we will neither water down the analysis of jihad to suit those modernists who oppose any notions of legitimate religious struggle and conflict, nor disregard, as do the 'fundamentalists', the intellectual and spiritual heritage of Islam which has defined for traditional Muslims the validity, but also the limitations, of the lesser jihad.

In carrying out this study we propose to examine those verses of the Qur'an that deal with fighting, as well as those which define those who are to be fought against in jihad. We will also provide, along with this textual analysis of Qur'anic doctrines of war, an historical analysis of the actual forms of the earliest jihad and the conduct of the *mujāhidūn*, the fighters of jihad, as exemplified by the Prophet of Islam and his successors, the Rightly-guided Caliphs, given that their actions have served for Muslims as an indispensable example to clarify Qur'anic pronouncements.[133] In this way, we hope to avoid both the etherialisation of jihad by Muslim apologists, and the distortion of the tradition at the hands of the fundamentalists. Lastly, we will examine fundamentalist interpretations of jihad and compare them with the traditional understanding of jihad in the early Qur'anic commentaries and the actual history of Islam.

'Do Not Take Christians and Jews as Awliyā''

Following the events of September 11th there is one verse of the Qur'an which has often been quoted by radio announcers, talk show hosts, and fundamentalists in both the East and the West. Before we deal with the actual issue of warfare or military jihad, it is necessary to say something about this verse which, if not understood correctly, can bias any further examination. This verse appears in chapter 5, verse 51 of the Qur'an:

> *O, you who believe [in the message of Muḥammad], do not take Jews and Christians as awliyā'. They are awliyā' to one another, and the one among you who turns to them is of them. Truly, God does not guide wrongdoing folk.* (*Al-Mā'idah*, 5:51)

The word *awliyā'* (sing. *walī*), which we left above in the original Arabic, has been commonly translated into English as 'friends'.[134] Given this translation, the verse appears to be a very clear statement opposing what we might term 'normative' or 'kindly relations' between Muslims and non-Muslims; but when we look at the traditional Qur'anic commentaries of medieval times, which discuss the events surrounding the revelation of this verse, the modern translation becomes suspect.

But before examining this issue in depth, it is necessary to clarify the importance of verse context in the Qur'an. Here a comparison between the Biblical text and the Qur'an is helpful.

Comparing the Bible and the Qur'an, we can use certain images to illustrate some of the major stylistic differences between the two sacred scriptures. We could say, for example, that the Bible is like a flowing stream; when one reads the text there is a constant contextualisation of the various verses, stories, chapters, and books. One begins reading with the story of Genesis, the creation of the world and the first man and woman, and then proceeds on through time, moving into the stories of the early patriarchs, then the later Hebrew judges and prophets, the coming of Christ, the post-Jesus community of the apostles, and finally the end of the world in the Book of Revelation. As one reads the Bible there is a historical context established for each of the major stories and events which enables the reader to situate what is being said within time and space, and indeed priority. The orientation of events as related to the chapters and verses is made explicit through the historical flow of the stories and, in the case of the New Testament, the eventual culmination of the text and all history.

In contrast, if we were to use an image to illustrate the Qur'anic revelation, it would be that of an individual standing upon a mountain at night as lightning flashes on him and in a valley below.[135] As this individual looks out upon the landscape shrouded in darkness, he would see sudden flashes, sudden illuminations of different portions of the mountain and the valley, but there would not appear to be any immediate relationship between these different illuminated regions, surrounded as they were by vast shadows. Of course, a relationship does exist between the different areas illuminated by the lightning, but that relationship is not explicit. It is hidden amid the darkness. This is something like the situation that is faced by the reader upon first examining the Qur'an. One will often read sections of the text and wonder what is the relationship between the various pronouncements that one encounters, for the Qur'an does not tell 'stories' as the Western reader is accustomed to from the Biblical tradition. In fact, there is only one full-length story in the Qur'anic text, in the chapter on the prophet Joseph. The rest of the Qur'an is a series of verses grouped into chapters and sections, and often two verses right next to one another will actually refer to two completely different events in the life of the early Islamic community. It is for this reason that the Qur'anic commentary tradition (*tafsīr*) deals so extensively with what is known in Arabic as *asbāb al-nuzūl*, or the occasions for God revealing particular Qur'anic verses. Without reference to these occasions of revelation most of the verses of the Qur'an would be susceptible to any and all forms of interpretation. This issue of the need for knowledge of the commentary tradition is, of course, further complicated—for those unable to read the original Arabic text—by translations, which often add yet another layer of difficulty for coming to terms with the meaning of the verses. When we examine verse 5:51, we encounter both these problems of context and translation.

The difficulties in understanding verse 5:51 begin with the translation of the Arabic word *awliyā'*, commonly rendered as 'friends'. In the context of this verse, the word *awliyā'* does not mean friends at all, as we use the term in English, and we know this from examining the occasion for its revelation. While it is true that *awliyā'* can mean friends, it has additional meanings such as 'guardians', 'protectors' and even 'legal guardians'. When we consult the traditional commentaries on the Qur'an, we are told that this verse was revealed at a particularly delicate moment in the life of the early Muslim community. To understand this verse it is thus necessary to explain the existential situation of the Muslims at this time in Arabia.

Before *Al-Mā'idah*, 5:51 was revealed, the Prophet of Islam and the Muslims had only recently migrated as a community from Mecca to Medina, some 400 kilometres to the north. They had done so, according to Islamic histories, due to the persecution to which they were subjected at the hands of their fellow tribesmen and relatives in Mecca. Most Meccans worshipped many idols as gods and feared the rising interest in the message of Muhammad ﷺ within the city, even though he was himself a son of Mecca. The Meccans feared the growing presence of the Muslims amongst them because the Muslims claimed that there was only one true God, who had no physical image, and who required of men virtue, generosity, and fair and kind treatment of the weaker members of society. This simple message, in fact, threatened to overturn the order of Meccan society, based as it was upon the worship of multiple gods and the privilege of the strong and the wealthy. It also threatened to disrupt the economic benefits of this privilege, the annual pilgrimage season, when peoples from all over Arabia would come to worship their many idols/gods at the Ka'bah—a cubical structure which the Qur'an claims was originally built by Abraham and his son Ishmael as a temple to the one God, before the decadence of religion in Arabia.[136] The message of Islam threatened to replace the social and economic system of Meccan polytheism with the worship of the one God, Who—as in the stories of the Old Testament—would not allow that others be worshiped alongside Him. In this difficult environment the Prophet of Islam peacefully preached the message of monotheism and virtue, but he and his small band of followers were eventually driven from the city by torture, embargo, threats of assassination, and various other forms of humiliation and abuse. The Muslims then migrated to Medina where the Prophet had been invited to come and live in safety with his followers and where the main Arab tribes of the city had willingly accepted his message and authority.

According to one of the earliest and most famous Qur'anic commentators, al-Tabari (225–310 AH/839–923 CE), it was not long after this migration to Medina that verse 5:51 was revealed. Specifically, al-Tabari tells us that this verse came down around the time of the battle of Badr (2 AH/623 CE) or perhaps after the battle of Uhud (3 AH/625 CE).[137] In these early days the Muslim community constituted no more than a few hundred people and had already left the city of Mecca; yet the Meccans continued to attempt to confront them militarily, and these two early battles, as well as others, were crucial events in the history of the early Islamic community. Militarily, the Meccans were a far more powerful force than the Muslims and they had allies throughout Arabia. Given the small numbers of Muslims, the Prophet and his fledgling community faced the real possibility of utter annihilation should they lose any of these early conflicts. Al-Tabari tells us that within this highly charged environment some members of the Muslim community wanted to make individual alliances with other non-Muslim tribes in the region. Within Medina there were Jewish tribes who constituted a powerful presence in the town and who were on good terms with the Meccans, and to the north of the city there were also Christian Arab tribes. Some Muslims saw the possibility of making alliances with one or more of these groups as a way of guaranteeing their own survival should the Meccan armies ultimately triumph. This was the stark reality of Arabia at that time; it was only through the protection of one's tribe or alliances with other tribes or clans that one's individual security was insured.

From the perspective of Islam, however, the Prophet realised that a young community, faced with great peril, could not allow such dissension in the ranks of the faithful as would be created by various individuals making bonds of loyalty with other groups not committed to the Islamic message. Indeed, from the Islamic point of view such actions, had they been allowed, would have been a kind of communal suicide that would have seriously undermined Muslim unity, broken the morale of the community (*ummah*), and perhaps caused the many individuals making such alliances to lack fortitude in the face of danger.

Bearing these historical issues in mind, it becomes obvious that the translation of *awliyā'* as 'friends' is incorrect. It should be rendered, in accord with another of its traditional Arabic meanings, as 'protectors' or 'guardians' in the strict military sense of these terms. The verse should be read as, *Do not take Christians and Jews as your protectors. They are protectors to one another....* This is the true message of the verse, and the appropriateness of this understanding is supported by the fact that the Qur'an does not oppose simple kindness between peoples, as is clear from verse *Al-Mumtaḥanah*, 60:8, to which we shall now turn.

'To Deal Kindly and Justly'

Verse 60:8 says, *God does not forbid that you should deal kindly and justly with those who do not fight you for the sake of [your] religion or drive you out of your homes. Truly, God loves those who are just* (*Al-Mumtaḥanah*, 60:8). Al-Tabari tells us that this verse was revealed on the occasion of an incident involving the half-sister of one of the Prophet's wives.[138] According to him, Asma' bint Abi Bakr, who was a Muslim living in Medina, received some gifts from her mother, Qutaylah, who lived in Mecca. Qutaylah had refused to convert to Islam and continued to practice the idolatrous ways of the Meccans. Asma' said, upon receiving the gifts, that she would not accept them, given that they came from one who had rejected the message of Islam and indeed one who had chosen to live among the arch-enemies of the Muslims; but then the above Qur'anic verse was revealed to the Prophet, indicating that there was no need to be ungracious towards the one who gave these gifts, even though she had rejected the message of the Prophet and was living with the enemies of Islam.

Al-Tabari goes even further in his analysis of the verse by criticising those Muslims who say that 60:8 was later abrogated by another Qur'anic verse which says, *Slay the idolaters wherever you find them'* (*Al-Tawbah*, 9:5).[139] Al-Tabari says that the most proper interpretation of verse 60:8 is that God commanded kindness and justice to be shown 'amongst all of the kinds of communities and creeds' (*min jamīʿ asnāf al-milāl wa'l-adyān*) and did not specify by His words some communities to the exclusion of others. Al-Tabari says that here God speaks in general of any group that does not openly fight against the Muslims or drive them out of their homes, and that the opinion that this kindness was abrogated by later Qur'anic statements makes no sense (*lā maʿnā li-qawl man qāla dhālik mansūkh*).[140] This understanding may seem to be in contradiction with our previous statement that the Meccans were indeed at war with the Muslims; however, Qutaylah, being a woman, could not technically be considered a combatant according to Islamic law. Indeed, this shows the essential distinction between combatants and non-combatants in the rules of Muslim warfare. This distinction, as we see from the example of Qutaylah, is to be upheld even in the context of engagement with an actively hostile enemy, as were the Meccans. Therefore, Islam does not oppose friendship and kindness between peoples who are not at war with one another and, even in the case of war, clear distinctions are to be made between 'those who fight' and 'those who do not fight'. We shall examine this principle further in the next section.

'Slay Them Wherever You Find Them'

Another verse that is related to jihad, and also deals with the subject of those against whom jihad is to be waged, is 2:190–1. According to many accounts, these verses represents the first command given by God to the Muslims to carry out military jihad,[141] but this command had specific limitations placed upon it, as we shall see. The Qur'anic text reads as follows:

> *Fight in the way of God against those who fight you, but transgress not the limits. Truly, God does not love the transgressors [of limits]. / And slay them wherever you find them, and turn them out from where they have turned you out.* (*Al-Baqarah*, 2:190–1)

Al-Tabari tells us that this verse is not to be read as a carte blanche to attack any and all non-Muslim peoples; rather, he says, the verse was revealed specifically in relation to fighting the idolaters of Mecca, who are referred to in Arabic sources by the technical term *mushrikūn* or *mushrikīn* (sing. *mushrik*).[142] This term comes from a three-letter Arabic root 'sh-r-k' which means 'to associate' or 'take a partner unto something', and the word *mushrikūn* literally means 'those who take a partner unto God', that is to say 'polytheists' or 'idolaters'. It should be noted that from the point of view of Islamic law, this injunction to perform jihad against the polytheists does not pertain to either Jews or Christians. Neither Jews nor Christians are ever referred to within the Qur'an by the terms *mushrik* or *mushrikūn*. They have, in fact, a very different status according to the Qur'an, which often refers to the two groups together by the technical term *Ahl al-Kitāb* or 'People of the Book', meaning people who have been given a scripture by God other than the Muslims. We shall discuss the status of Jews and Christians later, but what is important to recognise here is that this call to jihad was revealed in relation to a specific group of people, the idolaters of Mecca, and within a specific context, a context of persecution and the driving of Muslims from their homes in Mecca because of their religion. Indeed, this understanding is accepted not only by al-Tabari but, he says, it is the view of most Qur'an interpreters.[143]

In addition to this context for the first military jihad, there were also limits placed upon the early Muslims who carried out jihad against the *mushrikūn*. Verse 2:190 speaks of *fight[ing] in the way of God* but also of not transgressing the 'limits'. What are these limits? Al-Tabari gives many accounts detailing the limits placed upon the *mujāhidūn*. He says, for instance, that the cousin of the Prophet of Islam, Ibn 'Abbas, commented upon verse 2:190 as follows: 'Do not kill women, or children, or the old, or the one who greets you with peace, or [the one who] restrains his hand [from hurting you], and if you do this then you have transgressed'.[144] Another tradition related by al-Tabari comes from the Umayyad Caliph 'Umar ibn 'Abd al-'Aziz or 'Umar II (99/717–101/720 CE), who explained the meaning of 2:191 as: '... do not fight he who does not fight you, that is to say women, children, and monks.'[145]

These statements quoted by al-Tabari are very much in keeping with other commands given specifically by the Prophet and the Rightly-guided Caliphs (Abu Bakr, 'Umar, 'Uthman and 'Ali) to the Muslim armies involved in jihad. These commands are noted in the various hadith collections, i.e., records of the sayings of the Prophet and his companions, which along with the Qur'an form the basis for determining the Islamic nature of any act. Some examples of these hadith are:

> Nafi' reported that the Prophet of God ﷺ found women killed in some battles, and he condemned such an act and prohibited the killing of women and children.[146]
>
> When Abu Bakr al-Siddīq [the trusted friend of the Prophet and first of the Rightly-guided Caliphs] sent an army to Syria, he went on foot with Yazid ibn Abu Sufyan who was the commander of a quarter of the forces.... [Abu Bakr said to him:] 'I instruct you in ten matters: Do not kill women, children, the old, or the infirm; do not cut down fruit bearing trees; do not destroy any town; do not cut the gums of sheep or camels except for the purpose of eating; do not burn date-trees nor submerge them; do not steal from booty and do not be cowardly.'[147]
>
> [The Umayyad Caliph] 'Umar ibn 'Abd al-'Aziz wrote to one of his administrators: We have learnt that whenever the Prophet of God ﷺ sent out a force, he used to command them, 'Fight, taking the name of the Lord. You are fighting in the cause of the Lord with people who have disbelieved and rejected the Lord. Do not commit theft; do not break vows; do not cut ears and noses; do not kill women and children. Communicate this to your armies.'[148]
>
> Once when Rabah ibn Rabi'ah went forth with the Messenger of Allah, he and [the] companions of the Prophet passed

> by a woman who had been slain. The Messenger halted and said: 'She is not one who would have fought'. Thereupon, he looked at the men and said to one of them: 'Run after Khālid Ibn al-Walid[149] [and tell him] that he must not slay children, serfs, or women.'[150]

Such statements are common throughout the hadith collections and leave little doubt as to the limits set upon the military jihad, regardless of the enemy that is faced.

'Perform Jihad against the Kāfirūn'

As we noted earlier, the Qur'an does not speak of Jews or Christians as *mushrikūn* or polytheists. Therefore, none of the verses of the Qur'an that pertain to fighting the *mushrikūn* pertain to them. However, it must be admitted that the Qur'an does, within a limited context, speak of Jews and Christians as *kāfirūn*, a term often translated into English as 'unbelievers', although its literal meaning is, 'Those who cover over [the truth]' in some form or another. Unfortunately, the common translation of this term as 'unbelievers' gives it nuances of meaning from Western cultural history that do not necessarily apply to the original Arabic, such as the fact that 'unbelief' in English is synonymous with 'atheism'. In Arabic, however, *kufr* or 'covering' does not necessarily refer to lack of faith but to a lack of correct thinking on one or more aspects of faith. In fact Muslims can also be *kāfirūn*. For instance, according to the traditional commentaries, verse 9:49, *There are some who say, 'Give me leave to stay behind and do not tempt me.' Surely they have fallen into temptation already and hell encompasses the unbelievers (kāfirūn)* (*Al-Tawbah*, 9:49) refers to those Muslims who refused to respond to the Prophet's call to go on an expedition to Tabuk.[151]

The important question that could be asked, however, is: Does the Qur'an not speak about fighting against the *kāfirūn*, such as in the verse *O Messenger, perform jihad against the unbelievers (kāfirūn) and the hypocrites (munāfiqūn)* (*Al-Tawbah*, 9:73)? Does this verse not imply an essential militancy between Muslims on the one hand, and Jews and Christians on the other? In answering these questions we must refer to both Qur'anic pronouncements and to the historical actions of the early Muslims in jihad. We will deal with the issues of the Qur'an first and then turn, in the next section, to what the Muslims actually did in jihad.

When we look at the comments of al-Tabari regarding verse 9:73, as well as those of Ibn Kathir (d. 774 AH/1372 CE), perhaps the most famous of Sunni Qur'an commentators, both seem to condone the idea that this verse relates to violent or military jihad. Both make a distinction, however, between the two types of jihad mentioned in verse 9:73: jihad against the *kāfirūn*, and jihad against the *munāfiqūn*. Each states that the jihad against the *munāfiqūn* or hypocrites—i.e., those Muslims who knowingly disobey the commands of God—is *bi'l-lisān*, meaning 'with the tongue'. That is to say, one should reprimand the Muslim hypocrites with critical speech, not with physical violence. Whereas, in regard to the *kāfirūn*, both commentators make reference to the idea that the jihad against them is *bi'l-ṣayf*, or 'by the sword'.[152] This may seem to suggest that violent suppression of Jews and Christians is demanded, since we have already mentioned that both Jews and Christians—though never called *mushrikūn*—are sometimes referred to as *kāfirūn*. But before drawing this conclusion we must look more closely at how the Qur'an defines the *kāfirūn*. Here it is useful to refer to a series of Qur'anic verses referring to the 'People of the Book' such as *Al-Bayyinah*, 98:1, 98:6; *Al-Mā'idah*, 5:78; and *Al-Baqarah*, 2:105.

Verse 98:1 reads: *Those who disbelieved (kafarū) among (min) the People of the Book and the polytheists (mushrikūn) would not have left off erring until the clear truth came to them* (*Al-Bayyinah*, 98:1). This verse clearly indicates that 'to disbelieve' is not a characteristic belonging to all Jews and Christians or People of the Book. Instead, it declares that disbelief is a characteristic of some 'among' the People of the Book. This limiting of the declaration of unbelief is established by the Arabic preposition *min*, which serves to distinguish a distinct species within a genus, namely, those unbelievers present within the larger believing Jewish and Christian communities. This delimitation is also to be seen in verse 98:6 which says, *Those who disbelieved (kafarū) among the People of the Book are in Hellfire* (*Al-Bayyinah*, 98:6). Verses 5:78 and 2:105 are yet further examples of this qualifying and limiting of *kufr* or 'unbelief' in regard to the People of the Book. They state, respectively:

> *Those who disbelieved (kafarū) among the Tribe of Israel were cursed by the tongue of David and Jesus, son of Mary.* (*Al-Mā'idah*, 5:78)
>
> *Neither those who disbelieved (kafarū) among the People of the Book, nor the polytheists (mushrikūn), love that anything good should be sent down to you from your Lord.* (*Al-Baqarah*, 2:105)

We see in these verses that the Qur'anic perspective, as regards the followers of faiths other than Islam, is a subtle one, not simply a blanket condemnation of all non-Muslims. It is important to recall here the words of verses 113–5 of chapter 3 of the Qur'an, which say:

> *Not all of them are alike. Of the People of the Book are a group that stand (in prayer), rehearse the signs of God throughout the night and prostrate. / They believe in God and the Last Day; they enjoin what is right and forbid what is wrong, and they hasten in (all) good works. These are among the righteous. / Of the good that they do, nothing will be rejected of them, and God knows the God-fearing ones.* (*Āl 'Imrān*, 3:113–5)

Keeping these Qur'anic distinctions in mind, the injunction to fight the *kāfirūn* by the sword does not then apply to all Jews and Christians, but only to some 'among' them. But this raises the question, who, among the Jews and Christians, are the Muslims to fight? To answer this question we must now turn to the historical facts of the jihad of the first Muslims.

The Jihad of the First Muslims

It is perhaps best to begin our examination of historical jihad by recalling that the first jihad in Islam was not martial and had nothing to do with violence. The first jihad is referred to in the Qur'an in verse 25:52, which states, *Do not obey the unbelievers (kāfirūn), but strive against them (jāhidhum) with it, a great striving* (*Al-Furqān*, 25:52). This somewhat enigmatic verse, traditionally understood to have been revealed at Mecca, i.e., before any divine decree had been given as regards performance of military jihad (which came only later in the Medinan period), speaks of striving against the unbelievers by way of 'it'. Both al-Tabari and Ibn Kathir relate traditions from Ibn 'Abbās and from Ibn Zayd ibn Harith, the son of the Prophet's adopted son, telling us that this 'it'—the means by which to carry out jihad—is the Qur'an itself.[153] In other words, the earliest command to jihad was a kind of preaching of the Qur'an to the Meccans, or perhaps a taking solace or refuge in the divine word from the persecutions that the Muslims were experiencing at that time in Mecca. It was not military in nature. This brings up our first point regarding the historical form of military jihad and what may be its most misrepresented feature: the notion that the religion of Islam was spread through military force, that Jews, Christians, and other peoples of the Middle East, Asia, and Africa were forced to convert to Islam on pain of death.

'There is No Compulsion in Religion'

It has been a common view in the West, even to this day, to say that the religion of Islam spread through conquest. Although this Orientalist theory is now being shown to be a fallacy by modern scholarship,[154] it is important to mention that the peaceful spread of Islam throughout most of the Middle East,[155] Asia, and Africa was in fact due to principles flowing from the Qur'anic revelation itself. Here and in the next section we will discuss some of these principles, beginning with the injunction found in verse 2:256 which says, *There is no compulsion in religion* (*Al-Baqarah*, 2:256). Our commentators tell us that this verse was revealed during one of three possible situations.

The first possible context for the revelation of 2:256 has to do with a practice that was fairly common among the women of Medina before Islam came to the city. Our commentators tell us that if a woman did not have any living sons, she would sometimes make a promise that if she gave birth to a child and the child lived, she would raise the child in the faith of one of the Jewish tribes of the city.[156] Apparently this practice was somewhat popular; we know this from the events following another of the early military engagements of Islamic history: the siege of the fortress of the Medinan Jewish tribe of Nadir (4 AH/625 CE). The reason for the siege, according to Islamic sources, was that the Banu Nadir had broken an alliance that they had concluded with the Prophet by secretly planning to assassinate him. [157] As a result of this treason, the Muslims besieged the Banu Nadir for some ten days in their fortress just south of Medina. At the end of this siege the Banu Nadir accepted a punishment of exile from the region of Medina and the tribe left with their wealth packed on their camels, some heading north to the town of Khaybar, others going on further to Syria. Some of the Medinan Muslims protested the punishment of exile, saying to the Prophet: 'Our sons and brothers are among them!'[158] Indeed, some of the children of the Medinans had been raised within the Jewish faith and were living with their adopted clan. In response to the dissatisfaction of the Medinan Muslims the words of the Qur'an were revealed: *There is no compulsion in religion, for truth has been made clear from error,* meaning essentially that these 'sons and brothers' had made their choice to stay loyal to a treacherous group against the Prophet, as well as against their own Muslim relatives, and were party to a plan to murder God's messenger. In this way, the words of verse *Al-Baqarah*, 2:256, although harsh from a certain point of view, also reveal an essential principle within the Muslim faith: no one can be compelled to accept a religion, be it Islam or any other faith. This particular narration of the context of 2:256 is highly significant for delineating the attitude of Muslims on this issue, occurring as it does during the jihad of the siege of the Banu Nadir and rejecting, within that context, any compulsion in religion.

Another variant on this same story speaks of the people of Medina desiring to compel those of their 'sons and brothers' affiliated with another Jewish tribe in the city, the Banu Qurayzah, into accepting Islam. This version (whose number of narrations in the sources is much fewer than that of the Banu Nadir narrations) makes no mention of there being any hostilities at that time between the Muslims and the Jews, but only recounts the desire of the Medinan Muslims to force their Jewish relatives into Islam. In these narrations the Prophet responds to their desire to compel their family members with the words of 2:256,[159] again affirming the absolute necessity of freedom in choosing one's faith.

This principle is also brought out in relation to a third possible context for the revelation of verse 2:256. This is said to be the conversion to Christianity of the sons of Abu'l-Ḥusayn, a companion of the Prophet. The story is told that the two sons of Abu'l-Ḥuṣayn were converted in Medina by Christian merchants visiting the city from Syria. They then returned to Syria with the merchants.[160] Upon hearing of what his sons had done, Abu'l-Ḥuṣayn went to the Prophet and asked for permission to pursue them and bring them back. The Prophet then recited to him, *There is no compulsion in religion....* After Abū'l-Ḥuṣayn heard the words of the revelation, the narration concludes, 'So he let them go their way' (*fa-khallī sabīlahumā*).[161]

Regardless of the version of the story that we examine, the message is always the same—to choose one's own religion is a free choice whether in time of peace or war. Ibn Kathir's commentary upon 2:256 also reflects this fact when he says:

> God, the Exalted, said, '*There is no compulsion in religion*,' that is to say, you do not compel anyone to enter the religion of Islam. Truly it is made clear [and] evident. It [Islam] is not in need such that one compel anyone to enter it. Rather, the one whom God guides to Islam and expands his breast and illuminates his vision, he enters into it by way of clear proof. It is of no use to enter the religion as one compelled by force.[162]

Although these words are hardly ambiguous, we should also note that there have been those in the Islamic tradition who have tried to say that this Qur'anic verse was later abrogated, but this is not the opinion of either of our commentators. Both al-Tabari and Ibn Kathir note that 2:256 has never been abrogated by any other verse(s) of the Qur'an and that although 2:256 descended in regard to a particular case (*khaṣṣ*), i.e., in regard to either the Jews of Medina or the Christians from Syria, nevertheless, its application is general (*'amm*).[163] This is to say, the verse applies to all People of the Book, who should be free from being compelled to accept Islam.[164]

'Had God not Repelled some Men by Means of Others ...'

A related issue which goes beyond the simple idea of not forcing anyone into Islam is the fact that one of the essential and expressed elements of the earliest military jihad was the protection of the rights of worship of the People of the Book, i.e., not simply avoiding using force to bring them into Islam, but actively using force to preserve and defend their houses of worship. This characteristic of the military jihad is mentioned in verses 22:39–40 and, as we shall see, it is confirmed by many historical examples.

We noted earlier that verses 2:190–1 are sometimes claimed to be the first verses revealed relating to military jihad. This claim is also made for verses 22:39–40.[165] It is, of course, impossible to determine on the basis of the narrations given in the sources which group of verses is truly the first to speak of military jihad, but the Islamic tradition in general has simply accepted ambiguity on this issue. Verses 22:39–40 say:

> *Permission is given to those who are fought because they have been wronged. Surely, God is able to give them victory. / Those who have been expelled from their homes unjustly only because they said: 'Our Lord is God.' And if it were not that God repelled some people by means of others, then monasteries, churches, synagogues, and mosques, wherein the Name of God is mentioned much would surely have been pulled down. Verily, God will help those who help Him. Truly, God is powerful and mighty. (Al-Ḥajj, 22: 39–40)*

Our commentators tell us that these verses were revealed just as the Prophet and his companions were leaving Mecca and migrating to Medina.[166] Both al-Tabari and Ibn Kathir relay the words of Abu Bakr al-Ṣiddiq upon hearing the new revelation. He is reported to have said, 'I knew [when I heard it] that it would be fighting (*qitāl*) [between the Muslims and the Meccans].'[167] It is also interesting to note that al-Tabari relates traditions that state that the meaning of the phrase '*if it were not that God repelled some people by means of others*' is 'if it were not for fighting and jihad' and 'if it were not for fighting and jihad in the way of God.'[168] Furthermore, Ibn Kathir relates that many famous early figures of Islam 'such as Ibn 'Abbas, Mujahid, 'Urwah ibn al-Zubayr, Zayd ibn Aslam, Muqatil ibn Hayyan, Qatadah and others' also said that 'this is the first verse revealed concerning jihad'.[169] These commentaries are particularly important because all of them refer to the fact that jihad is to be understood, in its earliest sense, as a means by which 'monasteries, churches, synagogues, and mosques' are to be preserved and protected.[170] The call to jihad then was not for the destruction of faiths other than Islam; rather, one of its essential aspects was the preservation of places of worship belonging to the monotheistic faiths and protecting them against those polytheists—in this case the idolaters of Mecca—who might endanger them.

Some Applications of Qur'anic Principles to the Military Jihad

When we turn to the many examples of the early military jihad found in the sources, we see that the Muslim armies were actually quite consistent in their application of the Qur'anic doctrines mentioned in 22:39–40 and 2:256. Although the historical record does not speak definitively about the issue of whether or not these endeavours were strictly defensive—for as with all such undertakings, they involved both elements of true religious fervor and righteousness, as well as issues of the realpolitik of the time—what can be said rather definitively is that the Muslim forces, in carrying out the early jihad, did act in accordance with the limits established by the Qur'an and Hadith. We know this from the examination of the accounts presented in the various Islamic histories, such as al-Tabari's universal history, *Tārīkh al-rusul wa al-mulūk*, as well as other important historical works that specialise in the events of the early jihad, such as Baladhuri's (d. 279 AH/892 CE) *Futūḥ al-buldān* or 'Openings of the Nations'. In these accounts, there is clear evidence of the importance Muslims attached to the idea of 'no compulsion in religion', as well as to the preservation of the places of worship of the People of the Book. Baladhuri, for instance, recounts a text written by the Prophet to the Christian community of Najran in southern Arabia guaranteeing them certain social and religious rights under Islamic rule. The text reads:

> Najran and their followers are entitled to the protection of Allah and to the security of Muhammad the Prophet, the Messenger of Allah, which security shall involve their persons, religion, lands, and possessions, including those of them who are absent as well as those who are present, their camels, messengers, and images [*amthilah*, a reference to crosses and icons]. The state they previously held shall not be changed, nor shall any of their religious services or images be changed. No attempt shall be made to turn a bishop, a monk from his office as a monk, nor the sexton of a church from his office.[171]

Both al-Tabari and Baladhuri make many references to similar treaties concluded between Muslim commanders during the early jihad effort and the various populations that fell under Islamic political control. Indeed, such examples are to be found on every major front of the Islamic conquests from Persia to Egypt and all areas in between.

Within the region of Syria, we have the example of the companion of the Prophet and commander of Muslim forces Abu 'Ubaydah ibn al-Jarrah, who concluded an agreement with the Christian population of Aleppo granting them safety for 'their lives, their possessions, city wall, churches, homes, and the fort'. Abu 'Ubaydah is said to have concluded similar treaties at Antioch,[172] Ma'arrat Ma'rin,[173] Ḥoms,[174]Qinnasrin,[175] and Baalbek.[176]

Baladhuri reports that after the surrender of Damascus, Khalid ibn al-Walid wrote for the inhabitants of the city a document stating:

> In the Name of Allah, the Compassionate, the Merciful. This is what Khalid would grant to the inhabitants of Damascus, if he enters therein: he promises to give them security for their lives, property, and churches. Their city shall not be demolished; neither shall any Moslem be quartered in their houses. Thereunto we give to them the pact of Allah and the protection of his Prophet, the caliphs and the 'Believers'. So long as they pay the poll tax,[177] nothing but good shall befall them.[178]

In addition to these accounts, al-Tabari records the 'Covenant of 'Umar', a document apparently addressed to the people of the city of Jerusalem, which was conquered in the year 15 AH/636 CE. The document states:

> This is the assurance of safety (*amān*) which the servant of God 'Umar, the Commander of the Faithful, has granted to the people of Jerusalem. He has given them an assurance of safety for themselves, for their property, their churches, their crosses, the sick and the healthy of the city, and for all the rituals that belong to their religion. Their churches will not be inhabited [by Muslims] and will not be destroyed. Neither they, nor the land on which they stand, nor their crosses, nor their property will be damaged. They will not be forcibly converted.... The people of Jerusalem must pay the poll tax like the people of [other] cities, and they must expel the Byzantines and the robbers....[179]

These conditions, respecting Christian practices and places of worship, were also given to other towns throughout Palestine, according to al-Tabari.[180]

In regard to the Armenian front, we have references to treaties made with Jewish and Christian as well as Zoroastrian inhabitants of the region. It is noteworthy that both al-Tabari and Ibn Kathir in their Qur'an commentaries mention Zoroastrians (*al-majūs*) within the classification of 'People of the Book'[181]—Zoroastrianism being the other major faith, besides Judaism and Christianity, that was encountered by the Muslim armies as they spread out of Arabia and which, like Judaism and Christianity, possessed a sacred text. Baladhuri mentions the treaty concluded by the companion of the Prophet, Habib ibn Maslamah al-Fihri (d. 42 AH/662 CE), with the people of the town of Dabil which states:

> In the Name of Allah, the Compassionate, the Merciful. This is a treaty of Habib ibn Maslamah with the Christians, Magians [i.e., Zoroastrians], and Jews of Dabil, including those present and absent. I have granted for you safety for your lives, possessions, churches, places of worship, and city wall. Thus ye are safe and we are bound to fulfil our covenant, so long as ye fulfil yours and pay the poll tax...[182]

In addition to this, al-Tabari mentions treaties that the Muslims made with the Armenians of Al-Bab and Muqan in the Caucasus Mountains guaranteeing 'their possessions, their persons, [and] their religion'.[183]

When we turn to the region of Persia, Baladhuri mentions two agreements, one with the people of Rayy,[184] and the other with the people of Azerbaijan.[185] The texts of each of these agreements guarantees the safety of the lives of the inhabitants, as well as offering a promise not to 'raze any of their fire temples', a reference to Zoroastrian *ātashkādas*. In al-Tabari's history as well, treaties are recounted involving the town of Qumis,[186] the peoples of Dihistan in the province of Jurjan,[187] and the people of Azerbaijan,[188] each treaty granting 'safety ... for their religion'.

Finally, in Egypt we can point to the example of 'Amr ibn al-'Ās, a companion of the Prophet and the commander of Muslim forces on the Egyptian front. He concluded a treaty with the Bishop of Alexandria on the orders of the Caliph 'Umar, guaranteeing the safety of the city and agreeing to return certain Christian captives taken by the Muslims after an initial skirmish. According to al-Tabari, 'Umar's instructions to 'Amr were as follows:

> … propose to the ruler of Alexandria that he give you the *jizyah* in the understanding that those of their people who were taken prisoner and who are still in your care be offered the choice between Islam and the religion of their own people. Should any one of them opt for Islam, then he belongs to the Muslims, with the same privileges and obligations as they. And he who opts for the religion of his own people has to pay the same *jizyah* as will be imposed on his co-religionists.[189]

'Amr also concluded an agreement with Abu Maryam, the Metropolitan of Mi'r. Al-Tabari quotes 'Amr's words in an apparent face to face meeting with the Metropolitan: 'We call upon you to embrace Islam. He who is willing to do so will be like one of us. To him who refuses, we suggest that he pay the *jizyah* and we will give him ample protection. Our Prophet … has determined that we keep you from harm…. If you accept our proposition, we will give you constant protection.'[190] Al-Tabari then quotes the actual text of the treaty agreed to between them as follows:

> In the Name of God, the Compassionate, the Merciful.
>
> This is the text of the covenant that 'Amr b. al-'Ās has granted the people of Mi'r concerning immunity for themselves, their religion, their possessions, churches, crucifixes, as well as their land and their waterways…. It is incumbent upon the people of Mi'r, if they agree on the terms of this covenant and when the rise of the Nile water comes to a halt to afford the *jizyah*…. He who chooses [not to agree to these terms but] to depart will enjoy immunity, until he has reached his destination where he can be safe, or has moved out of the territory where our authority prevails.[191]

With these treaties in mind we can now return to a question which we raised earlier: Who, in the opinion of the early Muslims, were the People of the Book that had to be fought? In short, given this picture of the history, the answer to this question is that those who were to be fought among the People of the Book were only those who refused to submit to Islamic political authority, i.e., who refused to pay the poll tax (*jizyah*). The Muslims made no hair-splitting theological determinations regarding the issue of 'true belief', as some might think is implied in certain Qur'anic verses that we quoted earlier. All People of the Book were simply treated as 'believers' within their respective religious communities, regardless of whether they followed, for instance, in the case of Christianity, a Monophysite, Arian, Jacobite, Nestorian, or Catholic rite. There was no litmus test of faith which the Muslims applied to determine true belief on the part of the people who came under their political control, other than the self-declarations of those people themselves to be Jews, Christians, or Zoroastrians, and their willingness to pay the *jizyah*.[192] The earliest *mujāhidūn*, the Prophet, his companions, and their immediate successors, essentially placed all People of the Book under the general category of 'faith'. This fact played itself out not only in terms of treaties concluded between Muslims and non-Muslims, which as we have seen demonstrate no theological scrutiny of non-Muslim communities, but also in terms of the very composition of the 'Muslim' forces involved in the jihad, to which we will now turn.

The Composition of the Forces of Jihad

In relation to the practice of the military jihad we can see that Islam's universal perspective on faith also had an important effect on the make-up of the 'Muslim' armies. Here we can point to the fact that military jihad was not seen as the exclusive prerogative of Muslims. This is particularly true during the formative years of the Islamic conquests, i.e., from the first command to military jihad in Medina through the early Umayyad period. Again, this is made clear in various treaties the Muslims concluded with both the Jewish and Christian populations of the Near East at this time. Perhaps the most famous of these treaties is the Constitution of Medina, which was composed during the lifetime of the Prophet himself and which speaks of the Jews and Muslims fighting together as one ummah or community.

The Constitution of Medina

The Constitution of Medina, recorded in Ibn Ishaq's (d. 151 AH/768 CE) *Sīrat Rasūl Allāh* (*The Biography of the Messenger of God*), the most important historical account of the life of the Prophet, indicates that jihad was for any community willing to fight alongside the Muslims (with the exceptions of polytheists). Ibn Ishaq prefaces his account of the Constitution by saying:

> The Messenger of God ﷺ [composed] a writing between the Emigrants and the *Anṣār*,[193] in which he made a treaty and covenant with the Jews, confirmed their religion and possessions, and gave them certain rights and duties.[194]

The text of the treaty then follows:

> In the Name of God, the Compassionate, the Merciful.
>
> This is a writing of Muhammad the prophet between the believers and Muslims of Quraysh and Yathrib[195] and those who follow them and are attached to them *and who crusade (jāhada) along with them.* They are a single community distinct from other people.... Whosoever of the Jews follows us has the (same) help and support..., so long as they are not wronged [by him] and he does not help [others] against them.[196] [emphasis added]

Here we see that the participation in 'military jihad', translated above as 'crusade', is open to those 'attached' to the Prophet and the Muslims, and that together they constitute a 'single community' (*ummah wāḥidah*) in the face of all others. It is interesting to note that the claim that animosity has always existed between Muslims and Jews does not accord with this very early document dealing with military cooperation and mutual protection between the two communities.[197] Indeed the treaty seems not only to form a basis for an important military alliance between the Muslim and Jewish communities, but it also anticipates orderly and peaceful interactions on a general social level. Thus the constitution goes on to say:

> The Jews bear expenses along with the believers so long as they continue at war. The Jews of Banu 'Awf are a community (*ummah*) along with the believers. To the Jews their religion (*dīn*) and to the Muslims their religion. [This applies] both to their clients and to themselves, with the exception of anyone who has done wrong or acted treacherously; he brings evil only on himself and on his household. For the Jews of Banu'n-Najjar the like of what is for the Jews of the Banu 'Awf. For the Jews of Banu'l-Harith the like.... For the Jews of Banu Sa'idah the like.... For the Jews of Banu Jusham the

> like.... For the Jews of Banu'l-Aws the like.... For the Jews of Banu Tha'labah the like of what is for the Jews of Banu 'Awf....[198]

Another portion of the document speaks even more directly to the social attitudes that should form the basis of interactions between the two communities:

> Between them [Muslims and Jews] there is help (*naṣr*) against whoever wars against the people of this document. Between them is sincere friendship (*naṣḥ wa-naṣīḥah*) and honourable dealing, not treachery. A man is not guilty of treachery through [the act of] his confederate. There is help for the person wronged.[199]

What this document shows is that early in the life of the Islamic community, there was the anticipation of normal and 'friendly' relations between the Jews and Muslims and indeed, help between them in terms of war. These ideas are also supported by the authenticity generally accorded to the Constitution by modern scholarship. In terms of this authenticity, both the language and the content of the document suggest that it is an early piece of work, i.e., pre-Umayyad.[200] This is due to the fact that later falsifiers, writing during the time of the Umayyads or the Abbasids, would not likely have included non-Muslims as members of the ummah (a term later reserved for the Muslim community exclusively), nor retained the other articles of the document (from which we did not quote) that speak against the Quraysh,[201] nor made such prevalent and constant use of the term *mu'minūn* (believers) rather than *muslimūn* to refer to the followers of the Prophet and his message.[202] Both Julius Wellhausen and Leone Caetani placed the writing of the document sometime before the battle of Badr. Hubert Grimme argued for a date just after Badr, and W. Montgomery Watt, a date following siege of the Banu Qurayẓah (5 AH/627 CE).[203] In any case, it is clear that we are dealing here with a document whose early date of composition is claimed both from within and from without the tradition, suggesting a high degree of reliability that it does indeed express early Islamic attitudes toward the openness of the institution of military jihad.

Christians in Jihad

Another important point regarding the armies of jihad is that traditional Islamic histories give accounts of Christians taking part in some of the early battles alongside the Muslim armies. This is discussed by Fred Donner in his book *The Early Islamic Conquests*. He notes that, according to Muslim historical sources, in the very early period of jihad, Christian Arabs from tribes such as the Banu Ṭayyi' of Najd, the Banu al-Namir ibn Qasiu of the upper Euphrates river valley, and the Banu Lakhm participated in the jihad with the Muslim armies.[204] Other allusions to this kind of activity can be found in al-Tabari's *Tārīkh* where he notes, for instance, a treaty signed during the reign of the caliph 'Umar by Suraqah ibn 'Amr in 22 AH/642 CE. Suraqah was a commander of Muslim forces in Armenia, which was predominantly Christian. The treaty discusses the poll tax which the Christian population is to pay to the Islamic government, unless they are willing to supply soldiers to the jihad effort, in which case the poll tax would be cancelled.[205] In addition to this account, Baladhuri notes many other agreements in the *Futūḥ al-buldān* concluded by Muslim commanders with the Christian populations of various regions. Such is the case of the *Jarājimah*, a Christian people from the town of Jurjumah.[206] This town had been under the control of the patrician and governor of Antioch but surrendered to the Muslim armies, commanded by Habib ibn Maslamah al-Fihri, when they attacked the town. Baladhuri recounts the terms of the peace between Habib and the Jarajimah as follows:

Terms were made providing that al-Jarajimah would act as helpers to the Moslems, and as spies and frontier garrison in Mount al-Lukam. On the other hand it was stipulated that they pay no tax, and that they keep for themselves the booty they take from the enemy in case they fight with the Moslems.[207]

Here jihad is an endeavour open to the Christian Jarajimah. Another treaty concluded with them during the reign of the Umayyad Caliph al-Walid ibn 'Abd al-Malik (86–96 AH/705–15 CE), states:

> *Al-Jarājimah* may settle wherever they wish in Syria...; neither they nor any of their children or women should be compelled to leave Christianity; they may put on Moslem

> dress; and no poll tax may be assessed on them, their children, or women. On the other hand, they should take part in the Moslem campaigns and be allowed to keep for themselves the booty from those whom they kill…; and the same amount taken from the possessions of the Moslems should be taken [as tax] from their articles of trade and the possessions of the wealthy among them.[208]

These agreements, along with the many others that we have noted in the previous sections, in addition to revealing something of the martial applications of Islam's universal perspective on faith, also demonstrate that historically jihad was directed against those who stood in opposition to the political authority of the Islamic state. It was not directed against a people simply because they professed a faith other than Islam. The point of the jihad was not to establish a world populated only by Muslims; it was to create a social order in which the freedom to practice the worship of God was guaranteed, for Muslims as well as for the People of the Book. Although military jihad had as its goal the establishment of this Islamic authority, there were also certain essential and religiously unavoidable limitations placed upon the means to achieving this goal. These limitations were defined by the injunctions of the Qur'an and the Hadith and manifested, as well as clarified, by the conduct of the earliest *mujāhidūn*, the Prophet, and his companions. These teachings and examples have served as an indispensable guide to Muslims throughout their 1400-year history, not only in terms of jihad but in relation to all matters of faith. When we look at the attempts of certain contemporary figures to revive the military jihad, their words and actions must always be judged by way of the limits and examples mentioned in the early tradition. This is the only way to determine the essential 'Islamicity' of their claims and to know if their actions constitute some form of reprehensible (*makrūh*) or forbidden (*ḥarām*) innovation (*bid'a*) upon the tradition.[209] Muslims have always been cautioned to exercise the utmost care when introducing new interpretations or practices, as a famous hadith of the Prophet states: 'Beware of newly invented matters, for every invented matter is an innovation, every innovation is a going astray, and every going astray is in Hellfire.'[210]

Some Contemporary Fundamentalist Interpretations of Jihad

To begin our analysis it is perhaps best to start with the form of the jihad envisaged by the modern fundamentalists; that is to say, is the form of this jihad consistent with the established principles of the Islamic faith or not? It has been claimed that the jihad which Muslims must now wage involves killing Americans and their allies, civilian and military. Any such declaration would immediately place the endeavour outside the bounds of true jihad whose limits, as we noted earlier, would clearly exclude, for instance, attacks upon women and children. In fact, the categories of 'civilian' and 'military' often used by these extremists are somewhat alien to the Islamic tradition which always speaks on this issue of warfare in terms of 'those who fight against the Muslims' and 'those who do not', the tradition being unanimous in defining 'those who do not' as women and children, with other categories such as monks and the elderly often included. Therefore, the declarations making 'lawful' the indiscriminate killing of civilians unequivocally transgress the limits of warfare defined in the traditional sources. Indeed, some claim that now is the time for a new *fiqh* or jurisprudence in Islam that would leave behind such traditional constraints.[211] Some have even attempted to cast their arguments in the guise of religion by calling their declarations of jihad fatwas[212] and by quoting liberally from the Qur'an. Of course, the determination of the 'Islamicity' of any fatwa must be in relation to its content, and yet if we analyse the Qur'anic verses chosen by extremists to justify their own exegesis, it reveals that, far from being representatives of traditional Islam and the 'pious forefathers' (*salaf*) of the Muslim community, their perspective is actually what we might call the 'other side of the coin' of modernism, due to its near total disregard for the established contexts of the verses they quote.[213]

One verse often mentioned in this regard is verse 9:5:

> *But when the forbidden months are past, then fight and slay the polytheists [mushrikūn] wherever you find them, seize them, beleaguer them, and lie in wait for them in every stratagem [of war]* (*Al-Tawbah*, 9:5).

It is interesting that this verse should be cited in the context of calls for Muslims to fight Jews and Christians, particularly since this verse has nothing to do with the issue of the People of the Book. As we mentioned earlier, the Qur'an does not refer to Jews and Christians as *mushrikūn* but reserves this term for the idolatrous Arabs of Muhammad's ﷺ time. In the case of verse 9:5, however, we are not dealing with a reference to the idolaters of Mecca specifically because, according to tradition, the ninth chapter of the Qur'an was revealed after the conquest of Mecca by the Muslims, that is to say, at a time when there were no longer any polytheists in the city as a result of conversion to Islam. The *mushrikūn* referred to in verse 9:5 are therefore the Arab polytheists/idolaters who remained in other parts of Arabia not yet under Muslim control. This being the case, the use of 9:5 would represent a misappropriation of this verse to an end other than the one intended from its established traditional context of fighting the pagan Arabs.

Other verses which have become popular proof texts for the jihadist position are 9:36 and 2:193. The verses are, respectively: *And fight the polytheists [mushrikūn] together as they fight you together* (*Al- Tawbah*, 9:36), and *Fight them [i.e., the mushrikūn] until there is no more oppression and religion is for God* (*Al-Baqarah*, 2:193). These verses have been cited as direct support for killing civilians, yet both these verses, as with verse 9:5, refer directly to fighting the *mushrikūn*, not Jews or Christians and certainly not civilians. Neither al-Ṭabari nor Ibn Kathir have much to say regarding 9:36, except to emphasise that the Muslims should act together or in unison during warfare against the polytheists. The injunction to 'fight the polytheists together as they fight you together', which has sometimes been taken to mean that Muslims should respond in kind to the attacks of an enemy, cannot be understood as an invitation to transgress the established Islamic rules of warfare. It is telling in this regard that al-Ṭabari and Ibn Kathir only refer in their comments on 9:36 to the verse's meaning in relation to the 'unity' of the ummah, and do not mention issues of responding in kind to offenses, which would seem to be a subject worthy of at least some comment, if indeed that was the verse's intended meaning.

In terms of verse 2:193, Ibn Kathir sees it as part of a series of related verses beginning with 2:190. Like al-Ṭabari, he mentions that these verses refer to the first military jihad against the *mushrikūn* of

Mecca, and he also emphasises the fact that these verses are in no way an invitation to kill non-combatants, even those who live among the communities of the enemies of Islam. Like al-Ṭabari, Ibn Kathir in his comments quotes many narrations about the 'transgressing of limits' in warfare, such as the words of the famous Qur'an commentator and theologian Hasan al-Basri (d. 728 CE), who said that the acts which transgress the limits of war are:

> ... mutilation (*muthla*), [imposing] thirst (*ghulūl*), the killing of women (*nisā'*), children (*ṣibyān*), and the old (*shuyūkh*)—the ones who have no judgment for themselves (*lā ra'yy lahum*), and no fighters are among them, [the killing of] monks and hermits (*aṣḥāb al-ṣawāmi'*), the burning of trees, and the killing animals for other than the welfare [of eating].'[214]

In addition to this, Ibn Kathir mentions various sayings of the Prophet with meanings similar to the words of Hasan al-Basri, such as:

> When he [the Prophet] dispatched his armies, he said, 'Go in the Name of God! Fight in the way of God [against] the ones who disbelieve in God! Do not act brutally![215] Do not exceed the proper bounds! Do not mutilate! Do not kill children or hermits!'[216]

As if such statements were not enough, from the Islamic point of view, to reject the indiscriminate violence endorsed by many fundamentalists, Ibn Kathir also relays another hadith in which the Prophet tells the story of a community of people who were weak and poor and were being fought by a stronger group who showed animosity and harshness towards them. The Prophet says that the weaker group was eventually given help by God to overcome their enemies, but in their success, these weak ones became oppressors of those who had first tried to oppress them. He concludes with the words, 'And God was displeased with them till the Day of Resurrection'. The meaning of this prophetic story says Ibn Kathir, is: 'When they [the weak] possessed power over the strong, then they committed outrageous/unlawful/brutal acts (*a'tadū*) against them ... and God was displeased with them by reason of this brutality (*i'tidā'*)'. Thus, Ibn Kathir points out an important principle of warfare in Islam: acts of brutality committed against Muslims are not an excuse for

Muslims to respond in kind. This idea, so clear in the traditional sources, stands in direct contrast to the positions of the fundamentalists, which through their use of Qur'anic citations seek to hide what ultimately can only be described as disobedience to these teachings of the Prophet.

Another Qur'anic verse often quoted is 4:75:

> *And why should you not fight in the way of God and those who are weak—men, women, and children, whose cry has been: 'Our Lord, rescue us from this town, whose people are oppressors, and raise for us, from you, one who will help.'* (*Al-Nisā'*, 4:75)

This verse has been mentioned as justification for open warfare against the West and to inspire Muslims to fight the United States and its allies who threaten the Muslim lands in particular. According to our commentators, however, the reason for the revelation of 4:75 was the fact that even after the Prophet had made his migration to Medina, there were still some Muslims who remained in Mecca although they could not practice their religion, and some Meccans who wished to be Muslims but would not convert out of fear of their fellow tribesmen.[217] In both cases these difficulties were due to the weakness of these people vis-à-vis the polytheistic members of their own clans who sought to oppress them with threats and even torture. Therefore, verse 4:75 was revealed to call the Muslims of Medina to a twofold jihad: (1) to free their brethren who were left behind in Mecca from religious oppression, and (2) to give those Meccans who desired to convert the ability to do so without fear of reprisals from the enemies of Islam. This clearly established context is very different from the manner in which the verse is understood by extremists, for the least that can be said is that in the West, unlike many places in the Islamic world itself, Muslims are basically free to worship as they see fit, nor is there any attempt to stop men or women from converting to Islam. Clearly then, the use of 4:75 as a proof text for jihad against the West and America is at best disingenuous considering the traditional understanding of the circumstances surrounding its revelation.

In addition to these verses, some cite verses 3:139 and 4:89 in their call for each Muslim to kill Americans and plunder their wealth *in any place he finds them*. Verse 3:139, which says, *Do not lose heart, and do not be sad. For you will gain mastery if you are believers* (*Āl 'Imrān*, 3:139) like so many misplaced quotations, actually occurs in the context of the fight against the Meccan polytheists at the battle of Uhud, while *Al-Nisā'*, 4:89 refers to the *munafiqūn* or 'hypocrites' among the early Islamic community. The *munafiqūn*, as mentioned earlier, were those Muslims who disobeyed God's commands knowingly. Many of them converted to Islam only out of a sense of the advantage that could be gained from not openly opposing the Prophet while his power was waxing. Secretly they hoped for and worked toward victory for the polytheists. It is in regard to these traitors within the Muslim community that the verse speaks with such harshness, not in reference to those outside of the ummah. One last verse that is popular in modern jihadist literature is verse 9:38:

> *O you who believe, what is the matter with you that when you are asked to go forth in the way of God, you cling heavily to the Earth. Do you prefer the life of this world to the Hereafter?... Unless you go forth, He will punish you with a grievous torment and put others in your place.* (*Al-Tawbah*, 9:38)

According to our commentators, this verse relates to the military expedition (*ghazwah*) led by the Prophet to Tabuk, a region in what is today northwestern Saudi Arabia. During this expedition the Muslims went out in search of Byzantine military in the region. It is said that the Muslims stayed, manoeuvring in the field some ten days, but did not encounter any Byzantine forces. As regards the use of this verse, it has been quoted with the hope of encouraging Muslims today to 'go forth' against the United States and its allies, as the early *mujāhidūn* did against another world power, the Byzantines. The expedition to Tabuk, however, did not constitute some kind of special case in which the Islamic limits of warfare were neglected. Although the Muslims potentially would be facing a foe far more capable and powerful than any they had yet encountered, namely, the standing army of the Byzantine Empire which had only recently conquered much of Persia, this did not constitute an excuse for transgression. Despite the danger, at no time in the expedition did the Prophet ever give orders to his army to transgress or discard the limits set upon jihad. Therefore, any such use of this verse within the context of encouraging such transgression is inconsistent with the historical reality of the *ghazwah* to Tabuk. In fact, the expedition was an occasion for establishing treaties of protection very similar to those we have mentioned in previous sections of this essay, those concluded with the people of Ayla and the Christians of Duma.[218]

In the case of each of these verses we have cited, extremists have tried to apply them in ways which entail clear innovations from their generally accepted meanings. Such 'exegesis' not only goes against basic aspects of the science of Qur'anic commentary, it also introduces innovation into the very practice of Islam itself, by making jihad into a path of unbounded bloodshed. In this manner, the 'fundamentalists' violate the fundamental principles of warfare in Islam and betray the example of the Prophet, as well as that of the first Muslims engaged in jihad, and as Reza Shah-Kazemi shows in a following essay, many generations into the modern era. In fact their teachings are a not-so-subtle perversion of the very Islam they claim to want to preserve. So systematic is their disregard of the facts of early Islamic history and the circumstances surrounding the revelations of the Qur'an that one is left wondering what of Islam, other than a name, would they claim to save?

Conclusion

We have attempted to show in this paper that, properly understood, the traditional doctrine of jihad leaves no room for militant acts like those perpetrated against the United States on September 11th. Those who carried out these crimes in the name of God and the Prophet, in fact, followed neither God nor the Prophet, but followed their own imaginings about religion without any serious understanding of the traditional sources of the Islamic faith. No textual justifications for their acts can be found in the Qur'an, nor can one cite examples of such brutality and slaughter of innocents from the life of the Prophet or the military jihad of the early decades of Islam. The notion of a militant Islam cannot be supported by any educated reading of the source materials, be they the Qur'an and its commentaries, the Hadith tradition, or the early Islamic historical works. On the contrary, what is clear when looking at these texts is the remarkable degree of acceptance and, indeed, respect that was shown to non-Muslims, Jews and Christians in particular, at a time—the early medieval period—when tolerance and acceptance of religious differences were hardly well known attitudes. Even in cases of warfare, the Muslim armies acted with remarkable dignity and principle, irrespective of the weakness or strength of their opposition. In short, the early Islamic community was characterised not by militancy, but primarily by moderation and restraint.

These traits were not in spite of the religion of Islam but because of it. This can be seen in the Qur'an in Chapter 2, verse 143, where God says to the Muslims, *We have made you a middle people* (*Al-Baqarah*, 2:143), that is, a people who avoid extremes, and in another famous verse which says, ... *and He [God] has set the Balance [of all things]. Do not transgress the Balance!'* (*Al-Raḥmān*, 55:7-8). Traditional Muslims saw all of life in terms of balance, from simple daily activities to fighting and jihad. Each activity had its limits and rules because God had set the balance for all things. It has primarily been certain modernised Muslims, whose influences are not the traditional teachings of the faith, but the attitudes and excesses of modernity (only cloaked with turbans and beards), who have transgressed all limits and disregarded the Balance that is true Islam.

Originally published by World Wisdom in Islam, Fundamentalism and the Betrayal of Tradition. *Reproduced with the kind permission of the author and World Wisdom Press.*

CHAPTER FIVE

THE SPIRIT OF JIHAD[219]

Dr Reza Shah-Kazemi

> When we think how few men of real religion there are, how small the number of defenders and champions of the truth—when one sees ignorant persons imagining that the principle of Islam is hardness, severity, extravagance and barbarity—it is time to repeat these words: *Patience is beautiful, and God is the source of all succour. (Sabr jamīl, wa Allāhu al-mustaʿān—Yūsuf*, 12:18)
>
> Emir Abd al-Qadir al-Jaza'iri[220]

If these words were true in 1860, when the emir wrote them, they are sadly even truer today. In the aftermath of the earth-shaking events of September 11 many in the West and in the Muslim world are rightly appalled by the fact that the mass murder perpetrated on that day is being hailed by some Muslims as an act of jihad. Only the most deluded souls could regard the suicide attacks as having been launched by *mujāhidīn*, striking a blow in the name of Islam against 'legitimate targets' in the heartland of 'the enemy'. Despite its evident falsity, the image of Islam conveyed by this disfiguration of Islamic principles is not easily dislodged from the popular imagination in the West. There is an unhealthy and dangerous convergence of perception between, on the one hand, those—albeit a tiny minority—in the Muslim world who see the attacks as part of a necessary anti-western jihad, and on the other, those in the West—unfortunately, not such a tiny minority—who likewise see the attacks as the logical expression of an inherently militant religious tradition, one that is irrevocably opposed to the West.

Although of the utmost importance in principle, it appears to matter little in practice that Muslim scholars have pointed out that the terror attacks are totally devoid of any legitimacy in terms of Islamic law and morality. The relevant legal principles—that jihad can only be proclaimed by the most authoritative scholar of jurisprudence in the land in question; that there were no grounds for waging a jihad in the given situation; that, even within a legitimate jihad, the use of fire as a weapon is prohibited; that the inviolability of non-combatants is always to be strictly observed; that suicide is prohibited in Islam—these principles, and others, have been properly stressed by the appropriate shari'ah experts; and they have been duly amplified by leaders and statesmen in the Muslim world and the West. Nonetheless, here in the West, the abiding image of 'Islamic jihad' seems to be determined not so much by legal niceties as by images and stereotypes; in particular, in the immediate aftermath of the attacks, the potent juxtaposition of two scenes: the apocalyptic carnage at 'Ground Zero', where the Twin Towers used to stand, and mobs of enraged Muslims bellowing anti-western slogans to the refrain of *Allāhu Akbar*.

In such a situation, where the traditional spirit of Islam, and the meaning, role and significance of jihad within it, are being distorted beyond recognition, it behoves all those who stand opposed both to media stereotypes of jihadism and to those misguided fanatics who provide the material for the stereotypes to denounce in the strongest possible terms all forms of terrorism that masquerade as jihad. Many, though, will understandably be asking the question: if this is not jihad, then what is true jihad? They should be given an answer.[221]

Whilst it would be a relatively straightforward task to cite traditional Islamic principles which reveal the totally un-Islamic nature of this ideology of jihadism, we believe that a critique on this plane of principle will be much more effective if it is complemented with images, actions, deeds, personalities, and episodes that exemplify the principles in question, thereby putting flesh and blood on the bare bones of theory. The salience of intellectual argument, especially in the domain being considered here, is immeasurably deepened through corroboration by historically recorded cases in which the spirit of authentic jihad is vividly enacted; and the pretensions of the self-styled warriors of Islam can be more acutely perceived in the light cast by true *mujāhidīn*.

There is a rich treasure of chivalry in Muslim history from which to draw for this purpose. What follows is a series of scenes drawn from this tradition which might serve as illustrations of key Qur'anic and prophetic values which pertain to principled warfare. For it is one thing to quote Qur'anic verses, and quite another to see them embodied.

As regards the virtue of chivalry itself, it is no exaggeration to say that, throughout the Middle Ages, the very name 'Saladin' (Salah al-Din al-Ayyubi) was a byword for chivalry, and this remains to some extent true even to this day. The contemporary chronicles—by Muslims and Christians alike—which describe his campaigns and his consistent fidelity to the most noble principles of dignified warfare speak volumes. Again and again, often in the face of treachery from his adversaries, Saladin responded with magnanimity. Suffice it to draw attention to his forbearance, mercy, and generosity at the moment of his greatest triumph: the reconquest of Jerusalem on Friday 2 October, 1187, a memorable day indeed, being 27 of Rajab, the anniversary of the Prophet's *Laylat al-Miʿrāj*, his ascent through the heavens from Jerusalem itself. After detailing many acts of kindness and charity, the Christian chronicler Ernoul writes:

> Then I shall tell you of the great courtesy which Saladin showed to the wives and daughters of knights, who had fled to Jerusalem when their lords were killed or made prisoners in battle. When these ladies were ransomed and had come forth from Jerusalem, they assembled and went before Saladin crying mercy. When Saladin saw them he asked who they were and what they sought. And it was told him that they were the dames and damsels of knights who had been taken or killed in battle. Then he asked what they wished, and they answered for God's sake have pity on them; for the husbands of some were in prison, and of others were dead, and they had lost their lands, and in the name of God let him counsel and help them. When Saladin saw them weeping he had great compassion for them, and wept himself for pity. And he bade the ladies whose husbands were alive to tell him where they were captives, and as soon as he could go to the prisons he would set them free. And all were released wherever they were found. After that he commanded that to the dames and damsels whose lords were dead there should be handsomely distributed from his own treasure, to some more and others less, according to their estate. And he gave them so much that they gave praise to God and published abroad the kindness and honour which Saladin had done to them.[222]

Saladin's magnanimity at this defining moment of history will always be contrasted with the barbaric sacking of the city and indiscriminate murder of its inhabitants by the Christian Crusaders in 1099. His lesson of mercy has been immortalised in the words of his biographer, Stanley Lane-Poole:

> One recalls the savage conquest by the first Crusaders in 1099, when Godfrey and Tancred rode through streets choked with the dead and the dying, when defenceless Moslems were tortured, burnt, and shot down in cold blood on the towers and roof of the Temple, when the blood of wanton massacre defiled the honour of Christendom and stained the scene where once the gospel of love and mercy had been preached. 'Blessed are the merciful, for they shall obtain mercy' was a forgotten beatitude when the Christians made shambles of the Holy City. Fortunate were the merciless, for they obtained mercy at the hands of the Moslem Sultan ... If the taking of Jerusalem were the only fact known about Saladin, it were enough to prove him the most chivalrous and great-hearted conqueror of his own, and perhaps of any, age.[223]

Saladin, though exceptional, was but expressing essentially Islamic principles of conduct, as laid down by the Qur'an and the Prophet. These principles of conduct were exemplified in another telling incident which occurred some fifty years before Saladin's victory: a mass conversion of Christians to Islam took place, as a direct result of the exercise of the cardinal Muslim virtue of compassion. A Christian monk, Odo of Deuil, has bequeathed to history a valuable record of the event; being openly antagonistic to the Islamic faith, his account is all the more reliable. After being defeated by the Turks in Phyrgia in 543 AH/1147 CE, the remnants of Louis VII's army, together with a few thousand pilgrims, reached the port of Attalia. The sick, the wounded and the pilgrims had to be left behind by Louis, who gave his Greek allies 500 marks to take care of these people until reinforcements arrived. The Greeks stole away with the money, abandoning the pilgrims and the wounded to the ravages of starvation and disease, and fully expecting those who survived to be finished off by the Turks. However, when the Turks arrived and saw the plight of the defenceless pilgrims, they took pity on them, fed and watered them, and tended to their needs. This act of compassion resulted in the wholesale conversion of the pilgrims to Islam. Odo comments:

> Avoiding their co-religionists who had been so cruel to them, they went in safety among the infidels who had compassion upon them … Oh kindness more cruel than all treachery! They gave them bread but robbed them of their faith, though it is certain that, contented with the services they [the Muslims] performed, they compelled no one among them to renounce his religion.[224]

The last point is crucial in respect of two key Islamic principles: that no one is ever to be forced into converting to Islam; and that virtue must be exercised with no expectation of reward. On the one hand, *There is no compulsion in religion* (*Al-Baqarah*, 2:256), and on the other, the righteous are those who *feed, for love of Him, the needy, the orphan, the captive,* [saying] *we feed you only for the sake of God; we desire neither reward nor thanks from you* (*Al-Insān*, 76:8–9).

Mercy, compassion, and forbearance are certainly key aspects of the authentic spirit of jihad; it is not simply a question of fierceness in war, it is much more about knowing when fighting is unavoidable, how the fight is to be conducted, and to exercise, whenever possible, the virtues of mercy and gentleness. The following verses are relevant in this regard:

> *Warfare is ordained for you, though it is hateful unto you.* (*Al-Baqarah*, 2:216)
>
> *Muhammad is the messenger of God; and those with him are fierce against the disbelievers, and merciful amongst themselves.* (*Al-Fatḥ*, 48:29)
>
> *And fight in the way of God those who fight you, but do not commit aggression. God loves not the aggressors.* (*Al-Baqarah*, 2:190)
>
> *The Prophet is told in the Qur'an: It was by the mercy of God that thou was lenient to them; if thou had been stern and fierce of heart they would have dispersed from around thee.* (*Āl 'Imrān*, 3:159)

Repeatedly in the Qur'an one is brought back to the overriding imperative of manifesting mercy and compassion wherever possible. This is a principle that relates not so much to legalism and as to the deepest nature of things, for, in the Islamic perspective, compassion is the very essence of the Real. A famous saying of the Prophet tells us that, written on the very Throne of God are the words, 'My mercy takes precedence over My wrath'. Mercy and compassion (*raḥmah*) express the fundamental nature of God. Therefore nothing can escape from divine mercy: *My compassion encompasses all things* (*Al-'Arāf*, 7:156). The name of God, *al-Raḥmān*, is coterminous with Allah: *Call upon Allāh or call upon al-Raḥmān* (*Al-'Isrā'*, 17:10). The divine creative force is, again and again in the Qur'an, identified with *al-Raḥmān*; and the principle of revelation itself, likewise, is identified with this same divine quality. The chapter of the Qur'an named *Al-Raḥmān* (55) begins thus: *Al-Raḥmān, taught the Qur'an, created man.*

This 'ontological imperative' of mercy must always be borne in mind when considering any issue connected with warfare in Islam. The examples of merciful magnanimity given above are not only to be seen as instances of individual virtue, but also, and above all, as natural fruits of this ontological imperative; and no one manifested this imperative so fully as the Prophet himself. Indeed, Saladin's magnanimity at Jerusalem can be seen as an echo of the Prophet's conduct at his conquest of Mecca. As the huge Muslim army approached Mecca in triumphal procession, a Muslim leader, Sa'd ibn Ubada, to whom the Prophet had given his standard, called out to Abu Sufyan, leader of the Quraysh of Mecca, who knew that there was no chance of resisting this army:

> 'O Abu Sufyan, this is the day of slaughter! The day when the inviolable shall be violated! The day of God's abasement of Quraysh.' … 'O Messenger of God,' cried Abu Sufyan when he came within earshot, 'hast thou commanded the slaying of thy people?—and he repeated to him what Sa'd had said. 'I adjure thee by God,' he added, on behalf of thy people, for thou art of all men the greatest in filial piety, the most merciful, the most beneficent.' 'This is the day of mercy,' said the Prophet, 'the day on which God hath exalted Quraysh.'[225]

The Quraysh, having full reason to be fearful, given the intensity—and the barbarity—of their persecution of the early Muslims, and their continuing hostility and warfare against them after the enforced migration of the Muslims to Medina, were granted a general amnesty; many erstwhile enemies were thereby converted into stalwart Muslims.

This noble conduct embodied the spirit of the following verse: *The good deed and the evil deed are not alike. Repel the evil deed with one which is better, then lo! He, between whom and thee there was enmity* [will become] *as though he were a bosom friend.* (*Fuṣṣilat* 41: 34)

The principle of *no compulsion in religion* was referred to above. It is to be noted that, contrary to the still prevalent misconception that Islam was spread by the sword, the military campaigns and conquests of the Muslim armies were on the whole carried out in such an exemplary manner that the conquered peoples became attracted by the religion which so impressively disciplined its armies, and whose adherents so scrupulously respected the principle of freedom of worship. Paradoxically, the very freedom and respect given by the Muslim conquerors to believers of different faith communities intensified the process of conversion to Islam. Arnold's classic work *The Preaching of Islam* remains one of the best refutations of the idea that Islam was spread by forcible conversion. His comprehensive account of the spread of Islam in all the major regions of what is now the Muslim world demonstrates beyond doubt that the growth and spread of the religion was of an essentially peaceful nature, the two most important factors in accounting for conversion to Islam being Sufism and trade. The mystic and the merchant, in other words, were the most successful missionaries of Islam.

One telling document cited in his work sheds light on the nature of the mass conversion of one group, the Christians of the Persian province of Khurasan, and may be taken as indicative of the conditions under which Christians, and non-Muslims in general, converted to Islam. This is the letter of the Nestorian Patriarch, Isho-yabh III to Simeon, Metropolitan of Rev-Ardashir, Primate of Persia:

> Alas, alas! Out of so many thousands who bore the name of Christians, not even one single victim was consecrated unto God by the shedding of his blood for the true faith … (the Arabs) attack not the Christian faith, but on the contrary, they favour our religion, do honour to our priests and the saints of our Lord and confer benefits on churches and monasteries. Why then have your people of Merv abandoned their faith for the sake of these Arabs?[226]

This honouring of Christian priests, saints, churches and monasteries flows directly from the practice of the Prophet ﷺ—witness, among other things, the treaty he concluded with the monks of St Catherine's monastery in Sinai;[227] it is likewise rooted in clear verses relating to the inviolability of all places *wherein the name of God is oft-invoked.* Indeed, in the verse giving permission to the Muslims to begin to fight back in self-defence against the Meccans, the need to protect all such places of worship, and not just mosques, is tied to the reason for the necessity of warfare:

> *Permission [to fight] is given to those who are being fought, for they have been wronged, and surely God is able to give them victory; those who have been expelled from their homes unjustly, only because they said: Our Lord is God. Had God not driven back some by means of others, monasteries, churches, synagogues and mosques—wherein the name of God is oft-invoked—would assuredly have been destroyed.* (*Al-Ḥajj*, 22: 39–40)

The long and well-authenticated tradition of tolerance in Islam springs directly from the spirit of this and many other verses of similar import. We observe one of the most striking historical expressions of this tradition of tolerance—striking in the contrast it provides with the intolerance that so frequently characterised the Christian tradition—in the fate of Spanish Jewry under Islamic rule. Before looking at this particular case, we should note that, in general terms, active, systematic persecution of Jews is virtually unknown under Muslim rule. It is important to stress this fact in the strongest possible terms in the present context, and to debunk the pernicious lie that is circulating in our times, the lie that there is in Islam an inherent, deep-rooted, theologically sanctioned hostility to Judaism. One must not regard the present anger on the part of most Muslims against particular policies of the state of Israel as some atavistic resurgence of a putative anti-Semitism ingrained in the Islamic view of the world. Today, it is the extremists on both sides—that is the 'jihadists' and the Zionists—who share an interest in promoting this myth of an intrinsically and eternally anti-Jewish Islam; it is of the utmost importance to show the falsity of this notion.

One should also add here that it is not just the 'moderates' on both sides who come together, for the sake of peace and justice, in opposing this false characterisation of Muslim-Jewish relations; it is also the lovers of traditional, orthodox Judaism that come together, from all religions, to denounce, for the sake of veracity, that deviation from Judaism which Zionism is. Thus we find such groups as the Naturai Karta—traditional Jews opposed to Zionism on irrefutable theological grounds—joining hands with Muslim human rights groups to defend the legitimate rights of the Palestinians against the injustices perpetrated against them in the Holy Land. One must take care to distinguish, therefore, not only between Judaism and Zionism, but also between legitimate opposition to particular policies of the state of Israel—policies that reflect and embody Zionist aspirations in different degrees—and illegitimate jihad against Jews or Westerners simply on account of the fact that they are Jews or Westerners. The first expresses a legitimate grievance; the second makes of this grievance the pretext for terrorism.

As regards the refutation of the myth that Muslim-Jewish relations have traditionally been antagonistic and oppressive, a cursory perusal of the historical record suffices. Even so fierce a critic of Islam as Bernard Lewis cannot but confirm the facts of history as regards the true character of Muslim-Jewish relations until recent times. In his book *The Jews of Islam*, he writes that even though there was a certain level of discrimination against Jews and Christians under Muslim rule, 'Persecution, that is to say, violent and active repression, was rare and atypical. Jews and Christians under Muslim rule were not normally called upon to suffer martyrdom for their faith. They were not often obliged to make the choice, which confronted Muslims and Jews in reconquered Spain, between exile, apostasy and death. They were not subject to any major territorial or occupational restrictions, such as were the common lot of Jews in premodern Europe.'[228] He then adds the important point that this pattern of tolerance continued to characterise the nature of Muslim rule vis-à-vis Jews and Christians until modern times, with very minor exceptions.

It is not out of place to note here that the phenomenon of anti-Semitism has absolutely nothing to do with Islam. It was, as Schleifer notes, 'Church Triumphant'—that is the Byzantine Church which triumphed over the Roman Empire, and founded its new capital in Constantinople in the fourth century—it was this Church that was to 'unleash upon the world the phenomenon of anti-Semitism. For if we are to differentiate between the vicissitudes which any minority community may endure, and a principled and systematic hostility, then one can boldly state, with the consensus of modern historians, that anti-Semitism originated as a Christian phenomenon.'[229]

The story of anti-Semitism in Europe—the violent episodes of what today would be labelled ethnic cleansing—is too well known to need repeating here. But it should be borne in mind that at the same time as the Christian West was indulging in periodic anti-Jewish pogroms, the Jews were experiencing what some Jewish historians themselves have termed a kind of golden age under Muslim rule. As Erwin Rosenthal writes, 'The Talmudic age apart, there is perhaps no more formative and positive time in our long and chequered history than that under the empire of Islam.'[230]

One particularly rich episode in this golden period was experienced by the Jews of Muslim Spain. As has been abundantly attested by historical records, the Jews enjoyed not just freedom from oppression, but also an extraordinary revival of cultural, religious, theological and mystical creativity. As Titus Burckhardt writes, 'The greatest beneficiaries of Islamic rule were the Jews, for in Spain (*sephārād* in Hebrew) they enjoyed their finest intellectual flowering since their dispersal from Palestine to foreign lands.'[231] Such great Jewish luminaries as Maimonides and Ibn Gabirol wrote their philosophical works in Arabic, and were fully 'at home' in Muslim Spain.[232] With the expulsion, murder or forced conversion of all Muslims and Jews following the *reconquista* of Spain—brought to completion with the fall of Granada in 1492—it was to the Ottomans that the exiled Jews turned for refuge and protection. They were welcomed in Muslim lands throughout North Africa, joining the settled and prosperous Jewish communities already there, while also establishing new Jewish communities.

It was at this time also that Jews were suffering intense persecution in central Europe; they likewise looked to the Muslim Ottomans for refuge. Many Jews fleeing from persecution in central Europe would have received letters like the following, from Rabbi Isaac Tzarfati, who reached the Ottomans just before their capture of Constantinople in 1453. This is what he replied to those Jews of central Europe who were calling out for help:

> Listen, my brethren, to the counsel I will give you. I too was born in Germany and studied Torah with the German rabbis. I was driven out of my native country and came to the Turkish land, which is blessed by God and filled with all good things. Here I found rest and happiness … Here in the land of the Turks we have nothing to complain of. We are not oppressed with heavy taxes, and our commerce is free and unhindered … every one of us lives in peace and freedom. Here the Jew is not compelled to wear a yellow hat as a badge of shame, as is the case in Germany, where even wealth and great fortune are a curse for the Jew because he therewith arouses jealousy among the Christians … Arise, my brethren, gird up your loins, collect your forces, and come to us. Here you will be free of your enemies, here you will find rest …[233]

Given the fact that so much of today's jihadist propaganda is directed against Jews, it is important to stress that this tolerance of Jews under Muslim rule is one expression of an underlying theological harmony between the two religions—a harmony that is conspicuously absent when one compares Christian and Jewish theology. Islam was never considered the messianic fulfilment of Judaism, as was Christianity; it was put forward as a restoration of that primordial Abrahamic faith of which both Judaism and Christianity were alike expressions. Islam calls adherents of both faiths back to that pristine monotheism; far from rejecting their prophets, the Qur'an asserts that all the prophets came with one and the same message, and that therefore there should be no distinction made between any of them:

> *Say: We believe in God and that which is revealed unto us, and that which is revealed unto Abraham and Ishmael and Isaac and Jacob and the tribes, and that which was given unto Moses and Jesus and the prophets from their Lord. We make no distinction between any of them, and unto Him we have submitted. (Āl 'Imrān, 3:84)*

The consequences of this acceptance of the pre-Qur'anic scriptures—albeit conditioned by the need to beware of certain distortions (*taḥrīf*), distortions which, however, the Qur'an does not specify—these consequences were far-reaching as regards theological relations between Muslims and Jews. As the Jewish scholar Mark Cohen notes: 'Rabbinic exegesis of the Bible—so repugnant to Christian theologians—

bothered Muslim clerics only insofar as it distorted pristine Abrahamic monotheism. Thus the Islamic polemic against the rabbis was much less virulent and had far less serious repercussions. The Talmud was burned in Paris, not in Cairo or Baghdad.'[234]

Therefore, the refusal of the Jews to follow the shari'ah was not a challenge to Islamic belief; this in contrast to the Jewish rejection of Christ as messiah, which not only challenged a cardinal tenet of Christian dogma, it also deeply insulted Christian faith and sensibility. Whereas in Christendom, the Jews were reviled as the killers of Jesus, in Islam, the Jews were 'protected', as *ahl al-dhimmah*, by the very law that they refused to follow for themselves. To quote Cohen again, 'More secure than their brethren in the Christian West, the Jews of Islam took a correspondingly more conciliatory view of their masters. In Europe, the Jews nurtured a pronounced hatred for the Christians, whom they considered to be idolators, subject to the anti-pagan discriminatory provisions of the ancient Mishnah … The Jews of Islam had a markedly different attitude towards the religion of their masters. Staunch Muslim opposition to polytheism convinced Jewish thinkers like Maimonides of Islam's unimpeachable monotheism. This essentially 'tolerant' view of Islam echoed Islam's own respect for the Jewish "people of the Book"…'[235]

The tolerance extended by Islam to Jews (and, indeed, all believers, including Hindus, Buddhists and Zoroastrians) should be seen, again, not as arising only out of a sense of virtue or justice or expediency on the part of the majority of the rulers and dynasties throughout Muslim history—and thus as some kind of interesting historical prefiguration of modern, secular tolerance; rather, the fact that this phenomenon of Muslim tolerance is so clearly defined must be seen as organically connected to the spirit of the Qur'anic revelation, a spirit grasped in depth by traditional Muslims, and deliberately ignored or subverted by modern 'jihadists'. This spirit is well expressed in the following verses:

> *Truly those who believe, and the Jews, and the Christians, and the Sabeans—whoever believes in God and the Last Day and performs virtuous deeds—surely their reward is with their Lord, and no fear shall come upon them, neither shall they grieve.* (*Al-Baqarah*, 2: 62)
>
> *Of the People of the Scripture there is a staunch community*

> *who recite the revelations of God in the watches of the night, falling prostrate. / They believe in God and the Last Day, and enjoin right conduct and forbid indecency, and vie with one another in good works. These are of the righteous. / And whatever good they do, they will not be denied it; and God knows the pious.* (*Āl ʿImrān*, 3: 113–4)

The lifeblood of terrorism is hatred; and this hatred is often in turn the disfigured expression of grievance—a grievance that may be legitimate. In the present day, few doubt that the ongoing injustices in Palestine and other parts of the Muslim world give rise to legitimate grievances, but there is nothing in Islam that justifies the killing or injuring of civilians, nor of perpetrating any excess as a result of hatred, even if that hatred is based on legitimate grievances. The pursuit of justice must be conducted in accordance with justice; the means should not undermine the end:

> *O ye who believe, be upright for God, witnesses in justice; and let not hatred of a people cause you to be unjust. Be just—that is closer to piety.* (*Al-Māʾidah*, 5:8)

The principle here established is perfectly exemplified in the conduct of Emir Abd al-Qadir, leader of the Algerian Muslims in their heroic resistance to French colonial aggression between 1830 and 1847. The French were guilty of the most barbaric crimes in their '*mission civilisatrice*'; the emir responded not with bitter vengefulness and enraged fury but with dispassionate propriety and principled warfare. At a time when the French were indiscriminately massacring entire tribes, when they were offering their soldiers a ten franc reward for every pair of Arab ears, and when severed Arab heads were regarded as trophies of war, the emir manifested his magnanimity, his unflinching adherence to Islamic principle, and his refusal to stoop to the level of his 'civilised' adversaries, by issuing the following edict:

> Every Arab who captures alive a French soldier will receive as reward eight douros … Every Arab who has in his possession a Frenchman is bound to treat him well and to conduct him to either the khalifa or the emir himself, as soon as possible. In cases where the prisoner complains of ill treatment, the Arab will have no right to any reward.[236]

When asked what the reward was for a severed French head, the emir replied: twenty-five blows of the baton on the soles of the feet. One understands why General Bugeaud, governor-general of Algeria, referred to the emir not only as 'a man of genius whom history should place alongside Jugurtha', but also as 'a kind of prophet, the hope of all fervent Muslims'.[237] When he was finally defeated and brought to France, before being exiled to Damascus, the emir received hundreds of French admirers who had heard of his bravery and his nobility; the visitors by whom he was most deeply touched, though, were French officers who came to thank him for the treatment they received at his hands when they were his prisoners in Algeria.[238]

Also highly relevant to our theme is the emir's famous defence of Christians in Damascus in 1860. Now defeated and in exile, the emir spent his time praying and teaching. When civil war broke out between the Druze and the Christians in Lebanon, the emir heard that there were signs of an impending attack on the Christians of Damascus. He wrote letters to all the Druze shaykhs, requesting them not to 'make offensive movements against a place with the inhabitants of which you have never before been at enmity'. Here we have an expression of the cardinal principle of warfare in Islam: never to initiate hostilities. *And fight in the way of God those who fight you, but do not commit aggression. God loves not the aggressors* (*Al-Baqarah*, 2: 190).[239]

The emir's letters proved to no avail. When the Druze were approaching the Christian quarters of the city, the emir confronted them, urging them to observe the rules of religion and of human justice.

> 'What,' they shouted, 'you, the great slayer of Christians, are you come out to prevent us from slaying them in our turn? Away!'
>
> 'If I slew the Christians,' he shouted in reply, 'it was ever in accordance with our law—the Christians who had declared war against me, and were arrayed in arms against our faith.'[240]

This had no effect upon the mob. In the end, the emir and his small band of followers sought out the terrified Christians, giving them refuge, first in his own home, and then, as the numbers grew, in the citadel. It is estimated that no less than fifteen thousand Christians were saved by the emir in this action; it is important to note that in this number were included all the ambassadors and consuls of the European powers. As Churchill prosaically puts it:

> All the representatives of the Christian powers then residing in Damascus, without one single exception, had owed their lives to him. Strange and unparalleled destiny! An Arab had thrown his guardian aegis over the outraged majesty of Europe. A descendant of the Prophet had sheltered and protected the Spouse of Christ.[241]

The French consul, representative of the state that was still very much in the process of colonising the emir's homeland, owed his life to the emir; for this true warrior of Islam, there was no bitterness, resentment or revenge, only the duty to protect the innocent, and all the 'People of the Book' who lived peacefully within the lands of Islam. It is difficult to conceive of a greater contrast than that between the emir's conduct and the present-day self-styled *mujāhidīn*, who indiscriminately portray the West as the enemy tout court, and perpetrate correspondingly illegitimate acts against Westerners. The emir's action exemplifies well the Qur'anic verse:

> *God forbids you not from dealing kindly and justly with those who fought not against you on account of your religion, nor drove you out of your homes. Truly God loves those who are just.* (*Al-Mumtaḥanah*, 60:8)

It is interesting to note that another great warrior of Islam, Imam Shamil of Dagestan, hero of the wars against Russian imperialism,[242] wrote a letter to the emir when he heard of his defence of the Christians. He praised the emir for his noble act, thanking God that there were still Muslims who behaved according to the spiritual ideals of Islam:

> I was astonished at the blindness of the functionaries who have plunged into such excesses, forgetful of the words of the Prophet ﷺ, 'Whoever shall be unjust towards a tributary,[243] who shall do him wrong, who shall lay on him any charge beyond his means, and finally who shall deprive him of anything without his own consent, it is I who will be his accuser in the day of judgement'.[244]

While the emir fought French colonialism militarily, in the following century another great Sufi master in Algeria, Shaykh Ahmad al-Alawi, chose to resist with a peaceful strategy, but one which pertained no less to jihad, in the principal sense of the term. One has to remember that the literal meaning of the word jihad is 'effort' or struggle, and that the 'greater' jihad was defined by the Prophet as the *jihad al-nafs*, the struggle against the soul. The priority thus accorded to inward, spiritual effort over all outward endeavours must never be lost sight of in any examination of jihad. Physical fighting is the 'lesser' jihad, and only has meaning in the context of that unremitting combat against inner vices, the devil within, that has been called the greater jihad.

One contemporary Sufi master vividly contrasts the kind of inner warfare that characterises the true 'warriors of the spirit' from the mass of ordinary believers. He does so in connection with the Qur'anic distinction, within the category of those who are saved in the hereafter, between the *companions of the right* (*aṣḥāb al-yamīn*) and *the foremost* (*al-sābiqūn*) (*Al-Wāqi'ah*, 56: 8–10):

> Every Muslim is at war with the devil. As regards *those of the right*, however, this warfare is desultory and intermittent, with many armistices and many compromises. Moreover the devil is aware that as fallen men they are already to a certain extent within his grasp, and having by definition no faith in the Divine Mercy, he cannot foresee that they will escape from his clutches in the life to come. But as regards *the foremost*, he feels them actually throwing off his domination in the present, and they even carry the war into his territory. The result is a terrible retaliation ...[245]

The individual's moral and spiritual effort in this inner struggle is a necessary but not sufficient condition for victory; only by means of heaven-sent weapons can the war be won: sacred rites, meditations, incantations, invocations—all of which are summed up in the term 'remembrance of God'. In this light, the strategy of Shaykh al-Alawi can be better appreciated. It was to put first things first, concentrating on the 'one thing needful' and leaving the rest in God's hands. It might be seen, extrinsically, as an application, on the plane of society, of the following esoteric principle, enunciated by one of his spiritual forbears, Mulay Ali al-Jamal: 'The true way to hurt the enemy is to be occupied with the love of the Friend; on the other hand, if you engage in war with the enemy, he will have obtained what he wanted from you, and at the same time you will have lost the opportunity of loving the Friend.'[246]

Shaykh al-Alawi concentrated on this love of the Friend, and of all those values connected to this imperative of remembrance, doing so to the exclusion of other, more overt forms of resistance, military and political, against the French. The Shaykh's spiritual radiance extended not just to a few disciples but also, through his many *muqaddams*, to hundreds of thousands of Muslims whose piety was deepened in ways that are immeasurable.[247] The Shaykh was not directly concerned with political means of liberating his land from the yoke of French rule, for this was but a secondary aspect of the situation: the underlying aim of the French '*mission civilisatrice*' in Algeria was to forge the Algerian personality in the image of French culture,[248] so in the measure that one perceives that the real danger of colonialism was cultural and psychological rather than just territorial and political, the spiritual indomitability of the Shaykh and his many followers assumes the dimensions of a signal victory. The French could make no inroads into a mentality that remained inextricably rooted in the spiritual tradition of Islam.

Lest this approach be regarded as a prescription for unconditional quietism, one should note that the great warrior, the emir himself, would have had no difficulty whatsoever in asserting its validity, for even while outwardly engaging with the enemy on the battlefield, he was never for a moment distracted from his remembrance of the 'Friend'. It was without bitterness and rage that he fought, and this explains the absence of any resentment towards the French when he was defeated by them, submitting to the manifest will of God with the same contemplative resignation with which he went into battle with them in the first place. One may suspect us of romanticising somewhat, and of overstating the emir's capacity to deal with the exigencies of a brutal war whilst simultaneously plumbing the depths of contemplative experience; it is therefore useful to present the following account, written by a Frenchman, Léon Roche, who entered the inner circle of the emir's entourage by pretending to have converted to Islam. During the siege of Ayn Madi in 1838, Roche was traumatised by the fighting and killing, and sought out the emir; entering his tent, he pleaded with the emir to help him.

> He calmed me and had me drink an infusion of *schiehh* (a kind of absynthe common in the desert). He supported my head, which I could no longer hold up, on one of his knees. He was squatting in the Arab fashion. I was stretched out at his side. He placed his hands on my head, from which he had removed the *haik* and the *chechias*, and under this gentle touch I soon fell asleep. I awoke well into the night. I opened my eyes and felt revived. The smoky wick of an Arab lamp barely lit the vast tent of the amir. He was standing three steps away from me. He thought I was asleep. His two arms were raised to the height of his head, fully displaying his milky white *bernous* and *haik* which fell in superb folds. His beautiful blue eyes, lined with black lashes, were raised. His lips, slightly open, seemed to be still reciting a prayer but nevertheless were motionless. He had come to an ecstatic state. His aspirations towards heaven were such that he seemed no longer to touch the earth. I had on occasion been granted the honour of sleeping in Abd al-Kader's tent and I had seen him in prayer and been struck by his mystical transports, but on this night he represented for me the most striking image of faith. Thus must the great saints of Christianity have prayed.[249]

From this account one sees that the following 'official' description of the emir, given as the conclusion to a pamphlet defining army regulations in 1839, was not simply pious propaganda:

> Il Hadj Abdel Kader cares not for this world, and withdraws from it as much as his avocations permit … He rises in the middle of the night to recommend his own soul and the souls of his followers to God. His chief pleasure is in praying to God with fasting, that his sins may be forgiven … When he administers justice, he hears complaints with the greatest patience … When he preaches, his words bring tears to all eyes, and melt the hardest hearts.[250]

This remarkable combination of roles—warrior and saint, preacher and judge—recalls perhaps the greatest model of all Muslim *mujāhidīn*, Ali ibn Abi Talib, son-in-law and cousin of the Prophet, the fourth caliph of Islam and first Shi'i imam, unrivalled hero of all the early battles of Islam. The Prophet ﷺ said: 'I am the city of knowledge and Ali is its gate'. He also said, in a hadith bearing the highest degree of authenticity (*mutawātir*): '*For whoever has me as his master (mawlā), Ali is his master.*' And the Prophet ﷺ referred to Ali as having the same rank in relation to him as Aaron had in relation to Moses, except that Ali was not a prophet. This paragon of wisdom and virtue stands forth as the most compelling holy warrior in the Islamic tradition. As Frithjof Schuon puts it, 'Ali appears above all as the "Solar Hero", he is the "Lion" of God; he personifies the combination of physical heroism on the field of battle with a sanctity wholly detached from the things of the world; he is the personification of the wisdom, both impassive and combative, which the Bagavad-Gita teaches.'[251]

One of the great lessons of principled warfare, of 'fighting in the path of God', imparted by Ali was immortalised by Rumi in his poetic rendering of the famous incident in which Ali sheathed his sword instead of finishing off his defeated enemy, who had spat at him in a last gesture of defiance. Although the immediate spiritual significance of the action is clearly Ali's refusal to kill on the basis of personal anger—the warrior must be detached from self, and fight wholly for God—it is also given a deeper metaphysical meaning by Rumi. In his *Mathnawi*, Rumi turns the incident into a sublime commentary on the Qur'anic verse, *Ye slew them not, but God slew them. And thou* (Muhammad) *didst not throw when thou threwest, but God threw* (*Al-Anfāl*, 8:17). The last part of the verse refers to the throwing by the Prophet of a handful of dust in the direction of the enemy before a battle. But the verse as a whole alludes to the reality that the true, ontological agent of all actions is God Himself; man's actions are good only if he is conscious of this, and insofar as he is effaced in this consciousness. Rumi puts the following words into the mouth of Ali, who replies to the question of the baffled, defeated warrior on the ground: why did you not kill me?

> He said, 'I am wielding the sword for God's sake, I am the servant of God, I am not under the command of the body.
>
> I am the Lion of God, I am not the lion of my passion: my deed bears witness to my religion.
>
> In war I am (manifesting the truth of) thou didst not throw when thou threwest: I am (but) as the sword, and the wielder is the (Divine) Sun.

> I have removed the baggage of self out of the way, I have deemed (what is) other than God to be non-existence.
>
> I am a shadow, the Sun is my lord; I am the chamberlain, I am not the curtain (which prevents approach) to Him.
>
> I am filled with the pearls of union, like a (jewelled) sword: in battle I make (men) living, not slain.[252]
>
> Blood does not cover the sheen of my sword: how should the wind sweep away my clouds?
>
> I am not a straw, I am a mountain of forbearance and patience and justice: how should the fierce wind carry off the mountain?'[253]

The true warrior of Islam smites the neck of his own anger with the sword of forbearance;[254] the false warrior strikes at the neck of his enemy with the sword of his own unbridled ego. For the first, the spirit of Islam determines jihad; for the second, bitter anger, masquerading as jihad, determines Islam. The contrast between the two could hardly be clearer.

The episodes recounted here as illustrations of authentic jihad should be seen not as representing some unattainably sublime ideal, but as expressive of the sacred norm in the Islamic tradition of warfare; this norm may not always have been applied in practice—one can always find deviations and transgressions—but it was continuously upheld in principle, and, more often than not, gave rise to the kind of chivalry, heroism and nobility of which we have offered a few of the more striking and famous examples here.

This sacred norm stood out clearly for all to see, buttressed by the values and institutions of traditional Muslim society. It can still be discerned today, for those who look hard enough, through the clouds of passion and ideology. The emir bewailed the paucity of 'champions of truth' in his time; in our own time, we are confronted with an even more grotesque spectacle: the champions of authentic jihad being blown to pieces by suicide bombers claiming to be martyrs for the faith. One of the truly great *mujāhidīn* in the war against the Soviet invaders in Afghanistan, Ahmed Shah Massoud, fell victim to a treacherous attack by two fellow Muslims, in what was evidently the first stage of the operation that destroyed the World Trade Center. It was a strategic imperative for the planners of the operation to rid the land of its most charismatic leader; a hero who could credibly be used by the West as a figurehead for the revenge attack on Afghanistan that was provoked, anticipated, and hoped for, by the terrorists. But, politics aside, the reason why Massoud was so popular was precisely his fidelity to the values of noble warfare in Islam; and it was this very fidelity to that tradition that made him a dangerous enemy of the terrorists—more dangerous, it may be said, than that more abstract enemy, 'the West'. To present the indiscriminate murder of Western civilians as jihad, the values of true jihad needed to be dead and buried.

The murder of Massoud was thus doubly symbolic: he embodied the traditional spirit of jihad that needed to be destroyed by those who wished to assume its ruptured mantle; and it was only through suicide—subverting one's own soul—that this destruction, or rather, this apparent destruction, could be perpetrated. The destruction is only apparent in that, on the one hand:

> *They destroy [but] themselves, they who would ready a pit of fire fiercely burning [for all who have attained to faith].* (*Al-Burūj*, 85:4–5) [255]

And on the other hand:

> *Say not of those who are slain in the path of God: They are dead. Nay, they are alive, though ye perceive not.* (*Al-Baqarah*, 2:154)

Finally, let it be noted that, while it is indeed true that the martyr is promised paradise, a *shahīd* is one whose death truly bears 'witness' (*shahādah*) to the truth of God. It is consciousness of the truth that must animate and articulate the spirit of one who 'fights in the Path of God'; fighting for any cause other than the truth cannot be called a jihad, just as one who dies fighting in such a cause cannot be called a 'martyr'. Only he is a martyr who can say with utter sincerity:

> *Truly my prayer and my sacrifice, my living and my dying are for God, Lord of all creation.* (*Al-An'ām*, 6:162)

CHAPTER SIX

A FATWA ON JIHAD

HE Shaykh Ali Gomaa
(Former Grand Mufti of Egypt)

The concept of jihad in Islam is one of the topics that causes the most confusion and is surrounded by a cacophony aiming at equating jihad with mass murder and random shooting sprees.

All concepts have roots in a group of beliefs that nourish the concept into full bloom. By applying this definition to jihad, we would find that its roots are not the same as infamous propaganda would have us believe, namely that Islam instils bloodlust and a desire to terrorise people and massacre them in cold blood or convert them at the point of a sword.

The Relationship between Jihad and Islam

The roots of jihad are in Islam, and to understand the concept we need to take a broader look at the message of Islam and the messenger who carried it from heaven to earth. Muslims consider the Prophet Muhammad ﷺ to be the carrier of the last revelation from God to all mankind. This idea gives rise to the universality of Islam which does not confine itself to a certain place or limit itself to a specific time, nor, more importantly target a particular race or ethnicity, be it Arab or Turk or Anglo-Saxon or Asian. The reality is that Islam transcends the boundaries of space, time and race to encompass all of humanity in its fold.

The most important characteristic of the Prophet Muhammad ﷺ mentioned in the Holy Qur'an, is that he is a 'mercy' to the worlds. The idea that the Prophet Muhammad ﷺ was sent by God to be a mercy to the worlds reinforces the universal characteristic of the message of Islam, as the Prophet is not a mercy to Muslims alone but to all people, animals, plants, stones, indeed to all creatures; this is what is meant by 'all the worlds'.

This overarching characteristic of the Prophet being a mercy to all the worlds encompasses all the concepts and/or ideologies which stem from Islam and are promoted by it, including the concept of jihad.

The Linguistic Origin of Jihad

Before delving deeply into the concept of jihad, it is vital to define the term itself its root in the Arabic language. The word jihad comes from the root j/h/d, which in Arabic means to exert the most effort. This definition is general: as one can exert effort in studying or fulfilling goals and ambitions in a variety of areas.

In Islam the idea of exerting effort has two levels, a major level and a minor one. The major level of jihad is *jihad al-nafs* or struggling against one's lower self and its demeaning lustful desires. This jihad is the hardest because it needs discipline and hard work. The lesser, or minor jihad, is *al-qitāl* or armed struggle. This is the jihad that has been attacked by unjust and misleading propaganda in an effort to equate it with mere bloodshed.

Qur'anic Verses and Prophetic Traditions on jihad

Keeping in mind that 'mercy' is the backbone and root of all Islamic legislation and rulings, one must understand that jihad is no different. God in the Qur'an and the Prophet Muhammad ﷺ in his prophetic traditions have laid out the purpose of jihad, and laid down the rulings and foundational bases which condition this concept, and through which it can be defined.

God says in the Holy Qur'an:

> *We ordained for the children of Israel that if any one kills a person—unless it be for murder or for spreading mischief in the land—it would be as if he killed the whole people, and if anyone saved a life, it would be as if he saved the life of all people.* (*Al-Mā'idah*, 5: 32)

The Qur'an forbids murder whilst extolling the sanctity of human life,

> *Life, which Allah has made sacred* (*Al-An'ām*, 6: 151)

God also says in the Holy Qur'an:

> *Fight in the cause of Allah those who fight you but do not transgress limits; For Allah loveth not transgressors.* (*Al-Baqarah*, 2: 190)

In his commentary, Imam al-Taher Ibn 'Ashur reported through Ibn 'Abbas and 'Umar Ibn 'Abdul 'Aziz and Mujahid that this verse is definite and has not been abrogated. He went on to say: 'the purport is to fight those who are set to fight you, i.e. do not attack the old, women or children.'

Sulaymān Ibn Burayda narrated through his father that whenever the Prophet used to send an army to battle, he would brief its commander and remind him to fear Allah in his actions and those with him and say: 'Fight in the name of Allah, fight those (who fight you) from among the disbelievers and do not exceed your limits, do not transgress, deceive, mutilate [the dead] and do not kill a child.' (Al-Tirmidhi)

Ibn 'Umar ﷺ said: 'I saw the messenger of Allah ﷺ circling the Ka'bah saying: "How great and sacred you are, and how pleasant your fragrance! By He in whose hand is the life of Mohammed, the sanctity of a believer, his property, life and to think well of him is greater in the sight of Allah than yours."' (Ibn Majah). Consider also: 'The first cases to be adjudicated against on the Day of Judgment will be those of bloodshed' (Bukhari), and his strikingly stark threat that: 'Whoever kills one (non-Muslim) under contract (of Muslim protection) will never smell the scent of paradise' (Ibn Majah).

The Purpose of Jihad in Islam

The purpose or the aim of jihad or conducting wars for the sake of God is as follows:

1) Self-defence and fighting back against aggression.
2) Alleviating religious persecution and establishing freedom of religion so that people may have the opportunity to think freely and practice their religious convictions.

The Conditions and the Rulings for Jihad

1) The nobility of purpose, meaning that no personal interests or private gains should be the aim behind which jihad is being waged.
2) Fighting should be only against combatants not defenceless civilians who are not in the battlefield and are not equipped or trained to be engaged in combat.
3) The killing or harming of women and children is strictly

prohibited. Al-Bukhari and Muslim reported through Abdullah ibn 'Umar ﷺ that a woman was found dead in one of the battles fought by the Prophet ﷺ; thereupon he condemned killing women and children. Another phrasing of the hadith states: 'The Messenger of Allah ﷺ forbade killing women and children.' Imam al-Nawawi said: 'There is a scholarly consensus on putting this hadith in practice as long as the women and children do not fight [the Muslims]. If they do, the majority of scholars maintain that they should be killed' (*Sharḥ* Muslim 12/48).

4) Preserving the lives of captives and treating them humanely.
5) Preserving the environment, which includes a prohibition on killing animals or cutting trees or destroying harvests or polluting rivers or wells or demolishing houses.
6) Preserving religious freedom for worshippers in their homes, churches or synagogues.
7) Killing and attacking people by surprise is prohibited. Abu Hurayrah ﷺ narrated that the Messenger of Allah ﷺ said: 'A believer is not to kill [others]. Faith is a deterrent to killing.' Ibn al-Athir said: 'Killing [here] means taking others by surprise and killing them while they are unprepared' (*Al-Nihāyah fī Gharīb al-Ḥadīth wa al-Athār* 3/775). The hadith means that faith is a deterrent to attacking others suddenly while they are unprepared. The Prophet's words: 'A believer is not to attack [others] by surprise' is a clear prohibition against deception in combat.
8) Permission to enter a country is considered a non-verbal security agreement not to cause corruption in the host country. Imam al-Khurqi said in his *Mukhtasr*: 'Whoever enters enemy lands in safety is not allowed to cheat them of their money.' Commenting on this statement, Ibn Qudama said that 'it is prohibited to betray them [non-Muslims in non-Muslim countries] because there is an unspoken covenant to enter in safety on the condition that the person who seeks permission to enter a foreign country does not betray or oppress them. So whoever enters our lands in safety and betrays us violates this security agreement. This is prohibited because it involves treachery which is forbidden in our religion' (Al-Mughnī 9/237).

9) The enemy must be from among those whom Muslims are permitted to fight, rather than the enemy with whom Muslims have a truce. It is impermissible to attack the enemy under the cover of night because it is a violation of the security pact between them in terms of lives, wealth, and honour.
10) It is impermissible to use human shields save in a state of war and under specific conditions detailed by jurists. (Bahr Ra'iq 80/5, Hashiyat ibn 'Abn Abdin 223/3, Rawdat al Talibin 239/10, Mughnī al Muhtaj 223/4, Mughnī ibn Qudama 449/8, 386/10).

Who Has the Right to Call for Jihad and Declare War?

1) The principle in war is that it should be launched with the authorisation of, and under the banner of, the Muslim ruler; it is imperative that the decision to declare war be based on his own reasoning, and his subjects must obey him. A ruler is authorised to declare war due to his knowledge of evident and hidden matters, the consequences of actions and the interest of his people. For this reason, a ruler is authorised to declare war and agree to domestic or international treaties as soon as he assumes office. In turn, he does not issue decisions based on (personal) whims.

   The Muslim ruler declares war only after consulting specialists in every relevant field, such as technical and military specialists and political consultants who are indispensable to military strategy. The luminary al-Bahuti said in *Sharḥ Muntahā al-Iradāt*: 'It is prohibited to [launch an] attack without the ruler's permission because he is responsible for making the decision of declaring war. [This is because] he has access to all the information pertaining to the enemy. [His permission is mandatory] except if [Muslims] are taken by surprise by non-Muslim enemies and fear their threat. [Only] then is it permissible to fight the attackers without the ruler's permission because of the general benefit therein.'
2) Breach of international agreements and treaties: Islamic states must abide by the agreements and treaties that they have acknowledged and entered into of their own accord; standing

firmly with the international community towards achieving global peace and security (only) to the extent of the commitment of the signatory countries. Allah says:

O you who believe, fulfill [all] contracts (*Al-Mā'idah*, 5:1)

In the above verse, the term 'contract' refers to all commitments between two parties on a particular issue. In his interpretation of the above verse, the erudite Tunisian scholar, Ibn 'Ashur says: '"Contracts" in this verse refers to one of a genus denoting the totality [of contracts]. It includes covenants that Muslims made with their Lord such as to follow the shari'ah … pacts of allegiance between the believers and the Prophet ﷺ, not to associate partners with Allah, steal, or commit fornication … agreements between Muslims and non-Muslims … and agreements between one Muslim and another' (*Al-Tahrīr wa al-Tanwīr*, 6/74).

Amr ibn 'Awf al-Muzna ﷺ narrates that the Prophet ﷺ said: 'Muslims are bound by the conditions [they stipulate] except those that are unlawful or those that make unlawful matters lawful' (reported by al-Tirmidhi).

Commenting on this hadith, al-Jass said: 'It is a general obligation to fulfil all the conditions man holds himself to as long as there is nothing (in Islamic law) to restrict them.' (*Aḥkām al-Qur'ān*, 2/418)

Ali ﷺ narrated that the Prophet ﷺ said: 'The protection granted by the weakest Muslim to a non-Muslim is tantamount to that of the entire [community]. Whosoever violates it incurs the curse of Allah, the angels, and all the people.' (Reported by al-Bukhari)

Abdullah ibn 'Umar ﷺ narrated that the Prophet ﷺ said: 'The signs of hypocrisy are four: when he is entrusted with something he betrays the trust, when he speaks he lies, when he makes a promise he breaks it, when he quarrels he behaves in an immoral manner. Whoever possesses all four is a hypocrite and whoever possesses one of them possesses an element of hypocrisy until he gives it up.' (Reported by al-Bukhari in his *Ṣaḥīḥ*).

'Umar ibn al-Hamq al-Khaza'i narrated that the Prophet ﷺ said: 'If a man entrusts another with his life and is killed by him, I have nothing to do with the murderer, even if the murdered man were a non-Muslim' (Reported by al-Bayhaqi). Consequently, the parties to international treaties and agreements are committed to end war and enjoy a state of peace by virtue of the agreement they entered into. Allah Almighty says: *And if they incline towards peace, then incline to it [also] and rely upon Allah. Indeed, it is He who is the Hearing, the Knowing* (*Al-Anfāl*, 8:61).

Free Choice vs. Coerced Conversion

The concept of 'free choice' is central in the teachings of Islam as God stated in the Qur'an that 'there is no coercion in religion'. Muslims grasped this concept well and realised that God does not want the mere submission of bodies but the real surrender of hearts. The heart is the main target of God's Message because mercy is the all-encompassing nature of Islam, and the heart is where it resides.

In contemplating these stipulations we would find that none of the current incidents of terrorism which happen to involve Muslims claiming to be performing jihad are actually jihad, because they fail to meet any of the conditions laid out above. The sole aim of stipulating these conditions is to ensure that the concept of mercy and justice are at the forefront of Muslims' hearts and minds while conducting warfare.

The aim of jihad is not to steal people's property or to shed their blood or to alter their values and force them to convert. The aim is to free people from persecution so they may have the opportunity to think freely and choose their religion based on informed decisions.

All of the these terrorist attacks have probably one thing in common: the cowardice of the perpetrators who betray and target civilians and cause nothing but the bloodshed of innocents, Muslim and non-Muslim.

What breaks the heart the most is that while jihad in Islam teaches Muslims to be noble knights who defend the rights of the weak and fight back against transgressors who are warriors in combat, today we find the people who claim that they are performing jihad and attach themselves to this noble concept are those who are the furthest from Islam and jihad in letter and spirit.

The true noble knight jihadist is the one who lays the foundation of justice and freedom for all people, regardless of their personal religious convictions. Therefore, the concept of jihad being a legitimate war is a true and well-defined one even by our modern definitions of just wars according to the United Nations' charter on wars.

The Prophet Muhammad ﷺ was the role model who applied the different concepts of mercy, justice and freedom laid down in the Qur'an. He showed Muslims how to conduct and abide by these concepts practically.

The Prophet Muhammad ﷺ and Jihad

Before delving directly into the Prophet's conquests and contemplating the way it which they were conducted and the goals they strived to achieve, we need to take a broader look at the concept of war in ancient times and how it is a social phenomenon as old as humanity itself.

It is innate in human beings to preserve their lives and fend off death. The survival instinct causes human beings to defend what belongs to them even if this leads to struggle and combat in order to survive.

This primitive level of fighting for the basic needs of life, such as food or shelter, can become more sophisticated and develop into a higher level of war, such as the wars that are waged for gaining freedom or restoring dignity or fighting oppression.

Moving to the holy books and divine scriptures, namely the Torah and the Bible, we find that new reasons were added for waging war, reasons more advanced in nature and more civilisational in purpose. These new types of war were not waged to secure food for the next day, but with the aim of alleviating injustice and securing freedom of worship for all people, and helping the helpless and destitute.

Humanity witnessed a shift in the paradigm of conducting wars, which now aimed to move away from fulfilling the needs of the 'self' towards fulfilling 'divine ideals' for which people are ready to sacrifice their lives.

This shift in paradigm continued in the tradition of Islam and took the name of jihad. In jihad one finds himself or herself more than ready to sacrifice his life for his religious beliefs and for fulfilling a higher calling that advocates alleviating injustice and persecution and establishing freedom of religion and thought.

When the Prophet Muhammad ﷺ immigrated to Medina and established the nascent Muslim state after suffering thirteen years of violent opposition and anguish, the tribe of Quraysh in Mecca was angry at the huge success that the message of Islam had achieved, without coercion or bloodshed. The Quraysh felt threatened by the new power of Islam which would undermine their authority in Mecca, where idol worship was the centre of religious life and where the Quraysh were the religious leaders whom people from the rest of Arabia would come to visit and present their offerings.

Muslims patiently endured persecution for thirteen years in Mecca and abided by the Prophet's command to not respond to the aggression which they endured at the hands of the Meccan idolaters. When the Muslims emigrated to Medina and established their new state, they found themselves in a position where they had to defend the boundaries of their nascent state against the attacks of Quraysh who hoped to destroy this new religion in its infancy. It was at this time that God permitted Muslims to fight back against those who fought them, and to protect themselves against aggression. This indicates that jihad in the sense of armed struggle was not a self-embedded concept which originated with Islam. It is more likely that the circumstances into which the nascent Islamic state was born gave rise to jihad.

These same circumstances surrounded the message of the Prophet Jesus who called the Jews to peace and reform, even though they hunted him down and wanted to crucify him, except that in the Prophet Muhammad's ﷺ case, God saved his Prophet ﷺ from his persecutors.

Jihad vs. Terrorism

Terrorism, therefore, cannot be the outcome of any proper understanding of religion. It is, rather, a manifestation of the immorality of people with cruel hearts, arrogant souls, and warped logic. Islam by its nature is a religion of moderation, not of extremes. In his famous saying, the Prophet of Islam advised Muslims to always choose the middle ground and not seek extremes on either side. This moderation in religion means that one neither exaggerates, transgressing the limits set by God, nor neglects them altogether, thereby falling short of His expectations. While calling upon all Muslims to exercise moderation with all permissible things, Islam clearly and categorically rejects all forms of extremism, including *ghulū* (excessiveness), *tanatu'* (zealotry) and *tashaddud* (extreme practices). These forms of extremism do not find a home in Islamic teachings, because Islam recognises that extremism is morally flawed and unproductive. It is against human nature, and has always been a short-lived phenomenon which does not work.

The problem faced by Muslims today—and indeed religious communities across the globe—relates to the issue of authority. In both Islam and other religions we are witnessing a phenomenon in which laypeople without a sound foundation in religious learning have attempted to set themselves up as religious authorities, even though they lack the scholarly qualifications for making valid interpretations of religious law and morality. In many cases, they have been facilitated in this by the proliferation of new media and irresponsibly sensationalistic journalism. It is this eccentric and rebellious attitude towards religion that clears the way for extremist interpretations of Islam that have no basis in reality. None of these extremists have been educated in Islam in genuine centers of Islamic learning. They are, rather, products of troubled environments and have subscribed to distorted and misguided interpretations of Islam that have no basis in traditional Islamic doctrine. Their aim is purely political—to create havoc and chaos in the world.

Unfortunately, terrorists often invoke the Islamic concept of jihad to justify their crimes. This has led to much confusion and the tendency to misinterpret this important Islamic idea by linking it to violence and aggression. Military jihad, by contrast, is the antithesis of terrorism. It is a just war of the sort that can be found in every religious law and civil code. As the Qur'an says, *Fight in the way of God against those who fight against you, but avoid aggression for God does not like the aggressor. But if they cease [fighting], then God is Forgiving, Merciful.* This statement has been repeated many times throughout the second chapter of the Qur'an and forms the fundamental parameters for the Islamic law of warfare: namely, that it is permissible only for the purpose of repelling an attack, and protecting one's self, one's home and one's family.

Terrorism does not come close to fulfilling any of the many conditions which are necessary for a just jihad. Among these is the fact that war can only be launched upon the authorisation of the Muslim ruler, after consultation with specialists and consultants. Vigilantism has been clearly forbidden throughout Muslim history.

Similarly, terrorism involves killing people and taking them by surprise. The Prophet has instructed: 'A believer is not to kill [others]. Faith is a deterrent to killing.' Similarly, he has said: 'A believer is not to attack [others] by surprise.' Clearly, terrorists can only accomplish their goals by going against these Islamic teachings, which are fundamental to the type of chivalrous character Muslims must always exhibit, whether in wartime or during periods of peace.

Moreover, terrorism kills and harms women and children. A tradition of the Prophet relates that a woman was found dead in one of the battles. The Prophet found out about this, and thereupon forbade the killing of women and children. Another phrasing of this hadith states: 'The Messenger of Allah ﷺ forbade killing women and children.' The great scholar of Islam, Imam al-Nawawi commented on this: 'There is a scholarly consensus on acting on this tradition as long as the women and children do not fight.' It is clear once more that this is counter to the practice of terrorists.

As such, it is clearly a mistake to label the terrorists practitioners of jihad, or *mujāhidīn*. This is a lofty Islamic concept which bears no resemblance to the lawlessness practiced by terrorists.

The word commonly used in modern Arabic for terrorism, *irhāb*, though an improvement, also poses its own set of problems. Indeed, *irhāb* and the related Arabic root (r/h/b) often contain positive resonances for those conversant with classical Islamic vocabulary. For example, the Qur'an uses a word in the semantic range spawned by (r/h/b) to explain the proper awe with which humans ought to relate to God. *O Children of Israel, remember my favour wherewith I favoured you; and fulfill my covenant and I shall fulfill your covenant, and have awe of Me* (*Al-Baqarah*, 2:40). Similarly, the Qur'an uses a related word (*rahbān*) to refer to monks and monasticism (*rahbaniyyah*), and their manner of interacting with the Divine. Finally, and more concretely, the root (r/h/b) is used to refer to a praiseworthy deterrence against those enemies who would seek to aggressively intimidate the Muslim community. *Make ready for them whatever force you can and of horses tethered that you may thereby awe the enemy of God and your enemy* (*Al-Anfāl*, 8:60). This term therefore is often used to refer to a concept of deterrence aimed at securing an advantage that will lead to peace with an enemy that would otherwise transgress against the Muslim community.

The term *irjāf* as the proper translation into Arabic for terrorism is preferable. This word, which denotes subversion and scaremongering to bring quaking and commotion to society is derived from the root (r/j/f), which means to quake, tremble, be in violent motion, convulse, or shake. This term occurs in the Qur'an in this context in one telling verse: *Now; if the hypocrites do not give over, and those in whose hearts there is sickness and they make commotion (murjifūn) in the city, We shall assuredly urge thee against them.* (*Al-Aḥzāb*, 33:60). In the context of this verse, al-Qurtubi, the renowned thirteenth-century Qur'anic commentator and Maliki jurist, explains the meaning of *irjāf* with respect to 'shaking of the hearts (*taḥrīk al-qulūb*),' noting the root's corresponding application to 'the shaking of the earth (*rajafat al-arḍ*)'. Within an Islamic context, connecting this metaphor of creating commotion on earth (*murjifūn*) with that of shaking hearts (*taḥrīk al-qulīb*) connotes that those who do wrong are in fact acting against the wishes of the Divine.

The term *murjifūn* (singular, *murjif*), as well as the equivalent rendering *irjāfiyyūn* (singular, *irjāfi*), is a far better translation of terrorists ... Of course, there are multiple ways to bring about such intense commotion to society, but all of these fall under the term *irjāf*. From a linguistic perspective, the term unambiguously connotes the cowardice, deceit, and betrayal associated with terrorism in striking from behind.

CHAPTER SEVEN

BODY COUNT: A Comparative Quantitative Study of Mass Killings in History[256]

Dr Naveed Sheikh

Introduction

In his seminal work *The Clash of Civilizations and the Remaking of World Order* (1996), Harvard political scientist Samuel Huntington reformulated Arnold Toynbee's understanding of history as driven not only by impersonal material structures—territory, capital, population, and natural resources—but equally by interpersonal ideational structures such as culture, identity, communal solidarity and civilizational association. This perception seemed supported by empirical observation, and soon filled the intellectual and political lacunae which had attained particular salience in the wake of the collapse of Soviet-backed communism. Oftentimes, the reinstatement of religion—as the single most stable ideational structure in human history—was referred to as 'the revenge of God', but for social scientists and historians alike it became impossible to scientifically isolate the divine variable from terrestrial imperatives in the muddled socio-political praxes of earthlings. A casual observation, nonetheless, would suggest that discursive constructions about God (in politics, shorthand for absolute truth) have been a necessary corollary to nearly all conflictual formations, from the sub-state to the trans-state levels. The intensity of this linkage, and its constancy, is tested in this study.

Objectives

The present study attempts to quantify the human death toll of religious and political violence throughout the last two millennia and relate these to religio-cultural civilisations. Adopting a modified version of Huntington's civilisational taxonomy, the study progresses along the following lines: First, a comprehensive data list of over 3,000 violent clashes in history, 0–2008 CE was developed. We then proceeded to identify 276 of the most violent conflicts in history, all with estimated human death tolls over 10,000, and ranked them by death toll. The result was then organised along civilisational lines, in order to attain a comparative understanding of socio-religiously conditioned violence. The findings are represented in four tables, leading to a comparative evaluation of violence in different religious and civilizational traditions

Methodology

The study has first produced an aggregate list of major violent conflicts in the last two millennia, incorporating four categories of violence, namely war, civil war, democide, and structural violence. This shows the extent to which violence has been an almost universal form of 'doing politics' in all parts of the inhabited world for as long as history has been recorded. The study then proceeded to quantify the death tolls in the most violent episodes to produce a list of the most violent conflicts in the last two millennia. These conflicts were then organised along civilisational lines, thereby quantitatively delineating the frequency of major conflict per civilisation. Separately, we analysed genocidal violence (which may have been part of war or democide in the first analysis) to seek to gauge the level of intensity of violence.

Definitions

CIVILISATIONS: The social construct of civilisation denotes the historically conditioned and intersubjectively shared norms—cultural, religious and societal—whereby a substantial group of people develop a common cultural in-group identity by means of socialisation, pacific interaction and isomorphism. Civilisations are aggregates of local and regional cultures and are bound by shared religious or ethical values.

WAR: War is understood as large-scale acts of aggression and violence between two different (but equal) political units, such as states. According to Clausewitz's classic, *On War*, warfare has three dimensions: political objectives, strategy, and popular passion, whereas the equilibrium between the three (by way of the subordination of passion to strategy and strategy to policy objectives) determines the success or otherwise of any mission. Quantitatively, statisticians insist that the death toll must exceed 1,000 direct deaths (combat related and collateral) in order for an armed conflict to count as a war. Subcategories include interstate wars, continental wars, colonial wars.

CIVIL WAR: Civil wars are systematised acts of violence perpetuated mutually by members of the same nation. By nation in turn is understood adherence to the same ethno-linguistic group or, in modern times, members of the same territorial state. Subcategories include revolutions, rebellions, ethnic strife.

DEMOCIDE: Democide is meant to convey politically motivated murder by government forces or institutions. It can take collective forms (most notably in the form of genocide or lesser forms of mass murder) or individual forms (such as the systematic liquidation of opposition figures or political/ethnic threats to the established order). Democide is, moreover, enacted not only in direct action but also in 'Structural Violence'.

GENOCIDE: Genocide is a form of democide, where the aggressor aims to eliminate a substantial portion of an ethnic, linguistic, or religious group from a substantial territory.

STRUCTURAL VIOLENCE: As opposed to direct violence (direct physical harm), structural violence is a concept promoted by Scandinavian Peace Research to denote the violence perpetuated by malign structure—whether they be of institutional or normative character (for example apartheid as institution vs. racism as norm). Structural violence is thus the suffering which follows from exploitative or repressive forms of social or political organisation.

World Civilisations

The social construct of 'civilisation' conveys a meaning of common identity. This identity, in turn, entails shared social norms, societal values and cultural mores—all repeatedly iterated in public discourses and institutions of socialisation. Organised religion thus emerges as the chief signifier of civilisation, both directly (as the repository of identity and values) and indirectly (as shaper of institutions and discourses). While a 'civilisation' is not coterminous with a religion, the latter is a necessary (but not sufficient) component of the former. Where religion is relatively homogenous (as in much of the Muslim world), we allow for the conceptualisation of a single civilisation in the name of Islam (or the ummah, the Muslim community in a global sense). Likewise, 'associate' members of the Muslim civilisation are found in Africa as well as Europe. The difference between a core member and an associate member of a civilisation is the civilisational identity's location on a spectrum from contestedness to hegemony. Likewise, some civilisations (as the Primal-Indigenous) may simply be a residual category, which lacks formal association and membership.

The following seven civilisations are suggested and their respective locales indicated:

CIVILISATION	LOCALE
Antitheist	Communist block
Buddhist	East Asia, parts of South Asia
Christian	Europe, the Americas, parts of Africa
Indic	India, Nepal, Mauritius
Islamic	Middle East, parts of Asia, parts of Africa
Primal-Indigenous	Parts of Africa, the Americas before colonialism
Sinic	China, some neighbouring states

Table 1: A Death-Toll Ranking of Major Violent Conflict (0–2008 CE)

A note on methodology: estimating the death toll of conflicts is often fraught with dangers that derive both from the absence of data as well as its (un)reliability. Governments or other political groups often have vested interests in suppressing information or releasing partial or misleading information which either exaggerates or omits death figures. The problem is augmented by the longevity of the present study, as the reliability of information tends to deteriorate over time. We have in each case attempted to corroborate numbers from several sources and estimated a reasonable range, supported by scholarly accounts. Although it generally holds true that the older the conflict, the less reliable the data, even recent events sometimes have death toll estimates that differ by a factor of ten (for example Operation Desert Storm of 1991). Where possible, we have tried to narrow down the range, but on occasions the range has been set wide in order to accommodate diverse opinions and sources. A second-order problem arises from a monocausal allocation of blame for acts of political violence, which often emerge out of complex historical and political antecedents. Here we have not classed all engaged parties as belligerent, but simply those who have initiated hostilities in a given event. In particularly complex cases, two or more parties have been deemed to be equally responsible (and the figure is tabulated by dividing by two, three or more as appropriate). If a war is a colonial war, the coloniser or imperial power has by definition been classed as the belligerent power, and likewise in cases of democide, rebellions, revolts, and mutinies, the power-holder has by default been held responsible for any ensuing violence, unless the counter-hegemonic group has engaged in direct action against third parties (e.g. terror tactics).

Event	Estimated Death Toll (>10 million)	Event Type	Belligerent Civilisation
World War II (1939–45)	55,000,000–72,000,000	War, Democide	Christian, Buddhist
People's Republic of China (1949–1975)	44,500,000–77,000,000	Democide	Antitheist

Three Kingdoms Wars (220–80)	40,000,000	War	Sinic
Soviet Reign (1923–54)	38,000,000–55,000,000	Democide	Antitheist
An Shi Rebellion (755–63)	36,000,000	Civil War	Buddhist
Mongol Conquests (from 1207)	30,000,000–50,000,000	War	Primal-Indigenous
Manchu conquest of Ming China (1616–62)	25,000,000	War	Sinic
Tai Ping Rebellion (China, 1851–64)	20,000,000–50,000,000	Civil War	Sinic, Christian
World War I (1914–18)	15,000,000–66,000,000	War	Christian
Second Sino-Japanese War (1931–45)	15,000,000–22,000,00	War	Buddhist
Extermination of Native Americans (C16th-19th)	13,000,000–16,000,000	Structural	Christian
Nationalist China (1928–49)	10,075,000	Civil War	Sinic

<table>
<tr><td>Conquests of Timur the Lame (1360–1405)</td><td>7,000,000–20,000,000</td><td>War</td><td>Islamic</td></tr>
<tr><th>Event</th><th>Estimated Death Toll (>2 million)</th><th>Event Type</th><th>Belligerent Civilisation</th></tr>
<tr><td>Russian Civil War (1917–22)</td><td>5,000,000–9,000,000</td><td>Civil War</td><td>Christian, Antitheist</td></tr>
<tr><td>Conquests of Menelik II Ethiopia (1882–98)</td><td>5,000,000</td><td>War</td><td>Christian</td></tr>
<tr><td>Congo Free State colonial war (1885–1908)</td><td>4,500,000–12,000,000</td><td>War</td><td>Christian</td></tr>
<tr><td>Dungan Revolt (1862–1877)</td><td>4,000,000</td><td>Civil War</td><td>Sinic</td></tr>
<tr><td>Second Congo War (1998–2007)</td><td>3,800,000–5,400,000</td><td>War</td><td>Christian</td></tr>
<tr><td>Napoleonic Wars (1804–15)</td><td>3,500,000–6,000,000</td><td>War</td><td>Christian</td></tr>
<tr><td>China Mao Soviets (1923–49)</td><td>3,500,000</td><td>Democide</td><td>Antitheist</td></tr>
<tr><td>Thirty Years' War (1618–48)</td><td>3,000,000–8,000,000</td><td>War</td><td>Christian</td></tr>
</table>

<table>
<tr><td>Yellow Turban Rebellion (China, 184–205)</td><td>3,000,000–7,000,000</td><td>Civil War</td><td>Sinic</td></tr>
<tr><td>Korean War (1950–3)</td><td>2,500,000–5,040,000</td><td>War</td><td>Christian, Antitheist</td></tr>
<tr><td>Transatlantic Slave Trade (17th to 19th centuries)</td><td>2,400,000–4,300,000</td><td>Structural Violence</td><td>Christian</td></tr>
<tr><td>Vietnam War (1945–75)</td><td>2,300,000–5,100,000</td><td>War</td><td>Christian, Antitheist</td></tr>
<tr><td>French Wars of Religion (1562–98)</td><td>2,000,000–4,000,000</td><td>Civil War</td><td>Christian</td></tr>
<tr><td>Mahmud of Ghazni's invasions, India (1001–08) (1000-1027)</td><td>2,000,000</td><td>War</td><td>Islamic</td></tr>
<tr><th>Event</th><th>Estimated Death Toll (>1 million)</th><th>Event Type</th><th>Belligerent Civilisation</th></tr>
<tr><td>Post-War Expulsion of Germans (1945–7)</td><td>2,100,000–3,000,000</td><td>Democide</td><td>Christian</td></tr>
<tr><td>Cambodia, Khmer Rouge (1975–9)</td><td>1,700,000–2,035,000</td><td>Democide</td><td>Antitheist</td></tr>
<tr><td>North Korea (1948–87)</td><td>1,500,000–1,600,000</td><td>Democide</td><td>Antitheist</td></tr>
</table>

Afghan Civil War (1979–ongoing)	1,500,000–2,000,000	Civil War	Islamic
Arab Slave Trade (7th to 19th centuries)	1,400,000–2,000,000	Structural Violence	Islamic
Chinese Civil War (1928–1949)	1,300,000–6,200,000	Civil War	Sinic
Bengali War of Independence	1,100,000	War	Islamic
Mexican Revolution (1910–20)	1,000,000–2,000,000	Civil War	Christian
Shaka's conquests (1816–28)	1,000,000–2,000,000	Civil War	Primal-Indigenous
Soviet Afghan intervention (1979–89)	1,000,000–1,500,000	War	Antitheist
Nigerian Civil War (1967–70), Biafran	1,000,000–1,200,000	Civil War	Islamic, Christian
Iran-Iraq War (1980–88)	1,000,000	War	Islamic
Japanese invasions of Korea (1592–8)	1,000,000	War	Buddhist

<table>
<tr><td>Second Sudanese Civil War (1983–2005)</td><td>1,000,000</td><td>Civil War</td><td>Islamic, Christian</td></tr>
<tr><td>Crusades (1095-1272)</td><td>1,000,000</td><td>War</td><td>Christian</td></tr>
<tr><td>Aztec Atrocities</td><td>1,000,000+</td><td>Structural Violence</td><td>Primal-Indigenous</td></tr>
<tr><td>Panthay Rebellion (1856–73)</td><td>1,000,000</td><td>Civil War</td><td>Sinic</td></tr>
<tr><th>Event</th><th>Estimated Death Toll (>500,000)</th><th>Event Type</th><th>Belligerent Civilisation</th></tr>
<tr><td>Mozambique Civil War (1976–93)</td><td>900,000–1,000,000</td><td>Civil War</td><td>Christian, Islamic, PI</td></tr>
<tr><td>Seven Years' War (1756–1763)</td><td>868,000–1,400,000</td><td>War</td><td>Christian</td></tr>
<tr><td>Rwandan Civil War (1990–4)</td><td>800,000–1,000,000</td><td>Genocide, Civil War</td><td>Christian</td></tr>
<tr><td>Congo Civil War (1991–1997)</td><td>800,000</td><td>Civil War</td><td>Christian</td></tr>
<tr><td>Great Irish Famine (1845–52)</td><td>750,000–1,500,000</td><td>Structural Violence</td><td>Christian</td></tr>
</table>

Indonesia political/ ethnic strife (1965–87)	729,000–1,000,000	Democide, Civil War	Islamic
Iraq War (2003–Present)	614,000–1,100,000	War	Christian
Russian-Circassian War (1763-1864)	600,000-1,500,000	War	Christian
First Jewish-Roman War (66–73)	600,000–1,300,000	War	Primal-Indigenous
Qing-Dzungar War (1755–57)	600,000–800,000	War	Sinic, Buddhist
Second Jewish-Roman War (Bar Kokhba 132–135)	580,000	War	Primal-Indigenous
Eritrean War of Independence (1961–91)	570,000	War	Christian, Islamic
Algerian War of Independence (1954–1962)	550,000–1,000,000	War	Christian
Somali Civil War (1988 –)	550,000	Civil War	Islamic
Thuggee Cult Murders (17th to 19th centuries)	500,000–2,000,000	Ritual Murder	Indic

<table>
<tr><td>Suttee (4th to 19th centuries)</td><td>500,000–800,000</td><td>Structural Violence</td><td>Indic</td></tr>
<tr><td>Partition of India (1947)</td><td>500,000–1,000,000</td><td>Civil War</td><td>Islamic, Indic</td></tr>
<tr><td>Angolan Civil War (1975–2002)</td><td>500,000–550,000</td><td>Civil War</td><td>Christian, Primal</td></tr>
<tr><td>First Sudanese Civil War (1955–72)</td><td>500,000</td><td>Civil War</td><td>Islamic, Christian</td></tr>
<tr><th>Event</th><th>Estimated Death Toll (>250,000)</th><th>Event Type</th><th>Belligerent Civilisation</th></tr>
<tr><td>War of the Triple Alliance, Paraguay (1864–1870)</td><td>350,000–610,000</td><td>War</td><td>Christian</td></tr>
<tr><td>Miao, Nien and Muslim Rebellions (1850–77)</td><td>450,000</td><td>Civil War</td><td>Sinic</td></tr>
<tr><td>Darfur conflict (2003–ongoing)</td><td>400,000</td><td>Civil war, Democide</td><td>Islamic</td></tr>
<tr><td>War of the Spanish Succession (1701–14)</td><td>400,000–700,000</td><td>Civil War</td><td>Christian</td></tr>
<tr><td>Second Burundi Civil War (1993)</td><td>400,000</td><td>Civil War</td><td>Christian</td></tr>
</table>

Continuation War (1941–4)	371,000	War	Christian
French Revolutionary Wars (1792–1802)	350,000–663,000	War	Christian
Spanish Civil War (1936–1939)	350,000–500,000	Civil War	Christian
Great Northern War (1700–1721)	350,000–400,000	War	Christian
Portuguese Colonialism (1900–25)	325,000	War	Christian
American Civil War (1861–5)	365,000–618,000	Civil War	Christian
Wars of the Three Kingdoms (1639–51)	315,000–735,000	War	Christian
Caucasian War (from 1817)	300,000–1,500,000	War	Christian, Islamic
Ugandan Civil War (1979–86)	300,000–500,000	Civil War	Christian
French Conquest of Algeria (1839–47)	300,000	War	Christian

Mexican Yucatan Maya Campaign (1847–55)	300,000	Civil War	Christian
Idi Amin's Regime (1972–9)	300,000	Democide	Islamic
Abyssinian War (1935–41)	275,000–400,000	War	Christian
French Revolution (1793–4)	263,000–600,000	Civil War	Christian
Philippine-American War (1898–1913)	255,000–1,120,000	War	Christian
Ethiopian Civil Wars (1962–91)	230,000–1,400,000	Civil War	Christian
Albigensian Crusade (1208-1244)	250,000-1,000,000	War	Christian
Indian extermination, Brazil (1900 et seq.)	250,000–500,000	War, Democide	Christian
Iraq under Saddam Hussein (1979–2003)	250,000–1,300,000	Democide	Antitheist
Cuban Revolution (1895–8)	250,000–300,000	War	Christian

Event	Estimated Death Toll (>100,000)	Event Type	Belligerent Civilisation
Bosnian War (1992–5)	220,000	War, Civil War	Christian
Liberian Civil War (1989–97)	220,000	Civil War	PI, Christian
Russo-Turkish War (1877–8)	215,000–285,000	War	Christian, Islamic
Bangladesh Liberation War (1971)	200,000–2,800,000	War, Democide	Islamic
Warlord era in China (1917–28)	200,000–800,000	War	Sinic
Yugoslavia under Tito (1944–87)	200,000–572,000	Democide	Antitheist
East Timor (1975–99)	200,000–250,000	Democide, Civil War	Islamic
First Congo War (1996–7)	200,000	Civil War	Christian
Franco-Prussian War (1870–1)	185,000–204,000	War	Christian

Sierra Leone Civil War (1991–2002)	180,000–200,000	Civil War	Christian
La Violencia (1948–58)	180,000–300,000	Civil War	Christian
Maji-Maji Revolt, German East Africa (1905–7)	175,000–250,000	War	Christian
Mexican War of Independence (1810–21)	150,000–400,000	War	Christian
Communist Vietnam (1975 et seq)	165,000–460,000	Democide	Antitheist
Haitian Revolution (1791–1804)	160,000–350,000	War	Christian
Algerian Civil War (1991 et seq)	160,000–200,000	Civil War	Islamic
Mindanao Conflict (1969–ongoing)	160,000+	Civil War	Islamic, Christian
Lebanese Civil War (1975–90)	150,000–162,000	Civil War	Islamic, Christian
Second Liberian Civil War (1999–2003)	150,000	Civil War	Primal, Christian

Russo-Japanese War (1904–05)	130,000–150,000	War	Buddhist
Russo-Turkish War (1828–9)	130,000–191,000	War	Christian, Islamic
Winter War (1939–40)	148,000–1,000,000	War	Christian
Ten Years' War Cuba (1868–78)	200,000	War	Christian
Balkan Wars (1912–3)	140,000–225,000	War	Christian, Islamic
Guatemaltec Civil War (1960–96)	140,000–200,000	Civil War	Christian
Portuguese Colonial Wars	140,000	War	Christian
Eritrean-Ethiopian War (1998–2000)	125,000–190,000	War	Christian, Islamic
Great Turkish War (1683-1699)	120,000–384,000	War	Islamic, Christian
War of the Austrian Succession (1740–8)	120,000–359,000	War	Christian

Sichuan Revolt of the Peasants (1755–7)	120,000	Civil War	Sinic
Chaco War (1932–5)	100,500	War	Christian
North Yemen Civil War (1962–70)	100,000–150,000	Civil War	Islamic
War of the Two Brothers, Inca (1531–2)	100,000 –1,000,000	Civil War	Primal-Indigenous
Christian New Guinea (1984–)	100,000–400,000	Democide	Islamic
Indonesian invasion of East Timor (1975–8)	100,000–200,000	Democide	Islamic
Al-Anfal Campaign (1986–9)	100,000–180,000	Democide	Islamic
Franco's regime (1939–75)	100,000–160,000	Democide, Civil War	Christian
Libya-Italian Wars (1911–31)	100,000–125,000	War	Christian
Persian Gulf War (1991)	100,000	War	Christian, Islamic

Thousand Days War (1899–1901)	100,000–150,000	Civil War	Christian
Peasants' War (1524–5)	100,000	Civil War	Christian
Mad Mullah Jihad, Somalia (1899–1920)	100,000	War	Islamic, Christian
Battle of Las Navas de Tolosa (1212)	100,000	War	Christian
Imperial Russia (1900–17)	100,000	Democide	Christian
Russo-Polish War (1918–20)	100,000	War	Christian
Tyrone's Rebellion/Nine Year's War (1594–1603)	100,000–130,000	War	Christian
White Lotus Rebellion (179–1805)	100,000	Civil War	Sinic
Crimean War (1854–6)	105,000–277,000	War	Christian, Islamic

Event	Est. Death Toll (>50,000)	Event Type	Belligerent Civilisation
Second Chechen War (1999 et seq.)	80,000–210,000	War	Christian, Islamic
Battle of Alarcos (1195)	80,000–150,000	War	Christian
Equatorial Guinea (1968–79)	80,000	War	Primal Indigenous
Siege of Isfahan (1722)	80,000	War	Islamic
Greek War of Independence (1821–9)	75,000–120,000	War	Islamic
Indonesian National Revolution	75,000–205,000	War, Civil War	Christian, Islamic
El Salvador Civil War (1980–92)	75,000	Civil War	Christian
Second Boer War (1898–1902)	75,000	War	Christian
Greco-Turkish War (1919–22)	75,000–250,000	War	Christian, Islamic

Boxer Rebellion (1899–1901)	70,000–115,000	War	Christian, Sinic
Boudica's uprising (60–1)	70,000	War	Primal-Indigenous
Aceh War (1873–1914)	70,000	War	Christian
Russo-Austro-Turkish War (1787–91)	64,000–192,000	War	Islamic
Mozambican War of Independence (1964-1974)	63,500	War	Christian
Mau Mau Uprising (1952–60)	61,185	War	Christian
First Chechen War (1994–6)	60,000–200,000	War	Christian
Romania (1948–89)	60,000–150,000	Democide	Antitheist
Sri Lanka/Tamil conflict (1983–)	60,000–65,000	Civil War	Indic, Buddhist
Tupac Amaru Rebellion (1780–83)	60,000–80,000	War	Christian

Nicaraguan Rebellion (1972–91)	60,000	Civil War	Christian
Battle of Yarmouk (636)	55,000–70,000	War	Islamic
Egyptian-Ottoman War (1805–11)	56,000	War	Islamic
Angolan War of Independence	52,000–80,000	War	Christian
First Burundi Civil War (1972)	50,000–300,000	Civil War	Christian
Tajik Civil War (1992–7)	50,000–60,000	Civil War	Islamic
Wars of the Roses (1455–85)	50,000	Civil War	Christian
Opium Wars (1839–50)	50,000	War	Christian
Siege of Tabriz (1725)	50,000	War	Islamic
Byzantine-Rashidun War (634)	50,000	War	Islamic

Event	Estimated Death Toll (>20,000)	Event Type	Belligerent Civilisation
Greek Civil War (1945–9)	45,000–160,000	Civil War	Christian
Russo-Turkish War (1806–12)	45,000–170,000	War	Islamic
Kashmiri insurgency (1989–)	41,000–100,000	Civil War	Indic, Islamic
Herero Genocide (1904–7)	45,000–60,000	Democide	Christian
Witch Hunts (15th–17th centuries)	40,000–60,000	Democide	Christian
Maratha-Afghan War (1760–1)	40,000	War	Islamic
Bulgarian Uprising (1875–7)	40,000	War	Islamic
Second Riffian War (1921–6)	40,000–100,000	War	Christian
Nader Shah's Invasion of India (1738)	40,400–70,000	War	Islamic

Battle of Siffin (657)	40,000–65,000	Civil War	Islamic
Chad under Habre regime (1982–90)	40,000	Democide	Primal-Indigenous
South Vietnam under Diem (1955–63)	39,000	Democide	Buddhist
Russo-Austro-Turkish War (1736–9)	38,000	War	Islamic, Christian
Grand Columbia Wars of Independence (1810-21)	37,000–120,000	War	Christian
Finnish Civil War (1918)	36,000	Civil War	Christian
Mongolia under Communists (1936 et seq)	35,000	Democide	Christian, Buddhist
Java War (1825–30)	35,000–180,000	War	Christian
Siege of Malta (1565)	35,000–45,000	War	Islamic
Sandinista Rebellion (1972–9)	35,000–40,000	Civil War	Christian

Peru's Shining Path insurrections (1980 et seq)	45,000–69,000	Civil War	Antitheist
Battle of Nihawand (642)	43,000–65,000	War	Islamic
Ukrainian Pogroms (1919–21)	30,000–70,000	Democide	Christian
First Carlist War, Spain (1832–40)	33,000–125,000	Civil War	Christian
Vietnamese Persecution of Christians (1832-1887)	33,000–41,000	Democide	Buddhist
Rashidun-Sassanid War (633)	32,000–40,000	War	Islamic
Contra Rebellion (1981–90)	30,000–57,000	Civil War	Christian
Irish Uprising (1798)	30,000–40,000	Civil War	Christian
U.S. Invasion of Afghanistan (2001–2)	30,000–50,000	War	Christian, Islamic
Mozambique Anti-Colonial War (1961–75)	30,000–60,000	War	Christian

Bulgaria under Communism (1948–53)	30,00–50,000	Democide	Antitheist
Canudos War (1896–7)	30,000	Democide	Christian
Turko-Syrian Wars (1831–2, 1839–40)	30,000	War	Islamic
Poland under Communism (1948 et seq)	30,000	Democide	Antitheist
Argentina under Military (1976–83)	30,000	Democide	Christian
Turkey/PKK conflict (1984–)	40,000	Civil War, Democide	Islamic
Sino-Vietnamese War (1979)	30,000	War	Sinic, Antitheist
Rhodesian Bush War (1964–79)	30,000	War	Christian
El Salvador Peasant Revolt (1931–2)	30,000	Civil War	Christian
Seven Weeks' War (1866)	27,900–79,000	War	Christian

Bulavin's Rebellion (1707–9)	28,000	Civil War	Christian
Zulu Conflict (1856)	27,000	Civil War	Primal-Indigenous
Venetian-Austro-Turkish War (1714–8)	27,000–45,000	War	Islamic
American War of Independence (1775–83)	25,300–37,300	War	Christian
Indo-Pakistani War of 1971 (December 1971)	23,384	War	Islamic, Indic
Nagorno-Karabakh War (1988–94)	23,000	War	Christian, Islamic
Australian Frontier Wars (1788–1921)	23,000	War	Christian
Venezuelan Federal War (1859–63)	20,000–50,000	Civil War	Christian
Franco-Mexican War (1862–7)	20,000–50,000	War	Christian
Pugachov Revolt (1773–4)	20,000	Civil War	Christian

<table>
<tr><td>Six-Day War (1967)</td><td>22,000</td><td>War</td><td>Christian</td></tr>
<tr><td>War of the Quadruple Alliance (1718–20)</td><td>20,000–25,000</td><td>War</td><td>Christian</td></tr>
<tr><td>Italo-Turkish War (1911–2)</td><td>20,000</td><td>War</td><td>Christian, Islamic</td></tr>
<tr><td>Siege of Erevan (1723)</td><td>20,000</td><td>War</td><td>Islamic</td></tr>
<tr><td>Burmese-Chinese War (1765–1769)</td><td>20,000</td><td>War</td><td>Buddhist</td></tr>
<tr><td>Portuguese Civil War (1829–34)</td><td>20,000</td><td>Civil War</td><td>Christian</td></tr>
<tr><td>British-Afghan War (1838–42)</td><td>20,000–30,000</td><td>War</td><td>Islamic</td></tr>
<tr><td>Persian massacres of Bahais (1848–54)</td><td>20,000</td><td>Democide</td><td>Islamic</td></tr>
<tr><th>Event</th><th>Estimated Death Toll (>10,000)</th><th>Event Type</th><th>Belligerent Civilisation</th></tr>
<tr><td>Righteous Army Uprising, Korea (1907–12)</td><td>18,000</td><td>War</td><td>Buddhist</td></tr>
</table>

Transvaal Revolt (1880–1)	18,000	War	Christian
Paris Commune (1871)	17,000–23,000	Democide	Christian
Sikh Uprising (1982–91)	16,000–20,000	Civil War	Indic
Iran under the Pahlevis (1953–1979)	16,000	Democide	Islamic
Anglo-Burmese War (1823–6)	15,000–20,000	War	Christian
War of Italian Unification (1859)	15,000–22,500	Civil War	Christian
Polish Insurrection (1830–2)	15,000–21,000	War	Christian
Guinea-Bissau War of Independence (1963-1974)	15,000	War	Christian
Sino-Japanese War (1894–5)	15,000	War	Buddhist, Sinic
Christian-Druze Wars, Lebanon (1860)	15,000	Civil War	Christian, Unclassified

War of the Pacific (1879–84)	14,000–55,000	War	Christian
Hungarian Insurrection (1703–11)	14,000–43,000	War	Christian
Battle of Walaya (633)	14,000–22,000	War	Islamic
South Africa under Apartheid	14,000–19,000	Democide	Christian
Russo-Turkish War (1768–74)	14,000–20,000	War	Christian, Islamic
Mexican-American War (1846–8)	13,000–49,000	War	Christian
Namibia Civil War	13,000-20,000	Civil War	Christian
South Yemen Civil War (1986)	13,000	Civil War	Islamic
Bouganville Revolt, Papua New Guinea (1989–98)	13,000	Civil War	Christian
Czechoslovakia under Communism	13,000–60,000	Democide	Antitheist

Nepal Civil War (1996–2006)	12,700	Civil War	Indic
Sino-French War (1884–5)	12,000	War	Christian
Battle of Poitiers (732)	12,000	War	Islamic
Ottoman Invasion of Persia (1727)	12,000	War	Islamic
Batavia Massacres (1740)	10,000–12,000	Civil War	Christian
Israeli War against Palestine	12,000–19,000	War	Jewish, Islamic
Yom Kippur War (1973)	11,500–16,000	War	Islamic, Jewish
Malayan Emergency (1948–1960)	11,053	War	Christian, Islamic
Madagascar Revolt (1947)	11,000–60,000	Civil War	Christian
Battle of Sekigahara (1600)	11,000–32,000	Civil War	Buddhist

Croatian War of Independence (1991–5)	11,000–16,000	War	Christian
Hama Massacre, Syria (1982)	10,000–25,000	Democide	Islamic
Anglo-American War (1812–5)	11,000–20,000	War	Christian
Kanto Massacres, Japan (1923)	10,000–20,000	Democide	Buddhist
Haitian Massacres, Dominican Republic (1937)	10,000–20,000	Democide, Civil War	Christian
Congo-Brazzaville Coup and Civil War (1997–9)	10,000–20,000	Civil War	Christian
Massacres of the Janissaries (after 1826)	10,000–20,000	Democide	Islamic
Spanish-Moroccan War (1907–11)	10,000–15,000	War	Christian
Western Sahara (1975 et seq)	10,000–16,000	War, Democide	Islamic
Cameroon Insurrection	10,000–15,000	War	Christian

Seapoy Mutiny (1857)	10,000–15,000	Civil War	Christian
Argentine Civil War (1845–51)	10,000	Civil War	Christian
Amadu's Jihad (1810–8)	10,000	Civil War	Islamic
Mexico (1926–30)	10,000	Civil War	Christian
Russo-Swedish War (1741–3)	10,000	War	Christian
Tay Son Revolution, Annam (1772–1802)	10,000	Civil War	Sinic
Anglo-Sikh Wars (1846–8)	10,000	War	Christian
Spanish-American War (1898)	10,000	War	Christian
Indo-Pakistani War of 1965	8,000–15,000	War	Islamic, Indic

Key Findings and Analysis

Table 2: Death-Toll of Major Violent Conflict (0–2008 CE)

Civilisation	Minimum Death Toll	Maximum Death Toll	Median Death Toll
Antitheist	95,908,000	152,911,000	124,409,500
Buddhist	80,116,000	95,777,500	87,946,750
Christian	119,423,000	236,660,500	178,041,750
Indic	1,344,500	3,434,000	2,389,250
Islamic	21,224,000	40,813,000	31,018,500
Primal-Indigenous	34,232,000	56,890,000	45,561,000
Sinic	95,612,500	120,235,000	107,923,750
Total	**447,860,000**	**706,721,000**	**577,290,500**

INTERPRETING THE RESULTS: Our findings show that, using the entire data set for the period 0–2008, politically and religiously motivated violence has cost between 447.86 million and 706.72 million lives. The **Christian** civilisation's share of this is the largest with between 119.42 million and 236.66 million victims (median 178.04 million). In second place is the **Antitheist** civilisation which has contributed with a median figure of 124.41 million deaths. The **Sinic** civilisation is third with 107.92 million deaths (median). Fourth is the **Buddhist** civilisation with ca. 87.95 million deaths. Fifth is the **Primal-Indigenous** civilisation with 45.56 million deaths. Sixth is the **Islamic** civilisation with 31.02 million deaths. Finally, seventh and last, is the **Indic** civilisation with just under 2.39 million deaths.

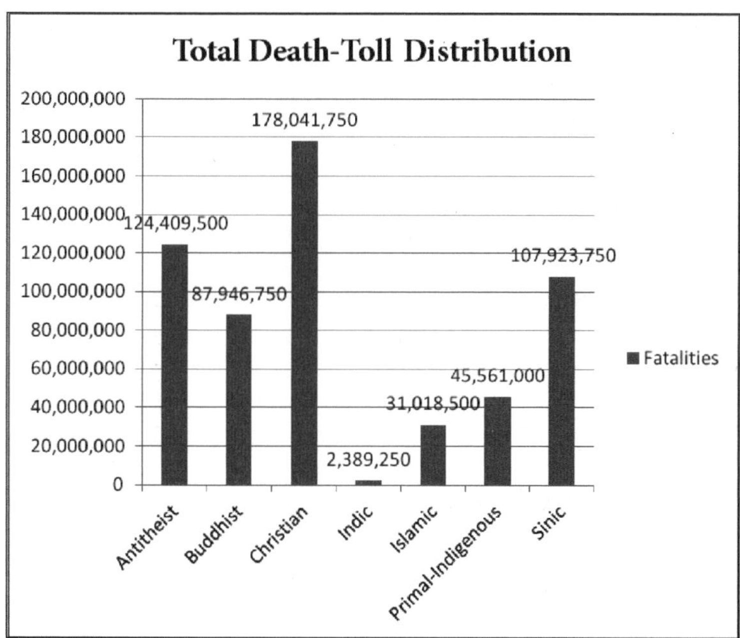

TABLE 3: DETAILED RESULTS

	No. of Events	Rank	Median Death Toll	Rank
Antitheist	18 (5.66%)	3	124,409,500	2 (21.55%)
Buddhist	15 (4.72%)	5	87,946,750	4 (15.23%)
Christian	166 (52.2%)	1	178,041,750	1 (30.84%)
Indic	9 (2.83%)	7	2,389,250	7 (0.41%)
Islamic	79 (24.84%)	2	31,018,500	6 (5.37%)
Primal-Indigenous	14 (4.40%)	6	45,561,000	5 (7.89%)
Sinic	17 (5.35%)	4	107,923,750	3 (18.69%)
Total	**318**		**577,290,500**	

INTERPRETING TABLE 3: The above table shows two sets of ranking, one based on frequency (the number of incidents in which a given civilisation has been involved in violent episodes) and one based on intensity (the number of killed in those episodes). In terms of frequency of bellicosity, the most belligerent civilisations are: (1) Christian, (2) Islamic, (3) Antitheist, and (4) Sinic. The Christian civilisation accounts for over 50 percent of all incidents, whereas the Muslim accounts for just under 25 percent, the Antitheist and Sinic civilisations are down to nearly a fifth of the latter at just over five percent. In terms of intensity, calculated on the basis of death toll, however, the ranking is very different. Here the ranking is as follows: (1) Christian, (2) Antitheist, (3) Sinic, and (4) Buddhist. In terms of death toll, the Christian civilisation accounts for over 30 percent of all killed, the Antitheist for over 21 percent, the Sinic for nearly 19 percent, and the Buddhist for approximately 15 percent. The Primal-Indigenous category is nearly half of that and the Islamic is down at under six percent. The findings are illustrated below:

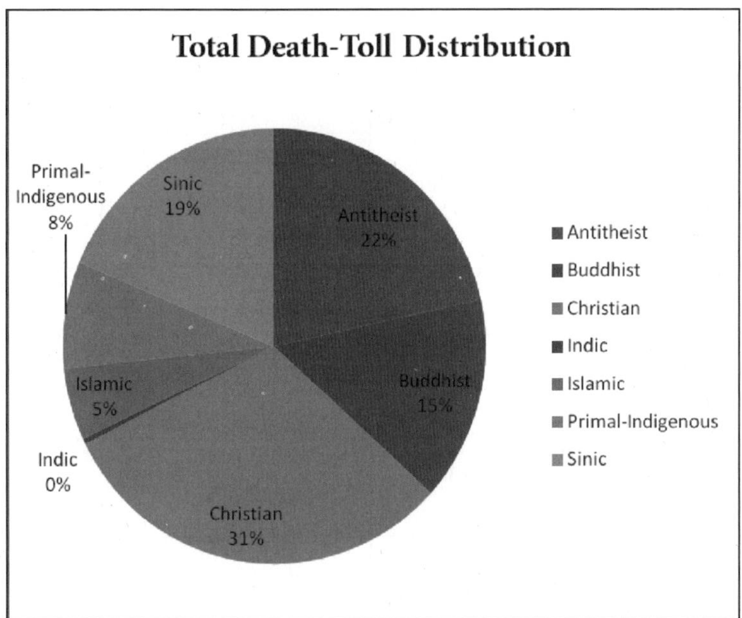

Table 4: Mass Killings, Massacres and Genocide in History (By Death Toll)

Date	Event	Perpetrators	Victims	Median Death toll	Civilisation
1835	Moriori Genocide	Maoris	Morioris	1,500	Primal-Indigenous
1995	Srebrenica Massacre	Serbs	Bosniaks	8,000	Christian
1854–64	Yuki Genocide	Californian settlers	Yuki Indians	10,000	Christian
1904–7	Herero & Namaqua Genocide	Germany	Herero & Namaqua	45,000	Christian
1919–21	Ukrainian Pogroms	Ukraine nationalists	Jews	50,000	Christian
1963	West Papuan Genocide	Indonesia	Papuans	100,000	Islamic
1986–8	Anfal Campaign	Baathist Iraq	Kurds	140,000	Islamic
1972	Burundi Genocide	Tutsi	Hutu	175,000	Christian

1975–99	East Timor Genocide	Indonesia	East Timorese	200,000	Islamic
1937–8	Rape of Nanking	Imperial Japan	Chinese	300,000	Buddhist
1914–23	Pontic Greek Killings	Young Turks	Greek Minorities	180,000	Islamic
1864–67	Circassian Genocide	Czarist Russia	Circassians	400,000	Christian
1919–20	Don Cossack Genocide	Soviet Russia	Don Cossack	400,000	Antitheist
1993	Burundi Genocide	Hutu	Tutsi	400,000	Christian
2003–8	Darfur Conflict	Janjaweed, Sudan	Darfur tribes	400,000	Islamic
1941–5	Serb Genocide	Ustasha	Serbs, Jews, homosexuals	465,000	Christian
1899–1902	American-Philippine War	USA	Filipinos	600,000	Christian
1208–44	Albigensian Crusade	Roman Church	Cathars	625,000	Christian

1915–23	Armenian Deaths during Forced Migration	Young Turks	Armenians	200,000	Islamic
1994	Rwandan Genocide	Hutu	Tutsi	900,000	Christian
1856–73	Panthay Rebellion	Qing Dynasty	Hui Muslims	1,000,000	Sinic
1975–9	Cambodian Genocide	Khmer Rouge	Cambodian Populus	1,850,000	Antitheist
1862–77	Dungan Revolt	Qing Dynasty	Hui Muslims	4,000 000	Sinic
1493–6	Hispaniola Genocide	Columbus	Arawaks	5,000,000	Christian
1933	Holodomor Famine	Soviet Russia	Ukrainian/ Kazakh	6,000,000	Antitheist
1880–1910	Congo Free State	Belgium	Congolese	8,250,000	Christian
1940–5	Nazi Genocides	Nazi Germany	Jews, Slavs, Roma, homosexuals	16,315,000	Christian

Key Findings and Analysis

Table 5: Mass Killings, Massacres and Genocide (0–2008 CE)

	No. of Events	Rank	Median Death Toll	Rank
Antitheist	3 (11.11%)	3	8,250,000 (17.18%)	2
Buddhist	1 (3.70%)	5/6	300,000 (0.62%)	5
Christian	14 (51.85%)	1	33,243,000 (69.24%)	1
Indic	0 (0%)	7	0 (0%)	7
Islamic	6 (22.22%)	2	1,220,000 (2.54%)	4
Primal-Indigenous	1(3.70%)	5/6	1,500 (0.00%)	6
Sinic	2 (7.41%)	4	5,000,000 (10.41%)	3
Total	**27**		**48, 014,500**	

INTERPRETING TABLE 5: Mass killings, massacres and genocides are instances of political violence, driven by hateful aggression and strategies of wilful elimination. Our list of 27 mass killings and genocides in world history, with a total death toll of 48.01 million, displays some remarkable facts: The Christian civilisation has been the most genocidal, accounting for 14 instances of mass killings and genocides with over 33 million deaths. As the total deaths derived from genocides are just over 48 million, the Christian share is over 2/3 of all genocide deaths. Although the Islamic civilisation is second in numbers of mass killings, the Antitheist group as well as the Sinic civilisation has higher death tolls at respectively 8.25 million and 5.00 million, whereas the Islamic civilisation's death toll is 1.22 million. The Antitheist and Sinic civilisations rank, respectively third and fourth in terms of acts of mass killings, whereas the Buddhist and Primal-Indigenous civilisations share the fifth place with a single instance of mass killing and genocide in each civilisation (although the Buddhist cost 300,000 lives, whereas the death toll in the Primal-Indigenous category was the lowest in the genocide category with 1,500 deaths). The Indic civilisation is not known to have perpetrated any mass killing or genocide after year 0.

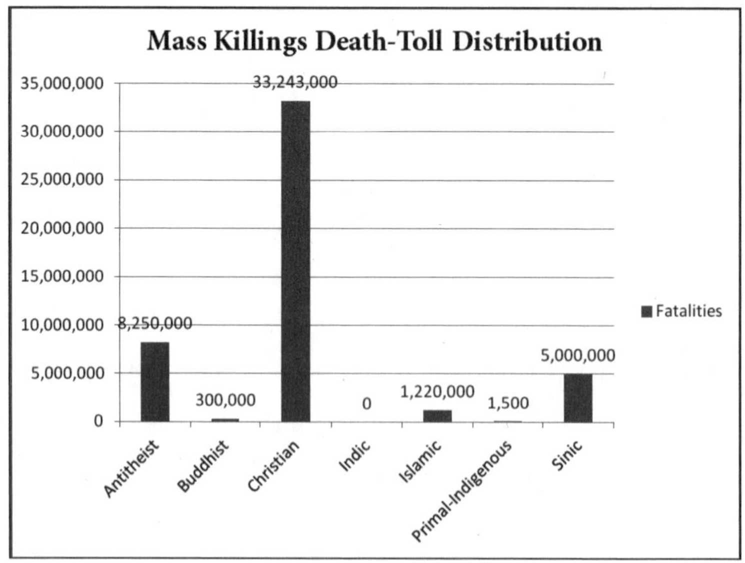

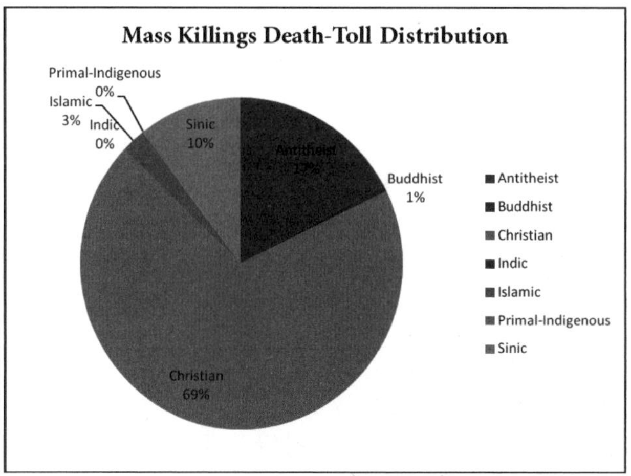

Conclusions

The present study has, on the basis of empirical examination of political violence in the last two millennia, made some startling findings.

1) We have found that the total death toll from acts of political violence (war, civil war, democide, and structural violence) has been between 447.86 million and 706.72 million in the years 0–2008. The median figure amounts to 577.29.
2) The distribution of the median death toll is illustrated below, expressed first in absolute figures and next in percentage of the total.

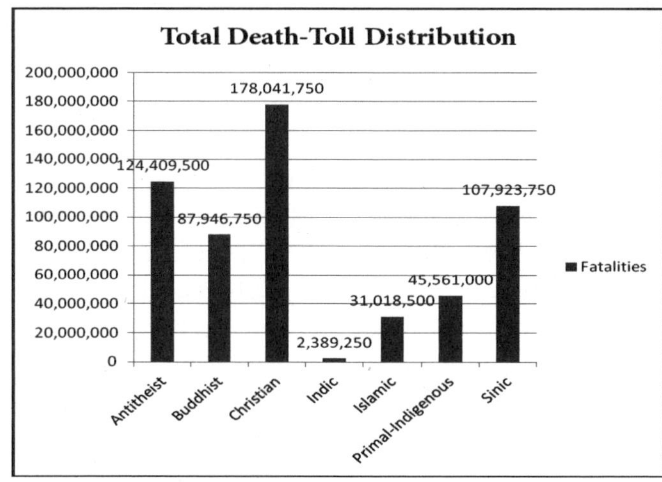

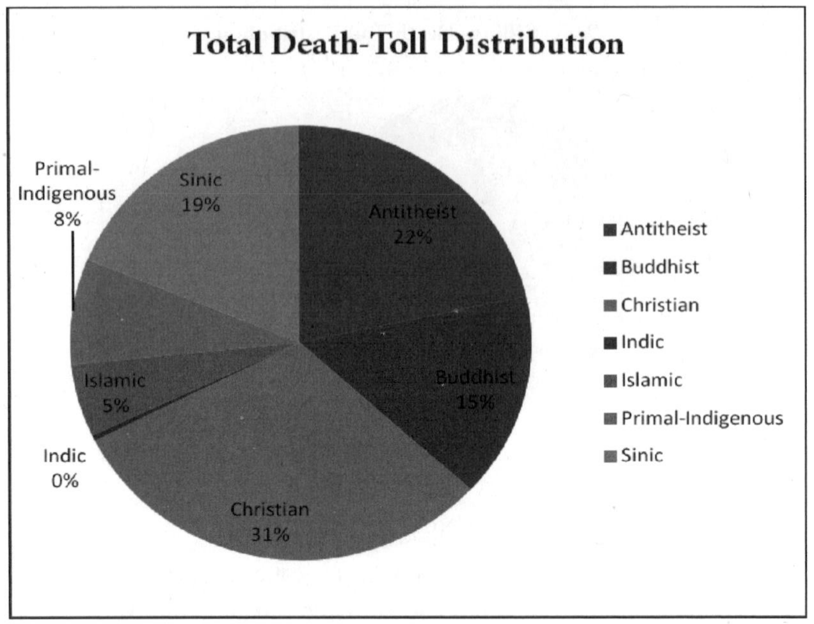

3) Of these 577.29 million fatalities, 48.01 million are genocidal deaths.
4) In comparative terms, we have found the open secret of world history to be that Christian societies in history have been the most bellicose on all counts: they are responsible for the highest number of death in world history, between 119.42 and 236.66 million (median: 178.04 million). This is over 30 percent of global fatalities for the period 0–2008 CE. In terms of number of instances of political violence, the Christian share is even higher, accounting for 166 events out of 318 in total (52.2 percent). Thus more than half of all major acts of political violence can be attributed to various Christian states and communities in history. Finally, in terms of genocides too the Christian world has perpetrated more than half of all genocides (14 out of 27, or 51.85 percent). Still, these 14 genocides have had a total death toll of 33.24 million, a whopping 69.24 percent of all genocide deaths. What is called the Christian world, therefore, emerges as the most violent and genocidal in world history.

5) Christian apologetics often charge anti-religious ideologies with perpetrating more violence than religious civilisations. Taking a broad view of history, rather than a perspective constrained to the Cold War period, our study does not confirm this hypothesis. Instead, the Antitheist world is second in terms of death toll contributions, ranging from 95.91 million to 152.91 million (a mean of 124.41 million, amounting to 21.55 percent of the total death toll across civilisations over the time period 0–2008 CE). As these deaths are spread over a mere 18 events, it is true that the average death toll per event is higher than in any other civilisational category. In terms of genocidal events, the Antitheist category is overall second as well, having produced 8.25 million deaths, again over relatively few events: namely three.
6) The Sinic civilisation is the third most violent civilisation, both in terms of overall death-toll (at 107.92 million, or 18.69 percent of total deaths) and in terms of genocidal deaths (at 5.00 million or 10.41 percent of total genocide deaths).With the Communist Revolution in China, the Sinic civilisation largely merged into the Antitheist civilisation, just as Communist Eastern Europe was part of the Antitheist civilisational category until it rejoined the Christian civilisation after the Cold War. Had this not been the case, the Sinic civilisation could have surpassed the Christian as the most belligerent civilisation.
7) The Muslim world has, before and after 9/11, been on the receiving end of media charges of violence and bigotry. This may be due to the large number of events in which the Muslim world has been involved: 79 acts of political violence, including six of genocidal character (in both instances ranking second in terms of number of events). However, in terms of death toll the Muslim world's share of death toll is ranked at the bottom, with only the Indic civilisation as more pacific. The Islamic death toll of 31.02 million (mean figure) amounts to 5.39 percent of the total world death toll, and is thus around a sixth of the Christian world's share and around a quarter of the Antitheist contribution. In the genocide category, however, the Islamic death toll is somewhat lower at 2.54 percent.

8) Contrary to the Islamic civilisation, the Buddhist world has enjoined an exceptionally good press in the West. Yet, the Buddhist contribution to the world death toll is almost three times the Islamic, at 87.95 million (or 15.23 percent of the total death toll). It should be noted that many instances of violence from the Buddhist civilisation derive from Japanese actions, including the sole engagement of genocidal violence with the death toll of 300,000.
9) Finally, the Indic civilisation is the most pacific civilisation with no instance of genocidal violence (despite the Bombay and Gujurat Riots in recent years). It is at the bottom of all tables, with only nine instances of large-scale political violence, out of 318, and less than half a percentage of the total death toll (although that remains a sizeable 2.39 million).

TABLE 6: THE GROWTH OF RELIGIOUS CIVILISATIONS (IN MILLIONS)

Year	World Population	Sinic	Christian	Primal	Indic	Islamic	Buddhist	Antitheist
1	213 million	53	0	87	24	0	19	
200	223 million	59	3	89	29	0	24	
400	198 million	55	16	69	26	0	28	
600	203 million	45	21	64	32	0	34	
800	222 million	50	26	47	43	11	39	
1000	276 million	66	35	44	52	23	43	

1100	311 million	98	40	42	66	32	45	
1200	380 million	115	53	40	73	44	46	
1300	396 million	86	76	37	77	52	44	
1400	362 million	81	60	34	82	56	40	
1500	443 million	108	81	40	93	71	42	
1600	562 million	146	106	41	104	98	48	
1700	645 million	160	131	46	122	114	57	4
1800	927 million	292	219	54	132	162	73	18
1850	1,221 million	384	332	65	158	215	96	32
1900	1,645 million	435	552	71	193	282	107	50
1950	2,514 million	405	887	62	410	478	167	100
1975	4,068 million	390	1,333	59	637	852	228	555
2000	6,000 million	661	1,972	76	816	1,290	390	600
2010	6,800 million	739	2,219	78	842	1,588	449	662

Table 7: Religious Civilisations in Proportion to World Population

Year	World Population	Sinic	Christian	Primal	Indic	Islamic	Buddhist	Antitheist
1	213 million	24.9%	0%	40.8%	11.3%	0%	8.9%	0%
200	223 million	28.3%	1.4%	39.9%	13.0%	0%	10.8%	0%
400	198 million	26.7%	8.1%	36.4%	12.1%	0%	15.7%	0%
600	203 million	22.2%	10.3%	31.5%	15.7%	0%	16.7%	0%
800	222 million	22.5%	11.7%	21.2%	19.4%	5.0%	17.6%	0%
1000	276 million	23.9%	12.8%	15.9%	18.8%	8.3%	15.6%	0%
1100	311 million	31.5%	12.9%	13.5%	21.2%	10.3%	14.5%	0%
1200	380 million	30.3%	13.9%	10.5%	19.2%	11.6%	12.1%	0%
1300	396 million	21.7%	19.2%	9.3%	19.4%	13.1%	11.1%	0%
1400	362 million	22.4%	16.6%	9.4%	22.6%	15.5%	11.0%	0%
1500	443 million	24.4%	18.3%	9.0%	21.0%	16.0%	9.5%	0%
1600	562 million	26.0%	18.9%	7.3%	18.5%	17.4%	8.5%	0%

1700	645 million	24.8%	20.3%	7.1%	15.5%	17.7%	8.8%	0.6%
1800	927 million	31.5%	23.6%	5.8%	13.6%	17.5%	7.9%	1.9%
1850	1,221 million	33.2%	27.2%	5.3%	12.9%	17.6%	7.7%	2.6%
1900	1,645 million	26.4%	33.6%	4.3%	11.7%	17.9%	7.1%	3.0%
1950	2,514 million	16.1%	35.3%	2.5%	16.3%	19.0%	6.6%	4.0%
1975	4,068 million	9.6%	32.8%	1.5%	15.7%	20.9%	5.6%	13.6%
2000	6,000 million	11.0%	32.9%	1.2%	13.6%	21.5%	6.5%	10.0%
2010	6,800 million	10.9%	32.6%	1.1%	12.4%	23.3%	6.6%	9.7%

DISCUSSION: The demographic balance between the world civilisations has seen several tectonic shifts in the last 2,000 years. In the period 0–800, ethno-tribal belief systems, here known as Primal-Indigenous religions, were the chief socio-religion dispensation among humankind. As the Christianisation of Europe merged with the Islamisation of the Middle East and North Africa, the Primal-Indigenous dominance was weakened. This gave way to the Sinic civilisation, which became the numerically largest, followed until the turn of the millennium closely by the Indic civilisation. The Sinic civilisation remained the dominant until medical advances in Europe resulted in decreased child mortality, courtesy of the Industrial Revolution, and by 1870 Christendom was the largest civilisation, a privilege it retains till this day.

However, while all civilisations are increasing in absolute terms, as a result of population growth, only Islam is growing in relative terms. Future projections anticipate that Islam will attain parity with Christianity by 2050, as Islam is the only civilisation whose growth rate is in excess of the generic growth rate of the world population at large. Islam has not before reached parity with Christianity, with the exception of narrowing the gap considerably around the time of the Black Death in Europe (a gap which since widened, even with the 30-Year War in Europe).

The most dramatic decline over the two thousand years is found in the Primal-Indigenous group, where evangelisation and death at the hand of colonialists entirely eradicated parochial forms of religiosity. Buddhism, too, has seen considerable demographic decline; from having been more numerous than Hindus, Buddhists suffered from loss of dynastic support in India and the spread of Islam in central Asia. Likewise, the Communist takeover of China sounded the death-knell of Sinic civilisation which quickly deteriorated. Like the Sinic civilisation, the Buddhist too suffered from the institutional imposition of Antitheism, a blow which either is still to recover from, even as Antitheism has recently seen a decline with the fall of the Soviet Bloc.

Originally published as Body Count *by the Royal Aal al-Bayt Institute for Islamic Thought as a booklet in 2009 (some figures in this chapter have been updated for this publication).*

PART II: PEACE AND ITS PRACTICE

CHAPTER EIGHT

ISLAM AND PEACE: A Survey of The Sources of Peace in the Islamic Tradition

Professor Ibrahim Kalin

Is Religion a Source of Violence?

This question haunts the minds of many people concerned about religion in one way or another. For the critics of religion, the answer is usually in the affirmative, and it is easy to cite examples from history. From Rene Girard's depiction of ritual sacrifices as violent proclivities in religions to the exclusivist claims of different faith traditions,[257] one can easily conclude that religions produce violence at both social and theological levels. As is often done, one may take the Crusades or the inquisition in medieval Europe or jihad movements in Islamic history and describe the respective histories of these traditions as nothing more than a history of war, conflict, violence, schism, persecution. The premeditated conclusion is unequivocal: the more religious people are, the more violent they tend to be. The solution therefore lies in the desacralisation of the world. Religions, and some among them in particular, need to be secularised and modernised to rid themselves of their violent essence and violent legacy.[258]

At the other end of the spectrum is the believer who sees religious violence as an oxymoron at best and the mutilation of his/her religious faith at worst. Religions do not call for violence. Religious teachings are peaceful at their base, meant to re-establish the primordial harmony between heaven and earth, between the Creator and the created. But specific religious teachings and feelings are manipulated to instigate violence for political gains. Violence is committed in the name of religion but not condoned by it. The only valid criticism the secularist can raise against religion is that religions have not developed effective ways of protecting themselves from such manipulations and abuses. As Juergensmeyer has shown in his extensive survey of religious violence in the modern period, violence does not recognise religious and cultural boundaries and can easily find a home in the most sublime and innocuous teachings of world religions[259]. At any rate, religions are vulnerable when they fail to find ways of preventing the use of force in their names. This becomes especially acute when they fall short of inculcating a consciousness of peace and non-violence in the minds and hearts of their followers. In short, religion per se cannot be seen as a source of violence. Only some of its bad practitioners can be held accountable.

Both views have strong cases and make important points about religion and violence. Both, however, are equally mistaken in resorting to a fixed definition of religion. And both views reduce the immense variety of religious practices to a particular tradition and, furthermore, to a particular faction or historic moment in that tradition. In speaking of Islam and violence or Hinduism and war, the usual method is to look at the sacred scriptures and compare and contrast them with historical realities that flow from their practice, or lack thereof. We highlight those moments where there are discrepancies between text and history as the breaking points in the history of that religion, viz., moments when the community has not lived up to the standards of the religion as demanded by the text.

Although there is some benefit to be gained from this approach, it fails to see the ways in which religious texts are interpreted and made part of the day-to-day experience of particular religious communities. Instead of looking at how religiously binding texts are read, revealed and enriched within the concrete experiences of the community, we separate text from history and somehow assume historical immunity for the text and/or textual basis for *all* history.

This is not to deny the centrality of the scripture. In the case of Islam, the Qur'an, together with the Sunnah of the Prophet of Islam, is and remains the main source of the Islamic *Weltanschauung*. After all, the numerous interpretations that we may talk about are interpretations of the Qur'an, the one text that is the subject of variant readings from the Sufis and Hanbalis to the Wahhabis and the modernists. The fact that the Prophetic Sunnah is part of the Islamic worldview and religious life, without which we cannot understand a good part of the Qur'an, can be seen as confirming the significance of reading the scripture within the concrete experiences of the Muslim community. This was in fact how the first Muslims, who became the spiritual and moral examples of later generations, learnt about the Qur'an, under the guidance and tutorship of the Prophet.

In this sense, Islamic history is not alien to the idea of reading religiously binding texts primarily within the context of a living and 'evolving' tradition. This is why the Sunnah was part of the Islamic law from the outset and this is how the tradition of transmitted sciences (*al-'ulūm al-naqliyyah*), dealing primarily with 'religious sciences', came about, namely, by looking at how the previous generations of Muslims understood the Qur'an and the Hadith. Taken out of this context, Qur'anic verses become abstruse, abstract, and impenetrable for the non-Muslim, or for anyone who is indifferent to this tradition and, by virtue of this, may be misled into thinking that a good part of Islamic history has come about in spite of the Qur'an, not because of it.

I deemed it necessary to insert these few words of caution and 'methodology' for the following reasons. Much of the current debate about Islam and violence is beset by the kind of problems that we see in the secularist and apologetic readings of the scriptural sources of Islam. Those who consider Islam as a religion that essentially condones violence for its theological beliefs and political aims pick certain verses from the Qur'an, link them to cases of communal and political violence in Islamic history, and conclude that Qur'anic teachings provide justification for unjust use of violence. While the same can be done practically about any religion, Islam has enjoyed much more fanfare than any other religion for the last thousand years or so. The apologist makes the same mistake but in a different way when he rejects all history as misguided, failing to see the ways in which the Qur'an, or the Bible or the Rig Vedas, can *easily*, if not legitimately, be read to resort to violence for intra- and inter-religious violence. This is where the hermeneutics of the text (in the sense of both *tafsīr* and *ta'wīl*) becomes absolutely necessary: it is not that the text itself is violent but that it lends itself to multiple readings, some of which are bound to be peaceful and some violent.

The second problem is the exclusive focus of the current literature on the legal and juristic aspects of peace and violence in Islam. Use of violence, conduct of war, treatment of combatants and prisoners of war, international law, etc. are discussed within a strictly legal context, and the classical Islamic literature on the subject is called upon to provide answers. Although this is an important and useful exercise, it falls short of addressing deeper philosophical and spiritual issues that must be included in any discussion of religion and peace. This is true especially in the case of Islam, for two main reasons. First of all, the legal views of peace and violence in the classical period were articulated and applied in the light of the overall teachings and aims of Islamic law (*maqāṣid al-sharīʿah*). The *maqāṣid* provided a context within which the strict legality of the law was blended into the necessities and realities of communal life. Political conflicts couched in the language of juridical edicts remained political conflicts, and were never extended to a war of religions between Islam or Christianity, Judaism, Hinduism or African religions, which Muslims encountered throughout their history. It should come to us as no surprise that the fatwa of a jurist of a particular school of law allowing the use of force against a Christian ruler was not interpreted as an excuse for attacking one's Christian or Jewish neighbour.

Secondly, the spiritual and ethical teachings of the Qur'an and the Sunnah underpin everything Islamic *in principle*, and this applies mutatis mutandis to the question of peace and violence. The legal injunctions (*aḥkām*) of the Qur'an concerning peace and war are part of a larger set of spiritual and moral principles. The ultimate goal of Islam is to create a moral and just society in which individuals can pursue a spiritual life, and in which the toll of living collectively, from economic exploitation and misuse of political authority to the suppression of other people, can be brought under control to the extent possible in any human society. Without taking into account this larger picture, we will fail to see how Islam advocates a positive concept of peace as opposed to a merely negative one, and how its political and legal precepts, which are exploited so wildly and irrationally by both the secular and religious fundamentalists of our day, lead to the creation and sustaining of a just and ethical social order.

With these caveats in mind, this paper has two interrelated goals.

The first is to analyse the ways in which the Islamic tradition can be said to advocate a positive concept of peace. This will be contrasted with 'negative peace', defined conventionally as absence of war and conflict. It will be argued that positive peace involves the *presence* of certain qualities and conditions that aim to make peace a principal *state* of harmony and equilibrium rather than a mere *event* of political settlement. This requires a close examination of the philosophical assumptions of the Islamic tradition which have shaped the experience of Muslim societies vis-à-vis the peoples of other faiths and cultures. These philosophical suppositions are naturally grounded in the ethical and spiritual teachings of Islam, and without considering their relevance for the cultural and political experience of Muslims with the 'other', we can neither do justice to the Islamic tradition, which spans a vast area in both space and time, nor avoid the pitfalls of historical reductionism and essentialism, which are so rampant in the current discussions of the subject.

This brings us to the second goal of the paper. Here I will argue that an adequate analysis of peace and war in the Islamic tradition entails more than fixating the views of some Muslim jurists of the ninth and tenth centuries as the definitive position of 'orthodox' Islam and thus reducing the Islamic modus operandi of dealing with non-Muslims to a concept of 'holy war'. With some exceptions,[260] the ever growing literature of Islam and peace has been concerned predominantly with the legal aspects of declaring war (jihad) against Muslim and/or non-Muslim states, treatment of the *ahl al-dhimmah* under the shari'ah, and expanding the territories of the Islamic state. This has obscured, to say the least, the larger context within which such legal opinions were discussed, interpreted and evolved from one century to the next, and from one cultural-political era to another.

I therefore propose to look at the concept of peace in the Islamic tradition in four interrelated contexts. The first is the metaphysical-spiritual context in which peace (*salām*) as one of the names of God is seen as an essential part of God's creation and assigned a substantive value. The second is the philosophical-theological context within which the question of evil (*shar*) is addressed as a cosmic, ethical, and social problem. Discussions of theodicy among Muslim theologians and philosophers provide one of the most profound analyses of the question of evil, injustice, mishap, violence and their place in the 'great chain of being'. I shall provide a brief summary to show how a proper understanding of peace in the Islamic tradition is bound to take us to the larger questions of good and evil. The third is the political-legal context, which is the proper locus of classical legal and juristic discussions of war, rebellion, oppression, and political (dis)order. This area has been the exclusive focus of current literature on the subject and promises to be an engaging and long-standing debate in the Muslim world. The fourth is the socio-cultural context, which would reveal the parameters of the Muslim experience of religious and cultural diversity with communities of other faiths and cultural traditions.

As will become clear in the following pages, all of these levels are interdependent and call for a larger context within which the questions of peace and violence have been articulated and negotiated by a multitude of scholars, philosophers, jurists, mystics, political leaders, and various Muslim communities. The Islamic tradition provides ample material for contemporary Muslim societies to deal with issues of peace, religious diversity and social justice, all of which, needless to say, require urgent attention. Furthermore, the present challenge of Muslim societies is not only to deal with these issues as internal affairs but also to contribute to the fostering of a global culture of peace and coexistence. Before turning to the Islamic tradition, however, a few words of definition are in order, to clarify the meaning of positive peace.

Peace as a Substantive Value

Peace as a substantive and positive concept entails the presence of certain conditions that make it an enduring *state* of harmony, integrity, contentment, equilibrium, repose, and moderation. This can be contrasted with negative peace that denotes the absence of conflict and discord. Even though negative peace is indispensable to prevent communal violence, border disputes or international conflicts, substantive-positive peace calls for a comprehensive outlook to address the deeper causes of conflict, hate, strife, destruction, brutality, and violence. As Lee states, it also provides a genuine measure and set of values by which peace and justice can be established beyond the short-term interests of individuals, communities or states.[261] This is critical for the construction of peace as a substantive value because defining peace as the privation of violence and conflict turns it into a concept that is instrumental and accidental at best, and relative and irrelevant at worst. In addition, the positive-substantive notion of peace shifts the focus from preventing conflict, violence, and strife to a willingness to generate balance, justice, cooperation, dialogue, and coexistence as the primary terms of a discourse of peace. Instead of defining peace with what it is not and forcing common sense logic to its limit, we may well opt for generating a philosophical ground based on the presence and endurance, rather than absence, of certain qualities and conditions that make peace a substantive reality of human life.[262]

Furthermore, relegating the discourse of peace to social conflict and its prevention runs the risk of neglecting the individual, who is the sine qua non of collective and communal peace. This is where the 'spiritual individualism' of Islam versus its social collectivism enters the picture: the individual must be endowed with the necessary qualities that make peace an enduring reality, not only in the public sphere but also in the private domain of the individual. The Qur'anic ideal of creating a beautiful soul that is at peace with itself and the larger reality of which it is a part brings ethics and spirituality right into the heart of the discourse of positive peace. Peace as a substantive value thus extends to the domain of both ethics and aesthetics, for it is one of the conditions that bring about peace in the soul, and resists the temptations of discord, restlessness, ugliness, pettiness, and vulgarity. At this point, we may remember that the key Qur'anic term *iḥsān* carries the meanings of virtue, beauty, goodness, comportment, proportion, comeliness, and 'doing what is beautiful' all at once. The active particle *muḥsin* denotes the person who does what is good, desired, and beautiful.[263]

In this regard, peace is not a mere state of passivity. On the contrary, it is being fully active against the menace of evil, destruction, and turmoil that may come from within or from without. As Collingwood points out, peace is a 'dynamic thing',[264] and requires consciousness and vigilance, a constant state of awareness that one must engage in spiritual and intellectual jihad to ensure that differences and conflicts within and across the collective traditions do not become grounds for violence and oppression. Furthermore, positive peace involves the analysis of various forms of aggression including individual, institutional and structural violence.

Peace as a substantive concept is also based on justice (*'adl*); for peace is predicated upon the availability of equal rights and opportunities for all to realise their goals and potentials. One of the meanings of the word justice in Arabic is to be 'straight' and 'equitable', i.e., to be straightforward, trustworthy, and fair in one's dealings with others.[265] Such an attitude brings about a state of balance, accord, and trust, and goes beyond the limits of formal justice dispensed by the juridical system. Defined in the broadest terms, justice encompasses a vast domain of relations and interactions from taking care of one's body to international law. Like peace, justice is one of the Divine names, and takes on a substantive importance in view of its central role in Islamic theology as well as law. Peace can be conceived as an enduring state of harmony, trust, and coexistence only when coupled and supported with justice because it also means being secure from all that is morally evil and destructive.[266] Thus the Qur'an combines justice with *iḥsān* when it commands its followers to act with 'justice and good manner' (*bi'l-'adl wa'l-iḥsān*) (*Al-Naḥl*, 16:90).[267]

The Spiritual-Metaphysical Context: God as Peace (al-Salām)

The conditions that are conducive to a state of peace mentioned above are primarily spiritual and have larger implications for the cosmos, the individual, and society. Here I shall focus on three premises that are directly relevant to our examination. The first pertains to peace as a Divine name (*al-Salām*) (*Al-Ḥashr*, 59:23). The Qur'anic concept of God is founded upon a robust monotheism, and God's transcendence (*tanzīh*) is emphasised in both the canonical sources and in the intellectual tradition. To this absolutely one and transcendent God belong 'all the beautiful names' (*Al-A'rāf*, 7:180, *Al-Ḥashr*, 59:24), i.e., the names of beauty (*jamāl*), majesty (*jalāl*), and perfection (*kamāl*). It is these names that prevent God from becoming an utterly unreachable and 'wholly other' deity. Divine names represent God's face turned towards the world and are the vessels of finding God in and through His creation.

The names of beauty take precedence over the names of majesty because God says that *my mercy has encompassed everything* (*Al-A'rāf*, 7: 156) and *God has written mercy upon Himself* (*Al-An'ām*, 6:12, 54).

This is also supported by a famous hadith of the Prophet according to which 'God is beautiful and loves beauty'. In this sense, God is as much transcendent, incomparable and beyond as He is immanent, comparable (*tashbīh*) and close.[268] As the ultimate source of peace, God transcends all opposites and tensions, is the permanent state of repose and tranquility, and calls His servants to the *abode of peace* (*Dār al-Salām*) (*Yūnus*, 10:25). *It is He who from high on has sent [sends] down inner peace and repose (sakīnah) upon the hearts of the believers*, says the Qur'an (*Al-Fatḥ*, 48:4). The proper abode of peace is the hearts (*qulūb*), which are *satisfied only by the remembrance of God (dhikr Allāh)* (*Al-Ra'd*, 13:28). By linking the heart, man's centre, to God's remembrance, the Qur'an establishes a strong link between theology and spiritual psychology.

In addition to the Qur'anic exegetes, the Sufis in particular are fond of explaining the 'mystery of creation' by referring to a 'sacred saying' (*hadīth qudsī*) attributed to the Prophet of Islam: 'I was a hidden treasure. I wanted (lit. 'loved') to be known and created the universe (lit. 'creation'[269]).' The key words 'love' (*ḥubb, maḥabbah*) and 'know' (*ma'rifah*) underlie a fundamental aspect of the Sufi metaphysics of creation: Divine love and desire to be known is the raison d'être of all existence. Ibn al-'Arabi says that God's *love for His servants is identical with the origination of their engendered existence … the relation of God's love to them is the same as the fact that He is with them wherever they are* (*Al-Ḥadīd*, 57:4), whether in the state of their nonexistence or the state of their *wujūd* … they are the objects of His knowledge. He witnesses them and loves them never-endingly.[270] Commenting on the above saying, Dawud al-Qaysari, the fourteenth century Turkish Sufi philosopher and the first university president of the newly established Ottoman state, says that 'God has written love upon Himself. There is no doubt that the kind of love that is related to the manifestation of [His] perfections follows from the love of His Essence, which is the source of the love of [His Names and] Qualities that have become the reason for the unveiling of all existents and the connection of the species of spiritual and corporeal bodies.'[271]

The second premise is related to what traditional philosophy calls 'the great chain of being' (*dā'irat al-wujūd*). In the cosmic scale of things, the universe is the 'best of all possible worlds' because, first, it is actual, which implies completion and plenitude over and against potentiality, and, second, its built-in order derives its sustenance from the Creator. The natural world is in a constant state of peace because according to the Qur'an it is 'muslim' (with a small m) in that it surrenders (*taslīm*) itself to the will of God and thus rises above all tension and discord (*Āl 'Imrān*, 3:83; *Al-Tawbah*, 9:53; *Al-Ra'd*, 13:15; *Fuṣṣilat*, 41:11). In its normative depiction of natural phenomena, the Qur'an talks about stars and trees as *prostrating before God* (*Al-Raḥmān*, 55:6) and says that *all that is in the heavens and on earth extols His glory* (*Al-Ḥashr*, 59:24). By acknowledging God's unity and praising His name, man joins the natural world in a substantive way—a process that underscores the essential link between the *anthropos* and the *cosmos* or the microcosm and the macrocosm. The intrinsic commonality and unity between the human as 'subject' and the universe as 'object' has been called the 'anthropo-cosmic vision'.[272] The thrust of this view is that the *anthropos* and the *cosmos* cannot be disjoined from one another and that the man-versus-nature dichotomy is a false one. Moreover, the world has been given to the children of Adam as a 'trust' (*amānah*) as they are charged with the responsibility of standing witness to God's creation, mercy, and justice on earth. Conceiving nature in terms of harmony, measure, order and balance points to a common and persistent attitude towards the non-human world in Islamic thought, and has profound implications for the construction of peace as a principle of the cosmos.[273]

The third principle pertains to man's natural state and his place within the larger context of existence. Even though the Qur'an occasionally describes the fallen nature of man in gruesome terms and presents man as weak, forgetful, treacherous, hasty, ignorant, ungrateful, hostile, and egotistic (cf., *inter alia*, *Ibrāhīm*, 14:34; *Al- Isrā'*, 17:11; *Al-Kahf*, 18:54; *Al-Ḥajj*, 22:66; *Al-Aḥzāb*, 33:72; *Al-Zukhruf*, 43:15; and *Al-'Ādiyāt*, 100:6), these qualities are eventually considered deviations from man's essential nature (*fitrah*), who has been created in the 'most beautiful form' (*aḥsan taqwīm*) (*Al-Tīn*, 95:4), both physically and spiritually. This metaphysical optimism defines human beings as 'God's vicegerent on earth' (*khalīfat Allāh fī'l-'arḍ*) as the Qur'an says, or, to use a metaphor from Christianity, as the 'pontifex', the bridge between heaven and earth.[274] The *fiṭrah* (*Al-Rūm*, 30:30), the primordial nature according to which God has created all humanity, is essentially a moral and spiritual substance drawn to the good and 'God-consciousness' (*taqwā'*) whereas its imperfections and 'excessiveness' (*fujūr*) (*Al-Shams*, 91:8) are 'accidental' qualities to be subsumed under the soul's struggle to do good (*al-birr*) and transcend its subliminal desires through his intelligence and moral will.

The Philosophical-Theological Context: Evil and the Best of All Possible Worlds

In the context of theology and philosophy, questions of peace and violence are treated under the rubric of good and evil (*ḥusn/khayr* and *sharr/qubḥ*). War, conflict, violence, injustice, discord, and the like are seen as extensions of the general problem of evil. Muslim philosophers and theologians have been interested in theodicy from the very beginning, and for good reasons, because the basic question of theodicy goes to the heart of religion: how can a just and perfect God allow evil and destruction in a world which He says He has created in perfect balance, with a purpose, and for the well-being of His servants? We can rephrase the question in the present context as follows: why is there so much violence, turmoil and oppression rather than peace, harmony and justice in the world? Does evil, of which violence is an offshoot, belong to the essential nature of things or is it an accident that arises only as the privation of goodness?

These questions have given rise to a long and interesting debate about evil among theologians. One particular aspect of this debate, known as the 'best of all possible worlds' (*aḥsān al-niẓām*) argument,[275] deserves closer attention as it is relevant to the formulation of a positive concept of peace. The classical statement of the problem pertains to Divine justice and power on the one hand, and the Greek notions of potentiality and actuality on the other. The fundamental question is whether this world in which we live is the best that God could have created. Since, from a moral point of view, the world is imperfect because there is evil and injustice in it, we have to either admit that God was not able to create a better and more perfect world or concede that He did not create a better world by will as part of the Divine economy of creation. Obviously, the first alternative calls into question God's omnipotence (*qudrah*) whereas the second jeopardises His wisdom and justice (*'adālah*). Following another line of discussion in Kalam, we can reformulate the question as a tension between God's nature and will: can God go against His own nature, which is just, if He wants to, or is it that His will cannot supersede His nature? Still, can God contradict Himself? If we say yes, then we attribute imperfection to God and if we say no, then we limit Him.

Even the most modest attempt to analyse these questions within the context of Kalam debates will take us too far afield. What is directly related to our examination here is how the concepts of evil, injustice, oppression and their variations are seen as the 'accidental outcomes' of the world of contingencies in which we live. True, the weaknesses and frailties of human beings contribute enormously to the creation and exacerbation of evil, and it is only reasonable to take a 'situational' position and attribute evil to ourselves rather than to the Divine. In fact, this is what the Qur'an holds vis-à-vis evil and man's accountability: *Whatever good happens to you, it is from God; and whatever evil befalls you, it is from your own self/soul* (*Al-Nisā'*, 4: 79; cf. also *Āl 'Imrān*, 3:165). The best of all possible worlds argument, however, shifts the focus from particular instances of individual or structural violence to the phenomenon of evil itself whereby we gain a deeper insight into how evil arises in the first place.

We may reasonably argue that evil is part of the Divine economy of creation and thus necessary. In a moral sense, it is part of Divine economy because it is what we are tested with (cf. *Al-Anbiyā'*, 21:36; *Al-Kahf*, 18:9). Without evil, there would be no accountability and thus no freedom.[276] Mulla Sadra calls this a necessity of Divine providence (*al-'ināyah*) and the 'concomitant of the ultimate *telos* of goodness' (*al-ghāyat al-khayriyyah*).[277] In an ontological sense, it is a necessity because the world is by definition imperfect, the ultimate perfection belonging to God, and the world is not God. That is why God has not created 'all beings as pure goodness'.[278] Evil as limitation and imperfection is an outcome of the first act of separation between the Divine and the non-divine or what Muslim theologians call *mā siwā Allāh* (*all that is other than God*). Ultimately, however, *all is from God* (*Al-Nisā'*, 4:78). This implies that evil as the 'contrastive manifestation of the good'[279] ceases to be evil and contributes to the 'greater good', which is what the best of all possible world argument asserts. In a rather paradoxical way, one cannot object to the existence of evil itself because it is what makes the world possible. But this does not absolve us of the moral duty of fighting against individual cases of evil. Nor does it make evil an essential nature of things because it was God's decision to create the world with a meaning and purpose in the first place. In short, evil remains contingent and transient, and this assumption extends to the next world.[280]

The notion of evil as an ontological necessity-cum-contingency has important implications for how we look at the world and its 'evil' side. From a psychological point of view, the acceptance of evil as a transient yet necessary phenomenon prevents us from becoming petty and bitter in the face of all that is blemished, wicked, imperfect, and tainted.[281] It gives us a sense of moral security against the onslaught of evil, which can and must be fought with a firm belief in the ultimate supremacy of the good. It also enables us to see the world as it is and for what it is, and strive to make it a better place in terms of moral and spiritual perfection. From a religious point of view, this underscores the relative nature of evil: something that may appear evil to us may not be evil, and vice versa, when everything is placed within a larger framework. Thus the Qur'an says that *it may well be that you hate a thing while it is good (khayr) for you, and it may well be that you love a thing while it is bad (sharr) for you. And God knows, and you know not* (*Al-Baqarah*, 2:216). Mulla Sadra applies this principle to 'natural evils', and says that even death, corruption (*al-fasād*) and the like are necessary and needed for the order of the world (*al-niẓām*) when they occur 'by nature and not by force or accident'.[282]

The best of all possible worlds argument is also related to the scheme of actuality and potentiality which Muslim philosophers and theologians have adopted from Aristotle. The argument goes as follows. This world in which we live is certainly one of the possibilities that the Divine has brought into actuality. In this sense, the world is pure contingency (*imkān*) and hung between existence and non-existence. From the point of view of its present actuality, however, the world is perfect and necessary because actuality implies plenitude and perfection whereas potentiality is privation and non-existence.[283] The sense of perfection in this context is both ontological and cosmological. It is ontological because existence is superior to non-existence and whatever is in the sphere of potentiality remains so until it is brought into actuality by an agent which itself is already actual. It is cosmological because, as stated before, the world has been created with care, order, and beauty, which the Qur'an invites its readers to look at as the signs of God (*ayāt Allāh* or *vestigia Dei* as it was called by the Scholastics). The perfect state of the cosmos is presented as a model for the establishment of a just social order. It then follows that evil is a phenomenon of this world, but not something that defines the essential nature of things.

An important outcome of this point of view is to identify evil as a rationally discernible phenomenon. This may appear to be a simple truism. Nevertheless, it is a powerful position against the notion of evil as a mysterious, mythical or even cosmological fact over which human beings have no control. Evil is something that can be discerned by the intellect and correct reasoning and, of course, with the help of revelation.[284] and this places tremendous responsibility on our shoulders vis-à-vis the evil that may come from within or from without. One may disagree with Mu'tazilite theologians for pushing the sovereignty of human freedom to the point of endangering God's omniscience and omnipotency. In fact, this was what had prompted al-Ash'ari, once a Mu'tazilite himself, to carry out his own *i'tizāl* and lay the foundations of Ash'arism. He and his followers believed that good and evil were ultimately determined by the Divine law (*al-sharī'ah*), leaving no space for the independent judgment of human reason (*al-'aql*). Paradoxically, however, the moral voluntarism of the Ash'arites agrees with Mu'tazilite rationalism in underscoring the relative and contingent nature of evil: whether determined by reason or revelation, evil is the privation of good and does not represent the essential nature of things.

Muslim philosophers assert the same point through what we might call the ontological argument. In addition to the fact that actuality is perfection over potentiality, existence (*al-wujūd*) is pure goodness (*khayr maḥḍ, summun bonum*). All beings that exist partake of this ontological goodness. Since God is the only Necessary being (*wājib al-wujūd*) by its essence, and 'in all regards', this perfection ultimately belongs to Him. According to Ibn Sina, evil has no enduring essence and appears only as the privation (*'adām*) of goodness:

> Every being that is necessary by itself is pure goodness and pure perfection. Goodness (*al-khayr*), in short, is that which

> everything desires and by which everything's being is completed. But evil has no essence; it is either the nonexistence of a substance or the nonexistence of the state of goodness (*ṣalāḥ*) for a substance. Thus existence is pure goodness, and the perfection of existence is the goodness of existence. Existence is pure goodness when it is not accompanied by non-existence, the non-existence of a substance, or the non-existence of something from that substance and it is in perpetual actuality. As for the existent contingent by itself, it is not pure goodness because its essence does not necessitate its existence by itself. Thus its essence allows for non-existence. Anything that allows for non-existence in some respect is not free from evil and imperfection in all respects. Hence pure goodness is nothing but existence that is necessary by its own essence.[285]

Elaborating on the same idea, Mulla Sadra argues that good and evil cannot be regarded opposites for 'one is the non-existence of the other; therefore goodness is existence or the perfection of existence and evil is the absence of existence or the non-existence of the perfection of existence'.[286] By defining good and evil in terms of existence and non-existence, Sadra shifts the focus from a moralistic to a primarily ontological framework. Like Ibn Sina, Sadra defines goodness as the essential nature of the present world order for it is an existent, viz., something positive. This leads Sadra to conclude that goodness permeates the world order at its foundation. In spite of the existence of such natural evils as death and famine, 'what is more and permanent is the desired goodness in nature'.[287] Once evil is relativised, it is easier to defend this world as the best of all possible worlds. This is what Sadra does when he says that 'the universe in *its totality* (*bi-kulliyatihi*) is the most perfect of all that may be and the most noble of all that can be conceived'.[288]

The Political-Legal Context: Law and Its Vicissitudes

The shari'ah rules concerning war, peace, jihad, religious minorities, and the religio-political divisions of *Dār al-Islām*, *Dār al-Ṣulḥ/'Ahd*, and *Dār al-Ḥarb* constitute an important component of the Islamic law of nations. Their contextual and historical interpretation presents a significant challenge to the modern scholars of Islam on the one hand, and the Muslims themselves on the other. In analysing the views of the jurists on these issues from the second Islamic century onwards, an extremely common tendency is to fixate specific legal rulings by certain jurists as the 'orthodox' view of Islam applicable to all times and places. While it is granted that Islamic law is based on the ultimate authority of the Qur'an and the Sunnah, the shari'ah as legal code is structured in such a way as to allow considerable freedom and leeway for Muslim scholars and communities to adjust themselves to different times and circumstances. The early generations of Muslim scholars, jurists (*fuqahā'*), Qur'anic commentators (*mufassirūn*), traditionists (*muhaddithūn*), and historians have made extensive use of this simple fact, paving the way for the rise and flourishing of various schools of law and legal opinions in Islam. This 'adoptionist' and resilient nature of the shari'ah, however, has been grossly overlooked and understated not only in Western scholarship but also in the Islamic world. In the present context, this has led to the oft-repeated conclusion that the teachings of the shari'ah and, by derivation, Islam itself do not warrant a substantive notion of peace and a culture of coexistence.[289]

To analyse the legal-political aspects of traditional shari'ah rulings concerning war and peace, I shall limit myself to three interrelated issues. The first is the Muslim community's right to defend itself against internal or external aggression and the transition of the first Muslim community from the overt 'pacifism' of Mecca to the 'activism' of Medina. This issue necessarily raises the question of jihad as an offensive or defensive war and its relation to what is called *jus ad bellum* in the Western tradition. The second is the political context of the legal injunctions of certain jurists, namely Imam Shafi'i (d. 820 CE) and the Hanafi jurist Sarakhsi (d. 1090 CE), concerning the legitimacy of the territorial expansion of Muslim states on religious grounds. Some contemporary scholars have disproportionately overstated Shafi'i's justificatory remarks about launching jihad against non-Muslim territories on the basis of their belief system. The third issue is the treatment of religious minorities, i.e. the dhimmis under the Islamic law and its relevance for religious diversity and cultural pluralism in the Islamic tradition.

To begin with the first, a major concern of the Prophet of Islam in Mecca was to ensure the security and integrity of the nascent Muslim community as a religio-political unit. This concern eventually led to the historic migration of the Prophet and his followers to Medina in

622 CE after a decade of pressure, sanctions, persecution, torture, and a foiled attempt to kill the Prophet himself. During this period, the community's right to defend itself against the Meccan polytheists was mostly exercised in what we would call today pacifist and non-violent means of resistance. Even though the Prophet was in close contact with the Meccan leaders to spread his message as well as to protect his small yet highly dedicated group of followers, his tireless negotiations did not mitigate the aggressive policies of Meccans against the growing Muslim community. The transition from the robust pacifism of Mecca to the political activism of Medina took place when the permission to fight was given with the verses *Al-Ḥajj*, 22:38–40:

> *Verily, God will ward off [all evil] from those who attain to faith: [and] verily, God does not love anyone who betrays his trust and is bereft of gratitude. Permission [to fight] is given to those against whom war is being wrongfully waged—and, verily, God has indeed the power to succor them--: those who have been driven from their homelands against all right or no other reason than their saying, 'Our Sustainer is God!' For, if God had not enabled people to defend themselves against one another, [all] monasteries and churches and synagogues and mosques—in [[all of] which God's name is abundantly extolled—would surely have been destroyed. (trans. M. Asad)*

This and other verses (*Al-Baqarah*, 2:190–3) define clearly the reasons for taking up arms to defend religious freedom and set the conditions of just war (*jus ad bellum*) in self-defence. That the verse, revealed in the first year of the Hijrah, refers to the grave wrongdoing against Muslims and their eviction from their homeland for professing the new faith confirms that the migration of the Prophet was the last stage of the forceful expulsion of the Muslim community from Mecca. This was a turning point for the attitudes and ensuing tactics of the Prophet and his followers to protect themselves against the Meccans. The subsequent battles fought between the Meccans and the Medinans, from Badr to Handak until the Prophet's triumphant return to Mecca. were based on the same principles of religious freedom, collective solidarity, and political unity. In addition to enunciating the conditions of just war, the above verse defines religious freedom as a universal cause for all the three Abrahamic faiths. Like any other political unit, communities tied with a bond of faith have the right and, in fact, the responsibility of securing their existence and integrity against the threats of persecution and eventual extinction. As I shall discuss below, this ecumenical attitude towards the religious freedom of all faith communities was a major factor in the Prophet's signing of a number of treatises with the Jews, Christians and Zoroastrians of the Arabian Peninsula as well as the treatment of religious minorities under the shari'ah.[290]

The construction of jihad as armed struggle to expand the borders of *Dār al-Islām* and, by derivation, subsume all *Dār al-Ḥarb* under the Islamic dominion is found in some of the jurists of the ninth and tenth centuries. Among those, we can mention Shafi'i and Sarakhsi who interpreted jihad as the duty of the Muslim ruler to fight against the lands defined as the 'territory of war'. Shafi'i formulated his expansionist theory of jihad as a religious duty at a time when Muslim states were engaged in prolonged military conflicts with non-Muslim territories and had become mostly successful in extending their borders. While these jurists had justified fighting against non-Muslims on account of their disbelief (*kufr*) rather than self-defence, they were also adamant on the observation of *jus in bello* norms, i.e., avoiding excessiveness, accepting truce, sparing the lives of non-combatants, women, children, etc.[291] In spite of these conditions, the views of Shafi'i and his followers represent a shift from the Qur'anic notion of self-defence to armed struggle to bring about the conversion of non-Muslims. Having said that, two points need to be mentioned.

First of all, the views of Shafi'i and Sarakhsi do not represent the majority, let alone the 'orthodox', stance of the jurists. The common tendency to present this particular definition of jihad as the mainstream position of Islam not only disregards the views of Abu Hanifah, Malik ibn Anas, Abu Yusuf, Shaybani, Awzai, Ibn Rushd, Ibn Taymiyyah, Ibn Qayyim al-Jawziyyah and others but also ignores the historical and contextual nature of such juridical rulings.[292] The same holds true for Muslim political philosophers and theologians who take a different position on the bifurcationist framework of *Dār al-Islām* versus *Dār al-Ḥarb*.[293] Moreover, these rulings were by and large the jurists' response to the de facto situation of the military conquests of Muslim states rather than their cause. Certain jurists begin to stress such reconciliatory terms as *Dār al-ʿAhd* ('the Land of the Covenant') and *Dār al-Ṣulḥ* ('the Land of Peace') during and after the eleventh and twelfth centuries when the Muslim states were confronted with political realities other than unabated conquest and resounding victories. This change in tone and emphasis, however, was not a completely novel phenomenon for the concept of *Dār al-Ṣulḥ* can be traced back to the treaty that the Prophet had signed with the Christian population of Najran when he was in Medina.[294] As I shall discuss below, this treaty, whose text has been preserved, lays the foundations of making peace with non-Muslim communities. In addition, the policy of giving *amān* (safe conduct), i.e., contractual protection for non-Muslims residing or travelling in Muslim territories, was a common practice. Such people were known as *mustaʾmīn*, and to grant them this status was not only the prerogative of the head of state or the *ʿulamāʾ* but also individuals, both men and women.[295]

Secondly, the idea of bringing the world under the reign of *Dār al-Islām* by military means and territorial expansion should be seen within the context of the geo-political conditions of the classical Islamic world. The medieval imperial world order, of which Muslim states were a part, was based on the idea of continuously expanding one's borders because 'conquest' (*fatḥ*) provided economic, political and demographic stability. In this sense, as Hitti points out, 'the Islam that conquered the northern regions was not the Islamic religion but the Islamic state … it was Arabianism and not Muhammadanism that triumphed first'.[296] In a world in which one was either a 'conqueror' or 'conquered', the triumphant Muslim states depended heavily on the expansion of their territories against both their Muslim rivals and non-Muslim enemies. The historic march of Muslim armies into territories once under non-Muslim rule was not jihad in the religious sense of the term, but an outcome of the power struggle to which all political establishments, Muslim or non-Muslim, were subject.

This is further made clear by the fact that territorial expansion and military conquest did not always and necessarily mean conversion. Beginning with the early history of Islam, conversion through persuasion and 'calling' (*daʿwah*) was encouraged, and a multitude of methods were put in place to facilitate the conversion of individuals and masses through peaceful means. Conversion by force, which would make Islam a proselytising religion, however, was not imposed as a policy either by the *'ulamā'* or the rulers. Furthermore, conversion was not a condition to become part of the Muslim community to gain religious freedom, receive protection, and possess property under the Islamic law. The considerably protean concept of the *dhimmī* allowed religious minorities to maintain their traditions and resist any attempts at forceful conversion. Since Islam does not ordain a missionary establishment, the agents of conversion responsible for the enormously successful and unprecedented spread of Islam were multifarious and extended from the Arab traders and the Sufis to the development of Islamic communal institutions.[297] Otherwise we cannot explain the en masse conversion of various ethnic, religious and cultural communities to Islam by the military prowess of a handful of Muslim groups in Anatolia, Iran, Africa or India.

Paradoxically, the policies of religious tolerance secured both the rights of religious minorities and the loyalties of new converts. In a manner that was simply unimaginable in the Christian kingdoms of Europe at the time, Jews, Christians, Sabeans and Hindus had access to considerably high state posts from the time of Mu'awiyah (661–680 CE) to the dissolution of the Ottoman Empire at the beginning of the twentieth century. Jewish and Christian scientists, physicians, accountants, counsellors and statesmen were employed at Umayad courts. St John the Damascene, one of the most influential figures of the Eastern Orthodox Church and the author of the earliest anti-Islamic polemics, and his father Ibn Mansur held positions under the Caliph Abd al-Malik (685-705).[298] During the Buwayhid era in Persia, the vizier of the powerful Persian king Adud al-Dawlah (949-982), Nasr ibn Harun was a Christian.[299] We find similar cases in India and the Ottoman Empire where the vertical mobility of religious minorities in state affairs was a common phenomenon. Even the *devshirme* system of the Ottomans, which has been criticised and labelled as a form of forced conversion, provided religious minorities with unfettered access to the highest government positions. Three grand viziers of Suleiman the Magnificent, the most powerful Ottoman sultan, were of Christian origin: Ibrahim Pasha was a Greek and an able diplomat and commander; Rustem Pasha was a Bulgarian and had handled the treasury with utmost competence;

and the celebrated Sokollu Mehmet Pasha was a Slav from Bosnia and had served in his youth as an acolyte in a Serbian church.[300] Among these, the case of Sokollu is probably the most interesting for it shows the extent to which the *devshirme* system eventually worked to the benefit of Christian communities under Ottoman rule. Although Sokollu embraced Islam and became one of the most powerful men of his time, he kept close contact with his brother who was an important religious figure in Bosnia and helped him with his status as the grand vizier.

In the light of these points, we have to make a distinction between jihad as 'just war' and jihad as 'holy war',[301] which brings us to our third issue. Just war refers to a community's right to defend itself against aggression and oppression. It is defensive in nature whereas 'holy war' entails converting everybody into one's religion by force, armed struggle, territorial expansion, and other means. In the first sense, jihad is an extension of the *jus ad bellum* tradition and can be seen as a necessity to protect justice, freedom and order. In this regard, the position taken by the Qur'an and the Prophet concerning the use of force against oppression by Muslims and non-Muslims alike is essentially a realist one and aims at putting strict conditions for regulating war and using force.[302] The guiding principle is that of fighting against aggression, which is 'to fight in the way of God', and not to be the aggressors: *Fight (qatilu, lit. 'kill') in the way of God against those who fight against you, but do not transgress the limits. Verily, God does not love aggressors* (*Al-Baqarah*, 2:190; Cf. also *Al-Nisā'*, 4:91 and *Al-Tawbah*, 9:36). Both the classical and modern commentators have interpreted the command not to 'transgress' (*lā ta'adadu*) as avoiding war and hostilities in the first place, resorting to armed struggle only to defend one's freedom, and, once forced to fight, sparing the lives of noncombatants that include women, children, and the elderly.[303]

Contrary to what Khadduri claims,[304] the global bifurcation of *Dār al-Islām* and *Dār al-Ḥarb* does not translate into a 'holy war' nor a 'permanent state of war' between Muslims and non-Muslims. No figure can illustrate this point better than Ibn Taymiyyah (d. 1327 CE) whose views have been widely distorted and exploited to lend legitimacy to extremist interpretations of the classical Islamic law of nations. Even though Ibn Taymiyyah lived through the destruction wrought upon the Islamic world by the Mongols and could have been expected to take a more belligerent stance against the 'infidels', he was unequivocal in stating that Muslims could wage war only against those who attacked them. The idea of initiating unprovoked war to convert people to Islam, namely to engage in 'holy war', belies the religion itself because, according to Ibn Taymiyyah, 'if the unbeliever were to be killed unless he becomes a Muslim, such an action would constitute the greatest compulsion in religion', which would be contrary to the Qur'anic principle that *there is no compulsion in religion* (*A-Baqarah*, 2:256).[305] Ibn Taymiyyah's famous student Ibn Qayyim al-Jawziyyah reiterates the same principle when he says that 'fighting (*qatl*) is permitted on account of war (*ḥarb*), not on account of disbelief (*kufr*)'.[306]

This extended meaning of jihad as *jus ad bellum*, i.e., armed struggle in self-defence can also be seen in the anti-colonialist resistance movements of the modern period. In the eighteenth and nineteenth centuries, calls for jihad were issued across the Islamic world to fight against colonialism. For the anti-colonialist resistance movements of this period, jihad functioned, first, as the religious basis of fighting against colonialism and, second, as a powerful way of mobilising people to join the resistance forces. Among others, the Barelvi family in India, Shaykh Shamil in Chechenya, Shaykh 'Abd al-Qadir al-Jazairi in Algeria, the Mahdi family in the Sudan, Ahmad 'Urabi in Egypt, and the Sanusiyyah order in Libya fought against European colonial powers.[307] It was during this period of resistance that jihad took a cultural tone in the sense that the fight against colonial powers was seen as both a military and religio-cultural struggle. Despite the enormous difficulties faced by Muslim scholars, leaders, merchants, and villagers in Egypt, Africa, India and other places, the jihad calls against the European armies did not lead to an all-out war against local non-Muslim communities. Even in cases where the Muslim population had to bear the full brunt of colonialism, extreme care was taken not to label local non-Muslims as the enemy because of their religious and cultural affiliation with European colonial powers. When, for instance, the Sanusi call for 'jihad against all unbelievers' caused a sense of urgency among the Christians in Egypt, Muslim scholars responded by saying that jihad in Libya was directed at the Italian aggressors, not all Westerners or Christians.[308]

Since jihad as armed struggle was fought against the invasion of European powers, it was not difficult for it to take religious and cultural tones. Napoleon's attempt to paint himself as a 'defender of Islam' when he invaded Egypt in 1798, for instance, was seen by the celebrated Egyptian historian Abd al-Rahman al-Jabarti (1754–1825) as no more than outright lies expected only from an 'infidel' (*kāfir*). In his letter to local Egyptian leaders, imams and scholars, Napoleon said that he 'more than the Mamluks, serve[s] God—may He be praised and exalted—and revere[s] His Prophet Muhammad and the glorious Qur'an' and that the 'French are also faithful Muslims'.[309] For Jabarti and his generation, this was yet another fact confirming the necessity of launching jihad against the '*afranj*' (the French, i.e., Europeans). This sense of jihad as anti-colonialist struggle has not completely disappeared from the minds of some Muslims in the post-colonial period. In fact, the modern calls for jihad as 'holy war' by such Muslim extremists as Abd al-Salam Faraj—who wrote the celebrated *al-Fariḍat al-ghai'bah* (*The Neglected Duty*)[310] presumably justifying the assassination of Anwar Sadat in 1981—and Osama bin Laden are as much the product of their strict and ahistorical reading of the classical shari'ah sources as the legacy of colonialism.

Lastly, I would like to turn briefly to the status of religious minorities under Islamic law. As mentioned before, the dhimmi status granted the religious minorities and especially Jews and Christians under Muslim rule some measure of economic and political protection, freedom of worship, right to own property, and, in some cases, access to high government positions. The religious-legal basis of the notion of the dhimmi goes back to the time of the Prophet. While the status of dhimmi was initially given to Jews, Christians, Sabeans and Zoroastrians, its scope was later extended to include all non-Muslims living under Islam.[311] A similar course of action was followed in India when Muhammad b. al-Qasim, the first Muslim commander to set foot on Indian soil in the eighth century, compared Hindus to Jews, Christians and Zoroastrians and declared them as part of the *ahl al-dhimmah*.[312] This decision, which was later sanctioned by the Hanafi jurists, was a momentous event in the development of the Muslim attitude towards the religions of India. This politico-legal ruling could be seen as laying the foundations of the Hindu-Muslim mode of cultural coexistence, which I shall discuss below.

That the Prophet and his companions were lenient towards the People of the Book is not only attested by the communal relationships that developed between Muslims and non-Muslims in Medina, but also recorded in a number of treatises signed by the Prophet. The 'Medinan Constitution' (*wathīqat al-madinah*), for instance, recognises the Jews of Banu 'Awf, Banu al-Najar, Banu Tha'laba and others as a distinct community with 'their own religion'.[313] Another treatise signed with the People of the Book of Najran reads as follows:

> They [People of the Book] shall have the protection of Allah and the promise of Muhammad, the Apostle of Allah, that they shall be secured; their lives, property, lands, creed, those absent and those present, their families, their churches, and all that they possess. No bishop or monk shall be displaced from his parish or monastery, no priest shall be forced to abandon his priestly life. No hardships or humiliation shall be imposed on them nor shall their land be occupied by [our] army. Those who seek justice shall have it: there will be no oppressors nor oppressed.[314]

The privileges given to dhimmis included things that were prohibited for Muslims such as breeding pigs and producing alcohol, which were not outlawed for Christians. The religious tax called *jizyah* was the main economic responsibility of the dhimmis under the shari'ah. Contrary to a common belief, the primary goal of the *jizyah* tax was not the 'humiliation' of the People of the Book. While many contemporary translations of the Qur'an translate the words *wa hum saghīrūn* as 'so that they will be humiliated', Ibn Qayyim al-Jawziyyah, who has written the most extensive work on the People of the Book, understands it as securing the allegiance of the People of the Book to laws pertaining to them (*aḥkām al-millah*). Instead, *wa hum saghīrūn* should be understood, says Ibn Qayyim, as making all subjects of the state obey the law and, in the case of the People of the Book, pay the *jizyah*.[315]

According to Abu Yusuf, one of the foremost authorities of the Hanafi school of law, *jizyah* was '48 dirhams on the wealthy, 24 on the middle class and 12 dirhams on the poor ploughman-peasant and manual worker'. According to Shafi'i, the *jizyah* is one dinar for the poor and four dinars for the rich.[316] It is collected once a year and may be paid in kind, i.e., as 'goods and similar property which is accepted according to its value'.[317] Those who cannot afford to pay it are not forced to do so.[318] The exempted also include women, children, the elderly and the sick.[319] To the best of our knowledge, the *jizyah* tax was not a significant source of income for the state[320], and it exempted the dhimmis from military service. In some cases, the *jizyah* was postponed or abandoned altogether by the head of the state as we see in India under the reigns of Akbar, Jahangir and Shah Jahan.[321] The *jizyah* was a compensation for the protection of the dhimmis by the state against any type of aggression from Muslims or non-Muslims. This is attested by the fact that the poll taxes were returned to the dhimmis when the Muslim state had been unable to provide the security of its non-Muslim minorities.[322] In most cases, the *jizyah* was imposed not as individual tax like the *kharāj* but as collective tribute on eligible dhimmis.[323]

While Ibn Qayyim al-Jawziyya's famous work on the dhimmis contains many rulings that present a condescending view of non-Muslims and advocate policies of humiliation against them,[324] many other jurists were insistent on treating the dhimmis with equity and justice. As people 'under the protection of the Prophet', Jews, Christians and other religious minorities were not to be forced to pay more than they could afford nor to be intimidated and oppressed because of their religious affiliations. Advising Harun al-Rashid (d. 803 CE), the famous Abbasid caliph, on the treatment of the dhimmis, Abu Yusuf exhorts him to 'treat with leniency those under the protection of our Prophet Muhammad, and not allow that more than what is due to be taken from them or more than they are able to pay, and that nothing should be confiscated from their properties without legal justification'.[325] In making this strong advice to the caliph, Abu Yusuf narrates a tradition of the Prophet in which the Prophet says that 'he who robs a dhimmi or imposes on him more than he can bear will have me as his opponent'. Another well-known case is the execution on the order of the Prophet of a Muslim who had killed a dhimmi. In response to this incident, the Prophet has said that 'it is most appropriate that I live up fully to my (promise of) protection'.[326]

These and other rules concerning the dhimmis show that Islam accepts the reality of the 'religious other' in terms of a de jure reality rather than as a matter of political exigency. The underlying principle behind this attitude of accommodation is that the interests of human beings are served better in peace than in conflict. To reveal the extent of the Islamic theology of peace and cultural pluralism, we need to look at the cultural attitudes and practices of Muslim societies vis-à-vis other communities, to which we now turn.

The Socio-Cultural Context: Confrontation, Coexistence and Peace

Islam does not prescribe a particular form of cultural identity. There are both doctrinal and historical reasons for this. The absence of a central religious authority or clergy in the Islamic tradition pre-empts authoritarianism as a model of negotiating religious affairs in the public sphere. This is attested by the multiplicity of schools of law as well as the notorious differences of opinion among them. This fact, often stated by Muslims with a sense of pride, however, does not negate the presence of established and commonly accepted views in the Islamic tradition. Assuming that there is a set of beliefs and practices that we may legitimately consider as mainstream and orthodox, it is based on the consensus of the community over the generations rather than a centralised body of legal rulings. The incremental process of establishing orthodox etiquettes is not the monopoly of the *'ulamā'*. Rather, it is shaped by a multitude of social agents that include men of letters, dervishes, saints, 'heretics', bards and folk singers, storytellers, political leaders, rulers, scientists, artists, traders, diplomats, philosophers, and theologians. While it is true that the dissemination of religious authority on the one hand and the malleability of cultural expressions in Muslim societies on the other has challenged centralism and authoritarianism, it has also raised the question of legitimacy and authenticity. Some, including the Wahhabis and some Orientalists, have called this a deviation from the norms of the religion, arguing that Islamic history has been not so much 'Islamic' as antinomian. Even if we admit that there are presumably overt discrepancies between what the ulama envision as a perfect shari'ah society and the cultural practices of Muslim societies, it is a healthy tension and functions as a mechanism of checks and balances against the strictly text-based, relatively abstract, and reductively legalistic approach of the jurists.

In creating their cultural orthopraxies, Muslim communities were functioning within the framework of the ethical universalism of the Qur'an and the Sunnah. The Qur'anic call to enjoin what is good and praised (*ma'rūf*) and forbid what is morally evil and disliked (*munkār*) is not a culture-specific injunction. It is addressed to all peoples regardless of their religious affiliations. The Prophet is considered a perfect example (*uswah ḥasanah*) for all humanity in his fight against all that is evil and oppressive and in defence of all that is praiseworthy and virtuous, whatever their origin might be. The notion of 'middle community' (*ummah wasaṭah)* (*Al-Baqarah*, 2:143) supports the same ethical universalism: *And thus We willed you to be a community of the middle way, so that [with your lives] you might bear witness to the truth before all mankind, and that the Apostle might bear witness to it before you* (trans. M. Asad). The aim of this ethical-spiritual universalism is to create an open society based on moral values, not on the received traditions of one tribe, city, or nation. This is in tandem with the fact that the Qur'an positions itself against the cultural localism and tribal parochialism of pre-Islamic Arabia—a rule that has been an invariable factor in the rapid spread of Islam outside the Arabic cultural zone. Once established as major cultural units, Muslim societies articulated this ethical universalism into various societal mechanisms by which the ideal of creating a virtuous and just human habitat could be realised. The politics of gaining status and social ascendancy in the Islamic context is thus based on the acquisition of two universal qualities: knowledge (*'ilm*) and virtue (*faḍīlah* and *iḥsān*). Both of these qualities are implicit in the Qur'anic notion of *taqwā* (*Al-Ḥujurāt*, 49:13), God-consciousness, which is the ultimate criterion of 'nobility' among people. In a broad sense, this forms the basis of an Islamic meritocracy whereby every member of society is urged to contribute to the creation of a moral and just social order. As the few examples below will show, the Muslim philosophers and scientists regarded seeking knowledge and leading a virtuous life as the basis of their interest in other cultures and traditions.

Historically, as the borders of the Islamic world expanded outside and beyond the Arabian Peninsula, Muslims became heir to all of the major cultural traditions of the time. The Graeco-Roman heritage through the Byzantine Empire and the pre-Islamic Persian culture through the Sasanids were the first two important traditions that Muslims encountered in less than a century after the death of the Prophet. This was followed by Mesopotamian, Indian, black African, central Asian, Chinese, and finally Malay-Indonesian civilisations in the fifteenth and sixteenth centuries.[327] The rapid establishment of the different cultural zones of the Islamic world went hand in hand with the rise of the numerous schools of law, Kalam, philosophy, and Sufi orders, generating a remarkable tapestry of cultural diversity within and across the *Dār al-Islām*.[328] In spite of occasional sectarian conflicts such as the *miḥnah* incident in the third/ninth century[329] or the Kadizade movement in the Ottoman Empire in the tenth/sixteenth century,[330] traditional Muslim societies succeeded in creating a stable and peaceful habitat in which both Muslim and non-Muslim members of the ummah contributed to the cultivation of a world civilisation in such diverse fields as arts, sciences, trade and architecture. The notion of cultural and religious coexistence that came about in this milieu was not merely based on the temporary absence of conflict and confrontation between Islamic and non-Islamic elements. Its positive character was nurtured and sustained by the inclusivist attitude of Muslims towards other cultures and religious traditions, which makes Islamic civilisation simultaneously both Islamic and 'Islamicate'.[331]

There is a plethora of examples in the history of Islam to illustrate the cultural ecumenism of Muslim societies. We may begin with the attitude of Muslim philosophers towards pre-Islamic traditions of learning. For the early Muslim philosophers, scholars, and scientists, the search for truth was both within and beyond religious boundaries. The Prophet's famous exhortations to 'seek knowledge even if it is in China'[332] and 'wisdom is a Muslim's lost [treasure]. He takes it wherever he finds it'[333] were frequently referred to by the philosophers of the intellectual sciences (*'ulūm 'aqliyyah*) interested in Greek-Alexandrian thought as well as the scholars of transmitted sciences (*'ulūm naqliyyah*) specialised in such disciplines as hadith, Qur'anic commentary, and jurisprudence (*fiqh*). Even though some later scholars have opposed philosophical sciences, especially its strictly Aristotelian version, and defined knowledge (*al-'ilm*) as 'religious science', this did not obstruct the steady development of philosophy and science in the Islamic world.

Contrary to Goldziher's attempt to present the critical views of certain Hanbalite jurists on the 'ancient sciences' (*'ulum al-awā'il*), meaning Greek philosophy and science, as the 'orthodox' Muslim position,[334] anti-intellectualism remained largely parochial to the traditionists (*al-muḥaddithūn*) who were as much opposed to the lore of pre-Islamic times as to Kalam and doctrinal Sufism. For the overwhelming majority of the Muslim intelligentsia, the universality of truth was the guiding principle and ground of their quest for knowledge. No one has stated this point better than al-Kindi, 'the philosopher of the Arabs'.

> We owe great thanks to those who have imparted to us even a small measure of truth, let alone those who have taught us more, since they have given us a share in the fruits of their reflection and simplified the complex questions bearing on the nature of reality. If they had not provided us with those premises that pave the way to truth, we would have been unable, despite our assiduous lifelong investigations, to find those true primary principles from which the conclusions of our obscure inquiries have resulted, and which have taken generation upon generation to come to light heretofore.[335]

That al-Kindi's attitude in the above quote was emblematic of his generation and later Muslim scholars is attested by Sa'id al-Andalusi who has divided nations (*umam*) according to their contribution to knowledge and science (*al-'ilm*). He states this point in unequivocal terms when he says that:

> We have determined that all nations, in spite of their differences and the diversities of their convictions, form *tabaqatayn* [two categories]. One *tabaqah* has cultivated science, given rise to the art of knowledge, and propagated the various aspects of scientific information; the other *tabaqah* did not contribute enough to science to deserve the honour of association or inclusion in the family of scientifically productive nations.[336]

The belief that truth transcends the contingencies of history was the conviction of educated classes across the Islamic world as they studied the countless schools of thought, both Islamic and pre-Islamic, producing an extensive literature on the history of ideas. The long list of scholars interested in intellectual history before and after Islam included, inter alia, Ibn al-Qifti, al-Mubashshir ibn Fatik, Abu Sulayman al-Sijistani, Sa'id al-Andalusi, Ibn al-Nadim, al-Jahiz, and Ibn Abi Usaybi'ah as well as such major writers of the *Milal* tradition as Shahrastani, Baghdadi and Ibn Hazm.[337] Among these works, the Egyptian *amir* Abu al-Wafa al-Mubashshir ibn Fatik's *Mukhtār al-ḥikām wa maḥāsin al-kilām* was noticed very early by medieval Europeans, translated into Latin and other languages, and, in fact, became the first book printed by William Caxton in England in the fifteenth century as *The Dicts and Sayings of the Philosophers*.[338] The continuity of humanity's search for truth had a normative value for most of these writers in that their quest for knowledge was part of a larger tradition to which every seeker of knowledge belonged. When Hasan ibn Sahl, for instance, was asked why he always invoked the views of those who came before him (*kalām al-awā'il*), he answered that 'because it [i.e. those views] has been passed down before us; had it been unworthy and imperfect, it would have never reached us and gained [universal] approval'.[339]

The concept of 'perennial philosophy' (*al-ḥikmat al-khālidah*) enjoyed a similar prestige due to the same notion of truth and its persistence in history. Suhrawardi, the founder of the school of Illumination (*ishrāq*) made a strong case for the perennity of certain philosophical questions and the answers given of them when he said:

> Do not think that wisdom has existed only in these recent times [i.e., the pre-Islamic Persian and Greek philosophers]. No, the world is never bereft of wisdom and the person who possesses it with arguments and self-evident proofs. He is God's vicegerent on His earth, and this shall be so as long as the heavens and the earth exist.[340]

Apart from the sublime world of the intellectuals, the Islamic concept of cultural pluralism was extended to virtually all minorities living in the lands of Islam. The experience of *convivencia* among Jews, Christians, and Muslims in Andalusia was a result of the Islamic notion of cultural inclusivism.[341] While the Jews of Europe were subject to woeful vilifications and persecutions during the Middle Ages, a major Jewish intellectual tradition had developed under the Muslim rule and included such prominent figures of medieval Jewish thought as Saadiah Gaon al-Fayyumi, Ibn Gabirol, Judah Halevi, Maimonides, Ibn Kammunah,

Ibn Paquda, and Gersonides (Levi ben Gershom). This resulted in a unique interaction between medieval Jewish philosophy on the one hand, and Islamic philosophy, Kalam, and Sufism on the other.[342]

In the subcontinent of India, a cultural syncreticism developed between Hindu and Muslim cultures. From the translation of Indian astronomical works into Arabic as early as the eighth century to Biruni's historic study of India and Amir Khusraw's formulation of an Islamic identity in the Indian cultural environment, a vast literature came into being, generating a unique mode of symbiosis between the two worlds on social, philosophical, and artistic levels. Perhaps the most important figure to illustrate this is Dara Shikuh (1615–1659), the famous Mughal prince and son of Shah Jahan. Dara Shikuh translated and authored two important works dealing with Hinduism from an Islamic point of view. He made a translation of the Bhagavad Gita and some fifty Upanishads into Persian as *Sirr-i akbar* ('Great Mystery'), which he interpreted in light of the school of Advaita-Vedanta or the non-dualism of Shankaracharya.[343] In making his case for the translation, Dara Shikuh says that he 'read the Old and the New Testaments and the Psalms of David and other scriptures but the discourse on *Tawḥīd* found in them was brief and in a summary form'. He then turned to the Upanishads 'which is undoubtedly the first heavenly Book and the fountainhead of the ocean of monotheism, and, in accordance with or rather an elucidation of the Kur'an'.[344] Dara Shikuh also wrote a treatise called *Majmā' al-baḥrayn*, referring to the Qur'anic verse *Maryam,*19:60, in which he attempted a monotheistic interpretation of Hinduism. In tandem with his 'universalist' outlook, he defined his work as 'a collection of the truth and wisdom of two Truth-knowing (*haqq-shinas*) groups', referring to Muslims and Hindus.[345] In addition to Dara Shikuh, we may also refer to the sixteenth century Persian philosopher Mir Findiriski, who is reported to have met a number of Hindu mystics during his travels to India, and translated and wrote a commentary on the Hindu mystical and philosophical text *Yoga-Vasishtha*[346].

Such modes of cultural coexistence would have been impossible without the recognition of the diversity of cultures and societies as part of human existence. The Qur'an takes up this issue in several places. Working towards a common good is made conditional upon the existence of different communities:

> *Unto every one of you We have appointed a [different] law and way of life. And if God had so willed, He could surely have made you all one single community: but [He willed it otherwise] in order to test by means of what He has vouchsafed unto you. Vie, then, with one another in doing good works!* (*Al-Mā'idah*, 5:48; also *Hūd*, 11:118)

This theme is further developed in the following verse. This time the emphasis is on the civic responsibility of 'knowing one another'.

> *O humans! Behold, We have created you all out of a male and a female, and have made you into nations and tribes so that you might come to know one another. Verily, the noblest of you in the sight of God is the one who is most deeply conscious of Him. Behold, God is all-knowing, all-aware.* (*Al-Ḥujurāt*, 49:13)

The examples from the history of Islamic culture briefly analysed above are neither scarce nor contrary to the norm. Even though the fundamentalists, for lack of a better term, consider cases of cultural symbiosis and syncretism in the Islamic world as deviations from an idealised and essentially ideological construct of Islam, both the Islamic intellectual tradition and Muslim societies have envisaged peace as a cross-cultural and inter-communal value.

I have argued in the preceding pages that a proper examination of the Islamic concept of peace takes us beyond the minimal definition of peace as absence of conflict, and certainly beyond the limited sphere of law. In a broad sense, the Islamic tradition has articulated a concept of peace that extends from metaphysics and cosmology to law and culture. We cannot possibly understand the experience of Muslim societies with the cultural and religious other(s) without taking into account these elements. The relevance of this tradition for the present day Muslim world requires little explanation. Today numerous Muslim intellectuals, scholars and leaders from Bosnia, Turkey and Egypt to Iran, Malaysia and the United States are engaged in constructing an Islamic political ethics that is compatible with the Islamic tradition as well as responsive to the challenges of the modern world. Questions of war and peace, communal violence, terrorism, international relations, constitutional and participatory democracy, pluralism, openness, civility and the attitude towards the religious other are being discussed from a multitude of perspectives, and the views expressed are by no means uniform and homogenous. There is, however, an emerging consensus on upholding peace as a value in itself regardless of the political state of Muslim countries and communities across the globe.

In conclusion, we should emphasise the significance of this consensus in the present context. Muslim communities can no longer address issues of conflict and violence without developing a proper ethics of peace. While most of the factional conflicts in the Islamic world can be resolved through non-violent means, the lack of a comprehensive discourse of peace supported by a network of scholars, intellectuals, leaders, activists, and state agencies, pre-empts the possibility of preventing communal strife and use of force. Conflicts in our age have become both local and global, making the distinction between the two a blurred one. We can no longer speak of local and national conflicts without considering their international implications nor can we ignore the impact of global trends and relations on local issues. The Kashmir problem or the Israeli-Palestinian conflict defy the conventional notions of interstate and/or territorial disputes. This presents a particular challenge to contemporary Muslim political thought in its transition from the large political units of the empire and its constellation states to the current system of nation states on the one hand, and globalisation on the other. It remains to be seen what the weakening of the nation state model will bring to Muslim societies in their struggle to cope with the current challenges of economic and cultural globalisation. Be that as it may, achieving a culture of peace is an urgent need for Muslim communities in their inter-communal relations as well as their relations with other societies.

Originally published as 'Islam and Peace: A Survey of the Sources of Peace in the Islamic Tradition', Islamic Studies *44:3 (2005), pp. 327–62.*

CHAPTER NINE

THE CONCEPT OF PEACE/SECURITY (*SALM*) IN ISLAM

Dr Karim Douglas Crow

Overview

The conception of سلم *salm* 'peace/security' in early Islamic sources is re-examined by exploiting early linguistic materials in the Qur'an and Hadith. The most essential value at the heart of Islam may be characterised as 'security/peace' (see Qur'anic terms *silm* and *salm*). This data on what Islam teaches about peace and security may now be aligned with the contemporary understanding linking human security to wider developmental and societal needs. The double thrust of the Islamic understanding of 'peace' is evident: social and communal, and individual and salvational. The current concern with human security finds ample support in Muslim thought and experience.

> *'Man lā yarḥamu, lā yurḥam'.* 'One who does not practice compassion' [show loving/kindness] toward others—is not shown merciful/compassion (by God).

God's Messenger Muhammad (Recorded in: Muslim, *K. al-Faḍā'il, bāb raḥmatihi Ṣ al-ṣibyān wa l-'iyāl* §5979; Abū Dawūd, *K. al-Adab, bāb fī qublati l-rajuli waladih* §5218; al-Tirmidhi, *K. al-Barr wa l-Ṣilah, bāb mā jā'a fī raḥmati l-wālid* §1911. Tradition states that the Prophet uttered this after al-Aqra' b. Habis witnessed him kissing his grandson, and then told the Prophet: 'I have ten children and never kissed even one of them.')

Introduction

It is frequently held that the religion of Islam was first presented and understood as a salvational practice of peace through outward submission and inner surrender. Today this assertion is radically questioned by many non-Muslims, who emphasise the combative role of a militant faith intent on conquest and dominion—a medieval European perception now cultivated among intelligence and security establishments countering terrorism. How should we properly understand the original context and meaning of peace in Islam? Inherent in its historical appearance was an integral connection of peacemaking with security. This linkage may aid us to grasp the intent and conception of an authentic Islamic understanding of peace. It becomes relevant now to take into account the current appreciation of the role of religion in establishing and promoting human security. We mean the concept of 'human security' in its dialogic relations linking the field of development and that of security and conflict studies, including peace and conflict resolution studies.

Human Security

This term appeared in mainstream development circles with the 1994 global *Human Development Report*,[347] and was the subject of a 2003 Global Commission co-chaired by Sadako Ogata and Nobel Laureate Amartya Sen.[348] Yet this notion previously had its own proponents and critics within security studies among scholars who for decades argued the pros and cons of expanding the notion of 'security'. Some have argued that the concept of security should be broadened to include underdevelopment as a threat. Yet a realist school rejects the inclusion of social, human and economic threats in the same category as 'national security'.[349] Traditionally security has been defined as a function of protection of the interests of the state. Until recently interstate relations—whether cooperative, competitive or complementary—remained confined to a function of nation states, with foreign policy and diplomacy conceived as a defining characteristic of the state in the international system. The *self-interest of the nation state* determined the concept of 'security'—defined in the limiting terms of 'state security' as perceived by ruling elites and power brokers who frequently identify their vision of state interests with their own economic and political preferences, namely their own self-interest.

However, many critics and human rights practitioners maintain that this privileging of state and elite interests is an overly narrow, state-centric and ultimately counterproductive conceptualisation of true security. These critics perceive that it is the level of the individual and his or her innate rights that most needs protection from perceived threats.[350] Such privileging of the individual might also be extended further to embrace the well-being of the collectivity or the community. If security is conceived as a response to threats, then the perception of what constitutes 'threat' may also need revisiting—e.g. by taking into account the ecological-planetary and socio-economic dimensions of human existence. Many security establishments now accept a widened concept of 'non-traditional security' embracing natural disasters and ecological degradation. As the need to find concerted, collective responses to new threats became increasingly clear, human security conceived in terms of the link between security and development became a topic of reform agendas during 2004–2005 in the United Nations and in regional organisations such as the European Union and the Association of Southeast Asian Nations (ASEAN).

A fundamental value and activity taught by Islam is 'security/peace'. In classical Arabic usage the term *salm* 'peacemaking' denotes the opposite of *ḥarb* 'war'.[351] The very name of the faith *al-Islām* may be understood to signify the safety and security experienced in acts of mutual harmony and concord between humans, springing out of the inner peace between individual creatures and their Creator. This name *al-Islām* points to the real purpose and source of true security: to draw closer to the ultimate origin of Peace—namely ALLAH. To better appreciate this conjunction of security with peace requires one to re-examine the early employment of these terms paying attention to their linguistic features and conceptual aura. Thereby one may be enabled to recover the basis upon which Islamic peace is grounded.

SECURITY-PEACE

There exists an intimate connection between the term *al-Islām* with peacemaking and human security, confirmed by linguistic and Qur'anic evidence. The concept of peace is primarily associated with Arabic verbal nouns derived from the root *S–L–M* (base form: *salima/yaslamu*). The main nouns from this base form are *salāmah*, *salm* & *silm*, and *salām*. In classical Arabic the term *salm* 'peacemaking' denotes the opposite of *ḥarb* 'war'. Verbal forms II *sallama* (lit. 'to make/render salutations of peace and security'—or to make the *taslīm*[352]), as well as form IV *aslama* ('to deliver up, surrender, give oneself up to') may also signify *inqāda* 'to follow/obey, yield, submit'; the verbal noun is *islām* while its active participle is *muslim* (m.) and *muslimah* (f.). Yet widespread contemporary Arabic usage of *salām* (literally: 'salutations conveying assurance of safety and peaceful security') generally understands it to connote 'peace'—whether positive or negative peace.[353] Although the main nouns from the base form (*salāmah*, *salm* and *silm*, and also *salām*) often converge in meaning and might even be used interchangeably in a loose sense, they also exhibit specific distinctions whose scrutiny yields significant insights.

Furthermore, the semantic scope of several other verbal roots overlaps in meaning with *salima*, whereby *salāmah* or *salām* may be equivalent to *amān*/surety, as well as *ṣulḥ*/conciliation; although the root *S–L–M* possesses an undeniable primacy.[354] We provide here a very brief conspectus of related notions whose semantic fields overlap conceptually and comprise significant extensions of meaning for peace in Islamic understanding.

Ṣ–L–Ḥ : *ṣulḥ* and *ṣalāḥ* and *iṣlāḥ* 'conciliation' and 'peacemaking' in resolving conflict between individuals or groups to ensure the harmony of the wider community. *Ṣulḥ* forms one of the pillars of peace in Islamic thought and practice, carrying the meanings of reconciliation, peacemaking, making amends and reforming, as well as moral rectitude and integrity/righteousness. When employed with its object—*iṣlāḥ lahum*, or *iṣlāḥ baynahum* and *ṣalāḥ dhāt al-bayn*—the expression connotes 'promoting well-being', 'setting aright', or peacemaking. This practice is central to Qur'anic teaching on ending conflict: *aṣliḥu dhāti baynikum/ and do you rightly dispose-order the case that is between you and be of one accord in unison*; or quite simply 'peacemaking'.[355] Muslims must be of one accord after divisions over spilt blood, disputed property or rivalries, and they are urged to act reciprocally with justice and equity (*al-muqsiṭūn*).

It is vital to appreciate that this notion of *ṣulḥ* & *iṣlāḥ* in Qur'anic usage is conceptually opposed to both *fasād* ('corruption', 'depravity' or 'stirring up dissension'—i.e. insecurity); as well as to *isrāf* (wasteful extravagance, sinful excess), for the peacemaker *muṣliḥ* is the opposite of the *musrif* 'profligate' and of the *mufsid* 'depraved'.[356] The *mufsid* is one who instigates *fasād* among others by seeking to spread insecurity, disorder, corruption and injustice, and thereby exceeds proper bounds (*musrif* & *isrāf*). Such iniquity is always paired with *iṣlāḥ*—wholesome order, self-reformation and righteous conduct which God intends humans to exhibit: *Create not disorder in the land after it was set in order/wa lā tufsidū fī l-arḍi ba'da iṣlāḥihā* (*Al-A'rāf*, 7:56), which may also be rendered *Create not insecurity in the land after it was made secure*.[357]

Prophetic utterances amplify and emphasise the centrality of this practice of conciliation and peacemaking. A well-known hadith narrated by the Companion Abu Ayyub al-Ansari states: 'The most meritorious act-of-charity (*afḍalu l-ṣadaqah*) is 'peacemaking' between conflicting parties.'[358] The Prophet is also reported to have instructed him: 'O Abū Ayyūb, truly let me tell you that by means of which God exalts one's reward and effaces sins: to walk in the cause of 'peacemaking' between people when they are mutually hating and stirring up dissension; it is an act of charity God loves being implemented.' In an oft-repeated tradition, Abu l-Dardā' reports the Prophet stating: 'Truly, let me tell you what is better than fasting and prayer and alms-giving: 'peacemaking' between conflicting parties (*ṣalāḥu dhāt al-bayn*); while 'stirring-up-dissension' between conflicting parties (*fasādu dhāt al-bayn*) is severing.'[359] The Prophet also strongly warned against backbiting and malicious gossip (*al-'iḍḍah* and *al-namīmah*) which provokes dissension and conflict between people, especially between wife and husband; while he affirmed that a lie may only be tolerated in three circumstances: in war, between husband and wife in order to effect reconciliation, and for 'peacemaking' between conflicting parties.[360]

A–M–N : *amn* and *amān* and *amānah,* 'safety – security – assurance of peace'; also *īmān* 'faith, secure belief (safeguarding from perdition)'. Verb *amina* (and *i'tamanahu*) denotes providing assurance of safety and security to a person, and conveys protection from harm and injury. Exhibiting security is a mark of reliable trustworthiness, itself viewed as a distinguishing characteristic of faith *īmān*. The utterance of the Prophet confirms this association: 'There is no faith for one who is untrustworthy/*lā īmāna li-man lā amānata lahu*.' In *Sūrat Al-An'ām*, 6:81–2, the term *amn* is used twice by Abraham to denote 'security' and 'peace', where true faith is free of injustice (*ẓulm*). While the legal application of *amān* or public security in the external political sphere is well known, the extension of *islām* into the interior domain of faith *īmān* is a crucial pairing all too often overlooked.

There were differing views among the legal and the theological schools on whether *īmān* was distinct from, or higher in value than, *islām*. The theological debate over conflating *islām* and *īmān* derives from the old Murji'ite position in the early doctrinal disputes over the status of the sinner, and the status of works for faith; yet the doctrinal consensus remains the necessity of works for *īmān*.[361] For the jurists, *islām* generally denotes the double 'confession of faith' (*al-shahādatayn*), being annexed to and complementary with faith (*īmān*). *Islām* is what is manifested by word or deed, and by means of which one's blood becomes secure from being shed. All Muslims agree that by embracing *islām* one departs from unfaith (*al-kufr*), and that it is the necessary precondition for applying laws of inheritance, validating marriage, legitimating prayer, alms tax, fasting, and pilgrimage.[362] In specific legal contexts juristic employment of the term *al-islām* echoed several archaic associations of related terms: *aslama amrahu ilayhi* ('delegate, entrust'); *aslama fī l-bay'* and *ta'āmala bi-l-salāmi* ('gave a down payment or security'); and the transaction procedure termed 'forward payment' *salam* سلم which involves paying a 'security' deposit to ensure future goods or services. Here the notion of security (safely securing delivery) is quite apparent. Legal usage also made definite equivalences between key terms: *al-ṣalāḥ = al-salāmah min al-'aybi; al-tasālum = al-taṣāluḥ;* and *al-ṣulḥ = al-silm* ('ending the state of war').

Ṣ–B–R : *ṣabr* 'long-suffering patience'—endurance of suffering for a higher cause. This fundamental virtue has a strong link with *jihad* ('total striving'), opening out on the pursuit of external security, conveying the sense of conscious sacrifice and suffering for a higher cause (which is the essence of non-violent action).

In numerous verses it is strongly emphasised that those who repent and act rightly by undertaking 'peacemaking' (*aṣlaḥū*) shall be rewarded and receive God's Compassionate forgiveness: e.g. *Al-Baqarah*, 2:160, 2:224; *Al-An'ām*, 6:48 (cf. *Al-Baqarah*, 2:62 & 69; *Al-Mā'idah*, 5:69); *Al-Anfāl*, 8:1; *Al-Shūrā*, 42:40, as well as *Al-Aḥzāb*, 33:70–1).

All these closely related concepts amplify the meanings of 'safety–security–faith/salvation' flowing from inward and outward resignation, or submission (*islām*). The total context requires one to align all such terms together for the full range of meaning to manifest, disclosing the comprehensive quality of the understanding of peace. *Islām* is inextricably bound up with the experience of safety and security at the individual moral level, and at the communal level of society and polity. A famous utterance of the Prophet confirms this most fundamental aspect of its meaning: 'The muslim is one from whom the Muslims are securely-safe from (harmful effects of) his tongue and his hand/ *al-muslimu man salima l-muslimūna min lisānihi wa yadih.*'[363] The core meaning 'safety from harm' and 'security from evil' is evident.

The Greeting of Peace (al-salāmu 'alaykum)

A distinctive characteristic of Muslims is the exchange of greetings, saluting one another with *al-Salāmu 'alaykum!* along with the response … *wa 'alaykum al-salām!*—usually translated as 'Peace be upon you!' and 'And upon you Peace!' (actually a shortened form of the complete phrase, see below.) Here *salām* is normally understood today as 'peace', while its sense might better be rendered: 'greetings of security-peace'.[364] This greeting is known as *taḥīyat al-islām,* 'the salutation of Islam',—conveying the hope for another person that God grant them a long successful life of peace secure from harm. A closer examination of this important phrase so frequently expressed on the lips of Muslims, confirms how inseparable the conceptions of security and peace are in Islamic experience.

Greetings in Prayer

A parallel use of this famous greeting occurs at the very conclusion of Islam's ritual prayer with the double salutation of *taslīm*,[365] first to one's right and then to the left, marking the completion of the formal *ṣalāt*. The act of *taslīm* involves dual repetition of the full phrase: *al-salāmu 'alaykum wa raḥmatu Allahi wa barakātuhu/Peace-Security be upon you, and God's Mercy and His Blessing.* The frequently uttered eulogy praising God's Messenger Muhammad—*May God bless him and give him peace/allā llāhu 'alayhi wa sallama*—conveys sincere benedictions and hopes that our Prophet enjoy the highest reward and beatitude in the Hereafter, namely in Paradise. Recall that *Dār al-Salām* ('The Abode of Peace-Security') refers to paradise—*Yūnus*, 10:25 states: *wa Allāhu yad'ū ilā dāri l-salāmi wa yahdī man yashā'u ilā ṣirāṭ mustaqīm/God invites to the Abode of Peace-Security and He guides whom He wills upon a straight path.* The faithful who gain entry to paradise by working good deeds attain to friendship with God, as *Sūrat Al-An'ām*, 6:127 states: *For them is the Abode of Peace with their Lord, and He is their Friend on account of what they performed.*

The *taslīm* is always preceded by the 'benediction of salutations', *al-taḥīyāt*,[366] forming an integral part of the ritual prayers, in which greetings and praises are pronounced upon God, while 'salutations of peace' are declared upon the Prophet and upon the righteous worshippers of God. In its fullest form at the end of the cycle of prostrations (two at dawn; three at sunset; or four at noon, mid-afternoon and eve),[367] it includes the portion of benedictions termed *al-tashahhud*—where the witnessing to God's Oneness and His Messenger is declared. It is noteworthy that these *taḥīyāt* voice 'salutations of peace' (both *al-salāmu* v*alayka,* and *al-salāmu 'alaynā*) upon the Prophet and one's fellow worshippers—but not specifically salutations upon God.

There remains another frequently repeated utterance closely associated with the *Taslīm* which completes the daily prayers, namely the supplication offered by the individual upon consummating each of the five daily prayers, affirming God as the ultimate source and origin of all peace. This beautiful invocation is not obligatory yet highly recommended, being known in Islamic tradition as the personal practice of God's Messenger and recorded in authoritative hadith:

> 'O God, You are Peace-Security (al-Salām), You are the Source of Peace, and Peace properly belongs to You.[368] So greet us Lord with the salutation 'Peace!' [fa-ḥayyinā rabbanā bi-l-salāmi], and admit us into the Paradise Gar-

> den the Abode of Peace. Blessed and Exalted are You our Lord, Possessor of Splendour and Reverence. (Text in the version reported by al-Tirmidhi and al-Nasai.)

The Muslim aspiration for peaceful security in this world and ultimate salvation and security in the hereafter is echoed in this prophetic supplication. This supports the reality that peace and security together involve both material and spiritual factors in the most inclusive sense. We may observe that here again, 'salutations of peace' are not uttered specifically upon God, although the word *salām* occurs five times. Here the phrase 'so greet us Lord with the salutation "Peace!"' intends our beseeching God to include us among the faithful admitted to paradise, and to whom He extends His glorious salutation of 'peace-security'.

This meaning is clearly established by related verses in the Qur'an affirming that the greatest boon the inhabitants of paradise may receive from God is His saluting them by the salutation of '*Peace!*': (*Yā Sīn*, 36:58), (*They will be greeted with*:) '*Peace!*'—*a word* (*of greeting*) *from the Merciful Lord*; and *Yūnus*, 10:9–10 portrays the faithful who perform good works as guided by God to Paradise, where: …*Their supplication therein shall be*, '*Glory be to Thee O God!*' and their salute to one another therein shall be '*Peace!*'. The highest degree of the faithful in paradise are 'the foremost', *al-sābiqūn*, who merit the outstanding grace described in *Al-Wāqi'ah* 56:25–6 whereby *They will hear therein no vain or sinful speech, only the word of salutation—'Peace, Peace!'*. Our highest hope and aspiration should be to reach the place where only the greetings and declarations of peace are uttered. Muslims are bidden to strive to achieve peace, just as they implore God to grant them peace.

Safety and Security

The Arab Jewish rabbi ʿAbdallah Ibn Salam, who embraced Islam soon after the Prophet Muhammad ﷺ migrated to Medina, described his very first encounter with God's Messenger in this way:[369]

> When the Prophet ﷺ arrived people crowded around him and I was among them. When his face became clearly visible, I knew that his face was not that of a liar. The first thing I heard him say was: 'Spread (the salutations of) "Peace", and feed the hungry food, and observe the bonds

> of kinship, and pray (night-vigils) while people are asleep! Thereby may you enter paradise with "peaceful/security". [The final phrase could also be rendered: '...enter Paradise greeted by (God's salutation of:) "Peace!"'[370]]

This unique utterance captures with beautiful concision several essential ethical values at the heart of Islam taught by the Prophet, and it is striking that in such an extremely brief catechism the term *salām* occurs twice. This reinforces the essential relevance of the term for Islam and requires little comment, save to recall that the phrase *Dār al-Salām* ('Abode of Peace/Security') refers to paradise: *wa Allahu yad'ū ilā dāri l-salāmi wa yahdī man yashā'u ilā ṣirāṭ* mustaqīm (*Yūnus*, 10:25, and compare *Al-An'ām*, 6:127).

Arabic morphologic–linguistic sources emphasise that *islām* as the name for the religious polity established by the Prophet Muhammad ﷺ is etymologically derived from *al-salāmah,* 'safety/security from harm/ evil' and 'avoidance of defects/vices'.[371] This conjunction with *al-salāmah* is very close to, or perhaps even coincides with, the notion of providing assurance of safety and security from harm conveyed by the greeting 'salutations of security/peace'—conveying the assurance and guarantee of peaceful intent and security from ultimate harm and evil. The authoritative eighth century Iraqi philologist Khalil b. Aḥmad (d. 179 AH) who authored the first etymological dictionary in Arabic, clarifies the link with the salutation *al-salāmu 'alaykum* instituted by Islam:

> *Al-salām* conveys the meaning of *al-salāmah*, so the saying by the people '*al-salāmu 'alaykum*' denotes '*al-salāmah from God be upon you*'. It is further stated that *al-Salām* is a name among God's Names; and it is said that (*al-Salām*) is God.[372] Thus if one says '*al-salāmu 'alaykum*' it may mean '*God is above you*' ... The term *al-islām* denotes 'seeking conformity *al-istislām* to God's command', denoting submission to His obedience and acceptance of His bidding/ *al-inqiyād li-ṭā'atihi wa l-qabūl li-amrih.*

Khalil was among the first to employ *inqiyād* ('submission' or 'self-resignation') as a main synonym for *al-islām*, something frequently repeated until the present day. Verbal *sallama* (as in *sallama amrahu ilā llāhi*/to resign oneself [one's cause or affair] to God), and verbal *aslama* (as in *aslama nafsahu* [*amrahu*] *ilā llāhi*/commit oneself, resign oneself to God's bidding), came by extension to signify 'to enter into the religion-polity of *al-Islām*' or 'enter into peace/security *al-salm*'. Furthermore, the nouns from the base form *silm* as well as *salm* were taken to be homonyms for *islām:* the religious polity and salvational faith-ethic originated by God's Messenger Muhammad.

This archaic linguistic analysis tracing the name of the faith *al-Islām* to the notion *al-salāmah*, 'safety/security from harm/evil', (understood as synonymous with *al-salām* 'salutations of security/peace') was indirectly supported by exegetes of the Qur'an who often asserted that God is named *al-Salām* on account of being free of defects and faults.[373] They observed that in the tongue of revelation God is not denominated *salīm* nor *sālim*, but only *al-Salām*. Nevertheless, a cogent critique of this earlier linguistic and exegetical consensus was offered by the twelfth century CE Andalusian scholar al-Suhayli (d. 581 AH) in his *Al-Rawḍ al-'Unf* regarding the *taḥīyah* (salutations of safety/security) and *al-Salām* as a Divine Name.[374] Suhayli based his interpretation squarely upon utterances of the majority of companions and early Muslim authorities, pointing to an alternative understanding overlooked in most contemporary discussion.

Suhaylī asserts: '*al-salām* سلام denotes one from whom others are safe/secure (*man sulima min-hu*), while *al-sālim* سالم denotes one who is safe/secure from others (*man salima min ghayrihi*)'. He argues that Qur'anic commentators have displaced the former with the latter's meaning, thereby contradicting the utterances of the pious forebears (*salaf*) who taught that *al-salāmah* سلامة is one quality among the characteristic-traits of *al-salām*. The presence of the *tā' marbūṭah* ة on *salāmah* points to a greater conceptual difference endowing this term with far more encompassing significance (just as with *al-jalāl* and *al-jalālah*). Therefore, in the *tashahhud* (the bearing witness to God as source of peace, pronounced after closing *taslīm* of ritual prayer) one does not utter: '*al-salāmu 'alā llāhi min 'ibādihi/salutations of safety/ security upon God from His servants*'. Yet *al-salām* is sought for and beseeched *from* God by His servants, as petition through prayer and gratitude for bounty; and this explains the form of this term in the *taḥīyah* or salute which man renders towards God—'...*wa min-hu al-salām*/and from Him (we seek bounty of) safety/security'.

Now Suhayli invokes an interesting proof text to support his view: the report in Ibn Hisham's *Sīrah* regarding the very early incident of prophetic revelation when Gabriel the Angel of revelation instructed God's Messenger Muhammad to convey to his wife Khadījah the salute or greeting from God—'*al-salāmu min rabbi-hā*/salutations of safety/security from her Lord'.[375]

> The Prophet said: 'O Khadījah, this is Gabriel, he extends salutations-of-peace from your Lord!' So Khadījah replied: 'God is Peace—and from Him comes 'safety/security'—and may salutations of safety/security be upon Gabriel/*Al-lahu l-Salāmu wa min-hu l-salāmu wa 'alā Jibrīli l-salām*.'

As Suhayli observes,[376] Khadījah rightly uttered: 'God is *al-salām* Peace'—because the term *al-salām* on the tongue of the creature is a petition for safety/security from the source of all security and safety; it cannot be an assertion of God's need for security from any harm. Therefore, states Suhayli, 'the meaning of her utterance 'God is *al-salām*' was her wisely thinking: "How can I respond to the divine salutation by my saying: 'Upon Him peace' [*'alayhi l-salām*/may security-safety be upon God], since safety/security comes from Him, and is beseeched of Him, and it is bestowed by Him?! But upon Gabriel [a created being] may there be safety/security."'

Indeed, Suhayli strongly emphasises that God, as *al-Salām* (Peace), must not be burdened with any defect or any fear of harm or injury, nor any variation or shortcoming—rather God bestows His care enclosing the entire creation (all creatures) within safety and security from harm or defect, due to His providential wise order. Thus God may be called 'Peace' on account of His being the ultimate source and goal of safety/security. One may conclude from this insightful passage by observing that *islām* primally mediates the notion of 'affording security from harm/injury to another', as well as 'resignation affording safety and peace/security to oneself'.

Peacemaking

One should pay closer attention to *salm* which is both masculine and feminine, and may be taken as either singular or plural. It was generally held that *al-silm* is equivalent or closely parallels *al-salm*. In the Qur'an's second chapter *Al-Baqarah*, 2:208, *yā ayyuhā l-lladhīna āmanū adkhulū fī l-silmi kāffat/O you who believe, enter ye into silm all-together*, it is clear that *silm* ('peace/reconciliation') is employed either as an attribute of faith *īmān*, and/or as synonymous with the religious polity of *islām*. Exegetes recognised the possibility of both readings in 2:208: either as *silm* (= *al-islām*), or as *salm* (= *al-ṣulḥ*, with confirmatory reference to *Al-Ḥujarāt*, 49:9).[377] Tabari's treatment of this marked difference of interpretation is quite informative, citing the authorities among Companions and Successors for both views. Those who read *al-silm* to denote the religious polity *islām* included Ibn ʿAbbas, Mujahid, al-Dahhak and al-Suddi as well as the majority of Kufan Qur'an reciters. Yet some understood *al-silm* here in the sense of *al-ṣulḥ*, 'peaceful-reconciliation'. However most of the Hijazi reciters read it with *fatḥah* as *al-salm*, construing its meaning as *al-ṣulḥ*, and/or *al-musālamah* [verbal noun of III], connoting abstention from war-making accompanied by payment of the poll tax (*jizyah*). Tabari argues for the preponderant reading *al-silm* as signifying the religious polity *al-islām* with an eye for its occasion of revelation. Addressing the 'believers' (*mu'minūn*), it makes no sense for God to bid them enter into *ṣulḥ* or *musālamah* since faithful Muslims obedient to the Prophet Muhammad ﷺ would not be in a state of war or enmity against God. This verse must therefore be addressing those 'faithful' who believed in previous prophets, and whom God expressly bid to recognize and acknowledge Muhammad as God's Messenger—given that faith in God is inseparable from acceptance of His Messenger and the message the Prophet Muhammad ﷺ conveys.

Tabari then provides plausible reasons for understanding *Sūrat Al-Baqarah*, 2:208 to have been sent down with reference to a party of the *Ahl al-Kitāb* who were being persuaded to embrace the totality of religious practice imposed by Islām. Even here there were different views among early authorities. Ibn ʿAbbas, Mujahid, and al-Dahhak upheld a general meaning covering the 'People of the Book' urging them to accept all obligatory practices imposed by God through His Messenger. However ʿIkrimah (a *mawlā* of Ibn ʿAbbas) asserted that this verse was sent down regarding leading Medinan Jews who had embraced Islam,[378] and who nevertheless requested of the Prophet permission to observe the Sabbath as a night of prayer vigil (in addition to the Islamic Friday) being a day sanctified by the Torah. Tabari concludes that *Al-Baqarah*, 2:208 applies to both the Muslim faithful who followed God's Messenger Muhammad ﷺ, as well as believing converts from among the 'People of the Book', all urged to observe the totality of obligatory practices and limits enjoined by God in His revelation to the Prophet. The *ta'wīl* attributed to Mujahid (*... adkhulū fī l-a'māli kāffat*)[379] serves to confirm Tabari's consensus judgement, a model of his critical method of *al-tafsīr bi-l-ma'thūr*.

Nevertheless, in *Sūrat Al-Anfāl*, 8:61 the term *salm* clearly denotes 'peace/making' as the antonym of 'war/bloodshed':

> ...wa in janaḥū li-l-salmi fa-ajnaḥ la-hā wa tawakkal ʿalā llāhi innahu huwa l-samīʿu l-ʿalīmu/*yet if they then incline toward peace, then do you likewise incline, and rely utterly on* God *[O Muhammad] for* He *is All-Hearing All-Knowing.*

Here in *Al-Anfāl*, 8:61, *al-salm* 'peace/making' may best be construed in the sense of *al-ṣulḥ*.[380] This directive for *al-ṣulḥ* is conditioned upon the best interests of the Muslims: that *al-Islām* be manifested over unbelief. The unspoken directive implied at the beginning of this verse is explicitly supplied by Tabarī: 'when you suspect deceit and duplicity, then deal with them in the same manner by announcing hostilities'. Otherwise, there is no divine bidding to initiate peacemaking, but only to respond in kind when the opposing party itself initiates peacemaking overtures. Likewise in *Sūrat Muḥammad*, 47:35 (*...wa tad'ū ilā l-salmi...*), where God in fact bids His Messenger to refrain from peacemaking with those of unbelief. Tabari had earlier remarked: '*As for initiating the inviting them to peaceful/reconciliation/ al-ṣulḥ, this is not found in the Qur'an*.'[381] Therefore, the initiative for peacemaking in the conflict with those of unbelief (Arab pagans) is entirely dependent upon their intentions and actions, an eminently practical and soberly cautious position. If the opposing party freely inclines to peaceful-reconciliation (negotiating a treaty), or accepts to render *jizyah* and/or subjugation, then *al-salm* 'peacemaking' (i.e., *al-ṣulḥ*) is divinely bidden. There must always be a peaceful response in response to a peacemaking initiative offered by the opposing party.

Tabari next raises a very important point of dissension among early commentators over whether *Al-Anfāl,* 8:61 bidding *al-ṣulḥ* had been abrogated by one or another of the 'fighting' verses bidding the faithful to combat the pagans (*al-mushrikūn*) unequivocally without respite — namely *Sūrat Al-Tawbah*, 9:5, 29, 36.[382] According to many reputable early authorities among the successors including Qatadah, ʿIkrimah, al-Suddi, Ibn Zayd and al-Hasan al-Basri, after the sending down of the *barā'ah* verse terminating pagan observances sometime in year 8 AH the earlier divine bidding to respond peacefully to peacemaking initiatives had been cancelled or abrogated (*nasakhah*), and divine bidding now enjoined unmitigated fighting against them until they made submission and proclaimed 'There is no divinity save The Divinity!'. In other words, these great successors maintained that *Al-Anfāl,* 8:61 was abrogated by a universal call upon the Muslims to pursue *jihad*. Now Tabari explicitly asserts that such an interpretation: '...has no evidence in Revelation, nor in Prophetic practice, nor in the innate human constitution of reason!'[383] This is indeed a very strong statement seemingly contravening a semi-consensus of the second generation Muslim scholars, and it must be heeded with full appreciation of Tabari's deep knowledge of all three factors he mentioned.[384] He strongly denies the widespread allegation that the divine bidding to respond to peaceful initiatives of peacemaking with corresponding peaceful conciliation was ever actually cancelled. The reason again is securely based on his expert knowledge of the 'occasions of revelation': the revealed verse *Al-Anfāl,* 8:61: *yet if they then incline toward peace, then do you likewise incline*, was sent down with regard to the Jewish tribe of Banu Qurayzah[385] (who thus belonged to the 'People of the Book'). Whereas the verse in *Al-Tawbah*, 9:5 *so fight the idolaters wherever you come across them,* was sent down regarding the pagan Arabs who served idols and fiercely resisted Muhammad's mission—from whom acceptance of *jizyah* was not permitted! Therefore, neither of these two verses could conceivably cancel the other, for both actually continued to be in full force given that they refer to two different groups in conflict or rivalry with the Medinan Muslim community, and who were treated with distinctly dissimilar policies. Similarly, a *ta'wīl* attributed to Mujahid is cited to confirm this interpretation, along with a supporting statement from Ibn Ishaq.[386]

Submit! You shall be Secure

These limited samples drawn from the wealth of exegetical literature alert us to lessons to be drawn for proper understanding of *al-salm* as the chief Islamic term for peacemaking. Such materials must be coordinated with corresponding insights drawn from early historical and literary sources, including the letters dispatched by the Prophet to neighbouring rulers and chiefs, as well as significant utterances by leading companions defining *islām* in relation to *īmān*—particularly several proclamations by the fourth Caliph ʿAlī b. Abi Talib which deserve extended attention. We will quickly draw attention to the Muslim historical tradition that dates the dispatching by the Prophet Muhammad of emissaries bearing letters to the great powers of his era (*ilā mulūk al-ʿajam*) late in year 6 AH (or possibly early in year 7). This was after the pact of Hudaybiyah during the interval of the *hudnah* or truce between the pagan Meccans and Muslims. These documents have not been properly scrutinised by occidental scholars for the historical data they shed on the initial spread of Islam, nor for the Prophet Muhammad's geostrategic policy. Generally they are dismissed in western Islamic studies as 'obvious forgeries' of the Umayyad era. These documents actually demand careful scrutiny, and have been unjustly maligned and neglected by non-Muslim scholars. Nevertheless, recent research on the linguistic, epigraphic and epistolary reality of the Near East and Arabia during the fourth to the seventh centuries CE may open the door to a fresh evaluation of these documents.[387] The relevant letters occur in early sources (Ibn Saʿd, Abu ʿUbayd al-Qasim b. Sallam, etc.) and were later gathered in more extensive compilations such as the fourteenth century CE Ibn Hudaydah's *al-Miṣbāḥ al-Muḍī* (vol. II *mukātabāt* pp. 3–323).[388]

The texts of the letters alleged to have been sent to the four great rulers of Abyssinia, Egypt, Byzantium and Sasanian Iran (as well as to a number of lesser authorities in the Arabian peninsula and Near East), all repeat in closely parallel form a similar phrase, usually at the start of the Prophet's actual message after the introductory address:

> *Aslim! Taslam*/ Submit!—You shall be secure. *Or*: Enter into *Islām!* [Be at peace!]—You shall achieve peace/security (from injury/harm and threat of conflict).

Is it possible to understand by this terse pregnant phrase reference to both the external political relation, and at the same time the interior religious condition of acceptance of the authority of God's Messenger mediating divine guidance inducing assurance of salvation? If these powerful rulers chose to recognise the authority and power of the Prophet heading the religious polity of *al-Islām* (centered in the Medinan ummah) and the dominion of the One God, they join the salvific community and gain worldly *and* other-worldly security.

Captive of Divinity

Before completing this concise review of the primary significance of *salm* we may draw attention to a little-noted connotation reflecting an archaic reality with direct bearing on the religion *al-Islām*. In ancient Semitic usage one finds a prevalence of theophorous names where the human is designated the 'client' or 'devotee' [*lit.* 'captive'] of the god. Cognate employment in Hebrew and Phoenician of names denoting the 'client of El' (*gêr*/c.f. Arabic *jār*) are frequent, as with the parallel term *taym* 'devotee' or 'lover' (Arabic *taym allāh*). This has a particularly striking parallel in Palmyrene with the proper name *Salm*. It is worth citing the great Scottish Arabist W. Robertson Smith on this convergence, perhaps the first scholar to point explicitly to its bearing on Arabic Islamic usage.[389]

> In Arabic proper, where the relation of protector and protected had a great development, and whole clans were wont to attach themselves as dependants to a more powerful tribe, the conception of god and worshipper as patron and client appears to have been specially predominant… . To the same conception may be assigned the proper name *salm*, 'submission', shortened from such theophorous forms as the Palymyrene *salm al-Lāt*, 'submission to Lāt', and corresponding to the religious use of the verb *istalama*, 'he made his peace', to designate the ceremony of kissing, stroking, or embracing the sacred stone at the Caaba… .

(According to the authority of Professor Ihsan ʿAbbas, the name *salām* [or perhaps *salm*?] occurred in pre-Islamic poetry as the designation of a particular divinity; regrettably we have not been able to pursue his hint further.[390]) One may invoke the common appellation *'abd Allāh* 'servant of God' ['captive' of the Divinity?], signifying the status of dependence and obligation involved in worship and service of the divine (*ʿibādah*). In other words, it is advisable to avoid some common associations evoked by the English 'submission' or 'surrender' when apprehending the proper meaning for *islām*. The supreme divinity conceived as King, Lord or Master naturally provoked the notion of the human subject as servant, resigned captive or submissive worshipper. The 'submission' involved is voluntary and freely rendered, while simultaneously bearing a communal political import.

A fundamental consideration to be kept in mind: 'The parallelism in ancient society between religious and political institutions is complete', for both spheres are conceived as being 'parts of one whole of social custom'.[391] This observation is a truism for the early Islamic reality, yet is often overlooked by contemporary Euro-American thinkers who frequently lapse into the assumption projected by Enlightenment modernity of the necessary or preferred separation of the religious from the political realm. The idea of a religion being accepted by voluntary submission, expressed by the name *al-Islām*, may not be divorced from the strategic political and cultural conditions through which it emerged in history. Religion was in that era accompanied by political rights and unfolded historically against the background of political power.[392]

Was the primordial religious polity of *Islām* centered primarily on the search for dominion and authority in this world? If the argument that Islām embraces simultaneously a religious polity and a salvational faith is valid, then what of its inner salvific dimension nurtured in the heart and mind of the individual believer? More investigation into the nexus of *islām* as both a religious polity and sociopolitical community born in historical context, and the deeply lived experience of individuals who have their presence and world view moulded by that historical community, has to be accomplished if we are to bring clarity to the quest for an authentic understanding of peace. The dual components of establishing a polity and nurturing a living faith coexist at a very deep level.

The relevance of religious ideals to human security appears to find a particularly compelling example in Islam. This invites more intensive exploration, and should be integrated with current concerns about deepening the understanding of security to include spiritual and ethical components. Complementing the emphasis on just polity and an equitable social order, Islamic teachings offer specific ideals and practices for active reconciliation between individuals and groups. Islam thereby sought a balance between the political dictates of justice and equity, and those of human clemency, harmony, and selfless love embraced by the notion of *al-iḥsān* 'surpassing goodness':

> *Surely God enjoins justice and the 'doing-good-to-others' [al-'adl wa l-iḥsān], and giving (to others) like unto (one's own) kin, and forbids indecency and manifest evil and unjust oppression.* (*Al-Naḥl*, 16:90)

CHAPTER TEN

HUMAN DIGNITY FROM AN ISLAMIC PERSPECTIVE

Professor Mohammad Hashim Kamali

Dignity is a composite concept that can embrace a variety of objective values and those which may be relative and subjective in the context of particular legal and cultural traditions. The values that dignity subsumes are also liable to change with new developments in science and technology, as well as with the mobility and interaction of peoples and cultures. Broadly speaking, from a legal perspective, human dignity connotes inviolability of the human person, recognition of a set of rights and obligations and guarantee of safe conduct by others, including the society and state. Juristic positions and human dignity also tend to have implications on a global scale as to whether the world communities and cultures accord dignity and inviolability to the other concerning Islam and Muslims are divided. Islam recognises dignity as an inherent right to all human beings regardless of colour and creed. This being the basic position, a certain level of internal disagreement in the Islamic juristic thought itself does not exist, just as negative trends in Muslim-non-Muslim relations have been on the increase in recent years that have altogether added to apprehension and scepticism on both sides.

This text explores human dignity through a study of the Qur'an and Hadith (sayings of the Prophet Muhammad), the two most authoritative sources of Islam that profoundly influence the Muslim psyche and conduct in almost all Muslim communities. Then follows a brief review of the juristic positions of the leading schools of Islamic law on the subject, and then concluding remarks on the effect of these guidelines on the realities of Muslim life.

Since the subject before us occupies a substantial number of Qur'anic passages and Hadith reports, I shall divide them into a few clusters around the following themes:

1) Direct scriptural evidence on human dignity.
2) Passages in the Qur'an and Hadith that characterise the God-Man relationship.
3) Evidence of concern to relations of human beings among themselves, within and outside the fold of Islam.
4) A brief review of the position of leading schools of Islamic jurisprudence.
5) The impact of these guidelines on the realities of Muslim life.

Textual Evidence on Human Dignity

The most explicit affirmation of human dignity (*karāmah*) is found in God's illustrious speech in the Qur'an, in a general and unqualified declaration: *We have bestowed dignity on the children of Adam (laqad karramnā banī Adama) ... and conferred upon them special favours above the greater part of Our creation (Al-'Isrā',* 17:70).

The reference to *the greater part of Our creation* in this verse is explained elsewhere in parts of the Qur'an where the text elaborates the manifestations of human dignity by declaring, for instance, the spiritual ranking of human beings above those of the angels on one hand and the devil (Iblis) on the other. In one such passage *(Al-A'rāf,* 7:11), the angels and Iblis were asked to bow down to Adam but only the angels bowed down, not so Iblis. Iblis asserted its own superiority, as the text recounts: *You created Adam from [humble] clay and created me from fire!* God's displeasure with this response was then conveyed in a question to Iblis: *what prevents thee from prostrating thyself to one whom I created with My Own Hand ?* (*Ṣād*, 38:75–6).

The subject is then taken up again in another context where God declared His intention to the angels that *I am about to appoint a vicegerent in the earth.* The angels protested, as the text goes, and said: *we extol and glorify Thee*, whereas Man is prone to corruption and bloodshed. Then the angels were told: *surely I know what you know not.* This is immediately followed by the affirmation: *And God taught Adam the names of all things...* (*Al-Baqarah*, 2:30–2), which would seem to suggest that knowledge and the capacity to learn are relevant to the dignity and nobility of humans. A level of intimacy and closeness is also shown in God's affirmation that *I created (Adam) with My own Hand.* For in most other places where a reference occurs to God's creation, it is often said that God commands or wills so and so and it becomes. But even more explicitly, this intimacy is shown in God's illustrious affirmation: *And I breathed into him (Adam) of My Own spirit* (*Ṣād*,38:72).

The spiritual superiority of humankind in the foregoing verses is then further supplemented by references to their physical constitution in places, for example, where it is declared: *Indeed, We created humankind in the best of forms;* and *We fashioned you in the best of images...* (*Al-Tīn*, 95:12; *Al-Taghābun*, 64:3). It is reported in a hadith that the Prophet stood one day in front of the Ka'bah, the holiest of all places known to Islam, and said in a symbolic language:

> 'You are most pure and most dignified, but the One in whose hands Muhammad's life reposes, the sanctity and honour of a believer, his life and his property, is far greater in the eyes of God'.[393]

The Qur'anic vision of dignity for the human race as depicted in these passages has been upheld, more specifically, in its references to the Muslim community, whom God has ranked in honour (*al-'izzah*) next to His own illustrious Self and that of His Messenger, Muhammad (*Al-Munāfiqūn*, 63:8). The Qur'anic designation of the Muslim community is also that of *a community of moderation* (*ummatan wasatan*, *Al-Baqarah*, 2:143), committed to the promotion of good and rejection of evil (*Āl 'Imrān*, 3:110), dedicated to the vindication of truth and justice (*Āl 'Imrān*, 3:103). To quote the Holy Book: *The believers, both men and women, are friends and protectors of one another; they enjoin good and they forbid evil.* (*Al-Tawbah*, 9:71) This is translated more pragmatically in the following hadith: 'If any of you sees something evil, he should set it right with his hand; if he is unable to do so, then with his tongue, and if he is unable to do even that, then (let him denounce it) in his heart. But this is the weakest form of faith.'[394] We may add here the point that there is no evidence anywhere in the sources to say that non-Muslims may not participate in the promotion of good or prevention and rejection of evil.[395] In two of his other sayings, the Prophet ﷺ is also quoted to have said: 'the best part of faith is to have beautiful manners';[396] and that: 'I have been sent in order to perfect moral virtues (among you).'[397]

The overall picture that emerges is summed up in the Qur'an commentator al-Alusi's observation that 'everyone and all members of the human race, including the pious and the sinner, are endowed with dignity'.[398] Twentieth century Muslim jurists and commentators have also gone on record to note that dignity is not earned by meritorious conduct; it is established as an expression of God's grace; and also that dignity is a natural and absolute right which inheres in every human person as of the moment of birth. It is God-given and natural; hence no individual nor state may take it away from anyone. As for the question whether dignity also remains intact of a criminal, the general answer provided is in the affirmative with the proviso, however, that it is partially compromised to the extent that a court decision on punishment may be enforced, even if punishment involves some erosion of dignity, but beyond that the personal dignity of prisoners must also be protected and observed. It follows then that prisoners should not be subjected to arbitrary and humiliating treatment nor to deprivation of their basic needs.[399]

Rights and obligations are a manifestation of human dignity in all major legal traditions and the shari'ah is no exception. There may be some differences of orientation among legal systems, but as far as Islamic law is concerned the emphasis is not so much on rights and obligations as it is on justice. A balanced approach to rights and duties should thus be realised through impartial justice. Yet for reasons that orated, Islamic law tends to be more emphatic on duties than rights.[400] I have advanced the view that human dignity provides a more objective basis of a modern doctrine of human rights in Islam, in preference perhaps, to the rights-based approach of the contemporary human rights discourse that places a much greater emphasis on rights compared to obligations. My research further indicates, however, that a duty-based approach to human rights is also not in total harmony with the Qur'anic conception of justice.[401]

Critics have voiced the view that dignity is a moral rather than a legal concept, and that violation of human dignity is not the same as violation of an entrenched right. Thus according to one observer, 'To violate a right goes well beyond merely falling short of some high moral standard'.[402] A partial response to this is that the five universals objectives of the shari'ah, known as *al-darūriyyāt* (to which a sixth, namely personal honour (*al-'irḍ*) was subsequently added), do take human dignity into a rights-based concept. I shall have more to say on this in my examination of juristic positions below.[403]

God-Man Relationship

The Qur'an is expressive, in a variety of places and contexts, of God's love for humanity, so much so that it becomes a characteristic feature of this relationship. This aspect of the God-Man relationship has not, however, received a balanced treatment in many of the Orientalist works I have seen, which are preoccupied with themes such as God's absolute power, God as an unrelenting judge, man as the servant of God and so forth.[404] A similar tendency is noted even among the Muslim commentators of the Qur'an, especially in the *tafsīr bi'l-ma'thūr* (precedent-based interpretation) genre of *tafsīr*, such as those of Ibn Jarir al-Tabari (d.923), Jalal al-Din al-Suyuti (d. 1505) and the works also of many shari'ah jurists who envision a somewhat distant and impersonal God that accentuates His majesty, imperium and justice much more than His intimacy and love for human beings.[405] This tendency in *tafsīr* and *fiqh* works has not remained unnoticed and has invoked criticism from many a leading Sufi and mystic of Islam. The Sufis have taken the jurists and even the Qur'an commentators to task for their preoccupation with a rule-based religion, for downsizing God's love (*maḥabbah*) for humankind, and for the latter's devotion to Him, that so unmistakeably feature in the Qur'an and Hadith. The Sufis are well-known for their rich and effusive expression of a profound devotion *('ishq)* through which God and humankind relate to one another. We believe love (*mahabbah*) and mercy (*raḥmah*) animate all aspects of God's relations with humankind and that God conferred dignity (*karāmah*) on human beings as a manifestation of His unbounded love.

God's love is manifested in His oft repeated expression of mercy for humanity in the Qur'an,[406] in His expression of trust in the nobility of Man, endowing mankind with the faculty of reason and bestowing on them immense capacity for knowledge and understanding.[407] God's expression of trust is also manifested in His appointment of humankind as His vicegerent in the earth (*Al-Baqarah*, 2:30–2), and His recurrent affirmation on the subjugation of the heavens and the earth for human benefit.[408] Other manifestations of favour are found in the Divine providence of availing to humankind the enjoyments of this life and its adornments, espoused with reminders that they should not neglect their fair share in them.[409] In an address to the Prophet Muhammad, God speaks in such terms: *When My servants ask you about Me, say that I am indeed close to them and I listen to the prayer of every supplicant when he calls on Me;* and *Surely We have created Man; We know the promptings of his heart, and We are nearer to him even than his jugular vein* (*Al-Baqarah*, 2:186; *Qāf*, 50:16). In a long Qudsi hadith (a variety of hadith wherein God speaks directly without the Prophet's intermediation) that al-Bukhari has recorded from Abu Hurayrah, God the Most High said:

> *One who offends any of My friends is like declaring war against Me… and My servant gets closer to Me through good deeds until I love him, and when I love him, I become like his ear by which he hears, and like the eye by which he sees, like his hand by which he reaches out, and I walk with him; when he asks Me, I give, and when he seeks protection through Me, I protect him.*[410]

These and other similar pronouncements may be seen as God's unconditional expressions of love and grace for humanity, which may be distinguished from other expressions that contemplate certain behaviour patterns, as are reviewed below.

In numerous places the Qur'an is expressive of God's love, in its typical phrase, *inn Allāh yuḥibbu* ('God loves') those who are good to others (*inna Allāh yuḥibbu al-muḥsinīn,* (*Al-Baqarah*, 2:195)); those who are just in their dealings with others (*al-muqsitīn*, *Al-Mā'idah*, 5:42), those who remain patient in the face of adversity (*al-ṣābirīn,* (*Āl 'Imrān,* 3:146)), those who are conscious of Him (*al-muttaqin*, (*Al-Tawbah*, 9:4)), those who observe purity and cleanliness (*al-mutaṭahhirīn*, (*Al-Baqarah,* 2:222)), those who repent and return to Him (*al-tawwabīn*, (*Al-Baqarah,* 2:222)), those who place their trust in Him (*al-mutawakkilīn*, (*Āl 'Imrān,* 3:159)) and so forth. In an unusually candid language, God has elsewhere addressed His beloved Prophet Moses in these terms: *And I cast My love over you in order that you may be reared under My eye* (*Ṭā Hā*, 20:39).

This theme is pursued further in other places where God's love is denied in the typical phrase *inna Allāha lā yuḥibbu* ('God loves not') to the aggressors, to the unjust, to those who spread corruption, to the arrogant and the boastful, the deniers of faith in Him, the treacherous, the prodigals and so forth.[411] Yet the Qur'anic dictum is varied in its expressions when it declares, for example, in another verse: *O My servants who have transgressed against their souls! Despair not of the mercy of God, for God forgives all sins. He is most forgiving, most merciful.* (*Al-Zumar*, 39:53).

Other manifestations of God-Man relations in the Qur'an are found in the affirmation and grant of freedom and moral autonomy for human beings (*Al-Rūm*, 30:30); in its declaration that *there shall be no compulsion in religion* (*Al-Baqarah*, 2:256); and again: *Let whosoever wills, believe, and whosoever wills, disbelieve* (*Al-Kahf*, 18:29). The Qur'an also declared in an address to the Prophet: *anyone who accepts guidance does so for his own good, but one who wantonly goes astray, then tell him that 'I am only a warner'.* (*Al-Naml*, 27:92)

Relations among Fellow Humans

The Qur'anic vision of humankind is that of a single fraternity which is endorsed by the affirmation of the unity and equality of all of its members. Thus in a reference to the creation of humankind it is provided: *God created you from a single soul (khalaqakum min nafsin wāḥidatin) and created its mate of the same (kind) and created from them multitudes of men and women....* Then they are all enjoined, in the same verse, to *observe the ties of kinship (al-arḥām) among yourselves* (*Al-Nisā'*, 4:1).

It is significant that the text accentuates the bonds of fraternity among humans with the expression *al-arḥām* (ties of kinship), a term usually employed in the Qur'an in the context of family relations and inheritance.[412] Another point of note in this passage is its phrase *He created you form a single soul,* which also occurs identically elsewhere in the text (*Al-Zumar*, 39:6), both implying that Eve was, not as it is sometimes erroneously claimed, created from Adam's rib, but created in a like manner of the essence of that single soul. This single soul emanates, it seems, in God's own illustrious spirit, hence its dignified origin of the highest order. What is in common between Adam and Eve is this soul, implied by the reference to it in the female singular (i.e. *minhā*—in the phrase *wa khalaqa minhā zawjahā*—and created from it its pair), which could not be a reference to Adam, but to that single soul. The Prophet Muhammad has endorsed this message of unity and equality in the following hadith: 'O people! Your Creator is one; you are from the same ancestor; all of you are from Adam, and Adam was created from earth.'[413] In the matter of reward and punishment, the Qur'an declares men and women absolutely equal,[414] and there is no notion of an original sin in the Qur'an either. In sum, since Islam subscribes to a broad human fraternity of equals, 'there could be no affront to the human dignity of any single person without there being an affront to the dignity of all'.[415] Since dignity is God-given, no human person or … has the authority to deny it to anyone nor to deprive another human being of his or her dignity.

The Qur'an views marriage as a basis of friendship and compassion (*muwaddah wa raḥmah)* where spouses find tranquillity and companionship and they are a 'protective garment' to each other's dignity and honour.[416] Parents are elevated to a position almost of divinity, and offspring is enjoined to treat them, in words and in deeds, with utmost dignity, in the spirit of benevolence (*iḥsān)* and submission (*Al-Isrā'*, 17:23). The text places special emphasis on being grateful to one's mother (*Luqmān*, 31:14). Parents are also enjoined to observe the natural ties of love and affection with their children, who are the adornments of life and a litmus test also of failure and success. The most meritorious legacy anyone can leave behind is a virtuous offspring (*Al-Kahf*, 18:46).

As for the dignified encounter and treatment of one's fellow humans, the Qur'an in numerous places enjoins affection and fraternity with everyone, within and outside the family, especially to one's neighbours. The believers are declared as brethren to one another (*Al-Ḥujurāt*, 49:15) and enjoined, in unqualified language, to speak to everyone with courtesy and tact (*Al-Baqarah*, 2:83); and then again *when you speak, speak with justice; … and in pursuit of righteousness* (*Al-An'ām*, 6:52; *Al-Aḥzāb*, 33:70). In numerous places, the text warns the believer, indeed all people, to avoid harbouring ill-feeling, rancour, suspicion, backbiting and espionage against one another.

In their dealing with non-Muslims and followers of other faiths, Muslims are enjoined to do justice and be good to them so long as they do not resort to acts of hostility and oppression against them (*Al-Mumtaḥanah*, 60:8). In the matter of engaging in disputation and discourse with non-Muslims, the believers are further directed to *reason with them in the best manner possible;* and *argue not with the followers of Scripture except in the fairest manner* (*Al-Naḥl*, 16:125, *Al-'Ankabūt*, 29:46).The general guideline that applies to everyone is also set in such terms that *there shall be no hostility except against the oppressors* (*Al-Baqarah*, 2:193). An act of aggression may be punished with its equivalent but no more than that (*Al-Baqarah*, 2:194). The text, moreover, enjoins everyone to *avoid aggression, for God loves not the aggressors* (*Al-Baqarah*, 2:190), but those who exercise patience and forgiveness will have their rewards from God (*Al-Naḥl*, 16:126). The Prophet has added his voice in confirmation to say: 'people are God's children and those dearest to Him are the one's who treat His children kindly.'[417] He also said: 'whoever believes in God and the Last Day, let him speak when he has something good to say, or else remain silent.'[418] In another hadith, the Prophet has been quoted to have said: 'God will punish (in the hereafter) those who punish people in this world.'[419]

Another manifestation of human dignity in Islam is the grant of moral autonomy to the people, as in the renowned hadith: 'There is no obedience in transgression; obedience is due only in righteous conduct.'[420] The Prophet is reported to have declared further that: 'The best form of jihad is to tell a word of truth to a tyrannical ruler.'[421]

Juristic Positions

Three interrelated concepts of Islamic law of relevance to human dignity that are featured in the scholastic jurisprudence of the leading schools (*madhāhib*) are *'iṣmah* (inviolability), humanity and personhood (*ādamiyyah*) and the five (or six) universals collectively known as al-*ḍarūriyyāt*, as previously mentioned. These are life, intellect, religion, family, property, and honour, which constitute the overriding goals and values of Islam that must be protected as a matter of priority by all concerned. [422] The two basic positions that are taken on these objectives and principles may be labelled respectively as universalist and communalist. The universalist camp is spearheaded by the Hanafi school of law, whereas the preponderant view of the other leading schools tends to take communalist postures on these concepts. The Hanafi school commands the widest following in present day Muslim countries, compared to any of the other leading schools, namely the Shafi'i, Maliki, Hanbali and the Shi'ah: About fifty percent of the world's Muslims are followers of the Hanafi school. The universalists take an affirmative stance on the recognition of *'iṣmah* for all humans regardless of religion, gender, race and the like. Human dignity is thus a natural endowment that everyone obtains by the mere fact of being human. Everyone's dignity, life, property and other rights are sacrosanct and inviolable, without any discrimination. Full and equal protection is therefore extended to all alike.

The communalist position maintains, on the other hand, that *'iṣmah* is established not by the fact of one's being a human, but by being a believer in Islam. Non-Muslims are consequently not qualified for *'iṣmah* unless they make a treaty with the Muslim state and secure their protection by virtue of a commitment (*dhimmah*). This view is spearheaded by the Imam al-Shafi'i (d. 820 CE) and has also found support with the other leading imams, namely Ahmad Ibn Hanbal (d. 855), Malik (d. 795) Daud al-Zahiri (d. 885) and the Shi'ite scholars such as al-Tusi (d. 1274) and his contemporary 'Allamah al-Hilli. They advanced the argument that the injunction on fighting the disbelievers in the Qur'an and Hadith is couched in a general language which supersedes the grant of *'iṣmah* to them.[423] Recep Senturk has drawn the conclusion from his research that the category of universal human rights that exists in the Hanafi concept of *adamiyyah* does not hold in the legal thought of the advocates of the communalist position, who have generally relied on the religiously defined categories of Muslims and non-Muslims.[424]

Imam Abu Hanifah (d. 767), the leading advocate of the universalist position, established a nexus between *ādamiyyah* and *'iṣmah* and maintained that being a progeny of Adam, whether Muslim or not, creates the legal basis for possession of both. His position is summarised in the phrase, *al-'ismah bi'l-ādamiyyah*—inviolability inherent in being human. Abu Hanifah's understanding of the Qur'an and hadith on fighting the disbelievers maintains that they are on the whole contextual, often referring to warlike situations and active military engagement between the pagans of Mecca and the nascent Muslim community of the time.[425] 'A human's religious choice must also be honoured,' wrote al-Sarakhsi (d.1090), 'even if it is contrary to Islamic teaching.' Sarakhsi further observed that everyone's life must be protected because only a living person can respond to the Divine call of religion, and his faculty of reason must be protected too, as this too is the only means by which he can understand and determine values. Everyone's mind must be honoured and protected 'even if they oppose the way we think'.[426] Al-Sarakhsi went on to add that freedom and the right to own property are endowed in humans from the moment of birth. The insane child and the sane adult stand on the same footing, in so far as these rights are concerned. This is how personhood is established in a human being, to create in him the capacity to bear rights and obligations.[427]

Another prominent Hanafi jurist, al-Marghinani, criticised the communalist view and wrote that the argument of al-Shafi'i to take religion as the criterion of *'iṣmah* is unacceptable. This is because 'protection is attached, not to Islam, but to the person', as it is the person who is the audience of religion and the carrier of obligations imposed by the law. People would be unable to receive the message and give a meaningful response to it unless they were immune from aggression in the first place. The person is, therefore, the original locus of protection, which means that *'iṣmah* inheres in all human beings.[428]

Ibn 'Abidin (d. 1834 CE), another leading voice in the Hanafi school, confirmed the universalist position of the school of his following and wrote that 'a human being is honoured, even if he is a non-Muslim (*al-ādamī mukarram wa law kāfiran*)'.[429] We are required to protect the sanctity of all humanity. Muslims must therefore defend the *'iṣmah* and the human rights of non-Muslims. Hence, each individual, community and state bears the responsibility to protect the *'iṣmah* of all human beings.

The universalist position crossed the boundaries of the Hanafi school of jurisprudence and gained followers from other schools. Many leading figures, including Abu Hamid al-Ghazali from the Shafi'i school, Ibn Rushd al-Qurtubi, Ibrahim al-Shatibi, and Ibn 'Ashur from the Maliki school, Ibn Taymiyyah and Ibn Qayyim al-Jawziyyah from the Hanbali, and Javad Mughniyyeh from the Ja'fari Shi'ite school have supported the universalist position on human dignity and *'iṣmah*.[430]

The Hanafi school remained influential until early the twentieth century, but European colonialism and the role it played in the fall of the Ottoman state, as well as the subsequent rise of the contemporary 'Islamic' states have negatively impacted the universalist doctrine. The communalist position consequently found renewed support in the views of many prominent scholars in the Arabian Peninsula, Egypt, North Africa and Iran. The universalist position suffered a steady decline and it remains conspicuously absent in the modern discourse of human rights in the Muslim world. Muslim jurists and commentators of recent times tend to be supportive of the universality of human rights, which they tend to assert, however, not through the scholastic approaches reviewed above but through direct recourse to the sources evidence of the Qur'an and Sunnah.[431]

Concluding Remarks

If one were to broadly characterise Islamic and Western cultures one might say Islam, generally, accentuates human dignity whereas Western culture tends to emphasise liberty. It is a question obviously of relative emphasis, as Western culture also puts a high premium on dignity. Bedouin culture in the history of the Arabs had a highly developed sense of personal honour and customary methodology that revolved around the preservation of dignity. Manliness and nobility of character (*murū'ah*), hospitality and honouring one's guest, and also a greater stress on one's obligation to others than on one's own rights, characterised Arab culture, and to a large extent also the teachings of Islam. These dignitarian concepts also penetrated other Muslim communities and cultures outside the Arabian peninsula and had enormous consequences on the gender question and issues of war and peace. In cases where Muslims were in rebellion against the status quo, a substantial cultural reason for the rebellion has been a perceived collective dignity. Ali Mazrui has rightly alluded, in a 2002 interview, to the relevance of this factor in the rebellion of Muslims in Chechnya, Palestine, Macedonia, Kashmir, Kosovo and even Nigeria.

Without wishing to embrace Huntington's articulation of the clash of civilisations in a broad sweep, a clash of cultures did occur, in my view, when, addressing the Taliban, then President Bush used the language of ultimatum when he said: 'Just hand over Osama bin Laden and his thugs. There is nothing to talk about.' He did not give the Taliban a line of dignified retreat, and the rest is a chronology of escalating violence in so many places as we have seen.

The Muslim public is also anxious to know whether the West accepts the dignity and inviolability of the different other. The course of post 9/11 events and divergent voices emerging in the United States and Europe have not helped provide the needed assurance. What seems certain, however, is that neither side can give that assurance unilaterally. Yet a sense of realism over the configuration of economic and military power would suggest that the initiative, and the burden of rectifying the deficit in understanding, fall more heavily on the West. There is a need for wider recognition of the best values of each culture and religion to give fresh impetus to the prospects of a more peaceful world, and for the Muslims to give reality to the Qur'anic address (*Al-Ḥujurāt*, 49:13), from where diversity and pluralism of peoples and nations should be used as bases of better understanding and recognition, among themselves and the wider reaches of human fraternity.

CHAPTER ELEVEN

THE PEOPLE OF THE BOOK IN THE QUR'AN

Professor Ismail Albayrak

Abstract

Muslims' understanding of the Qur'an has shaped their communal interfaith perceptions. This article selects the various Qur'anic verses that have influenced Muslims in relating to people of other faiths. The prime concern of this paper is to show how even the Qur'anic verses that might sound harsh to the ears of other faith groups can be read with sensitivity and understanding in the modern world. To accomplish this, the article provides an historical analysis of the relevant Qur'anic verses, together with some current discussions on the issue. The Qur'an, speaking generally, seems more germane to cultural and social plurality than to theological pluralism or dogmatic syncretism. In addition, the Qur'an considers doing good—or competing in doing good—as vital in the life of people of different faith groups. Nonetheless, the Qur'an accepts the People of the Book as they are and does not close the door to their exercise of religious freedom.

Introduction

This paper deals with two issues: How does the Qur'an present the People of the Book in both the Meccan and the Medinan surahs and how have the Muslims understood the relevant passages in contemporary and pre-contemporary times. Although it is difficult to do full justice to this important and complex subject within the confines of an article, I will start by studying the attitude of the pre-Islamic Arabs towards those whom the Qur'an calls the People of the Book, the attitude as reflected in the Qur'an, in the pre-contemporary *tafsīr* works, and finally in the writings of Muslim scholars in our own time. This will be followed by a general reappraisal of the subject.

To start with, it is important to note that the concept of *Ahl al-Kitāb* (the People of the Book) in the Qur'an is characterised by a degree of lack of rigidity, an overall attitude of amity and even a degree of respect. Generally speaking, the expression began to be used in the late Meccan and continued to be used in the Medinan surahs and occurs thirty-one times in the Qur'an as a whole. Besides this expression, there are also other expressions by which the Qur'an refers to the People of the Book, such as *alladhīna utū al-kitāb* ('those who have received the Book'),[432] *ātaynāhum al-kitāb* ('those unto whom We have given the Book'),[433] *utū nasīban min al-kitāb* ('those who were given a portion of the Book'),[434] *wa awrathnā al-kitāb/alladhīna urithū al-kitāb* ('We gave the Book as inheritance unto those'/'those who were made to inherit the Book'),[435] *wa man 'indahu 'ilm al-kitāb* ('whosoever has [true] knowledge of the Book'),[436] *alladhīna yaqra'ūn al-kitāb* ('those who read the Book'),[437] *fa'salū ahl al-dhikr* ('ask the followers of the Remembrance').[438] Since a special status has been conferred on the People of the Book in the Qur'an, they are also addressed in it by other titles. The Qur'an names the Jewish people as *yahūd*,[439] *hūdan*,[440] *alladhīna hādū*[441] and *banū Isrā'īl*.[442] The term *naṣārā*, which refers exclusively to Christians in the Qur'an, is mentioned fourteen times.[443] This term regularly occurs together with the expression *yahūd* and its derivates in the Qur'an. Besides this common term, an interesting expression is used to address the Christians, namely *ahl al-Injīl* ('the People of the Gospel').[444] The name *ḥawāriyyūn* is mentioned five times in the Qur'an, for the followers of Jesus ﷺ during his lifetime, all of them occurring in the Medinan surahs.[445]

Furthermore, the Qur'an mentions two other groups, the Sabeans in three places and the Zoroastrians (*Majus*) in one place.[446] Although the Prophet Muhammad ﷺ had no personal contact with the Sabeans, there is a hadith that the Zoroastrians should be accorded the status of the People of the Book.[447] However, most scholars have regarded both Sabeans and Zoroastrians as *ahl al-dhimmah* of the Muslim state. In brief, the boundaries of *Ahl al-Kitāb* in the Qur'an are not clearly defined but it is safe to assume that a distinct status is generally given to the Jews and Christians due to their religious beliefs. The Qur'an *Al-An'ām*, 6:156,[448] in my opinion, strongly supports this conclusion.

In terms of the Holy Scriptures, the Qur'an mentions the *Tawrah* (Torah),[449] *Zabūr* (Psalms),[450] *Injīl* (Gospel),[451] *al-ṣuḥuf al-ūlā* (the earlier sheets),[452] and the *ṣuḥuf* (sheets) of Abraham and Moses.[453]

The People of the Book in Pre-Islamic Arabia

It is well known that before the advent of Islam, the Arabs were familiar with the phrase *Ahl al-Kitāb* (the People of the Book). It is also known that the terms referring to both Jews and Christians occur in pre-Islamic poetry.[454] The word *Yahūd* is used in the poetry of the *Jāhiliyyah* period but it appears in the Qur'an during the Medinan period. Interestingly, the expression *banū Isrā'īl* is not found in pre-Islamic poetry although, as we know, it occurs many a time in the Qur'an. Clearly, this indicates that the Qur'an does not follow any particular pattern known in Arabia in this regard. This is important though it is quite often not noted.

Concerning the Christian population in Mecca and Medina, the Muslim sources mention a few individuals rather than a considerable community. In Mecca, the majority of these individuals were slaves,[455] while in Medina they seem to have numbered no more than fifty. Nonetheless, it is known that there were many Christians living in different parts of the Arabian peninsula.[456] Furthermore, we also come across some reports which show that there were Christian merchants who came to Mecca to conduct business, but they were not allowed to stay there too long, as the Meccan pagans feared they might convert the native population to Christianity,[457] and so drove them away. Similarly, there appear to have been only a few Jews in Mecca, whereas there seems to have been a substantial Jewish population near Medina, although their origin in Arabia is quite obscure. The Islamic sources put the number of Jewish clans in Medina at twenty.[458] Since the Jews were knowledgeable about the scripture, the native Arabs generally held the Jews of Medina in respect.[459]

The Prophet's Meccan Period

When the Prophet Muhammad ﷺ began to receive revelation and embarked on his mission as a Prophet, his first addressees were Meccan pagans. For this reason, the early Qur'anic passages focus primarily on critiquing polytheism. This does not mean, however, that the Qur'an makes no mention of the People of the Book until the Medinan period. There are many verses here and there concerning the People of the Book in the Meccan surahs. Besides the narratives regarding the earlier Prophets عليهم السلام and their communities, there are some verses which give specific information about the beliefs and practices of the People of the Book.

Before going into the details of these verses, it would be pertinent to note that the Qur'an, which is primarily meant to be a guidance to mankind, is a unique book and does not follow the conventional style of systematic works of theology or law. An analysis of the Qur'anic narratives shows that emphasis is placed on their dogmatic, spiritual, ethical and didactic aspects without necessarily trying to give a historical account of the events of the past in a chronological order. If we look at the Qur'an from this perspective we will notice that many highly respected Biblical figures are mentioned in it as *ṣaliḥūn* ('righteous')[460] before the advent of the Prophet Muhammad ﷺ, and that accordingly God sent a revelation to him to confirm the previous revelations (*Fāṭir*, 35:31). Considering itself to be a part of this revelatory tradition, the Qur'an is always on the side of the People of the Book as against the Meccan pagans.[461] Furthermore, when the Meccan pagans used the deification of Jesus عليه السلام as a pretext to support the idolatrous worship of angels, the Qur'an warned them.[462] God declares in the Qur'an: *My righteous slaves will inherit the earth* (*Al-Anbiyā'*, 21:105).[463] Thus the People of the Book are seen in the Qur'an as the Muslims' natural allies. For this reason, the Qur'an counsels the Meccan unbelievers, who doubted that Divine revelation could be made to any mortal, to ask the people of the Remembrance (*ahl al-dhikr*),[464] namely the Bible, and those *who have been reading the Book before you.*[465] This might seem to some as somewhat ambiguous, but the Qur'anic verses such as *Al-A'rāf*, 7:159 and 7:168 draw our attention to the existence of pious people among the People of the Book.

To be able to comprehend the relationship between the People of the Book and the Muslims of the early Meccan period, it is enough to recall the occasion of revelation of *Sūrat Al-Rūm* (surah 30). To put it succinctly, there were protracted hostilities between the Persians and the Byzantines. The Byzantines were Christians and so the Muslims were, relatively speaking, sympathetic to them. On the other hand, the Meccan pagans sympathised with the Persians due to their denial of God's unity. When the Persians conquered Syria and Palestine, and even occupied Jerusalem in 615 CE (that is, in the fifth year of Muhammad's Prophethood), the Muslims were unhappy. They suffered not only from the persecution and cruelty of the pagans, but were also distressed by their exultant boasting about the victory of the Persians. Consequently, *Sūrat Al-Rūm* was revealed to inform the Muslims that the Byzantines would be victorious within a few years. The Qur'anic prediction was fulfilled nine years later.[466]

During this difficult period the Prophet ﷺ asked some Muslims to take refuge with the Emperor of Abyssinia. This reinforced the close relationship between the Muslims and the People of the Book. Another verse which shows the Qur'anic preference for the People of the Book over the pagans is *Al-Isrā'*, 17:107:

> *Believe therein or believe not, lo! those who were given knowledge before it, when it is read unto them, fall down prostrate on their faces, adoring.*

The relationship between the People of the Book and the Muslims as reflected in the Meccan surah*s* is not limited to the aforementioned verses. At this juncture we should remember the verses of *Sūrat Al-Ra'd* which indicate the attitude of the People of the Book towards Muslims. Although there is considerable difference of opinion regarding the period in which this surah was revealed, scholars are generally inclined to the view that it is a Meccan surah but contains a few verses that were revealed in Medina. According to verse *Al-Ra'd*,13:36, the People of the Book rejoice in the revelation of the Qur'an. However, there are also others among them who deny the validity of parts of it. In the following three verses the Qur'an states that it is an ordinance in the Arabic tongue, and that the Prophet ﷺ should follow its teaching rather than the desires of people, for if he were to follow their desires there would be none to protect him. It is also emphasised that it was not given to any apostle to produce revelation save at God's behest (*Al-Ra'd*, 13:38). This verse ends with the statement that every age has its revelation, *li kulli ajalin kitāb.* The key verse in this passage is 13:39: *God annuls or confirms whatever*

He wills, for with Him is the source of all revelation (wa 'indahu umm al-kitāb). The earlier exegetes explain this as referring to the succession of the Divine messages culminating in, and ending with, the revelation of the Qur'an.[467]

Furthermore, the Qur'an pays attention to the differences among the followers of the earlier revelations who were divided by a schism. Some welcomed the new revelation while others denied it. These verses also indicate that the Qur'anic criticism of the People of the Book had already begun at Mecca. The Qur'an sometimes criticised the Jews for their *wrongdoings against themselves*, that is, for committing sins (*Al-Naḥl*, 16:118) and the Christians for their disagreements about the nature of Jesus ﷺ (*Maryam*, 19:36–7). God created humankind as a single community, but later they began to hold divergent views (*Yūnus*, 10:19). Nevertheless, *If He had wished He could have made all humankind one single community* (*Hūd*, 11:118). Interestingly, the divergent views appeared only after they had come to know the truth.

> *And had it not been for a decree that had already gone forth from your Sustainer (postponing all decision until a term set by God) it had been judged between them in respect of that wherein they differ* (*Yūnus*, 10:19).

Despite the fact that Muslims and the People of the Book belonged to the same revelatory tradition, the Qur'anic criticism of the conflicts and disputes among the People of the Book gradually increases. The Qur'an confirms the truth, warning the evildoers and bringing glad tidings to the doers of good and also explaining matters to the People of the Book on questions regarding which they held divergent views.[468] This gives the Qur'an a position of authority, enabling it to determine what is genuine and what is false in the earlier revelations. This high status of the Qur'an reaches its peak with the late Meccan verse of *Surat Al-A'rāf*, 7:157. In this verse the People of the Book are asked to follow the unlettered Prophet who was described in the Torah and the Gospel. The following verse, however, declares from the mouth of the Prophet Muhammad ﷺ that he is an Apostle of God to all of mankind (*Al-A'rāf*, 7:158).[469] But this universal call does not imply that the People of the Book would be forced to accept the call of the Qur'an. In another late Meccan verse (*Al-'Ankabūt*, 29:46) the Qur'an teaches Muslims how they should treat the People of the Book and how they should explain their religious message to them:

> *And do not argue with the followers of earlier revelation otherwise than in a most kindly manner. And say we believe in that which has been bestowed from on high upon us, as well as that which has been bestowed upon you, for our God and your God is one and the same.*

Although some exegetes think that this verse is abrogated,[470] it seems from the Qur'an's general context that this is hardly plausible. The function of this late Meccan *surah* is to draw attention to what unites the People of the Book and the Muslims.

We will now turn to an examination of the verses about the People of the Book revealed during the Medinan period of the Prophet's life.

The Prophet's Medinan Period

It has been observed that with the migration to Medina, the number of passages concerning the People of the Book increases. The long surahs such as *Al-Baqarah (*surah 2), which significantly deals with the Jews; *Āl 'Imrān (*surah 3) which contains many passages about the Christians; and *Al-Nisā'* (surah 4), *Al-Mā'idah* (surah 5) and *Al-Tawbah* (surah 9), which pay almost equal attention to both Christians and Jews, were revealed in Medina. The most probable reason for this was the Prophet's direct interaction with these communities in Medina. Not surprisingly, the Qur'anic discourse about the People of the Book changes in accordance with the nature of their relationship with the Muslims.

It is well known that when the Prophet Muhammad ﷺ came to Medina, he found many Jews there besides the Arab converts to Islam and the pagans. After building a mosque, establishing brotherhood between the Meccan immigrants and the Medinan Muslims, fixing the boundaries of Medina and counting its population, the most important achievement of the Prophet ﷺ was to conclude an agreement with the different segments of the population living in the region. We are referring here to the famous Medinan Pact *(Mithāq al-Madinah*). The document shows how a diverse community can live together in unity. According to Muhammed Hamidullah's edited text, Article 25 of the pact enshrines the freedom of religion and autonomy by saying: 'unto

Jews their religion and unto Muslims their religion'. In addition, the article also describes the Jews of Banu 'Awf as an independent community, like the Muslims.[471]

Since there was no significant Christian community in Medina, the pact does not mention them. However, when the Muslims later encountered various Christian groups in the years following the Hijrah, they also concluded agreements with them. When we look at the earlier Medinan surahs and the Prophet's traditions, we find that the Muslims considered the People of the Book to be their fellows in religion and in general tried, where no divine commandments existed, to behave in the same way as the Jews and Christians did in their daily lives. As a result of this fellowship, the Muslims followed the hairstyle of the Jews rather than Arab pagans,[472] and faced Jerusalem in their prayers for a period of nearly sixteen months. Moreover, when the Prophet ﷺ noted *Ahl al-Kitāb,* especially Jews fasting on the tenth of Muharram, he asked the Muslims to fast on the tenth of Muharram because we are closer to Moses ﵇ than them. However, the Prophet ﷺ later advised the Muslims to fast on the ninth and tenth or tenth and eleventh to make themselves distinct from the Jews.[473] The Qur'an also allowed the Muslims to eat the animals sacrificed by the People of the Book, to marry their women and to eat from their dishes.[474] This indicates that a clear distinction was made between the People of the Book and the Arab pagans. Since the scriptures of the People of the Book contained some authentic revelation and some people might commit the error of falsifying them, the Prophet ﷺ said: 'Do not confirm the People of the Book, and [at the same time] do not accuse them of falsehood, but say 'We believe in what has been revealed to us and what has been revealed unto you and Our deity and your deity is One, and we do submit to Him."[475] On the basis of this close relationship, the Prophet declared that he was the man closest to the son of Mary.[476] Furthermore, the Prophet ﷺ mentioned the Prophets ﵇ as brothers who have the same father but different mothers.[477]

Be that as it may, we do not claim that Islam always preserves its neutral position towards the People of the Book. Since Muslims' self-understanding is related, at least partly, to their attitudes towards the People of the Book, we find many traditions concerning the Prophet's invitation to them to accept Islam. It is recorded that the Prophet ﷺ went to Bayt al-Midras (House of Midrash) to ask them to accept whatever was common between them, or invite Jewish scholars to a discussion.[478] However, with the exception of a few individuals, the Jewish community in Medina did not respond positively, and several of them even adopted a hostile attitude towards Muslims.

Thus the Jews of Medina, as one of the major components of the collectivity called *Ahl al-Kitāb*, came in for criticism in the early Medinan verses. In my opinion, the first serious criticism against them was after the choice of Ka'bah as the Muslims' direction of prayer (*Al-Baqarah*, 2:145). This is followed by other criticisms of the Jews. The Qur'an frequently reminds them of their ancestors' mistakes with regard to God and the Prophets عليهم السلام. It also enumerates the sins they committed against God and the wrongs they perpetrated against the Prophet Muhammad ﷺ and the Muslims. Before coming to the series of errors committed by the People of the Book, especially by the Jews, attention needs to be drawn to an important point: the failure to see the distinction between the Qur'an's criticisms of the Jews in general and its censure of the Jews who were the contemporaries of the Prophet Muhammad ﷺ. This failure to make the distinction, however, presumably prevents many Muslim scholars from properly appreciating the Qur'anic view of the Jews. Consequently, some of them generalise the local beliefs or practices of the Jews while others localise their general beliefs or practices. In other words, some people hold the view the Jews of the Prophet's time to be part of the integral entity in history, and portray their practices and beliefs as though they are characteristic of the whole Jewish tradition irrespective of time and space. On the other hand, others place great emphasis on their local characteristics, portraying them as Arabian Jews in isolation from the main Jewish body; consequently every belief and practice of theirs is considered to have a predominantly local character with little to do with the mainstream Jewish tradition. Some examples of the Qur'anic criticism of the Jews' local beliefs and practices are as follows: hostility towards the Angel Gabriel (*Al-Baqarah*, 2:97), their claim that Ezra/'Uzayr was God's son (*Al-Tawbah*, 9:30), their belief in the revelation made to them alongside denial of God's other revelations or all revelations

(*Al-Baqarah*, 2:91; *Al-Ḥāqqah*, 69:91), belief in idols and false deities (*Al-Nisā'*, 4:51).

According to the Islamic sources—the Qur'an, Hadith, *Siyar, Maghāzi* and *Tārīkh*—the violation of treaties by the Jews of Medina created, within a few years, a great deal of tension between the Jews and the Muslims. This increasing strain in Jewish-Muslim relations is reflected in various verses. The Qur'anic narrative enumerates the misdeeds of the contemporary Jews as well as of their forefathers: they were disinclined to sacrifice the cow (*Al-Baqarah*, 2:67–73); they worshipped the golden calf (*Al-Baqarah*, 2:54; *Al-A'rāf*, 7:148; *Ṭā Hā*, 20:88); they disregarded their promise (*Al-Baqarah*, 2:83); they corrupted their religion *to acquire a trifling gain* (*Al-Baqarah*, 2:79); they ill-treated Moses عليه السلام (*Al-Nisā'*, 4:154); they rejected the Prophets عليهم السلام (*Al-Baqarah*, 2:146); they attempted to kill the Prophets عليهم السلام (*Al-Baqarah*, 2:87); their hearts were hardened or covered (*Al-Baqarah*, 2:74; 2:88); they forbade what God had permitted (*Āl 'Imrān*, 3:93–4); they wanted to see God (*Al-Baqarah*, 2:55); they claimed to be God's children (*Al-Mā'idah*, 5:18); they claimed that fire would touch them for only a limited number of days (*Al-Baqarah*, 2:80); they broke the Sabbath law (*Al-Nisā'*, 4:154); they corrupted the Scripture (*Al-Baqarah*, 2:70);[479] they took rabbis as their Lords (*Al-Tawbah*, 9:31); and they denied the last Prophet ﷺ although he confirmed the Torah (*Al-Baqarah*, 2:87).

Although some of these criticisms are also directed against the Christians, the Jews are judged quite severely for their blasphemous statement about Mary, Jesus' mother (*Al-Nisā'*, 4:156). The Qur'anic criticism of the Jews who rejected the Prophets عليهم السلام especially Jesus عليه السلام, clearly suggests that the Muslims considered the earlier Prophets عليهم السلام, including Moses and Jesus عليهما السلام, to be their own Prophets.

In the middle of the Medinan period, the main Jewish tribes were expelled from Medina because of their violation of the agreements they had made with the Prophet ﷺ. Their expulsion coincided with the establishment of the Muslims' religious and political integration.[480]

During the second phase of the Prophet's life in Medina, the relationship between the Muslims and the Christians grew significantly. Within a few years, the Prophet ﷺ sent envoys to the neighbouring states, which were generally Christian, and began receiving their ambassadors in

Medina. One of the important results of this relationship was to make Muslims more familiar with the religious beliefs and practices of the Christians in Arabia. This interaction is clearly depicted in the Qur'an. In contrast to its many criticisms of Jews, especially from an ethical perspective,[481] the Qur'an criticises the Christians for their adherence to certain exaggerated dogmas. The concept of the Trinity and the elevation of their monks and religious leaders, virtually making them lords besides God are the most salient examples of their exaggeration. [482]

We are now in a position to consider the Medinan verses concerning the People of the Book. Similar to some Meccan verses, a number of Medinan verses also state that mankind was once one community but after clear proofs had come to them they differed.[483] In verse *Al-Mā'idah*, 5:48 it is said that *if Allah had willed He could have made mankind one community.* Having accepted the difference as a fact of life, the Qur'an talks about six groups: Muslims, Jews, Christians, Sabeans (*Al-Baqarah*, 2:62; *Al-Mā'idah*, 5:69), Zoroastrians and idolaters (*Al-Ḥajj*, 22:17).[484] Now, the Qur'anic attitude as regards the idolaters is quite unambiguous. However, concerning the status of the Jews and Christians (see *Al-Baqarah*, 2:62; *Al-Mā'idah*, 5:69) it is worth noting that both early and modern Muslim scholars made great efforts to explain them. The plain meaning of the verses (*Al-Baqarah*, 2 :62; *Al-Mā'idah*, 5:69) is that, besides Muslims, the followers of the Jewish, Christian, or Sabean faiths who believe in One God and the hereafter and do right will have their reward with God. 'Abdullah Yusuf 'Ali translates *Al-Baqarah*, 2:62 as: *those who believe (in the Qur'an), and those who follow the Jewish (scriptures), and the Christians and the Sabeans—Any who believe in Allah and the Last Day, and work righteousness, shall have their reward with their Lord.* The exegetes of the pre-modern period generally consider this verse to mean that the Jews and Christians who achieved salvation with the pious believers are those who lived before the advent of Islam, or that they were those individuals who converted to Islam after the advent of the Prophet Muhammad ﷺ.[485] They also argue that the context of these verses supports this conclusion. Furthermore, a tradition narrated by 'Abd Allah ibn 'Abbas (d. 68/687) says that when the Prophet ﷺ recited verse *Āl 'Imrān*, 3:85: *And if anyone desires a religion other than Islam (submission to Allah), never will it be accepted from him, and he will be a loser in the hereafter*, then he started to recite the verse *Al-Baqarah*, 2:62.[486] This displays the exegetes' general stance regarding the salvation of the People of the Book. In other words, according to these exegetes, the People of the Book are required to accept Islam to achieve salvation. So the verses which laid down only a few conditions for salvation should be read in the light of other verses which require the acceptance of Islam. In short, they believed that the verse *Al-Baqarah*, 2:62 can be properly understood in the light of *Āl 'Imrān* 3:85.[487]

Nonetheless, besides the verses (*Al-Baqarah*, 2:62; *Al-Mā'idah*, 5:69) which seem to lay down the minimum conditions for salvation and comprise only three things, there are other verses which affirm that the People of the Book are not all alike, and that there are upright people among them (*Āl 'Imrān* 3:113-114). According to these verses, these followers of the earlier revelations recite God's messages through the night, prostrate themselves, enjoin the doing of what is good, forbid the doing of what is wrong and vie with one another in good works. The pre-modern exegetes exhibit a similar attitude towards these verses and identify these pious people as those who had converted to Islam.[488] Nevertheless, they are troubled by the expression *Ahl al-Kitāb* in the verse, and indeed the validity of the above-mentioned interpretation seems seriously problematic. The question is: if the reference is to the converted Muslims, why does the Qur'an refer to them as the People of the Book? Once again, the classical exegetes hold the view that this is due to their having been Jews or Christians before conversion. However, the literal meaning of the verse, which is regarded as ambiguous by al-Tabari, identifies these people as the followers of the earlier Scriptures.[489] Other Qur'anic verses (such as *Al-Baqarah*, 2:101, 148; *Āl 'Imrān*, 3:78/*farīq*), (*Āl 'Imrān*, 3:69, *72/ṭā'ifah*), (*Al-Baqarah*, 2:109; *Al-Mā'idah*, 5:66, 80–1/*kathīr*), and (*Āl 'Imrān* 3:110/ *akthar*) also indicate that all followers of the earlier revelations are not alike.[490]

Concerning the status of the People of the Book, certain passages (see *Al-Mā'idah*, 5:42–3, 47, 66) are worthy of attention. The main theme of these verses is the observance of the judgement of the Torah and the Gospel. If the People of the Book do not put the judgments of these Books into practice they will be evildoers. Although in *Al-Mā'idah*,

5:66 there is a clear reference to the necessity of the judgment of the Qur'an besides that of the Torah and the Gospel, in other verses, for example, *Al-Mā'idah*, 5:42–3, 47, only the Torah and the Gospel are mentioned. The exegetes' understanding of these verses is, however, quite different from some of their modern counterparts and they are again inclined to a kind of exclusivism. For example, in the interpretation of *Al-Mā'idah*, 5:66, they explain the meaning of the observance of the judgment of the Gospel as follows: 'They promised to obey the last Prophet ﷺ in their scripture. Thus the observance of the judgment of the Gospel means to fulfil this promise.'[491] The great exegete Fakhr al-Din Muhammad b. 'Umar al-Razi (d. 606 AH/1210 CE) poses the following question with regard to the interpretation of *Al-Mā'idah*, 5:43-47: 'After the Qur'an, is it possible to obey the rules of the Gospel?' In answering it, he offers three comments. First, similarly to the way in which Nasir al-Din 'Abd Allah b. 'Umar al- Baydawi (d. 685/1282) understands this verse, Razi believes that the observance of the judgment of the Gospel means that Christians should obey the verses which indicate the Prophethood of Muhammad ﷺ. Secondly, they should put into effect the rules which have not been abrogated by the Qur'an, and finally, they should confirm, without alteration or distortion, what God has sent in the Gospel.[492]

Ibn Kathir's comments are also in line with al-Razi's.[493] The question as to why these exegetes are in favour of an exclusivist interpretation of these seemingly inclusivist or to some extent pluralistically-oriented verses needs to be addressed. In my opinion, the prime motive behind this inclination is the existence of other verses which indicate that belief in the Prophethood of Muhammad ﷺ is necessary. *Āl 'Imrān*, 3:199 explicitly states that some of the People of the Book believe in what has been revealed to the Prophet Muhammad ﷺ and what was revealed to them. Similarly, *Al-Nisā'*, 4:162 states that those who are firm in knowledge believe in the revelation sent to the Prophet Muhammad ﷺ. The reason why the Prophet Muhammad ﷺ was raised is explained in *Al-Mā'idah*, 5:19: *O People of the Book! Now, after a long time during which no apostles have appeared, there has come unto you Our Messenger to make (the truth) clear to you, lest you say 'no bearer of glad tidings has come unto us, nor any warner.' For now there has come unto you a bearer of glad tidings and a warner*. The exegetes see these verses as a clear proof of Muhammad's Prophethood, and of the Qur'anic revelation having been made so as to rectify the distorted religion of the People of the Book.[494] Al-Tabari says that the last Prophet ﷺ brought the *Furqān* in order to distinguish between truth and falsehood.[495] If the People of the Book accept Muhammad ﷺ as God's Prophet, God will give them twofold of His mercy (*Al-Ḥadīd*, 57:28). According to al-Baydawi, this twofold mercy is the reward for their belief in the Prophethood of Muhammad ﷺ. Al-Tabari, however, considers the meaning to be that their belief in Muhammad's Prophethood will perfect their faith.[496]

Interestingly, when the Qur'an deals with non-Muslims in these verses, it generally uses the expression *Ahl al-Kitāb* as if it is drawing the believers' attention to similarities rather than to differences. Thus Islam, on the one hand, invites them to accept a common word, that is, *tawḥīd,* and on the other, provides the bases to bring both Christians and Jews closer to its teaching. In addition, the verse which occurs in the middle of *Sūrat Al-Baqarah* (2:143) suggests that the Muslim community is the community of the middle way, which bears witness to the truth before all nations by maintaining an equitable balance between extreme positions.[497] Clearly, these verses call people to believe in the Qur'an and Muhammad ﷺ. The verses also accord a privileged position to the Muslim community, who bear the responsibility of conveying the final message to others. Chronologically speaking, this reaches its peak in *Āl 'Imrān*, 3:64: *Say: 'People of the Book! Come now to a word common between us and you, that we serve none but God, and that we associate not aught with Him, and that some of us do not take others as Lords, apart from God.' And if they turn their backs, say: 'Bear witness that we are Muslims.'* [498] The subjects of this verse, according al-Tabari and others commentators, were either the Jews living in the environs of Medina or the Christians of Najran.[499] However, if we take the previous verses into account it seems that the main addressees are Christians. It is also narrated that when the Prophet ﷺ sent a letter to Heraclius (r. 610–41 CE), he recorded this verse on the back of the letter.[500] It is clear from the Qur'anic verses that neither the Jews nor the Christians gave a positive response, because the following verses (*Āl 'Imrān*, 3:67–8) reject the claim of Jews and Christians who associated Abraham ﷺ exclusively with their own religion. The Qur'an reminds them that the people who have the best claim to Abraham ﷺ are those who follow him, as does the Prophet (Muhammad) ﷺ and those who believe in him (that is, the Muslims). Abraham was not a Jew, nor yet a Christian; but he was an upright man who had surrendered (to Allah), that is, 'was a Muslim' and not of the idolaters.[501]

These are in general late Medinan verses and their tone is quite severe, which is understandable in view of the high degree of tension in the relations between the Muslims and the People of the Book at the time. This is manifest, for instance, in *Al-Mā'idah*, 5:51, where the Muslims are asked not to take the Jews and Christians as their allies.[502] The early exegetes understand this verse generally in the context of not trusting non-Muslims in religious matters. Others, who associate alliance or friendship with intimate confidence, explain the verse as enjoining Muslims not to give away the secrets of the Muslim state to Jews and Christians.[503] Nonetheless, these approaches do not prevent Muslim scholars from appreciating the virtues and merits of the People of the Book.[504] In brief, the Qur'an does not altogether reject friendship between Muslims and the People of the Book.

Here it is pertinent to draw attention to the approach of a contemporary Muslim activist and scholar, Bediuzzaman Said Nursi [Badiʿ al- Zaman Saʿid Nursi] (d. 1379 AH/1960 CE) to the *Al-Mā'idah*, 5:51: 'Just as not all of the characteristics of an individual Muslim necessarily reflect the teaching of Islam, so also, not all of the qualities of individual Jews or Christians reflect unbelief.' He also asks the question: 'Can a Muslim love a Christian or Jew?' After noting the marriage of a Muslim man to a woman of the People of the Book, he replies, 'Of course, yes. He should love her.'[505]

Another late Medinan surah in the Qur'an which records the tension between the Muslims and the People of the Book is *Sūrat Al-Tawbah* (surah 9). This surah was revealed during a military expedition and clearly reflects the non-Muslims' alliance against the Muslims. An interesting aspect of this situation is illustrated in *Al-Tawbah*, 9:29: *Fight those who believe not in Allah nor the Last Day, nor hold that which hath been forbidden by Allah and His Messenger, nor acknowledge the Religion of truth, from among the People of the Book, until they pay the jizyah with willing submission, and feel themselves subdued.*[506] The verse cannot be understood unless it is considered as part of an integral whole. Thus one should read it in its historical context and in the light of other related verses.

Modern Muslim Scholarship Concerning the Qur'anic View of the People of the Book

The pressures of modernism and secularism are, broadly speaking, diminishing the force of religion in the public sphere. We find that pluralism has gone hand in hand with secularism. Although religious and social pluralism has not been seriously addressed, it has now become a basic feature of modern Muslim and non-Muslim societies. It is clear from an examination of the scholarship relating to the relevant Qur'anic texts and the Prophetic traditions that, both in the modern and pre-modern periods, Muslim scholarship has supported social and cultural pluralism, which seeks to ensure the harmonious coexistence of diverse religious communities and protect the rights and freedoms of the followers of all religions. The same, however, cannot be said for pluralism in the domain of dogma and theology, pluralism in the sense that all religions are on the same level of truth as regards their beliefs. As distinguished from the generality of classical Muslim scholars, several modern scholars look at different religions from a pluralistic perspective. Although the view of a great number of contemporary Muslim thinkers on this issue remains in line with that of their predecessors, some intellectuals tend to go beyond the confines of the traditional framework. They are inclined to the view that if non-Muslims observe the minimum conditions of the principles of faith (such as belief in One God and in the Day of Judgment, and performance of righteous acts) they will be saved from punishment in the hereafter.

One instance of this approach is the one provided by Musa Jar Allah (d. 1949) who lived all his life in a multi-religious community in Russia. In his work *Rahmeti ilahiye Burhanlari* (The Evidences of God's Mercy) written in 1911, he argues, basing his opinion on verse *Al-Zumar*, 39:53,[507] that God's mercy will embrace everyone because the word *'ibādī* used in this verse is not specific but general.[508] Nevertheless, in my opinion modern Muslim thinkers, including the late Fazlur Rahman

(d. 1408 AH/1988 CE), continue to have problems with some implications of pluralism. To take another instance, in their interpretation of verse *Āl 'Imrān*, 3:113: *They are not alike.* Muhammad 'Abduh (d. 1323/1905) and his favourite disciple, Muhammad Rashid Rida (d. 1354/1935) argued that the classical exegetes failed to understand how a non-Muslim could be saved even if he or she believes in the basic principles of religion (belief in God, and the hereafter, and performance of good deeds), and so the generality of scholars identified these praised Jews and Christians with the converted Muslims. Moreover, 'Abduh and Rida see no contradiction between the partly distorted natures of the Torah and the Gospel and the righteous attitude of one group among the People of the Book. There are some Prophetic traditions which are authentic, and some weak or fabricated, but whoever follows them is called a practitioner of the tradition. On this basis Rida believes that the truly pious and religious people are known only to God, therefore no one, whether Muslim or non-Muslim, is justified in practising 'religious nationalism' (*al-qawmiyyah al-dīniyyah)* concerning the question of ultimate salvation.[509] This shows that, at least in principle, Rida is apparently not opposed to dogmatic pluralism.

The Indian Shi'ite scholar Hasan 'Askari (d. 1398/1978), who was influenced by Muslim mystics, also supported the idea of pluralism.[510] Another famous scholar from Pakistan, the late Fazlur Rahman, who spent most of his life in the West, also discussed the issue quite elaborately. According to Fazlur Rahman, the vast majority of Muslim commentators of the Qur'an avoid giving the obvious meaning of the verses (*Al-Baqarah*, 2:62; *Al-Mā'idah*, 5:69) which assure that whoever (no matter whether they are Muslims, Jews, Christians, or Sabeans) believe in God and the Last Day, and do good deeds will be saved. The Qur'an, Fazlur Rahman says, gives its final answer to the problem of pluralism in verse *Al-Mā'idah*, 5:48. Briefly, humankind was a single unity, but this unity was later split up in accordance with God's plan. Thus the Muslim community is recognised as one among the several communities.[511]

Using Fazlur Rahman's approach as the starting point, a few Turkish academics point out that the Qur'an was not revealed to abrogate the previous Scriptures but to confirm them. Thus, the Qur'an asks the

People of the Book to take the notion of *tawḥīd* seriously, but does not ask them to abandon their own religion. These scholars give numerous examples to show that the teachings of the People of the Book are in accord with the basic principles of faith and ethics and differ only in their implementation. They also seek to make a distinction between two Islams: one is established by the consensus of Muslim scholars, the other is the universal Islam preached by all the Prophets ﷺ who came to different nations at different times. According to them, the failure to see this distinction has confused Muslim scholarship concerning the verses about the People of the Book. They think that most of the Qur'anic criticism of the People of the Book is valid for all times. For this reason they argue that belief in the Prophethood of Muhammad ﷺ is not an essential part of *tawḥīd* and salvation.[512]

Today many Muslims feel that this pluralistic approach represents an extreme liberalism in Islamic thought which cannot be easily accepted by the vast majority of Muslims. It is worth noting that like their Christian counterparts, those Muslim intellectuals who promote the idea of dogmatic pluralism, that is, those who suggest that regardless of the soundness of their dogma/belief, followers of all religions will attain salvation if their conduct is righteous, are a small minority.

Before closing this section, I would like to highlight the attitude of two Turkish scholars towards the People of the Book in Muslim tradition. These scholars are Said Nursi and Fethullah Gulen, whose teachings are being enthusiastically welcomed in Turkey. Nursi, whose life spanned the Ottoman and Republican eras, lived in very difficult times for Muslims. However, he never lost his hope that religions would flourish again in the near future. He sincerely asked the believers, both Muslims and Christians, to come together and work together: 'The believers should now unite, not only with their Muslim brothers but also with truly religious and pious Christians, disregarding questions of dispute and not arguing over them. For absolute disbelief (atheism) is on the attack.'[513] Nursi's emphasis on Muslim-Christian cooperation was supported by many Prophetic traditions which indicate that Muslims will enjoy peace with the pious Christians towards the end of time. This unity will ensure security, and they will fight together against the common enemy, namely irreligiosity.[514] To encourage this common endeavour, Nursi re-formulates the expression *Ahl al-Kitāb* into *Ahl al-Maktab* (the literate people).[515] This important reinterpretation should not be seen as simply a semantic contribution. Nursi, with utmost sincerity, calls Christians the people literate in modern science, whose knowledge enables them to fight against the disbelief which stems from secularism rooted in modern science. Thus Nursi believes in a close dialogue with Christians and thinks that true humanity, dignity and justice can only be established by a mutual understanding based on cooperation between these revealed religions. In saying so, however, Nursi does not imply that there are no differences between Islam and Christianity, or that the differences which exist are not significant. For there are indeed important differences between the two. However, what Nursi is trying to do, as Thomas Michael points out, is to show that concentrating obsessively on these differences can blind both Muslims and Christians to the even more important common task which they share, that of offering the modern world a vision of human life and society in which God is central and God's will is the normative basis of moral values.[516]

In line with Nursi, Fathullah Gulen, a contemporary Turkish thinker and religious scholar, believes in the importance of dialogue with the People of the Book. His starting point in this regard is *basmalah* (the initial phrase of Qur'anic surahs). He sees in this phrase God's most recurrent attributes, namely His being *the Compassionate and the Merciful/ al-Rahmān, al-Rahīm*. These words, according to Gulen, require human beings to show compassion not only to their fellows but to all living beings.[517] For Gulen, this is a natural conclusion to be drawn from one of God's most beautiful names, *al-Wadūd* (The Loving One). Thus he holds the view that dialogue is the most important aspect of Islamic ethics. This, however, should be carried out in complete sincerity, using a constructive approach and without claiming one's superiority over the other.[518] Accepting every individual in his or her own situation is one of Gulen's most frequent mottos. Gulen's aim is to prepare different religious communities to learn how to live together in mutual respect and in peace. The serious criticism of both Christians and Jews in the Qur'an, Gulen says, needs to be viewed in its historical context. This historical reading, according to Gulen, will allow Muslims to re-establish healthier relationships with other communities, both religious and non-religious.[519] Nonetheless, Gulen's emphasis seems to be on the cultural and social aspects of pluralism rather than on the dogmatic aspect.

Conclusion

The contents of the Qur'an concerning the People of the Book are quite rich. There are various verses which deal with their fundamental beliefs, practices, and moral principles, and with several important Biblical figures. As a matter of fact, it is possible to find more references to some of these issues and figures in the Qur'an than in the Gospels and the Hebrew Bible.

Leaving aside the polemical works, it is clear that Western scholarship is interested in the Qur'anic presentation of the People of the Book. We must admit, however, that generally speaking, Western scholars' understandings of these views are discordant with those of Muslims. The main reason for this, especially in relation to the apparent points of similarity, lies in their Western methodology, namely using the terminology and criteria extraneous to Islam to analyse the Qur'anic text. The result can be astonishing: some find incarnation in the Qur'an and some see references to the original sin. Others, having considered the differences on the semantic level, argue that the Qur'an confirms the legitimacy of the Trinity.[520] Some non-Muslim scholars who have a strong religious background find the Qur'anic theology extremely inflexible.[521] As followers of the earlier Scriptures, both Jews and Christians tend to think that any endorsement on their part of the authenticity of the Qur'an and the Prophethood of Muhammad ﷺ would be tantamount to a denial of their own faith. This group among the non-Muslim scholars consists of those who see the claims of all Scriptures to truth to be relative, and consider no religion superior or inferior to another. From an Islamic perspective, none of these approaches seems helpful.

When we examine Muslim scholarship, with the exception of a few scholars of the present time, we find the preponderant majority of Muslim scholars to have very little disagreement on the question of dogmatic pluralism. In the pre-modern period, only a few Muslims were interested in the Bible. It is clear from their works that they were not well acquainted with the contents of either the Hebrew Bible or the New Testament.[522] It is important to note that Muslims' understanding of the People of the Book is determined by the Qur'an and the Prophetic traditions. In the Qur'an and the Prophet's sayings, however, we find many assessments of the Prophet's contemporaries rather than a general evaluation of the People of the Book. It is true that the Qur'an attributes various negative moral and theological attributes to the Jews and Christians. But the Qur'an also accepts that spiritual depth exists in those communities. Above all, the People of the Book enjoy a specific religious status given to them by the Qur'an. It is obvious that in every religious community, there are sincere and insincere people. What the Muslim exegetes did was to disregard the historical context of the verses critical of the Jews and the Christians and too easily apply the negative characteristics mentioned in the Qur'an to the People of the Book for all times and places. They unfortunately display piecemeal approaches to the Qur'an rather than treating it in an integral manner. In addition, like their non-Muslim counterparts, they also evaluate both Judaism and Christianity according to the criteria of their own religion and react with horror to some controversial issues such as division in the Godhead, annulment of the Prophetic immunity from sin, the status of the verbal inspiration of the Scriptures, and so on. These scholars' attitude towards the People of the Book is confessional in that they reject the possibility that any other religion can provide salvation.

Others, by contrast, seem to be inclined towards religious pluralism, disregarding some unbridgeable dogmatic differences. Their focus is on the universality of Divinity, the relativity of faith and the compassion of God which enable them to promote pluralism. Nonetheless, their approach is not free from problems. Moreover, the views of these scholars are generally not welcomed by the preponderant majority of Muslims. Another group of Muslims, however, disregards controversial questions and concentrates on what the believing communities can do. In modern society, all kinds of religious people coexist within the same city, street, university, classroom, factory and so on. So this group tries to find ways of constructively coming to grips with religious diversity in the overall framework of social harmony and understanding.

Here it would be pertinent to consider one of the most important Qur'anic terms, namely *ta'āruf*. The meaning of the verse *Al-Ḥujurāt*, 49:13 where this term occurs is as follows: *O mankind! We have created you from a male and female, and have made you nations and tribes that you may know one another. Lo! the noblest of you, in the sight of Allah, is the best in conduct (taqwā)....* It is safe to assume that one of the key words of the Qur'an concerning plurality lies in this verse. *Ta'aruf* (knowing each other) should be reconsidered in the context of the need to find common grounds for the coexistence of diverse religious communities. It provides a key that could open the door to interfaith dialogue. Here the Qur'an draws attention to equality with regards to biology and to a dignity common to all. Thus no one is justified in boasting of an inherent superiority over others. Furthermore, the idea of superiority is criticised in another key verse (*Al-Nisā'*, 4:123) which says: *It will not be in accordance with your desires, nor the desires of the People of the Book. He who does wrong will have the recompense thereof, and will not find against Allah any protecting friend or helper.* So, true salvation should be looked for in *taqwa*, and only God knows to what extent each person has *taqwa*. Thus the answer to the question of how the adherents of the three Abrahamic traditions could become allies lies in the degree of sincerity of intention (*taqwa*) that they bring to bear on their effort to know and understand each other *(ta'aruf)* and contributing to common good. The limits of *ta'aruf* however, are described by another verse (*Al-Baqarah*, 2:256) *There is no compulsion in religion. The right direction is henceforth distinct from error.*[523] According to this verse, no one should pressure others to accept a certain religious faith. Those who do so commit a grievous wrong. It is also important to note that this verse also enjoins Muslims to protect the basic rights of others, especially their religious freedom. This is the realm of *ta'aruf* and it should apply not only to the believing communities, but also to non-believers. And God knows best *(wa Allāhu a'lam).*

© *Ismail Albayrak*

CHAPTER TWELVE

DHIMMĪ AND MUSTA'MIN: A JURISTIC AND HISTORICAL PERSPECTIVE

Professor Mohammad Hashim Kamali

Executive Summary

This chapter begins with a brief explanation of the meaning and concept of *dhimmī* and *musta'min* and continues with a review of the source evidence and *fiqh* provisions on the subject. Then follows a historical analysis of events and developments that impacted the *fiqh* discourse on the position of dhimmis. The chapter continues with a critical examination of the *fiqh* rules in an attempt to renegotiate the impact of historical changes on them: the rules of *fiqh* were a construct of a certain era that no longer obtained, and that, in turn, raised the question as to whether these rules should also be revised. The post-colonial period and independence movement in the Muslim world brought about momentous changes, which were reflected, for the most part, in the ensuing constitutions and laws of nationality and citizenship. A certain disparity arose, as a result, between these and their counterparts in *fiqh*. The chapter draws attention to some of these developments, and advances reform proposals that address the position of dhimmis as equal citizens. The proposed reforms also seek to close the gap between the *fiqh* provisions and the applied laws of Muslim countries.

A Review of Fiqh Provisions

Non-Muslim residents of a Muslim majority state are divided into two categories, namely those who have taken permanent residence and the Muslim state is committed to their protection (i.e. the dhimmis), and the musta'mins, those who come to the Islamic lands for temporary residence. *Dhimmī* is a derivative of *dhimmah*, which means commitment, and it applies to those who enter a contract, known as *'aqd al-dhimmah*, which entails mutual commitment on their part and on the part of the Islamic government. This is why the dhimmīs are also known as *al-mu'āhidūn*, or covenantees. They commit themselves to loyalty and the state is in return committed to their protection and support. The contract of *dhimmah* basically entitles non-Muslim citizens to equal rights and obligations to those of their Muslim compatriots. It is a permanent contract which can only be concluded by the head of state or his representative, and once concluded, it cannot be revoked, but the law provides for certain eventualities whereby the contract may be terminated.

Dhimmah is binding and permanent as far as Muslims are concerned, but it is revocable as far as the non-Muslim party is concerned. The Hanafi school of law has, however, confined the grounds of revocation to three, namely when the *dhimmī* embraces Islam; when he joins the enemies; and when he or she acts in consort and jointly declares war on the Muslims. Outside these three situations the contract of *dhimmah* is not revocable even when the *dhimmī* commits blasphemy, refuses to pay the poll-tax (*jizyah*) or commits murder, adultery and theft. This is the Hanafi view-point, but the majority of Sunni and Shi'i jurists have held refusal to pay the *jizyah* as a ground for revocation of the contract of *dhimmah*.

All non-Muslim residents, whether temporary or permanent, are required to submit to the authority of the Islamic government and observance of its laws, except for personal and customary matters such as marriage, divorce, and inheritance, where the shari'ah allows them to practice their own customary laws and traditions.[524] The dhimmis are entitled to retain and practice their own religion without any hindrance, and should they choose, at any point in time, to embrace Islam, their status of *dhimmah* is automatically terminated and they become full-fledged citizens as of that time. Notwithstanding some juristic rulings to the contrary, the position has prevailed that the status of *dhimmah* may be conferred not only on Christians and Jews, known as the *Ahl al-Kitāb*, but on all non-Muslims, indeed anyone who applies for it regardless of religious following.[525]

The basic requirement of acquiring the *dhimmī* status is to take domicile in the Muslim territory and pay a poll tax. I shall presently attempt to address some *jizyah*-related issues in the context especially of contemporary conditions. Suffice it to note at this point that the lawful government and the *ūlū al-amr* (those in charge of community affairs) may specify the requirements of conferring citizenship on non-Muslim applicants in the light of prevailing conditions, considerations of fairness and considerations of public interest (*marabaḥah*)—all within the framework of a *sharī'ah*-oriented policy (*siyāsah shar'iyyah*).[526] The Muslim state is authorised to enact appropriate rules and procedures that apply to the various modes of conferment of citizenship. It can be conferred, under the applied laws of the present-day Muslim countries, through birth, naturalisation, marriage, domicile, grant on application, reintegration, subjugation, acquisition of territory and so forth.[527]

The *musta'minūn* (lit. those who enjoy safe conduct) are aliens who are granted safe conduct to facilitate their entry and temporary stay in Muslim territories. They are admitted by permission and passport on the basis of contract, known as *'aqd al-amān*, or contract of safe conduct. The *musta'min* thus enjoys the same rights that are recognised for the *dhimmī*, except that he or she is not required to pay the *jizyah* if the period of stay is less than one year. The contract of *amān* guarantees safe conduct to the person and property of the *musta'min* and to his family. The *musta'min* enjoys total freedom of movement within Muslim territories and that includes, according to the Hanafi, but not the Shafi'i and Hanbali schools, freedom to visit and enter the mosques, and also residence in the vicinity of Ka'bah in Mecca for three days without any prior permission. The *musta'mins* are under similar obligations, as are the dhimmīs, to observe the laws of the land. Unlike the contract of *dhimmah,* which is permanent, *amān* is temporary and revocable by the authorities. Again, unlike *dhimmah,* which is only offered by the state authorities, *amān* can be offered and concluded both by the state authorities and any Muslim citizen, men and women alike.[528] The procedure of giving *aman* is very simple and there is no disagreement among the Muslim jurists on it. Once the intention of the person requesting *amān* is known, regardless of the language spoken, any word or sign of approval is enough to confer the status of *amān*.[529]

With the exception of the Hanafis, who are of the view that safe conduct to aliens may be granted by both the Muslim and non-Muslim citizens (the latter with permission of the authorities), the majority have confined this right to Muslim citizens only.[530] This is yet another instance perhaps where the more egalitarian position of the Hanafi school is preferable and could be adopted by a simple permission that the head of state might extend to non-Muslim citizens.

Basic authority for *amān* is found in the Qur'anic verse which provides in an address to the believers: *If one of the idolaters seeks your protection, protect him so that he hears the word of God, then convey him to his place of safety* (*Al-Tawbah*, 9:6).

The general (*'amm*) declaration of this text is then confirmed and endorsed in a renowned hadith which provides:

> The lives of Muslims are equal (in respect of retaliation and diyyah) and they are a unity against their opponents. When the least among them offers safe conduct to someone, it becomes a commitment on all of them.[531]

Muslim women are equally entitled to grant *amān* to aliens who enter the Muslim territory for non-hostile purposes. This is confirmed in a clear hadith where the Prophet ﷺ endorsed the *amān* that Umm Hānī, the daughter of Abu Talib, had granted to one of the pagan Arabs on the day of the conquest of Mecca. Umm Hānī's brother had wanted to kill this man, at which time she went to the Prophet and informed him about it, and the Prophet addressed her by saying 'we protect the one to whom you have offered protection O Umm Hānī'.[532]

The status of *amān* might be repudiated by the head of state or his representative at any time if it is discovered that the *musta'min* has used it for harmful purposes, or when termination is deemed to be in the best interest of the community. The *amān* normally terminates when its period is expired or when the *musta'min* leaves the Muslim territory (i.e. *Dār al-Islām*—as was known before the advent of nation state). If he or she wanted to return to *Dār al-Islām*, he or she would need to obtain another *amān*.[533] The dhimmis and musta'mins lose all claim to protection and their status is revoked in the following two situations: 1) when they leave the Muslim state and go over to the enemies, and 2) when they openly revolt against the Muslim government and try to sabotage it.[534]

The majority of Muslim jurists have held that it is not permissible to compel a *dhimmī* or a *musta'min* to profess Islam. As for the belligerent (*ḥarbī*) who is actively at war with the Muslims, although the majority have held forced conversion permissible in their case, the preferred view is that of a minority group of jurists who considered it impermissible to compel anyone into Islam. Wahbah al-Zuhayli and ʿAbd al-Wahhab Khallaf, who discussed both these views also considered the latter as preferable. For there is clearly a difference between the permissibility of fighting the *ḥarbīs* to repel their aggression and mischief, and compelling or subjugating any of them to embrace Islam. This would be unreasonable as it cannot lead to a valid outcome.[535]

The wife, under the *fiqh* rules, automatically acquires the citizenship of the country of her husband. Thus if a non-Muslim alien woman marries a Muslim or even a non-Muslim citizen of the Muslim state, she becomes the citizen of that state. The husband on the other hand does not acquire the status of his wife. This would mean that when a non-Muslim alien marries a woman who is the subject of a Muslim state, he does not automatically become the subject of that state. But the husband may apply for naturalisation which the authorities may grant. Muslim jurists have not suggested a probationary period, but it is a discretionary matter for the government to determine whether the applicant should reside for a certain period and have a clean record of upright conduct during that time as a prerequisite for conferment of citizenship status.[536] Having discussed the *fiqhī* position on dhimmis, I now briefly discuss the impact of historical developments and the extent to which they affect the legal status of the *ahl al-dhimmah*.

From Dhimmī to Muwāṭin (Compatriot): An Historical Sketch

As already noted, *dhimmī* is a derivative of *dhimmah*, a contract that is concluded between two parties. It is not an enactment or *ḥukm* of *sharīʿah* of permanent standing, and has no independent existence unless it is created by the contracting parties. *Dhimmah* comes into existence when the parties to it are in existence. In historical terms the *dhimmah* came to an end, as Salim el-Awa has rightly observed, with the onset of colonial rule in the Muslim lands, because the original parties who entered the covenant of *dhimmah* no longer existed, hence in juristic terms neither the *dhimmah* nor its bearer, the *dhimmī*, existed any longer. This was because the western colonial state did not apply the regime of *dhimmah* and no *dhimmī* status could therefore be said to exist as of that time. The whole concept of *dhimmah* has therefore been replaced and substituted by the new legal regime of *muwāṭanah* (citizenship) that came into being under the laws and constitutions of the newly independent Muslim state.[537] Although Muslim jurists have identified *dhimmah* as a permanent contract, that provision takes for granted its valid conclusion in the first place; it cannot exist, in other words, unless it is concluded in the first place, and it comes to an end and is dissolved under certain conditions which the jurists have also specified.

Muwāṭanah, on the other hand, is not a contract, rather it is a permanent status consisting of a relationship between a person and a place that gives rise to certain rights and obligations. *Muwāṭanah* inheres in a person by the fact of birth and residence which need not be created through an agreement with another party. It comes into being, in other words, when its grounds are present, without which it would not exist. *Muwāṭanah* in the sense of a legal relationship is not a new concept as its origins can be traced back to the time of the Prophet Muhammad ﷺ when it was for the first time created under the Constitution of Medina. The Prophet signed this document with the residents of Medina and those who migrated from Mecca to Medina. The non-Muslim parties who ratified this document consisted of Jews and pagans, and the document that was signed as a result was a constitutional instrument that articulated the rights and responsibilities of the citizens, or the *muwāṭinīn*, of Medina. The Constitution of Medina regulated the relations between the newly created Islamic government under the Prophet's leadership and the citizens of that state, both Muslim and non-Muslim. 'The *muwāṭanah* that was created as a result was not based in any particular religion.'[538] For this was a constitution and not a bilateral contract which articulated the structure of relations in the Medinan society under its new government.

The contract of *dhimmah* that Muslim jurists later formalised was neither uniform nor well defined. The *dhimmah* contract that was defined and articulated in *fiqh* manuals was basically a creation of necessity of the times of conquest. Each time the Muslim rulers conquered a territory, they had to deal with two groups of people, one of whom accepted the new religion and acquired the same rights and duties as the Muslims enjoyed themselves. The second group was those who chose to retain their religion; the Muslim rulers acquired responsibility to adjudicate their disputes and protect their rights and properties. It was in response to this need that Muslim jurists constructed the contract of *dhimmah* in line, more or less, with the agreement that the Prophet had concluded with the Christians of Najran and the people of Bahrain.[539] To these prototypes the Muslim rulers added provisions as they deemed necessary in the light of circumstances in each particular locality and case. Basically the Muslim rulers entered provisions that recognised the religious freedom of the conquered people and a certain protection of their rights. But they also imposed a poll tax which was payable once a year at a rate similar to that of *zakāh* (poor tax). Non-Muslims were exempt from payment of *zakāh*, but were instead required to *jizyah* at an equivalent rate. But even these basic provisions were adjusted at times when such seemed appropriate under the circumstances—as discussed below.

Early Muslim rulers have at times entered *dhimmah* agreements which eliminated the *jizyah* altogether—as in the agreement entered during the time of the second caliph ʿUmar with the Turkish tribe of Jarajimah which welcomed the Muslim forces and declared its dislike of the Romans, but stipulated that its members be allowed to remain Christian; this was agreed. The tribe also agreed to help the Muslims in the event of any military engagement with the Romans. The Muslim party agreed in return to protect the tribe and also relieved its members from payment of *jizyah*.

A similar example of a variant *dhimmah* arrangement was the peace agreement that the Muslims signed with the people of Cyprus, who did not offer resistance. In return the Muslim party agreed not to levy the *jizyah* on them. Another example of this was the agreement that ʿAmr b. al-ʿĀs, Caliph ʿUmar's governor, signed with the Copts of Egypt when his forces besieged and eventually conquered Egypt. There was no mention of *jizyah* in the treaty that was subsequently signed.[540]

When the Muslim forces entered Jerusalem in the time of the caliph ʿUmar, its Christian residents refused to surrender the key to its fortress except to the caliph himself, on the condition that no Jewish settlers would be allowed to reside in their area. The caliph wrote them a letter and agreed to their proposed conditions and also granted them safe conduct without imposing any *jizyah*.[541]

It is worth mentioning that *dhimmah* provided a formula by which the Muslim conquerors established a pattern of relations with the people they ruled, but there was considerable variation in the terms of the particular agreements that were subsequently negotiated and concluded.[542]

Dhimmis as Equal Citizens

Then came the era of struggle for independence from western colonialism and the many long years of confrontation that followed. The anti-colonialist campaign was conducted with the participation of all the *muwāṭinīn* in the former colonies; Muslims and non-Muslims struggled side by side and all made sacrifices. When they won that campaign and gained independence for their homelands, they sought to regulate their national life through a national charter and constitution. One of the major gains of this struggle that was articulated in many of their constitutions was equality before the law for all citizens. This development was not dissimilar perhaps to what led to the signing of the Constitution of Medina during the Prophet's lifetime, under which , as earlier noted, all the signatories, including the Jews of course, were accorded equal status.

The *dhimmah* as a contract and a legal instrument came to an end with the colonial domination of Muslim lands. After the collapse of colonialism a new state was formed which was not a successor to any of the previous regimes—neither to the colonial state, nor to the Islamic state that might have existed preceding it. The *dhimmī* status also terminated as a result. The non-Muslims that live in Muslim communities today are people who have fought for their country and continue to defend it through participation in the army and security forces. There is consequently no *dhimmah* in the Muslim state of today, as it has to all intents and purposes been replaced by *muwāṭanah* (citizenship) and the entitlement as a result of all to equal rights and obligations without any discrimination. Under its concept of ratiocination (*ta'līl*), which is concerned with the *ratio decidendi* and effective cause (*'illah*) of the rules (*aḥkām*) of shari'ah, a rational *ḥukm* collapses when the *'illah* on which it stands also collapses and the *ḥukm* in question may then be substituted with another as the new situation may indicate.[543]

With reference to Egypt, Tariq al-Bishri has underscored the common cause of the Egyptian nation by recounting the events of the liberation movement in the late nineteenth century. Slogans such as 'Egypt for the Egyptians' and 'brotherhood of compatriots' came from the pens of al-Ṭahtawi and others. When the National Homeland Party (*al-Ḥizb al-waṭanī al-ahlī*) was formed on the eve of the 'Urābiyyah revolution in 1879, it was stipulated in section five of its manifesto that 'Christians and Jews and everyone who protects Egypt and speaks its language may join this party, which shall not look at their differences of creed, knowing that they are all brethren and have equal rights in politics and legislation'.[544]

This was an eminently egalitarian call, one that united all Egyptians for the defence and liberation of their homeland, charting out the formation of a national society based on the historical experience of its people. This was not a sudden development but an historical pattern which was put to the test once again by developments in post-World War One years where two types of identity for Egypt were commonly debated. People talked of an Islamic community within the framework of the Ottoman Caliphate, just as they talked about the Egyptian society and nation as a smaller unit in its own right. The question typically posed was whether the one took priority over the other. The answer clearly emerged in favour of the Egyptian nation and society, due in large measure to the national campaign against British colonialism.[545]

Situations in Egypt and elsewhere in the Muslim world were also influenced by developments in the Ottoman Empire. Legal reforms under the Ottomans were first introduced under the Tanzimat, which culminated in the two imperial edicts of 1839 and 1856 as discussed earlier. Promulgated under European pressure, they established equality before the law for all the sultan's subjects. In Egypt, the *jizyah* was abolished by the Khedive Sa'id in 1855, followed in 1856 by a large scale recruitment of Copts into military service. Fifty years later, the Revolution of 1919 seemed to signal the victory of equality and national unity over religious segregation and communalism.

The principle of equality was soon after enshrined in the Egyptian Constitution of 1923 which proclaimed Islam as the official religion, but which stopped short of establishing the rule of sharī'ah as the applied law of the land. Nor did this constitution provide for a system of proportional representation for non-Muslim minorities. This was the opposite of the Lebanese experience where the administrative system was based on proportional representation, which had the negative effect, however, of boosting communalism (*ṭā'ifiyyah*) that led to a civil war in the 1950s. Although right up to the time of Egypt's formal independence in 1922, Copts continued to fulfil important functions in the administration and economy as well as in the cultural sphere, they had either been discredited because of their association with the occupying power, or else brought into controversy with the new Egyptian Islamic middle class.[546]

Conclusion

I may bring this essay to a close by quoting Muhammad al-Talibi, who criticised the late Iranian leader Ayatollah Khomeini's treatise, *al-ḥukūmah al-Islāmiyyah* (Islamic government), which advocated the return of *dhimmah* and *kharāj* (land tax based on differentiation between Muslims and non-Muslims) to be imposed on non-Muslims. Talibi posed the question: which *dhimmah* is it that one can talk about in today's conditions? What about the forty percent of the world's Muslims who live under the rule of non-Islamic governments? Should they also be given a reciprocal treatment and considered as dhimmis under non-Muslim rule? And then the question over the factual determination of this status—as to who is under whose protection—arises in countries such as Lebanon and Israel. 'It is an irony of our time that in today's world and in the context of the prevailing balance of economic and military power that the Muslims are the real dhimmis.'[547] To talk therefore of *dhimmah, jizyah* and *kharāj* is to turn away from reality. We now live in the era of human rights and it is in this context that the Muslims should see themselves in their own societies and regulate their relations with the non-Muslims on precisely the same basis.

Although al-Talibi has not said it, a *fiqhi* justification for this view can be sought under the reciprocal treatment formula. Relations with foreign powers and non-Muslim-majority countries are thus to be conducted under the Islamic law guideline of *mu'āmalah bi'l-mithl* (lit. like for like treatment) provided it does not entail engagement in any unlawful activities.

The vast majority of present-day Muslim countries have introduced new constitutions in the post-colonial period, which generally uphold the principles of equality and government under the rule of law. The structure of relations among Muslim and non-Muslim citizens in these countries are now governed by their existing constitutional guidelines, which on the whole, prescribe equal rights and duties for all citizens. Hence those parts of the *fiqh* rules that differentiated among citizens based on the religion of their following would be hard to justify under the new constitutions. Thus it is proposed that human dignity, equality and justice should now replace those differentiations, as these principles have, in any case, a stronger grounding in the broader structure of Islamic values and textual injunctions of the Qur'an and Sunnah.

PART III

BEYOND PEACE: FORBEARANCE, MERCY, COMPASSION AND LOVE

CHAPTER THIRTEEN

THE UNCOMMONALITY OF 'A COMMON WORD'

Dr Joseph Lumbard

Introduction

November 4, 2008 was an historic day. Not only did it mark a new chapter in the long and complicated history of race relations in the United States, it also marked an historic event in the long and multi-faceted relationship between Islam and Christianity. For the first time in the history of Muslim-Christian relations, a delegation of twenty-nine Catholic cardinals, bishops and scholars met with twenty-nine leading Muslim authorities and scholars representing some of the most established figures in the Sunni and Shiʿite worlds. After two days of meetings that it is hoped will mark the first in a series of seminars held once every three years by the newly established Catholic-Muslim Forum, they issued a fifteen-point final declaration that included an appeal for the defence of religious minorities and a call for Muslims and Christians to work together in promoting peace the world over. The declaration read, 'We profess that Catholics and Muslims are called to be instruments of love and harmony among believers, and for humanity as a whole, renouncing any oppression, aggressive violence and terrorism, especially that committed in the name of religion, and upholding the principle of justice for all.'[548] In his comments at the final session, Pope Benedict XVI affirmed that Muslims and Christians share moral values and should defend them together:

> There is a great and vast field in which we can act together in defending and promoting the moral values which are part of our common heritage. We should thus work together in promoting genuine respect for the dignity of the human

> person and fundamental human rights, even though our anthropological visions and our theologies justify this in different ways.[549]

Time alone will let us know if this is indeed a watershed event in the history of interfaith understanding between Christians and Muslims. Nonetheless, the fact that this and other meetings among the world's religious leaders are taking place at all is historic. There is no previous record of leading Muslim authorities representing all branches of Islam engaging the Vatican as a single voice. That it is now happening should be cause for hope; for when two civilisations come to a greater appreciation of the humanity and the concerns of one another, there is much less probability of misunderstandings, mistrust and the violence that can arise therefrom. At the very least, dialogue is better than indifference. At the very best, the collective moral voice of the world's two largest religious communities may help to prevent another Bosnia, another Iraq, or another Sudan. As Seyyed Hossein Nasr said in his closing comments to the first seminar of the Catholic-Muslim Forum:

> Whether we are Christians or Muslims, we are beckoned by our religions to seek peace. As people of religion meeting here at the centre of Catholicism, let us dedicate ourselves to mutual understanding, not as diplomats, but as sincere religious scholars and authorities standing before God and responsible to him beyond all worldly authority.[550]

The Beginning

This historic Muslim-Christian exchange began in earnest on 13 October, 2007, when 138 Muslim scholars from all corners of the world, representing every branch of Islam, including such figures as the grand muftis of Bosnia, Egypt, Syria, Jordan, Oman, Bahrain and even Russia, delivered a fifteen-page letter entitled *A Common Word Between Us and You* to the leaders of Christian churches and denominations throughout the world. Originally composed by Prince Ghazi bin Muhammad of Jordan in consultation with traditional Islamic scholars and under the auspices of King Abdullah II of Jordan, this letter was met with responses from Christian leaders the world over, ranging from independent scholars to the Vatican, the World Council of Churches, the Archbishop of Canterbury, and the

Patriarch of Russia, among many others.[551] The most public response was a letter initially signed by over 300 Christian leaders and scholars entitled *Loving God and Neighbor Together: A Christian Response to 'A Common Word Between Us and You'* that was organised by the Yale Center for Faith & Culture and the Yale Divinity School and published in the *New York Times* on 17 November, 2007. The most substantial theological response was penned by the then Archbishop of Canterbury, the Most Reverend and Right Honourable Dr Rowan Williams, after prolonged consultation with Christian church leaders from several Orthodox churches, the Roman Catholic church, and a range of Protestant and evangelical churches. The Archbishop's response displays a subtle understanding of the limitations inherent to such a dialogue, and the possibilities to which it opens. Since the initial launch the number of Muslims scholars who have signed *A Common Word* has grown to more than 300, with more than 460 Islamic organisations and associations now endorsing it, and there are now over 500 signatories to *A Christian Response* in addition to dozens of additional Christian responses.

The initial letter and the many responses to it have given rise to a series of conferences between Muslim and Christian leaders. The first conference, 'Loving God and Neighbor in Word and Deed: Implications for Christians and Muslims', focused upon theological issues and was held at Yale University between 24–31 July, 2008. The second, 'A Common Word and Future Christian-Muslim Engagement', focused on scripture and was convened by the Anglican Archbishop and hosted by the Cambridge Inter-Faith Programme at the University of Cambridge on 13 and 14 October, 2008, with a final meeting at Lambeth Palace on 15 October, 2008. The third was the first seminar of the Catholic-Muslim Forum hosted by the Vatican, from 4–6 November, 2008. A second seminar of the Muslim-Catholic Forum was held at the Baptism Site in Jordan in November 2011. The fourth major conference, '*A Common Word Between Us and You*: A Global Agenda for Change', held at Georgetown University in October 2009, focused upon the geopolitical implications of the *Common Word* initiative. Smaller conferences that continue the work of these initial conferences have been held in Jordan (September 2010) and at the University of South Carolina (March 2009), the Evangelical Theological Society,

Los Angeles (November 2011), Georgetown University (2011) and Yale University (2011).

The United Nations (UN) Resolution to declare a worldwide interfaith harmony week for the first week of February every year is an important development that would not have been possible without the *Common Word* initiative.[552] Like *A Common Word*, the interfaith harmony week calls upon religious leaders and followers the world over to employ the teachings of their respective traditions to promote peace and understanding of other religions. As Prince Ghazi bin Muhammad stated when presenting the proposal for an interfaith harmony week to the UN General Assembly:

> The misuse or abuse of religions can thus be a cause of world strife, whereas religions should be a great foundation for facilitating world peace. The remedy for this problem can only come from the world's religions themselves. Religions must be part of the solution, not part of the problem.[553]

In addition, *A Common Word Between Us and You* was the central impetus for the Wamp-Ellison Resolution adopted in the US House of Representatives on 23 September, 2008. The official summary explains that the resolution

> Expresses the sense of Congress that the United States: (1) supports the spirit of peace and desire for unity displayed in interfaith dialogue among leaders of the three Abrahamic faiths; (2) encourages the many people of faith around the world who reject terrorism and extremism to join these and similar efforts to build a common bond based on peace, reconciliation, and tolerance; and (3) appreciates those voices around the world who condemn terrorism, intolerance, genocide, and ethnic and religious hatred, and instead commit themselves to a global peace anchored in respect and understanding among adherents of the three Abrahamic faiths.[554]

The Common Word initiative has had a significant trickledown effect in many religious communities. It has given rise to grass roots and community level initiatives as far apart as Bangladesh, Indonesia, Canada and the United States. Development has begun on a joint website supported by the Royal Aal al-Bayt Institute for Islamic Thought, Yale

University and Lambeth Palace that will recommend books in several languages so that members of each faith can read about the other faith as presented by its adherents, rather than its opponents. Discussions are also underway for the development of a multi-university student drive *Common Word* initiative in the United States.

In many instances these projects are a direct continuation of the practical accomplishments that have arisen from the conferences at Yale University, Cambridge University, the Vatican, and Georgetown University. In other instances these initiatives have arisen as a spontaneous response from international organisations and local religious communities. Together they indicate that *A Common Word* has become a global movement that continues to gain traction. As such, it has also become a subject of scholarly investigation with several books and articles having resulted from it.[555]

The Evolution of 'A Common Word'

When discussing the development of the *Common Word* initiative, many look to the polemical comments in *Faith, Reason and the University: Memories and Reflections*, a lecture delivered by Pope Benedict XVI at the University of Regensburg on 12 September, 2007, to mark its inception.[556] Others look to the initial Muslim response, entitled *An Open Letter to His Holiness Pope Benedict XVI*, issued one month later, while others look to *A Common Word between Us and You*. It must, however, be emphasised that the Catholic-Muslim Forum is only one aspect of this Christian-Muslim dialogue. In addition, it would be disingenuous to suggest that the Pope's Regensburg address, wherein Islam was presented as a religion of violence and irrationality, was an invitation to dialogue.[557] In fact the Vatican made no response to the open letter that sought to clarify the misunderstandings of the Regensburg lecture other than a perfunctory courtesy visit to Prince Ghazi bin Muhammad, who had initiated the response.

The Vatican's initial response to *A Common Word* also appears to have been miscalculated. In contrast to the positive responses that will be examined in greater detail below, Cardinal Jean-Louis Tauran, President of the Pontifical Council for Inter-religious Dialogue, went so far as to say that theological dialogue with Muslims would be difficult because 'Muslims do not accept that one can question the Qur'an, because it was written, they say, by dictation from God. With such an absolute interpretation, it is difficult to discuss the contents of faith.'[558] It is remarkable that the president of any council for interreligious dialogue would be so dismissive of Islam's rich and diverse hermeneutical tradition, wherein every word of the Qur'an is seen as having multiple layers of meaning. Cardinal Tauran's statement is akin to Muslims saying that they cannot have dialogue with Christians so long as Christians maintain that Jesus is the Son of God. Cardinal Tauran also cast doubt upon the sincerity of the document and the efficacy of dialogue, saying, '...but some questions remain when we speak of the love of God, are we speaking about the same love?'[559] The Vatican's opposition to open dialogue with Muslims appears to have changed after the publication of the response orchestrated by the Yale Center for Faith & Culture, *Loving God and Neighbor Together: A Christian Response to 'A Common Word Between Us and You'*. Only two days after the appearance of this letter, the Vatican Secretary of State, Cardinal Tarcisio Bertone, sent a reply to Prince Ghazi bin Muhammad on behalf of the Pope. Soon thereafter arrangements were underway for the formation of the Catholic-Muslim Forum. In this respect it seems that the positive response of so many other churches and Christian leaders may have forced the Vatican's hand.

While the Regensburg address may have been an unintended efficient or proximate cause for this exchange, it did not serve as its source. The source of this movement lies in the mechanisms for dialogue that Muslim scholars have been developing since 2003. Many who have followed the process from before its inception would put the starting point in July 2005 with the Amman Conference entitled 'The International Islamic Conference: True Islam and Its Role in Modern Society', organised by the Royal Aal al-Bayt Institute for Islamic Thought in Jordan, under the Patronage of King Abdullah II. This ground-breaking conference marked the beginning of a process whereby Muslim scholars representing all schools of Islamic law and theology employed international consensus to address the challenges that face the whole of the Islamic world. In this way, an intra-Islamic initiative laid the groundwork for this interfaith initiative.

To understand the genesis of *A Common Word*, it is thus important that one take into account the accomplishments of the Amman

Conference of July 2005. On the one hand, the lead-up to the Amman conference established the mechanisms by which consensus could be reached among Muslim scholars of all branches. And on the other hand, the final declaration of the Amman Conference answers one of the main objections that many have had to *A Common Word*, those who claim that Muslims need to denounce extremism before there can be true dialogue. Michael Gonyea expresses such concerns in *The American Thinker*, when he writes of the Catholic-Muslim Forum, 'If in the upcoming forum a broad cross section of Muslim leaders can be self-critical, if they can condemn the extremists, ...Christians will embrace them.'[560] Such self-critical condemnation had in fact been achieved several years earlier in what Fareed Zakaria referred to as 'a frontal attack on Al Qaeda's theological methods'.[561]

This frontal attack consists of three basic dimensions. Supported by seventeen fatwas from leading Sunni and Shi'ite authorities, it first established broad support for the eight schools of traditional Islamic law. This in itself was historic, as both Shi'ites and Sunnis came together to publicly affirm the validity of one another's schools of law. They also emphasised that the schools of law are not regressive, but in fact moderate the religion by providing essential checks and balances. The second prong in this attack was to deny the legitimacy of *takfīr*, or apostasising others. The third was a reiteration of the traditional qualifications for issuing a fatwa. To outside observers this may seem to be a simple academic exercise, but it is in fact essential; for every act of terrorism that takes the name of Islam is preceded by an attempt at justification in Islamic terms. Within traditional Islam this is usually done through fatwas.[562] Demonstrating the illegitimacy of fatwas that call for wanton violence thus strikes at the very root of extremist interpretations of Islam. That is to say that the problem of extremist interpretations of Islam is a textual, methodological problem that requires a textual, methodological solution. For no one commits terrorist acts without being convinced that terrorism is justified. Such justification requires a fatwa. The fatwa must be issued by one who is willing to distort the texts and sidestep the methodologies of classical Islamic law. Only by eradicating this pattern can one eradicate extremist interpretations of Islam and their attendant violence. The final declaration of the Amman

Conference and the collection of fatwas employed to support it was thus a crucial step in a true 'war on terrorism' in which Muslims and non-Muslims can work hand in hand.[563] Rather than striking at the branches of radical Islamism, it struck a blow to its ideological roots. The Amman Conference was thus noteworthy for its innovative approach to building consensus across a broad spectrum of Muslim scholars, and for its repudiation of the extremist interpretations of Islam. This laid the necessary foundations for a broad based inter-religious exchange in which influential *ulamā'* from across the Islamic spectrum would be willing to participate and which they would be willing to endorse.

The Message of 'A Common Word'

A Common Word Between Us and You bears many similarities to the final declaration of the Amman Conference of 2005. It employs the same form of consensus, addresses matters of crucial concern to the global Muslim community, and is grounded in classical Islamic teachings while building upon them. Like the final declaration of the Amman Conference, the initial *Common Word* letter was ratified at a conference in Jordan. The final form of the letter was presented at a conference in September 2007 entitled 'Love in the Qur'an' held by The Royal Aal al-Bayt Institute for Islamic Thought in Jordan under the Patronage of King Abdullah II. As the *Common Word* website states, 'Never before have Muslims delivered this kind of definitive consensus statement on Christianity. Rather than engage in polemic, the signatories have adopted the traditional and mainstream Islamic position of respecting the Christian scripture and calling Christians to be more, not less, faithful to it.'[564]

To effectively analyse this initial letter and the dialogue to which it has given rise, we must first allow the document to speak for itself. It begins:

> Muslims and Christians together make up well over half of the world's population. Without peace and justice between these two religious communities, there can be no meaningful peace in the world. The future of the world depends on peace between Muslims and Christians. The basis for this peace and understanding already exists.
>
> It is part of the very foundational principles of both faiths: love of the One God, and love of the neighbour. These principles

> are found over and over again in the sacred texts of Islam and Christianity. The Unity of God, the necessity of love for Him, and the necessity of love of the neighbour is thus the common ground between Islam and Christianity.[565]

The letter continues by citing verses from both the Bible and the Qur'an to demonstrate the manner in which these principles are underlined in scripture:

> *Of God's Unity, God says in the Holy Qur'an: Say: He is God, the One! / God, the Self-Sufficient Besought of all!* (*Al-Ikhlāṣ*, 112:1–2). Of the necessity of love for God, God says in the Holy Qur'an: *So invoke the Name of thy Lord and devote thyself to Him with complete devotion* (*Al-Muzzammil*, 73:8). Of the necessity of love for the neighbour, the Prophet Muhammad said: 'None of you has faith until you love for your neighbour what you love for yourself.' In the New Testament, Jesus Christ said: 'Hear, O Israel, the Lord our God, the Lord is One. / And you shall love the Lord your God with all your heart, with all your soul, with all your mind, and with all your strength.' This is the first commandment. And the second, like it, is this: 'You shall love your neighbour as yourself. There is no other commandment greater than these.' (Mark 12:29–31)[566]

A Common Word Between Us and You then calls for dialogue and cooperation based upon these two principles—love of the One God and love of the neighbour—which it refers to as the two 'greatest commandments' of the Bible. In this vein it states:

> Whilst Islam and Christianity are obviously different religions—and whilst there is no minimising some of their formal differences—it is clear that the Two Greatest Commandments are an area of common ground and a link between the Qur'an, the Torah, and the New Testament.[567]

The letter concludes by saying, 'So let our differences not cause hatred and strife between us. Let us vie with each other only in righteousness and good works. Let us respect each other, be fair, just and kind to one another and live in sincere peace, harmony and mutual goodwill.'[568]

The title of the letter derives from a Qur'anic verse that commands Muslims to issue the following call to Christians (and to Jews—the 'People of Scripture' as they are known in the Qur'an), *Say, 'O People of Scripture! Come to a common word between us and you: that we shall worship none but God, and that we shall ascribe no partner unto Him, and that none of us shall take others for lords beside God*' (*Āl 'Imrān*, 3:64). A similar verse is cited at the beginning of the letter: *Call unto the way of thy Lord with wisdom and fair exhortation, and contend with them in the fairest manner. Truly thy Lord is Best Aware of him who strayeth from His way and He is Best Aware of those who go aright* (*Al-Naḥl*, 16:125). Drawing upon these and other verses, *A Common Word Between Us and You* proposes that dialogue and even contention in the fairest manner are incumbent upon Muslims, and that the principles of devotion to the one God and love of the neighbour are the strongest possible basis for mutual understanding, efficacious dialogue, and cooperation between Christianity and Islam, because they stem from the theological core of each religion. But unlike many other interfaith efforts, it does not seek to syncretise or to proselytise. Participants in this initiative have even taken pains to emphasise the need for recognising the fundamental differences between the two traditions. Rather than watering down theological positions in the name of cooperation and thus bringing Christian and Muslim communities together at their margins, it asks both communities to speak from what is central and authoritative to each.

One of the letter's chief aims, according to the press release that accompanied it, is to provide a 'common constitution' and a definitive theological common ground for the work of myriad groups and associations around the world who are carrying out interfaith dialogue. It points out that many of these groups are unaware of each other's efforts and often duplicate each other's work. By providing an authoritative 'Christian-Muslim Constitution' grounded in scripture, the letter aims to unify and unite the forces working towards interfaith peace and harmony. The final section of the letter proposes that this is not a matter of choice but of responsibility:

> Finding common ground between Muslims and Christians is not simply a matter for polite ecumenical dialogue between selected religious leaders. Christianity and Islam are the largest and second largest religions in the world and in history. Christians and Muslims reportedly make up over a third and over a fifth of humanity respectively. Together they make

> up more than fifty-five percent of the world's population, making the relationship between these two religious communities the most important factor in contributing to meaningful peace around the world. If Muslims and Christians are not at peace, the world cannot be at peace. With the terrible weaponry of the modern world; with Muslims and Christians intertwined everywhere as never before, no side can unilaterally win a conflict between more than half of the world's inhabitants. Thus our common future is at stake. The very survival of the world itself is perhaps at stake.[569]

Some have ascribed ulterior motives to *A Common Word*, suggesting that its signatories and proponents intended to foist Muslim theology upon Christians, to reduce Islam and Christianity to an artificial union, to form a Muslim-Christian alliance against Judaism, or even to lull Christians into a false sense of complacency. But there has thus far been nothing in the movement that would support such contentions. As Prince Ghazi bin Muhammad explains:

> We had honestly ... only one motive: peace. We were aiming to try to spread peace and harmony between Christians and Muslims all over the world, not through governments and treaties but on the all-important popular and mass level, through the world's most influential popular leaders precisely—that is to say through the leaders of the two religions. We wanted to stop the drumbeat of what we feared was a growing popular consensus (on both sides) for worldwide (and thus cataclysmic and perhaps apocalyptic) Muslim-Christian jihad/crusade. We were keenly aware, however, that peace efforts required also another element: knowledge. We thus aimed to try to spread proper basic knowledge of our religion in order to correct and abate the constant and unjust vilification of Islam, in the West especially.[570]

Christian Responses to 'A Common Word'

The Christian responses to a Common Word have covered the full spectrum. The majority have been very positive, with only a few cynical or dismissive responses. As there have been more than seventy separate responses from bishops, priests, councils and individual scholars, and as several of these responses have led to dialogues on many levels, each cannot be analysed here. I will instead focus upon the aforementioned responses from the Yale Center for Faith and Culture at the Yale University Divinity School, the Archbishop of Canterbury and the Vatican, for each of these has already borne fruit and each has the institutional backing to continue into the future. I will also draw attention to the response of the World Council of Churches (WCC), as it represents the widest and most diverse body of Christian denominations to have fully supported the initiative and subsequent developments, such as establishment of the World Interfaith Harmony Week.

Yale University Divinity School

The first broad based Christian response to *A Common Word* was organised by Miroslav Volf and Joseph Cummings of the Yale Center for Faith & Culture at the Yale Divinity School. Signed by over 300 Christian leaders and scholars, *Loving God and Neighbor Together: A Christian Response to 'A Common Word Between Us and You'* reaffirms the fundamental thrust behind *A Common Word*, saying, 'Peaceful relations between Muslims and Christians stand as one of the central challenges of this century...' and that it is incumbent upon all who truly claim to uphold the values of these traditions to work together to meet this challenge.[571] It then reaffirms the centrality of the two commandments that were the focus of *A Common Word*, and in language that closely reflects that of *A Common Word*, concludes by saying:

> 'Let this common ground'—the dual common ground of love of God and of neighbour—'be the basis of all future interfaith dialogue between us' which your courageous letter urges. Indeed, in the generosity with which the letter is written you embody what you call for. We most heartily agree. Abandoning all 'hatred and strife', we must engage in interfaith dialogue as those who seek each other's good, for the one God unceasingly seeks our good. Indeed, together with you we believe that we need to move beyond 'a polite ecumenical dialogue between selected religious leaders' and work diligently together to reshape relations between our communities and our nations so that they genuinely reflect our common love for God and for one another.[572]

Even before this letter was released, talks were underway for a conference and workshop that would bring Muslim and Christian theologians, evangelicals in particular, into greater dialogue. The conference and workshop, entitled 'Loving God and Neighbor in Word and Deed: Implications for Christians and Muslims', took place at Yale University from 24–31 July, 2008. Several of the papers were published in *A Common Word: Muslims and Christians on Loving God and Neighbor* edited by Prince Ghazi bin Muhammad and Miroslav Volf, Director of the Yale Center for Faith and Culture.[573] The workshop, on 24–28 July, involved approximately sixty Christian and Muslim scholars, along with three Jewish scholars. The discussions, undertaken through the presentation of scholarly papers and through panels and informal conversations, focused on five major areas: 'Love of God', 'Love of Neighbour', 'Love and Speech about the Other', 'Love and World Poverty', and 'God is Loving'. The larger conference, 28–31 July, began with an address from Senator John Kerry. It included approximately eighty Muslim participants, eighty Christian participants, and seven Jewish participants, extending the discussions of the scholarly workshop to a larger group of scholars and leaders.

While some of the participants, such as the Grand Mufti of Bosnia, Seyyed Hossein Nasr, David Burrell, and the members of the Yale Center for Faith and Culture were veterans of inter-religious dialogue, many participants were new to interfaith gatherings. Even participants who were veterans of such gatherings remarked that the theological depth of discussion in the workshops was beyond any inter-religious dialogue in which they had previously engaged.[574] The depth of these discussions helped move the dialogue beyond the platitudes that often plague such encounters. The participation of many figures that are new to inter-religious exchanges demonstrated the breadth of this movement. The inclusion of important religious figures, such as Leith Anderson, who was then president of the National Association of Evangelicals and Ingrid Mattson, who was then president of the Islamic Society of North America, and the opening address from Senator John Kerry demonstrate the ability of this initiative to move those who shape public opinion.

Perhaps the most noteworthy aspect of the conference is that it brought together evangelical Christians and traditional Muslims, two communities that have had little exposure to one another and often view one another with suspicion. In one keynote session of the conference, a leading Muslim scholar and televangelist (for lack of a better word) from the Arab world, Habib Ali al-Jifri, and a leading televangelist from the United States, Rev. Dr Robert Schuller, the founding pastor of the Crystal Cathedral who is known for his internationally broadcast 'Hour of Power', shared the same stage. This was an historic encounter in which two preachers from opposite ends of the world who have the ability to move millions within their religious communities, a traditional Islamic community and an American evangelical community that many believe to be in a clash with one another, spoke from the same podium and conveyed the same message. Never before have an international leader of the American evangelical movement and an international leader of traditional Islamic communities shared the same stage.

The final statement of the Yale Conference, which was agreed upon by all participants, reiterated the content of the previous letters, recognising that Islam and Christianity share 'an essential common ground' and 'a common Abrahamic heritage'.[575] Reaffirming the commitment to promote peace, the final statement declared, '... ours is an effort to ensure that religions heal rather than wound, nourish the human soul rather than poison human relations. These Two Commandments teach us both what we must demand of ourselves and what we should expect from the other in what we *do*, what we *say*, and what we *are*.'[576] The Final Declaration also recognised that each religion affirms Divine unity and that Divine love is central to the whole of the Judeo-Christian-Islamic tradition. In addition it recognised that Christians and Muslims alike must not deny one another basic rights, nor tolerate the denigration or desecration of that which is central to either religion. The first point is of central importance to countering the claims of fringe Islamic groups that Christians worship multiple gods, a key factor in the argument of those who wish to declare them unbelievers. The second point helps to address the misunderstandings that arose in the wake of the Danish cartoon controversy and the more recent eruption over 'The Innocence of Muslims' video trailer. It lays the foundations for Muslim and Christian leaders to confront insults against either community with one voice, and thus avoid the violence that sometimes ensues in the wake of such effrontery.

The participants also discussed practical issues such as 'world poverty, the wars in Iraq and Afghanistan, the situation in Palestine and Israel, the dangers of further wars, and the freedom of religion'.[577] In addition, the organisers committed to establishing mechanisms whereby the principles agreed upon could be conveyed to their respective communities. These include a website with recommended reading lists, the publication of study materials addressed to religious communities and setting aside a week every year wherein each community would seek to emphasise the good in the other community. The latter served as the catalyst for the aforementioned proposal to the United Nations to declare an annual worldwide interfaith harmony week.

While 'Loving God and Neighbor Together: A Christian Response to *A Common Word Between Us and You*' and the Yale Conference received wide acclaim, some responses have also revealed the tensions to which dialogue between Muslims and Christians can give rise. This is most evident in the response of John Piper, a prominent evangelical pastor and author, who released a video criticising 'Loving God and Neighbor Together' for failing to accentuate the unique nature of Jesus as the saviour sent for 'the propitiation of our sins'.[578] Piper goes so far as to say that the Islamic rejection of the Christian teaching regarding Jesus indicates that Muslims and Christians do not worship the same God and that Muslims shall thus be 'cast out into utter darkness'. Such criticisms have led some prominent evangelicals who signed 'Loving God and Neighbor Together' and who attended the first Yale conference in 2008 to explain their responses and modify their endorsements. Citing the difficulties of creating a document upon which everyone could agree, Leith Anderson writes, 'While I am listed as the President of the National Association of Evangelicals, I added my name as an individual and not as an institution.'[579]

Such responses allude to tensions within the evangelical community itself, as some within the evangelical movement are hesitant to embrace any dialogue that would admit to common ground between Muslims and Christians. Others think that engaging Muslims in such dialogue is the best approach to gain access and evangelise in the Muslim world. This intra-evangelical debate was evident at the sixty-first annual meeting of the Evangelical Theological Society in November of 2009, where

Joseph Cumming, the main impetus behind 'Loving God and Neighbor Together', along with Donald Smedley, a signatory to the same document, participated on a panel with John Piper and Albert Mohler, President of the Southern Baptist Theological Seminary and a prominent evangelical pastor and radio host, and two Muslim signatories to *A Common Word*, Professors Caner Dagli and Joseph Lumbard.[580] The discussion shed light on the subtle theological differences that 'Loving God and Neighbor Together' revealed.

The Archbishop of Canterbury and Lambeth Palace

While the response organised by the Yale Divinity School was a strong affirmation of *A Common Word* and was made all the more effective by the signatures of over 300 Christian scholars, the response from the Archbishop of Canterbury, *A Common Word for the Common Good*, has been the most trenchant and perspicacious response to date. Though written as a letter from the Archbishop himself to the signatories of *A Common Word*, the response was generated through extensive discussion between the Archbishop and leaders of the Eastern, Greek and Russian Orthodox Churches, the Roman Catholic Church, and leaders from other Protestant denominations. The Archbishop first met with academics and church leaders in advance of a larger meeting in June 2008 to discuss drafting a response to *A Common Word*. There was unanimous support among the academics and church leaders present for the archbishop to send a letter to Muslim leaders. He then wrote the final letter after further consultation with members at the meeting in June 2008.

A Common Word for the Common Good begins by reaffirming the open spirit of *A Common Word* and acknowledging that though the ways of understanding the Divine are different, Christianity and Islam are not mutually unintelligible and that they speak enough of a common language to address the concerns of humanity together. The Archbishop notes that such a dialogue can invite us to 'think afresh about the foundations of our convictions',[581] and then focuses upon five areas where continued cooperation can bear fruit: focus upon love and praise of God; love of neighbour that is rooted in love of God; grounding of this interfaith exchange in scriptures so that both traditions speak from that which is central and authoritative to each; respecting and discussing differences to avoid mutual fear and suspicion; and honouring a shared responsibility towards humanity and creation.

The subtle explanations of the Christian understanding of love offered by the Archbishop deserve extensive theological discussion that is beyond the scope of this survey. Suffice to say that he takes the opportunity to explain the manner in which Trinitarian theology leads many Christians to a deeper appreciation of the workings of love within the Divine Itself and that this is the foundation for love of the neighbour and of the stranger as the proper response to the gift of love from God. This discussion lays the foundation for an explanation of the deleterious nature of religious violence that exposes the theological hypocrisy that lies at the heart of extremist religious violence of any stripe:

> The idea that any action, however extreme or disruptive or even murderous, is justified if it averts failure or defeat of a particular belief or a particular religious group is not really consistent with the conviction that our failure does not mean God's failure. Indeed, it reveals a fundamental lack of conviction in the eternity and sufficiency of the object of faith.[582]

Based upon this observation, the Archbishop argues, 'Religious violence suggests an underlying religious insecurity'.[583] Keeping in mind that the Divine has no need of human 'protection' can then lead to the awareness 'that to try and compel religious allegiance through violence is really a way of seeking to replace divine power with human'.[584] This serves as the foundation for a vision of what can be accomplished through an extended dialogue between Muslims and Christian leaders:

> What we need as a vision for our dialogue is to break the current cycles of violence, to show the world that faith and faith alone can truly ground a commitment to peace which definitively abandons the tempting but lethal cycle of retaliation in which we simply imitate each other's violence.[585]

In this way he offers the hope that 'our religious convictions can be a vehicle for creating peace where it is absent'.[586] This does not oblige Muslims and Christians to reject their own truth claims or come to some neutral agreement in areas of theological dispute. Rather it seeks to demonstrate the manner in which transcendent truth claims can serve to expose the self-serving nature of all attempts to justify violence in the name of one ideology or another. This subtle analysis of the ideological roots of human violence and the ability of religion to counter it demonstrates the potential influence that the *Common Word* initiative can have. As the Archbishop observes:

> Our voice in the conversation of society will be the stronger for being a joint one. If we are to be true to the dual commandment of love, we need to find ways of being far more effective in influencing our societies to follow the way of God in promoting that which leads to human flourishing—honesty and faithfulness in public and private relationships, in business as in marriage and family life; the recognition that a person's value is not an economic matter; the clear recognition that neither material wealth nor entertainment can secure a true and deep-rooted human fulfilment.[587]

An essential component of the Archbishop's letter that is not as fully addressed in other communiqués in this exchange is the need to understand and respect the different nature of scripture within each tradition. As he writes:

> ...for us as for you reading the scriptures is a constant source of inspiration, nurture and correction, and this makes it very appropriate for Christians and Muslims to listen to one another, and question one another, in the course of reading and interpreting the texts from which we have learned of God's will and purposes.[588]

It is fitting that the Archbishop should have brought these observations to light, as the conference hosted at Cambridge University with a final meeting at Lambeth Palace from 13–15 October, 2008 concentrated upon scripture and interpretation. While the Yale University Conference hosted hundreds of scholars from around the world and addressed most facets of the *Common Word* initiative, the conference convened by the Archbishop was limited to fifteen representatives from each faith tradition. Among these were some of the most prominent signatories, such as Abdullah bin Bayyah, whom many regard as the most knowledgeable living scholar of Sunni Islam, and Ramadan Buti, one of the most respected Sunni Muslim scholars in Syria today, who have not attended any other events associated with the *Common Word* initiative.

As with the Yale conference, the conference at Lambeth palace produced a final declaration that reaffirmed the core principles of *A Common Word*, love of God and love of neighbour. The document was, however, only signed by Ali Gomaa, the Grand Mufti of Egypt, and by the Archbishop. While reaffirming the central tenets of the others, this communiqué also offered a joint condemnation of the persecution of religious groups in Iraq, with a specific focus upon the recent persecution of Christian minorities. In the spirit of the conference, it also spoke in glowing terms of the experience of reading scripture together in a spirit of openness and cooperation:

> One of the most moving elements of our encounter has been the opportunity to study together passages from our scriptures. We have felt ourselves to have been together before God and this has given us each a greater appreciation for the richness of the other's heritage as well as an awareness of the potential value in being joined by Jewish believers in a journey of mutual discovery and attentiveness to the texts we hold sacred. We wish to repeat the experience of a shared study of scriptural texts as one of the ways in which we can come, concretely, to develop our understanding of how the other understands and lives their own faith. We commend this experience to others.[589]

For those who have been involved with interfaith dialogue and movements such as the scriptural reasoning project, this is not a remarkable observation in and of itself. But it adds greater significance and influence to the scriptural reasoning movement when the Grand Mufti of Egypt and the Archbishop of Canterbury join with imams and priests to encourage their followers to read the Bible and the Qur'an together. Muslims and Christians learning to read their scriptures in relation to one another rather than in opposition, and learning how the other communities understand their own texts could bear unimagined fruits for future generations, especially when they are encouraged to do so by the religious authorities whom they most respect. This emphasis upon the possibilities inherent to scriptural reasoning indicates one of the important ways in which academics have played an important role in working together with religious leaders to shape the *Common Word* initiative. One hopes that this encouragement will help a broader audience apply the tools of comparative scriptural inquiry that the scriptural reasoning movement has developed over the past fifteen years.[590]

The Vatican

While the response coordinated by the Yale Divinity School and the letter written by the Archbishop of Canterbury have been overwhelmingly positive, the responses from the Vatican have been mixed. Statements by Cardinal Tauran have indicated that the Vatican would prefer to focus upon the development of the Catholic-Muslim Forum in conjunction with the *Common Word* initiative, rather than it being dispersed into other international interfaith initiatives, such as that initiated by King Abdullah bin Abdul Aziz Al Saud. As noted above, the Vatican response to *A Common Word* was not at first positive, and the Vatican did not appear receptive to official dialogue with Muslims until it became apparent that other Churches had engaged *A Common Word*.

Given the multiple declarations regarding inter-religious dialogue and interfaith relations that have been issued by the Vatican, beginning with *Nostra Aetate* in 1965, the Muslim-Catholic exchange must first be viewed in this broader context. Recognising the tensions to which religious misunderstanding can give rise, *Nostra Aetate* sought to outline that which is common to all religions, especially the Abrahamic traditions:

> The Church regards with esteem also the Muslims. They adore the one God, living and subsisting in Himself, merciful and all-powerful, the Creator of heaven and earth, who has spoken to men; they take pains to submit wholeheartedly to even His inscrutable decrees, just as Abraham, with whom the faith of Islam takes pleasure in linking itself, submitted to God. Though they do not acknowledge Jesus as God, they revere Him as a prophet. They also honour Mary, His virgin Mother; at times they even call on her with devotion. In addition, they await the day of judgement when God will give their deserts to all those who have been raised from the dead.
>
> The sacred Council now pleads with all to forget the past, and urges that a sincere effort be made to achieve mutual

> understanding; for the benefit of all, let them together preserve and promote peace, liberty, social justice and moral values. (*Nostra Aetate*, 3)

In this vein, *Nostra Aetate* marked a momentous step forward in the official Catholic approach to people of other faith traditions and the reconciliation of traditional Catholic orthodoxy with modern pluralism. Nonetheless, although the Vatican has afforded greater recognition to Judaism and Islam, it continues to maintain that one can only be saved through a relationship with Christ that is mediated through 'the Church' (*Dominus Iesus*, § 20). Regarding the prayers and rituals of other faiths, the Vatican has gone so far as to declare:

> Indeed, some prayers and rituals of the other religions may assume a role of preparation for the Gospel, in that they are occasions or pedagogical helps in which the human heart is prompted to be open to the action of God. One cannot attribute to these, however, a divine origin or an *ex opere operato* salvific efficacy, which is proper to the Christian sacraments. Furthermore, it cannot be overlooked that other rituals, insofar as they depend on superstitions or other errors, constitute an obstacle to salvation. (*Dominus Iesus*, § 21)

In other words, other religions can be tolerated, but only in so far as they are a step towards full salvation in Christ. Viewed in relation to one another, *Nostra Aetate* and *Dominus Iesus* appear to say that error cannot be tolerated in and of itself, but that people who are in error still have rights that must be respected. Especially those who are well meaning and seek God, even be it in a manner that the Church considers imperfect. Following upon *Nostra Aetate*, the late Pope John Paul II made unprecedented overtures towards other Christian denominations and towards people of other faiths, especially Jews and Muslims. Regarding Muslims he declared, 'We Christians joyfully recognise the religious values we have in common with Islam. Today I would like to repeat what I said to young Muslims some years ago in Casablanca: "We believe in the same God, the one God, the living God, the God who created the world and brings his creatures to their perfection."'[591]

In contrast to Pope John Paul II's positive embrace of Muslims, many have sensed a different tone in the statements of Pope Benedict

XVI, especially in his assertions that Europe is a Christian continent and in the unfortunate comments of his Regensburg address. In this context, many Muslims felt it necessary to engage the Catholic Church in the hopes of maintaining relations more similar to those that had been enjoyed during the tenure of John Paul II. It in this vein that *An Open Letter to His Holiness Pope Benedict XVI* was delivered one month after the Regensburg Lecture was written. After correcting the factual errors of the Regensburg address, the letter states:

> Christianity and Islam are the largest and second largest religions in the world and in history. Christians and Muslims reportedly make up over a third and over a fifth of humanity respectively. Together they make up more than fifty-five percent of the world's population, making the relationship between these two religious communities the most important factor in contributing to meaningful peace around the world. As the leader of over a billion Catholics and moral example for many others around the globe, yours is arguably the single most influential voice in continuing to move this relationship forward in the direction of mutual understanding. We share your desire for frank and sincere dialogue, and recognise its importance in an increasingly interconnected world. Upon this sincere and frank dialogue we hope to continue to build peaceful and friendly relationships based upon mutual respect, justice, and what is common in essence in our shared Abrahamic tradition, particularly 'the two greatest commandments' in Mark 12:29–31 (and, in varying form, in Matthew 22:37–40), that, the Lord our God is One Lord; / And thou shalt love the Lord thy God with all thy heart, and with all thy soul, and with all thy understanding, and with all thy strength: this is the first commandment. / And the second commandment is like, namely this, Thou shalt love thy neighbour as thyself. There is none other commandment greater than these.[592]

The lack of response to this letter and the lack of media coverage it received, while many unproductive and counterproductive reactions were reported, frustrated some Muslims. The desire to alleviate this frustration and to proactively prevent another Regensburg address by the Pope or by other Christian leaders gave rise to the *Common Word* initiative in order to 'move the dialogue toward the direction of mutual understanding'. The first impression is that this objective has been achieved, for in his remarks on the final day of the first seminar of the Catholic-Muslim Forum, Pope Benedict XVI sounded more like John Paul II:

> I am well aware that Muslims and Christians have different approaches in matters regarding God. Yet we can and must be worshippers of the one God who created us and is concerned about each person in every corner of the world. Together we must show, by our mutual respect and solidarity, that we consider ourselves members of one family: the family that God has loved and gathered together from the creation of the world to the end of human history.[593]

While acknowledging that Muslims and Christians conceive of God in different ways and have a different understanding of the precise nature of the relation between the Divine and the human, he affirmed that they can nonetheless work together for the good of all humanity:

> There is a great and vast field in which we can act together in defending and promoting the moral values which are part of our common heritage. Only by starting with the recognition of the centrality of the person and the dignity of each human being, respecting and defending life which is the gift of God, and is thus sacred for Christians and for Muslims alike—only on the basis of this recognition, can we find a common ground for building a more fraternal world, a world in which confrontations and differences are peacefully settled, and the devastating power of ideologies is neutralised.[594]

Though he did not apologise for the remarks of the Regensburg address, Pope Benedict XVI did embrace the call for understanding that had been issued in the initial open letter addressed to him:

> Dear friends, let us unite our efforts, animated by good will, in order to overcome all misunderstanding and disagreements. Let us resolve to overcome past prejudices and to correct the often distorted images of the other which even today can create difficulties in our relations; let us work with one another to educate all people, especially the young, to build a common future.[595]

None of these remarks are ground-breaking. They are nonetheless significant because they indicate that *A Common Word Between Us and You* has succeeded in countering the deleterious effects of the

Regensburg address and in bringing Muslims and Christians into the type of dialogue to which *Nostra Aetate* opened and which Pope John Paul II had embraced. The cycle of recriminations to which the Regensburg address initially gave rise has thus been averted, and for the time being Catholics and Muslims are engaged in real dialogue rather than juxtaposed monologues. The second seminar of the Catholic-Muslim Forum, held in Jordan at the Baptism Site of Jesus on the river Jordan, developed upon the issues addressed by the first seminar and expanded upon the developments of other conferences. Whatever direction it may take, it is significant that Muslims and Catholics have committed themselves to a forum wherein they will be able to express their differences and work towards establishing better understanding between Muslims and Catholics. This will provide an open channel whereby unfortunate misunderstandings, such as those created by the Regensburg address, can be avoided and whereby, if they do arise, they can be addressed before any negative consequences are realised.

World Council of Churches

The responses from the Yale Divinity School, the Archbishop of Canterbury and the Vatican have given rise to more interaction between Muslims and Christians than have any others. But one should also take note of the response issued by the World Council of Churches (WCC), *Learning to Explore Love Together: Suggestions to the Churches for Responding to 'A Common Word'*. Acknowledging their commitment to 'fresh thinking about the relationship between Islam and Christianity', the letter of the WCC encourages member churches to recognise the serious intent of *A Common Word* and 'prayerfully consider its invitation to dialogue and cooperation'.[596] The Council then proposes that it will 'create a joint *planning group* to prepare steps towards common action, and seek Muslim and Christian initiatives of dialogue and cooperation at both regional and global levels'.[597]

After committing to this 'prayerful response' in the first page and a half, the remainder of *Learning to Explore Love Together* provides a thoughtful outline of the issues and difficulties that confront Muslim-Christian dialogue, noting that 'signs of similarity must be held in tension with real divergences and hard to reconcile differences'.[598] It then touches upon two central questions of Muslim-Christian dialogue:

the relationship between *tawḥīd* and trinity, and the understanding of God's word as revealed in Jesus and the Qur'an. Regarding the first it asks, 'Are these contradictory doctrines, as the history of engagement between the two faiths attests, or is there a way in which they can be seen as complementary insights into the mystery of God?' Regarding the latter it asks:

> Similarly, while both Muslims and Christians claim to receive revelation from God, what is meant when Muslims claim to perceive the will of God revealed in the Qur'an—what has been called the Word of God become book, and what is meant when Christians claim to perceive God's self revealed in Jesus Christ—who is called the Word of God become flesh?[599]

Although the response from the World Council of Churches has not yet led to the same type of high-level interaction that those of the Vatican, Lambeth Palace and Yale the Divinity School have initiated, it is significant that the broadest and most inclusive international Christian organisation has encouraged its 349 member churches in more than 100 countries to participate in this movement. This can be an important step in helping Muslims and Christians to 'strive to reach the point at which they can recognise and endorse what they hold in common with sufficient integrity to allow them to work together in the world'.[600] It is also of fundamental importance for the continued success of World Interfaith Harmony Week.

Analysis

Outside of the official participants, the *Common Word* initiative has received some criticism, though the response has been overwhelmingly positive. Though few outside the movement initially grasped its potential significance—what the Grand Mufti of Egypt Ali Gomaa has referred to as 'something of a small miracle'[601]—some are beginning to recognise the power that Muslims and Christians coming together for the common good can have. In the English speaking press one can now find over 700 articles addressing various aspects of the initiative. While this might seem substantial, it is but a drop when compared to the coverage of the Regensburg address, the Danish cartoon fiasco, or the 'Innocence of Muslims' video trailer about each of which tens of thousands of articles have been written. Given the secular inclinations of the mainstream media, it is not surprising that the vast majority of reporters are unable to distinguish the *Common Word* movement from other interfaith initiatives and see what promise it may hold.

Three central features make *A Common Word Between Us and You* and the ongoing exchange a crucial, promising and historic step in Muslim-Christian dialogue: the grounding in scripture; the acceptance of theological differences; and the participation of religious leaders of the highest rank. As seen in the passages of *A Common Word* cited above, this dialogue has been grounded in scripture from its inception, and has even sought to expand the manner in which some Qur'anic verses are interpreted. The title is drawn from the famous verse, *Say, 'O People of the Scripture! Come now to a word common between us and you, that we worship none but God and that we do not associate anything with Him, and do not take each other for lords, beside God'* (*Āl 'Imrān*, 3:64). Several scholars have noted that this verse is usually interpreted in a polemical context and employed to support polemical objectives. The interpretive history of *Āl 'Imrān*, 3:64 is indeed polemical. Muhammad ibn Jarir al-Ṭabari (d. 310/923), the dean of Qur'anic exegesis, Fakhr al-Din al-Razi (d. 606/1210), Abu 'Qasim al-Zamakhshari (d. 538/1144), al-Baghawī (d. 516/1122) and other influential exegetes tended to view this verse as a challenge to Christians.[602] Nonetheless, as with most verses of the Qur'an, there are many ways of understanding it. Other exegetes have seen *Āl 'Imrān*, 3:64 as an allusion to fundamental principles that all Abrahamic faiths are believed to share in common, saying of the phrase 'a common word', 'that is the Torah, the Gospel, and the Qur'an do not differ regarding it, or there is no differentiation regarding it among the revealed religions (*sharā'i'*).'[603] And as the eighteenth century Moroccan scholar Ahmad ibn 'Ajibah (d. 1224/1809) says in his commentary on the verse, 'The paths are many and the goal is one, and it is pure unity (*tawḥīd*)'.[604] Thus while the polemical strand of interpreting *Āl 'Imrān*, 3:64 may predominate in Islamic history, it is certainly not the only interpretive strand.

It is significant that many of the world's leading Islamic scholars have chosen to emphasise the more universal implications of *Āl*

'Imrān, 3:64 over the polemical interpretations. For it represents an integral component of this dialogue. Each community has taken it upon themselves to tell the other how they understand the sources of their own tradition, while listening as leaders of the other community explains how they understand the sources and tenets of their respective traditions. As the Final Declaration of the Yale Conference states, '*A Common Word* is rooted in our sacred texts, arising from within, not imposed from without'.[605] And as Archbishop Rowan Williams has written in his response to *A Common Word*, '... for both faiths, scripture provides the basic tools for speaking of God, and it is in attending to how we use our holy texts that we often discover most truly the nature of each other's faith.'[606] This is an essential observation, for Christians and Muslims often find it difficult to relate to the theological subtleties of one another's faiths and are rarely swayed by references to great theologians that proponents of other religions may esteem. But given the centrality of scripture in their own tradition, they are able to relate to the centrality of scripture in another tradition. In this way, scripture provides one of the best platforms for Muslim and Christian dialogue. Unfortunately, members of each tradition all too often refuse to afford another scripture the same leniency they have learned to give their own. They are thus less patient and less willing to allow the apparent naiveties, inconsistencies and contradictions of a scripture outside their own unfold into the profundities that they have come to expect of their own scriptural traditions. If, however, Muslims and Christians are able to read their scriptures together, they may come to see that in reading the scriptures of another tradition against that tradition, they have committed the very same errors of which they accuse the other tradition when it cites their scriptures against them. Comparative scriptural inquiry also has the potential to highlight dimensions of one's own scripture by showing them in another light.

The second feature that distinguishes the *Common Word* movement is that the dialogue has not sought to ignore or deny theological differences, but rather to acknowledge and even embrace them. To paraphrase Archbishop Rowan Williams, this is to say that the dialogue does not seek to bring Christian and Muslim communities together at the margins of their historic identities, but by speaking from what is central and authoritative to each.[607] In this way, the *Common Word* initiative avoids a major pitfall of much interfaith dialogue, wherein well-meaning believers barter away central tenets of their communities' creeds in the hopes of finding a common ground that is in reality a least common denominator. As if one were to say, 'I'll give up the uncreated Qur'an, if you drop the Trinity.' In the name of violating neither religion, this form of dialogue undermines religion as such, by accepting two unspoken premises: 1) that religions cannot reach common ground on religious terms; and (2) that in the modern period all people of religion must yield to the principles of secular humanism. This form of dialogue dilutes religion. It thus leads many to reject inter-religious dialogue as antithetical to the teachings of their own faith, or as a Trojan horse by which its central tenets will be undermined. This can in turn lead to greater misunderstanding and mistrust. In addressing this issue, Prince Ghazi bin Muhammad has said of the initiative, '... I would like to say also that *A Common Word* does not signal that Muslims are prepared to deviate from or concede one iota of any their convictions in reaching out to Christians—nor, I expect, the opposite. Let us be crystal clear: *A Common Word* is about equal peace, NOT about capitulation.'[608]

The third feature that sets *A Common Word* apart from other interfaith initiatives is that it has the backing of many of the highest-ranking religious authorities in both the Christian world and the Islamic world. On the Muslim side this includes figures such as Ahmad El-Tayyeb, the Shaykh of al-Azhar, Abdullah bin Bayyah, Ramadan Buti, Ayatollah Muhaqqiq-i Damad, regarded by many as one of the leading Shiʿite theologians of his generation, and the Grand Muftis of Egypt, Syria, Jordan, Bosnia, Oman, and Russia, among many others. On the Christian side, this includes the Pope, the Archbishop of Canterbury, the head of the National Association of Evangelicals, and the heads of most international Churches. The history of Christian-Muslim relations has never witnessed collaboration among authorities of this stature. In the extended version of his final address at the first seminar of the Catholic-Muslim Forum, Seyyed Hossein Nasr underlines the importance of their participation when he writes:

> In this effort to reorient ourselves toward each other, all of us, Christian and Muslim alike, can play a role. But there is no doubt that the main responsibility lies on the shoulders of religious leaders, thinkers and scholars, those whom we call *'ulamā'* in Islam. Those who are guides and trailblazers in religious matters must come forward and seek to bring about understanding to those in their own communities who hearken to their call. They should bring about further knowledge about the other whom they should present as friend, not enemy, to be loved and not vilified.[609]

The involvement of such leaders has many ramifications and was central to the establishment of United Nations Interfaith Harmony Week. It is also likely that the *Common Word* initiative served as a catalyst for the interfaith initiative launched by King Abdullah bin Abdul Aziz AlSaud. But most importantly the participants in this initiative are the people who influence what is said on Friday and Sunday in mosques and churches, what is taught in schools, and what is heard on television. If these leaders are committed to this exchange, the message of *A Common Word* has the potential to change the way that Christians and Muslims conceptualise and approach one another throughout the world.

Summary and Conclusions

Despite the significant features mentioned above, it should be stressed that the crucial theological issues that divide Christians and Muslims have not yet been fully discussed in the exchanges brought about by *A Common Word* and that they may never be fully addressed in the context of the *Common Word* initiative. For this is not at its heart a theological exchange. *A Common Word Between Us and You* is an initiative that seeks to promote peace by alleviating misunderstandings between Christians and Muslims through an emphasis on the love of God, devotion to the One God, and love of neighbour. In this way it allows the participants to maintain theological differences in creative tension while asserting what they hold in common and working for the greater good. As the World Council of Churches has expressed it:

> [Muslims and Christians] should make it a priority to understand how the precious heritages the each hold can direct and even impel them to work together for justice and peace,

> recognising their joint goals and responding to the call of the One they worship and obey to come together not only in a common word but also in common action for the greater glory of God and the well-being of all.[610]

Theological discussions may develop in the future, and this may be a role the Royal Academy can play in this dialogue; for those who do not represent large constituencies risk less when venturing new approaches to the faith. Perhaps in this way academics and theologians can help others to imagine what might be gained if Muslims and Christians sought to define themselves in relation to one another rather than in opposition.

One can hope that the spirit of this exchange will continue to be one of 'vying in good works' in accord with the Qur'anic verse cited in *A Common Word*: *Perhaps God will create friendship between you and those you consider your enemies.* (*Al-Mumtaḥanah*, 60:7) As Daniel Madigan SJ observes in his response to *A Common Word*, 'Where love replaces enmity, it is surely God at work, not just us'.[611] Let us hope that it can be so. For this interfaith endeavour is not only important for relations between Islam and Christianity, it is important for the response of religion to the forces of bigotry, terrorism and extremism. Some have argued that to avoid violent clashes between nations and peoples, religion must be abandoned altogether. But in the twentieth century—the bloodiest of human history—ideological conflicts and their attendant wars have demonstrated that it is humanity, not religion, which is responsible for the atrocities of the past and the present. Many employ religion to justify reckless ideologies and wanton violence. But in so doing they betray the very teachings of the religions they propose to represent. Perhaps by reaffirming the ethical teachings of their traditions together, Christians and Muslims can employ their collective moral voice to address injustices committed against peoples of all faiths.

The exchange initiated by *A Common Word* will not answer all of the questions that arise from religious diversity, nor will it ameliorate all of the tensions that arise from theological disputes and misunderstandings. It could, however, offer reflections that will transfer the positive effects of Christian-Muslim dialogue from the pens and lips of theologians to the *minbar* and the pulpit, from where it can also reach into the schools and streets. Agreement may not always be reached, but by continuing to approach each other in good faith, Muslims and Christians can take important steps towards eradicating the extremism that corrodes from within and divides from without. Perhaps in this way, *A Common Word* can be one small step towards realising the vision of the Prophet Isaiah, 'The nations will beat their swords into plowshares and their spears into pruning hooks. Nation will not take up sword against nation, nor will they train for war anymore' (Isaiah 2:4).

This is an updated version of a paper originally published by Brandeis University Crown Center, Crown Papers, *Crown Paper 3, October 2009.*

CHAPTER FOURTEEN

DIVINE LOVE AND MERCY IN THE QUR'AN

HRH Prince Ghazi bin Muhammad

Love as a Divine Quality

God speaks of His love many times in the Holy Qur'an. He mentions those whom He loves, such as, for example, those who rely on Him:

> *And when you are resolved, rely on God; for God loves those who rely [upon Him].* (*Āl 'Imrān*, 3:159)

However, God's Love is not merely one of God's acts or actions, but one of God's very Own Divine Qualities or Names. This can be seen by the many Divine Names in the Holy Qur'an which denote God's loving qualities, such as: 'The Gentle'—*Al-Laṭīf*; 'The Kind'—*Al-Ra'ūf*; 'The Generous'—*Al-Karīm*; The Forbearing—*Al-Ḥalīm*; 'The Absolutely Reliable'—*Al-Wakīl*; The Friend—*Al-Walī*; The Good—*Al-Barr*; 'The Forgiving'—*Al-Ghafūr*; 'The Forgiver'—*Al-Ghaffār*; 'The Granter and Accepter of Repentance'—*Al-Tawwāb*; and 'The Pardoner'—*Al-'Afū*), and in particular by His Name 'The Loving' (*Al-Wadūd*), which occurs twice in the Holy Qur'an:

> *And ask forgiveness of your Lord, then repent to Him. Truly my Lord is Merciful, Loving.* (*Hūd*, 11:90)

> *And He is the Forgiving, the Loving.* (*Al-Burūj*, 85:14)

Here we see the connection between love and mercy: the Divine Name 'The Loving' is mentioned alongside the Divine Names 'The Merciful' and 'The Forgiving' in the two Qur'anic verses (and never without them), indicating that God's Love is inseparable from His Mercy.[612] Thus Love comes with Mercy, and Mercy comes with Love.

Indeed, some of God's other Divine Names which indicate the

'gentle' Divine Qualities—such as the Divine Name 'The Kind' (*Al-Ra'ūf*), which occurs in the Holy Qur'an ten times,[613] and certain other Names as previously mentioned—also imply *both* God's Love and His Mercy together. We may even say that Mercy engenders Love; for the word *raḥmah* ('mercy') is derived from *raḥm* ('womb'), and God says in a *Ḥadīth Qudsī* (that is, a hadith where the Messenger of God ﷺ is quoting God Himself as Speaker):

> *'I am God (Allāh), I am The Compassionate One (Al-Raḥmān). I created the womb (raḥm) and named it after My Name. He who keeps its ties, I shall keep [my ties with] him; and he who cuts its ties, I shall cut him off [from Me].'*[614]

Indeed, if we reflect on the womb, we will realise that the womb produces mercy just as it produces children, because when a child is born from the womb he or she already naturally enjoys his or her mother's love. This is a law of nature: mercy produces love, even though love has special qualities which mercy does not necessarily share.

The natural connection between love and mercy is not confined to the keeping of family ties alone, for God also alludes to the connection between affection—which is a form of love—with mercy, in the following verse:

> *And of His signs is that He created for you from yourselves mates that you might find peace by their side, and He ordained between you affection (mawaddah) and mercy. Surely in that there are signs for a people who reflect.* (*Al-Rūm*, 30:21)

Love and Mercy as of the Divine Essence

God equates His Name 'The Compassionate' (*Al-Rahmān*) with His Divine Name 'God' (*Allāh*) in His words:

> *Say: 'Invoke God or invoke the Compassionate One; whichever you invoke, to Him belong the Most Beautiful Names'....* (*Al-Isrā'*, 17:110)

Since the Divine Name *Allāh* refers to the Divine Essence, this means that Divine Mercy is of the very Divine Essence—the Godhead or the Self—Itself, without and before any relation to any created being. This is also proved by God's words:

> *...He has prescribed for Himself (nafsihi—His Self) mercy....* (*Al-An'ām*, 6:12)

And His words:

> *...Your Lord has prescribed for Himself (nafsihi—His Self) mercy....* (*Al-An'ām*, 6:54)

Thus God has made mercy incumbent upon Himself or rather His Self—the Arabic word *nafsihi* means both Himself (reflexively) and 'His Self' (thus referring to the Divine Essence or Self or Godhead)—which is to say that Divine Mercy is of the Divine Essence Itself. God's Mercy is thus incumbent on God by His own very Being. Consequently, God is bound by Himself to be Merciful, and His Mercy embraces everything. This is affirmed by His words:

> *...My mercy embraces all things.... (Al-A'rāf, 7:156)*

Moreover, this is what the angels affirm when they pray for forgiveness for the believers:

> *... Our Lord, You embrace all things in [Your] mercy and knowledge...* (*Ghāfir*, 40:7)

We must also mention that every one of the 114 chapters of the Holy Qur'an begins with the sacred formula *In the Name of God, the Compassionate, the Merciful* (*Bism Allāh Al-Raḥmān Al-Raḥīm*') except the ninth (*Sūrat Al-Tawbah*)—albeit that Islamic scholars point out that the 'missing' *basmallah* of *Sūrat Al-Tawbah* reappears in *Sūrat Al-Naml* wherein God says:

> *... And lo! it is: In the Name of God, the Compassionate, the Merciful.* (*Al-Naml*, 27:30)

Thus the fact that practically every chapter in the Holy Qur'an begins with *In the Name of God, the Compassionate, the Merciful* further indicates the connection between the Divine Name 'God' (*Allāh*) and mercy.[615]

All of this allows us to say that since Divine Love, like Divine Mercy, is a Divine Quality; and since God's Loving is inseparable from His Mercy; and since Divine Mercy is of the very Divine Essence Itself, then we can conclude that Divine Love, like Divine Mercy, is of the Divine Essence Itself, as well as being a Divine Quality. This is seen in the *Āyat al-Kursī*—which the Messenger of God ﷺ called 'the greatest verse in the Holy Qur'an'[616]—which speaks of the Divine Essence, and of the Qualities of God in relation to His Creation. God says:

> *God, there is no god, except Him, The Living (Al-Ḥayy), The Eternal Sustainer (Al-Qayyūm). Slumber does not seize Him, neither sleep; to Him belongs all that is in the heavens and the earth; who is there, that shall intercede with Him save by His leave? He knows what lies before them, and what is after them; and they encompass nothing of His knowledge, save such as He wills. His throne embraces the heavens and the earth; the preserving of them wearies Him not; He is The Sublime, The Tremendous.* (*Al-Baqarah*, 2:255)

After mentioning two of His Names (*Al-Ḥayy* and *Al-Qayyum*) and some of His Qualities, God says: *who is there, that shall intercede with Him save by His leave?* Now intercession is evidently a function and a reflection of mercy, so we understand from this sacred verse not only that Divine Mercy is of the Divine Essence, but also that all mercy—even the mercy of God's creatures to each other—is ultimately from God, for it is *by His leave*. Indeed, God says:

> *And how many an angel there is in the heavens whose intercession cannot avail in any way except after God gives permission for whomever He wills, and He is satisfied.* (*Al-Najm*, 53:26)

> *And warn therewith those who fear they shall be gathered to their Lord: apart from Him they have no protector and no intercessor so that they might fear [God].* (*Al-An'ām*, 6:51)

> *God is He Who created the heavens and the earth and whatever is between them in six days, then He presided upon the Throne. You do not have besides Him any protector or intercessor. Will you not then remember?* (*Al-Sajdah*, 32:4)

> *Or have they taken besides God intercessors? Say: 'What! even though they have no power whatever and are unable to comprehend?' / Say: 'All intercession belongs [solely] to God. To Him belongs the kingdom of the heavens and the earth; then to Him you will be brought back'.* (*Al-Zumar*, 39:43–4)

Muslim scholars and exegetes have disagreed about the exact differences between 'The Compassionate' (*Al-Raḥmān*) and 'The Merciful' (*Al-Raḥīm*), but they all affirm that the Divine Name 'The Compassionate' does not require an object, whilst the Divine Name 'The

Merciful' does require an object to receive the mercy. This means that 'The Compassionate' is compassionate in His Essence, and 'The Merciful' is merciful in His actions. However, since love comes with mercy, and since mercy exists in both the Divine Names 'The Compassionate' and 'The Merciful', then love too is implied in both the Divine Names 'The Compassionate' and 'The Merciful'. Thus God's Love is twice implied—along with the double mention of Divine Mercy—at the beginning of the Holy Qur'an itself and the beginning of every one of its 114 chapters except the ninth (which is later compensated for).[617]

QUESTION: Since God's Mercy embraces all things (*My mercy embraces all things*); and since God *has prescribed for Himself mercy*; and since God's Mercy outstrips His wrath (according to the *Ḥadīth Qudsī* which says: '*My mercy outstrips My wrath*'), then how can God punish sinners with painful and severe punishment for their sins? God says:

> *The Jews and Christians say: 'We are the sons of God and His beloved ones'. Say: 'Why then does He chastise you for your sins? Nay; you are mortals from among those He created. He forgives whom He wills, and He chastises whom He wills'. For to God belongs the kingdom of the heavens and of the earth, and all that is between them; to Him is the journey's end.* (*Al-Mā'idah*, 5:18)
>
> *And whoever slays a believer deliberately, his requital is Hell, abiding therein, and God is angry with him and has cursed him, and has prepared for him a mighty chastisement.* (*Al-Nisā'*, 4:93)

Fakhr al-Din al-Razi says:

> There are many opinions about His words *My mercy embraces all things*. It is said that *My mercy embraces all things* means that His Mercy in the life of the lower world is granted universally to all, whilst in the hereafter it is granted only to the believers. This is indicated by [proceeding] His words: *and so I shall prescribe it for those who are God-fearing.*[618]

And Qurtubi says, commenting on this verse:

> His words *My mercy embraces all things* are universal, meaning infinite; meaning that it will not fail to reach all those to whom it applies. It is said that it means that [His Mercy] embraces all in creation, in that even animals have mercy and

> affection for their young. Some exegetes say that all beings were given hope by this verse, even Iblis [Satan], who said, 'I am a thing!' But then God says: *and so I shall prescribe it for those who are God-fearing.*[619]

In any case, God says: *My mercy embraces all things.* He does not say: 'My tenderness embraces all things', but rather (elsewhere): *God is Tender with His servants. He provides for whomever He will. And He is the Strong, the Mighty* (*Al-Shūra*, 42:19). God, then, is tender with His servants in a general way, and *He provides for whomever He will.* This does not mean for all, and does not mean that His tenderness—and therefore gentleness—embraces all things all the time, otherwise there would never be any suffering or pain in the world. There is thus a big difference between mercy and tenderness. Indeed, we may have mercy on something by temporarily doing something harsh to it to save it from something even worse and more permanent (as, for example, does the surgeon or veterinarian who performs surgery); yet this mercy (or this surgery) might not be that gentle or involve any tenderness at all. God's Mercy embracing all things thus does not mean that nothing will ever suffer, but that God will guide every existing thing to what will enable it to suffer the least; and God knows best.

Love as the Root of Creation

God created human beings *out of* His Mercy, for He says:

> *The Compassionate One / has taught the Qur'an. / He created man, / teaching him [coherent] speech. (Al-Rahmān, 55:1–4)*

And He says:

> *Had your Lord willed, He would have made humankind one community, but they continue to differ, / except those on whom your Lord has mercy; and for that did He create them...* (*Hūd*, 11:118–9)

Fakhr al-Din al-Razi says about God's words *and for that did He create them*:

> There are three opinions about these words. The first opinion: Ibn 'Abbas ﷺ said: 'He created them for mercy'; and this is the opinion of the majority of Mu'tazilites, who say that it cannot be that God created them so that they would differ.

> There are several proofs for this: firstly, pronouns should be assumed to refer to their nearest possible antecedent, and the nearest possible antecedent here is 'mercy', whilst 'to differ' is further away. Secondly, had He created them to differ and wanted them to believe this, He could not then punish them for it, since they would be obeying Him by differing. Thirdly, if we understand the verse in this way, it is in harmony with what He says elsewhere: *and I did not create the jinn and humankind except that they may worship Me* (*Al-Dhāriyāt*, 51:56). If it is said, 'If the meaning were that He created them because of His Mercy, the pronoun "that" would be feminine in Arabic (since *raḥmah* ["mercy"] is a feminine noun in Arabic), not masculine,' we respond that the feminine status of the word *raḥmah* is not a true feminine, since the word means 'favour' and 'forgiveness' [respectively *faḍl* and *ghufrān* in Arabic, which are both masculine], as He says: *Said he, 'This* [*hādhā*—a masculine pronoun] *is a mercy* (*raḥmah*) *from my Lord'...* (*Al-Kahf*, 18:98), and He says: *... surely the mercy* (*raḥmah*) *of God is near* (*qarīb*, masculine adjective) *to the virtuous* (*Al-A'rāf*, 7:56). The second opinion is that these words mean that He created them so that they would differ. The third opinion, which is the most satisfactory one, is that He created the people of mercy for mercy, and the people of differing for differing.[620]

We believe that the opinion of Ibn 'Abbas is the one that corresponds best with the literal meaning of the verse. Indeed, we cannot ignore the opinion of Ibn 'Abbas—who learnt the Holy Qur'an personally from his cousin the Prophet Muhammad ﷺ himself—even if al-Razi does not concur. Moreover, as al-Razi himself says, linguistically speaking, the word *raḥmah* may be considered either feminine or masculine—and therefore the word 'that' can indeed refer to it. At most, it might be said—to accommodate al-Razi's opinion—that God created people as such for mercy, but also created them as 'people of differing' for differing and 'people of mercy' for mercy—in other words, that God wants to grant His Mercy to everyone, but created them free and thus allowed them not to choose His Mercy. However, this seems an unnecessary, complicated quibble with Ibn 'Abbas's commentary. Moreover, logically speaking, God prescribes Mercy for Himself:

> *...Your Lord has prescribed for Himself mercy...* (*Al-An'ām*, 6:54)

And this Mercy is linked to the very creation of the heavens and the earth:

> *Say: 'To whom belongs what is in the heavens and in the earth?' Say: 'To God.' He has prescribed for Himself mercy. He will surely gather you together on the Day of Resurrection of which there is no doubt. Those who have forfeited their own souls, they do not believe.* (*Al-An'ām*, 6:12)

And the Messenger of God ﷺ said:

> When God created the world, He wrote above His Throne: My mercy outstrips My wrath. '[621]

How, then, could God have 'created the people of differing for differing', as al-Razi says, and not for mercy? Rather, God created human beings *for* His mercy but some of them 'differed', and as a result of this they closed themselves off from Divine mercy, despite the vastness of His mercy about which God says: *My mercy embraces all things...* (*Al-A'rāf*, 7:156).[622]

Furthermore, how could God have created 'the people of differing' for 'differing', when God has actually stated the reason for creation elsewhere in the Holy Qur'an, and it is precisely not for 'differing' as such. God says:

> *And I did not create the jinn and humankind except that they may worship Me* (*Al-Dhāriyāt*, 51:56)

Now the worship of God is a mercy, and it leads to more mercy; and God does not say here that He created some of humanity and the jinn for worship, and others for something else (i.e. 'differing'), but rather that He created them *all* for worshipping Him, and therefore for attaining His Mercy. Indeed, there are more than twenty-five verses in the Holy Qur'an which indicate that God created human beings for mercy, and for that which leads to mercy. Thus God says He created human beings to be God-fearing:

> *O people, worship your Lord Who created you and those that were before you, so that you may be God-fearing.* (*Al-Baqarah*, 2:21)

And 'to know the names of all things', for He says:

> *And when your Lord said to the angels, 'I am appointing on*

> *earth a vicegerent', they said, 'What, will You appoint therein one who will do corruption therein and shed blood, while we glorify You with praise and sanctify You?'; He said, 'Assuredly, I know what you know not'. / And He taught Adam the names, all of them; then He presented them to the angels and said, 'Now tell Me the names of these if you speak truly'.* (*Al-Baqarah*, 2:30-31)

And He created human beings 'to reward them with the best reward', for He says:

> *And to God belongs whatever is in the heavens and whatever is in the earth that He may requite those who do evil for what they have done, and reward those who are virtuous with the best [reward].* (*Al-Najm*, 53:31)

And 'to test which of them is best in conduct', for God says:

> *[He] Who created death and life, that He may try you [to see] which of you is best in conduct, and He is the Mighty, the Forgiving (Al-Mulk, 67:2)*

And 'to reward those who believe and perform good deeds', for God says:

> *To Him is the return of all of you: God's promise, in truth. Truly He originates creation, then recreates it that He may requite those who believe and perform righteous deeds, justly. And those who disbelieve, for them will be a draught of boiling water and a painful chastisement because they disbelieved.* (*Yūnus*, 10:4)

And 'so that human beings may be certain about the encounter with God', for He says:

> *God is He Who raised up the heavens without visible supports then presided upon the Throne and disposed the sun and the moon, each one moving, until [the conclusion of] an appointed time. He directs the command. He details the signs so that you might be certain of the encounter with your Lord.* (*Al-Ra'd*, 13:2)

And 'so that human beings may seek His favour, give thanks to Him, reflect on His signs, understand them and be guided', for God says:

> *He created the heavens and the earth with the Truth. Exalted be He above what they associate. / He created man from a drop of fluid, yet behold! he is disputatious, openly. / And the cattle, He created them for you. In them there is warmth, as well as [other] uses, and of them you eat; / and for you there is in them beauty, when you bring them [home] to rest, and when you drive them forth to pasture. / And they bear your burdens to a land which you could not reach, save with great trouble to yourselves. Indeed your Lord is Gentle, Merciful. / And [He created] horses and mules and asses, that you may ride them, and for adornment; and He creates what you do not know. / And God's is the direction of the way, and some of them are deviant. And had He willed, He would have guided you all. / He it is Who sends down water from the heaven, whence you have drink, and whence are trees, whereat you let your animals graze. / With it He makes the crops grow for you, and olives and date-palms and vines and all kinds of fruit. Surely in that there is a sign for people who reflect. / And He disposed for you the night and the day, and the sun and the moon and the stars are disposed by His command. Surely in that there are signs for people who understand. / And whatever He has created for you in the earth, diverse in hue. Surely in that there is a sign for people who remember. / And He it is Who disposed the sea, that you may eat from it fresh meat, and bring forth from it ornaments which you wear. And you see the ships ploughing therein; and that you may seek of His favour, and that you might be thankful. / And He cast into the earth firm mountains, lest it should shake with you, and rivers and ways so that you might be guided /—and landmarks [as well], and by the stars, they are guided.* (Al-Naḥl, 16:3–16)

And so that human beings remember Him and thank Him, for God says:

> *And He it is Who made the night and day [to appear] in succession for him who desires to remember or desires to be thankful.* (Al-Furqān, 25:62)

And so that human beings supplicate Him, for God says:

> *Say, 'My Lord would not be concerned with you were it not for your supplications. But you have denied, and so that will remain binding.'* (Al-Furqān, 25:7)

And 'so that He might relent to the believing men and women', for God says:

> *So that God may chastise the hypocrites, men and women, and the idolaters, men and women, and that God may relent to the believing men and believing women. And God is Forgiving, Merciful.* (*Al-Aḥzāb*, 33:73)

And 'so that human beings may complete an appointed term, and understand', for God says:

> *He it is Who created you from dust, then from a drop [of sperm], then from a blood clot, then He brings you forth as infants, then that you may come of age, then that you may become aged, though there are some of you who die earlier, and that you may complete an appointed term that perhaps you might understand.* (*Ghāfir*, 40:67)

And 'so that human beings might seek God's favour, and thank Him, and reflect upon His signs', for God says:

> *God it is Who disposed for you the sea so that the ships may sail upon it by His command, and that you may seek of His favour, and that perhaps you may give thanks. / And He has disposed for you whatever is in the heavens, and whatever is in the earth, all being from Him. Surely in that there are signs for a people who reflect.* (*Al-Jāthiyah*, 45:12–3)

And 'to requite each soul justly', for God says:

> *And God created the heavens and the earth with the truth and so that every soul may be requited for what it has earned, and they will not be wronged.* (*Al-Jāthiyah*, 45:22)

And 'so that human beings may come to know one another', for God says:

> *O humankind! We have indeed created you from a male and a female, and made you nations and tribes that you may come to know one another. Truly the noblest of you in the sight of God is the most God-fearing among you. Truly God is Knower, Aware.* (*Al-Ḥujurāt*, 49:13)

And 'so that human beings might have insight and be people of remembrance and penitence', for God says:

As an insight and a reminder for every penitent servant. (*Qāf*, 50:8)

And 'so that human beings might keep the balance with justice', for God says:

The Compassionate One / has taught the Qur'an. / He created man, / teaching him [coherent] speech. / The sun and the moon follow a reckoning, / and the grass and the trees prostrate. / And He has raised the heaven and set up the balance, / [declaring] that you should not contravene with regard to the balance. / And observe the weights with justice and do not skimp the balance. (*Al-Raḥmān*, 55:1-9)

And 'so that human beings might be guided to the way, and be grateful to God', for God says:

Verily We created man from a drop of mixed fluid, so that We may test him. So We made him hearing, seeing. / Verily We have guided him to the way, whether he be grateful or ungrateful. (*Al-Insān*, 76:2-3)

And that 'God created the earth as sustenance for human beings', for God says:

Are you harder to create or the heaven which He has built? / He made it rise high and levelled it, / and darkened its night, and brought forth its day; / and after that He spread out the earth; / from it He has brought forth its waters and its pastures, / and has set firm the mountains / as a [source of] sustenance for you and your flocks. (*Al-Nāzi'āt*, 79:27–33)

What all these verses have in common is the fact that God creates human beings, gives them freedom and tests them in this life so that they might attain His Mercy, although those who fail and do evil things are requited for their own evil deeds.

It should also be mentioned that in addition to all the verses from the Holy Qur'an cited above there are twenty-five other verses in the Holy Qur'an in which God describes the wisdom behind His creating *certain parts* of creation (and not all of it). These parts of creation were *specifically* made for the service of humanity, to help achieve their purpose in life, which is to attain God's Mercy by worshipping Him. These verses include, for example:

> *It is He Who made the earth tractable for you, so walk in its flanks and eat of His provision; and to Him is the resurrection.* (*Al-Mulk*, 67:15)[623]

Thus it is clear and beyond doubt that God created human beings and the world *out of mercy* and *for mercy*; and since Divine Mercy is inseparable from Divine Love (as we have already just seen), this means that the world and human beings were created *out of love* and *for love* as well.

QUESTION: If the world and human beings were created *out of* mercy, and thus love, and *for* mercy and thus love, then how can it be that God does not love certain (evil) people?

As discussed elsewhere, the only creatures and things which God does not love are the evildoers and disbelievers and certain evil deeds. The answer to this question is therefore limited to an examination of the states of the evildoers, disbelievers and certain evil deeds with respect to God's Love and Mercy.

As regards evildoers and the disbelievers, God in His Mercy and Love created them in a state of primordial purity, and in the best stature and the best form.[624] God says:

> *By the fig and the olive, / and [by] the Mount Sinai, / and [by] this secure land, / Verily We created man in the best stature. / Then, We reduced him to the lowest of the low, / except those who believe and perform righteous deeds, for they shall have an unfailing reward. / So what makes you deny thereafter the Judgement? / Is not God the fairest of all judges?* (*Al-Tīn*, 95:1–8)

> *God it is Who made for you the earth as a [stable] abode and the heaven as a canopy. And He formed you and perfected your forms, and provided you with [all] the wholesome things. That then is God, your Lord, so blessed be God, the Lord of the Worlds.* (*Ghāfir*, 40:64)

> *He created the heavens and the earth with the truth, and He shaped you and made your shapes excellent; and to Him is the journey's end.* (*Al-Taghābun*, 64:3)

> *O man! What has deceived you with regard to your generous Lord? / Who created you, then made you upright, then proportioned you, / assembling you in whatever form He wishes?* (*Al-Infiṭār*, 82:6–8)

But this does not mean that God, who created human beings *in the best of statures*, still loves them if and after they become *the lowest of the low*. Abu Hurayrah ﷺ reported that the Messenger of God ﷺ said:

> *'Every child is born primordially pure, and then his parents make him Jewish, or Christian, or Magian ....'*[625]

And 'Iyad ibn Majashi'i reported that the Messenger of God ﷺ said:

> *'God Almighty says: ... And I created all My servants in a righteous state, and then demons came to them and drew them away from their religion....'*[626]

This means that although God created human beings out of mercy, He made them free and able to choose between good and evil. God says:

> *Verily We have guided him to the way, whether he be grateful or ungrateful.* (*Al-Insān*, 76:3)
>
> *And We guided him to the two paths.* (*Al-Balad*, 90:10)
>
> *And as for Thamud, We offered them guidance, but they preferred blindness to guidance. So the thunderbolt of the humiliating chastisement seized them on account of what they used to earn.* (*Fuṣṣilat*, 41:17)

If a person chooses goodness, virtue, or the like, then God will love him or her more. However, if they choose the way of evil and sin, and close themselves off from God's guidance, then they will not attain God's Mercy and Love. Thus God—out of mercy and love—creates people free, but some use this freedom to choose not to accept God's Mercy and Love. The inevitable price to be paid for freedom is the possibility of evil and thus the rejection of God's Mercy. Indeed, God cites the Prophet Noah in the Holy Qur'an saying:

> *He said, 'O my people, have you considered if I am [acting] upon a clear proof from my Lord and He has given me mercy from Him, and you have remained blind to it, can we force it on you, even though you are averse to it?'* (*Hūd*, 11:28)

It is thus not a question of God not loving evil people and acts, but rather of evil people freely refusing to be loved by God. And God knows best.

God's Love for Humanity in General

God's favour (*faḍl*) is an aspect of His Mercy, and Divine Mercy itself—as we saw earlier—is inseparable from Divine Love. Hence we must mention here God's completely gratuitous favour upon humanity in general as an aspect of God's Love.

After creating human beings from dust, God breathed His spirit into him:

> *So when I have proportioned him, and breathed in him My spirit, then fall down in prostration before him!* (*Ṣād*, 38:72)

> *Who beautified everything that He created. And He began the creation of man from clay, / then He made his progeny from an extract of a base fluid, / then He proportioned him, and breathed into him of His spirit. And He made for you hearing, and sight and hearts. Little thanks do you give.* (*Al-Sajdah*, 32:7–9)

> *And when your Lord said to the angels, 'Indeed I am going to create a mortal out of dry clay [drawn] from malleable mud. / So, when I have proportioned him and breathed of My spirit in him, fall down in prostration before him!' / And so the angels prostrated, all of them together, / except Iblis, he refused to be among those prostrating. / He [said]: 'O Iblis what is wrong with you that you are not among those prostrating?' / Said he, 'I was not about to prostrate myself before a mortal whom You have created out of a dry clay [drawn] from malleable mud.' / Said He, 'Then be gone from hence; for you are indeed accursed.'* (*Al-Ḥijr*, 15:28–34)

And God created human beings in the best of forms (*sūrah*):

> *God it is Who made for you the earth as a [stable] abode and the heaven as a canopy. And He formed you and perfected your forms, and provided you with [all] the wholesome things. That then is God, your Lord, so blessed be God, the Lord of the Worlds.* (*Ghāfir*, 40:64)

> *He created the heavens and the earth with the truth, and He shaped you and made your forms excellent; and to Him is the journey's end.* (*Al-Taghābun*, 64:3)

> *O man! What has deceived you with regard to your generous Lord? / Who created you, then made you upright, then proportioned you, / assembling you in whatever form He wishes?* (*Al-Infiṭār*, 82:6–8)

And God created human beings in the best of statures (*taqwīm*):

> *By the fig and the olive, / and [by] the Mount Sinai, / and [by] this secure land, / Verily We created man in the best of statures. / Then, We reduced him to the lowest of the low, / except those who believe and perform righteous deeds, for they shall have an unfailing reward. / So what makes you deny thereafter the Judgment? / Is not God the fairest of all judges?* (*Al-Tīn*, 95:1–8)

And He created human beings in the primordial state of purity (*fiṭrah ḥanīfah*):

> *Nay, but those who do evil follow their own desires without any knowledge. So who will guide him whom God has led astray? And they have no helpers. / So set your purpose for religion, as a ḥanīf—a nature (fitrah) given by God, upon which He originated humankind. There is no changing God's creation. That is the upright religion, but most people do not know.* (*Al-Rūm*, 30:29–30)

> *So by God's spirit; by the best of forms; by the best of statures; and by the primordial state of purity, God has favoured or preferred (faḍḍala) humanity in general above many other creatures.*[627] God says:

> *And verily We have honoured the Children of Adam, and carried them over land and sea, and provided them with good things; and We have preferred (faḍḍalnahum) them above many of those whom We created with a marked preferment.* (*Al-Isrā'*, 17:70)

Indeed, by these favours, God has ennobled human beings above even the angels, and made them His vicegerent on earth:

> *And We created you, then shaped you, then said to the angels: 'Prostrate yourselves before Adam!' So they fell prostrate, all save Iblis [Lucifer], he was not of those who make prostration.* (*Al-A'rāf*, 7:11)

> *He it is Who created for you all that is in the earth; then He turned to heaven and levelled them seven heavens and He has knowledge of all things. / And when your Lord said to the*

> *angels, 'I am appointing on earth a vicegerent,' they said, 'What, will You appoint therein one who will do corruption therein and shed blood, while we glorify You with praise and sanctify You?'; He said, 'Assuredly, I know what you know not.' / And He taught Adam the names, all of them; then He presented them to the angels and said, 'Now tell Me the names of these if you speak truly.' / They said, 'Glory be to You! We know not except what You have taught us. Surely You are the Knower, Wise.' / He said, 'Adam, tell them their names.'; And when he had told them their names He said, 'Did I not tell you that I know the Unseen in the heavens and the earth?, And I know what you reveal and what you were hiding.' / And when We said to the angels, 'Prostrate yourselves to Adam'; so they prostrated themselves, except Iblis, he refused and disdained; and so he became one of the disbelievers (kāfirīn).* (*Al-Baqarah*, 2:29–34) [628]

Through all these Divine favours, human beings were given a trust greater than could have been borne by the heavens, the earth and the mountains:

> *Indeed We offered the Trust to the heavens and the earth and the mountains, but they refused to bear it and were apprehensive of it; but man undertook it. Truly he is a wrongdoer, ignorant.*(*Al-Aḥzāb*, 33:72)

Finally, we must mention that in addition to all the gratuitous favours which God has granted every human being in general, He has also granted gratuitous graces (*ni'mah* pl. *ni'am*) to every single human being individually. God says:

> *And if you were to count God's grace you could never reckon it. Indeed God is Forgiving, Merciful.* (*Al-Naḥl*, 16:18)

> *Whatever grace you have, it is from God. Then when misfortune befalls you, to Him you cry for help.* (*Al-Naḥl*, 16:53)

> *Do you not see that God has disposed for you whatever is in the heavens and whatever is in the earth, and He has showered His graces upon you, [both] outwardly and inwardly? Yet among people there are those who dispute concerning God without any knowledge or guidance or an illuminating scripture.* (*Luqmān*, 31:20)

> *Each We supply [to] these and [to] those from your Lord's bounty. And your Lord's bounty is not confined.* (*Al-Isrā'*, 17:20)

God's Love for the Virtuous in Particular

As we have seen, God has greatly favoured human beings in general and individually—more than He has favoured other creatures. Divine favour comes from Divine Mercy, and Divine Mercy is inseparable from Divine Love. Thus God's great favour to human beings is also a result of His Love for them in general, or as such.

In addition to all that, God says that He loves people more if they follow the Messenger of God ﷺ:

> *Say: 'If you love God, follow me, and God will love you more (yuḥbibkum), and forgive you your sins; God is Forgiving, Merciful.'* (*Āl 'Imrān*, 3:31)

Moreover, God mentions that a people may come in the future whom God loves and who love God, and who are characterised by the following attributes:

> *O you who believe, whoever of you apostatises from his religion, God will assuredly bring a people whom He loves and who love Him: humble towards believers, stern towards disbelievers, struggling in the way of God, and fearing not the reproach of any reproacher. That is God's favour; He gives it to whom He will; and God is Embracing, Knowing.* (*Al-Mā'idah*, 5:54)

God also specifically mentions eight general kinds of people whom He says (in the present tense) that He 'loves'. They are as follows:

1) 'Those who rely' (on God) (*al-mutawakkilīn* or *al-mutawakkilūn*, depending on the word's grammatical case):

> *It was by the mercy of God that you were lenient with them; had you been harsh and fierce of heart, they would have dispersed from about you. So pardon them, and ask forgiveness for them, and consult them in the matter. And when you are resolved, rely on God; for God loves those who rely.* (*Āl 'Imrān*, 3:159)

2) 'Those who cleanse themselves' (*al-mutaṭahhirīn*) or 'purify themselves' (*al-muṭṭahhirīn*):

> *They will ask you about the monthly period. Say: 'It is an ailment; so part with women in the monthly period, and do not approach them until they are pure; when they have cleansed*

themselves, then come to them, as God has commanded you.' Truly, God loves those who repent, and He loves those who cleanse themselves. (*Al-Baqarah*, 2:222)

Never stand there. A mosque which was founded upon piety from the first day is worthier for you to stand therein; in it are men who love to purify themselves; and God loves those who purify themselves. (*Al-Tawbah*, 9:108)

3) 'Those who repent' (*al-tawwābīn*):

They will ask you about the monthly period. Say: 'It is an ailment; so part with women in the monthly period, and do not approach them until they are pure; when they have cleansed themselves, then come to them, as God has commanded you.' Truly, God loves those who repent, and He loves those who cleanse themselves. (*Al-Baqarah*, 2:222)

4) 'The just' (*al-muqsiṭīn*):

Listeners to calumny and consumers of unlawful gain. If they come to you, then judge between them or turn away from them. If you turn away from them, they cannot harm you at all; and if you judge, then judge justly between them; God loves the just. (*Al-Mā'idah*, 5:42)

And if two parties of believers fall to fighting, make peace between them. And if one of them aggresses against the other, fight the one which aggresses until it returns to God's ordinance. Then, if it returns, reconcile them, and act justly. Surely God loves the just. (*Al-Ḥujurāt*, 49:9)

God does not forbid you in regard to those who did not wage war against you on account of religion and did not expel you from your homes, that you should treat them kindly and deal with them justly. Surely God loves the just. (*Al-Mumtaḥanah*, 60:8)

5) 'Those who fight for His cause in ranks, as if they were a solid structure' (*al-ladhīna yuqātilūna fi sabīlihi ṣaffan ka'annahum bunyānun marṣūṣun*)[629]:

Indeed God loves those who fight for His cause in ranks, as if they were a solid structure. (*Al-Ṣaff*, 61:4)

6) 'The patient' (*al-ṣābirīn*):

How many a prophet has been killed and with him thou-

sands manifold [fought], but they fainted not in the face of what afflicted them in God's way; they neither weakened, nor did they humble themselves. And God loves the patient. (*Āl 'Imrān*, 3:146)

7) 'The God-fearing' (*al-muttaqīn*):

Nay, but whoever fulfils his covenant, and has fear, for truly God loves the God-fearing. (*Āl 'Imrān*, 3:76)

Excepting those of the idolaters with whom you have made a pact, and who have not diminished [their commitment to] you in anyway, nor supported anyone against you; [as for these] fulfil your pact with them until the term. Truly God loves the God-fearing. (*Al-Tawbah*, 9:4)

How can the idolaters have a pact with God and His Messenger, except for those with whom you made a pact at the Sacred Mosque? So long as they are true to you, be true to them. Truly God loves the God-fearing (*Al-Tawbah*, 9:7)

8) 'The virtuous' (*al-muḥsinīn*):

And spend in the way of God; and do not cast yourselves by your own hands into destruction; but be virtuous; God loves the virtuous. (*Al-Baqarah*, 2:195)

Who expend in prosperity and adversity, and restrain their rage, and pardon their fellow-men; and God loves those who are virtuous. (*Āl 'Imrān*, 3:134)

And God gave them the reward of this world, and the fairest reward of the Hereafter, and God loves the virtuous. (*Āl 'Imrān*, 3:148)

So because of their breaking their covenant, We cursed them and made their hearts hard; they distort words from their contexts; and they have forgotten a portion of what they were reminded of; and you will never cease to discover some treachery on their part, except for a few of them. Yet pardon them, and forgive; surely God loves the virtuous. (*Al-Mā'idah*, 5:13)

Those who believe and perform righteous deeds are not at fault in what they may have consumed, so long as they fear, and believed and performed righteous deeds, and then were God-fearing and believed, and then were God-fearing and virtuous; God loves the virtuous. (*Al-Mā'idah*, 5:93)

What do all these eight types of people have in common? The answer is that they are all characterised by certain good and virtuous characteristics of the soul. Reliance, purity, repentance, justice, fighting in God's cause, patience, fear of God and virtue are all good and virtuous characteristics of the soul. They are thus all aspects of 'beauty of soul' or of human beings' 'inner beauty'.[630] This confirms our definition of God's Love as the '*love of beauty*', as per the hadith wherein it is stated: 'God is beautiful, and He loves beauty.'[631]

However, 'virtue' (*iḥsān*) is more than one single good characteristic in the soul; it encompasses the entire soul and all its traits. This is evident from the 'hadith of Gabriel', which says: 'Virtue (*al-iḥsān*) means to worship God as though you see Him; for [even] if you see Him not, He assuredly sees you.'[632]

Sincere worship—as though we see God—requires the whole soul because people cannot be fully aware of God and worship Him as if they saw Him without giving Him all that they are with all their hearts, with all their souls, with all their minds and with all their strengths. God's Oneness and Absoluteness requires people's unanimity and totality. This is reflected in the root meaning of the word *iḥsān* ('virtue'): *iḥsān* comes from *ḥusn*, which means 'beauty', or 'the opposite of ugliness.'[633] Virtue, then, is the beauty of the soul, or human beings' inner beauty, in its entirety. This conforms perfectly to the description of God's Love as from the hadith, namely that God's Love is 'love for beauty'. Thus in all of the aforementioned verses (about those whom God loves), it is as though God were saying that He *particularly* loves those who adorn themselves with virtue or beauty of soul, in varying degrees; and God knows best.

Certainly, this is what we understand from God's words:

> *Say: 'If you love God, follow me, and God will love you more (yuḥbibkum), and forgive you your sins; God is Forgiving, Merciful.'* (*Āl 'Imrān*, 3:31)[634]

God 'loves more' (*yuḥbibkum*)—that is, God loves them greatly and loves them more than others[635]—those who follow the way of the Messenger of God ﷺ; and those who follow the way of the Messenger of God ﷺ are necessarily the righteous and the virtuous, because the Messenger of God ﷺ had a magnificent nature:

> *And assuredly you possess a magnificent nature.* (*Al-Qalam*, 68:4)

God's words '*Say: If you love God, follow me, and God will love you more*' imply that God does not necessarily promise His greatest Love to anyone but His Messenger ﷺ. As for everyone else, He promises to love them more if they follow the Sunnah, without necessarily promising them ultimate success therein. God knows best, but there may be herein a great mystery to the effect that the person who loves God and is loved by Him in the most perfect way is the Messenger of God ﷺ. This is also suggested by the fact that in the Holy Qur'an there is no other specific, individual mention of anyone who 'loves God and God loves him' in the present tense as such, and on the only occasion when this phrase is used, it is used in the future tense. This occurs in the following Qur'anic verse, which we have already cited:

> *O you who believe, whoever of you apostatises from his religion, God will assuredly bring a people whom He loves and who love Him: humble towards believers, stern towards disbelievers, struggling in the way of God, and fearing not the reproach of any reproacher. That is God's favour; He gives it to whom He will; and God is Embracing, Knowing.* (*Al-Mā'idah*, 5:54)

Howbeit, we will not discuss God's Love for His Messenger ﷺ here, and will content ourselves with this mere allusion to the subject.

Among the types of virtuous people mentioned above it appears that there are differences of degree and rank, for God mentions that He loves 'the virtuous' (*al-muḥsinūn*) five times in the Holy Qur'an; 'the God-fearing' (*al-muttaqūn*) and 'the just' (*al-muqsitūn*) three times each, and all the other categories of people once only.

On the other hand, God only specifically says that He is 'with' (*ma'*) 'the virtuous' (*al-muḥsinūn*), 'the God-fearing' (*al-muttaqūn*), and 'the patient' (*al-ṣābirūn*), and does not specifically say this about the other five categories mentioned. The meaning of 'God's Companionship' (literally: 'God's being with someone', *ma'iyyat Allāh*') is a delicate issue over which Muslim scholars have differed; but Muslim scholars have generally distinguished between two kinds of Divine Companionship in the Holy Qur'an:[636]

1) 'General Divine Companionship'. This refers to God's being with all things:

And We shall narrate to them with knowledge; for verily We were not absent. (*Al-A'rāf*, 7:7)

And with every group of people:

Have you not seen that God knows all that is in the heavens and all that is in the earth? No secret conversation of three takes place but He is their fourth [companion], nor of five but He is their sixth, nor of fewer than that or more but He is with them wherever they may be. Then He will inform them of what they did, on the Day of Resurrection. Assuredly God has knowledge of all things. (*Al-Mujādilah*, 58:7)

And even with the sinners:

They hide themselves from people, but they do not hide themselves from God; for He is with them while they plot at night with discourse displeasing to Him. God is ever Encompassing what they do. (*Al-Nisā'*, 4:108)

2) 'Special Divine Companionship'. This refers to God's being with the messengers, the prophets, and the believers in particular:

If you have sought a judgment, the judgment has now come to you; and if you desist, it will better for you. But if you return, We shall return, and your host will not avail you in any way, however numerous it be; and verily God is with the believers. (*Al-Anfāl*, 8:19)

God had made a covenant with the Children of Israel, and We raised up from among them twelve leaders. And God said: 'I am with you. Surely if you establish the prayer, and pay the alms, and believe in My messengers and succour them, and lend to God a goodly loan, I will absolve you of your evil deeds, and I will admit you to gardens underneath which rivers flow. So whoever of you disbelieves after that, surely he has strayed from the right way'. (*Al-Mā'idah*, 5:12)

It is He Who created the heavens and the earth in six days, then presided upon the Throne. He knows what enters the earth, and what issues from it, and what comes down from the heaven. And He is with you wherever you may be; and God is Seer of what you do. (*Al-Ḥadīd*, 57:4)

> *So do not falter, and [do not] call for peace when you have the upper hand; and God is with you, and He will not stint you in [the reward for] your works.* (*Muḥammad*, 47:35)
>
> *If you do not help him, [know that] God has already helped him, when the disbelievers drove him forth—the second of two; when the two were in the cave—when he said to his companion, 'Do not despair; verily God is with us.' Then God sent down His spirit of peace (sakīnatahu) upon him and supported him with legions you did not see; and He made the word of those who disbelieved the nethermost, and the Word of God was the uppermost. And God is Mighty, Wise.* (*Al-Tawbah*, 9:40)

And with Moses ﷺand Aaron ﷺ:

> *Said He, 'Certainly not! Go both of you with Our signs. We will indeed be with you, hearing.'* (*Al-Shu'arā'*, 26:15)
>
> *He said, 'Do not fear, for I shall be with the two of you, hearing and seeing.'* (*Ṭā Hā*, 20:46)

And with Moses ﷺindividually:

> *He said, 'Certainly not! Indeed I have my Lord with me. He will guide me.'* (*Al-Shu'arā'*, 26:62)

Thus there are two distinct kinds of 'God's Companionship'. Otherwise, what did the Messenger of God ﷺ mean by saying 'Do not despair; verily God is with us'? If there were no difference between God's being with His Messenger ﷺ and Abu Bakr ؓ inside the cave of Thawr, and God's being with the disbelievers who were trying to kill them outside the cave of Thawr, then these words would be redundant. Similarly, what did the Prophet Moses mean by saying 'Certainly not' (in answer to his people's saying that they would be caught by Pharaoh and his army)? If there is no difference between God's being with Moses and the Children of Israel and His being with Pharaoh and his army, then these words too would be redundant.

This leads us to distinguish between the five aforementioned types of people whom God loves but does not specifically say He is 'with' them (namely: 'those who rely'; 'those who purify themselves' or 'cleanse themselves'; 'those who repent'; 'the just', and 'those who fight for His cause in ranks, as if they were a solid structure'), and the three types of people whom God loves *and* whom God says He is with, namely:

1) 'The patient'[637] (*al-ṣābirīn*):

O you who believe, seek help through patience and prayer; surely God is with the patient. (*Al-Baqarah*, 2:153)

And when Saul went forth with the hosts, he said, 'God will try you with a river; whoever drinks of it, is not of me, and whoever tastes it not, he is of me, except for him who scoops up with his hand. But they drank of it, except a few of them; and when he crossed it, with those who believed, they said, 'We have no power today against Goliath and his troops.' Those who thought they would meet God, said, 'How often a little company has overcome a numerous one, by God's leave; and God is with the patient.' (*Al-Baqarah*, 2:249)

And obey God and His Messenger, and do not quarrel with one another, lest you falter and your strength fade; and be patient. Surely God is with the patient. (*Al-Anfāl*, 8:46)

Now God has lightened [the burden] for you, for He knows that there is weakness in you. So if there be a hundred of you, steadfast, they will overcome two hundred; and if there be a thousand of you, they will overcome two thousand by the leave of God. And God is with the patient. (*Al-Anfāl*, 8:66)

2) 'The God-fearing' (*al-muttaqīn*):

The sacred month for the sacred month; holy things demand retaliation; whoever commits aggression against you, then commit aggression against him in the manner that he aggressed against you; and fear God, and know that God is with the God-fearing. (*Al-Baqarah*, 2:194)

Verily the number of months with God is twelve months in the Book of God from the day that He created the heavens and the earth; four of them are sacred. That is the right religion. So do not wrong yourselves during them. And fight the idolaters altogether, even as they fight you altogether; and know that God is with the God-fearing. (*Al-Tawbah*, 9:36)

O you who believe, fight those of the [aggressive] disbelievers who are near to you, and let them find harshness in you, and know that God is with the God-fearing. (*Al-Tawbah*, 9:123)

3) 'The virtuous' (*al-muḥsinīn*):

But as for those who struggle for Our sake, We shall assuredly

> *guide them in Our ways, and truly God is indeed with the virtuous.* (*Al-'Ankabūt*, 29:69)

In addition to all the above, God mentions 'the virtuous' and 'the God-fearing'—and alludes to 'the patient'—all together in the following two passages in the Holy Qur'an:

> *So be patient, and your patience is only by [the help of] God. And do not grieve for them, nor be in distress because of that which they scheme. / Truly God is with those who fear [Him], and those who are virtuous.* (*Al-Naḥl*, 16:127–8)

> *They said: 'Is it really you, Joseph?' He said, 'I am [indeed] Joseph, and this is my brother. God has truly shown favour to us. Verily if one fears and is patient, God does not waste the wage of those who are virtuous.'* (*Yūsuf*, 12:90)

This means—and God knows best—that the three types of believers whom God loves ('the patient', 'the God-fearing' and 'the virtuous') are, as it were, a degree more distinguished than the other five types of believers whom God loves ('those who rely'; 'those who purify themselves' or 'cleanse themselves'; 'those who repent'; 'the just'; and 'those who fight for His cause in ranks, as if they were a solid structure').

This is remarkably confirmed in God's mention of those whom He rewards '*without reckoning*'—that is to say: without limit, and without any common measure with the good they have done—this reward obviously being an important indication of God's favour, if not His Love. In six different verses in the Holy Qur'an, God mentions rewarding *without reckoning*:

> *Decked out fair to the disbelievers is the life of this world; and they deride the believers; but those who fear (ittaqū) shall be above them on the Day of Resurrection; and God sustains whomever He will without reckoning.* (*Al-Baqarah*, 2:212)

> *You make the night to pass into the day and You make the day to pass into the night; You bring forth the living from the dead, and You bring forth the dead from the living, and You provide whom You will without reckoning.* (*Āl 'Imrān*, 3:27)

> *Her Lord accepted the child with gracious acceptance, and made her grow excellently, and Zachariah took charge of her. Whenever Zachariah went into the sanctuary, where she*

was, he found her with provisions. 'O Mary,' he said, 'Whence comes this to you?' She said, 'From God. Truly God provides for whomever He will without reckoning.' (*Āl 'Imrān*, 3:37)

[M]en whom neither trading, nor sale distracts from the remembrance of God and the observance of prayer and payment of the alms. They fear a day when hearts and eyes will be overturned, / so that God may reward them for the best of what they did, and give them more out of His favour; and God provides whomever He will without reckoning. (*Al-Nūr*, 24:37–8)

Say: 'O servants of Mine who believe! Fear (ittaqū) your Lord. For those who are virtuous (aḥsanū) in this world, there will be good, and God's earth is vast. Truly the steadfast (al-ṣābirūn) will be paid their reward in full without any reckoning.' (*Al-Zumar*, 39:10)

Whoever commits an evil deed shall not be requited except with the like of it; but whoever acts righteously, whether male or female, and is a believer—such shall be admitted into Paradise wherein they will be provided without any reckoning. (*Ghāfir*, 40:40)

The first verse alludes to 'the God-fearing' (*ittaqū*); the second verse does not define those who receive the reward *without reckoning*; the third verse concerns the Blessed Virgin Mary; the fourth verse refers to those who remember God constantly; the fifth verse refers to 'the patient', 'the God-fearing' and 'the virtuous'—all three of the virtues mentioned earlier together here in one verse; and the sixth and last verse refers to those who 'act righteously', which perhaps implies 'the virtuous' in action. In short, the only virtues that are specifically mentioned as being rewarded by God *without reckoning* are the same three virtues mentioned earlier—'the patient', 'the God-fearing' and 'the virtuous'—as 'the elite' among those whom God loves.[638]

There seems to be a hierarchy even within 'the patient', 'the God-fearing' and' the virtuous', with the latter two seeming to be slightly more excellent than the former: this is seen in the fact that the only promise that God has explicitly 'bound Himself' (*kāna 'alā rabbika wa'dan mas'ūlan*) as such to fulfil in the Holy Qur'an is to the 'God-fearing' (*al-muttaqūn*). God says:

> *Say: 'Is that better, or the Garden of Immortality which has been promised to the God-fearing, which will be their requital and journey's end?' / For them therein is that which they desire, forever and ever—a promise that your Lord has bound Himself to fulfil (kāna 'alā rabbika wa'dan mas'ūlan).'* (*Al-Furqān*, 25:15–6)

This of course is very significant, and is reminiscent of God's 'prescribing for Himself Mercy' (*Sūrat Al-An'ām*, 6:12 and 6:54), as something so important that God has deigned to 'make it incumbent upon Himself', because, in fact (as we have seen earlier) Divine Mercy is of the Divine Essence Itself. In other words, God loves 'the God-fearing' to the degree that rewarding them with the *Garden of Immortality* is necessitated by God's own Essence.[639]

On the other hand, the paramount importance of virtue (*iḥsān*) is seen in the use of the word 'indeed with' (*la-ma'*) in Gods words: a*nd truly God is indeed with the (la-ma') virtuous* (*Al-'Ankabūt*, 29:69), indicating additional emphasis on God's being with the virtuous. Furthermore, 'the virtuous'—and only 'the virtuous'—are described in the Holy Qur'an as being 'near to God's Mercy':

> *And work not corruption in the land, after it has been set right, and call upon Him in fear, and in hope—surely the mercy of God is near to the virtuous.* (*Al-A'rāf*, 7:56)

All of this confirms our earlier definition of 'virtue' as the combination and culmination of all the good character traits of the soul. In other words, God particularly loves those whose souls are beautiful and virtuous *according to the very measure of the level* of their beauty of soul and virtue. And the sum of virtue is synonymous with a sound (spiritual) heart, for God says:

> *The day when neither wealth nor children will avail, / except him who comes to God with a heart that is sound* (*Al-Shu'arā'*, 26:88–9)

Although God particularly loves the patient, the God-fearing and the virtuous, His Mercy embraces all things, as we have mentioned. To this it should be added that God's generous bounty reaches also all things and all people, whether they deserve it or not—the virtuous and the sinners—as a free gift from Him, for He says (referring to the people who only want this world and to the believers, as mentioned in the preceding verses):

> *Each We supply [to] these and [to] those from your Lord's bounty. And your Lord's bounty is not confined.* (*Al-Isrā'*, 17:20)

Even in the case of the most virtuous people, there is no common measure between God's grace and their worthiness to receive it:

> *And He gives you all that you ask of Him. And if you were to enumerate God's graces, you could never number them. Lo! man is verily a wrong-doer and unthankful!* (*Ibrāhīm*, 14:34)

> *Do you not see that God has disposed for you whatever is in the heavens and whatever is in the earth, and He has showered His graces upon you, [both] outwardly and inwardly? Yet among people there are those who dispute concerning God without any knowledge or guidance or an illuminating scripture.* (*Luqmān*, 31:20)

And even the evildoers, disbelievers, idolaters and hypocrites receive God's Mercy and bounty:

> *And if God were to take humankind to task for their wrongdoing, He would not leave upon it any living being; but He gives them respite until an appointed term; and when their term comes they will not defer it by a single hour nor advance it.* (*Al-Naḥl*, 16:61)

> *Were God to take humankind to task for what they have acquired, He would not leave on its surface a single creature. But He reprieves them to an appointed term. And when their term comes—then truly [they will know that] God is ever Seer of His servants.* (*Fāṭir*, 35:45)

Summary

In summary, in the Holy Qur'an love is a Divine Quality, and like mercy, it is of the Divine Essence Itself. Human beings—and indeed the universe itself—were created *out of* Divine Love, and *for* Divine Love. God's Love and Favour to humanity in general is a free gift, and all beyond reckoning, but God loves in particular those who are virtuous, to the degree that they are virtuous. Therefore, human beings must be virtuous—and thus loving and merciful—in order to receive more Divine Love and Mercy. The very purpose of our lives is to partake—through practicing virtue, love and mercy—of the Divine gifts of Grace, Love and Mercy.

Hence all praise belongs to God:

> *And He is God; there is no god except Him. To Him belongs [all] praise in the former and in the latter. And to Him belongs the judgement, and to Him you will be returned.* (*Al-Qaṣaṣ*, 28:70).

Reproduced and adjusted from Love in the Holy Qur'an *(Chapters 4, 5, and 7).*

CHAPTER FIFTEEN

LOVE OF OTHERS IN THE QUR'AN

(ALL HUMANITY, THE 'PEOPLE OF THE SCRIPTURE', BELIEVERS AND FRIENDS)

HRH Prince Ghazi bin Muhammad

God clarifies all the different kinds of love between human beings in the Qur'an. We have elsewhere extensively discussed[640] certain special kinds of inter-human love—love of the believers for the Prophets and other blessed personages; conjugal and sexual love and family love; in what follows we discuss general human love in the Qur'an: 'Love of Others' as such.

ALL HUMANITY

Because God's mercy '*embraces all things*' (*Al-A'rāf*, 7:156), He creates mercy and love between all people, albeit in differing degrees and with specific conditions. Perhaps one of the reasons for this is that every person is ultimately related to every other person, since all human beings are the progeny of Adam and Eve, and since all human beings are thus the 'sons [or daughters] of Adam' (*banī Ādam*').[641] This thus constitutes a degree of kinship, although distant (and kinship, as we have discussed elsewhere,[642] engenders and demands love). God reminds human beings of this in the Holy Qur'an, and warns them to fear God whenever they deal with their brothers and sisters from the womb (*raḥm*) of their common mother, Eve:

> *O people, fear your Lord, Who created you of a single soul, and from it created its mate, and from the pair of them scattered many men and women; and fear God by whom you claim [your rights] from one another and kinship ties (arḥam). Surely God has been watchful over you.* (*Al-Nisā'*, 4:1)

> *And He it is Who produced you from a single soul, such that some are established and some are deposited. Verily We have distinguished the signs for a people who understand.* (*Al-An'ām*, 6:98)

God also tells human beings that they were created, and they will be resurrected, as a single soul. Human beings thus share not only the same beginning but the same end as well:

> *Your creation and your resurrection are only as [that of] a single soul. Truly God is Hearer, Seer.* (*Luqmān*, 31:28)

Moreover, although God created human beings as different nations and tribes, they are nonetheless all equal before God. The only thing that differentiates one person from another in the sight of God is how God-fearing he or she is (and therefore how good they are):

> *O humankind! We have indeed created you from a male and a female, and made you nations and tribes that you may come to know one another. Truly the noblest of you in the sight of God is the most God-fearing among you. Truly God is Knower, Aware.* (*Al-Ḥujurāt*, 49:13)

Indeed, the ethnic and linguistic differences and variety between peoples and nations reflect divine wisdom and manifest divine 'signs' (*ayāt*) which people must respect, contemplate and appreciate:

> *And of His signs is the creation of the heavens and the earth and the differences of your tongues and your colours. Surely in that there are signs for all peoples.* (*Al-Rūm*, 30:22)

Human beings must value and rejoice in the way people differ. This is one of the meanings of *that you may come to know one another*, and God knows best. Moreover, God forbids the killing of any human soul, saying:

> *And do not slay the soul [whose life] God has made inviolable, except with due cause....* (*Al-Isrā'*, 17:33)

> *...do not slay the life which God has made sacred, except rightfully. This is what He has charged you with that perhaps you will understand.* (*Al-An'ām*, 6:151)

Furthermore, God values every single soul as if it were all humanity, when it comes to saving its life or not causing its death:

> *Because of that, We decreed for the Children of Israel that*

> *whoever slays a soul for other than a soul, or for corruption in the land, it shall be as if he had slain humankind altogether; and whoever saves the life of one, it shall be as if he had saved the life of all humankind. Our messengers have already come to them with clear proofs, but after that many of them still commit excesses in the land.* (*Al-Mā'idah*, 5:32)

Thus God commands Muslims in the Holy Qur'an not to aggress against any individual soul. God says:

> *And fight in the way of God with those who fight against you, but aggress not; God loves not the aggressors.* (*Al-Baqarah*, 2:190)

> *O you who believe, do not profane God's sacraments, nor the sacred month, nor the offering, nor the garlands; nor those repairing to the Sacred House, seeking favour from their Lord, and beatitude. But when you are discharged, then hunt for game. And let not hatred of a people that, barred you from the Sacred Mosque cause you to commit aggression. Help one another to righteousness and piety; do not help one another to sin and enmity. And fear God; surely God is severe in retribution.* (*Al-Mā'idah*, 5:2)

> *O you who believe, be upright before God, witnesses in equity. Let not hatred of a people cause you not to be just; be just, that is nearer to God-fearing. And fear God; surely God is aware of what you do.* (*Al-Mā'idah*, 5:8)

Muslims may not even commit verbal aggression against anyone, for God says:

> *Woe to every backbiter, [who is a] slanderer* (*Al-Humazah*, 104:1)

Nor even may Muslims insult anyone in their beliefs, even if they be idolaters:[643]

> *Do not revile those whom they call upon, besides God, lest they then revile God out of spite, through ignorance. So, We have adorned for every community their deeds; then to their Lord they shall return, and He will tell them what they used to do.* (*Al-An'ām*, 6:108)

Thus God commands Muslims to be peaceful and to be just towards every single human being, except those who wage war upon them, destroy their places of worship and drive them out of their homes (this being the sufficient justification for a just, defensive war in the Holy Qur'an[644]):

> *It may be that God will bring about between you and those of them with whom you are at enmity, affection. For God is Powerful, and God is Forgiving, Merciful. / God does not forbid you in regard to those who did not wage war against you on account of religion and did not expel you from your homes, that you should treat them kindly and deal with them justly. Assuredly God loves the just.* (*Al-Mumtaḥanah*, 60:7–8)

> *How can the idolaters have a pact with God and His Messenger, except for those with whom you made a pact at the Sacred Mosque? So long as they are true to you, be true to them. Truly God loves the God-fearing.* (*Al-Tawbah*, 9:7)

In addition to this, God enjoins mercy and empathy *upon all* human beings *to* all human beings and not merely to particular groups of people, in the following verse (although 'Ali ibn Abi Talib عليه السلام, the Lady Fatimah, Al-Hasan عليه السلام and Al-Husayn عليه السلام were all the specific cause of its revelation):

> *And they give food, despite [their] love of it to the needy, and the orphan, and the prisoner.* (*Al-Insān*, 76:8)

Fakr al-Din al-Razi comments, in his *Al-Tafsir al-Kabir*:

> His words, *And they give food, despite [their] love of it to the needy, and the orphan, and the prisoner*, refer to the story we have related in which 'Ali عليه السلام fed the needy, the orphan and the prisoner. Others say that the verse refers generally to all the pious people, and that 'giving food' symbolises all acts of kindness and benevolence towards the needy, of whatever kind, even if not giving food specifically.[645]

As if to confirm this, God mentions a prayer said by believers which evinces mercy even towards disbelievers:

> *Our Lord, do not make us a cause of beguilement for those who disbelieve, and forgive us. Our Lord, You are indeed the Mighty, the Wise'. / Verily there is for you in them a beautiful example, for those [of you] who hope for God and the Last Day. And whoever turns away, [should know*

> *that] God is the Independent, the Worthy of Praise.* (*Al-Mumtaḥanah*, 60:5–6)
>
> *So they said, 'In God we have put our trust. Our Lord, make us not a [cause of] temptation for the evildoing folk.'* (*Yūnus*, 10:85)

God also says:

> *And worship God, and associate nothing with Him. Be kind to parents, and near kindred, and to orphans, and to the needy, and to the neighbour who is near, and to the neighbour who is a stranger, and to the friend at your side, and to the wayfarer, and to what your right hands own. Surely God loves not the conceited, and the boastful.* (*Al-Nisā'*, 4:36)

In the Qur'anic Commentary *Tafsīr al-Jalālayn*, it is explained that *the neighbour who is near* means 'the one who is near to you either in terms of residence, or of family ties', and that *the neighbour who is a stranger* means 'the one who is distant from you, either in terms of residence, or of family ties'.[646] In other words, according to *Tafsīr al-Jalālayn*, the *neighbour* means every person on the face of the earth, whether Muslim or disbeliever.

Likewise, it is stated in the Qura'nic Commentary *Tafsīr al-Qurṭubī* that *the neighbour who is near* means the 'nearby neighbour', and that *the neighbour who is a stranger* means the 'unknown neighbour';[647] and God knows best.

The Messenger of God ﷺ emphasised this when he said: 'By Him in whose hand is my soul, no servant believes until he loves for his neighbour (or he said: 'his brother') what he loves for himself.'[648]

Similarly, the Messenger of God ﷺ said: 'The Compassionate One has mercy upon those who have mercy; have mercy upon those on earth, and He who is in Heaven will have mercy upon you.'[649]

The Messenger of God ﷺ also said: 'God does not have mercy on those who have no mercy on people.'[650]

Thus mercy and empathy should be shown to all people—every single human being—whether they be believers or not. And mercy and empathy towards all humanity, even disbelievers, necessarily means to forgive them, just as it means to forgive Muslims. God says:

> *Tell those who believe to forgive those who do not hope for*

the days of God that He may requite a people for what they used to earn. (*Al-Jāthiyah*, 45:14)

It was by the mercy of God that you were lenient with them; had you been harsh and fierce of heart, they would have dispersed from about you. So pardon them, and ask forgiveness for them, and consult them in the matter. And when you are resolved, rely on God; for God loves those who rely. (*Āl 'Imrān*, 3:159)

And forgiveness, in turn, means to pardon people. God says:

We did not create the heavens and the earth and all that is between them save with the Truth. And truly the Hour shall come. So pardon them with a gracious pardoning. / Truly your Lord, He is the Creator, the Knowing. (*Al-Ḥijr*, 15:85–6)

Then pardon them and say, 'Peace!' For they will [soon] come to know. (*Al-Zukhruf*, 43:89)

But verily he who is patient and forgives—surely that is [true] constancy in [such] affairs. (*Al-Shūrā*, 42:43)

And pardon and forgiveness are the way—or part of the way—of God's prophets, for the Prophet Joseph عليه السلام said:

They said: 'Is it really you, Joseph?' He said, 'I am [indeed] Joseph, and this is my brother. God has truly shown favour to us. Verily if one fears and endures, God does not waste the wage of those who are virtuous'. / They said, 'By God, truly God has preferred you over us, and indeed we have been erring'. / He said, 'There shall be no reproach on you this day. May God forgive you, and He is the Most Merciful of the merciful. (*Yūsuf*, 12:90–2)

Similarly, the Prophet Abraham عليه السلام said:

My Lord, truly they have led many of humankind astray. So whoever follows me, verily belongs with me, and whoever disobeys me, truly You are Forgiving, Merciful. (*Ibrāhīm*, 14:36)

Equally, the Prophet and Messenger of God Muhammad ﷺ pardoned the Meccans on the Day of the Conquest, saying:

'What say you, and what think you?' They said: 'We say: The son of a noble and generous brother, and the son of a noble and generous uncle.' The Messenger of God ﷺ said: 'I say, as Joseph said: There shall be no reproach upon you this day. May God

forgive you, and He is the Most Merciful of the merciful.' So they went out, as though they had been brought out of their graves.[651]

To pardon, in turn, means to stop oneself from growing angry. God says:

> *And vie with one another hastening to forgiveness from your Lord, and to a garden as wide as the heavens and the earth that has been prepared for those who fear. / Who expend in prosperity and adversity, and restrain their rage, and pardon their fellow men; and God loves those who are virtuous. / And who when they commit an indecency or wrong themselves, remember God, and pray forgiveness for their sins—and who shall forgive sins but God?—and who do not persist in what they did, knowing. / Those—their requital is forgiveness from their Lord, and Gardens beneath which rivers flow, abiding therein; excellent is the wage of those workers!* (Āl 'Imrān, 3:133–6)

> *So whatever you have been given is [but] the enjoyment of the life of this world. But what is with God is better and more lasting for those who believe and put their trust in their Lord, / and those who avoid grave sins and indecencies and [who], when they are angry, forgive, / and those who answer their Lord, and whose courses of action are [a matter of] counsel between them, and who, of what We have bestowed on them, expend, / and those who, when they suffer aggression defend themselves: / For the requital of an evil deed is an evil deed like it. But whoever pardons and reconciles, his reward will be with God. Truly He does not love wrongdoers. / And whoever defends himself after he has been wronged, for such, there will be no course [of action] against them. / A course [of action] is only [open] against those who wrong people and seek [to commit] in the earth what is not right. For such there will be a painful chastisement.* (Al-Shūrā, 42:36–42)

Furthermore, pardon on its own is not enough, for Muslims are asked to repay an ill turn with a good one, to 'turn the other cheek'. God says:

> *Ward off with that which is better the evil [act]. We know best what they allege.* (Al-Mu'minūn, 23:96)

> *And they are not equal, the good deed and the evil deed. Repel with that which is better then, behold, he between whom and*

> *you there was enmity will be as though he were a dear friend. / But none is granted it, except those who are steadfast; and none is granted it except one [deserving] of a great reward.* (*Fuṣṣilat*, 41:34–5)

> *And such as cement what God has commanded should be cemented, and fear their Lord, and dread an awful reckoning; / such as are patient, desiring their Lord's countenance; and maintain the prayer and expend of that which We have provided them, secretly and openly, and repel evil with good; those, theirs shall be the sequel of the [heavenly] Abode: / Gardens of Eden, which they shall enter along with those who were righteous from among their fathers and their spouses and their descendants; and the angels shall enter to them from every gate. / 'Peace be upon you for your patience'. How excellent is the sequel of the [heavenly] Abode!* (*Al-Ra'd*, 13:21–4)

> *And if you retaliate, retaliate with the like of what you have been made to suffer; and yet if you endure patiently, verily that is better for the patient.* (*Al-Naḥl*, 16:126)

> *And the [true] servants of the Compassionate One are those who walk upon the earth modestly, and who, when the ignorant address them, say [words of] peace.* (*Al-Furqān*, 25:63)

In summary: God has given each and every human being inalienable rights, and has obliged Muslims to have respect for all human beings; not to commit aggression against anyone; to be peaceful and to be just; to be merciful; to empathise with all human beings; to forgive them; to pardon them; to restrain themselves from anger; and even to repay evil deeds with kindness and 'turn the other cheek'—and to do this with all people, whoever they may be and regardless of their faith (or lack of it) all the time, so long as they are not first waging war against Muslims.

The 'People of the Scripture'

God has enjoined mercy, justice and forgiveness upon people in general, even as He has commanded people to be kind to all their neighbours, whether near or far, regardless of the neighbour's religion. God says:

> *And worship God, and associate nothing with Him. Be kind to parents, and near kindred, and to orphans, and to the needy, and to the neighbour who is near, and to the neighbour who is a stranger, and to the friend at your side, and to the wayfarer,*

and to what your right hands own. Surely God loves not the conceited, and the boastful. (*Al-Nisā'*, 4:36)

As we mentioned earlier, according to the commentaries of Qurtubi and the *Jalālayn*, 'the neighbour' means every human being whether near or far. It is worth adding here that Ibn Kathir says the following in his own commentary:

It is related from 'Ikrimah, Mujahid, Maymun ibn Mahran, Dahhak, Zayd ibn Aslam, Muqatil bin Hayyan, Qatada, and Nawf Bakkali (according to Abu Ishaq) that 'the neighbour who is near' means the Muslim, and 'the neighbour who is a stranger' means the Jew and the Christian.[652]

It is also worth mentioning that God calls the Christians of Najran 'believers', and curses those who tortured them, in the Holy Qur'an:

Perish the men of the ditch! / Of the fire abounding in fuel, / when they sat by it, / and they themselves were witnesses, to what they did to the believers. / And they ill-treated them for no other reason than that they believed in God, the Mighty, the Praised. (*Al-Burūj*, 85:4–8)

Qurtubi said, commenting on this verse:

This refers to those who made the ditches and cast into them the believers who dwelt in Najran in the time between Jesus ﷺ and Muhammad ﷺ; the narrators differ in their exact words, but the meaning of what they say is essentially the same.[653]

God also refers to the joy of the Muslims when the Christians of Byzantium defeated the pagan Persians:

Alif lām mīm. / The Byzantines have been vanquished / in the nearer [part of the] land. But they, after their vanquishing, shall be the victors / in a few years. To God belongs the command before and after, and on that day, the believers shall rejoice. (*Al-Rūm*, 30:1–4)

God knew full well of course that Muslims would later face the same Christians of Byzantium in battle (including at the Battle of Mu'tah during the Messenger's ﷺ own lifetime in 630 CE), yet He immortalised the Muslims' joy about the Christian victory over the idolaters in the Holy Qur'an. Moreover, God speaks of their victory in the form of a happy promise to the Muslims that would cause the Muslims to rejoice, and so this means that there is special affection between Muslims and Christians. Indeed, this is precisely what God promises in the following verse:

> *You will truly find the most hostile of people to those who believe to be the Jews and the idolaters; and you will truly find the nearest of them in love to those who believe to be those who say 'Verily, we are Christians'; that is because some of them are priests and monks, and because they are not proud.* (Al-Mā'idah, 5:82)

Although God warns His Messenger ﷺ about the hostility of some Jews towards him,[654] and praises Christians in this verse, in other verses God praises the Children of Israel (or at least the faithful and pious among them[655]) and says that they were His most favoured people:

> *O Children of Israel, remember My grace wherewith I graced you, and that I have favoured you above all the worlds.* (Al-Baqarah, 2:47)

> *He said, 'Shall I seek other than God as a god for you, when He has favoured you above all the worlds?'* (Al-A'rāf, 7:140)

> *And when Moses said to his people, 'O my people, remember God's favour to you, when He established among you prophets, and established you as kings, and gave you such as He had not given to any in all the worlds'.* (Al-Mā'idah, 5:20)

> *And verily We gave the Children of Israel the Scripture, and [the means of] judgement, and prophethood, and We provided them with the good things, and We favoured them above [all] worlds. / And We gave them clear illustrations of the commandment. And they did not differ, except after the knowledge had come to them, out of rivalry among themselves. Surely your Lord will judge between them on the Day of Resurrection concerning that in which they used to differ.* (Al-Jāthiyah, 45:16–7)

> *And verily We favoured them with a knowledge over [all] the worlds. / And We gave them signs in which there was a manifest trial.* (Al-Dukhān, 44:32–3)

> *And verily We gave Moses the Scripture; so do not be in doubt concerning the encounter with Him; and We appointed him a guidance for the Children of Israel. / And We appointed among them leaders who guided by Our command, when they had endured [patiently] and had conviction in Our signs. / Surely your*

> *Lord will judge between them on the Day of Resurrection concerning that wherein they used to differ.* (Al-Sajdah, 32:23–5)

Moreover, God tells Muslims that among all the People of the Scripture there are righteous and exemplary people (who should be admired):

> *Yet they are not all alike; some of the People of the Scripture are a community upright, who recite God's verses in the watches of the night, prostrating themselves. / They believe in God and in the Last Day, enjoining decency and forbidding indecency, vying with one another in good works; those are of the righteous. / And whatever good you do, you shall not be denied it, and God knows the God-fearing.* (Āl 'Imrān, 3:113–5)

> *And those who adhere to the Scripture, and have established prayer—verily We shall not let the wages of reformers go to waste.* (Al-A'rāf, 7:170)

In summary: God enjoins upon Muslims—in addition to having respect, justice and mercy in general towards all humanity—to have affection and admiration for the People of the Scripture in general (notably Christians and Jews). God says in the Holy Qur'an that the Jews were His most favoured people and that Muslims have a special affinity with Christians in particular; and God knows best.

The Believers

In addition to respect, justice, mercy, pardon, forgiveness,[656] kindness, affection and admiration, God requires believers to maintain special ties of brotherhood between them:

> *The believers are indeed brothers. Therefore [always] make peace between your brethren, and fear God, so that perhaps you might receive mercy.* (Al-Ḥujurāt, 49:10)

Thus God makes believers brothers (and sisters), and reminds them of the rights of this brotherhood by saying '*and fear God*'. God then makes His mercy conditional upon fearing Him and maintaining the bond of brotherhood and peace between believers. In other words, God says that He will have mercy on those who love their brethren in faith and keep peace with them and between them.

Now, 'brotherhood' means love—and nothing less than love—between believers:

And those who had settled in the hometown, and [had abided] in faith before them, love those who have emigrated to them, and do not find in their breasts any need of that which those [others] have been given, but prefer [others] to themselves, though they be in poverty. And whoever is saved from the avarice of his own soul, those—they are the successful. (*Al-Ḥashr*, 59:9)

In this beautiful verse, God Almighty makes it clear that the love that believers should have for one another is not a matter of mere sentiment that does not oblige the believer to *do* anything. Rather, this love presupposes a state of soul which sincerely and altruistically puts the good of others above oneself, and thus overcomes '*the avarice of his [or her] own soul*'.[657]

In summary: in addition to respect, justice, mercy, affection and kindness, God requires believers to love one another more than they love themselves. This love is what is sometimes called 'love for the sake of God' or 'love in God' (*al-ḥubb fi'Llāh*).

Friends

In addition to the brotherhood of faith just discussed, God mentions various degrees of friendship in the Holy Qur'an. 'Company' or 'companionship' (*ṣuḥbah*) is the lowest level of friendship, and God mentions it in many verses of the Holy Qur'an, such as the following two verses:

[Moses] said, 'If I ask you about anything after this, then do not keep me in your company (tuṣaḥibni), for truly you [will] have found from me' [sufficient] excuse. (*Al-Kahf*, 18:76)

O my two fellow-prisoners (saḥibayy al-sijni)!: Are several lords better, or God, the One, the Almighty? (*Yūsuf*, 12:39)

Generally, the word 'company' (*ṣuḥbah*) in the Holy Qur'an does not imply a special affection or friendship, but suggests the notion of fellowship or companionship in a particular thing. The 'companions of hell' (*aṣḥāb al-nār*) do not love one another, but they are together in hell:

He will say, 'Enter into the Fire among communities of jinn and humankind who passed away before you'. Every time a community enters, it curses its sister-community, until, when they have all followed one another there, the last of them shall say

> *to the first of them, 'Our Lord, these led us astray; so give them a double chastisement of the Fire.' He will say, 'For each will be double but you do not know'. / And the first of them shall say to the last of them, 'You have no advantage over us. So taste the chastisement for what you used to earn'.* (*Al-A'rāf*, 7:38–9)

Sometimes *ṣuḥbah* can simply mean 'ownership', as with *aṣḥāb al-fīl* ('*owners of an elephant*')—the army of the Abyssinian King Abrahah who owned an elephant and tried to attack the Ka'bah in pre-Islamic times. God says:

> *Have you not considered the way in which your Lord dealt with the Men of the Elephant (aṣḥāb al-fīl)?* (*Al-Fīl*, 105:1)

Despite this, the word 'company' (*ṣuḥbah*) can also mean 'friendship' and imply a certain kind of affection, as is the case in the following two verses:

> *If you do not help him, [know that] God has already helped him, when the disbelievers drove him forth—the second of two; when the two were in the cave—when he said to his companion, 'Do not despair; verily God is with us'. Then God sent down His spirit of peace (sakīnatahu) upon him and supported him with legions you did not see; and He made the word of those who disbelieved the nethermost, and the Word of God was the uppermost. And God is Mighty, Wise.* (*Al-Tawbah*, 9:40)

> *Or did you think that the Companions of the Cave and the Inscription were a [unique] marvel from among Our signs?* (*Al-Kahf*, 18:9)

Beyond 'companionship' lies 'friendship' (*ṣadāqah*). 'Friendship' (*ṣadāqah*) implies a specific level of sincere mutual love (*maḥabbah*) and brotherhood. God mentions 'friendship', clarifies its meaning, honours it, and grants it a special status by acknowledging it even in His Laws:

> *There is no blame upon the blind, nor any blame upon the lame, nor any blame upon the sick, nor upon yourselves if you eat from your own houses, or your fathers' houses, or your mothers' houses, or your brothers' houses, or your sisters' houses, or the houses of your paternal uncles or the houses of your paternal aunts, or the houses of your maternal uncles or the houses of your maternal aunts, or [from] that whereof you*

> *hold the keys, or [from] those of your [faithful] friends. You would not be at fault whether you eat together, or separately. But when you enter houses, bid peace to yourselves with a salutation from God, blessed and good. So God clarifies the signs for you that perhaps you might comprehend.* (*Al-Nūr*, 24:61)

Above 'friendship' we can discern 'close friendship' (*ṣadāqah ḥamīmiyyah*) in the Holy Qur'an, for God says:

> *Tell My servants who believe that they establish prayers and expend of that which We have provided them, secretly and openly, before a day comes wherein there will be neither bargaining, nor befriending (khilāl).* (*Ibrāhīm*, 14:31)
>
> *Nor any intimate friend.* (*Al-Shu'arā'*, 26:101)[658]

Finally, there is a degree of friendship that is even higher than 'close friendship' (*ṣadāqah ḥamīmiyyah*). God calls this *khullah* or 'intimate friendship'.[659] God says:

> *[Intimate] Friends (al-akhillā') will, on that day, be foes of one another, except for the God-fearing.* (*Al-Zukhruf*, 43:67)

In summary: God mentions, affirms and blesses four different degrees of 'friendship'—over and above the love which exists between believers—in the Holy Qur'an: (1) 'Company' or 'companionship' (*ṣuḥbah*); (2) 'friendship' (*ṣadāqah*); (3) 'close friendship' (*ṣadāqah ḥamīmiyya*), and (4) 'intimate friendship' (*khullah*). These constitute, in ascending order, the gamut of friendship between believers, and the highest degrees of (non-sexual) love between those who are not related;[660] and God knows best.

Reproduced and adjusted from Love in the Holy Qur'an *(Chapters 17). © HRH Prince Ghazi bin Muhammad, 2010*

CHAPTER SIXTEEN

MERCY IN THE HADITH

Shaykh Sayyid Hassan Saqqaf and
HRH Prince Ghazi bin Muhammad

INTRODUCTION

The *Ḥadīth*, sometimes called 'Traditions', are texts which relate the sayings and doings of the Prophet Muhammad ﷺ.

The corpus of these beautiful sayings are considered by Muslims to be second in spiritual and legal authority only to the Holy Qur'an. In what follows we cite around forty of the best known and best loved hadith about Divine Mercy and the necessity of human beings being merciful. These hadith are epitomised by the very inscription on God's throne—itself related in a hadith—'My mercy outstrips My wrath.'

Each section below quotes verses from the Qur'an, as the truths of the Qur'an give the hadith meaning and substance. The verses are cited with chapter and verse numbers, while the hadith citations refer to the numbering system of The Sunna Project's *Encyclopedia of Hadith*, prepared in cooperation with the scholars of al-Azhar, which includes *Ṣaḥīḥ al-Bukhārī*, *Ṣaḥīḥ Muslim*, *Sunan Abu Dāwud*, *Sunan al-Tirmidhī*, *Sunan al-Nasā'ī*, *Sunan Ibn Mājah*, and *Muwaṭṭa' Malik*. Generally only the words of the Prophet ﷺ are quoted, without the *isnād* or chain of transmission, but for some hadith the context or questions posed to the Prophet ﷺ are included. The Qur'an translations are based on Pickthall, with modifications.

Part One: Mercy, Which Outstrips

Mercy

From reciting the Qur'an to sitting at the table, Muslims begin their actions by saying *In the Name of God, the Compassionate, the Merciful.* This sacred formula, whose author is God, is based firstly on the supreme name *Allah*, then on the two names *al-Raḥmān* and *al-Raḥīm*, both of which derive from *raḥmah*, or mercy, a word which can also mean love, kindness, and compassion. God did not choose two names of wrath (*ghadab*) or even a balance between mercy and wrath, because with God there is no balance between mercy and wrath. Even wrath, from a certain point of view, is a kind of mercy for the believer, because it can purify his soul and help make him ready to enter paradise.

Among the Qur'anic verses which relate to mercy and compassion are the following, in which God says:

> *Say: Unto whom belongs whatsoever is in the heavens and the earth? Say: Unto God. He has prescribed for Himself mercy.* (*Al-Anʿām*, 6:12)

> *Your Lord has prescribed for Himself mercy, that whoso of you does evil through ignorance and repents afterward thereof and does right, (for him) lo! He is Forgiving, Compassionate.* (*Al-Anʿām*, 6:54)

> *My mercy embraces all things, therefore I shall ordain it for those who ward off (evil) and pay the poor-due, and those who believe Our revelations.* (*Al-Aʿrāf*, 7:156)

> *Lo! the mercy of God is near to the virtuous.* (*Al-Aʿrāf*, 7:56)

> *Announce, (O Muhammad) to My slaves that verily I am the Forgiving, the Compassionate.* (*Al-Ḥijr*, 15:49)

> *Those who bear the Throne, and all who are round about it, hymn the praises of their Lord and believe in Him and ask forgiveness for those who believe (saying): 'Our Lord! You comprehend all things in mercy and knowledge, therefore forgive those who repent and follow Your way. Ward off from them the punishment of hell.'* (*Ghāfir*, 40:7)

And from the hadith of the Prophet ﷺ:

> 'God says, Great and Glorious is He, "*My mercy outstrips my wrath.*"' (*Ṣaḥīḥ Muslim no. 7146, Kitāb al-Tawbah.)*

'God is not merciful to one who is not merciful to people.' *(Ṣaḥīḥ al-Bukhārī no. 7465, Kitāb al-Tawḥīd; Ṣaḥīḥ Muslim no. 6170, Kitab al-Faḍā'i.)*

The Messenger of God kissed (his grandson) Hasan, the son of 'Ali, while Aqra' bin Habis al-Tamimi was sitting nearby. Aqra' said, 'I have ten children and have not kissed any of them.' The Messenger of God looked at him and said, 'He who does not show mercy shall not be shown mercy.' *(Ṣaḥīḥ al-Bukhārī no. 6063, Kitāb al-Adab.)*

An old man came looking for the Prophet, and the people were slow in making way for him, so the Prophet said, 'He who is unkind to the young and disrespectful to the old is not one of us.' *(Sunan al-Tirmidhī no. 2043, Kitāb al-Birr wa'l-ṣilah.)*

'The merciful are shown mercy by the Merciful. Be merciful to those on earth, and He who is in heaven will be merciful to you. Kinship ties are connecting branches from the Merciful. Whoever maintains them will be maintained by God, and whoever cuts them will be cut off by God.' *(Sunan al-Tirmidhī no. 2049, Kitāb al-Birr wa'l-ṣilah.)*

'Ā'ishah (the wife of the Prophet) said, 'The Messenger of God never struck anything with his hand, neither woman nor servant. He only did so while struggling in the path of God. Nor did he ever do harm to a thing such as to take vengeance upon its owner. He only did so when God's sacred bounds were violated, and would take vengeance for God, Great and Glorious is He.' *(Ṣaḥīḥ Muslim no. 6195, Kitāb al-Faḍā'il.)*

'God made mercy one-hundred parts. He held back ninety-nine parts, and sent down one part to earth. It is from that part that creatures show mercy to each other, such that a mare will lift her hoof over her foal, fearing that she might harm him.' *(Ṣaḥīḥ al-Bukhārī no. 6066, Kitāb al-Adab.)*

'If the believer knew the punishment of God, he would never feel assured of His Garden, and if the unbeliever knew the mercy of God, he would never despair of His Garden.' *(Ṣaḥīḥ Muslim no. 7155, Kitāb al-Tawbah.)*

The Heart and the Intention

The heart is the centre of man, and is the place where mercy descends from God, and is the source from which man's mercy then manifests in the world. It is the heart that finds peace in the remembrance of God, and it is the heart into which the tranquility of God descends. Intention is inseparable from the heart, because the heart commands all the faculties of the human soul, and lives in the hereafter where we will experience the consequences of our intentions and actions in this life.

Among the Qur'anic verses which relate to the heart and intention are the following, in which God says:

> *And whosoever believes in God, He guides his heart. And God is Knower of all things.* (*Al-Taghābun*, 64:11)
>
> *(The Day of Judgment is): The day when wealth and sons avail not (any man), save him who brings unto God a whole heart.* (*Al-Shu'arā'*, 26:88–9)
>
> *Know that God comes in between the man and his own heart, and that He it is unto Whom you will be gathered.* (*Al-Anfāl*, 8:24)
>
> *(God guides those): Who have believed and whose hearts have rest in the remembrance of God. Verily in the remembrance of God do hearts find rest!* (*Al-Ra'd*, 13:28)
>
> *He it is Who sent down tranquillity into the hearts of the believers that they might add faith unto their faith.* (*Al-Fatḥ*, 48:4)
>
> *Is not the time ripe for the hearts of those who believe to submit to God's reminder?* (*Al-Ḥadīd*, 57:16)
>
> *For indeed it is not the eyes that grow blind, but it is the hearts, which are within the bosoms, that grow blind.* (*Al-Ḥajj*, 22:46)

And from the hadith of the Prophet ﷺ:

> 'Actions come only through intentions. Every man shall have what he intended. Whoever emigrates to attain something of this world, or to marry a woman, emigrates for what he emigrates for.' (*Ṣaḥīḥ al-Bukhārī no. 1, Kitāb Bad' al-Waḥy; Ṣaḥīḥ Muslim no. 5036, Kitāb al-Imārah*)
>
> 'No man shall enter the Garden so long as he has a mote's

weight of pride.' A man said, 'Men like to have beautiful clothes and sandals.' He said, 'God is beautiful and loves beauty. Pride is to disregard the truth and to scorn people'. *(Ṣaḥīḥ Muslim no. 275, Kitāb al-Īmān)*

'The permitted is clear, and the forbidden is clear. Between the two lie doubtful matters unknown to most people. Whoever is pious regarding doubtful matters is thereby thorough in his religion and his honour. As for he who falls into doubtful matters, he is like a shepherd who pastures around a sanctuary, on the verge of entering it. Every king has a sanctuary, and indeed God's sanctuary on earth is His sacred bounds. Behold! Within everybody is a piece of flesh: when it thrives, the whole body thrives, and when it rots, the whole body rots, and indeed that is the heart.' *(Ṣaḥīḥ al-Bukhārī no. 52, Kitāb al-Īmān; Ṣaḥīḥ Muslim no. 1599, Kitāb al-Musāqāh.)*

The Prophet said, 'God does not look at your bodies or at your forms, but looks at your hearts,' and he used his fingers to point at his chest. *(Ṣaḥīḥ Muslim no. 6707, Kitāb al-Birr wa'l-Ṣilah wa'l-Adāb)*

The Messenger of God used to say, 'O God, I seek refuge in Thee from a heart that is not humble, a prayer that goes unheard, a soul that is not satisfied, and knowledge that is of no use. I seek refuge in Thee from these four.' *(Sunan al-Tirmidhī no. 3819, Kitāb al-Da'awāt.)*

'The first person to be judged on the Day of Judgment will be a man who was martyred. He will be brought forth, shown the favours he enjoyed, and he will recognise them. He (God) will say, 'What did you do concerning these?' He will say, 'I fought for Your sake until I was martyred.' He will say, 'You have lied. Rather, you fought so that it would be said, "He was bold," and it was said.' Then it will be commanded that he be dragged along on his face until he is thrown into the Fire. Then there will be a man who acquired and dispensed knowledge and recited the Quran. He will be brought forth, shown the favours he enjoyed, and he will recognise them. He will say, 'What did you do concerning these?' He will say, 'I acquired and dispensed knowledge and recited the Quran for Your sake.' He will say, 'You have lied. Rather, you acquired knowledge so that

> it would be said, "He is learned," and you recited the Quran so that it would be said, "He is a reciter," and it was said.' Then it will be commanded that he be dragged along on his face until he is thrown into the Fire. Then there will be a man whom God enriched and gave all manner of wealth. He will be brought forth, shown the favours he enjoyed, and he will recognise them. He will say, 'What did you do concerning these?' He will say, 'I left no path upon which you ordered that a bestowal be made without giving something there for Your sake.' He will say, "You have lied. Rather, you did that so that it would be said, "He is generous," and it was said.' Then it will be commanded that he be dragged along on his face and then thrown into the Fire. '
> *(Ṣaḥīḥ Muslim no. 5032, Kitāb al-Imārah.)*

Piety and Righteousness

Piety (*taqwah*) and righteousness (*birr*) can be seen, from a certain perspective, as the expression of mercy in all aspects of our life. Indeed, when we show mercy we must not limit it to certain people, or to certain situations, but must let our kindness, love, and respect shine through in everything we do. This must originate from our mindfulness of God's mercy, and from reverential fear of His wrath should we choose the way of anger over the way of mercy.

Among the Qur'anic verses which relate to piety and righteousness are the following, in which God says:

> *O you who believe! When you conspire together, do not conspire together for crime and wrongdoing and disobedience toward the messenger, but conspire together for righteousness and piety, and keep your duty toward God, unto whom you will be gathered.* (*Al-Mujādilah*, 58:9)

> *O mankind! Lo! We have created you male and female, and have made you nations and tribes that you may know one another. Lo! the noblest of you, in the sight of God, is the most pious of you. Lo! God is Knower, Aware.* (*Al-Ḥujurāt*, 49:13)

> *So make provision for yourselves (Hereafter); for the best provision is piety. Therefore keep your duty unto Me, O people of understanding.* (*Al-Baqarah*, 2:197)

What (plea) have they that God should not punish them, when they debar (His servants) from the Inviolable Place of Worship, though they are not its fitting guardians. Its fitting guardians are the pious. But most of them know not. (*Al-Anfāl*, 8:34)

It is not righteousness that you turn your faces to the East and the West; but righteous is he who believes in God and the Last Day and the angels and the Scripture and the prophets; and gives wealth, for love of Him, to kinsfolk and to orphans and the needy and the wayfarer and to those who ask, and to set slaves free; and observes proper worship and pays the poor-due. And those who keep their treaty when they make one, and the patient in tribulation and adversity and time of stress. Such are they who are sincere. Such are the pious. (*Al-Baqarah*, 2:177)

You will not attain unto righteousness until you spend of that which you love. And whatsoever you spend, God is Aware thereof. (*Āl 'Imrān*, 3:92)

And from the hadith of the Prophet ﷺ:

'The best of you are those with the most virtuous character.' *(Ṣaḥīḥ al-Bukhārī no. 3599, Kitāb al-Manāqib.)*

'None of you believes until you desire for your brother what you desire for yourself.' *(Ṣaḥīḥ al-Bukhārī no. 13, Kitāb al-Īmān; Ṣaḥīḥ Muslim no. 179, Kitāb al-Īmān.)*

Speaking to his Companion Abu Hurayrah, the Prophet ﷺ said, 'Abu Hurayrah, be Godfearing so as to be the most worshipful of people, be content so as to be the richest of people, desire for people what you desire for yourself so as to be a believer, act virtuously with your neighbour so as to be a Muslim, and reduce your laughter, for excessive laughter kills the heart.' (*Sunan Ibn Mājah no. 4357, Kitāb al-Zuhd.)*

'Whoever relieves a believer's hardship in the world will have a hardship of the Day of Judgment relieved for him by God. Whoever eases a difficulty will be eased in the world and in the hereafter by God. Whoever covers a Muslim will be covered by God in the world and in the hereafter. God helps his slave as long as the slave helps his brother. Whoever travels a path to acquire knowledge will

> have his path to Paradise made easy by God. No group gathers together in a house of God, reciting the Book of God and studying it together, without tranquillity descending upon them, mercy enveloping them, the angels encircling them, and God remembering them with those around Him. One who is slowed by his actions will not be quickened by his lineage.' *(Ṣaḥīḥ Muslim no. 7028, Kitāb al-Dhikr wa'l-Du'ā'.)*

Forgiveness

Forgiveness comes from mercy, and for the fallen soul forgiveness is that aspect of mercy which saves. God promises us forgiveness for our sins, but we must do our part in trying to make amends for our faults. If we are sincere and repentant, we have no reason to despair of His mercy.

Among the Qur'anic verses which relate to forgiveness are the following, in which God says:

> *Lo! God does not pardon that partners should be ascribed unto Him. He pardons all, save that, to whom He will.* (*Al-Nisā'*, 4:116)

> *(The prophet Joseph said to his brothers): Have no fear this day! May God forgive you, and He is the Most Merciful of those who show mercy.* (*Yūsuf*, 12:92)

> *Say: 'O My slaves who have been prodigal to their own hurt! Despair not of the mercy of God, Who forgives all sins. Lo! He is the Forgiving, the Compassionate.'* (*Al-Zumar*, 39:53)

> *He is the Forgiving, the Loving.* (*Al-Burūj*, 85:14)

> *Lo! there was a party of My slaves who said: 'Our Lord! We believe, therefore forgive us and have mercy on us for You art Best of all who show mercy.'* (*Al-Mu'minūn*, 23:109)

> *And (O Muhammad) say: 'My Lord! Forgive and have mercy, for You art Best of all who show mercy.'* (*Al-Mu'minūn*, 23:118)

> *(The prophet Moses said, upon slaying the Egyptian): 'My Lord! Lo! I have wronged my soul, so forgive me.' Then He forgave him. Lo! He is the Forgiving, the Compassionate.* (*Al-Qaṣaṣ*, 28:16)

And from the hadith of the Prophet ﷺ:

> 'If none of you had any sins for God to forgive for you, God

> would bring forth a people with sins that he would forgive for them.' (Ṣaḥīḥ Muslim no. 7140, Kitāb al-Tawbah.)
>
> The Prophet said, 'A slave sinned and said, "O God, forgive me my sin." God, Blessed and Most High, said, "My servant sinned and knew that he has a Lord who forgives sins and punishes for them." Then he sinned again and said, "O Lord, forgive me my sin." God, Blessed and Most High, said, "My servant sinned and knew that he has a Lord who forgives sins and punishes for them." Then he sinned again and said, "O Lord, forgive me my sin." God, Blessed and Most High, said, "servant sinned and knew that he has a Lord who forgives sins and punishes for them. Do what you wish, for I have forgiven you."' *(Ṣaḥīḥ Muslim no. 7162, Kitāb al-Tawbah.)*
>
> The Prophet said that God said, 'Son of Adam, so long as you call upon Me and ask of Me, I shall forgive you for what you have done, and I shall not mind. Son of Adam, were your sins to reach the clouds of the sky and were you then to ask forgiveness of Me, I would forgive you. Son of Adam, were you to come to Me with faults nearly equalling the earth and were you then to meet Me, ascribing no partner to Me, I would bring you forgiveness nearly equalling the earth.' *(Sunan al-Tirmidhī no. 3885, Kitāb al-Da'awāt.)*

Part Two: Wrath, Which is Outstripped

Harm and Wrongdoing

It is fitting, when remembering Divine Mercy, to call to mind what opposes it. The Qur'anic term *ẓulm* can be translated as tyranny, wrongdoing, and darkness. The wrongdoer or tyrant chooses darkness over the light of God's mercy. His very act of doing harm to others or to himself is a turning away from that mercy. Indeed, from a certain point of view, God never withholds His mercy. It is we who enter into the shadows of our own souls, forgetting that the light of mercy is always shining regardless of what we do.

Among the Qur'anic verses which relate to harm and wrongdoing are the following, in which God says:

> *They wronged Us not, but they did wrong themselves.* (*Al-Baqarah*, 2:57)

Lo! God wrongs not mankind in anything; but mankind wrong themselves.(*Yūnus*, 10:44)

Whoso transgresses God 's limits, he verily wrongs his soul. (*Al-Ṭalāq*, 65:1)

Those who do wrong will come to know by what a (great) reverse they will be overturned! (*Al-Shu'arā'*, 26:227)

And from the hadith of the Prophet ﷺ:

It was said, 'Messenger of God, who is the best Muslim?' He said, 'He from whose tongue and hand Muslims are safe.' *(Ṣaḥīḥ Muslim no. 170, Kitāb al-Īmān; Ṣaḥīḥ al-Bukhārī no. 11, Kitāb al-Īmān.)*

God harms the one who harms, and God torments the one who torments. *(Sunan Abu Dāwud no. 3637, Kitāb al-Aqdiya; Sunan Ibn Mājah no. 2432, Kitāb al-Aḥkām.)*

'Let there be neither harming nor requital to harm'. *(Sunan Ibn Mājah no. 2430, Kitāb al-Aḥkām.)*

The Prophet said that God, Blessed and Most High, said, 'My slaves, I have forbidden tyranny for Myself, and have made it forbidden among you. So be not tyrants of one another.' *(Ṣaḥīḥ Muslim no. 6737, Kitāb al-Birr wa'l-Ṣilah wa'l-Adāb.)*

'Abusing a Muslim is a sin, and killing him is unbelief.' *(Ṣaḥīḥ al-Bukhārī no. 47, Kitāb al-Īmān; Ṣaḥīḥ Muslim no. 230, Kitāb al-Īmān.)*

The Prophet said, 'By God, he does not believe; by God, he does not believe; by God, he does not believe.' It was said, 'Who, Messenger of God?' He said, 'One whose neighbour does not feel safe from his trespasses.' *(Ṣaḥīḥ al-Bukhārī no. 6084, Kitāb al-Adab.)*

'May he who believes in God and the Last Day do no harm to his neighbour, and may he who believes in God and the Last Day honour his guest, and may he who believes in God and the Last Day say what is good or keep silent.' *(Ṣaḥīḥ al-Bukhārī no. 6087, Kitāb al-Adab.)*

'Do not envy one another, nor expose one another, nor be angry with one another, nor be disparate from one another, nor let one sell what belongs to another. Be slaves of God, in brotherhood. A Muslim is a Muslim's brother. He does

> not wrong him, abandon him, or mock him. Piety is here,' and he pointed to his chest three times, 'It is enough evil for a man to mock his Muslim brother. The blood, property, and honour of all Muslims is inviolable by all others.' *(Ṣaḥīḥ Muslim no. 6706, Kitāb al-Birr wa'l-Ṣilah wa'l-Adāb.)*

Bigotry and Takfīr

Often bigotry and *takfīr* (meaning to declare another person to be an unbeliever or *kāfir*) are disguises for the more fundamental sins of greed, jealousy, revenge, and the desire for power. *Takfīr* is a means by which a soul justifies its taking of an innocent life, when in reality such a person is merely covering his bloodlust and brutality with a pious veneer. He may fool himself into thinking that the human being he devalues has no right to life, property, or honour, but his judgment does not bind God, though God's judgment will bind *him*. Declaring another person to be an unbeliever, or to dehumanise him through any other form of bigotry and ideology, opens the door to the great sins of pride, avarice, and lust, which lead to theft, rape, and murder. *Takfīr* and bigotry are thus the very antithesis of mercy.

Among the Qur'anic verses which relate to bigotry and *takfīr* are the following, in which God says:

> *And hold fast, all of you together, to the cable of God, and do not separate. And remember God 's favour unto you: How you were enemies and He made friendship between your hearts so that you became as brothers by His grace; and (how) you were upon the brink of an abyss of fire, and He did save you from it. Thus God makes clear His revelations unto you, that perhaps you may be guided.* (*Āl 'Imrān*, 3:103)
>
> *Lo! As for those who sunder their religion and become schismatics, no concern at all have you with them. Their case will go to God, Who then will tell them what they used to do.* (*Al-An'ām*, 6:159)
>
> *O you who believe! When you go forth (to fight) in the way of God, be careful to discriminate, and say not unto one who offers you peace: 'You are not a believer,' seeking the chance profits of this life (so that you may despoil him). With God are plenteous spoils. Even thus (as he now is) were you before; but God has since then been gracious unto you. Therefore*

> *take care to discriminate. God is ever Informed of what you do.* (*Al-Nisā'*, 4:94)
>
> *The believers are nothing else than brothers. Therefore make peace between your brethren and observe your duty to God that perhaps you may obtain mercy.* (*Al-Ḥujurāt*, 49:10)

And from the hadith of the Prophet, ﷺ:

> A Companion of the Prophet related that, while on an expedition, 'I came upon a man who said, "There is no deity but God," and I ran him through. This occurred to me and so I mentioned it to the Prophet, and the Messenger of God said, "He said, 'There is no deity but God,' and you killed him?" I said, "He only said it out of fear of the sword." He said, "Did you open him up to see if his heart said it or not?" He kept repeating that until I wished that I had entered Islam that day.' *(Ṣaḥīḥ Muslim no. 287, Kitāb al-Īmān.)*
>
> 'Whosoever is killed under the banner of pride, calling to tribalism or aiding tribalism, has a killing from the days of ignorance.' *(Ṣaḥīḥ Muslim no. 4898, Kitāb al-Imārah.)*
>
> 'When a man declares his brother to be an unbeliever, one of them is deserving of it.' *(Ṣaḥīḥ Muslim no. 224, Kitāb al-Īmān.)*
>
> A man said to the Prophet, 'Counsel me.' He said, 'Do not get angry.' He repeated it a few times, and he said, 'Do not get angry.' (*Ṣaḥīḥ al-Bukhārī no. 6184, Kitāb al-Adab; Sunan al-Tirmidhī no. 2152, Kitāb al-Birr wa'l-Ṣilah.)*
>
> 'Whoever leaves off obedience and separates from the community and dies has died a death from the days of ignorance. Whosoever fights under the banner of pride, standing up for some faction or calling to some faction or helping some faction, and is then killed, has a killing from the days of ignorance. He who rises against my ummah (religious community), assaulting its righteousness, attacking it, not sparing its believers, and not keeping his covenants, is not of me, nor am I of him.' *(Ṣaḥīḥ Muslim no. 4892, Kitāb al-Īmārah.)*

War

Islamic law promulgates the most merciful and just principles governing the causes and conduct of war, despite the abuses and crimes which take place in the name of Islam. We can never rid ourselves completely of war, any more than we can remove all the evil from human souls. Indeed, it is this evil which causes war.

In Islam, there is no good in war for its own sake, and no glory in fighting for its own sake, because a man may fight for an evil end. A Muslim can and must be merciful at all times and in all situations, especially in war, but he must be pure of heart, fight for what is good and just, not for his own personal desires, and he must always obey the principles and rules set down by the *sharīʿah*.

Among the Qur'anic verses which relate to war are the following, in which God says:

> *Whosoever kills a human being for other than man-slaughter or corruption in the earth, it shall be as if he had killed all mankind.* (*Al-Māʾidah*, 5:32)

> *Whoso slays a believer on purpose, his reward is hell for ever. God is angry with him and He has cursed him and prepared for him an awful doom.* (*Al-Nisāʾ*, 4:93)

> *And if they incline to peace, incline you also to it, and trust in God.* (*Al-Anfāl*, 8:61)

And from the hadith of the Prophet ﷺ:

> 'The disappearance of the world is easier on God than the killing of a Muslim man.' *(Sunan al-Tirmidhī no. 1455, Kitāb al-Diyāt.)*

> 'Ever will the believer have latitude in his religion, so long as he does not draw inviolable blood.' *(Ṣaḥīḥ al-Bukhārī no. 6946, Kitāb al-Diyāt.)*

> 'If the denizens of heaven and earth were to conspire against the blood of a believer, God would throw them into the Fire.' *(Sunan al-Tirmidhī no. 1459, Kitāb al-Diyāt.)*

> 'The first thing to be judged between people is the matter of bloodshed.' *(Ṣaḥīḥ al-Bukhārī no. 6948, Kitāb al-Diyāt.)*

> A woman was found slain in one of the campaigns of the Messenger of God, whereupon the Messenger of God forbade the killing of women and children. *(Ṣaḥīḥ al-Bukhārī no. 3052, Kitāb al-Jihad; Ṣaḥīḥ Muslim no. 1744, Kitāb al-Jihad wa'l-Sayr.)*

> 'Abd al-Rahman bin Samurah was walking hand in hand

with Ibn 'Umar in one of the roads of Madinah when they came to a head that had been set up, upon which Ibn 'Umar said, 'This person's killer is in torment.' When they had passed it he said, 'I think this one is only in torment. I heard the Messenger of God say, "Whoever goes to kill a man of my ummah (religious community), let him say this, for the killer is in the Fire and the victim is in the Garden."' (*Sunan Abu Dāwud no. 4262, Kitāb al-Fitan.)*

Do not be hopeful of meeting the enemy, and ask God for well-being. *(Ṣaḥīḥ al-Bukhārī no. 7323, Kitāb al-Tamanni.)*

Corruption and Sedition

Harmony is a dimension of beauty, which is itself a manifestation of mercy. As surely as there is beauty and harmony in colour, shape, sound, and rhythm, so too is there harmony in human relations, and in the love connecting family, friends, and neighbours.

Through spreading corruption (*fasād*) in the earth and sowing the seeds of strife, we place fear in the place of hope, revenge in place of forgiveness, and destroy the beauty and harmony of human relations as surely as acid destroys a beautiful face, or a terrible screech a beautiful sound, or an earthquake a beautiful city. *Fitnah* is a word that can be translated as persecution, sedition, and trial, all of which can destroy the bonds we share as God's creatures, robbing us of our ability to show mercy to one another.

Among the Qur'anic verses which relate to corruption and sedition are the following, in which God says:

Sedition is worse than killing.... (*Al-Baqarah*, 2:191)

Sedition is more grievous than killing.... (*Al-Baqarah*, 2:217)

Lo! they who persecute believing men and believing women and do not repent, theirs verily will be the doom of hell, and theirs the doom of burning. (*Al-Burūj*, 85:10)

And guard yourselves against a chastisement which cannot fall exclusively on those of you who are wrong-doers. (*Al-Anfāl*, 8:25)

(The prophet Shu'ayb said): Wrong not mankind in their goods, and work not confusion in the earth after the fair

ordering thereof. That will be better for you, if you are believers. (*Al-A'rāf*, 7:85)

(The prophet Moses said): Lo! God upholds not the work of mischief-makers. (*Yūnus*, 10:81)

(Moses also said): Eat and drink of that which God has provided, and do not act corruptly, making mischief in the earth. (*Al-Baqarah*, 2:60)

Seek not corruption in the earth; lo! God loves not corrupters. (*Al-Qaṣaṣ*, 28:77)

And from the hadith of the Prophet ﷺ:

Ibn 'Umar said, 'The Prophet said, "O God, bless us in Sham, O God bless us in Yemen." It was said, "In Najd?" He said, "O God, bless us in Sham, O God bless us in Yemen." It was said, "O Messenger of God, in Najd?". I think the third time he said, "There will be earthquakes and sedition there, through which the horn of Satan will rise."' *(Ṣaḥīḥ al-Bukhārī no. 7183, Kitāb al-Fitan.)*

Abu Salamah and 'Ata' bin Yasar came to Abu Sa'id al- Khudri and asked whether he had heard the Prophet say anything about the 'hot wind' (ḥarūriyyah). He said, 'I do not know what the hot wind is. I heard the Prophet say, "Within this ummah (religious community) a people will come out"—he did not say, "from this ummah"—"whose prayers will be such that you hold your own prayers lowly. They will recite the Quran, but it will not reach past their throats—or their larynxes—and they will pass through this religion as an arrow passes through game. The shooter looks at his arrow, its head, the sinews, and the nock. Has any blood cleaved to it?" *(Ṣaḥīḥ al-Bukhārī no. 7017, Kitāb Istitabat al-Murtaddīn; Ṣaḥīḥ Muslim no. 2503, Kitāb al-Zakāh.)*

'God does not withdraw knowledge from the people, but takes the learned and with them knowledge disappears. What remains among the people are ignorant leaders who make religious decisions for them without knowledge. They misguide and are misguided.' *(Ṣaḥīḥ Muslim no. 6974, Kitāb al-'Ilm.)*

Asked about the verse, O you who believe! You have charge of your own souls. He who errs cannot injure you if you are rightly guided. (*Al-Mā'idah*, 5:105), the Prophet said, 'Indeed, command what is right, and forbid what is wrong, until you see avarice obeyed, passions followed, this worldly life preferred, and every man charmed by his own opinion. Then, it will be your duty to care for your own soul, and to leave the rest. There are days coming after you, when patience will be like clutching a live coal. He who does a thing in those days will have a reward akin to that of fifty men who do as you do.' He was asked, 'Messenger of God, fifty men from among us or among them?' He replied, 'Indeed, fifty of you.' *(Sunan al-Tirmidhī no. 3335, Kitāb Tafsīr al-Qur'ān.)*

Abu Darda' related that the Prophet gazed at the sky and said, 'These are times when knowledge is snatched away from the people such that they can cannot make use of it at all.' Ziyad bin Labid al-Ansari asked him, 'How can it be snatched away from us, as we recite the Quran? For by God we recite it, our women and children as well.' He said, 'Shame on you, Ziyad. I counted you among the learned of Madinah. The Torah and Gospel are with the Jews and Christians. Does it avail them anything?' *(Sunan al-Tirmidhī no. 2865, Kitāb al-'Ilm.)*

'The religion will gather itself up in the Hijaz as a snake gathers itself up in its burrow, and the religion will take refuge in the Hijaz as a goat does on a mountaintop. The religion began a stranger and is returning a stranger. Blessed be those who set right my Wont (sunnah) which the people corrupted.' *(Sunan al-Tirmidhī no. 2839, Kitāb al-Īmān.)*

Beware of excessiveness in religion. Those before you perished only for excessiveness in religion. *(Sunan al-Nasā'ī no. 3070, Kitāb Manāsik al-Ḥajj.)*

I leave you that which, if you hold to it, will never let you go astray. The first is greater than the second: the Book of God is a rope extended from heaven to earth, and my progeny, the people of my House. These two shall never be separated, even unto their arrival with me at the Pond. So take care how you disappoint me concerning them. *(Sunan al-Tirmidhī no. 4157, Kitāb al-Manāqib; a similar hadith is found in Ṣaḥīḥ Muslim no. 6378, Kitāb Faḍā'il al-Ṣaḥābah.)*

Originally published in 2007 by the Royal Aal al-Bayt Institute for Islamic Thought as a booklet entitled
Forty Hadith on Divine Mercy.

APPENDIX

THE CONDITIONS NECESSARY FOR JUST WAR IN THE HOLY QUR'AN

HRH Prince Ghazi bin Muhammad

War and combat require specific conditions in the Holy Qur'an, without which they are completely forbidden and illegitimate. Indeed, every single passage in the Qur'an which contains an injunction or permission for Muslims to wage a war or combat is immediately preceded or followed by a Qur'anic verse that:

A) explains that the war is defensive;
B) explains that without war there would be greater death and suffering, hence implying a just war is the lesser of two evils;
C) enjoins mercy and shows how to fight the war as mercifully as possible; and/or:
D) urges an end to the war when possible.

Moreover, there are a number of passages that seem to be sanctioning war but are actually:

E) informing Muslims of the reality, meaning and lessons of what happened in battles they had already fought (such as Badr, Uhud, the Trench or Hunayn) without this in itself necessarily constituting a legal injunction as such to fight in the future;
F) merely relating the stories of previous nations (usually the Children of Israel) and their wars, which—since they do not have the same sacred laws as Islam—do not apply to Muslims except by way of parable;
G) merely enjoining a 'struggle' (this is the actual meaning of jihad in Arabic) against unbelief and hypocrisy without this meaning physical combat as such;
H) warnings or predictions to the unbelievers or 'hypocrites' (the

'hypocrites' were those who pretended to be Muslims but were in fact not and were just waiting for an opportunity to hurt the Muslims from within—see *Sūrat Al-Munāfiqūn* (63)) without being declarations of war as such;

I) in fact condemning or at least eschewing combat in that context; and/or

J) specifically urging forbearance and patience, and not war.

There are also verses that do not relate to war as such and are in fact:

K) prescribing capital punishment for murder or other capital offences.

In what follows, we systematically go through all the passages in the Qur'an that seem to enjoin or permit war, and show that these verses are all in fact conditioned by the principles of self-defence, of justice, of proportionality, of preferring peace to war and above all by mercy—even whilst enjoining Muslims to win the wars they have no choice but to fight.

(The capital letters in the NOTES column relate to the explanations above.)

WAR VERSES	VERSES WITH CONDITIONS	NOTES
2: 54	2: 54	F; K.
2: 85–6	2: 84	F; I.
2: 178	2: 178–9	K: *Lex Talionis*: this verse does not relate to war but to murder.
2:191; 193–4	2: 190; 192–3	A; C; D.
2: 216–8	2: 217	A; B.
2: 244–6	2: 246	A; F.

2: 250–1; 253	2: 251	B; F: This passage follows on from the last one and thus A applies here as well.
3: 12–3	3: 12	H.
3: 111	3: 111	A.
3: 121–34	3: 128–9; 134	E: These verses refer to the Battle of Badr (2 AH/ 624 CE). In addition, verses 3:128–9 hold out the promise of God's forgiveness. J: v.134 commends forgiving and restraining oneself from anger.
3: 139–80	3: 149	B; E: It is to be noted also that this long passage in *Sūrat Āl 'Imrān* refers A: mostly to a defensive battle that has already occurred—the Battle of Uhud (3 AH/625 CE)—and that whilst it encourages Muslims to keep up the fight (vv. 139–48; 150–1; 156–63), and explains that it is to be viewed as a trial from God (vv. 140–3; 166–7; 179), it should be borne in mind that this battle was a defensive one.
4: 66	4: 66	G.
4: 71–104	4: 75; 86; 90; 94	This long passage touches on many important subjects, not merely war. A: The defensive justification for war is in verse 4: 75. C: in verse 4: 90; D: in verses 4: 86 and 94.

War Verses	Verses With Conditions	Notes
4: 141	4: 141	E.
5: 2	5: 2	I: verse 5:2 commands Muslims not to commit aggression even though their religious freedom has been prohibited.
5: 8–9	5: 8–9	I; C: 5: 8 commands Muslims to be just to their enemies even when they have cause to hate them.
5: 11	5: 11	B; E.
5: 21–6	5: 21–6	F.
5: 33–4	5: 33–4	C; K: verse 5:33 prescribes capital punishment for war crimes; 5: 34 offers amnesty.

5: 45	5: 45	F: K: *Lex Talionis*, but this verse merely states that it was prescribed in the Torah.
8: 1–19; 39–49; 56–75	8: 26; 30; 39; 61; 70-71.	The name of this surah is *Al-Anfāl* ('The Spoils of War') and it is largely about the Battle of Badr. E: in verses: 7–13; 17; 41–4; 67–71. The surah contains at least four injunctions to fight (12; 15; 16; 39), and also a commandment to prepare for war (60) and to undertake war even against superior numbers (65–6). A: All of the above is mitigated by verses 26 and 30, which make it clear that the war in question is a defensive war. Furthermore, A and D: Verses 19 and 39 make it clear that war will end when Muslims are no longer religiously persecuted. D: Verse 61 commands Muslims to make peace if they are offered it. Most remarkable of all, verse 45 spiritualises war and makes its very prosecution dependent on the remembrance of God. C: Verses 70–1 hold out the promise of amnesty for prisoners of war.

War Verses	Verses With Conditions	Notes
9: 1–29	9: 2; 4; 6; 13	This surah (*Al-Tawbah*, 'Repentance') is the only surah in the whole Qur'an which does not start with the Divine Names of Mercy (*al-Raḥmān, al-Raḥīm*) and perhaps the most warlike. Verse 5 is commonly thought of as the 'Sword Verse' declaring jihad. Verses 11–12 also reiterate the commandment to fight. D: However, verse 5—like verse 11—also offers peace for those who repent from waging war on Muslims, and verse 29 implies an end to war after surrender of the enemy. C: verses 1–5 give fair warning of the beginning of hostilities and offer temporary truces. A: It is above all verse 13 which makes clear that the war is in self-defence and that after the enemy not only started the war, but also broke a truce thereafter. E: Verses 24–5 are about the Battle of Hunayn (in Ta'if, 8AH/630 CE).

9: 38–47	9: 40	These verses call for war, but A: Verse 40 makes it clear that the unbelievers had started hostilities by attempting to kill the Prophet ﷺ and by forcing him (and the Muslim community) out of Mecca.
9: 73–4	9: 74	These verses contain a commandment to fight the unbelievers and the hypocrites, but the verses which follow (75-87) show K: that the fight was against treason and betrayal within Medina. C: Verse 74 also holds out the promise of forgiveness for repentance.
9: 88–96	9: 95	Verses 88–92 encourage and praise those who fight in God's way. E: Verses 93–6 relate what happened to Muslims in their recent struggles. D: Verse 95 allows for a cessation in the fighting.
9: 111–2	9: 112	Verse 111 promises paradise for those who are martyred. C: verse 112 shows that there are limits in warfare.

War Verses	Verses With Conditions	Notes
9: 117–23	9: 123	E: Verses 117–8 relate to past fighting. Verses 119–21 promise reward for fighting in God's way. Verse 122 is another remarkable verse because it values learning above fighting even during wartime. A: Verse 123 orders fighting against those enemies who are close (only).
16: 126	16: 126	J; C.
17: 5–8	17: 5–8	F.
17: 33	17: 33	I.
18: 74–5	Explained by 18: 65; 80–2.	F; K.
18: 86–8	18: 86–8	F; K.

22: 38–40	22: 39–40	These verses are the most important verses in the Qur'an related to war because they are the first verses that allowed the Muslims to fight (according to all the commentaries—see *Tafsīr al-Ṭabarī* and *Tafsīr al-Qurṭubī*). They must be cited in full: *Indeed God protects those who believe. Indeed God does not love the treacherous, the ungrateful. / Permission [to fight] is granted to those who have been attacked because they have been wronged. And God is truly able to help them; / those who were expelled from their homes without right, only because they said: 'Our Lord is God'. Were it not for God's causing some people to drive back others, destruction would have befallen the monasteries, and churches, and synagogues, and mosques in which God's Name is mentioned greatly. Assuredly God will help those who help Him. God is truly Strong, Mighty* (*Al-Ḥajj*, 22:38–40). After ten years of religious persecution, torture, murder and banishment, and an assassination attempt on the Prophet ﷺ himself in Mecca, in 622 CE the Prophet ﷺ and the Muslim community emigrated one by one to the city of Yathrib (Medina).

War Verses	Verses With Conditions	Notes
22: 38–40	22: 39–40	(This event marks the start of the Islamic calendar). From Medina, the Muslims were finally allowed by God to defend themselves. The first Caliph Abu Bakr Al-Siddiq ﷺ said: '[When I first heard this verse {v.39}] I knew there would be combat, and it was the first to be revealed [about combat]' (Tabari). These verses are remarkable because they show that a just war in Islam depends on: (1) being attacked first; (2) being wronged (and having been patient); (3) being expelled from one's homes and land; (4) being religiously persecuted merely for belief in God; and (5) having one's holy places (or the holy places of Jews and Christians) destroyed. Also, the fact that God grants 'permission'—and does not merely give a commandment to fight—shows that fighting is an exceptional state which requires a Divine exemption or 'special permission', and is thus not the preferred state of affairs. Hence this also shows that war may only be declared by the legitimate authority and ruler.

22: 58–60	22: 60	D; C.
22: 78	22: 78; see also 25:52	G: This verse calls for 'real jihad', but the commentators (see Tabari) on this verse are split as to whether the jihad in question is a moral jihad (as suggested by the previous verse and by verse 25:52 where the 'great jihad' is teaching the Qur'an) or physical war. The context and remainder of the verse suggest the former.
25: 52	25: 52	G: This is the verse of the 'great jihad': *So do not obey the disbelievers, but struggle against them* (jāhidhum) *therewith with a great jihad.* (*Al-Furqān*, 25:52). However, the great jihad is not physical combat but the moral jihad using the Qur'an. Thus the Prophet ﷺ said: 'We have returned from the Lesser Holy War (*al-Jihad al-Aṣghar*) to the Greater Holy War (*al-Jihad al-Akbar*)'. When asked what the Greater Holy War was, he replied: '[It is] the war against the ego [*nafs*]'. (Ahmad bin Hussein Al-Bayhaqi, *Kitāb al-Zuhd*, vol. 2, p. 165, no. 373).
26: 226	26: 226	A.
27: 18–28	27: 18–28	F.

War Verses	Verses With Conditions	Notes
29: 6	29: 6	G: This verse mentions jihad (for the soul), but like verse 25: 52, it is a peaceful jihad that is meant.
29: 8	29: 8	I; G: This verse mentions a peaceful jihad (struggle) but against Muslims, which they are to resist peacefully.
29: 10	29: 10	F.
29: 69	29: 69	I: This verse mentions a peaceful jihad (struggle) but against Muslims which they are to resist peacefully, like 29: 69.
30: 2–6	30: 2–6	F.
31: 5	31: 5	I: This verse mentions a peaceful jihad (struggle) but against Muslims which they are to resist peacefully, like 29: 69.
33: 9–27	33: 9–27	E: These verses are about what happened in the Battle of the Trench (Al-Khandaq) in 5 AH/627 CE.
33: 60–1	33: 60–1	H.

42: 39–43	42: 39–43	A: verse 39; verses 41–2. C and D: verse 40. J: verse 43. These verses summarise the Qur'an's attitude to war, and it is significant that they are from the Meccan period—that is to say, after war had already started (they are cited at the end of this text).
47: 4; 7	47: 1; 32; 34	This whole surah (*Sūrat Muḥammad*) has 'work' or 'deeds' (*'amal*) as its central theme, and indeed the word and its derivatives are mentioned at least nine times in the surah (the surah has 38 verses in total). Part of work (*'amal*) can be combat and verses 4, and 7 call for this. However, A: verses 47: 1, 32, 34 make it clear that combat occurs only after religious persecution. Verse 4, C: orders humane treatment of prisoners of war and either ransom or amnesty after war.
47: 20–3	47: 1; 32; 34	These verses (47: 20-23) are about reactions to the Qur'an's orders to fight but again they relate to A: verses 47: 1, 32, 34.

War Verses	Verses With Conditions	Notes
47: 25; 31–5	47: 1; 32; 34	These verses (47:25; 31–5) encourage combat, and verse 35 calls on the believers not to slacken or be fainthearted in war and cry for peace whilst they are winning, but again they relate to A: verses 47: 1, 32, 34.
48: 1–7	48: 1–7	E: These verses (48: 1–7) refer to the Pact of Hudaybiyyah (6 AH/ 628 CE), when the Prophet ﷺ and the Muslims went unarmed to Mecca and were turned back by their enemies, but made a pact with them so that they could return on pilgrimage the following year. God refers to this as a 'clear triumph' in verse 1, and it is this triumph that is referred to in the name of this Surah (*Sūrat Al-Fatḥ*).
48: 15–7	48: 15–7	H: These verses warn the hypocrites amongst the Bedouins.
48: 18–28	48: 18–28	E: These verses refer to the events around Hudaybiyyah, and (vv. 18–21; 27) predict future victory and the fall of Mecca (which happened in 10 AH/630 CE).
49: 9–10	49: 9–10.	C: verse 9. D: verse 10.

54: 44–5	54: 44	H. At the Battle of Badr the Prophet ﷺ recalled verse 45.
58: 5	58: 5	A.
58: 20-21	58: 22	A.
58: 22	58: 22	E. Al-Razi mentions in his Great Commentary (*Mafātīḥ al-Ghayb*) that that Ibn 'Abbas ؓ said that this verse commends Abu 'Ubaydah ؓ at the Battle of Uhud, and Ali ؓ, Abu Bakr ؓ and 'Umar ibn al-Khattab ؓ at the Battle of Badr.
59: 2–7	59: 2–7	E: verses 2–7; C: 3. These verses describe the struggle (in 4 AH/626 CE) with the Jewish tribe of Banu Nadir in Medina who betrayed the Muslims and tried to kill the Prophet ﷺ. Verse 5 is sometimes misinterpreted to permit the cutting down of palm trees (and thus scorched earth tactics), but in fact it permits only the cutting of the date stalks (līnah)—that is to say, of the dates themselves, without ruining future crops.

War Verses	Verses With Conditions	Notes
59: 11–5	59: 11–5	H: verses11–4; E: verse15. These verses describe the struggle (in 4 AH/626 CE) with Banu Nadir of Medina who betrayed the Muslims and tried to kill the Prophet ﷺ.
60: 1–8	60: 7–8	A.
61: 4	61: 4	H: This verse commends a manner of fighting in solid lines once there is a war, but does not itself call for war.
61: 8–13	60: 8	A: 60: 8
63: 8	63: 8	A; H.
66: 9	66: 9	G.
73: 20	73: 20	H.
100: 1–5	100: 1–5	H: These verses merely mention charging horses and imply their awesomeness.
105: 1–5	105: 1–5	F; I.

N.B.: There are a total of 114 surahs (chapters) in the Qur'an (of uneven length) with 6236 verses in total.

In addition to all these conditions for—and limitations of—war in the Qur'an, there are also a number of other verses in the Qur'an that condemn murder and violence. These include the following: *Āl 'Imrān*, 3:21–2; *Al-Nisā'*, 4:29–30 (hell is promised for murder); 4:92–3 (hell is promised for murder); 4:155; *Al-Mā'idah*, 5:71; 5:27–32 (5:32 mentions that God decreed in the Torah that murder of one soul is like killing all souls, and saving one soul is like saving all souls); *Al-An'ām*, 6:137; 6:140; 6:152 (6:151–2 resemble the Ten Commandments); *Al-Isrā'*, 17:33; *Al-Mumtaḥanah*, 60:12; *Al-Burūj*, 85:10 et al.

Thus, as will clearly be seen from all the above, the Qur'an categorically:

1) condemns all forms of murder;
2) does not enjoin or permit war except in self-defence (and 'self-defence' is conditional upon [A] being attacked first; [B] being wronged (and having been patient); [C] being expelled from one's homes and land; [D] being religiously persecuted merely for belief in God; and [E] having one's holy places—or the holy places of Jews and Christians—destroyed);
3) gives fair warning before hostilities;
4) respects agreements and truces and protects those who have made agreements and truces;
5) does not permit or enjoin war on other religious communities simply because they have different religious beliefs and
6) does not force opponents to convert to Islam;
7) protects non-Muslim holy sites (and hence also their occupants);
8) does not enjoin or permit total war or scorched earth tactics or the destruction of livestock and the environment;
9) does not allow killing of civilians or non-combatants, and especially protects clergy, women, children, the elderly or the infirm;
10) wages legitimate war as mercifully as possible and forbids all unwarranted brutality, even whilst aiming for a military victory;

11) orders humane treatment of prisoners of war, including meeting their essential needs, and their ransoming or exchange or being set free (if they teach ten Muslims to read or write or convert to Islam);
12) encourages peace and cessation of hostilities whenever possible during conflict;
13) regards war as the last option; and
14) makes it clear that only a legitimate ruler of the entire Muslim community may declare war.

In summary, war sanctioned by God in the Qur'an—the 'lesser jihad'—is a just and humane war, and it is waged only for morally justified self-defence and not for religious or ideological conquest. God says in the Qur'an:

> *... [A]nd those who, when they suffer aggression defend themselves: / For the requital of an evil deed is an evil deed like it. But whoever pardons and reconciles, his reward will be with God. Truly He does not like wrongdoers. / And whoever defends himself after he has been wronged, for such, there will be no course [of action] against them. / A course [of action] is only [open] against those who wrong people and seek [to commit] in the earth what is not right. For such there will be a painful chastisement. / But verily he who is patient and forgives—surely that is [true] constancy in [such] affairs.* (Al-Shūrā, 39–43).

NOTES

CONTENTS

[1] Originally published by the Royal Aal al-Bayt Institute for Islamic Thought as a separate booklet in 2007.

[2] Reproduced with the permission of the author and World Wisdom Press.

[3] Originally published in *Seasons: Semi-annual Journal of Zaytuna Institute*, Spring-Summer Reflections, 2005, vol. 2, no. 2, pp. 45-68.

[4] Originally published as *Body Count* by the Royal Aal al-Bayt Institute for Islamic Thought as a booklet in 2009.

[5] Reproduced (and adjusted) from *Love in the Holy Qur'an* (Chapters 4, 5, and 7) by H.R.H. Prince Ghazi bin Muhammad.

[6] Reproduced (and adjusted) from *Love in the Holy Qur'an* (Ch.17) by H.R.H. Prince Ghazi bin Muhammad.

[7] Originally published by the Royal Aal al-Bayt Institute for Islamic Thought as a booklet entitled *Forty Hadith on Divine Mercy* in 2007.

INTRODUCTION

[8] Seyyed Hossein Nasr, *The Heart of Islam: Enduring Values for Humanity* (New York, NY: Harper Collins Publishers Paperback Edition, 2004), p. 256.

[9] There are a number of English translations of the Qur'an; authors in this volume have not specified which they have used, and indeed in some cases may have provided their own translations. Some have translated the Divine Name '*Allah*' as 'God', and some have left it as '*Allah*'—we have respected this. The chapter and verse numbers refer to the original Arabic. We have also kept the authors' own preferences as regards modern or archaic English (in translating the Qur'an).

[10] The Arabic version reads '*al-mujāhidu man jāhada nafsahu.*' See 'Abd al-Rahman al-Mubarakfuri, *Tuḥfat al-Aḥwazi bi-Sharḥ Jāmi' al-Tirmidhī*, edited by 'Abd al-Rahman 'Uthman (Cairo: Maktaba'at al-Ma'rifah, n.d), hadith no. 1671.

[11] Ibn Majah, *Sunan Ibn Mājah, Kitāb al-fitan, bāb al-'amr bi'l-ma'rūf*, hadith no. 4011.

[12] Muslim, *Mukhtaṣar Ṣaḥîḥ Muslim*, edited by Nasir al-Din al-Albani (Kuwait (several editions)), p. 469, hadith no. 1756.

[13] Bukhari, *Ṣaḥīḥ al-Bukhārī*, hadith no. 2957.

[14] The second and the third categories, namely of jihad against the unbeliever and the hypocrites refer primarily to the idolaters (*mushrikūn*) of Mecca, and the hypocrites (*munāfiqūn*) of Medina respectively. There is ample evidence in the sources, as the book before us expounds, to the effect that no jihad may be waged to compel anyone into embracing Islam.

[15] Ibn Qayyim al-Jawziyyah, *Zād al-Ma'ad min Huda Khayr al-'Ibad*, as quoted in Muhammad Hisham Kabbani, 'Principles of leadership in War and peace' (2004) at www.islamicsupremecouncil.org/legal_rulings/Jihad/jihadwithadditions.pdf. A similar classification of jihad has been advanced by Ibn Rushd al-Kabir in *al-Muqaddimat al-Mumahhidāt*.

[16] Seyyed Hossein Nasr, *The Heart Of Islam: Enduring Values for Humanity*, p.262.

[17] Ali A Mazrui, 'The Ethics of War and Rhetorics of Politics: the West and the Rest,' *2 Islamic millennium Journal* (2002), p.1.

[18] Quoted by Anicee Van Engeland-Nourai, 'The Challenge of Fragmentation of International Humanitarian Law' in Bassiouni, ed., *Jihad and its Challenges*, p. 147; see also Seyyed Hossein Nasr, *The Heart of Islam*, p. 263.

[19] Quoted by Anicee Nourai, 'The Challenge of Fragmentation', p. 148.

[20] Nasr, *The Heart of Islam*, p. 263.

[21] Nikkie R. Kiddie, 'The Revolt of Islam—1700 to 1993' in Bryan S. Turner, ed., *Islam: Critical Concepts in Sociology* (Oxford: Routledge, 2003), vol. 2, p. 89.

CHAPTER 1

[22] What is meant by manifest coercion is coercion through physical force such as iron and fire; what is meant by surreptitious coercion is perceptible miracles to which one submits.

[23] This is different from his responsibility, and that of the caliphs who followed him, to carry out God's shari'ah within the Ummah (Muslim community).

[24] The *jizyah* is not, as some think, a sum paid in exchange for life or the right to refuse conversion to Islam. It is, as we have said, a symbol that signifies yielding, the desistance from warfare and impeding the *da'wah* and a token of participation in the affairs of the state in return for the protection of life and property. On page 35 of *Kitāb al-Kharāj*, Abu Yusuf writes: 'After Abu 'Ubaydah concluded a peace treaty with the people of Syria and had collected from them the *jizyah* and the tax for agrarian land (*kharāj*), he was informed that the Romans were readying for battle against him and that the situation had become critical for him and the Muslims. Abu 'Ubaydah then wrote to the governors of the cities with whom pacts had been concluded

that they must return the sums collected from *jizyah* and *kharāj* and say to their subjects: "We return to you your money because we have been informed that troops are being raised against us. In our agreement you stipulated that we protect you, but we are unable to do so. Therefore, we now return to you what we have taken from you, and we will abide by the stipulation and what has been written down, if God grants us victory over them."'

[25] Some people whose intent is to disparage Islam do not go beyond a superficial interpretation of the verse: *... fight those of the disbelievers who are near to you ....* They claim that Islam orders Muslims to fight unbelievers in general until they convert to Islam whether they commit aggression or not. They also claim that Islamic law (shari'ah) decrees this. The truth is that what is meant by the word 'disbelievers' in this verse and others is the warring polytheists who fought the Muslims, aggressed against them, expelled them from their homes, took their property and spread sedition among people regarding their faith. The morals of these polytheists have been described in the opening verses of *Sūrat Al-Tawbah*.

Further, what is meant by the word 'people' in the hadith: 'I have been ordered to fight the people ...' should be understood in the same manner. For according to consensus (*ijmā'*) on this hadith, warfare must cease if the enemies are Arab polytheists. As for other enemies, the war against them must cease on the condition that they ... *pay the jizyah tribute, readily being subdued.* Thus, these verses are in agreement and there is no contradiction between the Holy Qur'an and the Hadith and the aforementioned false allegation is dropped.

[26] These verses warn against violating treaties or conducting them in a manner in which one or both parties are not left feeling secure. The verses also warn against remaining under the mercy of a power that does not know peace or justice. They also warn against using treaties as an artful means to take advantage of the weak, who are compelled by circumstances to consent to them. History has proven that treaties conducted under these circumstances are ultimately corrupt and end badly. God says in the Holy Qur'an: *And do not make your oaths a [means of] deceit between you lest a foot should slip after being steady, and [lest] you should taste evil, forasmuch as you barred [people] from the way of God, and there be a tremendous chastisement for you.* (*Al-Naḥl*: 16:94). Compare then the teachings of these verses with the treaties conducted by modem nations which have ended up being disastrous to the world.

CHAPTER 2

[27] http://www.fbi.gov/stats-services/publications/terrorism-2002-2005/terror02_05. Scroll to the bottom for a chronological list commencing in 1980. Access date: 1 April 2011.

[28] Muslims make up 23 percent of the world's 6.8 billion humans. See the

Pew Forum on Religion & Public Life, *Mapping the Global Muslim Population: A Report on the Size and Distribution of the World's Muslim Population* (Washington, DC: Pew Research Center, October 2009), p. 1. Cf.:

http://pewforum.org/Mapping-the-Global-Muslim-Population.aspx. Access date: 1 April 2011.

[29] The King James Version of the Holy Bible contains 788,280 words: 609,269 in the Old Testament and 179,011 in the New Testament. Cf.: http://www.bible-believers.com/believers-org/kjv-stats.htm

[30] *Mapping the Global Muslim Population.*

[31] The very first word revealed to Muhammad was *Iqrā'*, which means 'recite' and the word *Qur'ān* itself originates from the root word *Qara'a*, which means 'to read out' or 'to recite'.

[32] The title of Mr Spencer's most controversial bestseller is: *The Truth about Muhammad, Founder of the World's Most Intolerant Religion* (Washington, DC: Regnery Press, 2006). Spencer's other books include: *Islam Unveiled: Disturbing Questions about the World's Fastest Growing Faith* (New York: Encounter Books, 2002); *The Myth of Islamic Tolerance: How Islamic Law treats Non-Muslims* (New York: Prometheus Books, 2005); *The Politically Incorrect Guide to Islam (And the Crusades)* (Regnery, 2005); *Religion of Peace? Why Christianity Is and Islam Isn't* (Regnery, 2007).

[33] Cf. the published works, journalism and Internet articles of Daniel Pipes, Benny Morris, David Horowitz, Bernard Lewis, Sam Harris, David Bukay and David Pryce-Jones, among others. I need to make my position clear. As a liberal and an academic I strongly support the liberal arts education model and the enhanced societal contributions made by critically educated minds. At the heart of my philosophy lies a passionate belief in the value of dialogue and debate. I therefore do not challenge the right of these scholars and pundits publicly to express their concerns about Islam, even though I do not share them.

[34] There are numerous English-language translations of the Qur'an which give slightly different wordings, but the translation that I consider most reliable, easiest to read and closest to the meaning of the Arabic text is: Shaykh-ul-Islam Dr Muhammad Tahir-ul-Qadri, *The Holy Qur'an (English Translation / Irfan-ul-Qur'an), 2009 edn* (Lahore: Minhaj-ul-Quran International, 2006). I also recommend the readability and reliability of Maulana Wahiduddin Khan's translation, *The Quran* (New Delhi: Goodword, 2009). Another very popular modern translation is the so-called Wahhabi translation: *Dr Muhammad Muhsin Khān and Dr Muhammad Taqī-ud-Din Al-Hilālī, Interpretation of the Meanings of the Noble Qur'ān in the English Language: A Summarised Version of At-Tabarī, Al-Qurtubī and Ibn Kathīr with Comments from Sahīh Al-Bukhārī: Summarised in One Volume* (Riyadh: Darussalam, 1996. Revised edition 2001). It must be pointed out, however, that this easy-to-read translation has not been immune from criticism, particularly with regard to many interpolations that seem to

provide a deliberately negative portrayal of Christians and Jews. For that reason I do not use it, and I believe others should read it, should they wish, with this caveat in mind. Cf. Khaleel Mohammed, 'Assessing English Translations of the Qur'an', *Middle East Quarterly*, vol. 12 no. 2 (Spring 2005), pp. 59–72.

[35] *Jizyah* was a tax levied by the Islamic state on non-Muslims. In return they gained exemption from military service and guarantees of safety within the state. This taxation arrangement, essentially a type of tribute, was a pre-Islamic practice merely continued by the Muslims. Cf. Majid Khadduri, *War and Peace in the Law of Islam* (Baltimore: Johns Hopkins Press, 1955), p. 178.

[36] Cf. Ibid., pp. 96, 163; Majid Khadduri, *The Islamic Conception of Justice* (Baltimore: Johns Hopkins University Press, 1984), p. 165. Spencer, ed., *The Myth of Islamic Tolerance*, pp. 43–4.

[37] Cf. Spencer, *The Politically Incorrect Guide to Islam*, p. 28. After negatively quoting a statement praising Muhammad as 'a hard fighter and a skillful military commander', Samuel P. Huntington writes that 'no one would say this about Christ or Buddha'. He adds that Islamic doctrines 'dictate war against unbelievers … The Koran and other statements of Muslim beliefs contain few prohibitions on violence, and a concept of non-violence is absent from Muslim doctrine and practice.' Huntington, *The Clash of Civilizations and the Remaking of World Order* (London: Simon & Schuster, 1996), p. 263.

[38] Deuteronomy 7: 1–3 and 20: 16–7.

[39] Polybius, *Histories*, XXXVIII.21.

[40] Sohail H. Hashmi, ed., *Islamic Political Ethics: Civil Society, Pluralism, and Conflict* (Princeton: Princeton University Press, 2002), p. 196.

[41] *Sūrat Sabā'*, 34:28; *Al-Zumar*, 39:41; and Al-*Tawkīr*, 81:27.

[42] Spencer, The Politically Incorrect Guide to Islam, pp. 24–6. Cf. also:http://www.answering-islam.org/Bailey/jihad.html

[43] Cf. David Bukay, 'Peace or Jihad: Abrogation in Islam', in *Middle East Quarterly* (Fall 2007), pp. 3–11, available online at:

http://www.meforum.org/1754/peace-or-jihad-abrogation-in-islam. Access date: 1 April 2011.

[44] Zakaria Bashier, *War and Peace in the Life of the Prophet Muhammad* (Markfield: The Islamic Foundation, 2006), pp. vii–viii; Khadduri, *War and Peace*, p. 105.

[45] Bukay, 'Peace or Jihad', cited above.

[46] http://www.pbs.org/newshour/terrorism/international/fatwa_1996.html. Access date: 1 April 2011.

[47] http://www.pbs.org/newshour/terrorism/international/fatwa_1998.html. Access date: 1 April 2011.

[48] This is clearly the judgement of prominent intellectual Tariq Ramadan. Cf. his biography, *The Messenger: The Meanings of the Life of Muhammad* (London: Penguin, 2007), p. 91.

[49] Bashier, *War and Peace*, p. 284. An interesting introductory book for anyone unfamiliar with Islam is Sohaib Nazeer Sultan's amusingly titled *The Koran for Dummies* (Hoboken: Wiley, 2004). Sultan makes the same point (pp. 278, 281) that the martial verse and the sword and those like it do not abrogate the more numerous peaceful, tolerant and inclusive verses.

[50] Bashier, *War and Peace*, p. 288.

[51] Louay Fatoohi, *Jihad in the Qur'an: The Truth from the Source* (Birmingham: Luna Plena, 2009). Email from Dr Louay Fatoohi to Dr Joel Hayward, 23 August 2010.

[52] Muhammad Abu Zahra, *Concept of War in Islam* (Cairo: Ministry of Waqf, 1961), p. 18, quoted in Hashmi, ed., *Islamic Political Ethics*, p. 208.

[53] Michael Fishbein, trans., *The History of al-Tabarī (Tā'rīkh al-rusūl wa'l-mulūk): vol. VIII: The Victory of Islam* (State University of New York Press, 1997), pp. 162–5; Bashier, War and Peace, pp. 224–6.

[54] *Tafsīr Ibn Kathīr*, vol. 4 (*Sūrat Al-'A'rāf* to the end of *Sūrat Yūnus*), (Riyadh: Darussalam, 2003.), pp. 371–5; Safiur-Rahman Al-Mubarakpuri, *The Sealed Nectar: Biography of the Noble Prophet*, 2002 edn (Riyadh: Darussalam, 1979), pp. 351–3; Lt. Gen. A. I. Akram, *The Sword of Allah: Khalid bin al-Waleed, His Life and Campaigns* (New Delhi: Adam, 2009), pp. 97–8; Bashier, *War and Peace*, pp. 237–8, 241.

[55] *Tafsīr Ibn Kathīr*, vol. 4, p. 371.

[56] W. Montgomery Watt, *Muhammad at Medina*, 2004 edn (Oxford University Press, 1956), p. 311; Ibn Kathir, *The Life of Muhammad* (Karachi: Darul-Ishaat, 2004), pp. 516, 522; Shaykh Muhammad al-Ghazālī, *A Thematic Commentary on the Qur'an* (Herndon: International Institute of Islamic Thought, 2000), p. 182.

[57] *Al-Tawbah*, 9:6.

[58] *Tafsīr Ibn Kathīr*, vol. 4, pp. 369ff.; Sayyid Ameenul Hasan Rizvi, *Battles by the Prophet in Light of the Qur'an* (Jeddah: Abul-Qasim, 2002), pp. 126–30.

[59] Ibn Kathir, *Life of Muhammad*, pp. 516, 522.

[60] Spencer, *Religion of Peace?*, p. 78.

[61] Although Ad-Dahhāk bin Muzāhim, as quoted by Isma'il ibn Kathīr (*Tafsīr Ibn Kathīr*, vol. 4, p. 377), sees this as a repudiation of Muhammad's pilgrimage agreements with all pagans, other early sources insist that this was not the case and that it would have reflected intolerance that Muhammad was not known to possess. Rizwi Faizer, 'Expeditions and Battles' in Jane Dammen McAuliffe, ed., *Encyclopaedia of the Qur'an* (Leiden and Boston: Brill, 2002), vol. II, p. 151.

[62] Fatoohi, *Jihad in the Qur'an*, p. 34.

[63] Hashmi, ed., *Islamic Political Ethics*, p. 201.

[64] Armstrong, *Islam*, p. 17.

[65] This is certainly the view of the influential eighth-century biographer, Ibn Ishaq: Alfred Guillaume trans., *The Life of Muhammad: A Translation of Ibn*

Ishaq's Sīrat Rasūl Allāh, 1967 edn (Oxford University Press, 1955), p. 212. For modern writers who agree, see: Fatoohi, *Jihad in the Qur'an*, p. 31; Karen Armstrong, *Muhammad: A Biography of the Prophet* (London: Phoenix, 1991. 2001 edition), p. 168; Martin Lings, *Muhammad: His Life based on the Earliest Sources*, Islamic Texts Society 2009 edn (London: George Allen & Unwin, 1983), p. 135; Al-Mubarakpuri, *The Sealed Nectar*, p. 183; Sohail H. Hashmi, 'Sunni Islam', in Gabriel Palmer-Fernandez, ed., *Encyclopedia of Religion and War* (London: Routledge, 2004), p. 217. Hashmi, ed., *Islamic Political Ethics*, p. 198.

[66] *Tafsīr Ibn Kathīr*, vol. 1 (Parts 1 and 2 (*Sūrat Al-Fātihah* to verse 252 of *Sūrat Al-Baqarah*)), p. 528.

[67] *Sūrat Al-Baqarah*, 2:193.

[68] Hashmi, ed., *Islamic Political Ethics*, p. 204.

[69] Bukhari, *Ṣaḥīḥ*, 3025, trans. Dr Muhammad Muhsin Khan, vol. 4, 2738 to 3648 (Riyadh: Darussalam, 1997), p. 164; Rizwi Faizer, ed., *The Life of Muhammad: Al-Wāqidī's Kitāb al-Maghāzī* (London: Routledge Studies in Classical Islam, 2010), p. 546.

[70] *Sūrat Al*-Baqarah, 2:216 and see *Al-Shūrā*, 42:41.

[71] *Al-Baqarah*, 2: 217, 2:191 and *Al-Nisā'*, 4:75–8.

[72] Bashier, *War and Peace*, pp. 229–33.

[73] Ibn Ishaq, p. 553; *The History of al-Tabarī*, vol. VIII, p. 182.

[74] Ibn Ishaq, p. 385; *The History of al-Tabarī*, vol. VIII, p. 182.

[75] Ibn Ishaq, p. 553; *The History of al-Tabarī*, vol. VIII, p. 183.

[76] *Sūrat Al-Mā'idah*, 5:45.

[77] Cf. *Al-Baqarah*, 2:194.

[78] Cf. *Al-Shūrā*, 42:40–3.

[79] Cf. Khadduri, *War and Peace*, pp. 96–8.

[80] Ibid., p. 98.

[81] Imam Muhammad Shirazi, *War, Peace and Non-violence: An Islamic Perspective* (London: Fountain Books, 2003 ed.), pp. 28–9.

[82] It even applied to the quarrels that the Qur'an criticises most: those between different Muslim groups. If one side aggressively 'transgressed beyond bounds', the other side was permitted to fight back in self-defence, but only until the aggressor desisted, at which point war was to end and reconciliation was to occur. Cf. *Al-Ḥujurāt*, 49:9–10.

[83] *Tafsīr Ibn Kathīr*, Volume 1, p. 528.

[84] Shirazi, *War, Peace and Non-violence*, p. 29.

[85] Hashmi, ed., *Islamic Political Ethics*, p. 211; Fred M. Donner, trans., *The History of al-Tabarī (Ta'rīkh al-rusul wa'l-mulūk): vol. X: The Conquest of Arabia* (State University of New York Press, 1993), p. 16.

[86] *Al-An*'ām, 6:151; *Al-Isrā'*, 17:33; *Al*-Furqān,25:68.

[87] *Al-Mā'idah*, 5:33–4.

[88] *Āl 'Imrān*, 3:134.

[89] Fatoohi, *Jihad in the Qur'an*, p. 73.

[90] Mathnawi I: 3721ff. published online at: http://www.dar-al-masnavi.org/n-I-3721.html

[91] *Al-Ḥujurāt*, 49:13. The clause in parentheses is a contextual explanation by the translator.

[92] Fatoohi, *Jihad in the Qur'an*, pp. 25–6.

[93] Fatoohi, *Jihad in the Qur'an*, p. 87.

[94] This hadith is found in the book *Kitāb al-Durar al-Muntathira fī al-Ahādith al-Mushtahira* by Jalal al-Deen al-Suyuti.

[95] http://www.winstonchurchill.org/learn/speeches/speeches-of-winston-churchill/1940-finest-hour/128-we-shall-fight-on-the-beaches

[96] Cf. Chapter V in Khadduri, *War and Peace.*

[97] Karen Armstrong, 'The True, Peaceful Face of Islam', *Time*, 23 September 2001, available online at:
http://www.time.com/time/magazine/article/0,9171,1101011001-175987,00.html. Access date: 1 April 2011.

CHAPTER 3

[98] An archival search of the New York Times for 'holy war' or 'jihad' shows that this term is still a standard translation of jihad, very often taking the form 'jihad, or holy war'. Or one can enter the term 'holy war' into a search on Google News and see that it is still a widespread translation of jihad. Even sympathetic and responsible authors perpetuate the equation between the two, such as Juan Cole, *Sacred Space and Holy War* (I. B. Tauris, 2002). The publishing world is full of provocative titles such as Peter Bergen's *Holy War, Inc.: Inside the Secret World of Osama bin Laden* (Free Press, 2002).

[99] This phrase even found its way into a speech by the Pope in September 2006, albeit in the form of a quotation from a Byzantine emperor. Though the Pope said he regretted the reaction, he never disavowed the statement nor did he apologise for it.

[100] This term was even used by President George W. Bush (in a speech before the National Endowment for Democracy in October 2005), and for a time became popular with certain right-wing intellectuals and media talking heads, though it fell out of favour after significant criticism as an empty propaganda term, having been used to describe people and groups as disparate as Al-Qaeda, the government of Iran, and Syria. The first is a stateless terrorist group who hate Shi'ites, the second is a Shi'a religious state, and the third is a secular state run by an Alawite elite ruling over a Sunni majority. The fact that one term means all these things signifies that it is devoid of any real content. The word 'fascism' evokes the idea of a malevolent global movement, wherein lies its power as a buzzword. Writing as far back as 1944, George Orwell, writing for the British

public, pointed out that the word fascist had become so nebulous and overused it lacked any precise meaning: 'Except for the relatively small number of Fascist sympathisers, almost any English person would accept 'bully' as a synonym for 'Fascist'. That is about as near to a definition as this much-abused word has come.' Little has changed in the use of this word. It is obvious that the vigilante rebels of Al-Qaeda have little in common with the military-industrial-state apparatus that was the core of twentieth century European fascism, possessing neither a military, industry, or state.

[101] 'Infidel' comes from the Latin *infidelis* meaning unfaithful. As a technical term in the Catholic Church it denoted those who were not baptised, such as Muslims or Jews. The word *kāfir* literally means 'to cover' and originally signified a kind of ingratitude, meaning that one 'covered over' the gifts or blessings one was given. It thus has the sense of denial and rejection. Practically speaking, it is used in a way similar to 'infidel', but with one crucial difference: by and large Muslims did not call non-Muslims *kāfir* unless they were pagan or atheist. It would be contradictory to call a Jew or Christian a *kāfir*, since the Qur'an often calls upon them to follow their own religion more faithfully (5:66, 5:68). Infidel goes back at least as far as the eleventh century *The Song of Roland* (*Chanson de Roland*), where the infidels are the Muslims in the Holy Land. It also appears in the King James Version in 2 Corinthians 6:15, *And what concord hath Christ with Belial? Or what part hath he that believeth with an infidel?* and 2 Corinthians 6:14–6 *But if any provide not for his own, and specially for those of his own house, he hath denied the faith, and is worse than an infidel.* This term is noteworthy because Muslims themselves almost never use the word 'infidel' to translate *kafir* (preferring 'unbeliever', 'disbeliever', 'denier'), yet critics of Islam regularly accuse Muslims of this or that view in relation to 'infidels'. For example, a contemporary convert to Christianity from Islam, Nonie Darwish, has written a book, *Now They Call Me Infidel* (Sentinel HC, 2006). Has anyone actually called her that specific word, or is it her own translation? The word 'infidel' effectively conjures the emotional impact of this term as a part of the West's collective memory, disregarding the fact that the term has no resonance for a Western Muslim, and means something significantly different from *kafir*. Another book by Ayaan Hirsi Ali, another former Muslim, bears the title *Infidel* (Free Press, 2007), implying that this is the label she now bears from some undefined group of Muslims. Actually, as an atheist the Latin-based word 'infidel' more strongly demarks her relationship with Christianity than with Islam.

[102] Often misunderstandings about the Qur'an can be easily cleared up by referring to the classical and recognised Qur'anic commentaries, such as those of al-Tabari (*Jāmiʿ al-bayān 'an ta'wīl āyat al-Qur'ān*), Fakhr al-Din Razi (*Mafātih al-Ghayb*, or *al-Tafsīr al-Kabīr*), Ibn Kathir (*Tafsir Ibn Kathir*), al-Qur-tubi (*al-Jāmiʿ li-ahkām al-Qur'ān*), al-Baydawi (*Tafsīr al-Baydawi*),

al-Zamakhshari (*al-Kashshāf ʿan Ḥaqā'iq al-Tanzīl*), and many others who are well known to the scholarly tradition, and which are our starting point. Though simply referring to such works is not sufficient in itself to arrive at a conclusive and binding knowledge of a particular issue, it is worth noting that many of those who speak about jihad and war never bother to make reference to the classical commentaries at all.

[103] Al-Nasa'i, *Sunan*, *Kitāb al-Baʿyah*, with similar hadith in Ibn Majah's *Sunan, Kitāb al-Fitan* and in the *Sunan* of Abu Dawud, *Kitāb al-Mulāhim.*

[104] Narrated by Daylami, with a similar hadith narrated by Tirmidhi in his *Sunan, Kitāb Faḍā'il al-*Jihad. See Muhammad Saʿid Ramadan al-Buti, *Al-Jihad fī'l-Islām* (Damascus: Dar al- Fikr, 2005) p. 21.

[105] Ibn Majah, *Sunan*, *Kitāb al-Adab.*

[106] Ibn Kathir relates that many famous early figures of Islam such as Ibn ʿAbbas, Mujahid, Muqatil ibn Hayyan, Qataadah and others said that this is the first verse revealed concerning jihad. *Tafsir al-Qur'ān al-ʿAẓīm*, vol.3, (Riyadh: Dar al-Salam, 1998), p.103.

[107] Ibid.

[108] Ibid.

[109] Ibid.

[110] The second caliph, ʿUmar ibn al-Khattab, had a Christian servant named Asbaq. When ʿUmar invited him to Islam, the servant refused, to which ʿUmar replied, quoting the Qur'an, 'There is no compulsion in religion,' and then said, 'Asbaq, if you were to accept Islam I would have entrusted you with some of the Muslims' affairs.' In another incident, ʿUmar said to an old woman who had not accepted Islam, 'Become Muslim, old woman, become Muslim. God sent Muhammad with the truth.' She replied, 'I am an old woman who is close to death.' Umar said, 'Dear God, bear witness!' and he recited: 'There is no compulsion in religion'. (Buti, p. 52)

[111] Once a polytheist asked Ali if they would be killed if one of them were to come to the Prophet with some need or to hear the Word of God. Ali replied in the negative, and quoted 9:6 on asylum for the polytheists. (Buti, p. 57 quoting from *al-Jāmiʿ li-aḥkām al-Qur'ān*, 8:76)

[112] Ibn Kathir, *Tafsīr al-Qur'ān al-ʿAẓīm* (Riyadh, 1998) pp.308–9. Many of the selections and translations of this section are taken from David Dakake, 'The Myth of a Militant Islam'. In Joseph Lumbard, ed., *Islam, Fundamentalism, and the Betrayal of Tradition*, (Bloomington, Indiana: World Wisdom, 2004), pp.3–37.

[113] See Ibn Taymiyyah, *al-Siyāsa al-Sharʿīyyah fī Islāh al-Raʿī wa'l-Raʿiyyah*, quoted in Peters, p.49. For a similar hadith see Bukhari 3052, *Kitāb al-Jihad.*

[114] The *Sunan* of Abu Dawud, *Kitāb al-Jihad.*

[115] Malik's *Muwatta'*, *Kitāb al-jihad.*

[116] Ibn Kathir, *Tafsīr*, vol.1, p.308.

[117] Baladhuri, *Futūh al-buldān*, trans. P. Hitti as *Origins of the Islamic State* (New York: AMS Press) vol.1, p.100.

[118] Ibid. p. 187.

[119] Al-Tabari, *The History of al-Tabari*, vol. XII: *The Battle of al-Qadissiyyah and the Conquest of Syria and Palestine*, trans. Y. Friedmann (Albany: SUNY Press, 1985), p.191.

[120] Baladhuri, vol.1, p.314.

[121] *Rawdat al-Ṭalibīn*, 10:315-16 (see Buti, p.133).

[122] Al-Mughni, 4:250 (see Buti, p.133).

[123] See Buti, p.134.

[124] From Nawawi's commentary upon the *Ṣaḥīḥ* of Muslim, 12:229 (see Buti, p.149).

[125] Muslim, *Ṣaḥīḥ* , *Kitāb al-Imārah.*

[126] Ibid., *Kitāb al-Imārah*

CHAPTER 4

[127] As regards women, for example, there are hadith that declare that the 'jihad of women' is making the pilgrimage (*ḥajj*) to Mecca. See Bukhari, *Ṣaḥīḥ al-Bukhārī* (Medina: Dār al-Fikr, n.d.), vol. 4, pp. 36, 83–4 (*Kitāb al-jihad*, hadith no. 43, 127, 128). There are also hadith concerning the various types of death that qualify one as a martyr (*shahīd*), i.e., as having died like a fighter in jihad. One such type of death is said to be the death of a woman in childbirth. Other traditions in *Ṣaḥīḥ al-Bukhārī* imply that women can fulfil the duty of jihad by attending to the wounded on the battlefield (see *Ṣaḥīḥ*, vol. 4, pp. 86–7, *ḥadīth* no. 131–4). See also Muslim, *Ṣaḥīḥ Muslim*, (printed with commentaries) (Beirut: Dār al-Kutub al-'Ilmiyya, 1978), vol. 5, pp. 153, 157.

[128] These are: 1) testifying that there is only one true God and that Muhammad is His messenger, 2) praying five times a day, 3) paying a charity tax every year, 4) fasting during the month of Ramadan, and 5) making a pilgrimage to Mecca once in one's life, if one has the means and the health to do so.

[129] See 'Aljunī, *Kashf al-khafā'* (Beirut: Dār Iḥyā' al-Turāth al-'Arabī, 1968), hadith no. 1362.

[130] It should be noted that 'outward jihad' is by no means only military in nature. The arena of outward jihad is the level of human action. It is not concerned with inner attitudes of the soul, such as sincerity and love (which constitute the realm of the inner jihad) but with proper outward action alone, as defined by the religious law (shari'ah).

[131] The word translated here as 'themselves', *anfusihim* in Arabic, may be more literally translated as 'their souls'. This demonstrates an essential Qur'anic perspective: the inner struggle (i.e., 'until they change *their souls*') takes precedence over the outer struggle (i.e., the particular state in which a people

exist at a given moment) and furthermore, that no amount of purely outward actions can overcome hypocrisy of soul.

[132] There are a few important exceptions to this categorisation. Among them are the articles of Khaled Abou El Fadl, 'The Place of Tolerance in Islam', in the book by the same title, J. Cohen and I. Lague, eds (Beacon Press, 2002); 'The Rules of Killing at War: An Inquiry into the Classical Sources', *Muslim World* 89, no. 2 (April 1999), and Sherman Jackson, 'Jihad and the Modern World', *The Journal of Islamic Law and Culture* (Spring/Summer 2002).

[133] For examples of how these traditional teachings were followed in later generations see Reza Shah-Kazemi's 'From the Spirituality of Jihad to the Ideology of Jihadism' in this volume.

[134] Although it is incorrect in this context, the six major translations of the Qur'an available in English, those of A. J. Arberry, Marmaduke Pickthall, N. J. Dawood, Yusuf Ali, Ahmad Ali, and El-Hilali/Khan, all translate the word *awliyā'* as 'friends'.

[135] We owe this image to Dr Seyyed Hossein Nasr.

[136] Qur'an 2:125-129.

[137] Al-Tabari, *Jāmi' al-bayān 'an ta'wīl āy al-qur'ān* (Beirut: Dār al-Fikr, 1995), vol. 4, pp. 372–3.

[138] Ibid., vol. 14, pp. 83–4.

[139] We will look more closely at verse *Al-Tawbah* 9:5 when we examine the fatwa of the World Islamic Front later in this essay.

[140] Al-Tabari, vol. 14, p. 84.

[141] Ibid., vol. 2, p. 258. It should be noted that there is another group of verses, 22:39–40 which is also considered to have been the first verses to speak about the military jihad. We shall have occasion to speak about this later in the essay.

[142] Ibid., vol. 2, p. 258.

[143] Ibid., vol. 2, p. 258.

[144] Ibid., vol. 2, p. 259.

[145] In addition, al-Tabari reports a second narration of these words of 'Umar ibn 'Abd al-'Aziz with only slight changes in phrasing, Ibid., vol. 2, p. 259.

146 See Malik ibn Anas, *Muwatta'*, trans. M. Rahimuddin (New Delhi: Tāj, 1985), p. 200 (*Kitāb al-jihad, ḥadīth* no. 957). See also Bukhari, *Ṣaḥīḥ*, vol. 4, pp. 159–60 (*Kitāb al-jihad, ḥadīth* no. 257–8), Abu Dawud, *Sunan Abī Dāwūd* (Beirut: Dār al-Kutub al-'Ilmiyya, 1996), vol. 2, p. 258 (*Kitāb al-jihad, ḥadīth* no. 2668), and Muslim, *Ṣaḥīḥ*, vol. 5, p. 56 (*Kitāb al-jihad*).

[147] Mālik, *Muwaṭta'*, p. 200 (*Kitāb al-jihad, ḥadīth* no. 958). Other similar instructions are given to the Muslim armies prohibiting the killing of children and the mutilating of bodies, see Muslim, *Ṣaḥīḥ*, vol. 5, pp. 46–50 (*Kitāb al-jihad*).

[148] Mālik, *Muwatta'*, p. 201 (*Kitāb al-jihad, ḥadīth* no. 959). A similar version

of this hadith in the *Sunan* of Abu Dawud mentions not killing the elderly, in addition to the categories of women and children, see Abu Dawud, *Sunan*, vol. 2, p. 243 (*Kitāb al-jihad, ḥadīth* no. 2614).

[149] Khalid ibn al-Walid (d. 22 AH/ 642 CE) was a companion of the Prophet and one of the famous early commanders of Muslim forces.

[150] Quoted from Ibn Rushd, '*Bidāyat al-mujtahid wa nihāyat al-muqtaṣid*', trans. Rudolph Peters in *Jihad in Mediaeval and Modern Islam* (Leiden: E. J. Brill, 1977), p. 17. For a similar version of this hadith see Abu Dawud, *Sunan*, vol. 2, p. 258 (*Kitāb al-jihad, ḥadīth* no. 2669).

[151] See Ibn Ishaq, *Sīrah Rasūl Allāh*, trans. A. Guillaume in *The Life of Muhammad* (Oxford: Oxford University Press, 1978), pp. 602–3.

[152] Al-Tabari, *Jāmi' al-bayān*, vol. 6, pp. 233–4; and Ibn Kathir, *Tafsīr al-Qur'ān al-'aẓīm*, vol. 2 (Riyadh: Dar al-Salam, 1998), pp. 488–9.

153 Al-Tabari, *Jāmi' al-bayān*, vol. 11, p. 30; Ibn Kathir, *Tafsīr*, vol. 3, p. 429.

[154] See for example R. Bulliet, *The Patricians of Nishapur* (Cambridge: Harvard University Press, 1972) and *Islam: The View from the Edge* (New York: Columbia University Press, 1994) where he speaks about the case of the conversion of the Persian plateau. Bulliet has carried out demographic studies showing that for three centuries following the Muslim's political conquest of the region the land of Iran still had a majority Zoroastrian population, in direct contradiction to any notions of forced conversion.

[155] It was only the polytheistic Arab tribes in the Arabian Peninsula who were compelled to enter Islam. Those Arab tribes who were already People of the Book were not forced to accept the religion. Numerous examples of this can be found in the histories, particularly in regard to the Christian Arabs. See the accounts of the Arabs of Najran (al-Tabari, *Tārīkh al-rusul wa al-mulūk*, vol. 1, edited by M. J. de Goeje (Leiden: E. J. Brill, 1964), pp. 1987–8 and p. 2162); the Banu Namir, Banu Iyad, and Banu Taghlib (al-Ṭabarī, *Ta'rīkh*, I, p. 2482 and pp. 2509–10), the Banu Ghassan (Baladhuri's *Futūḥ al-buldān*, trans. P. Hitti as *The Origins of the Islamic State*, vol. 1 (New York: AMS Press), p. 209); the Banu Salih ibn Hulwan (Balādhurī, *Origins*, vol. 1, p. 223); the Banu Tayyi' and the Arabs of the settlement of Hadir Halab (Balādhurī, *Origins*, vol. 1, p. 224); and the Arabs of Baalbek (Baladhuri, *Origins*, vol. 1, p. 198).

[156] Al-Tabari, *Jāmi' al-bayān*, vol. 3, p. 21; Ibn Kathir, *Tafsīr*, vol. 1, p. 417.

[157] We shall speak of this alliance known as the Constitution of Medina later in this essay.

[158] Al-Tabari, *Jāmi' al-bayān*, vol. 3, p. 22. See also Wahidi, *Asbāb al-nuzūl* (Beirut: 'Ālam al-Kutub, 1970), p. 58 and Abu Dawud, *Sunan*, vol. 2, pp. 262–3 (*Kitāb al-jihad, ḥadīth* no. 2682).

[159] See al-Tabari, *Jāmi' al-bayān*, vol. 3, p. 23.

[160] Al-Tabarī, *Jāmi' al-bayān*, vol. 3, p. 220; Ibn Kathir, *Tafsīr*, vol. 1, p. 417; Wahidi, *Asbāb al-nuzūl*, pp. 58–9.

[161] It should also be noted that in the case of one version of this story (see al-Tabarī, *Jāmiʿ al-bayān*, vol. 3, p. 22 and Wahidi, *Asbāb al-nuzūl*, pp. 58–9), the Prophet, after pronouncing the Qur'anic verse, says, 'God banish them! They are the first ones to disbelieve' (*abʿadahumā Allāh, hum awwal man kafara*). This statement requires some explanation and needs to be understood in the context of the time. It can be said from the Islamic point of view that the actions of Abu'l-Husayn's sons represent a grave error, because they were rejecting a prophet within his own lifetime, a prophet whom they knew personally. The actions of Abu'l-Husayn's sons represent a denial of the immediate presence of the truth, and this is very different than, for instance, someone choosing not to accept the message of Islam today; one who never had the chance to actually see the Prophet, who was the living embodiment of submission to God. Like the words of Christ, 'He who has seen me has seen the truth', the Prophet said, 'He who has seen me has seen his Lord,' thereby placing great responsibility on the shoulders of those who were privileged to encounter him. The strident words of the Prophet about the sons of Abu'l-Husayn need to be understood in this context.

[162] Ibn Kathir, *Tafsīr*, vol. 1, p. 416.

[163] Al-Tabari, *Jāmiʿ al-bayān*, vol. 3, p. 25; Ibn Kathir, *Tafsīr*, vol. 1, p. 417.

[164] Moreover this injunction is reflected elsewhere in the Qur'an, such as in the verse, *For each we have given a law and a way, and had God willed He could have made you one people, but that He might put you to the test in what He has given you [He has made you as you are]. So vie with one another in good works. To God will you all be brought back, and He will inform you about that wherein you differed* (*Al-Māʾidah*, 5:48). The universality and indeed acceptance of other 'ways' and 'laws' evident in this verse is to be seen even more directly in verse 2:62: *Those who say 'We are Jews' and 'We are Christians' and 'We are Sabians,' all who believe in God and the Last Day and do good works, they have their reward with their Lord and neither shall they fear nor grieve* (*Al-Baqarah*, 2:62). The word 'Sabians' may be a reference to the remnants of a group of followers of St John the Baptist, but in any case the message of this verse is very far from the fallacious notion that Islam denies the truth of other faiths. Indeed, the Qur'an demands that Jews and Christians judge according to what God has given them in the Torah and the Gospel. This is evident in the Qur'anic statement, *Truly, We revealed the Torah. In it is a guidance and light. By it the prophets who submitted [to God] judged the Jews ... with what they were entrusted of the Book of God, and they were witnesses to it. Therefore, fear not men, but fear Me. Sell not My signs for little gain. Whoever does not judge by that which God has revealed, those are the unbelievers. We ordained therein [within the Torah]: a life for a life, an eye for an eye, nose for a nose, an ear for an ear, a tooth for a tooth, and wounds for retaliation. But if any one remits it then it is a penance for him, and whosoever does not judge by that*

which God has revealed, they are wrongdoers (*Al-Mā'idah*, 5:44–5). In relation to the followers of the Gospel, the Qur'an says, *We sent him [Jesus] the Gospel. Therein is a guidance and a light.... Let the People of the Gospel judge by that which God has revealed therein. Whosoever does not judge by that which God has revealed, those are the corrupt* (*Al-Mā'idah*, 5: 46–7). Therefore, not only are the People of the Torah and of the Gospel not to be compelled to accept Islam, but they must, according to the Qur'an, be free to make their own decisions based upon what their scriptures reveal to them. Moreover, for them not to do so is displeasing to God.

[165] Al-Tabari, *Jāmi' al-bayān*, vol. 10, p. 227–8; Ibn Kathir, *Tafsīr*, vol. 3, p. 303.

[166] Al-Tabarī, *Jāmi' al-bayān*, vol. 10, p. 226; Ibn Kathir, *Tafsīr*, vol. 3, p. 302.

[167] Al-Tabari, *Jāmi' al-bayān*, vol. 10, p. 227; Ibn Kathir, *Tafsīr*, vol. 3, p. 303.

[168] Al-Tabari, *Jāmi' al-bayān*, vol. 10, p. 229.

[169] Ibn Kathir, *Tafsīr*, vol. 3, p. 303.

[170] Mahmoud Shaltut (d. 1963), the former Shaykh al-Azhar, arguably the most important exoteric authority in the Islamic world, commented upon these verses in his book *Al-Qur'an wa al-qitāl*, trans. Peters, *The Qur'an and Fighting* in *Jihad*, p. 43, as follows: 'These verses are, as we have said, the first verses of fighting. They are clear and do not contain even the slightest evidence of religious compulsion. On the contrary, they confirm that the practice that the people ward off each other is one of God's principles in creation, inevitable for the preservation of order and for the continuation of righteousness and civilisation. Were it not for this principle, the earth would have been ruined and all different places of worship would have been destroyed. This would have happened if powerful tyrants would have held sway over religions, free to abuse them without restraint and to force people to conversion, without anyone to interfere. These verses are not only concerned with Muslims, but have clearly a general impact....'

[171] Baladhuri, *Origins*, vol. 1, p. 100.

[172] Ibid., vol. 1, p. 227.

[173] Ibid., vol. 1, p. 229.

[174] Ibid., vol. 1, p. 187.

[175] Ibid., vol. 1, p. 223.

[176] Ibid., vol. 1, pp. 198-199.

[177] The poll tax or *jizyah* was required to be paid by the People of the Book to the Islamic state according to verse *Al-Tawbah*, 9:29 of the Qur'an and certain hadith. This tax, unlike feudal taxation in Europe, did not constitute an economic hardship for non-Muslims living under Muslim rule. The tax was seen as the legitimate right of the Islamic state, given that all peoples—Muslim and non-Muslim—benefited from the military protection of the state, the freedom of the roads, and trade, etc. Although the *jizyah* was paid by non-

Muslims, Muslims were also taxed through the *zakāt*, a required religious tax not levied on other communities. Since we have just mentioned verse 9:29 it is perhaps best to deal with it more thoroughly here, for it has been a source of great controversy and is often quoted by militant Muslims as well as Western detractors of Islam and not only for its mention of the issue of the *jizyah*. In full, verse 9:29 reads: *Fight against those who do not believe in God and Last Day (of Judgment) and do not forbid what God and His Messenger have forbidden and are not obedient to the Religion of Truth, (even) among those who have been given the Book, until they pay the jizyah out of hand and are humbled* (*Al-Tawbah*, 9:29). There is no doubt that most of the classical Muslim exegetes understood 9:29 as sanctioning the continuation of jihad beyond the conflict with the pre-Islamic Arab idolaters to include the *ahl al-kitāb*, and just as the early Israelites did not see the use of offensive military force by Moses or Joshua as something which negated the moral veracity of their religion, so too the early Muslims did not find the institutionalisation of jihad for the sake of obtaining the political hegemony of Islam to be a moral dilemma either. The Muslims in jihad, like the armies of the Israelites entering the Promised Land, saw themselves as engaged in a holy mission, not of a purely inward, spiritual nature, but a mission which also entailed bringing about a new society on Earth. In the case of the Israelites the new society was to be created in a specific place, the Promised Land, and participation in that society would be generally limited to a specific group of people, the Chosen People. Whereas in the case of the early Muslims, the society that was to be created would not be confined to a specific place or to a specific people. In fact, the specificity of the new Islamic polity would be precisely its universality; its general lack of ethnic and religious boundaries. This is not to say that the situation for religious minorities in the Islamic world was perfect by any means, but it was substantially better than the social climate that prevailed for Muslims and Jews within the lands of Christendom for example. For the sake of achieving this new society, 'bringing' to mankind the 'best' and, up to that moment, the most inclusive form of social order on Earth, the Muslims were willing to fight and die, just as the Jews were willing to do so for a new kind of life in the Promised Land. This willingness to do violence to establish certain kinds of social orders has certainly not come to an end even among nations today, but it should be understood that in both the Israelite and Islamic contexts spreading political control through violent means was something almost to be expected given the social conditions prevailing then in the ancient world. When Islam spread out of Arabia in the seventh century (and similarly in the time of Moses and Joshua), warfare and conflict were the normal state of affairs between nations and peoples. The state of nearly constant warfare was simply the way of the world and peace was the extraordinary and occasional exception to the rule. Today, in the modern world, the situation is somewhat reversed: we might say that peace is generally the norm and warfare, although not exactly extraordinary, is somewhat less of a constant than it was in ancient times. This fact has led the vast majority of Muslim scholars today to declare that continual, offensive jihad is no longer applicable to the contemporary situation and that jihad today is primarily *difāʾi* or defensive, because the world is itself is in a different state from what it was in the seventh century. Therefore, just as the militant acts of Moses and Joshua portrayed in the Hebrew Bible no longer play a direct role in how Jews actually practice Judaism today and these scriptural stories are relegated to 'ancient history', with largely symbolic and no longer literal significance in the lives of contemporary Jews, so too for the vast majority of Muslims verse 9:29 and other Qur'anic verses related to jihad are simply not of primary concern when they think about what it means to be a 'good Muslim' today. While *Al-Tawbah*, 9:29 is without doubt extremely significant in the formation of the early Islamic view of military jihad, the idea that it represents the final word on Muslim attitudes toward Jews, Christians and the uses of violence is like declaring that Medieval Papal pronouncements about the Crusades are the key to understanding Catholic feelings about Muslims and Jews today or like saying that Deuteronomy 20:10–8 exposes the true, inner attitude of Jews toward the presence of gentiles in the land of Israel. To even suggest such things would be absurd, but while we are aware of the complexities and nuances of our own Western cultural history, which enable us to reject out of hand the absurd, totalising claims just mentioned, when it comes to Islamic culture similar totalising proof-texting of the Qur'an and verses like 9:29 is somehow seen as a 'legitimate' encapsulation of 'the real truth about Islam and Muslims'. As regards those Muslim fundamentalists who quote 9:29 as their proof text for an 'eternal jihad' commanded by God against the *ahl al-kitāb*, it is remarkable with what ferocity they cling to any Qur'anic verses that deal with fighting and with what cavalierism they dismiss verses that speak positively of Jews and Christians (*Al-Baqarah*, 2:62; 2:111–2; 2:139; *Āl 'Imrān*, 3:113–5; 3:199; *Al-Māʾidah*, 5:44; 5:46–7; 5:69), as if they are able to determine with certainty which of God's words in the Qur'an He actually meant eternally and which of His words need to be understood as just nice Arabic words in the Qur'an devoid of contemporary relevance. To put it another way, many of these militant *jihadi*s seem to wish to reduce all 114 chapters of the Qur'an to one, namely chapter 9 (*Al-Tawbah*), which possesses a major share of the verses regarding fighting.

[178] Baladhuri, *Origins*, vol. 1, p. 187.

[179] Al-Tabari, *The History of al-Tabari, v. XII: The Battle of al-Qadisiyya and the Conquest of Syria and Palestine*, trans. Y. Friedmann (Albany: SUNY Press, 1985), p. 191. The use of the word 'Byzantines' here should not be conflated with 'Christians'. 'Byzantines' refers to those people who were the administrators of Byzantine authority in the lands that were now conquered by the Muslims. The

very fact that the word 'Byzantines' is used, and not 'Christians', is significant. This shows that it was not 'Christianity' but rather the political and military opposition of Byzantium that was at issue. It was because of this opposition that the Byzantines needed to be expelled. Byzantine administrators and officials, like the robbers also mentioned in the quotation, were a possible source of social unrest and political chaos. Just as there cannot be two kings ruling a single kingdom, the Muslims needed to remove any vestiges of Byzantine political authority in the lands they now controlled. This did not mean the removal of the vestiges of 'Christianity' from those lands, for the quotation itself also mentions preserving the rights of Christians to practice their faith and maintain their churches, crosses, etc., under the new Islamic government.

[180] Ibid., pp. 191–2. Al-Tabari indicates that similar letters were written to 'all the provinces' around Jerusalem as well as to the 'people of Lydda and all the people of Palestine'.

[181] Al-Tabari, *Jāmi' al-bayān*, vol. 3, pp. 24–5; Ibn Kathir, *Tafsīr*, vol. 2, pp. 457–8. This position has been generally agreed upon by most of the early scholars of Islamic law; see for instance the comments of Ibn Rushd in his *Bidāyat al-mujtahid*, in Peters, *Jihad*, p. 24.

[182] Baladhuri, *Origins*, vol. 1, p. 314.

[183] Al-Tabari, *The History of al-Ṭabarī, v. XIV: The Conquest of Iran*, trans. G. Rex Smith (Albany: SUNY Press, 1994), pp. 36–8.

[184] Baladhuri, *Origins*, vol. 2, p. 4

[185] Ibid., p. 20.

[186] Al-Tabari, *The History of al-Ṭabarī, v. XIV: The Conquest of Iran*, p. 28.

[187] Ibid., p. 29.

[188] Ibid., p. 33.

[189] Al-Tabari, *The History of al-Ṭabarī, v. XIII: The Conquest of Iraq, Southwestern Persia, and Egypt*, trans. G. H. A. Juynboll (Albany: SUNY Press, 1985), pp. 164–5.

[190] Ibid., pp. 167–8.

[191] Ibid., pp. 170-171.

[192] The issue as to whether the Muslims may accept the *jizyah* from the *mushrikūn* or polytheists, thereby granting them protected (*dhimmī*) status under the Islamic state, like the status of the People of the Book, has been debated by scholars of Islamic law. For various opinions on this issue see Ibn Rushd, *Bidāyat al-mujtahid*, in Peters, *Jihad*, pp. 24–5.

[193] These terms may need some explanation. The people of the city of Mecca were almost all members of an Arabic tribe known as Quraysh, and the Prophet and the vast majority of his early followers in Mecca were also members of this tribe. When the Prophet left Mecca for the city of Medina, an event known as the Hijrah or migration, those members of his community who journeyed with him were given the title of *muhājirūn* or 'emigrants'. As for the term *anṣār*, it

refers to those people of Medina who accepted the Islamic message and invited the Prophet and the emigrants to the city, giving them refuge from their situation of persecution in Mecca. For this reason these residents of Medina were given the title of *anṣār* or 'helpers,' due to the fact that they gave safe haven to the Prophet and the emigrants.

[194] W. M. Watt, *Muhammad at Medina* (Oxford: Clarendon Press, 1956), p. 221.

[195] The term Yathrib actually refers to the city of Medina. Before the time of Islam, Medina was called 'Yathrib'. The name 'Medina' came to be used later as a result of the fact that the city was eventually renamed *Madīnat al-Nabī* (The City of the Prophet). Today the city is simply referred to by the first part of this title, Medina, or 'The City'.

[196] Watt, *Muhammad*, p. 221.

[197] It may be asked if this pact of mutual protection does not contradict the point made earlier concerning verse *Al-Mā'idah*, 5:51. We stated that 5:51 essentially tells the Muslims not to take Jews (or Christians) as their 'protectors' in a military sense, and yet the Constitution seems to be doing just that by stating that between Muslims and Jews is 'help against whoever wars against the people of this document'. Is this not then taking Jews as 'protectors'? In answer to this question it needs to be said that the specific context of 5:51 is that of individual Muslims taking alliances with those outside the ummah in order to save their own individual lives and thereby endangering the unity and internal strength of the Muslims. It does not refer to a context in which the Muslims, as an *ummah*, agree to a treaty for the benefit and safety of the ummah as a whole. This issue points out the necessity of clearly understanding the *asbāb al-nuzūl* of Qur'anic passages. Without such understanding a mistake could be made such that all agreements of help or assistance between Muslims and non-Muslims would be seen as compromising Islam; but this is simply not the context of 5:51. Indeed if it were, it would compromise practically the entire early history of the jihad effort which is filled with agreements of protection and assistance, as we see with the constitution and as we shall see in other parts of this essay.

[198] Watt, *Muhammad*, p. 222.

[199] Ibid., p. 224.

[200] The Umayyad Dynasty ruled the Islamic world immediately following the end of the 'Rightly-guided caliphate' (40 AH/ 661 CE) until they were overthrown by the Abbasids in 132 AH/ 750 CE, who established their own dynasty, which ruled over all Muslim lands (in a nominal way from the fourth century AH/ tenth century CE onwards) until the Mongol conquest of their capital at Baghdad in the seventh century AH/ thirteenth century CE, at which time the last Abbasid caliph was killed.

[201] Such comments criticising the tribe of Quraysh would have been construed

by the Umayyads (see note 67) as a critique of their legitimacy, given that the Umayyad's drew their legitimacy from their status as descendants of one of the prominent clans of Quraysh. The importance that they placed upon this Qurayshi lineage was as a result of the fact that, within the tribe of Quraysh, they were not descendants of the immediate clan of the Prophet, i.e., the clan of Hashim, but of another clan within Quraysh, the clan of 'Abd Shams. Thus, it was not through their immediate clan but through their more distant Qurayshi heritage that they could claim a relation to the Prophetic substance of Muhammad.

[202] Although the Qur'an discusses both *mu'minūn* and *muslimūn* in referring to those who followed the message of Muhammad, most early theological and sectarian documents refer to members of the Islamic community as *mu'minūn* or 'believers', rather than *muslimūn* specifically. For example, the early sectarian writings of the Kharijites and Murji'ites always discussed issues of membership in the Islamic community in terms of 'believers' and non-believers, not in terms of Muslims and non-Muslims.

[203] Watt, *Muhammad*, pp. 225–7.

[204] Fred M. Donner, *The Early Islamic Conquests* (Princeton: Princeton University Press, 1981), p. 200.

[205] Al-Tabari, *The History of al-Ṭabarī, v. XIV*, p. 36. The text of the treaty is: 'In the name of God, the Compassionate, the Merciful. This is the safe-conduct Suraqah b. 'Amr, governor of the Commander of the Faithful, 'Umar b. al-Khattāb, has granted to Shahrbaraz, the inhabitants of Armenia, and the Armenians [in al-Bab]. [He grants] them safe-conduct for their persons, their possessions, and their religion lest they be harmed and so that nothing be taken from them. [The following is imposed] upon the people of Armenia and al-Abwab, those coming from distant parts and those who are local and those around them who have joined them: that they should participate in any military expedition, and carry out any task, actual or potential, that the governor considers to be for the good, providing that those who agree to this are exempt from tribute but [perform] military service. Military service shall be instead of their paying tribute. But those of them who are not needed for military service and who remain inactive have similar tribute obligations to the people of Azerbaijan [in general].... If they perform military service, they are exempt from [all] this.'

[206] Jurjumah was located in the border region between modern-day Syria and Turkey.

[207] Baladhuri, *Origins*, vol. 1, p. 246.

[208] Ibid., p. 249.

[209] For a full explanation of the traditional Islamic teachings on innovation (*bid'a*) see T. J. Winter's 'The Poverty of Fanaticism' in this volume.

[210] Al-Nawawi, *An-Nawawi's Forty Hadith*, trans. by E. Ibrahim and D. Johnson Davies (Malaysia: Polygraphic Press Sdn. Bhd., 1982), p. 94 (*ḥadīth no.* 28). This hadith is also to be found in the *Sunan* of Abu Dawud and the *Jāmi'*

of Tirmidhi. Other hadith related by al-Nawawi concerning the issue of innovation are: 'He who establishes (*aḥdatha*) something in this matter of ours that is not from it, it is rejected (*radd*)!' and 'The one who acts [in a way that is] not in agreement with our matter, it is rejected!' (see p. 40).

[211] We should not have the impression that modern fundamentalists represent the first time that the traditional Islamic limits of warfare have been disregarded. The Kharijite movement, whose roots go back to a religio-political dispute in the first Islamic century, represent one of the most famous examples of just such transgression. The Kharijites were perfectly willing to attack 'civilians', although their dispute was essentially with other members of the Muslim community rather than with non-Muslims. They declared a sentence of 'excommunication' (*barā'a*) upon anyone who did not accept their perspective on Islam. According to the Kharijites, such excommunicated people—men, women, and children—were afforded no protection under the laws of religion for their lives or property. Therefore, the Kharijites considered it perfectly legal to kill such persons. It is important to mention that throughout the early history of Islam the Kharijite position was condemned and even physically opposed by every major Muslim group, Sunni and Shi'ite.

[212] The choice of this word is a calculated political manoeuvre to co-opt the authority of the 1400-year Islamic legal tradition. Within the science of Islamic jurisprudence (*fiqh*), a *fatwa* refers to a religious opinion issued by a scholar of law (*sharī'ah*). Most fundamentalists have had no formal training in the study of Islamic law.

[213] For an examination of the relationship between modernism and fundamentalism, see Joseph E. B. Lumbard's 'The Decline of Knowledge and the Rise of Ideology in the Modern Islamic World' in '*Islam, Fundamentalism, and the Betrayal of Tradition: Essays by Western Muslim Scholars*', World Wisdom, 2004).

[214] Ibn Kathir, *Tafsīr*, vol. 1, p. 308.

[215] The command here in Arabic, *lā ta'tadū*, means 'not to act brutally', but it can also mean 'not to commit excess, outrage, unlawful action, or violate women'.

[216] Ibn Kathir, *Tafsir*, vol. 1, pp. 308–9.

[217] Al-Tabari, *Jāmi' al-bayān*, vol. 4, p. 220; Ibn Kathir, *Tafsīr*, vol. 1, p. 698.

[218] See Guillaume, *The Life of Muhammad*, pp 607–8.

CHAPTER 5

[219] This is an expanded version of an article first published in the journal *Sacred Web*, no.8, 2001.

[220] This statement was made in a letter written by the emir in 1860. Quoted in Charles Henry Churchill, *The Life of Abdel Kader* (London: Chapman and Hall, 1867), p.323.

221 One of the best answers to this question is contained in the series of essays on jihad by S.A. Schleifer. He mounts an excellent critique of the political reduction of jihad, using as his basis 'traditional Islamic consciousness', and including, as a case study of jihad conducted according to this consciousness, the little known *mujāhid* in the struggle against the colonisation of Palestine in the 1920s and 1930s, 'Izz al-Din al-Qassam. This case study forms part 1 of the series, which was published in the journal *Islamic Quarterly*, vol. XXIII, no.2 (1979); part 2, 'Jihad and Traditional Islamic Consciousness' is in vol. XXVII, no.4 (1983)_; part 3, is in vol.XXVIII, no.1 (1984); part 4, in vol.XXVIII, no.2 (1984); and part 5, in vol.XXVIII, no.3 (1984).

222 Quoted in Stanley Lane-Poole, *Saladin and the Fall of the Kingdom of Jerusalem* (Beirut: Khayats Oriental Reprints, 1964), p.232–3. (Originally published in London, 1898.) It is not irrelevant to note here that, as Titus Burckhardt says, the Christian 'knightly attitude towards women is Islamic in origin' (*Moorish Culture in Spain* (London: Allen & Unwin, 1972), p.93). Simonde de Sismondi, writing in the early nineteenth century, asserts that Arabic literature was the source of 'that tenderness and delicacy of sentiment and that reverential awe of women … which have operated so powerfully on our chivalrous feelings'. (*Histoire de la littérature du Midi de l'Europe*, quoted in R. Boase, *The Origin and Meaning of Courtly Love* (Manchester University Press, 1977), p.20.

223 Lane-Poole, op. cit., p.233–4.

224 Quoted in Thomas Arnold, *The Preaching of Islam* (London: Luzak, 1935), p.88–9.

225 Martin Lings, *Muhammad—His Life According to the Earliest Sources* (London: ITS and George Allen & Unwin, 1983), p.297–8.

226 *The Preaching of Islam*, op. cit., p.81–2.

227 A copy of the document is displayed to this day in the monastery, which is the oldest continually inhabited monastery in Christendom. See J. Bentley, *Secrets of Mount Sinai* (London: Orbis, 1985), pp.18–9.

228 Bernard Lewis, *The Jews of Islam* (Princeton University Press, 1984), p.8.

229 S.A. Schleifer, 'Jews and Muslims—A Hidden History', in *The Spirit of Palestine* (Barcelona: Zed, 1994), p.2.

230 Quoted in Schleifer, op.cit., p.5.

231 T. Burckhardt, *Moorish Culture in Spain* (London: George Allen and Unwin, 1972, pp.27–8.

232 Despite the fact that Maimonides suffered at the hands of the al-Mohhads, during a rare episode of persecution in Muslim Spain, the next stage of his career—as physician to Saladdin—manifested his continuing loyalty to Muslim rule.

233 Quoted in Schleifer, op.cit., p.8.

[234] Mark Cohen, 'Islam and the Jews: Myth, Counter-Myth, History', in *Jerusalem Quarterly*, no.38, 1986, p.135.

[235] Ibid.

[236] See Mohamed Chérif Sahli, *Abdelkader—Le Chevalier de la Foi* (Algiers: Entreprise algérienne de presse, 1967), p.131–2.

[237] Cited in Michel Chodkiewicz, *The Spiritual Writings of Amir 'Abd al-Kader* (Albany: State University of New York, 1995), p.2. This selection of texts from the emir's *Mawāqif* reveals well the other side of the emir: his inner spiritual life, lived out as a master of Sufism. In this work the emir comments on Qur'anic verses and hadith, as well as upon Ibn Arabi's writings, doing so from a rigorously esoteric perspective. Indeed, the emir was designated as the *wārith al-'ulūm al-akbariyyah*, inheritor of the Akbari sciences, those sciences pertaining to the Shaykh al-Akbar ('the greatest master'), Ibn Arabi. See pp.20–4 for this little known aspect of the emir's function.

[238] See Churchill, op. cit., p.295.

[239] See the important treatise by the late Shaykh of al-Azhar, Mahmud Shaltut (see Ch.1 in this volume), in which jihad in Islam is defined in entirely defensive terms. The treatise, *al-Qur'ān wa'l-Qitāl*, was first published in Cairo in 1948, and presented in translation by Peters under the title 'A Modernist Interpretation of Jihad: Mahmud Shaltut's Treatise, *Koran and Fighting*' in his book, *Jihad in Classical and Modern Islam* (Leiden: Brill, 1977), pp.59–101.

[240] Churchill, op. cit., p.314.

[241] Ibid., p.318.

[242] Like the emir, Imam Shamil was regarded with awe not only by his own followers, but also by the Russians; when he was finally defeated and taken to Russia, he was fêted as a hero. Although occasionally embroidered with romanticism, Lesley Blanch's *Sabres of Paradise* (New York, Caroll and Graf, 1960) conveys well the heroic aspect of Shamil's resistance. For a more scholarly account, see Moshe Gammer, *Muslim Resistance to the Tsar: Shamil and the Conquest of Chechnia and Daghestan* (London: Frank Cass, 1994); Chechnya. Our own *Crisis in Chechnia—Russian Imperialism, Chechen Nationalism and Militant Sufism* (London: Islamic World Report, 1995) offers an overview of the Chechen quest for independence from the eighteenth century through to the war of the mid-1990s, with a particular stress on the role of the Sufi brotherhoods in this quest.

[243] That is, a *dhimmī*, a non-Muslim who enjoys the *dhimmah,* or 'protection' of the Muslim state.

[244] Quoted in Churchill, op. cit., p.321–2.

[245] Abu Bakr Siraj ad-Din, *The Book of Certainty* (Cambridge: Islamic Texts Society, 1992), p.80. See also the essay by S.H. Nasr, 'The Spiritual Significance of Jihad', ch.1 of *Traditional Islam in the Modern World* (London: KPI, 1987);

and also 'Traditional Islam and Modernism', which remains one of the most important principal critiques of modernist and extremist thought in Islam.

[246] Quoted by the Shaykh al-Arabi al-Darqawi, founder of the Darqawi branch of the Shadhiliyya Sufi order. See *Letters of a Sufi Master*, trans. Titus Burckhardt (Bedfont, Middlesex: Perennial Books, 1969), p.9.

[247] See the essay by Omar Benaissa 'Sufism in the Colonial Period' in *Algeria: Revolution Revisited*, ed. R. Shah-Kazemi (London: Islamic World Report, 1996), for details of this religious influence of the *tariqa* of the Shaykh on Algerian society; and our own essay, 'From Sufism to Terrorism: The Distortion of Islam in the Political Culture of Algeria', in which several points made in the present article are amplified.

[248] Alexis de Tocqueville bitterly criticised the assimilationist policy of his government in Algeria. In a parliamentary report of 1847 he wrote that 'We should not at present push them along the path of our own European civilisation, but in their own ... We have cut down the number of charities [i.e. religious *waqf* institutions], let schools fall into ruin, closed the colleges [i.e. madrasas] ... the recruitment of the men of religion and of the [shari'ah] law has ceased. We have, in other words, made Muslim society far more miserable, disorganised, barbaric and ignorant than ever it was before it knew us.' Quoted in Charles-Robert Ageron, *Modern Algeria*, trans. Michael Brett (London: Hurst, 1991), p.21.

[249] Léon Roche, *Dix Ans à travers l'Islam* (Paris, 1904), p.140–1. Cited in M. Chodkiewicz, op. cit., p.4.

[250] Cited in Churchill, op. cit., p.137–8.

[251] Frithjof Schuon, *Islam and the Perennial Philosophy* (London: World of Islam Festival, 1976), p.101. Schuon also referred to Ali as the 'representative par excellence of Islamic esotericism'. *The Transcendent Unity of Religions* (London: Faber and Faber, 1953), p.59.

[252] Cf. the following verse in the Bhagavad-Gita: 'Who thinks that he can be a slayer, who thinks that he is slain, both these have no [right] knowledge: He slays not, is not slain.' *Hindu Scriptures*, trans. R.C. Zaehner (London: Dent, 1966), p.256.

[253] *The Mathnawi of Jalalu'ddin Rumi*, trans. R.A. Nicholson (London: Luzac, 1926), Book 1, p.205, lines 3787–94. The parentheses are inserted by Nicholson. See Schleifer's comments on Rumi's account of this episode in 'Jihad and Traditional Islamic Consciousness' op. cit., pp.197–9.

[254] As Rumi says, continuing Ali's discourse; see line 3800, p.207.

[255] We follow Muhammad Asad's translation of these elliptical verses. See his *The Message of the Qur'an*, Gibraltar: Dar al-Andalus, 1984, p.942.

CHAPTER 7

[256] The editors have edited this text slightly.

CHAPTER 8

[257] Rene Girard, *Violence and the Sacred*, trans. by Patrick Gregory (Baltimore: The Johns Hopkins University, 1979).

[258] This is the gist of Bernard Lewis' attacks on 'Islamic fundamentalism' in a number of highly publicised essays including 'The Roots of Muslim Rage', *The Atlantic Monthly* (September 1990), pp. 47–60 and 'Islam and Liberal Democracy', *The Atlantic Monthly* (February, 1993). Lewis considers 'Islamic fundamentalism', which he equates occasionally with terrorism, as arising out of the overtly religious and intolerant traditions of Islam. I have dealt with Lewis' arguments in my 'Roots of Misconception: Euro-American Perceptions of Islam Before and After 9/11' in Joseph Lumbard, ed., *Islam, Fundamentalism, and the Betrayal of Tradition* (Bloomington, IN: World Wisdom, 2004), pp. 143–87.

[259] Cf. Mark Juergensmeyer, *Terror in the Mind of God: The Global Rise of Religious Violence* (Berkeley and New York): Univeristy of California Press, 2000).

[260] One such exception to the rule is Richard Martin's essay 'The Religious Foundations of War, Peace, and Statecraft in Islam' in John Kelsay and James Turner Johnson, eds, *Just War and Jihad: Historical and Theoretical Perspectives on War and Peace in Western and Islamic Traditions* (New York: Greenwood Press, 1991), pp. 91–117.

[261] Cf. Steven Lee, 'A Positive Concept of Peace' in Peter Caws, ed., *The Causes of Quarrel: Essays on Peace, War, and Thomas Hobbes* (Boston: Beacon Press, 1989), pp. 183–4.

[262] Gray Cox, 'The Light at the End of the Tunnel and the Light in Which We May Walk: Two Concepts of Peace' in Caws, *ibid.*, pp. 162–3.

[263] The celebrated *ḥadīth jibrīl* confirms the same Qur'anic usage: '*Iḥsān* is to worship God as if you were to see Him; even if you see Him not, he sees you'. For an extensive analysis of *iḥsān* as articulated in the Islamic tradition, see Sachiko Murata and William Chittick, *The Vision of Islam* ,Paragon House, 1998), pp. 265–317.

[264] R. G. Collingwood, *The New Leviathan* (New York: Thomas Y. Crowell, 1971), p. 334.

[265] Ibn Manzur, *Lisān al-'arab*, XIII, pp. 457–8 and al-Tahanawi, *Kashshāf iṣṭilāḥāt al-funūn* (Beirut: Dar al-Kutub al-'Ilmiyya, 1998), III, pp. 288–9.

[266] Cf. Muhammad Asad, *The Message of the Qur'an*, p. 179, no. 46 commenting on the Qur'an *Al-An'ām*, 6:54: 'And when those who believe in Our messages come unto thee, say: "Peace be upon you. Your Sustainer has willed upon Himself the law of grace and mercy so that if any of you does a bad deed out of ignorance, and thereafter repents and lives righteously, He shall be [found] much-forgiving, a dispenser of grace."'

[267] On the basis of this verse, the tenth century philologist Abu Hilal al-'Askari

considers justice and *iḥsān* as synonyms. Cf. his *al-Furūq al-lughawiyyah*, p. 194, quoted in Franz Rosenthal, 'Political Justice and the Just Ruler' in Joel Kraemer and Ilai Alon, eds, *Religion and Government in the World of Islam* (Tel-Aviv: Tel-Aviv University, 1983), p. 97, no. 20.

[268] Like other Sufis, Ghazali subscribes to the notion of what Ibn al-'Arabi would later call the 'possessor of the two eyes' (*dhū'l-'aynayn*), viz., seeing God with the two eyes of transcendence (*tanzīh*) and immanence (*tashbīh*). Cf. Fadlou Shehadi, *Ghazali's Unique Unknowable God* (Leiden: E. J. Brill, 1964), pp. 8–10 and 51–5. For Ibn al-'Arabi's expression of the 'possessor of the two eyes', see William Chittick, *The Sufi Path of Knowledge* (Albany, State University of New York Press, 1989), pp. 361–2. The Mu'tazilite and Ash'arite theologians have a long history of controversy over the three major views of Divine names and qualities, i.e., *tanzīh, tashbīh*, and *ta'tīl* ('suspension'). Cf. Michel Allard, *Le problème des attributes divins dans la doctrine d'al-Aš'ari et des ses premiers grands disciples* (Beirut: Editions De L'Impirimerie Catholique, 1965), pp. 354–64.

[269] 'Ali b. Sultan Muhammad al-Harawi al-Qari, *al-Maṣnū' fī Ma'rifat al-ḥadīth al-Mawḍū'* (Riyadh: Maktabat al-Rushd, 1404 AH), 1:141.

[270] Quoted in William Chittick, *The Self-Disclosure of God: Principles of Ibn al-'Arabi's Cosmology* (Albany: State University of New York Press, 1998), p. 22.

[271] Dawud al-Qaysari, *Risālah fī ma'rifat al-maḥabbah al-ḥaqīqiyyah* in *al-Rasā'il*, edited by Mehmet Bayraktar (Kayseri: Kayseri Metropolitan Municipality, 1997), p. 138.

[272] The term has first been used by Mircea Eliade and adopted by Tu Weiming to describe the philosophical outlook of the Chinese traditions. For an application of the term to Islamic thought, see William Chittick, 'The Anthropocosmic Vision in Islamic Thought' in Ted Peters, Muzaffar Iqbal, Syed Nomanul Haq, eds, *God, Life, and the Cosmos* (Aldershot: Ashgate, 2002). pp. 125–52.

[273] Cf. Seyyed Hossein Nasr, *Religion and the Order of Nature* (Oxford: Oxford University Press, 1996), pp. 60–3.

[274] The classical Qur'an commentaries are almost unanimous on interpreting this 'khalifah' as Adam, i.e., humans in the generic sense. Cf. Jalal al-Din al-Mahalli and Jalal al-Din al-Suyuti, *Tafsīr al-Jalalayn* (Beirut: Mu'assasat al-Risalah, 1995), p. 6 and Ibn al-'Arabi, *al-Futūḥāt al-makkiyyah*, edited by M. 'Abd al-Rahman al-Mar'ashli, (Beirut: Dar Ihya' al-Turath al-'Arabi, 1997), vol. I, p. 169.

[275] Another formulation is *laysa fī'l-imkān abdā' mimmā kān*. Loosely translated, it states that 'there is nothing in the world of possibility more beautiful and perfect than what is in actuality'. This sentence, attributed to Ghazali, has led to a long controversy in Islamic thought. For an excellent survey of this debate in Islamic theology, see Eric L. Ormsby, *Theodicy in Islamic Thought: The Dispute over al-Ghazali's 'Best of All Possible Worlds'* (Princeton, NJ:

Princeton University Press, 1984). Cf. Also Ghazali, *Ihyā' 'ulūm al-dīn*, (Cairo: 1968), vol. IV, p. 321. The earliest formulation of the problem, however, can be traced back to Ibn Sina. See my 'Why Do Animals Eat Other Animals: Mulla Sadra on Theodicy' (forthcoming).

[276] Plantinga's 'free will defence' is based on this premise. Cf. Alvin Plantinga, 'The Free Will Defence' in *Philosophy in America*, Max Black, ed., reprinted in Baruch A. Broody, ed., *Readings in the Philosophy of Religion: An Analytical Approach* (New Jersey: Prentice-Hall, 1974), p. 187. See also his 'God, Evil, and the Metaphysics of Freedom' in Marilyn M. Adams and Robert M. Adams, eds, *The Problem of Evil* (Oxford: Oxford University Press, 1990), pp. 83–109.

[277] Mulla Sadra, *al-Ḥikmah al-muta'āliyah fi'l-asfār al-'aqliyyah al-'arba'ah*, (cited hereafter as *Asfār*) (Tehran, 1383, A. H.), II, 3, p. 72.

[278] Ibid., p. 78.

[279] Frithjof Schuon, *In the face of the Absolute* (Bloomington: World Wisdom Books, 1989), p. 39.

[280] This is the main reason why a good number of Sufis, philosophers, and some theologians believe that hellfire will be terminated whereas paradise will remain eternal. For the debate between the Mu'tazilites and the Ash'arites on this issue, see Sa'd al-Din al-Taftazani, *Sharḥ al-maqāṣid* (Beirut: 'Alam al-Kutub, 1989), vol. 5, pp. 131–40.

[281] Cf. the following verse: *Man never tires of asking for the good [things of life]; and if evil fortune touches him, he abandons all hope, giving himself up to despair. Yet whenever We let him taste some of Our grace after hardship has visited him, he is sure to say, 'This is but my due!'—and, 'I do not think that the Last Hour will ever come: but if [it should come, and] I should indeed be brought back unto my Sustainer, then, behold, the ultimate good awaits me with Him'* (*Fuṣṣilat*,41:49–50; trans. M. Asad).

[282] Sadra, *Asfār*, II, 3, pp. 92–3; also p. 77.

[283] Cf. Plotinus, The *Enneads*, V, IX, 5, p. 248, and Mulla Sadra, *Asfār*, I, 3, pp. 343–4. Baqillani considers the potential (*bi'l-quwwah*) as non-existent. See his *Kitāb al-tawḥīd*, p. 34–44, quoted in Franz Rosenthal, *Knowledge Triumphant: The Concept of Knowledge in Medieval Islam* (Leiden: E. J. Brill, 1970), p. 216.

[284] As the 'leader of the sceptics' (*imām al-mushakkikīn*), Fakhr al-Din al-Razi disagrees. His objection, however, clarifies another aspect of the discussion of theodicy in Islam. As Razi points out, there is no dispute over the fact that some actions are good and some others bad. The question is 'whether this is because of an attribute that belongs [essentially] to the action itself or this is not the case and it is solely as an injunction of the shari'ah [that actions and things are good or bad]'. Razi hastens to add that the Mu'tazilites opt the first view and 'our path', i.e., the Asha'rites believe in the second. Cf. Fakhr al-Din al-Razi, *al-Arba'īn fī usūl al-dīn* (Cairo: Maktabat al-Kulliyat al-Azhariyyah, 1986), vol. I, p. 346. For a defence of the same Ash'arite position, see Taftazani,

Sharḥ al-maqāṣid, vol. 4, p. 282 where it is asserted that human reason is in no place to judge what is good (*al-ḥusn*) and what is evil (*al-qubḥ*). For Sabziwari's defence of the Mu'tazilites, the philosophers, and the 'Imamiyyah' on the rationality of good and evil, see his gloss on Sadra's *Asfār*, II, 3, pp. 83–4.

[285] Ibn Sina, *Kitāb al-najāh*, edited by Majid Fakhry (Beirut: Dar al-Afaq al-Jadidah, 1985), p. 265; cf. also Ibn Sina, al-*Mubāḥathāt*, edited by Muhsin Bidarfar (Qom: Intisharat-i Bidar, 1413 AH), p. 301.

[286] Sadra, *Asfar*, II, 1, p. 113.

[287] *Asfār*, II, 3, p. 76. The intrinsic goodness of things in their natural-ontological state has given rise to a number of popular formulations of the problem, the most celebrated one being Merkez Efendi, the famous Ottoman scholar. When asked if he would change anything were he to have the 'centre' of the world at his hands, he replied that he would leave everything as it is, hence the name 'merkez' (centre).

[288] Sadra, *Asfār*, III, 2, pp. 114. See also ibid. II, 2, p. 114, III, 1, p. 256, III, 2, pp. 106–134. Sadra employs two arguments to defend the best of all possible worlds argument, which he calls the 'ontological' (*innī*) and 'causal' (*limmī*) methods (*manhaj*).

[289] This is what Tibi claims in his essentialist generalisations and oversimplifications about the Islamic pathos of peace and war. Cf. Bassam Tibi, 'War and Peace in Islam' in Terry Nardin, ed., *The Ethics of War and Peace: Religious and Secular Perspectives* (Princeton: Princeton University Press, 1996), pp. 128–145.

[290] Concerning the Zoroastrians and Sabeans and their being part of the People of the Book, Abu Yusuf narrates a number of traditions of the Prophet to show that they should be treated with justice and equality as the other dhimmis. The inclusion of the Zoroastrians among the dhimmis is inferred from the fact that the Prophet had collected *jizyah* from the Majus of Hajar. Cf. *Taxation in Islam: Abu Yusuf's Kitab al-kharāj*, trans. A. Ben Shemesh (Leiden: E. J. Brill, 1969), pp. 88–9.

[291] Some of these stipulations can be followed from Shaybani's Siyar; English translation by Majid Khadduri, *The Islamic Law of Nations: Shaybani's Siyar* (Baltimore: The John Hopkins University Press, 1966), pp. 75–94; also Muhammad Hamidullah, *The Muslim Conduct of State* (Lahore: S. Ashraf, 1961), pp. 205–8.

[292] Cf. 'Ṣulḥ', Encyclopedia of Islam (EI2), IX, 845a.

[293] As a representative text of the Ash'arite kalam, see Sa'd al-Din al-Taftazani, *Sharḥ al-maqāṣid*, vol. 5, pp. 232–320 where the long discussion of the imamate contains no references to jihad as conquering non-Muslim territories. See also Ibn Khaldun, *Muqaddimah*, trans. Franz Rosenthal, abridged by N. J. Dawood (Princeton: Princeton University Press, 1969), pp. 158–160 and Fakhr al-Din al-Razi, *al-Arba'īn fī usūl al-dīn*, vol. 2, pp. 255–70. The Muslim philosophers, especially al-Farabi, define jihad as just war and stress the virtues of the 'city'

(*madinah*) or the human habitat. Cf. Joel L. Kraemer, 'The *Jihad* of the *Falasifa*', Jerusalem Studies in Arabic and Islam, 10 (1987), p. 293 and 312. Butterworth holds the same view about al-Farabi's notion of warfare in his 'Al-Farabi's Statecraft: War and the Well-Ordered Regime' in James Turner Johnson and John Kelsay, eds, *Cross, Crescent, and Sword: The Justification and Limitation of War in Western and Islamic Tradition* (New York: Greenwood Press, 1990), pp. 79–100.

[294] Cf. 'Dar al-ṣulḥ', EI2, II, 131a.

[295] Shaybani, *Siyar*, pp. 158–194; also 'Amān', EI2, I, 429a.

[296] Philip K. Hitti, *History of the Arabs* (New York, St. Martin's Press, 1970), p. 145. Dozy makes a similar point when he says that 'the holy war is never imposed except only when the enemies of Islam are the aggressors. Otherwise, if we take into account the injunctions of the Qur'an, it is nothing but an interpretation of some theologians.' R. Dozy, *Essai sur l'histoire de l'Islamisme* (Leiden: Brill, 1879), p. 152.

[297] Cf. Richard Bulliet, 'Conversion to Islam and the Emergence of a Muslim Society in Iran' in Nehemia Levtzion, ed., *Conversion to Islam* (New York: Holmes and Meier Publishers, Inc., 1979), pp. 30–51. See also the introduction by the editor, p. 9.

[298] Cf. Daniel J. Sahas, *John of Damascus on Islam: The 'Heresy of the Ishmaelites'* (Leiden: E. J. Brill, 1972).

[299] T. W. Arnold, *The Preaching of Islam* (Delhi: Renaissance Publishing House, 1984; originally published in 1913), pp. 63–4.

[300] Cf. Lord Kinross, *The Ottoman Centuries: The Rise and Fall of the Turkish Empire* (New York: Morrow Quill, 1977), p. 259.

[301] Abdulaziz A. Sachedina, 'The Development of Jihad in Islamic Revelation and History', in *Cross, Crescent, and Sword*, p. 36.

[302] On the question of rebellion and irregular warfare (*aḥkām al-bughat*) in Islamic law, see Khaled Abou el Fadl, *Rebellion and Violence in Islamic Law* (Cambridge: Cambridge University Press, 2001). For a shorter synoptic account, see ibid., '*Ahkam al-Bughat*: Irregular Warfare and the Law of Rebellion in Islam' in Johnson and Kelsay, eds, *Cross, Crescent, and Sword*, pp. 149–176.

[303] Imam Shawkani, *Faḥt al-qadīr*, abridged by Sulayman 'Abd Allah al-Ashqar (Kuwait: Shirkat Dhat al-Salasal, 1988), p. 37; *Le Coran: 'Voila le Livre…'*, French translation and commentary by Yahya 'Alawi and Javad Hadidi (Qom: Centre pour la traduction du Saint Coran, 2000), pp. 318–9; Muhamad Asad, *The Message of the Qur'an* (Maktaba Jawahar ul uloom: Lahore, n.d.), p.41; Shaykh Muhammad al-Ghazali, *A Thematic Commentary on the Qur'an*, trans. by A. Shamis (Herndon: International Institute of Islamic Thought, 2000), pp. 18–9.

[304] In his *War and Peace in the Law of Islam* (Baltimore: The Johns Hopkins University Press, 1955) Majid Khadduri goes so far as to translate jihad as

'warfare' (p. 55) and 'permanent war' (p. 62), and claims that 'the universalism of Islam, in its all-embracing creed, is imposed on the believers as a continuous process of warfare, psychological and political if not strictly military' (p. 64). This belligerent view of jihad is hard to justify in the light of both the legal and cultural traditions of Islam discussed below.

[305] Ibn Taymiyyah, 'Qā'idah fī qitāl al-kuffār', from *Majmū' āt rasā'il*, p. 123, quoted in Majid Khadduri, *The Islamic Law of Nations*, p. 59.

[306] Ibn Qayyim al-Jawziyyah, *Aḥkām ahl al-dhimmah*, edited by Subhi al-Salih (Beirut: Dar al-'Ilm li'l-alamin, 1983, 3rd edn), vol. I, p. 17.

[307] Cf. John Voll, 'Renewal and Reform' in John Esposito, ed., *The Oxford History of Islam* (Oxford: Oxford University Press, 2000).

[308] Rudolph Peters, *Islam and Colonialism: The Doctrine of Jihad in Modern History* (The Hague: Mouton Publishers, 1979), p. 86. Peters' work presents an excellent survey of how jihad was reformulated as an anti-colonialist resistance idea in the modern period. See also Allan Christelow, *Muslim Law Courts and the French Colonial State in Algeria* (Princeton: Princeton University Press, 1985) for the struggle of Muslim jurists to continue the tradition of Islamic law under the French colonial system.

[309] *Al-Jabarti's Chronicle of the French Occupation*, trans. by Shmuel Moreh (Princeton: Markus Wiener Publishers, 1997), p. 26.

[310] Faraj's treatise has been translated by Johannes J. G. Jansen, *The Neglected Duty: The Creed of Sadat's Assassins and Islamic Resurgence in the Middle East* (New York: Macmillan Publishing Company, 1986), pp. 160–230.

[311] There is a consensus on this point among the Hanafi and Maliki schools of law as well as some Hanbali scholars. For references in Arabic, see Yohanan Friedmann, *Tolerance and Coercion in Islam: Interfaith Relations in the Muslim Tradition* (Cambridge: Cambridge University Press, 2003), pp. 85–6. For the inclusion of Zoroastrians among the People of the Book, see Friedmann, *Tolerance and Coercion*, pp. 72–6. Shafi'i considers the Sabeans, a community mentioned in the Qur'an, as a Christian group. Cf. Ibn Qayyim, *Aḥkām*, vol. I, p. 92.

[312] The incident is recorded in Baladhuri's *Futūḥ al-buldān*. Cf. Friedmann, *Tolerance and Coercion*, p. 85.

[313] The text of the Medinan treatise is preserved in Ibn Hisham's *Sīrah*. It is also published in Muhammad Hamidullah, *Documents sur la Diplomatie à l'Epoque du Prophète et des Khalifes Orthodoxes* (Paris, 1935), pp. 9–14. For an English translation, see Khadduri, *War and Peace*, pp. 206–9.

[314] Quoted in Khadduri, *War and Peace in the Law of Islam*, p. 179. The original text of the Najran treatise is quoted in Abu Yusuf, *Kitāb al-kharāj* and Baladhuri, *Futūḥ al-buldān*.

[315] Ibn Qayyim, *Aḥkām ahl al-dhimmah*, vol. I, p. 24.

[316] Ibn Qayyim, *Aḥkām ahl al-dhimmah*, vol. I, p. 26.

[317] Abu Yusuf, *Kitāb al-kharāj*, p. 84. Cf. Shaybani, *Siyar*, in Khadduri, *War and Peace*, p. 143.

[318] Ibn Qayyim, *Aḥkām ahl al-dhimmah*, vol. I., p. 32ff.

[319] Ibn Qayyim, *Aḥkām ahl al-dhimmah*, p. 42 and 49.

[320] This is not to deny that there were examples to the contrary. When one of the governors of ʿUmar ʿAbd al-ʿAziz asked permission to ʻcollect huge amounts of *jizyah* owed by Jews, Christians and Majus of al-Hira before they accepted Islam', ʿAbd al-ʿAziz responded by saying that ʻGod has sent the Prophet Muhammad to invite people to Islam and not as a tax collector'. This letter is quoted in Abu Yusuf, *Kitāb al-kharāj*, p. 90.

[321] Cf. Aziz Ahmad, *Studies in Islamic Culture in the Indian Environment* (Oxford: Oxford University Press, 1964), pp. 80–1.

[322] Abu Yusuf mentions the case of Abu ʿUbaydah returning the *jizyah* to the dhimmis of Homs when he was not able to provide protection for them against the Roman emperor Heraclius. Cf. the letter by Abu ʿUbayadah mentioned by Abu Yusuf, *Kitāb al-kharāj*, p. 150.

[323] Cf. Khadduri, *War and Peace*, pp. 188–9.

[324] These include some restrictive rulings on what the People of the Book could wear and what religious symbols they could display. Cf. A. S. Tritton, *The Caliphs and Their Non-Muslim Subjects* (London: Oxford University Press, 1930), chapters VII and VIII. As Tritton notes, however, such rulings were not implemented strictly and displayed considerable variety across the Islamic world. A case in point, which Tritton mentions (p. 121), is Salah al-Din al-Ayyubi who had some Christian officers working for him without following any strict dress code.

[325] Khadduri, *War and Peace*, p. 85.

[326] Quoted in Friedmann, *Tolerance and Coercion*, p. 40.

[327] The major and minor religions that the Islamic world encountered throughout its history make up a long list: the religious traditions of the pre-Islamic (*jāhiliyyah*) Arabs, Mazdeans in Mesopotamia, Iran, and Transoxania, Christians (of different communions like Nestorians in Mesopotamia and Iran, Monophysites in Syria, Egypt and Armenia, Orthodox Melkites in Syria, Orthodox Latins in North Africa), Jews in various places, Samaritans in Palastine, Mandaeans in south Mesopotamia, Harranians in north Mesopotamia, Manichaeans in Mesopotamia and Egypt, Buddhists and Hindus in Sind, tribal religions in Africa, pre-Islamic Turkic tribes, Buddhists in Sind and the Panjab, Hindus in the Punjab. Cf. J. Waardenburg, ʻWorld Religions as seen in the Light of Islam' in A. T. Welch and P. Cachia, eds, *Islam Past Influence and Present Challenge* (Edinburgh: Edinburgh University Press, 1979), pp. 248–9. See also J. Waardenburg, *Muslims and Others: Relations in Context* (Berlin and New York: Walter de Gruyter, 2003).

[328] The six cultural zones of the Islamic world comprise Arabic, Persian,

Turkish/Turkic, Indian, Malay-Indonesian, and African spheres of culture where the expression of Islam as a religious and cultural identity has been more heterogeneous and complex than the Christian, Hindu or Chinese worlds. For a discussion of these zones, see S. H. Nasr, *The Heart of Islam*, (San Francisco: HarperCollins, 2003), pp. 87–100.

[329] See for details, M. Hinds, 'Mihna' in Encyclopaedia of Islam, 2nd edn, 7:26.

[330] See Semiramis Cavusoglu, 'The Kadizadeli Movement: An Attempt at Seri'at-Minded Reform in the Ottoman Empire' (Unpublished Dissertation; Princeton University, 1990). Also see Madeline C Zilfi, 'Vaizan and Ulema in the Kadizadeli Era' Proceedings of the tenth Congress of the Turkish Historical Society (Ankara, 1994), pp.2493–500.

[331] Marshall Hodgson's suggestion of the term 'Islamicate' to express the hybrid and multifaceted nature of Islamic civilization is not completely without justification as many previously non-Islamic elements were incorporated into Islamic civilisation in a relatively short period of time. Cf. his *The Venture of Islam* (Chicago: The University of Chicago Press, 1974).

[332] See Al-Rabi' b. Habib al-Basari, *Musnad al-Imām al-Rabī', Bāb fī al-'Ilm wa ṭalabih wa Faḍlih.* This is also narrated by Abu Bakr Aamad b. 'Amre al-Bazzar in his *al-Baḥr al-Zukhkhar* also known as *Musnad al-Bazzar* (Beirut: Mu'assasat 'Ulum al-Qur'an, 1409 AH), 1:1775, where he claims that there is no foundation (*aṣl*) for this hadith.

[333] Abu 'Isa Muhammad Tirmidhi, *Sunan al-Tirmidhī, Kitāb al-'Ilm 'an Rasūl Allāh, Bāb mā Jā'a fī Faḍl al-Fiqh 'alā al-'Ibādah;* Ibn Majah, *Sunan Ibn Mājah, Kitāb al-Zuhd, Bāb al-ḥikmah.* This hadith has been transmitted in many hadith collections with some variations.

[334] Ignaz Goldziher, 'The Attitude of Orthodox Islam Toward the 'Ancient Sciences' in *Studies on Islam*, trans. and edited by M. L. Swartz, Oxford, 1981, pp. 185–215. For an important criticism of Goldziher's conceptualisation, see Dimitri Gutas, *Greek Thought, Arabic Culture* (London: Routledge, 1998), pp. 166–171.

[335] Ya'qub b. Ishaq Al-Kindi, *Rasā'il*, I, p. 97, quoted in Majid Fakhry, *A History of Islamic Philosophy* (New York: Columbia University Press, 1983), p. 70.

[336] Sa'ib b. Ahmad al-Andalusi, *Science in the Medieval World 'Book of the Categories of Nations'* (*Tabaqāt al-umam*) trans. S. I. Salem and A. Kumar, (Austin: The University of Texas Press, 1991), p. 6.

[337] Cf. Franz Rosenthal, *The Classical Heritage in Islam* (London: Routledge, 1975), pp. 25–51.

[338] The Arabic text of *al-Mukhtar* has been edited by A. Badawi (Beirut: The Arab Institute for Research and Publishing, 1980, 2nd edn) and see the original English translation by Curt F. Buhler (London: Oxford University Press, 1941).

[339] Quoted in Abu Sulayman al-Sijistani, *Muntakhab ṣiwan al-ḥikmah*, edited by D. M. Dunlop (The Hague: Mouton Publishers, 1979), p. 3.

[340] Shihab al-Din Yahya b. Habash al-Suhrawardi, *Ḥikmat al-Ishrāq* (*The Philosophy of Illumination*), edited and translated by John Walbridge and Hossein Ziai (Utah: Brigham Young University Press, 1999), p. 2.

[341] For Andalusia, see Anwar Chejne, *Muslim Spain: Its History and Culture* (Minneapolis: University of Minnesota Press, 1974) and Salma Khadra Jayyusi and Manuela Marin, eds, *The Legacy of Muslim Spain* (Leiden: E. J. Brill, 1992). For the concept of *convivencia* and the Jewish contributions to Andalusian civilization, see V. B. Mann, T. F. Glick, and J. D. Dodds, eds., *Convivencia: Jews, Muslims, and Christians in Medieval Spain* (New York: The Jewish Museum, 1992).

[342] See, among others, Arthur Hyman, 'Jewish Philosophy in the Islamic World' in S. H. Nasr and Oliver Leaman, eds, *History of Islamic Philosophy* (London: Routledge,), vol. I, pp. 677–95 and Paul B. Fenton, 'Judaism and Sufism', ibid., pp. 755–68.

[343] Cf. Aziz Ahmad, *Studies*, pp. 191–6; Annemarie Schimmel, *Islam in the Indian Subcontinent* (Leiden: E. J. Brill, 1980), pp. 99–100.

[344] From the Introduction to *Sirr-i akbar* quoted in *Majmā'-ul-baḥrayn or the Mingling of the Two Oceans by Prince Muhammad Dara Shikuh*, translated by M. Mahfuz-ul-Haq (Calcutta: The Asiatic Society, 1929), p. 13.

[345] *Majmā'-ul-baḥrayn*, p. 38.

[346] Fathullaj Mujtabai, *Hindu Muslim Cultural Relations* (New Delhi, 1978), p. 82; Edward G. Browne, *A Literary History of Persia* vol. IV, pp. 257–8.

CHAPTER 9

[347] UNDP, *Human Development Report 1994—New Dimensions of Human Security* (New York: Oxford University Press, 1994).

[348] Commission on Human Security, *Human Security Now: Final Report* (New York: CHS, 2003).

[349] See in particular David Baldwin, 'The Concept of Security', *Review of International Studies* 23/1 (1997) pp. 5–26; and John Baylis, 'International Security and Global Security in the Post-Cold War Era', in John Baylis & Steve Smith, eds., *The Globalization of World Politics. An Introduction to International Relations* (3rd edn, Oxford: Oxford University Press, 2005) pp. 297–324.

[350] Shahrbanou Tadjbakhsh, 'Human Security: Concepts, Application and Implication', *Etudes du CERI*, No.117–8, Paris, CERI (September 2005). See further: 'What is "Human Security"? Comments by 21 Authors', *Security Dialogue* 35/3 (2004) pp. 347–87.

[351] Al-Khalil b. Ahmad, *Kitāb al-ʿAyn*, s.v. *S-L-M* : *'al-salmu' ḍiddu l-ḥarb, wa yuqāl: al-salmu wa l-silmu wāḥid*/'peacemaking' is the antonym of war…; also s.v. *Ḥ-R-B* : *'al-ḥarbu' naqīḍu l-salm*/'war' is the opposite of peacemaking.

[352] At conclusion of ritual prayer, the *taslīm* is the double salutation to

right and left. See *Sūrat Al-Aḥzāb*, 33:56 …*ṣallū 'alayhi wa sallimū taslīm*.

[353] But note the current Arabic term for pacifism: *ḥubb al-silm*. Classical Juridical usage also equated *al-ṣulḥ* with *al-silm* 'ending the state of war'.

[354] We rely for what follows on the Qur'an, and classic lexicons s.v. *S-L-M*, including al-Khalil b. Aḥmad, *al-'Ayn;* al-Jawharī, *Ṣiḥāḥ;* Ibn Durayḍ, *al-Ishtiqāq;* Ibn Fāris, *Maqāyīs al-Lughah;* and Murtaḍā al-Zabīdī, *Lisān al-'Arab*. Relevant linguistic material may also be gleaned from major Exegetical/*Tafsīr* and Prophetic Biographical/*Sīrah* genres. Here we are very concise, it being understood that important details might be developed at greater depth.

[355] See *Sūrat al-Anfāl*, 8:1; *Al-Nisā'*; 4:35, 4:114; *Al-Ḥujurāt*, 49:9–10, etc.

[356] Indeed, the significance of the nexus of these fundamental opposing conceptual pairs demands a separate study in greater detail, linking this notion with the cluster of ideas derived from *amn* and *āminūn*, as opposed to *ẓulm* ('manifest injustice'). The richness and centrality of the *ṣulḥ* notion displays its true centre of gravity when the verses wherein it occurs are explored in the light of exegetical data preserved in the *tafsīr* and *asbāb al-nuzūl* literatures.

[357] The Qur'an presents this important teaching as the message of the previous prophets to their peoples; consult e.g. *Sūrat Al-Baqarah*, 2:220; *Al-A'rāf*, 7:85 and 142; and *Al-Naml*, 27:48 where the plotters against the Prophet Salih are portrayed as those *who spread corruption in the land and who would not reform / yufsidūna fī l-arḍi wa lā yuṣliḥūna*.

[358] See al-Hafiz Ahmad b. al-Husayn al-Bayhaqi, *Shu'ab al-īmān* [*Branches of Faith*], edited by M. S. Basyūnī Zaghlūl (Beirut: 1990) vol.VII pp. 487–97, for materials on peacemaking; this utterance is no. 11092, and the immediately following one no.11093.

[359] Ibid, no.11088 (as cited in Muslim, *Ṣaḥīḥ, via* 'Abd al-Razzāq … Abu Hurayrah); an alternative transmission (no. 11089) gives *bighḍah* 'hatred' in place of *fasādu dhāt al-bayn,* through al-Zuhri—Abu Idris al-Khawlani—as an utterance by Abu l-Dardā'. / This famous Prophetic utterance also frequently occurs cited by 'Ali b. Abī Talib in his deathbed testament to his two sons (the grandsons of Muhammad).

[360] Ibid,, nos11096–8; and pp. 491–7.

[361] Consult Toshihiko Izutsu, *The Concept of Belief in Islamic Theology: A Semantic Analysis of* Īmān *and* Islām (Keio University, 1965; rpr. Kuala Lumpur: Islamic Book Trust, 2006) on pp. 71–103 and 196–237.

[362] For the variety of juridical employment consult e.g. the juridical lexicon by Sa'di Abu Jayb, *al-Qāmūs al-Fiqhīyah lughat wa iṣṭilāḥ* (2nd pr., Damascus: Dār al-Fikr, 1988) pp.180–2.

[363] The great Kufan jurist Abu Hanifah (d. 150/767 CE) included this Prophetic utterance among his choice of five weightiest Prophetic *ḥadīth* crucial for faith.

[364] When the Prophet's paternal cousin Jaʿfar b. Abi Talib in 615 CE (seven years before the migration of the Prophet to Madinah in 622) described the essence of Islamic guidance to the Ethiopian Emperor al-Najāshī at his court in Axum, Jaʿfar emphasised this 'salutation of Islam' as a new practice specific to their religion taught them by Muḥammad.

[365] This word *taslīm* from verbal form II *sallama* ('to make or render salutations of peace-security'), most often refers to the formula of praise and blessing invariably invoked upon mentioning the Prophet Muhammad—see *Sūrat Al-Aḥzāb*, 33:56: *God and His angels make blessings upon the Prophet; O you who believe, do you also bless him and render him salutations of peace-security* / *...ṣallū ʿalayhi wa sallimū taslīm.*

[366] Singular *taḥīyah* (verbal-noun form II *ḥayyā* or *ḥayyiya*) denotes 'salutation, greeting' [i.e. *salām 'alayka*]; as well as 'security from death and evils', or 'everlasting existence'. Compare the familiar salute *ḥayyāka llāhu:* 'May God make thee secure from harm-evil'—or simply 'May God prolong thy life'.

[367] The *al-taḥīyāt* are uttered in short form after every second prostration, and in prolonged complete form (*tashahhud*) after the third or the fourth cycle of prostrations; except of course for the dawn prayer which consists of only two cycles.

[368] *Allāhumma Anta l-salām wa min-Ka l-salām wa ilay-Ka yaʿūdu l-salām...* . See what follows for a parallel tradition involving the Prophet's wife Khadijah.

[369] Ibn Hanbal, *Musnad* (Cairo: 1313) V p. 451 [no. 23272 in the recent edition]. This *ḥadīth* is only found in this source as far as I am aware. However, it should be observed that similar statements occur in Imāmī sources as an utterance assigned to 'Ali b. Abi Talib, as well as to Salman al-Farisi.

[370] *Ifshū l-salāma wa iṭma'ū l-ṭa'āma wa ṣilū l-arḥām wa ṣallū wa l-nās niyām, tadkhulū l-jannata bi-salām!* The alternative rendering *...greeted by God's salutation* '*Peace*'! has much to recommend it. / Recall that *salām* is often a synonym of *al-amān* ('surety') as well as *al-ṣulḥ* ('peace-making').

[371] For this and the following etymological data, consult sources specified in note 354 above; and also Ibn Abil-Hadid, *Sharḥ Nahj al-Balāghah* (old edition of Cairo) II p. 445.

[372] Compare the eulogy of divine names in *Sūrat Al-Ḥashr*, 59:23 *...al-Maliku l-Quddūsu l-Salāmu l-Mu'min;* further see our examination below of *Salām* as an archaic theomorphic name.

[373] *Al-salāmah min al-sū' wa l-ikhtilāl.* See the treatment of the Divine Name *al-Salām* in the genre of writings on God's Most Beautiful Names (*Asmā' Allāh al-Ḥusnā*). This valuable genre has to be integrated into what we are briefly sketching here.

[374] ʿAbd al-Rahman b. ʿAbdullah al-Suhayli, *al-Rawḍ al-ʿUnf*, edited by Majdī b. Manṣūr b. Sayyid al-Shūrā (Beirut: Dar al-Kutub al-ʿIlmiyah, n.d.) I

pp. 418–9. / *Rawḍ* is an important commentary upon the Prophet's Biography or *Sīrah* compiled by Ibn Hishām (d. 213 AH), who drew upon the famous early work by Ibn Isḥāq (d. 151 AH).

[375] Cited by Ibn Hisham on an unnamed authority; this *ḥadīth* on the phrase *Allāhu l-Salām* is also cited in al-Bukhārī, *Ṣaḥīḥ* IV p. 136; and in Muslim, *faḍā'il al-ṣaḥābah* no. 91 (through ʿA'ishah).

[376] al-Suhayli, *al-Rawḍ al-ʿUnf* I pp. 419–420.

[377] See e.g. Ibn Jarir al-Tabari, *Jāmi' al-Bayān fī Ta'wīl al-Qur'ān*, edited by Hani al-Hajj *et al.* (Cairo: al-Maktabat al-Tawfiqiyah, n.d.) II pp. 363–6. And al-Maturidi, *Ta'wīlāt al-Qur'ān* (Istanbul: 2005) I p. 412. We also signal here, without discussion, the occurrence of the term *al-salama* in *Sūrat Al-Nisā'* 4:86–91.

[378] Namely: Thaʿlabah, ʿAbdallah Ibn Salam, Ibn Yamin, Asad and Usayd ibnay Kaʿb, Shuʿbah b. ʿUmar, and Qays b. Zayd—all prominent Medinan Jews who accepted Islam and Muhammad's prophethood. Tabari's *isnād* for this statement by ʿIkramah is through Ibn Jurayj (another leading tradent from the circle of Ibn ʿAbbas); this is a singular tradition not supported by complementary reports, and might not inspire much confidence, which may explain why Tabari does not appear to place much weight on it. Nevertheless, it is of definite interest and cannot be dismissed out of hand, perhaps reflecting a Jewish reaction to the Muslim Friday day of rest being an explicit divergence from Israelite tradition. Keep in mind that the 'believers' in Medina under the Prophet included Jews and several Christians, as well as Arab Muslims.

[379] Tabari, *Jāmiʿ al-Bayān* II p. 365.

[380] Tabari, *Jāmiʿ al-Bayān* X pp. 35–7.

[381] Tabari, *Jāmiʿ al-Bayān* II p. 364: *ammā daʿā'uhum ilā l-ṣulḥi ibtidā' fa-ghayr mawjūd fī l-Qur'ān*. He is correct in this assertion.

[382] The famed 'sword' verses permitting combat against pagan idolaters are most often given as *Al-Baqarah*, 2:190, and/or *Al-Ḥajj*, 22:39.

[383] Tabari, *Jāmiʿ al-Bayān* X p. 36: *mā qālahu Qatādah wa man qāla mithla qawlihi min an hādhihi l-āyah mansūkhah, fa-qawlu lā dalālata 'alayhi min kitāb wa lā sunnat wa lā fiṭrata 'aql!* This appeal to inborn reason is not surprising coming from Tabari, whose juridical law rite the Jariri *madhhab* was noted for its rational orientation and thus condemned by Traditionalist Ḥanbalīs.

[384] Current scholarship on jihad has highlighted this divergence over the claimed abrogation of Meccan verses by later Medinan revelations. See e.g., Muhammad Saʿid Ramadan al-Buti, *al-Jihad fī l-Islām: kayfa nafhamuhu wa kayfa numārisuhu?*, 2nd revised ed., (Damascus: Dar al-Fikr, 1995).

[385] For the siege and subsequent execution of adult males of the Qurayzah tribe in upper Medina in year 5 AH, see concise overview with full list of sources given in Karim Crow, *Facing One Qiblah* (Singapore: Pustaka Nasional, 2005)—Appendix 'Jewish Tribes in Madīnah'.

[386] *Jāmi' al-Bayān* X p. 37.

[387] Consult e.g. Robert G. Hoyland, 'Arab kings, Arab tribes and the beginnings of Arab historical memory in late Roman epigraphy', in Hannah M Cotton et al., eds, *From Hellenism to Islam. Cultural and Linguistic Change in the Roman Near East* (Cambridge: Cambridge University Press, 2009) pp.374–400; R. G. Hoyland, *Arabia and the Arabs* (London: 2001), on pp. 96–103; and Hoyland, 'Epigraphy and the Emergence of Arab Identity', in P. Sijpesteign et al., eds, *From Andalusia to Khurasan: Documents from the Medieval Islamic World* (Leiden: Brill, 2007) pp. 219–42.

[388] See this invaluable compilation by the erudite Andalusian scholar Muhammad b. ʿAli b. Ahmad b. Ḥudaydah al-Ansari (d. 783 AH/ 1381 CE), *al-Miṣbāḥ al-Muḍī fī Kuttāb al-Nabī al-Ummī wa Rusulihi ilá Mulūk al-Arḍ min ʿArabī wa ʿAjamī*, edited by al-Shaykh Muhammad ʿAzim al-Din (2nd revised edn, Beirut: 'Alam al-Kutub, 1985; in 2 vols). The learned editor made use of Professor M. Hamidullah's fundamental study *Majmū'at al-Wathā'iq al-Siyāsīyah*, and supplemented significant references and relevant documentation drawn from the wealth of Hadith literature, with excellent indices. Certain textual details concerning these letters are to be found only in *al-Miṣbāḥ al-Muḍī*.

[389] W. Robertson Smith, *The Religion of the Semites* [1889] (2nd edn 1894; rpr. New York: Meridan, 1956) pp. 79–80. Observe the archaic meaning still reflected in classical Muslim legal usage of the term *al-salam = al-istislām* 'a prisoner captured apart from war'. / Palmyrene was one branch of old Arabic along with Nabataean, as well as the dialect of the Hijaz—the basis of Qur'anic Arabic.

[390] Personal communication in 1999, from my respected teacher Professor ʿAbbas in the year before his death in Amman; may God show him mercy.

[391] W. Robertson Smith, *Religion of the Semites* p. 20.

[392] Consult e.g. Subhash C. Inamdar, *Muhammad and the Rise of Islam: The Creation of Group Identity* (Madison. CT: Psychosocial Press, 2001), which provides a psycho-social model for the moulding of groups and their socio-historical impact on individuals and society.

CHAPTER 10

[393] 'Abd Allah al-Khatib al-Tabrizi, *Mishkāt al-Maṣābīḥ*, edited by Muhammad Nasir al-Din al-Albani, 2nd edn (Beirut: al-Maktab al-Islami, 1399/1979), vol. 2, hadith no. 2724.

[394] Muslim b. Hajjaj al-Nishapuri, *Mukhtasar Ṣaḥīḥ Muslim*, edited by M Nasir al-Din al-Albani, 2nd edn (Beirut: Dar al-Maktab al-Islami, 1404/1984), p.11, hadith no. 34.

[395] For further detail on the principle of *ḥisbah* (promotion of good and

prevention of evil) and the manner in which it is conducted see M. H. Kamali, *Freedom of Expression in Islam* (Cambridge: Islamic Texts Society, 1997), pp. 28–34.

[396] Tabrizi, *Mishkat*, vol.1, hadith no. 46.

[397] Ibid., vol.3, hadith no. 5097.

[398] Shihab al-Din al-Alusi, *Rīh al-M'ānī fī Tafsīr al-Qur'ān al-'Aẓīm* (Beirut: Dar al-Turath al-'Arabi, nd.), vol. XV, no. 117.

[399] For a roundup of opinion and references to Sayyid Qutb, Mustafa al-Siba'i, 'Abd al-Hakim Hasan al-'Ili, Ahmad Yusri, and Wahbah al-Zuhaili see Mohammad Hashim Kamali, *The Dignity of Man: an Islamic Perspective,* (Cambridge: Islamic Texts Society, 2002), pp. 1–2.

[400] For details on the subject of rights and duties in Islamic law, see M.H. Kamali, 'An Analysis of Rights in Islamic Law', *The American Journal of Islamic Social Sciences* 10 (1993), pp. 178–201. A summary of this examination can also be found in idem. *Freedom of Expression in Islam*, pp. 16–24.

[401] See my views on this and other aspects of the human rights discourse in Kamali, *The Dignity of Man*, pp. xv-xvi.

[402] Jack Donolly, 'Human Rights and Human Dignity: An Analytic Critique of non-Western Conceptions of Human Rights', *The American Political Science Review* 76 (June 1982), p. 304.

[403] I shall not engage into details here but merely point out that textbook writers number the *ḍarūriyyāt* into five, hence the phrase *al- ḍarūriyyāt al-khamsah*, to which the seventh century jurist Shihab al-Din al-Qarafi added a sixth, namely *al-'irḍ* (honour). Since this is a valid addition and has a Qur'anic basis, I refer to them as the six universals, namely of life, intellect, religion, family, property, and honour. See for details M.H. Kamali, *An Introduction to Shari'ah* (Kuala Lumpur: Ilmiah Publishers, 2006), ch. 6 'Goals and Purposes *(maqāṣid)* of Shari'ah: History and Methodology', pp. 115–33, at 118. A revised and enhanced edition of this book is due to be published by Oneworld Publication, Oxford, U.K.

[404] Cf. Dirk Bakker, *Man in the Qur'an* (Amsterdam: Drukkerij, 1965), p. 127 and passim. Bakker also quotes in support C. Snouk Hurgronje and Richard Bell. He has on the other hand discussed Montgomery Watt, H. Berkeland and others that variously characterised God-man relationship with mercy, guidance, creative power, and dominion etc.

[405] Cf. Muddathir 'Abd al-Rahim, '*Anmat al-Ḥubb fi'l-Qur'ān al-Karīm: Naẓrah Ijmāliyyah*', conference paper presented to the International Conference on 'al-Ḥubb fi'l-Qur'ān al-Karīm', (Manifestations of Love in the Noble Qur'an), organised by the Royal Academy of Jordan, 4–6 September 2007, p.6f.

[406] Cf., *Sūrat Al-Baqarah*, 2:263; *Al-A'rāf*, 7:156; *Al-Ḥijr*, 15:56; *Al-Zumar*, 39: 53 and passim.

[407] *Al-Baqarah* 2:164; *Āl 'Imrān*, 3:18; *Al-Nisā'*, 4:162; *Al-Ḥajj*, 22:54; *Al-Rūm*, 30:28; *Al-Mujādilah*, 58:11; *Fāṭir*, 35:88; *Ṣād*, 38:43; *Al-Zumar*, 39:9,18.

[408] Cf., *Luqmān*, 31:20; *Fāṭir*, 35:13; *Al-Mulk*, 67:15.

[409] *Al-A'rāf*, 7:10, 30; *Ibrāhīm*, 14:34 and *Al-Qaṣaṣ*, 28:77.

[410] Muhammad b.. Isma'il al-Bukhari, *Ṣaḥīḥ al-Bukhari*, *Kitāb al-Riqāq*, hadith no.6502.

[411] The Arabic terms used in the Qur'an are *al-mu'tadīn, al-ẓalimīn, al-mufsidīn, al-mustakbirīn, al- fakhūr, al-kāfirīn, al-kha'inīn, al-musrifīn* (*Al-Baqarah*, 2:195; *Al-Shūra*, 42:40; *Al-Baqarah*, 2:205; *Al-Naḥl*, 16:23; *Al-Nisā'*, 4:36; *Al-A'rāf*, 7:32; *Al-Anfāl*, 8:58; and *Al-An'ām*, 6:141 respectively).

[412] Al-Qaradawi's discussion of this and other related verses in the Qur'an leads him to the conclusion that Islam recognises two levels of fraternity, namely human fraternity (*al-ikhā' al-insāni*) and fraternity in faith (*al-ikhā' al-dīnī*). The latter does not weaken the former, rather it substantiates and endorses the wider fraternity of humankind: Yusuf al-Qaradawi, *al-Khasā'is al-'Ammah li'l-Islām* (Cairo: Maktabah Wahbah, 1409/1989), p. 84.

[413] From the Prophet's Farewell Sermon, Muslim, *Mukhtasar Ṣaḥīḥ Muslim*, p.186, hadith no. 707.

[414] *Āl 'Imrān*, 3:195; *Al-Naḥl*, 16:97.

[415] J. Weeramantry, *Islamic Jurisprudence: an International Perspective* (Basingstoke, U.K: Macmillan, 1988), p. 64.

[416] *Al-Anbiyā'*, 21:20; *Al-Baqarah*, 2:187.

[417] Al-Tabrizi, *Mishkāt*, vol.2, hadith no.4998.

[418] Muslim, *Mukhtasar Ṣaḥīḥ Muslim*, p. 476, hadith no.1794.

[419] Muslim, *Mukhtasar Ṣaḥīḥ Muslim*, p. 484, hadith no.1833.

[420] Al-Tabrizi, *Mishkāt*, vol.2, hadith no. 3665.

[421] Muhammad ibn Yazid al-Qazwini ibn Maja, *Sunan ibn Mājah* (Istanbul: Cagri Yayinlari, 1401/1981), *kitāb al-fitān; bāb 'amr bi'l-ma'rūf wa nahī 'an al-munkar.*

[422] For further detail on *ḍarūriyyat* also see M. H. Kamali 'Maqasid al-Shari'ah, the Objectives of Islamic Law', *Islamic Studies* 38 (1999), pp. 193–209. On the concept of *'iṣmah* see Baber Johansen, Contingency in a Sacred Law: Legal and Ethical Norms in the Muslim Fiqh (Leiden: Brill, 1999). For the emergence and development of concepts see also Recep Senturk, '*Ādamiyyah* and '*Iṣmah*: The Contested Relationship between Humanity and Human Rights in the Classical Islamic Law', *Turkish J. of Islamic Studies,* 8(2002), pp. 39–70.

[423] *Al-Tawbah*, 9:5 (a likely reference to the pagans of Mecca), and *Al-Anfāl*, 8:39 (permits fighting to end mischief and oppression).

[424] Recep Senturk, 'Sociology of Rights', (see the next footnote), p. 16.

[425] Cf. Abu al-Hassan Burhan al-Din al-Marghinani (d. 593 H/1296C.E), *al-Hidāyah Sharḥ Bidāyat* al-*Mubtadī,* edited by Muhammad Tamir et al. (Cairo: Dar al-Salam, 1420/2000), vol. II, no. 852; see also Recep Senturk, 'Sociology

of Rights: I Am Therefore I Have Rights: Human Rights in Islam Between Universalistic and Communalistic Perspectives', produced by the Berkeley Electronic Press, 2005: http:www.bepress.com/mwjhr/vol.12/iss1/art11.

[426] Abi Bakr Muammad b. Ahmad al-Sarakhsi, *Usūl al-Sarakhsi*, edited by Abu'l-Wafa al-Afghani (Istanbul: Kahraman Yay, 1984, 86).

[427] Ibid., 333–4.

[428] Abu al-Hassan Burhan al-Din al-Marghinani, *The Hedaya or Guide: a commentary on the Mussulman laws,* trans. Charles Hamilton (Karachi: Daru'l-Ishaat, 1989), II, 221.

[429] Muhammad Amin ibn 'Abidin, *Hashīyah ibn 'Abidin* (Cairo: Mustafa al-Babi al-Halabi, 1386/1966), vol. V, 58.

[430] Cf. Senturk, 'The Sociology of Rights', p. 16.

[431] The present writer has written extensively on the fundamental rights of the individual in Islam. See for details Mohammad Hashim Kamali, *The Right to Life, Security, Privacy and Ownership in Islam*, 2008, pp. xi+318, Idem, *The Right to Education, Work and Welfare in Islam*, 2010, pp, x and 294 and Idem, *Citizenship and Accountability of Government: An Islamic Perspective,* 2011, pp. x and 321. All three books published by Cambridge: Islamic Text Society.

CHAPTER 11

[432] *Sūrat Al-Baqarah*, 2:101, 144, 145; *Āl 'Imrān*, 3:19, 20, 100, 186, 187; *Al-Nisā'*, 4:47, 131; *Al-Mā'idah*, 5:5, 57; *Al-Ḥadīd*, 57:16; *Al-Muddaththir*, 74:31; *Al-Bayyinah*, 98:4.

[433] *Al-Baqarah*, 2: 121, 146; *Al-An'ām*, 6:20, 89, 114; *Al-Ra'd*, 13:36; *Al-Naml*, 27:52; *Al-'Ankabūt*, 29:47; *Al-Jāthiyah*, 45:16.

[434] *Āl 'Imrān*, 3:23; *Al-Nisā'*, 4: 44, 51.

[435] *Fāṭir*, 35:32; *Al-Shūrā*, 42:14.

[436] *Al-Ra'd*, 13:43.

[437] *Yūnus*, 10:94.

[438] *Al-Naḥl*, 16:43; *Al-Anbiyā'*, 21:7. Though *al-dhikr* is one of the names of the Qur'an, the pre-modern exegetes have generally identified *ahl al-dhikr* with either *ahl al-tawrah* or *ahl al-injīl* or both. See Isma'il b. 'Umar Ibn Kathir, *Tafsīr al-Qur'ān al-'Aẓīm* (Cairo: Matba'ah al-Istiqamah, 1375/1956), *Āl 'Imrān*, 3: 174, comments on *Al-Anbiyā'*, 21:7.

[439] This occurs nine times in the Qur'an only in the Medinan surahs (*Al-Baqarah*, 2:113 (twice), 120; *Āl 'Imrān*, 3: 67; *Al-Mā'idah*, 5: 18, 51, 64, 82; *Al-Tawbah*, 9:30).

[440] This occurs three times in *Sūrat Al-Baqarah* (*Al-Baqarah*, 2:111, 135, 140).

[441] This occurs ten times, mostly in the Medinan surahs (*Al-Baqarah*, 2: 62; *Al-Nisā'*, 4: 46, 160; *Al-Mā'idah,* 5: 41, 44, 69; *Al-An'ām*, 6: 146; *Al-Naḥl*, 16:118; *Al-Ḥajj*, 22:17; *Al-Jumu'ah*, 62:6).

[442] The phrase *banū/banī Isrā'īl* (the Children of Israel) is mentioned in the Qur'an forty times. The usage of this phrase is quite different from that of the above mentioned terms. The phrase *banū Isrā'īl* seems to indicate the Jewish race, whereas the term *yahūd* and its derivatives are generally used to address people of Jewish faith. These latter terms seem to have a pejorative connotation. See for further discussion, Omer Faruk Harman, 'Tefsir Geleneginde Yahudilere Baki'j' in his *Muslumanlar ve Diger Din Mensuplari* (Ankara: Turkiye Dinler Tarihi Dernegi Yayinlar, 2004), pp. 119–20. It is also interesting to note that the title of one of the Qur'anic surahs in the late Meccan period is *Banū Isrā'īl* (surah 17).

[443] Almost all of them occur in the Medinan surahs (*Al-Baqarah*, 2:62, 111, 113 (twice), 120, 135, 140; *Al-Mā'idah*, 5: 14, 18, 51, 69, 82; *Al-Tawbah*, 9:30; *Al-Ḥajj*, 22:17). In one place the term *naṣrāni* is mentioned (*Āl 'Imrān*, 3: 67).

[444] *Muḥammad*, 47: *Let the People of the Gospel judge by what Allah has revealed therein...*

[445] *Āl 'Imrān*, 3:52; *Al-Mā'idah*, 5:111, 112; *Al-Ṣaff*, 61:14 (twice).

[446] Sabeans: *Al-Baqarah*, 2:62; *Al-Mā'idah*, 5:69; *Al-Ḥajj*, 22:17. And Zoroastrians: *Al-Ḥajj*, 22:17.

[447] Malik b. Anas, *al-Muwatta'* (Istanbul: Çagri, 1992), 1: 244. Only the Zahiri school of thought holds the view that marriage with a Zoroastrian woman is legitimate. See Abu Muhammad 'All b. Ahmad Ibn Hazm, *al-Muhalla bi 'l-Athar* (Beirut: Dar al-Fikr, n.d.), 5: 413–4. Although the Hanafi jurist Abu Yusuf Ya'qub b. Ibrahim (d. 182/798) includes the Zoroastrians among *ahl al-dhimmah,* he does not see marrying their women to be legitimate. See his *Kitāb al-Kharaj* (Cairo: n.p., 1990), pp. 122, 128–30.

[448] *Al-An'ām*, 6:156: *Lest you should say: The Book was sent down only upon two parties* (*ṭā'ifatayn*) *before us, and we have indeed been heedless of their study.*

[449] *Tawrah* is mentioned eighteen times in the Qur'an; almost all occurring in the Medinan surahs (the single exception is the verse *Al-A'rāf*, 7:157 in the late Meccan *Surat Al-A'rāf*).

[450] *Zabūr* is mentioned three times, two of which are related to the Prophet David ﷺ. The plural form of the term *zabūr* (pl. *zubur)* occurs in seven places. Interestingly, most of these surahs are Meccan. Moreover, the late Dr Hamidullah thinks that the statements *zubur al-awwalīn* in *Al-Shu'arā*, 26:196 and *al-ṣuḥuf al-ūlā* in *Al-A'lā*, 87:18 refer to the Hindus' sacred texts. See Muhammad Hamidullah, *Le Saint Coran* (Beirut: Mu'assasat al-Risalah, n.d.), 2: 492, 804. However, this does not seem very plausible.

[451] *Injīl* is mentioned twelve times in the Qur'an; almost all occurring in the Medinan surahs (again, the single exception is in the late Meccan surah, *Al-A'rāf*, 7:157). It is also important to note that the Qur'an does not use the plural form 'Gospels'.

[452] *Al-A'lā*, 87:18. There are also some Prophetic traditions which say that

God sent *suhuf* (sheets) to the Prophets Adam (Adam) and to Shith who was a son of the Prophet Adam and Prophet Enoch (Idris) عليهم السلام. See Abu Hatim Muhammad b. Hibban al-Taymi, *Ṣaḥīḥ Ibn Ḥibbān bi Tartīb Ibn Balbān,* edited by Shu'ayb al-Arna'ut (Beirut: Mu'asasat al-Risalah, 1414/1993), 2: 76. See also, Abu Ja'far Muhammad b. Jarir al-Tabari, *Tarīkh al-Rusul wa al-Mulūk* (Beirut: Dar al-Kutub al-'Ilmiyyah, 1407 ah), 1: 96, 102.

[453] *Al-A'lā,* 87:19.

[454] Harman, 'Tafsir Geleneginde Yahudilere Bakis', p. 119.

[455] It is narrated that the Prophet Muhammad ﷺ met three of them, namely Ya'ish and Jabr from Banu Hadrami, and Bal'am whom he taught the Qur'an. Abu Ja'far Muhammad b. Jarir al-Tabari, *Jamī'al-Bayān 'an Ta'wīl Ayy al-Qur'ān* (Beirut: Dar al-Fikr 1988), 8: 177–8; 16:103.

[456] The majority of Christians lived in the tribes of Bakr b. Wa'il, Tayy, Khath'am, Kalb, Taghlib, etc. See Levent Ozturk, *Islam Toplumunda Birarada Yaşama Tecrubesi* (Istanbul: insan Pub., 1995), p. 25.

[457] Not only foreign Christians but also a few native (converted) Christians were warned by the Meccans not to interfere in the local people's religious life. For example, Abu Sufyan advised Umayyah b. Abi 'l-Salt not to lead laymen away from their forefathers' beliefs. It is also noted that when Zayd b. 'Amr b. Nufayl refused to accept idolatry, his brothers tortured him and sent him away from Mecca. See 'Abd al-Malik Ibn Hisham, *al- Sīrah al-Nabawiyyah* (Cairo: n.p., 1971), I: 246; Muhammad Rashid Rida, *al-Waḥy al-Muḥammadi* (Cairo: n.p., 1960), p. 75. It is also narrated that 'Amrah, the daughter of Mu'awiyah b. Mughirah b. Abi al-'As, married a Christian, Abu Najdah. Consequently, she was severely criticised by the Meccans. See Ahmad b Yahya b. Jabir al-Baladhuri, *Ansāb al-Ashrāf* edited by M. Schloessinger (Jerusalem: n.p., 1938), IV B: 169-170.

[458] According to historians, when the Prophet ﷺ came to Medina, the number of Jews there was around four thousand. See Muhammed Hamidullah, 'Medine'de Kurulan ilk Islam Devletinin Esas Tejkilat Yapisi ve Hz. Peygamber' in Vecdi Akyuz, ed., Vazettigi Yeryuzundeki ilk Yazili Anayasa', *Islam Anayasa Hukuku,* (Istanbul: Beyan Publishing House, 1995), p. 95.

[459] See Muhammed Hamidullah, *Islam Peygamberi,* trans. Salih Tug (Istanbul: Irfan Publishing House, 1990), 1: 187.

[460] See for example, *Maryam*, 19:1-72.

[461] *Is he (to be accounted equal with him) who relies on a clear proof from his Lord, and a witness from Him recites it, and before it was the Book of Moses, an example and a mercy?... Hūd,* 11:17.

[462] See *Muḥammad,* 47:57–9.

[463] This verse is the only explicit Biblical quotation (Psalms, 37:29) in the Qur'an.

[464] See *Al-An'ām*, 6: 43; *Al-Anbiyā',* 21:7.

[465] See *Maryam*, 19:94.

[466] See al-Tabari, *Jamīʿ al-Bayān*, 11: 16–20.

[467] Ismaʿil b. ʿUmar Ibn Kathir, *Tafsīr al-Qur'ān al-'Aẓīm*, 2: 221, comments on *Al-Raʿd*, 13:39.

[468] See *Sūrat Fāṭir*, 35:31; *Al-Aʿrāf*, 7:157. See *Al-Naml*, 27:76.

[469] There is another verse, *kāffatan* (*Sabā'*, 34:28), which shows that the message of the Qur'an and the Prophethood of Muhammad ﷺ are universal; his message is neither time-bound nor confined to any particular cultural milieu.

[470] See Ibn Kathir, *Tafsīr al-Qur'ān al-'Aẓīm*, 3: 415–6, comments on *Al-ʿAnkabūt*, 29:46.

[471] Dr Muhammad Hamidullah (d. 2002) and some Western scholars have called this pact the Medinan Constitution. The articles of the pact do not occur in toto in Hadith collections. According to Hamidullah, there are 52 articles, whereas Julius Wellhausen (d. 1918) believes that there are 47 articles. In addition to this, Hamidullah says that the Jews participated in this pact after the Muslims. Although there is some disagreement about the exact number of articles and content of the pact, it is generally accepted as an authentic document by a vast body of scholars. Unfortunately, however, the pact did not endure. See Hamidullah, 'Medine'de Kurulan ilk Islam Devletinin Esas Tejkilat ve Hz Peygamber'in Vazettigi Yeryuzundeki ilk Yazili Anayasa', pp. 100–4; Ahmet Bostanci, *Hz. Peygamber'in Gayri Muslimlerle Iliçkileri* (Istanbul: Ragbet Publishing House, 2001), pp. 31–6.

[472] It is narrated that the Prophet ﷺ preferred to follow the People of the Book instead of Meccan pagans in matters where there were no specific religious commandments. See Ahmad b. Hanbal, *Musnad Aḥmad, Bidāyatu Musnad* ʿAbd Allah b. ʿAbbas.

[473] Muhammad b. Ismaʿil al-Bukhari, *Ṣaḥīḥ al-Bukhārī, Kitāb al-Ṣiyām, Bāb Ṣiyām Yawm 'Ashūra'*.

[474] *Sūrat Al-Mā'idah*, 5:5. See also for a detailed analysis Davut Ayduz, *Tarih Boyunca Dinlerarasi Diyalog* (Istanbul: Ijik Pub., 2004), pp. 105–8.

[475] Muhammad b. Ismaʿil al-Bukhari, *Ṣaḥīḥ al-Bukhārī, Kitāb al-Anbiyā', Bāb mā Dhukira 'an Banī Isrā'īl*. It is also mentioned in ʿAbd al-Razzaq's *Muṣannaf*. There are various legal implications of this statement. According to some scholars, this hadith indicates a neutral status (neither forbidden nor recommended). However, many other scholars explain this hadith as 'there is no need to narrate from the Children of Israel'. ʿAli b. Muhammad Ibn Hajar al-ʿAsqalani, *Fatḥ al-Bārī Sharḥ Ṣaḥīḥ al-Bukhārī* (Cairo: Dar al-Fikr 1988), 10: 261. Regarding the belief in the existence of authentic words of God in the Torah and Gospels, it can be gauged from the fact that some Muslim scholars have discussed whether one should perform ablution before touching them. Abu al-Qasim ʿAbd al-Karim b. Muhammad al-Rafiʿi, *Fatḥ al-ʿAzīz*

Sharḥ al-Wājiz (Beirut: Dar al-Fikr, n.d.), 2: 108; Muhammad b. Salih b. Yusuf, *al-Inṣāf, Bāb Nawāqid al-Wuḍū'*, I: 364, <http://www.al-islam.com >. Furthermore, the notion of *shar' man qablanā* is worth mentioning. According to this rule, if the Qur'an and the Prophetic traditions (*aḥādith*) are silent on an issue, and this issue is explained in the scriptures of the Jews or Christians, Muslims should take them into consideration. 'Abd al-Wahhab al-Khallaf, *'Ilm Usūl al-Fiqh* (Istanbul: Eda Pub., 1991), pp. 92–3.

[476] Muslim b. al-Hajjaj, *Ṣaḥīḥ Muslim, Kitāb al-Faḍā'il, Bāb Faḍā'il 'Isa 'alayh al-salām.*

[477] Ibid.

[478] Muhammad b. Isma'il al-Bukhari, *Ṣaḥīḥ al-Bukhārī, Kitāb al-Jizyah wa 'l-Muwada'ah, Bāb Ikhrāj al-Yahūd min Jazīrat al-'Arab*, there are many reports in Hadith literature concerning the Prophet's visit to Bayt al-Midras.

[479] See *Sūrat Al-Baqarah*, 2:75, 79; *Al-Nisā'*, 4: 46, 48; *Al-Mā'idah*, 5:13, 16, 41, 45.

[480] Muslims are commanded to direct their faces to Mecca (Ka'bah) during their prayer, to fast in the month of Ramadan, to recite the *adhān* (call for prayer) to inform people about the time of prayer, and to start to attend regularly a Friday prayer. But these should not be seen merely as a tactic used by the Prophet ﷺ in order to achieve what he wanted.

[481] Such as their claim to be chosen by God, their love of life and their cowardice when called on to fight, their mocking God's rule and their frequent collaboration with hypocrites and idolaters against the Muslims.

[482] See *Sūrat Al-Nisā'*, 4:171–2; *Al-Mā'idah*, 5:17, 72–5, 77, 116. See *Al-Tawbah*, 9:31.

[483] See *Al-Baqarah*, 2:213.

[484] In his interpretation of this verse (*Al-Ḥajj*, 22:17) Mahmud b. 'Umar al-Zamakhshari is extremely exclusivist: 'There are five religions, four of which belong to Satan and the one to the Compassionate.' He did not consider idolaters to be a religious community. See Jar Allah Mahmud b. 'Umar al-Zamakhshari, *al-Kashshāf 'an Haqā'iq Ghawāmiḍ al-Tanzīl wa 'Oyoon al-'Aqawīl fi Wujooh al-Ta'wīl* (Beirut: Dar Ihya' al-Turath al-'Arabi, 1997), *3: 149.*

[485] The names of these individuals are: 'Abd Allah b. Salam, Najashi (Negus of Abyssinia), Tha'labah b. Shu'bah, Asad and Usayd, the two sons of Ka'b, Sa'yah b. 'Amr, Asad b. 'Ubayd. See al-Tabari, *Jamī' al-Bayān,* 3:52, comments on *Al-Baqarah*, 2:62. Concerning the occasion of revelation of this verse (*Al-Baqarah*, 2:62), Ibn Kathir notes that it was revealed due to Salman al-Farisi's inquiry about his pious Christian friends. According to Ibn Kathir, from the time of Moses عليه السلام to that of Jesus عليه السلام Judaism prevailed; from the time of Jesus عليه السلام to that of Muhammad ﷺ, Christianity prevailed, from the time of Muhammad ﷺ to the end of the world Islam will prevail. See Ibn Kathir, *Tafsīr al-Qur'ān al-'Aẓīm*, 1:71–2, comments on *Al-Baqarah*, 2:62.

[486] Ibid., 1: 171.

[487] See al-Tabari, *Jamī' al-Bayān,* 2: 155.

[488] See al-Tabari, *Jamī' al-Bayān* and Ibn Kathir, *Tafsīr al-Qur'ān al-'Aẓīm,* comments on *Al-Baqarah,* 2:62; *Al-Mā'idah,* 5:69 and *Āl 'Imrān,* 3:113.

[489] See al-Tabari, *Jamī' al-Bayān,* comments on *Al-Baqarah,* 2:62; *Al-Mā'idah,* 5:69 and *Āl 'Imrān,* 3:113.

[490] *Āl 'Imrān,* 3: 75 also offers an interesting example: *Among the People of the Book there is he who, if you trust him with a weight of treasure, will return it to you. And among them there is he who, if you trust him with a piece of gold (dīnār), he will not return it to you unless you keep standing over him.*

[491] Nasir al-Din 'Abd Allah b. 'Umar al-Baydawi, *Anwār al-Tanzīl wa Asrār al-Ta'wīl* (Beirut: Dar al-Kutub al-'Ilmiyyah, 1988), 1: 274, comments on *Al-Mā'idah,* 5: 66.

[492] See Fakhr al-Din Muhammad b. 'Umar al-Razi, *Mafātih al-Ghayb* (Beirut: Dar al-Fikr 1981), 12: 11, commenting on *Al-Mā'idah,* 5: 43–7.

[493] Ibn Kathir, *Tafsīr al-Qur'ān al-'Aẓīm,* comments on *Al-Mā'idah,* 5:43–7. Interestingly, the Qur'an also makes a fine distinction between the Jews and the Christians in *Al-Mā'idah,* 5:82: *You will find the most vehement of mankind in hostility to those who believe (to be) the Jews and the idolaters. And you will find the nearest of them in affection to those who believe (to be) those who say: Lo! We are Christians. That is because there are among them priests and monks, and because they are not proud.* On the basis of this verse, al-Zamakhshari says: 'Since the Jews are mentioned before idolaters, this shows that they go even farther.' Al-Zamakhshari, in *al-Kashshāf,* comments on *Al-Mā'idah,* 5:82. God's characterisation of the Christians as tender-hearted people who are moved to tears when they hear the Qur'an, however, is in accordance with what is reported concerning the Negus of Abyssinia or the envoy of Abyssinia who converted to Islam. Al-Tabari, on the other hand, says that this verse would be applicable to all those who bear these characteristics. See al-Tabari, *Jamī'al-Bayān,* comments on *Al-Mā'idah,* 5: 82.

[494] See Ibn Kathir, *Tafsīr al-Qur'ān al-'Aẓīm,* comments on *Al-Baqarah,* 2:68. They generally think that faith in God necessarily entails belief in Muhammad ﷺ because God has made this incumbent upon mankind.

[495] Al-Tabari, *Jamī'al-Bayān,* comments on *Āl 'Imrān,* 3:4.

[496] Ibid., comments on *Al-Mā'idah,* 5:19. al-Baydawi, *Anwār al-Tanzīl, Al-Baqarah,* 2:472, comments on *Al-Mā'idah,* 5:19.

[497] In line with this verse, *Āl 'Imrān,* 3:110 describes Muslims as the best community.

[498] There is another verse (*Āl 'Imrān,* 3: 61) in this surah which is called the verse of *mubāhalah* (trial by prayer). On the occasion of a dispute between the Prophet ﷺ and a deputation of the Christians of Najran who maintained that Jesus عليه السلام was the Son of God and therefore God incarnate, the Prophet ﷺ

summoned them together with their families to participate in and then invoke God's curse on those who lie. Although they refused to invoke God's curse on the liars proposed by the Prophet ﷺ, he concluded with them a treaty guaranteeing all their civic and religious freedoms. See al-Baydawi, *Anwār al-Tanzīl,* 1: 263, comments on *Āl 'Imrān*, 3:61; Muhammad Asad, *The Message of the Qur'an* (Gibraltar: Dar al-Andalus, 1980), p. 76, comments on *Āl 'Imrān*, 3:61.

[499] See Tabari, *Jamī'al-Bayān,* 6: 484, comments on *Āl 'Imrān*, 3:61.

[500] Abu 'Abd Allah Muhammad b. Ahmad al-Qurtubi, *al-Jamī' li Aḥkām al-Qur'ān* (Beirut: n. p., 1985), 4: 105, comments on *Āl 'Imrān*, 3:64.

[501] See *Āl 'Imrān*, 3:67.

[502] *O ye who believe take not the Jews and the Christians for your friends and protectors: they are but allies and protectors to each other. And he amongst you that turns to them (for protector) is of them. Verily Allah guideth not a people unjust.* (*Al-Mā'idah*, 5:51).

[503] Al-Baydawi, *Anwār al-Tanzīl,* 1: 270, comments on *Al-Mā'idah*, 5:51. It should be noted that this did not prevent the Muslim rulers from appointing both Jews and Christians to important positions in their realm.

[504] See for instance, Bediuzzaman Said Nursi, *Munazarat* (Istanbul: Yeni Asya, 1993), p. 32.

[505] Ibid., p. 71.

[506] *Jizyah* is no more and no less than an exemption tax in lieu of military service and in compensation for a covenant of protection accorded to such citizens by the Islamic state. See Asad, *The Message of the Qur'an,* p. 262.

[507] *Al-Zumar*, 39:53: *Say: O My slaves ('ibādī), who have been prodigal to their own hurt! Despair not of the mercy of Allah, Who forgives all sins. Lo! He is the Forgiving, the Merciful.* It will be noted that this goes way beyond the view that there are some minimal requirements for salvation: belief in God, in the Last Day, and acting righteously. This seems to suggest salvation for all, even for those who do not believe in God and the Last Day and do not care to act righteously.

[508] Quoted from Adnan Arslan 'Dini Çogulculuk Problemine Çozurn Onerisi', in *Muslumanlar ve Diger Din Mensuplari* (Ankara: Turkiye Dinler Tarihi Dernegi Pub. 2004), p. 348. The other verses on which Jar Allah frequently places great emphasis are: *Al-Mā'idah*, 5:117–8; *Al-Shūrā*, 42:5; *Qāf*, 50:29. Furthermore, he argues that hellfire is not eternal. See ibid., passim. Jalal al-Din Muhammad al-Rumi (d. 672/1273), Muhyi 'l-Din Muhammad b. 'Ali Ibn 'Arabi (d. 638/1240), Abu Sa'id Abu 'l-Khayr (d. 440/1049), Qutb al-Din 'Abd al-Haqq b. Ibrahim Ibn Sab'in (d. 669/1270), 'Abd al-Karim b. Hawazin al-Qushayri (d. 465/1072) are most frequently cited in this context.

[509] See Muhammad Rashid Rida, *Tafsīr al-Manār* (Beirut: Dar al-Ma'rifah, n.d.), 4: 71–74 commenting on *Āl 'Imrān*, 3:113.

[510] Kate Zebiri, *Muslims and Christians: Face to Face* (Oxford: Oneworld,

1997), p. 163. Some Muslim and non-Muslim intellectuals prefer to use some Sufis' arguments to support religious pluralism. Jalal al-Din Muhammad al-Rumi (d. 672/1273), Muhyi 'l-Din Muhammad b. 'Ali Ibn 'Arabi (d. 638/1240), Abu Sa'id Abu 'l-Khayr (d. 440/1049), Qutb al-Din 'Abd al-Haqq b. Ibrahim Ibn Sab'in (d. 669/1270), 'Abd al-Karim b. Hawazin al-Qushayri (d. 465/1072) are most frequently cited in this context. However, Keller's recent work proves the contrary. See Carl A. Keller, 'Perception of Other Religions in Sufism' in Jacques Waardenburg, ed., *Muslim Perceptions of Other Religions: A Historical Survey* (New York-Oxford: Oxford University Press, 1999), pp. 181–4.

[511] See Fazlur Rahman, *Major Themes of the Qur'an* (Minneapolis: Bibliotheca Islamica, 1991), pp. 165–7.

[512] See Suleyman Atej, 'Cennet Kimsenin Tekelinde Degildir' in *Islami Araçtirmalar Dergisi,* 3 (1989), pp. 7–24; Mehmet Okuyan-Mustafa Ozturk, 'Kur'an Verilerine Gore Otekinin Konumu' in Cafer Sadik Yaren, ed., *Islam ve Oteki* (Istanbul: Kaknus, 2001), pp. 163–216.

[513] Said Nursi, *Emirdag Lahikasi - I* (Istanbul: Envar, 1992), p. 206.

[514] See Said Nursi, *Şualar* (Istanbul: Envar, 1993), p. 587; There are some reports which say that at the end of time, Jesus (عليه السلام will come and act in accordance with the holy law of Islam or that Jesus عليه السلام will come and perform prayer *(salāh)* behind the *Mahdi.* See Ibn Majah, *Sunan, Kitāb al-Fitan, Bāb Fitnat al-Dajjāl wa Khurūj 'Isa ibn Maryam.* Nonetheless, Nursi does not talk about the Christians' complete conversion to Islam; rather, he thinks that the current Christianity will be purified in the face of reality, it will cast off its superstitions and unite with the truths of Islam. According to Nursi, this will be a transformation into a sort of Islam. See Said Nursi, *Şualar,* p. 587.

[515] See Said Nursi, *Sozler* (Istanbul: Sozler, 1993), p. 396.

[516] Thomas, Michel, 'Bediuzzaman Said Nursi'nin Dujuncesinde Musluman-Hiristiyan Diyalogu ve Ijbirligi', *International Bediuzzaman Said Nursi Conference,* Istanbul (September 1998).

[517] See Zeki Saritoprak and Sidney Griffith, 'Fethullah Gulen and the 'People of the Book': A Voice from Turkey for Interfaith Dialogue' in *The Muslim World,* vol. 95, no. 3 (2005), p. 333.

[518] See ibid., p. 334.

[519] See Selfuk Camci-Kudret Unal, *Hoşgoru ve Diyalog Iklimi* (Izmir: Merkur, 1999), p. 156.

[520] See Zebiri, Muslims and Christians: Face to Face, p. 166.

[521] See ibid., pp. 117–9.

[522] Muhammad Ibn Ishaq (d. 151/768), Abu 'Uthman 'Amr b. Bahr al-Jahiz (d. 255/868), 'Abd Allah b. Muslim Ibn Qutaybah (d. 276/889), Muhammad b. al-Tayyib al-Baqillani (d. 403/1013), 'Ali b. Ahmad Ibn Hazm (d. 456/1064), Imam al-Haramayn 'Abd al-Malik b. 'Abd Allah al- Juwayni (d. 478/1085), 'Abd al-Rahman b. Muhammad Ibn Khaldun (d. 808/1406) are exceptions.

[523] Concerning the occasion of revelation of this verse, it is mentioned that when the Medinan Arabs had no children, they vowed that if God gave them children they would give them to the Jews who would educate them religiously. And when they had children, they did this and gave their children to the Jews. Then the Prophet ﷺ came to Medina and a few years later, when the Jews left the city, they wanted to take these children with them. However, the children's parents tried to prevent this. The dispute was brought to the Prophet ﷺ, who decided that if the children adopted Judaism and wanted to go with their religious fellows they could go. See al-Tabari, *Jamī' al-Bayān,* 3: 14–18, comments on *Al-Baqarah,* 2:256.

CHAPTER 12

[524] ʿAbd Allah Basyuni, *Naẓariyyat al-Dawlah fi'l-Islām* (Beirut: al-Dar al-Jamiʿiyyah, 1986),p. 28; Sa'id Ramadan, *Islamic Law, Its Scope and Equity,* 2nd edn (Kuala Lumpur: Muslim Youth Movement of Malaysia, 1992), p. 165; Wahbah Zuhayli, *Al-Fiqh al-Islāmī wa-ʿAdillatuhuh,* 3rd edn (Damascus: Dār al-Fikr, 1409/1989), 8 vols, vol. iv, p. 435.

[525] ʿAbd al-Karim Zaydan, *Aḥkām Ahl al-Dimmah wa'l-Musta'minīn fī Dār al-Islām* (Baghdad: Maktabat al-Quds, 1963), p. 27; Rashid al-Ghannushi, *Ḥuquq al-Muwāṭanah, Ḥuquq Ghayr al-Muslim fi'l-Mujtamaʿa al-Islāmī,* 2nd edn (Herndon, VA & Tunis: Al-Maʿhad al-ʿUlamī li'l-Fikr al-Islāmī, 1413/1993), p. 57; Muhammad Hamidullah, *Muslim Conduct of State,* 3rd edn (Lahore: Shah Muhammad Ashraf, 1953), p. 118.

[526] See for details on *siyāsah sharʿiyyah,* article by Mohammad Hashim Kamali, '*Siyāsah shar'iyyah* or the Policies of Islamic Government' in *American Journal of Islamic Social Sciences,* 6 (1989), pp. 59–81.

[527] Ramadan, *Islamic Law,* 165–6.

[528] Cf. Basyuni, *Naẓariyyat al-Dawlah,* 28–9; Hamidullah, *Muslim Conduct of State,* p. 202; Zuhayli, *Al-Fiqh al-Islāmī,* vol. iv, p. 435.

[529] Zuḥaylī, *Al-Fiqh al-Islāmī,* vol. vi, p. 434; ʿAbd al-Qadir ʿAwdah, *Al-Tashrīʿ al-Jinā'ī al-Islāmī Muqāranan bi'l-Qānun al-Wāḍʿī* (Cairo: Maktabah Wahbah, 1401/1981), 2 vols, vol. I, p. 277; Majid Khadduri, *War and Peace in the Law of Islam* (Baltimore: The Johns Hopkins Press, 1955), p.164.

[530] Cf. Al-Ghannushi, *Ḥuquq al-Muwāṭanah,* p. 61; Muhammad Fathi ʿUthman, *Al-Fikr al-Qānunī al-Islāmī: Bayn Uṣūl al-Sharīʿah wa-Turāth al-Fiqh* (Cairo: Maktabat Wahbah, n.d.), p. 270.

[531] Muhammad b Ismā'īl Bukhārī, *Ṣaḥīḥ al-Bukhārī,* trans. Muhammad Muhsin Khan, (Lahore: Qazi Publications, 1979) 9 vols, iv, 102; Abu Dāwud, *Mukhtasar Sunan Abu Dāwud,* edited by Ahmad Muhammad Shakir and Hamid Muhammad al-Faqi. Beirut: Dar al-Marifah, hadith no. 195; Zuhayli, *al-Fiqh al-Islāmī,* vol. vi, p. 432.

532 Ya'qub b Ibrāhīm Abu Yusuf, *Kitāb al-Kharāj*, 5th edn (Cairo: al-Maṭba'ah al-Salafiyyah, 1396 AH), p. 244; Zuhayli, *al-Fiqh al-Islāmī*, vol. vi, p. 432.

533 Cf. Zuhayli, *al-Fiqh al-Islāmī*, vol. vi, p. 433; Khadduri, *War and Peace*, p. 168.

534 Cf. S. Abu 'l-A'la Mawdudi, *Islamic Law and Constitution*, trans. and edited by Khurshid Ahmad, (Lahore: Islamic Publications (Pvt.) Ltd., 1960), p.181.

535 Cf. Zuhayli, *Ḥaqq al-ḥurriyyah*, p. 147; See also 'Abd al-Wahhab Khallaf, *Al-Siyāsah Al-Shar'iyyah* (Cairo: al-Matba'ah al-Salafiyyah, 1350 AH), p. 35.

536 Al-Sarakhsī, Shams al-Dīn, *Sharḥ al-Siyar al-Kabīr*, vol. iv, p. 115; Hamidullah, *Muslim Conduct of State*, p. 119.

537 This was the subject of a lecture delivered in London by M Salim el-Awa, *'al-Muwāṭanah Hiya Asās al'Ilāqah Bayn al-Muslimīn wa-Ghayrihim'*, *Islam 21*, no. 20 (Dec 1999), p. 11.

538 Idem.

539 Cf. Abu al-Hasan Al-Baladhuri, *Fuṭuḥ al-Buldān*, edited by Riḍwān Muhammad Riḍwān (Beirut: Dār al-Kutub al-'Ilmiyyah, 1412/1991); cf. Zuhayli, *Ḥaqq al-ḥurriyyah*, p. 146.

540 Ibid., p.12; Abu Ja'far Muhammad Ibn Jarir Al-Tabari, *Tārīkh al-Umam wa'l-Muluk* (Cairo: al-Matba'ah al-Tijariyyah, 1358/1939), vol. iv, p. 229.

541 Ibid., p. 12; Baladhuri, *Fuṭuḥ al-Buldān*, p. 136.

542 Ibid., p.12.

543 See for details on *ta'līl* Mohammad Hashim Kamali, *Principles of Islamic Jurisprudence* (Cambridge: Islamic Texts Society, 3rd edn, 2003),pp. 279f.

544 Quoted in Tariq al-Bishri, *Bayn al-Islām wa'l-'Urubah* (Cairo: Dār al-Shuruq, 1418/1998), p. 92.

545 Ibid., p. 95.

546 Cf. Gudrun Kramer, 'Dhimmi or Citizen', in Jorgan Nielsen, ed., *The Christian-Muslim Frontier* (London: IB Tauris, 1998), pp. 37–8.

547 Muslim, *Ṣaḥīh Muslim*, hadith no. 2054.

CHAPTER 13

548 'Final Declaration of the first Seminar of the Catholic-Muslim Forum', Rome, 4–6 November, 2008, p. 3.

549 'Address of His Holiness Benedict XVI to Participants in the Seminar organised by the Catholic Muslim Forum', Vatican City, Clementine Hall, 6 November, 2008.

http://www.vatican.va/holy_father/benedict_xvi/speeches/2008/november/documents/hf_ben-xvi_spe_20081106_cath-islamic-leaders_en.html.

550 Seyyed Hossein Nasr, 'We And You—Let us Meet in God's Love', 1st Catholic-Muslim Forum Seminar, Vatican City, 6 November, 2008, p. 1.

551 The nature of these responses merits a study in and of itself. To see the

seventy different responses go to:
http://acommonword.com/index.php?lang=en&page=responses.

[552] See http://worldinterfaithharmonyweek.com/.

[553] http://worldinterfaithharmonyweek.com/newspost/h-r-h-prince-ghazi-bin-muhammad-delivers-kings-world-interfaith-harmony-week-proposal-at-un/.

[554] H. Con Res. 374. For an outline of the history of the resolution see http://thomas.loc.gov/cgi-bin/bdquery/z?d110:HC00374:@@@L&summ2=m&.

[555] The most important of these have been: Miroslav Volf, Ghazi bin Muhammad and Melissa Yarrington, eds, *A Common Word: Muslims and Christians on Loving God and Neighbor* (Grand Rapids: Wm. B. Eerdmans, 2009); and Waleed El-Ansary and David Linnan, eds, *Muslim and Christian Understanding: Theory and Application of 'A Common Word'* (New York: Palgrave Macmillan, 2010).

[556] This is the analysis offered by Samir Khalil Samir, SJ in 'Pope Benedict XVI and Dialogue with Muslims', *Annals Australasia* (January/February 2008), pp. 20–5.

[557] The entire Regensburg Lecture can be found on the Vatican website, http://www.vatican.va/holy_father/benedict_xvi/speeches/2006/september/documents/hf_ben-xvi_spe_20060912_university-regensburg_en.html. The polemical passage is as follows:

'I was reminded of all this recently, when I read the edition by Professor Theodore Khoury (Münster) of part of the dialogue carried on—perhaps in 1391 in the winter barracks near Ankara – by the erudite Byzantine emperor Manuel II Paleologus and an educated Persian on the subject of Christianity and Islam, and the truth of both. It was probably the emperor himself who set down this dialogue, during the siege of Constantinople between 1394 and 1402; and this would explain why his arguments are given in greater detail than the responses of the learned Persian.

'The dialogue ranges widely over the structures of faith contained in the Bible and in the Qur'an, and deals especially with the image of God and of man, while necessarily returning repeatedly to the relationship of the three Laws: the Old Testament, the New Testament, and the Qur'an. In this lecture I would like to discuss only one point—itself rather marginal to the dialogue itself—which, in the context of the issue of faith and reason, I found interesting and which can serve as the starting-point for my reflections on this issue.

'In the seventh conversation edited by Professor Khoury, the emperor touches on the theme of the jihad (holy war). The emperor must have known that surah 2, 256 reads: There is no compulsion in religion. It is one of the surahs of the early period, when Mohammed was still powerless and under threat.

'But naturally the emperor also knew the instructions, developed later and recorded in the Qur'an, concerning holy war. Without descending to details, such as the difference in treatment accorded to those who have the "Book" and the "infidels", he turns to his interlocutor somewhat brusquely with the central question on the relationship between religion and violence in general, in these words:

'"Show me just what Mohammed brought that was new, and there you will find things only evil and inhuman, such as his command to spread by the sword the faith he preached."

'The emperor goes on to explain in detail the reasons why spreading the faith through violence is something unreasonable. Violence is incompatible with the nature of God and the nature of the soul.

'God is not pleased by blood, and not acting reasonably is contrary to God's nature. Faith is born of the soul, not the body. Whoever would lead someone to faith needs the ability to speak well and to reason properly, without violence and threats ... To convince a reasonable soul, one does not need a strong arm, or weapons of any kind, or any other means of threatening a person with death....'

'The decisive statement in this argument against violent conversion is this: not to act in accordance with reason is contrary to God's nature. The editor, Theodore Khoury, observes: 'For the emperor, as a Byzantine shaped by Greek philosophy, this statement is self-evident. But for Muslim teaching, God is absolutely transcendent. His will is not bound up with any of our categories, even that of rationality.' Here Khoury quotes a work of the noted French Islamist R. Arnaldez, who points out that Ibn Hazn [sic] went so far as to state that God is not bound even by his own word, and that nothing would oblige him to reveal the truth to us. Were it God's will, we would even have to practice idolatry.'

[558] As quoted in 'Cardinal Praises Muslims for "Eloquent" Letter', 19 October, 2007. http://www.zenit.org/article-20787?l=english.

[559] Tom Heneghan, 'Vatican says Pope cannot sign collective response to Muslims', Reuters Blogs, 23 October, 2007.

http://blogs.reuters.com/faithworld/2007/10/23/vatican-says-pope-cannot-sign-response-to-muslims/.

[560] Michael Gonyea, 'Islam's Transcendent Challenge', *American Thinker*, 12 October 2008. http://www.americanthinker.com/2008/10/islams_transcendent_challenge.html.

[561] Fareed Zakaria, 'New hope: Defeating terror requires Muslim help and much more than force of arms', *Newsweek*, 18 July, 2005, US Edition.

http://www.fareedzakaria.com/articles/newsweek/071805.html. 'Now things are changing. The day before the London bombs, a conference of 180 top Muslim sheiks and imams, brought together under the auspices of Jordan's King Abdullah, issued a statement forbidding that any Muslim be declared takfi—an apostate [sic]. This is a frontal attack on Al Qaeda's theological methods. Declaring someone takfir—and thus sanctioning his or her death—is a favorite tactic of bin Laden and his ally in Iraq, Abu Mussab al-Zarqawi. The conference's statement was endorsed by ten fatwas from such big conservative scholars as

Tantawi; Iraq's Grand Ayatollah Ali Sistani; Egypt's mufti, Ali Jumaa, and the influential Al-Jazeera TV-shaykh, Yusuf al-Qaradawi. Signed by adherents of all schools of fiqh (Islamic jurisprudence), it also allows only qualified Muslim scholars to issue edicts. The Islamic Conference's statement, the first of its kind, is a rare show of unity among the religious establishment against terrorists and their scholarly allies.'

[562] For examples of the pseudo-fatwas issued by extremist elements see Bruce Lawrence, ed., *Messages to the World: The Statements of Osama bin Laden* (London & New York: Verso, 2005). One is most struck by the lack of questions; for a traditional fatwa is always an answer to a question. But in Bin Laden's instance proclamations are presented as fatwas.

[563] For the full text of the Final Declaration go to: http://ammanmessage.com/index.php?option=com_content&task=view&id=20&Itemid=34

[564] http://www.acommonword.com/

[565] *A Common Word Between Us and You* (Amman, The Royal Aal al-Bayt Institute For Islamic Thought, 2007), p. 2. For access to the original document see: http://www.acommonword.com/index.php?lang=en&page=downloads.

[566] Ibid., p. 2.

[567] Ibid., p. 12.

[568] Ibid., p. 16.

[569] Ibid., p. 16.

[570] Prince Ghazi bin Muhammad, '*A Common Word Between Us and You:* Theological Motives and Expectations', Acceptance Speech for the Eugen Biser Award Ceremony, 2 November, 2008, pp. 5–6.

[571] 'Loving God and Neighbor Together: A Christian Response to *A Common Word Between Us and You*', *New York Times*, 17 November, 2007.

[572] Ibid.

[573] Miroslav Volf, Ghazi bin Muhammad and Melissa Yarrington, eds, *A Common Word: Muslims and Christians on Loving God and Neighbor* (Grand Rapids: Wm. B. Eerdmans, 2009).

[574] From personal discussion with Reza Shah-Kazemi and Ibrahim Kalin, spokesperson for *A Common Word*, 26 July, 2008.

[575] 'Final Declaration of the Yale Common Word Conference', July 2008, p. 1.

[576] Ibid., p. 1.

[577] Ibid., p. 1.

[578] For John Piper's response to *A Common Word* see, http://www.desiringgod.org/Blog/1032_a_common_word_between_us/

[579] Leith Anderson, 'Signing the Letter to Islam'. http://www.nae.net/index.cfm?FUSEACTION=editor.page&pageID=500&IDcategory=1

[580] See: http://www.desiringgod.org/resource-library/conference-messages/evangelicals-and-a-common-word.

[581] Archbishop Rowan Williams, *A Common Word for the Common Good* (London: Lambeth Palace, 2008), p.2.

[582] Ibid., p. 12.

[583] Ibid., p. 12.

[584] Ibid., p. 13.

[585] Ibid., p. 13.

[586] Ibid., p. 14.

[587] Ibid., p. 14.

[588] Ibid., p. 16.

[589] The Most Reverend & Right Honourable Dr Rowan Williams and H.E. Shaykh Prof. Dr Ali Gomaa Mohamed Abdel Wahab, 'Communiqué from A Common Word conference', London, Lambeth Palace, 15 October, 2008.

[590] For an introduction to Scriptural Reasoning see : http://etext.lib.virginia.edu/journals/ssr/issues/volume2/number1

[591] *Insegnamenti*, VIII/2, [1985], p. 497, quoted during a general audience on 5 May, 1999.

[592] 'Open Letter to His Holiness Pope Benedict XVI', 13 October, 2006, p. 4.

[593] 'Address of His Holiness Benedict XVI to Participants in the Seminar organised by the Catholic Muslim Forum', Vatican City, Clementine Hall, 6 November, 2008.

[594] Ibid.

[595] Ibid.

[596] The World Council of Churches, 'Learning to Explore Love Together', p. 2: http://www.oikoumene.org/en/resources/documents/wcc-programmes/interreligious-dialogue-and-cooperation/interreligious-trust-and-respect/20-03-08-learning-to-explore-love-together.html.

[597] Ibid., p. 2.

[598] Ibid., p. 3.

[599] Ibid., p. 3.

[600] Ibid., p. 4.

[601] As quoted in an interview with Stryker McGuire, 'A Small Miracle', *Newsweek*, 21 October, 2008.

[602] Several scholars have raised this point, but the only thorough study is that of Gordon Nickel, '*A Common Word* in Context and Commentary', unpublished conference paper, Annual Meeting of the American Academy of Religion, Chicago, IL, 3 November, 2008.

[603] Mahmud b. 'Abdallah al-Alusi, *Rūḥ al-maʿānī fī tafsīr al-qur'ān al-karīm wa-l-sabaʿ al-mathānī* (Beirut: Dar Ehia al-Tourath al-Arabi, 1420/1999), vol. 3, p. 193.

[604] Aḥmad ibn 'Ajiba, *al-Baḥr al-madīd fī tafsīr al-qur'ān al-majīd* (Beirut: Dar al-Kotoob al-Ilmiyyah, 1426/2005), vol. 1, p. 330.

605 'Final Declaration of the Yale Common Word Conference', July 2008, p. 1.

606 Archbishop Rowan Williams, *A Common Word for the Common Good*, p. 3.

607 Ibid., p. 2.

608 Ghazi bin Muhammad, '*A Common Word Between Us and You:* Theological Motives and Expectations', pp. 8–9.

609 Seyyed Hossein Nasr, 'We and You—Let us Meet in God's Love', (expanded version), *Sophia: The Journal of Traditional Studies*, vol. 14, no. 2, (Winter 2009).

610 The World Council of Churches, 'Learning to Explore Love Together', p. 4.

611 Daniel Madigan, SJ, '*A Common Word Between Us and You*: Some initial Reflections', p. 7.

CHAPTER 14

612 Abu Hamid al-Ghazali (d. 505 AH) says the following about God's Name 'the Loving': 'The Loving (*Al-Wadūd*) is He who loves goodness for all creation, treats them with kindness and blesses them. *It is similar to the meaning of 'The Merciful'*, save that mercy is shown to those who are in dire need of mercy, and the actions of The Merciful require one who is weak and in need of mercy, whilst the actions of The Loving do not require this; rather, blessing in the first place is a fruit of love.' (Abu Hamid al-Ghazali, *Al-Maqṣad al-asnā fī sharḥ ma'ani asmā' Allāh al-ḥusnā*, p. 122.) And Fakhr al-Din al-Razi (d. 606 AH) said about God's Name 'the Loving': 'The Almighty says: *And He is the Forgiving, the Loving, and 'wudd' means 'love'*. The word *Wadūd* has two possible meanings: it may be an active participle, meaning 'He who loves', meaning that He loves them, as He says: *...a people whom He loves and who love Him...* (*Al-Mā'idah*, 5:54). When we say that He loves His servant, this means that He wants to send good things to him. Know that according to this understanding, love is similar to mercy; the difference between them is that mercy requires someone who is weak and in need of mercy, whilst love does not; rather, blessing in the first place is a fruit of love. The second possible meaning is that He is loving in the sense that He causes men to love one another, as He says: *...for them the Compassionate One shall appoint love* (*Maryam*, 19:96). A third possibility is that it [*Wadūd*] is a passive participle, morphologically similar to the words *hayūb* ("afraid") or *rakūb* ("mounted", as on a horse); in this case, God Almighty is beloved to the hearts of His friends because of the great favour He shows them.' (Fakhr al-Din al-Razi, *Sharḥ asmā' Allāh al-ḥusnā*, pp. 273–4).

613 *Al-Baqarah*, 2:143; *Al-Baqarah*, 2:207; *Āl 'Imrān*, 3:30; *Al-Tawbah*, 9:117; *Al-Nahl*, 16:7; *Al-Nahl*, 16:47; *Al-Mu'minūn*, 23:65; *Al-Nūr* 24:20; *Al-Ḥadīd*, 57:9; and *Al-Ḥashr*, 59:10.

614 Al-Tirmidhi, *Sunan*, *ḥadīth* no. 1907, *Kitāb al-birr wa al-ṣilah, Bāb mā jā' fī qāṭi'at al-raḥm.*

[615] In his book *Al-Insān al-kāmil*, the Muslim scholar ʿAbd al-Karim Jili (d. 805 AH) suggests that Mercy is the origin of God's Names and Qualities, and that God's Names proceed from the Quality of Mercy.

'The Mercy from the Divine Essence (*Al-Raḥmaniyyah*) is the manifestation of the realities of the Names and Qualities; it lies *between His essential qualities, such as the Names of the Essence, and those qualities which are directed towards created beings*, such as His being the Knower, the Omnipotent, the All-Hearing, and the other Qualities which have a connection to temporal beings .... The Name which is directly derived from the level of Mercy from the Divine Essence (*Al-Raḥmaniyyah*) is *Al-Raḥmān*, the Compassionate—a Name which refers to the Names of His Essence (*al-Asmā' al-Dhātiyyah*) and the Qualities of His Person (*al-Awṣāf al-Nafsiyyah*), which are seven in number: life, knowledge, omnipotence, will, speech, hearing and seeing ... This level [of Being] has this name because of how this all-enveloping mercy covers all the levels of Reality and creation; and it was because of its manifestation in the levels of Reality that the levels of creation came into existence. Thus mercy became universally present in all beings, from the Merciful Presence.' (Abd Al-Kareem al-Jili, *Al-Insān al-Kāmil*, p. 73).

[616] Muslim, *Saḥīḥ*, *ḥadīth* no. 810, *Kitāb ṣalāt al-musāfirīn wa qasraha, Bāb faḍl sūrat al-kahf wa āyat al-kursī.*

[617] God's Names *The Compassionate (Al-Raḥmān)* and *The Merciful (Al-Raḥīm)*: Muslim scholars have said many things about the meaning of God's Names *The Compassionate* and *The Merciful*. The following are amongst the most pertinent: Ibn Kathir says:'*The Compassionate* and *The Merciful* are two Divine Names derived from the word *raḥmah* ('mercy'); both are intensive morphological forms, but *The Compassionate* is more intensive than *The Merciful*. It is related that Jesus said: "The Compassionate is Compassionate in this life and the next, while the Merciful is Merciful in the next life." ... Abu Ali Farisi said: "*The Compassionate* is a universal name which encompasses all the forms of mercy, and only God may be called by this Name. *The Merciful* refers solely to the mercy God shows the believers, as He says: ...*And He is Merciful to the believers.* (*Al-Aḥzāb*, 33:43)". Ibn Abbas said that: "They are two gentle Names, one of which is gentler than the other: that is, suggestive of yet more mercy."... Ibn Mubarak said that *The Compassionate* is the One who gives when He is asked, whilst *The Merciful* is the One who becomes wrathful when He is not asked; this is derived from a hadith ... The Messenger of God ﷺ said: "If one does not ask of God, He becomes angry with one." I heard ʿAzrami say of the Names *The Compassionate, The Merciful* that God is Compassionate with all His creatures, and Merciful to the believers. They say that this is why God says: ... *Then [He] presided upon the Throne. The Compassionate One* (*Al-Furqān*, 25:59), and says: *The Compassionate One presided upon the Throne* (*Ṭā Hā*, 20:5). God thus links His presiding [over the Throne] to His Name

The Compassionate to indicate how His mercy envelops all His creation; and He says: *...And He is Merciful to the believers.* (*Al-Aḥzāb*, 33:43), singling them out with His Name *The Merciful*. They say that this implies that *The Compassionate* denotes the higher degree of mercy because it applies in both worlds to all His creatures, whilst *The Merciful* applies to the believers alone ... And His Name *The Compassionate* (*Al-Raḥmān*) is for Him alone, and no one else may be called this ... As for *The Merciful*, He describes another with this attribute when He says: *Verily there has come to you a messenger from among yourselves for whom it is grievous that you should suffer; who is full of concern for you, to the believers full of pity, merciful (raḥīm)* (*Al-Tawbah*, 9:128).' (Ibn Kathir, *Tafsīr al-Qur' ān al-'Aẓīm*, pp. 65–6).

Al-Ghazali says: '*The Compassionate (Al-Raḥmān)* and *The Merciful (Al-Raḥīm)* are both derived from the word 'mercy' (*raḥmah*), and mercy requires an object, and the object of mercy must be needy. Someone who meets a needy person's need unintentionally and without caring about the needy person is not called 'merciful'. The one who wishes to meet the needy person's need but does not do so when he is able to do is not called 'merciful', because if he really wanted to do it, he would. If he is unable to do so, he might be called 'merciful' because of his sympathy, but his mercy is incomplete. Perfect mercy means to shower the needy with goodness having the intention to take care of them. Universal mercy is that which is given to the deserving and the undeserving alike. God's mercy is thus both perfect and universal; it is perfect in that He wishes to meet the needs of the needy, and does so; and it is universal in that it encompasses both the deserving and the undeserving—in this lower world and in the hereafter—and it meets both dire needs and ordinary needs, as well as additional matters beyond this. He is truly the Absolutely Merciful.' (Ghazali, *Al-Maqṣad al-asnā fī sharḥ ma'ānī asmā' Allāh al-huṣnah*, p. 62).

Al-Razi says: 'Which of them is more intensive: *The Compassionate*, or *The Merciful*? Abu Salih related that Ibn Abbas said: '*The Compassionate* and *The Merciful* are two gentle Names, one of which is gentler than the other'; yet he did not state which is the gentlest. But Husayn bin Fadl al-Balkhi said: "This is a mistake on the part of the narrator, for gentleness (*riqqah*) is not a Divine Quality. The Prophet said: 'God is Kind (*rafīq*), and He loves kindness, and He gives for it that which He does not give for violence.'" Know that there is no doubt that both *The Compassionate (Al-Raḥmān)* and *The Merciful (Al-Raḥīm)* are derived from the word 'mercy' (*raḥmah*), and if one were not more intensive than the other they would be exact synonyms in every way without any distinction between them; and this is unlikely. Therefore we must understand that one of them is more intensive in meaning than the other. Beyond this, they differ: most say that *The Compassionate* implies greater mercy than *The Merciful*, and they give several arguments to support this.' (Al-Razi, *Sharḥ asmā' Allāh al-ḥusnā*, p. 162).

The common elements between all these definitions are:

(1) that *The Compassionate (Al-Raḥmān)* can only be used to describe God, whilst *Merciful (Al-Raḥīm)* can be used to describe both God and human beings.

(2) that the Name *The Compassionate* linguistically implies a greater 'amount' of mercy.

(3) that *The Merciful* requires an object, whilst *The Compassionate* does not require an object.

(4) that *The Compassionate* always comes before *The Merciful* whenever the two Names are mentioned together.

(5) that *The Compassionate* is virtually a synonym for the Name 'God' (*Allāh*) for God says: *Say: 'Invoke God or invoke the Compassionate One, whichever you invoke, to Him belong the Most Beautiful Names'...* (*Al-Isrā'*, 17:110)

(6) and, finally, that since *...He has prescribed for Himself mercy...* (*Al-An'ām*, 6:12), and since *The Compassionate* implies greater mercy than *The Merciful* and does not require an object, this means that *The Compassionate* is one of the Names of God's Essence, whilst *The Merciful* is one of the Names of His Qualities. And God knows best.

[618] Al-Razi, *Al-Tafsīr al-kabīr, Mafātih al-ghayb*, vol. 5, p. 379.

[619] Al-Qurtubi, *Tafsīr al-Qurtubi*, vol. 7, p. 261.

[620] Al-Razi, *Al-Tafsīr al-kabīr*, vol. 6, p. 412.

[621] Bukhari, *Saḥīḥ*, *ḥadīth* no. 7403; *Kitāb al-Tawḥīd, Bāb: Qawlihi ta'āla "Wa laqad sabaqat kalimatunā li-'ibādinā al-mursalīn'*.

[622] We should not neglect to mention here the *Hadith Qudsi*: *I was a hidden treasure, and I loved to be known, so I created humankind and made Myself known to them, and they knew Me.* The Hadith scholar 'Ajluni said about this hadith: 'Ibn Taymiyah said it is not a saying of the Prophet and that he did not know any chain or narration for it, whether strong or weak. Zarkashi, Hafiz Ibn Hajar (in *al-Laāli'*), Suyuti and others concurred. Al-Qari said: "But its meaning is correct and can be derived from God's words: *And I did not create the jinn and humankind except that they may worship Me*," that is, that they may know God, as Ibn 'Abbas ﷺ and others understood it. The way it is generally reported is: "*I was a hidden treasure and I loved to be known, so I created men, and through Me they knew Me.*" It is quoted very often by the Sufis, and they rely on it and have based some of their fundamental ideas on it.' ('Ajluni, *Kashf al-khafā'*, vol. 1, p. 132). However, Ibn Arabi declared—controversially perhaps—the hadith to be 'authentic according to personal disclosure' (*ṣaḥīḥ kashfan*); these are his words from *Al-Futuḥāt al-Makkiyyah*: 'In a *ḥadīth* which is authentic based on personal disclosure, but lacking an established chain of narration, the Messenger of God ﷺ reported that his Lord says words to the effect of: *I was a hidden treasure, and I loved to be known, so I created humankind and made Myself known to them, and they knew Me.*' (Muhyi al-Din Ibn al-Arabi, *Al-Futuḥāt al-Makkiyyah*, vol. 2, p. 393).

We do not wish to get into a discussion about the authenticity or weakness of this hadith—all the other hadiths that we quote in this work are sound—but we will say that the meaning of the hadith is sound, as maintained above by the hadith scholar 'Ali Al-Qari. And its meaning is that God created Human beings first of all out of His Love ('and I loved to be known'), and secondly out of His Mercy ('so I created humankind and made Myself known to them, and they knew Me'). There is no contradiction here between God's love and God's mercy, because as previously discussed, Divine love and Divine Mercy are inseparable.

[623] See also: *Al-Baqarah*, 2:185–7; *Al-An'ām*, 6:165; *Al-A'rāf*, 7:156; *Yūnus*, 10:5, 14, 67; *Ibrāhīm*, 14:32–4; *Al-Hijr*, 15:16–50; *Al-Naḥl*, 16:78–81; *Ṭā Hā*, 20:15, 53–4; *Al-Hajj*, 22:65; *Al-Mu'minūn*, 23:78–80; *Al-Furqān*, 25:10; *Al-Naml*, 27:60–64, 86; *Al-Qaṣaṣ*, 28:70–3; *Al-Rūm*, 30:46; *Luqmān*, 31:10–11, 31–2; *Al-Sajdah*, 32:7–9; *Faṭir*, 35:12-13; *Yā Sīn*, 36:80; *Ghāfir*, 40:64, 79–80; *Al-Fatḥ*, 48:4–9; *Al-Ṭalāq*, 65:12, 23--4; *Nūh*, 71:14–20.

[624] In the following chapter on God's Love for Humanity in General we explain at length and in detail how and with what God blesses human beings in general.

[625] Bukhari, *Ṣaḥīḥ*, *ḥadīth* no. 1385, *Kitāb al-Janā'iz, Bāb Mā qil fī awlād al-mushrikīn*; Muslim, *Ṣaḥīḥ*, *ḥadīth* no. 2658, *Kitāb al-Qadr, Bāb Ma'nā kull mawlūd yulad 'ala al-fitrah.*

[626] Muslim, *Ṣaḥīḥ*, *ḥadīth* no. 2865, *Kitāb al-Jannah, Bāb al-Ṣifāt allatī yu'raf bihā fī al-dunyā ahl al-jannah wa Kitāb al-Qadr, Bāb Ma'nā kull mawlūd yūlad 'alaal-fitratahl al-nār.*

[627] It will be noted here that whereas God favours or prefers (*faḍḍala*) each one of the Prophets *above all the worlds* (*Al-An'ām*, 6:85), and at one time preferred the Children of Israel *above all the worlds* (*Al-Jāthiyah*, 45:16–17; see also: *Al-Dukhān*, 44:32–3; *Al-Mā'idah*, 5:20; *Al-A'rāf*, 7:140), He only prefers humanity *above many of those whom We created* (*Al-Isrā'*, 17:70). God sheds light on this elsewhere in the Holy Qur'an, when He asks Iblis (Satan) why he did not prostrate himself before Adam: *He [God] said, 'O Iblis! What prevents you from prostrating before that which I have created with My own hands? Are you being arrogant, or are you of the Exalted (al-'Ālīn)?'* (*Ṣād*, 38:75).

There are thus those who are too exalted to prostrate to Adam (*al-Ālīn*). These are perhaps themselves *above the world* since God refers elsewhere to the *muqarrabūn*—the angels 'close to God'—(*Al-Nisā'*, 4:172). This perhaps explains why God says that He preferred the Children of Adam to *many of those whom We created* and not 'all' of those whom He created; and God knows best.

[628] See also: *Al-'rāf*, 7:12–27; *Al-Isrā'*, 17:61–5; *Al-Kahf*, 18:50; *Ṭā Hā*, 20:115–6; *Ṣād*, 38:71–85; *Yūnus*, 10:14; *Al-An'ām*, 6:165; *Fāṭir*, 35:39; *Al-Aḥzāb*, 33:73.

[629] At first glance the inclusion of *those who fight for His cause in ranks, as if they were a solid structure* among the kinds of people whom God loves might seem a little puzzling, especially given the more obvious virtues of the other

seven kinds. However, this is easily understood if the verses preceding this verse are remembered. God says: *O you who believe, why do you say what you do not do? / It is greatly loathsome to God that you say what you do not do. / Indeed God loves those who fight for His cause in ranks, as if they were a solid structure.* (*Al-Ṣaff*, 61:2–4) Thus fighting in God's cause *in ranks, as if they were a solid structure* is linked to doing 'what we say we will do'. In other words, it is linked to being completely sincere; having no trace of hypocrisy or hesitation, and thus being 'unanimous' (literally: 'of one soul'). Hence the *ranks* and *solid structure* are above all in people's own selves, in their own souls (*anfus*). God says: *Will you bid others to piety and forget yourselves (anfusakum), while you recite the Book? Do you not understand?* (*Al-Baqarah*, 2:44).

[630] Because of this, God loves thoroughness in acts and work. The Messenger of God ﷺ said: 'God loves that, when one of you does any work, he does it well.' (Tabarani, *Al-Mu'jam al-awsaṭ*, vol. 1, p. 275) Thoroughness is thus the work of the beautiful soul; and beautiful work comes from a beautiful soul. And God knows best.

[631] Muslim, *Ṣaḥīḥ*, *ḥadīth* no. 99, *Kitāb al-Imān*.

[632] Muslim, *Ṣaḥīḥ*, *ḥadīth* no. 1, *Kitāb al-Imān*.

[633] Zabidi, *Tāj al-'arūs*, vol. 18, p. 14.

[634] And the eight kinds of people whom God loves are those who follow the way of the Messenger of God ﷺ, and they are all included in the general sense of this Qur'anic verse.

[635] Raghib Al-Isfahani says: 'The meaning of "I greatly love (*ḥababtu*) so-and-so" is "I reached the core (*ḥabbah*) of his heart"; there are other expressions [in Arabic] with similar meanings, such as "I reached the skin of his heart", "I reached his liver", "I reached his inner heart".' (*Al-Mufradāt fī gharīb al-Qur'ān*, p. 112).

42 Naturally the fact of God's being 'with' these categories of people can be considered a special kind of love, for the Messenger of God ﷺ explained the relationship of love to company when he said: 'A person is with those they love.' (Bukhari, *Ṣaḥīḥ*, *ḥadīth* no. 6168, *Kitāb al-adab, Bāb 'Alamāt ḥubb Allāh*). And also when he replied to someone who said to him, 'I have prepared nothing for the Hour save that I love God and His Messenger': 'You shall be with those you love.' (Bukhari, *Ṣaḥīḥ*, *ḥadīth* no. 3688, *Kitāb al-Manāqib, Bāb Manāqib 'Umar ibn al-Khattab.*)

[636] Al-Qushayri says in his *Risalah*, p. 46: 'Ibn Shahin asked Junayd what "with [God]" means, and he said: ""With" has two meanings; God is with the prophets in the sense that He gives succour and protection, as God says: *He said, 'Do not fear, for I shall be with the two of you, hearing and seeing*; and He is with all people in the sense that He has complete knowledge of them, as God says: *No secret conversation of three takes place but He is their fourth.*" Ibn Shahin replied, "Someone such as you is fit to guide the Community to God!"'

[637] Perhaps the fact that God says four times in the Holy Qur'an that He is 'with' the patient indicates that patience requires perseverance before the patient person (*al-sābir*) reaches the level of virtue (*iḥsān*); God knows best.

[638] It is extremely instructive to consider how the three virtues of *taqwah*, *sabr* and *iḥsān* are depicted in the Holy Qur'an. In general, we may say that: (1) *taqwah* is the very reason for the creation (see *Al-Baqarah*, 2:21); that it is the essential message of the Prophets (see *Al-Shu'arā'*, 26:87, 106, 124, 142, 161, 177; and *Al-Ṣaffāt*, 37:124) and that the *muttaqīn* (those who have *taqwah*) are those who will be in paradise (this is repeated many times in the Holy Qur'an—see *Al-*A'rāf,7:128; *Hūd*, 11:49; *Al-Ḥijr*, 15:45; *Al-Naḥl*, 16:30-31; *Maryam*, 19:85; *Al-Shu'arā'*, 26:90; *Al-Qaṣaṣ*, 28:31; *Ṣād*, 38:49; *Dukhān*, 44:51; *Qāf*, 50:31; *Al-Dhāriyāt*, 51:17; *Al-Tūr*, 52:17; *Al-Qamr*, 54:55; *Al-Qalam*, 68:34; *Al-Mursalāt*, 77:41; *Al-A'lā*, 87:31). As regards: (2) *sabr*, it is also a virtue of those who will be in paradise (see *Al-Ra'd*, 13:43), but it is more often described as the virtue of the 'resolute' among the Messengers (see *Al-Aḥqāf*, 46:35, see also *Al-Naḥl*, 16:2 and *Al-Ma'ārij*, 70:5) and the greatest of the saints (see *Al-Kahf*, 18:68, 72, 75, 78, 82 and *Fuṣṣilat*, 41:35). Finally, as regards *iḥsān*, whilst it is also obviously a virtue of those who will be in paradise (see *Al-Mā'idah*, 5:85 and *Al-Dhāriyāt*, 51:16), it is more often described as a sublime and unsurpassable virtue (see *Al-Nisā'*, 4:125) for which there is an unfailing Divine reward (see *Al-Raḥmān*, 55:60); that is *the firmest handle ('urwah wuthqā*—see *Luqmān*, 31:22); that is never lost (see *Al-Tawbah*, 9:120; *Yūsuf*, 12:56; *Yūsuf*, 12:90; *Al-Ṣaffat*, 37:80, 105, 110, 121, 131; *Al-Zumar*, 39:34; *Al-Dhāriyāt*, 51:16); and that leads to perpetual increase (see *Al-Baqarah*, 2:58). Because it is the sum of virtue, it is also the virtue to be exercised towards parents, who in the Holy Qur'an are accorded the highest respect and consideration (see *Al-Baqarah*, 2:83; *Al-An'ām*, 6:151 and *Al-Isrā'*, 17:23). One might also say that *taqwah* is the sum total of piety—how a human being should be towards God; *iḥsān* is the sum of virtue—how human beings should be before other human beings, and *sabr* is how human beings should be in themselves—how they should face the human condition (although obviously all three virtues necessarily largely overlap). From a different point of view, one might even say that *sabr* relates more to the will and hence to fear (*makhāfah*) of God; *taqwah* relates more to the intelligence and hence knowledge (*ma'rifah*) of God, and *iḥsān* relates more to sentiment and hence love (*ḥubb*) of God; and God knows best.

[639] In his commentary on this verse (in *Mafātīh al-ghayb*), Fakhr al-Din al-Razi relates God's 'binding promise' (*wa'dan mas'ūla*) back to the supplication of the believers, and the supplication of the angels: *Our Lord, grant us what You have promised us through Your messengers, and abase us not on the Day of Resurrection. You will not fail the tryst* (*Āl 'Imrān*, 3:194). ....*Our Lord, You embrace all things in [Your] mercy and knowledge. So forgive those who repent and follow Your way and shield them from the chastisement of Hell-fire. / Our*

Lord, and admit them into the Gardens of Eden that which You have promised them, along with whoever were righteous among their fathers and their wives and their descendants. Surely You are the One Who is the Mighty, the Wise. (*Ghāfir*, 40:7–8). However, the extraordinary forwardness of these prayers—'reminding' God of His own promise, as it were, and cited by God Himself in the Holy Qur'an—only prove how God's own Essence has made His own promise binding upon Himself, if one may be permitted to phrase these things in such a manner; and God knows best.

CHAPTER 15

640 See: Ghazi bin Muhammad, *Love in the Holy Qur'an* (USA: Kazi Publications, 2011), Chapter 13: The Believer's Love for the Messenger of God ﷺ; Chapter 14: Love for the Family and Kin of the Messenger of God ﷺ; Chapter 16: Family Love; Chapter 18: Conjugal and Sexual Love.

641 This also means, naturally, that every human being is essentially God's vicegerent on earth, into which God breathed 'something' of His spirit (see the author's *Love in the Holy Quran*, Chapter 7: God's Love for Humanity).

642 See: Ghazi bin Muhammad, *Love in the Holy Qur'an*, Chapter 16: Family Love.

643 That is not to say obviously that the religion of Islam is sympathetic towards idolatry in any way—it is absolutely against it and refutes it completely in the very first Testimony of Faith (the *Shahādah*) that *There is no god but God* (*Lā illāha illa Allāh*)—but nevertheless, God allows everyone to choose their own religion freely, whatever it be, for He says:

There is no compulsion in religion. Rectitude has become clear from error; so whoever disbelieves in the false deity, and believes in God, has laid hold of the most firm handle, unbreaking; God is Hearing, Knowing. (*Al-Baqarah*, 2:256)

And say, 'The truth [that comes] from your Lord; so whoever will, let him believe, and whoever will, let him disbelieve'.... (*Al-Kahf*, 18:29)

Say: 'O disbelievers! / I do not worship what you worship, / and you do not worship what I worship, / nor will I worship what you have worshipped, / nor will you worship what I worship. / You have your religion and I have a religion'. (*Al-Kāfirūn*, 109:1–6)

So leave them to indulge and to play, until they encounter that day of theirs, which they are promised; (*Al-Ma'ārij, 70:42).*

644 God says: *Indeed God protects those who believe. Indeed God does not love the treacherous, the ungrateful. / Permission is granted to those who fight because they have been wronged. And God is truly able to help them; / those who were expelled from their homes without right, only because they said: 'Our Lord is God'. Were it not for God's causing some people to drive back others, destruction would have befallen the monasteries, and churches, and synagogues, and*

mosques in which God's Name is mentioned greatly. Assuredly God will help those who help Him. God is truly Strong, Mighty. (*Al-Hajj*, 22:38–40)

[645] Fakr al-Din al-Razi, *Al-Tafsīr al-kabīr*, vol. 10, p. 747.

[646] Jalal al-Din Mahalli and Jalal al-Din Suyuti, *Tafsīr al-Jalālayn*, p. 106.

[647] Al-Qurtubi, *Tafsīr al-Qurtubi*, vol. 5, p. 171.

[648] Muslim, *Ṣaḥīḥ*, *ḥadīth* no. 45, (related on the authority of Anas ibn Malik) *Kitāb al-Īmān; Bāb al-Dalīl ʿalā anna min khisāl al-imān an yuḥibb li-akhihi al-Muslim mā yuḥibb li-nafsih min khayr.* In another narration on the authority of Anas ibn Malik the Messenger of God said: 'None of you believes until he loves for his brother what he loves for himself.' (Bukhari, *Ṣaḥīḥ*, *ḥadīth* no. 13, *Kitāb al-Īmān; Bāb Min al-imān an yuḥibb li-akhihi mā yuḥibb li-nafsih).*

[649] Tirmidhi, *Sunan*, *ḥadīth* no. 1924, (related on the authority of ʿAbdullah ibn ʿAmr) *Kitāb al-birr wa al-ṣilah; Bāb Mā jā' fī raḥmat al-nās.*

[650] Bukhari, *Ṣaḥīḥ*, *ḥadīth* no. 7376, (related on the authority of Jarir ibn ʿAbdullah) *Kitāb al-Tawḥīd; Bāb Qawluhu taʿāla qul udʿu Allah aw udʿu al-Raḥmān.*

[651] Bayhaqi, *Al-Sunan al-kubrā*, vol. 9, p. 118.

[652] Abu al-Fida' Ismaʿil ibn ʿUmar ibn Kathir al-Qurashi al-Dimashqi, *Tafsīr al-Qur'ān al-ʿaẓīm*, p. 480.

[653] Abu al-Fida' Ismaʿil ibn ʿUmar ibn Kathir al-Qurashi al-Dimashqi, *Tafsīr al-Qur'ān al-ʿaẓīm*, p. 480.

[654] It is very important to point out here also that God addresses His Messenger ﷺ individually in this verse ('*You* [*innaka*, which means 'you' in the second person singular] *will truly find*'), and not the believers in general; that is to say then, that this hostility does not extend to all Jews and all Muslims, but rather between certain Jewish tribes and the Messenger of God ﷺ during his own lifetime.

[655] Thus God says:

So, for their breaking their covenant and disbelieving in the signs of God, and slaying the prophets wrongfully, and for their saying, 'Our hearts are covered up'—nay, but God sealed them for their disbelief; so they do not believe, except for a few. (*Al-Nisā'*, 4:155)

And verily you know that there were those among you who transgressed the Sabbath, and We said to them, 'Be apes, despised!' (*Al-Baqarah*, 2:65)

See also: *Al-Baqarah*, 2:78, 91; *Al-Mā'idah*, 5:60; *Al-Aʿrāf*, 7:166; and others verses in this regard.

[656] Indeed, God says: *And let not those who possess dignity and ease among you swear not to give to the near of kin and to the needy, and to fugitives for the cause of God. Let them forgive and show indulgence. Yearn ye not that God may forgive you ? God is Forgiving, Merciful.* (*Al-Nūr*, 24: 22).

[657] As such, Muslims are not even allowed to morally judge their fellow believers, much less drive them away. God says (relating the story of Noah عليه السلام):

The council of his people who disbelieved, said: 'We see you but a mortal like us, and we see not that any follow you save the vilest among us, [through] rash opinion. We do not see that you have any merit over us; nay, we deem you liars'. / He said, 'O my people, have you considered if I am [acting] upon a clear proof from my Lord and He has given me mercy from Him, and it has been obscured from you, can we compel you to it, while you are averse to it? / And O my people, I do not ask of you any wealth for this. My wage falls only upon God and I will not drive away those who believe; they shall surely meet their Lord. But I see you are a people who are ignorant. / And O my people, who would help me against God if I drive them away? Will you not then remember? / And I do not say to you, "I possess the treasure houses of God" nor, 'I have knowledge of the Unseen; nor do I say, "I am an angel". Nor do I say to those whom your eyes scorn that God will not give them any good—God knows best what is in their souls. Lo! then indeed I would be of the evildoers'. (*Hūd*, 11:27–31)

They said, 'Shall we believe in you, when it is the lowliest people who follow you?' / He said, 'And what do I know of what they may have been doing? / Their reckoning is only my Lord's concern, if only you were aware. / And I am not about to drive away the believers. / I am just a plain warner'. (*Al-Shu'arā'*, 26:111–5).

Accordingly, God tells the Prophet Muhammad ﷺ: *And do not drive away those who call upon their Lord at morning and evening desiring His countenance. You are not accountable for them in anything; nor are they accountable for you in anything, that you should drive them away and be of the evildoers.* (*Al-An'ām*, 6:52).

[658] See also the description of 'intimate friend' in the following verses: *Ghāfir*, 40:18; *Fuṣṣilat*, 41:34; *Al-Ḥaqqah*, 69:35; *Al-Ma' ārij*, 70:10).

[659] This kind of friendship might perhaps also be called a *walījah*—an intimate friendship, or literally a 'penetrating friendship'—which is only appropriate between believers. God says: *Or did you suppose that you would be left [in peace] when God does not yet know those of you who have struggled and have not taken, besides God and His Messenger and the believers, an intimate friend? And God is aware of what you do.* (*Al-Tawbah*, 9:16).

[660] It will be noted that we become friends in accordance with the goodness and inner beauty people show us, as we understand it at least—that is, if the friendship is sincere—and in accordance with the time we have spent with our friends (and thus in accordance with our experience of their inner beauty and their experience of ours).

Index to Qur'anic Quotations

INDEX